IN ANOTHER LIGHT
DANISH PAINTING IN THE NINETEENTH CENTURY

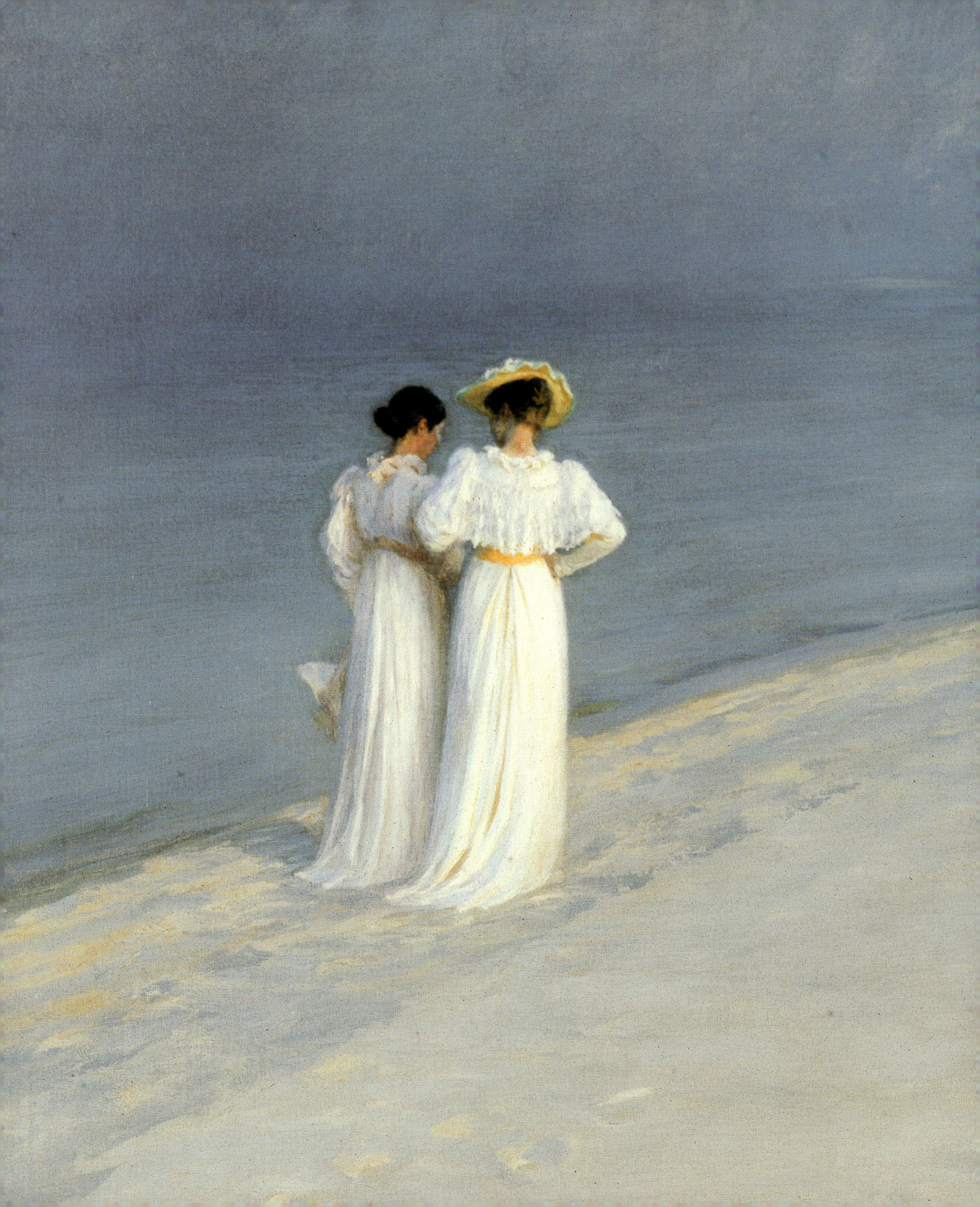

IN ANOTHER LIGHT

DANISH PAINTING IN THE NINETEENTH CENTURY

PATRICIA G. BERMAN

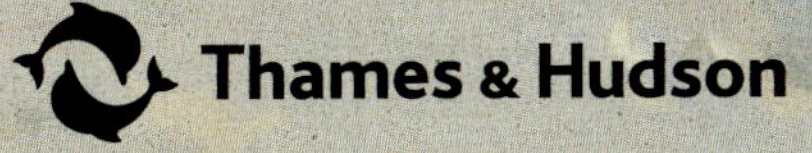

First published in the United Kingdom in 2007 by
Thames & Hudson Ltd, 181A High Holborn,
London WC1V 7QX

First paperback edition 2013
Reprinted 2019

British Library Cataloguing-in-Publication Data
A catalogue record for this book is available from the British Library

ISBN 978-0-500-29098-9

Printed and bound in Slovenia by DZS-Grafik d.o.o.

To find out about all our publications, please visit
www.thamesandhudson.com.
There you can subscribe to our e-newsletter, browse or download
our current catalogue, and buy any titles that are in print.

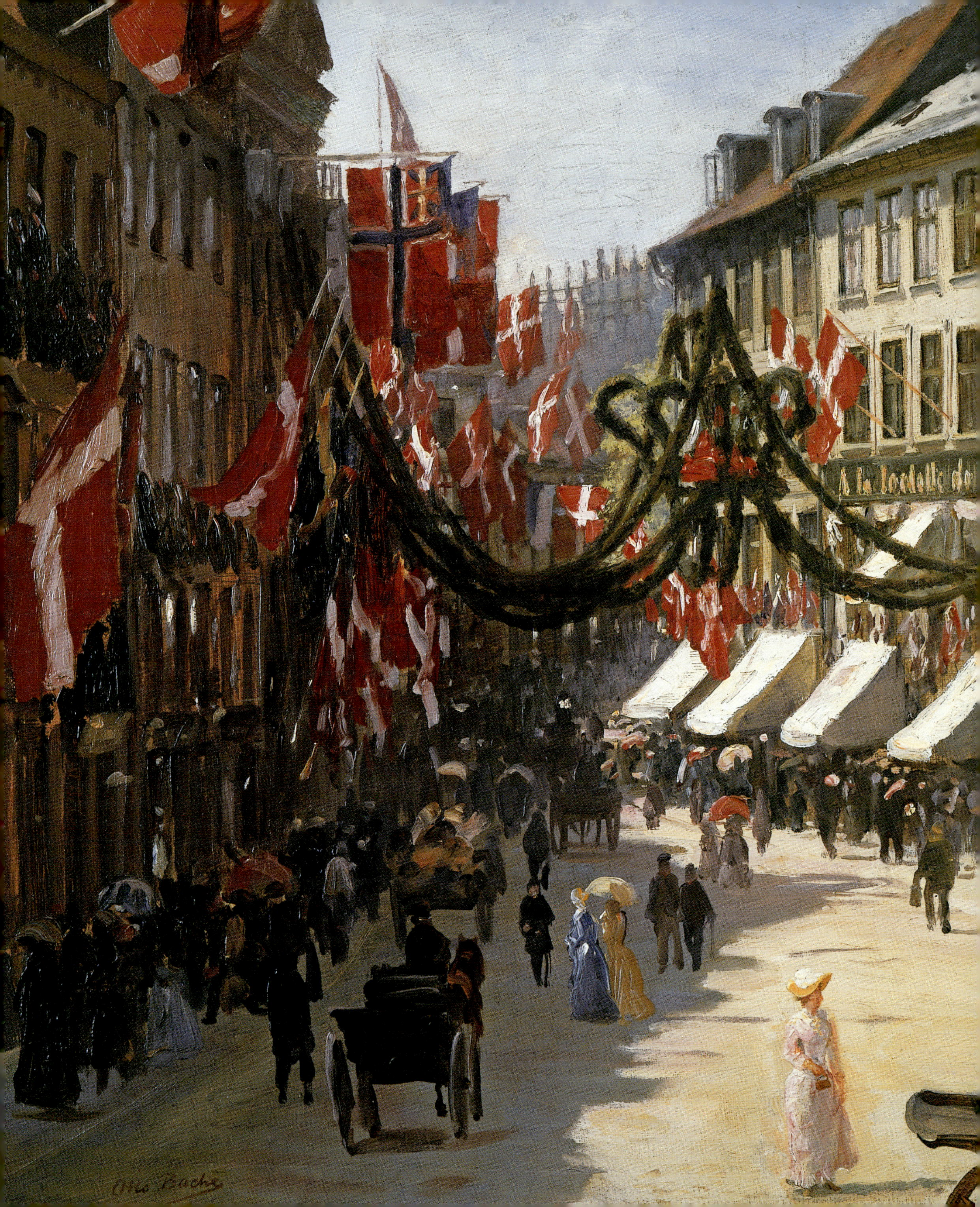
Otto Bache

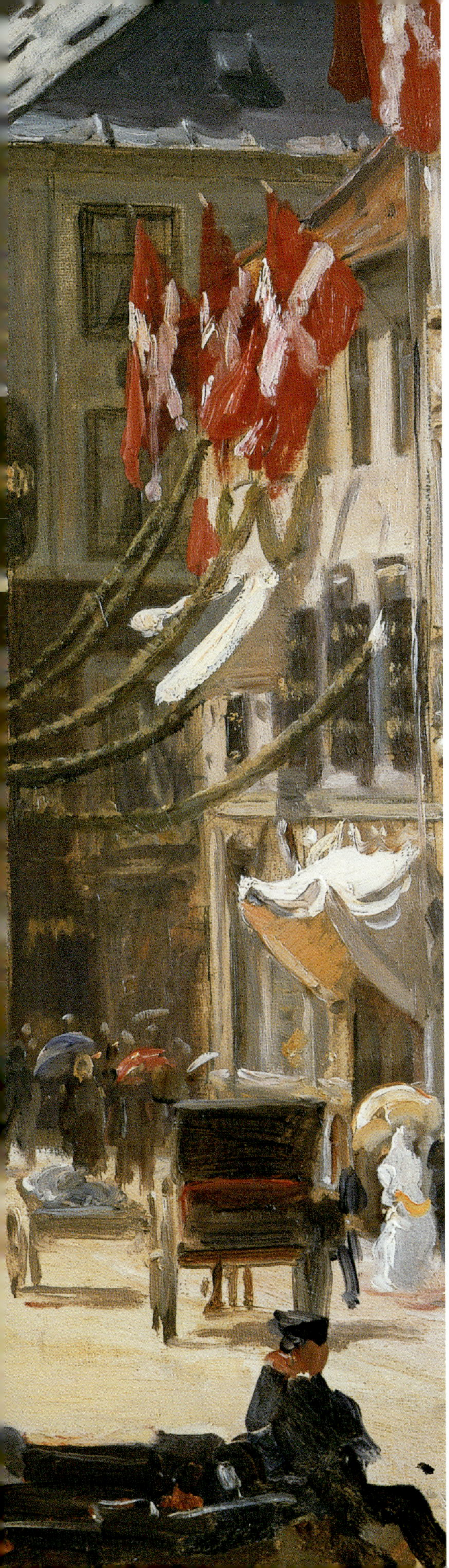

CONTENTS

INTRODUCTION

Danish painting of the nineteenth century is generally unknown to the non-Nordic art audience—a *terra incognita*.[1] However, once encountered, Danish art of the period turns out to be a site of aesthetic pleasure and cultural interest. A body of work often distinguished by its stark beauty, it evades easy categorization. The general understanding of nineteenth-century painting is shaped by the Parisian model of successive avant-gardes and well-defined movements advancing from Neoclassicism to Romanticism, Realism and Naturalism giving way to Impressionism, and Post-Impressionist experimentation leading inexorably toward abstraction. Such distinct movements and generational transformations are not apparent in Danish art. Instead, the history of Danish painting can be outlined as a series of subtle tensions between nationalism and internationalism, and as offering shifting affiliations with historical memory produced within a newly marginalized country on the edge of Europe. Between 1800 and 1900, the period under consideration, artists and critics, working in dialogue with international colleagues, often created unconventional work that presaged developments elsewhere in Europe precisely because of their precarious cultural position. The art of Denmark deviates from the accustomed French model, offering insights into the dynamics of smaller European nations in the era of emerging democratization, nationalism, and industrialization.[2]

Denmark was powerfully transformed during this period. It ceased to be the prosperous country that it had been in the eighteenth century. During the Napoleonic Wars, Denmark suffered a series of catastrophes, including the English bombardment of Copenhagen's harbor by the British in 1807 and the loss of its partner state Norway in 1814. Mounting antagonisms with Germany over the southern provinces of Schleswig and Holstein led to war in 1848–1850 and again in 1864 when Denmark was forced to cede those regions to the Prussian state. One of the oldest monarchies in the world, with a thousand year history, Denmark had been ruled by an absolutist king since 1660, but established a constitutional monarchy in 1849. Agrarian reforms of the late eighteenth century resulted in the dissolution of agricultural collectives and the emergence of a rural proletariat. Despite a population boom in the early nineteenth century that increased Denmark's size from under one million inhabitants in 1800 to 1.3 million in 1850, Denmark's loss of Norway and the southern provinces left the country truncated and under economic pressure.

The Danish intelligentsia responded to this instability by seeking a means of consolidating—of reinventing—a sense of national identity. Geographically dispersed across large and small islands in the North and Baltic Seas, largely rural, and increasingly distrustful of the official classes that had drawn the country into war, Denmark turned to a special set of myths, stories, and nationalistic strategies to shape a sense of collective coherence and continuity.[3] This desire for a stable and unique identity inflected the art of the century and shaped successive communities of artists who were invested in a mission to embody and express "Danishness." In a diminished country with a lingering sense of global importance, the visual arts were enlisted to bring prestige to the nation. During this period, the notion of Danish national identity itself underwent significant changes. In the late eighteenth century, it was associated with the absolutist monarchy, then with the rising middle class in the first half of the nineteenth century, then with the rural laboring classes at mid-century, and finally, at the end of the century, it was associated with the psychological world of an intellectual elite.

Each of the seven chapters of this book offers a single painting as a springboard for the examination of a period or generation in Denmark's art history, followed by a survey of allied works. It is hoped that this framework will elucidate both individual works of art and the broader social and historical issues within which they circulated. The chapters do not proceed strictly chronologically, but are instead organized by theme that corresponds to physical location. Chapter 1, "The Making of a Danish Tradition," frames the study, offering both a pre-history of nineteenth-century practices in Copenhagen and a look backward from the perspective of fin-de-siècle artist Vilhelm Hammershøi. Chapters 2, 3, and 4 examine the years between 1810 and 1850, the period that has been called Denmark's "Golden Age"—bracketed roughly by the Napoleonic Wars and the European-wide political turmoil of 1848. These three chapters explore interlocking and overlapping arenas of artistic production in those years: the Royal Academy in Copenhagen, the Danish community in Rome, and the topography and monuments of Denmark. Chapters 5 and 6, "Skagen and the Modern Breakthrough" and "The Free Exhibition and the Psychological Breakthrough," examine the period between 1850 and 1900, in which Danish artists explored modernity as a theme and an ideal. On the beaches at Skagen (northernmost Jutland) and in new avant-garde institutions in Copenhagen, artists adopted the metaphor of a "breakthrough"—an embrace of modernity—as articulated in the 1870s by the literary critic Georg Brandes. With chapter 7, the book concludes where it began, examining the historically self-conscious work of Vilhelm Hammershøi from the 1880s to World War I.

The paintings of the Golden Age, examined in the first half of the book, represent the materialization of Denmark's desire for stability after the Napoleonic Wars. These works often focused on themes drawn from everyday events and settings, both mirroring and propagating values of and for the emerging Danish middle class. They are often intimate canvases, painted with exceptional precision and an eye toward the capricious. In ambitious Golden Age works, such as Christen Købke's glowing, sentimental view of Frederiksborg Castle, north of Copenhagen (1835; fig. 62), or Christoffer Wilhelm Eckersberg's *'Asow', A Russian Ship of the Line*, (1828; fig. 72), the artists utilized rigorous systems of scientific measure to portray accurately the complex geometry and proportions of cables and masts on ships or the specific masonry and fenestration of the national castle, while at the same time creating heartstoppingly beautiful renderings of the most ephemeral atmospheric effects.

In these years, nationalist intellectuals called for the special analysis of their country's material culture, promoting a kind of internal or domestic Grand Tour. By mid-century, landscape paintings and images of rural labor came to dominate the consciousness of the Danish art world, as artists such as Thomas Lundbye (figs. 75–80) sought increasingly intimate and resonant sites of primal meaning located in myths of the generative earth. Typically bathed in a penetrating light and oriented toward odd, asymmetrical compositions that often provide a kind of hyper-attention to modest details, Golden Age paintings echoed scientific writings about the Danish landscape itself in the 1820s and 1830s. The land was understood to signify the Danish temperament, whose characteristics were sobriety, integrity, and resolve.

Toward the end of the century, as examined in chapters 5, 6, and 7, artists such as P. S. Krøyer (chapter 5) and J. F. Willumsen (chapter 6) began to seek and display greater cosmopolitanism. They engaged in, and made possible for others, international contact, and they endeavored to change Danish painting via an infusion of continental ideas and values. Within their generation, artists such as Vilhelm Hammershøi (chapter 7) began to practice increasingly inwardly turned modes of painting, expressing sensitive and sometimes ironic responses to Danish cultural history and topography. The tensions between individual achievement and a desire to serve a collective national purpose shaped Danish painting throughout.

One of the challenges of writing a survey book is to create a coherent notion of a national school of art while at the same time analyzing the myths and strategies of nation building that helped to form it. It is, of course, not possible to fully separate national traditions, particularly in the nineteenth century with the advent of successively sophisticated tourist conveyances, international exhibition apparatuses, and urban cosmopolitanism. What is at stake in such a study is the examination of national strategies of self-definition rather than a generalized notion of "Danishness" as an organic metaphor.

National identity is itself a question of curiosity in the case of Danish national figures, even those as fundamentally significant as C. W. Eckersberg (the so-called father of Danish painting) who was born in north Germany when it was part of Denmark, and of Johan Christian Dahl who was born in Norway, trained in Denmark, and who relocated to Dresden where he became a close associate of the German painter Caspar David Friedrich. Dahl is included in the canons of both German and Danish art, and he is known as the father of Norwegian landscape painting. The notion of fatherhood itself is an artifact of nationalist desire, identifying the nation and its art as a familial entity. The flexibility of identity is somewhat peculiar to Denmark, given the nation's shifting boundaries in the nineteenth century, but it is repeated in Poland, Finland, France, and other countries whose territories were abrogated by war and treaty. This book therefore surveys the artists, institutions, and achievements of a dispersed country endeavoring toward cohesion—a story of the nineteenth century filtered through another light.

HISTORIOGRAPHY

Danish painting of the nineteenth century is sparsely represented in collections outside Scandinavia and in English-language scholarship. It was, ironically, better known to the English world early in the last century, when the American-Scandinavian Foundation circulated a survey exhibition of Nordic painting to New York, Buffalo, Toledo, Chicago, and Boston in 1912–13. As critic Christian Brinton wrote at the time:

> The art of Denmark approaches more closely that of Holland than any other
> country, and, indeed, the land and its people at many points suggest a gradual
> refinement upon the Dutch, though possessing a combination of dreamy languor,
> delicate sensibility, and genuine good spirits rarely encountered anywhere else in
> the world…. Danish painting is at present … known through the fluid, almost
> monochromatic ambience of [Vilhelm] Hammershøi's interiors, the faithful
> transcriptions of rural scenes by [L. A.] Ring, and the poignant humanity of
> Ejnar Nielsen's austere and sober-toned character studies.[4]

Indeed, Danish painters not only fared well in the French Salons of the late nineteenth century, but they garnered great praise and attention at the international exhibitions of the turn of the century. If they were not exactly household names, at least Peter Severin Krøyer and Vilhelm Hammershøi had international profiles. However, by the mid-twentieth century, Danish painting was largely ignored in survey books and exhibitions, and it was the rare museum exhibition that included it. The last English-language survey book of Danish painting was published in 1976.[5]

All of that began to change in the 1980s, when a series of important exhibitions reintroduced Nordic painting of the late nineteenth century to foreign audiences.[6] The first and most important of these exhibitions was *Northern Light: Realism and Symbolism in Scandinavian Painting 1880–1910*, organized by Kirk Varnedoe. It traveled to the Brooklyn Museum, the Corcoran Gallery in Washington, the Minneapolis Institute of Arts, and the Gothenburg Art Museum.[7] Varnedoe noted social and cultural dynamics operating within the Nordic countries that conditioned a fundamentally different kind of work than that produced in France, then the ne plus ultra of nineteenth-century studies. He noted in particular the complex relationship between Realism (both in terms of style and as a strategy) and Symbolism, offering a revised view of the late nineteenth century. In this way, Varnedoe established a new area of analysis. Several exhibitions following his model were then organized in London, Paris, Stockholm, and Oslo.[8] By the early 1990s, the notion of a pan-Nordic set of formal, aesthetic, and cultural issues shaping local painting became accepted. Michelle Facos, writing about Swedish art, elaborated this research, modeling the important understanding that the arts of the nineteenth century are intermingled with the issues of national self-definition.[9]

An art historian who has consistently incorporated the close study of Danish art into a rich international context is Robert Rosenblum, whose foundational works *Transformations in Eighteenth-Century Art* (1967) and *Modern Art and the Northern Romantic Tradition* (1975) demonstrated the fundamental importance of at least a handful of Danish artists for the international art currents of the nineteenth and twentieth centuries.[10] Further, his co-authored survey volume *Nineteenth Century Art* (1984) and exhibition *1900: Art at the Crossroads* (ca. 2000) have "mainstreamed" Nordic art, folding the geographic margins into a reconceived artistic center.[11]

Several important exhibitions and publications further popularized the production of the Nordic countries in the English-language world. A 1984 exhibition, curated by Roald Nasgaard, entitled *The Mystic North: Symbolist Landscape Painting in Northern Europe and North America, 1890–1940*, at the Art Gallery of Ontario (Toronto), called attention to the significant ways in which Nordic landscape painting, with its emphasis on crystalline light and atmospheric effects, both paralleled and influenced North American landscape painting in the early twentieth century.[12] Neil Kent's two books, *The Triumph of Light in Nature: Nordic Art 1740–1940* (ca. 1987) and *The Soul of the North* (2000) also examine Danish art in dialogue with the arts of its Nordic neighbors. More recently, two important volumes by Torsten Gunnarsson have delved into the formal, philosophical, and cultural politics of Nordic landscape painting—his 1998 *Nordic Landscape Painting in the Nineteenth Century* and the 2006 exhibition catalogue *A Mirror of Nature: Nordic Landscape Painting 1840–1910*.[13] A study of incalculable value is Barbara Miller Lane's *National Romanticism and Modern Architecture in Germany and the Scandinavian Countries*, which analyzes pan-Northern theories and practices of nation building.[14] All of these exhibitions and studies have raised significant new interest in Danish and other Nordic painting.

Danish art as a distinct school has likewise garnered increasing attention through a series of exhibitions (and accompanying catalogues in English) in Los Angeles, London, Washington, D.C., New York, Toronto, and Cambridge, Massachusetts. The painter Vilhelm Hammershøi has also been the subject of several significant monographic exhibitions outside of Denmark, in Washington, D.C., New York, Paris, and Hamburg. In the United States, the collection of Ambassador John L. Loeb Jr. has also raised the critical profile of Danish nineteenth-century painting through its exhibition at the Busch-Reisinger Museum, Harvard University Art Museums in 1994, and at the Bruce Museum of Arts and Sciences in Greenwich, Connecticut, and the Frances Lehman Loeb Art Center at Vassar College in Poughkeepsie, New York, in 2005, and through the publication of Susanne Ludvigsen's scholarly catalogue.[15]

The present volume is indebted to these and other efforts to introduce and analyze Danish painting for an international audience. This book draws on and synthesizes the vast and rich body of Danish scholarship. Because the Danish language is not commonly read or spoken outside of Denmark, much of this crucial scholarship is unavailable to an English audience. The selected bibliography at the back of this volume offers sources in Danish, as well as in English and other languages.

ACKNOWLEDGMENTS

The insights of Michelle Facos and Alice Friedman were fundamental to the development of this book. It is also with immense gratitude that I acknowledge Robert Lubar, Kasper Monrad, Elisabeth Fabritius, Suzanne Ludvigsen, Thor Mednick, Niels Jul Nielsen, Anne Wichstrøm, Øivind Storm-Bjerke, and especially Sam Engelstad for their advice, and Kate Erickson and Jacob Engelstad for research assistance.

Ambassador John L. Loeb Jr. has for many years been a strong advocate for the reception of Danish art in the United States. Offering works from his substantial collection of Danish painting (the largest outside of Scandinavia) for public exhibition, and establishing lectureships and scholarships, he has increased the institutional visibility and public understanding of Danish painting in the United States. I am grateful for his support of this book, and for his generosity and interest in every phase of this project. Last, but by no means least, I thank Mark Magowan for the opportunity to write this book, for his support and insight, and Christopher Sweet for his patience and clarity.

In Another Light
Danish Painting in the Nineteenth Century

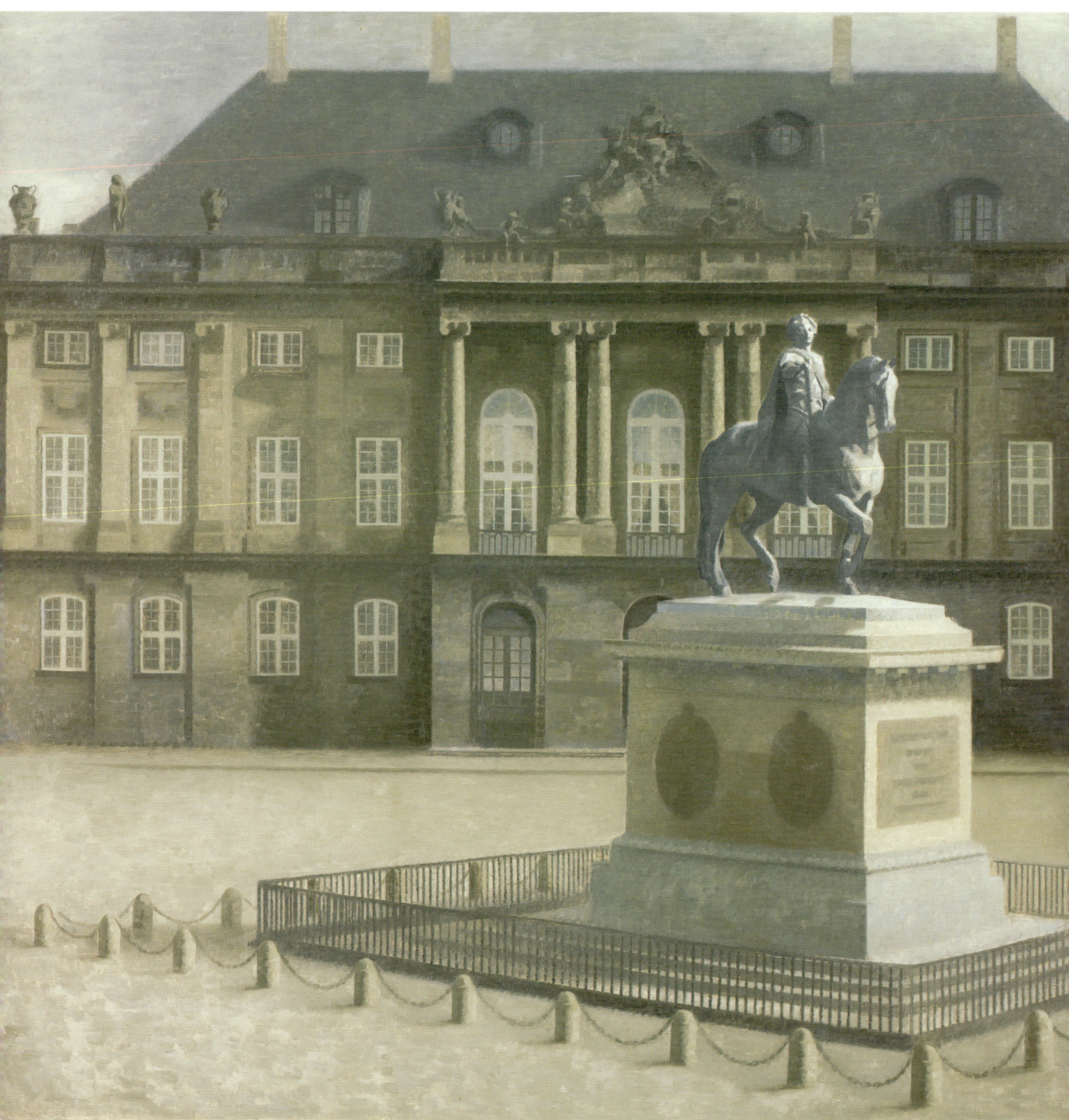

The Making of a Danish Tradition

IN 1896, VILHELM HAMMERSHØI (1864–1916), a founding member of Denmark's new and radical independent artists' organization, *Den Frie Udstilling* (The Independent Exhibition), painted a view of Copenhagen's Amalienborg palace complex (fig. 1). Seemingly veiled in light-infused fog, the palace pavilion and square are drained of local color and empty of activity. A gentle raking light emphasizes the classicizing elements of the façade and especially the massing and details of the equestrian statue, viewed obliquely, to the right. The occluded middle ground and compressed view of the sky invest this vast, open public space in the center of Copenhagen with a curious intimacy. The rigorously tight and neutralized palette and the lack of anecdotal incident, in fact, mark this as an eccentric view of the city, and one that intentionally suppresses any references to modernity. In fact, the muted light and skewed perspective obviate any historicist display, making this a view detached from both past and present.

In the late nineteenth century, Copenhagen was a city undergoing a remarkable transformation. Its changing urban fabric reflected its growth, modernization, and increasingly prominent popular social movements. Yet its skyline, punctuated by the spires of its historic state and religious buildings, spoke of past imperial might. From virtually any point within the central core of Copenhagen (fig. 2), the monuments to empire could be seen: the massive Frederik's Church (the so-called Marble Church, see chapter 4), one of the city's most elegant, and the Amalienborg Palace, alongside the harbor. A complex of four classicizing palaces designed by Royal Academy director Nikolai Eigtved (1701–1754) in the mid-eighteenth century, the Amalienborg was originally built for four noble families under King Frederik V (fig. 3). Two of the palaces were connected by a colonnade and became a royal residence after Christiansborg Palace, the previous royal residence, was destroyed by fire in 1794. Amalienborg was the centerpiece of Frederiksstad, a district of Copenhagen built by King Frederik V to commemorate in 1748 the three-hundredth anniversary of the Oldenburg family's ascent to the

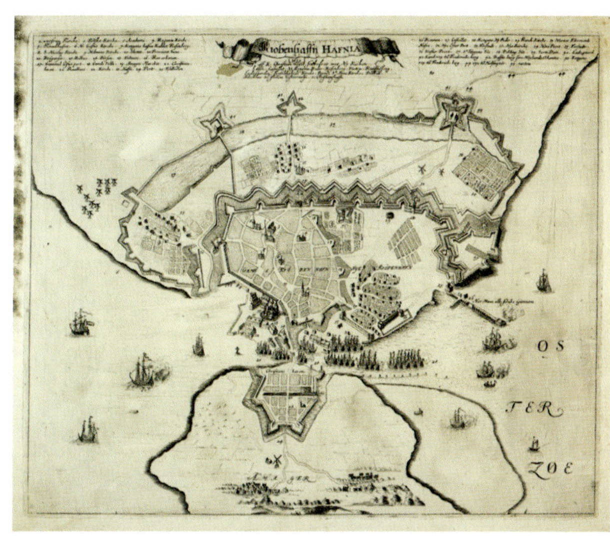

OPPOSITE

1.
Vilhelm Hammershøi
Amalienborg Square, Copenhagen 1896
Oil on canvas, 53¾ x 53¾ in.
(136.5 x 136.5 cm)
Statens Museum for Kunst,
Copenhagen

ABOVE

2.
Map of Copenhagen, as of 1659
Atlas Danicus
Royal Library, Copenhagen

throne of Denmark. One of the driving forces behind the project was Adam Gottlob Moltke (1710–1792), director of the Danish East India Company and one of the most powerful men in Denmark. Moltke commissioned the equestrian statue of Frederick V at the center of the complex by French sculptor Jacques-François-Joseph Saly (1717–1776). The foundation stone for the sculpture was laid in 1760, the centennial of political absolutism in Denmark. With its history embedded in imperial celebration, Amalienborg Square is a deeply resonant historical site, and one that was particularly poignant when Hammershøi chose to render his empty, static view of 1896, a century after it had become a royal residence. In its elegance and seeming abandonment, Hammershøi's *Amalienborg Square* encapsulates the history of the nation, its cultural aspirations, its decline, and its reinvention. It provides a view backwards to the achievements of the eighteenth century and registers the complexity of Denmark's national position. This chapter examines that history, particularly as it was shaped by artists Jens Juel and Nicolai Abildgaard, and as it was much later evoked by Hammershøi.

Located between the North and Baltic Seas, Denmark is small (approximately half the size of Maine) and dispersed across Jutland, the peninsula north of Germany, and over four hundred islands, fewer than one quarter of which are inhabited (fig. 4). A small country on the edge of Europe, Denmark and its culture may be seen today to be peripheral. Yet Denmark arose as a great imperial power in the twelfth century and was for centuries a vast and wealthy nation. In 1397, Denmark entered into the Kalmar Union with Norway and Sweden-Finland (then a political entity) that lasted until Sweden withdrew in 1523. For several centuries following the dissolution of the Kalmar Union, Denmark vied militarily with Sweden for domination within the Baltic region.

Throughout the late Middle Ages, the king of Denmark ruled the Skanian provinces (ceded to Sweden in 1658), Danish Estonia, and the Baltic island of Gotland (in present-day Sweden). The duchies of Schleswig and Holstein, in northern Germany, were also included in this large state, constituting what the historian Knud Jespersen calls an "enormous North Atlantic-Baltic empire, stretching from the North Cape to the River Elbe in the south—a distance just as great as that from the Elbe to Gibraltar."[1] Denmark's kings also held what Jespersen calls a "double position" as Dukes of Holstein. As such, their interests resided both within the Nordic nations and until 1806 to the south, with the Holy Roman Empire.

In 1536, Denmark entered a formal union with Norway and its colonies Iceland, Greenland, and the Faroe Islands. From the seventeenth century, Denmark also held colonial interests in Danish India (Tranquebar) until 1850, the Danish Gold Coast in Africa (roughly corresponding with Ghana) until 1850, and the Danish West Indies (the U.S. Virgin Islands) until 1917 via the Danish East India Company (founded 1616) and the West India Company (established in 1671, purchased by the government in 1754). These were among the wealthiest trading companies in Europe during the late Baroque period. Great wealth was generated by Denmark's natural resources, commodities, ports, and labor within its expanded boundaries. Denmark's strategic position, straddling the Baltic and the North Seas, was for centuries a source of the nation's power. Central to sea routes between the Baltic Sea and the Atlantic Ocean and between the Nordic counties and Central Europe, Denmark benefited from taxes levied in its ports.

Following the Lutheran Reformation, which began in the early sixteenth century, an economic boom spurred the construction of secular buildings and their decoration, largely inspired

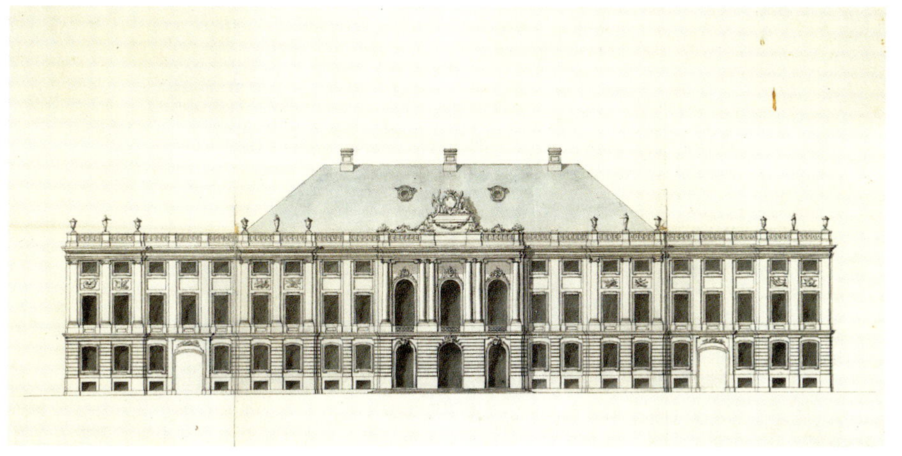

3.
Nicolai Eigtved
Façade of Amalienborg Palace, 1750–54
Kunstakademiets Collection of
Architectural Drawings, Copenhagen

by the art of the Netherlands. The royal castles built by Frederik II at Kronborg (1574–85) and Frederiksborg (begun 1560; fig. 5) represent the culmination of this period. In 1660, Frederik III established absolutism and Denmark was then ruled by a line of absolutist monarchs, who, along with their courts, commissioned ambitious architectural and artistic monuments and institutions as symbols of their political power up through the early nineteenth century. The end of the eighteenth century coincides with the end of this period of prosperity.

The beginning of the nineteenth century ushered in a period of sudden and extreme rupture for Denmark. Twice the British Navy threatened Copenhagen's harbor during the Napoleonic Wars, in 1801 and in 1807. The latter episode, the Second Battle of Copenhagen, was disastrous for Denmark. Over the course of several days of heavy bombardment, Denmark lost most of its merchant fleet, at the time one of the largest in the world, and the British navy commandeered its naval fleet. Over three hundred houses were destroyed by fire, more than a thousand were damaged, and the cathedral and university were burned. (Only twelve years earlier, in June 1795, nearly nine hundred fifty homes were lost to a fire that cut a large swath through the city.) Following the British bombardment of Copenhagen, previously neutral Denmark entered into an alliance with France that proved ruinous. In 1814, Denmark was compelled to cede its partner state Norway to Sweden under the treaty of Kiel, thus removing one of the sources of Denmark's wealth through the loss of Norway's merchant fleet as well as its rich timber and mineral resources, and, indeed, striking a blow to Denmark's sense of itself.[2] In the previous year, Denmark had been forced to declare bankruptcy, a legacy of the war, but also of financial mismanagement on the part of the government.[3]

After a period of national consolidation, Denmark was divided by war between 1848 and 1850, fueled by the dueling nationalisms of Denmark and the increasingly consolidated Germany. In 1849, the absolute monarchy was abolished and a constitution established. Denmark suffered another crushing defeat when it lost its southern provinces of Schleswig and Holstein to Otto von Bismarck's Prussia in 1864. With the loss of those territories, Denmark relinquished approximately one-third of its population. The once expansive absolutist kingdom struggled for its very survival as a nation in the latter part of the nineteenth century.

The very instability of this period gave rise to a consolidated effort in the visual arts to stabilize and magnify a sense of Danish identity. The first half of the nineteenth century has come to be known as Denmark's Golden Age. The very term Golden Age is a product of

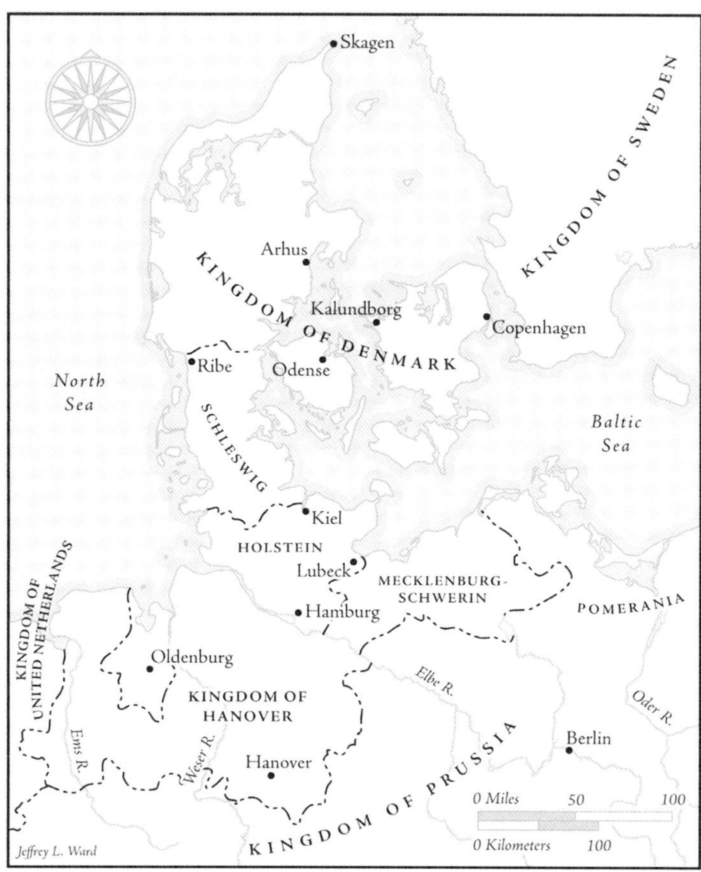

4.
Map of Denmark, ca. 1815

national identity formation. As Philip Conisbee notes, the phrase was applied retrospectively, in 1890, to the period between 1814 and 1848 by the Danish literary critic Valdemar Vedel (1865–1942).[4] Vedel's nostalgia for an ideal age, evoking as it did the Dutch Golden Age of painting as well, established the Danish past, before the revolutions and the national loss of the provinces of Schleswig and Holstein, as the utopian period in the nation's history. Danish artists of the nineteenth century were members of groups committed to this broad-based movement, even the seemingly disengaged Vilhelm Hammershøi.

Hammershøi painted *Amalienborg Square* at the end of this century of cataclysm and reinvention. It is one of the artist's many isolating and deadpan paintings of Denmark's official architecture, and, measuring four-and-a-half-feet square, it is one of his largest. The artist had researched the site and had secured permission to render it from the second-floor level of Levetzau's Palace (one of the four original palace pavilions constituting the Amalienborg), which had been used as the quarters of the Foreign Ministry.[5] A newspaper reported that Hammershøi endeavored "as far as possible to render the beautiful palace in its original and even more beautiful form before the pavilions were made higher."[6] The artist's intention, in a sense, to erase or purify history is further reflected in his decision to omit the complex's lampposts and to suppress all local detail. His is an ambivalent yet nostalgic view, rendering an irretrievable past through the liberties he took with the scale, color, and blurred illumination of the Amalienborg's physical space.

In this painting, the artist employed one of the chief motifs of Golden Age painting—public architecture (see for example Christen Købke's views of Frederiksborg Palace, chapter 4). He also reprised the official and therefore paradigmatic view of the palace published in the catalogue of the 1888 Nordic Exhibition in Copenhagen, a site of national prestige (fig. 6). Yet Hammershøi evokes these public images only to turn them back on themselves. As we shall see, as a painter and collector, Hammershøi looked back with irresolution to the beginning of the nineteenth century as a moment of a remarkable flowering in Danish artistic culture. It was at that time that a group of painters at the Royal Academy of Art in Copenhagen began to establish what became an internally acknowledged Danish School.

The history of the Royal Academy in the eighteenth century provides the backdrop to Danish art education and identity in the nineteenth century. The academy had been founded in 1754 under Frederik V. Prior to this time, the increasingly prominent Danish court had attracted painters from throughout Europe, particularly Netherlandish, Dutch, and German artists, to create portraits and decorative architectural ensembles. With the establishment of absolutism,

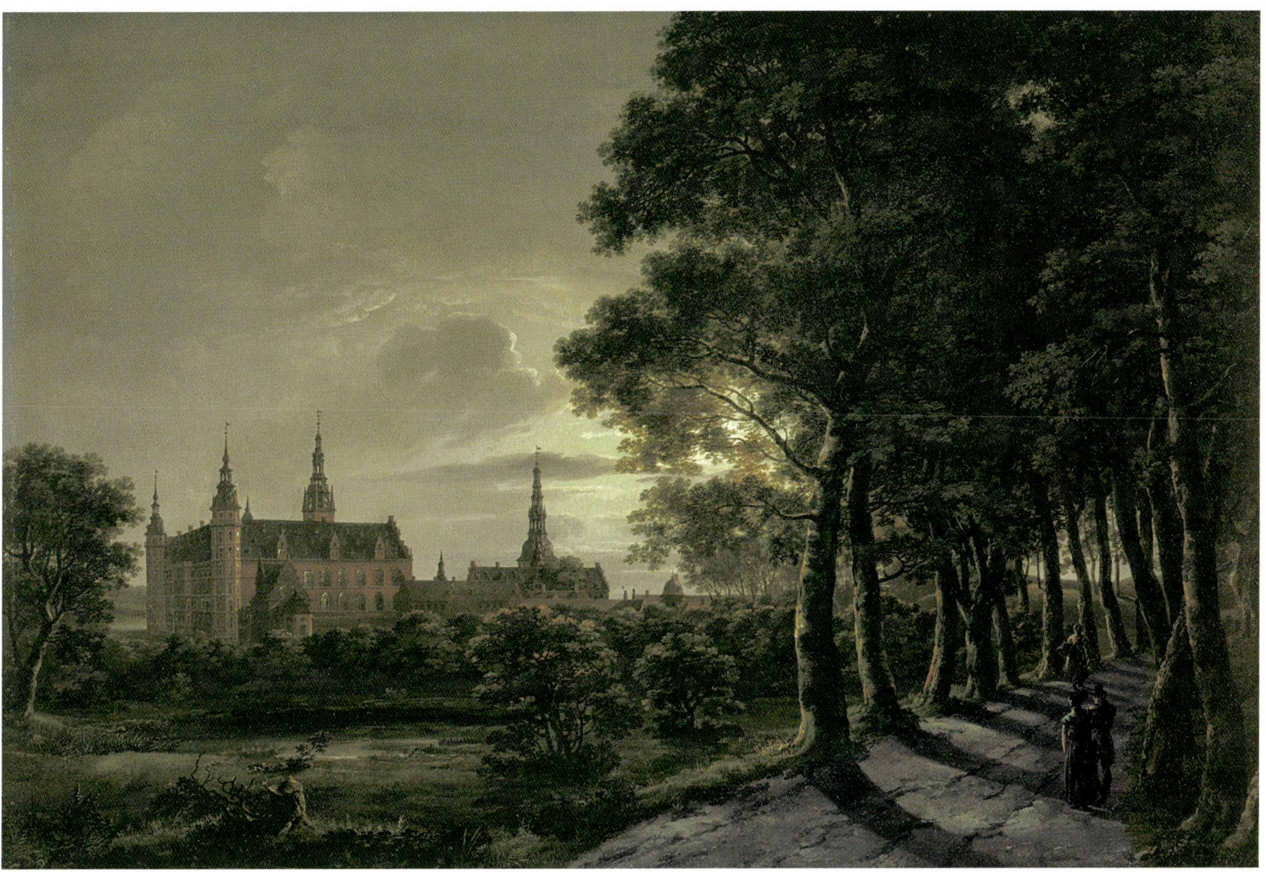

Lambert van Haven (1630–1695) was appointed chief master builder and inspector of pictures and sculpture, establishing the foundation for more centralized control of the arts in the service of the monarchy. Christian VI and Frederik V were particularly active patrons of the arts. In 1751 architect Niels Eigtved organized the Royal Danish Academy of Art. The institution received its charter several years later under Frederik V and moved into the Charlottenborg Palace where it remains to this day. Then called the Royal Danish Painting, Sculpture and Building Academy, the institution was organized along the model of the French Academy (founded 1648) with the purpose of educating artists and craftsmen within these three disciplines under one roof (see chapter 2). The academy represented the only official authority of the arts in Denmark. In the 1750s and 1760s, Adam Gottlieb Moltke, who commissioned the equestrian portrait of Frederik V, was the driving force behind the academy in the service of the absolutist monarchy. Moltke also amassed a large private collection that, in addition to the Royal Academy collection, offered European works for study by emerging Danish artists.

In 1771, during the reign of Christian VII, many foreign artists were effectively excluded from state patronage in an attempt to foster indigenous talent.[7] This reining in of the internationalism of the academy opened the path for local artists to assume new influence both within the institution and throughout the material culture of Denmark. Several artists trained within the academy in the later eighteenth century proved to be exemplary teachers and leaders. These artists laid the foundation for nineteenth-century Danish painting. Initially they produced work exclusively for the court but later they began to solicit the patronage of the bourgeoisie.

5.
Johan Christian Clausen Dahl
Frederiksborg Castle, 1817
Oil on canvas, 21¼ x 31⅛ in.
(54 x 79 cm)
Statens Museum for Kunst,
Copenhagen

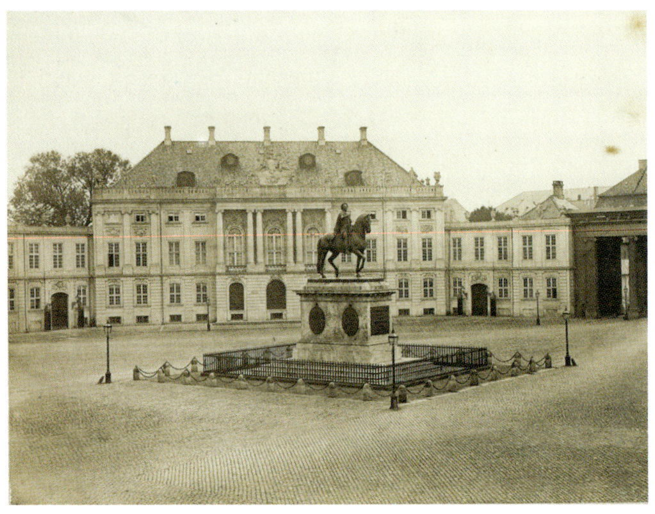

The most influential painters to emerge in the late eighteenth century were Nicolai Abildgaard and Jens Juel, both of whom introduced highly subjective interpretations of subject matter and formal rigor to their work. Jens Juel (1745–1802) was one of Denmark's greatest portraitists and its most prolific. Born into modest circumstances on the island of Funen, he showed such precociousness that his family sent him to Hamburg to study from 1760 to 1765. There he learned the fundamentals of painting from Johann Michael Gehrmann (d. 1770). From 1765 to 1766, he studied at the Royal Academy in Copenhagen, from which he received a "great" Gold Medal in 1771. Although this, the highest academic reward the institution could give, made him eligible for a substantial travel stipend, Juel was unable to travel as the limited funds available had already been committed to Nicolai Abildgaard.

However, Juel received private support from an "anonymous committee," which included Moltke, to travel to Rome.[8] In his letter of thanks to Moltke, he effused, "I shall journey straight to Italy, although this winter I chiefly intend to visit the best galleries in Germany," and promised to "apply all possible diligence in order to show myself worthy of the privilege of being such an extraordinary and fortunate scholar."[9]

Juel intended only to stop briefly in Germany but his trip extended to several years. He remained in Hamburg in the years 1772 to 1773 and in Dresden from 1773 to 1774. He finally arrived in Rome in the autumn of 1775, where, among other contacts, he joined up with Nicolai Abildgaard. There he copied the works of Raphael and, likely, also of Pompeo Batoni (1708–1787), Rome's leading portraitist.[10] Following his time in Rome, Juel traveled to Paris, then an international center for portrait painting and Neoclassical art, where he remained from mid-1776 to early 1777. He then spent nearly three years in Geneva where he met the naturalist and philosopher Charles Bonnet (1720–1793) and where he developed a reputation as a portraitist. Returning to Copenhagen in 1780, he used this cosmopolitan experience to forge a significant new academic manner, and he rapidly became Denmark's leading portrait painter. Juel was unanimously elected as a member of the Royal Danish Academy in 1782 and was appointed court portraitist to Christian VII. He became a professor in 1786 and director of the academy in 1795. His most prominent students were Caspar David Friedrich and Philipp Otto Runge, who were among a group of young north German artists to study in Copenhagen in the 1790s. Both artists later acknowledged their indebtedness to him (see chapter 2).

Juel had, from his early years at the academy, already amassed portrait commissions from among the Danish nobility.[11] His work from this period, as suggested by his self-portrait from around 1767–68 (fig. 7), reflected the softened features and shadowed backgrounds derived from his study in Hamburg. Emphasizing the luminosity of his skin set against the light-absorbing fabric of his scarf and jacket, Juel portrayed himself looking almost directly out toward the viewer. The subtly deflected gaze of his round eyes, however, suggests his self-surveillance in a mirror. Together with his upright posture and fluttering scarf, the cast of his eyes suggests the self-scrutiny of a highly self-conscious artist. The clarity of light, delicacy of color and touch, emphatic sensuality of the lips, and sense of psychological intimacy conveyed by the portrait were the hallmarks of his early Rococo-derived style.

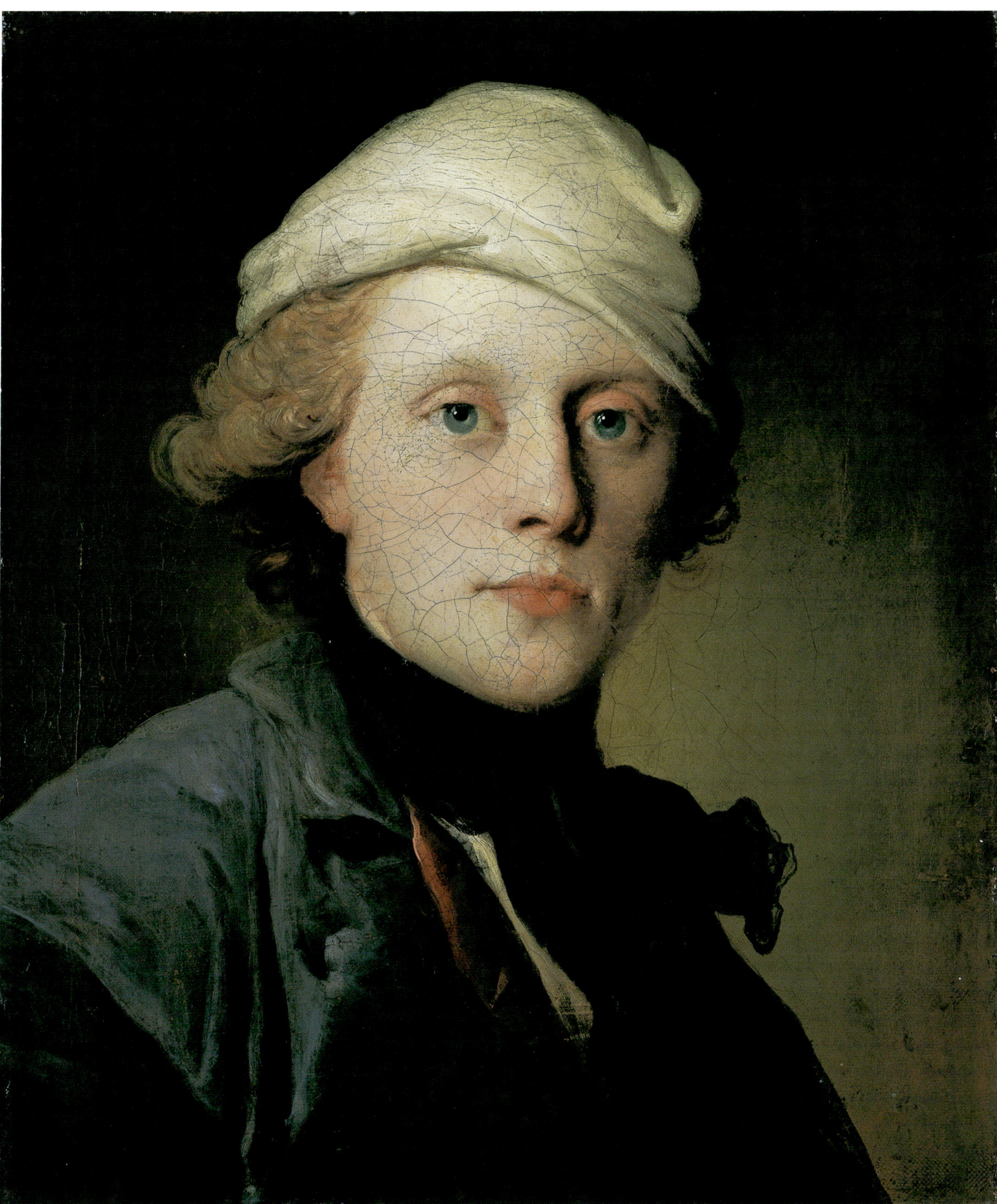

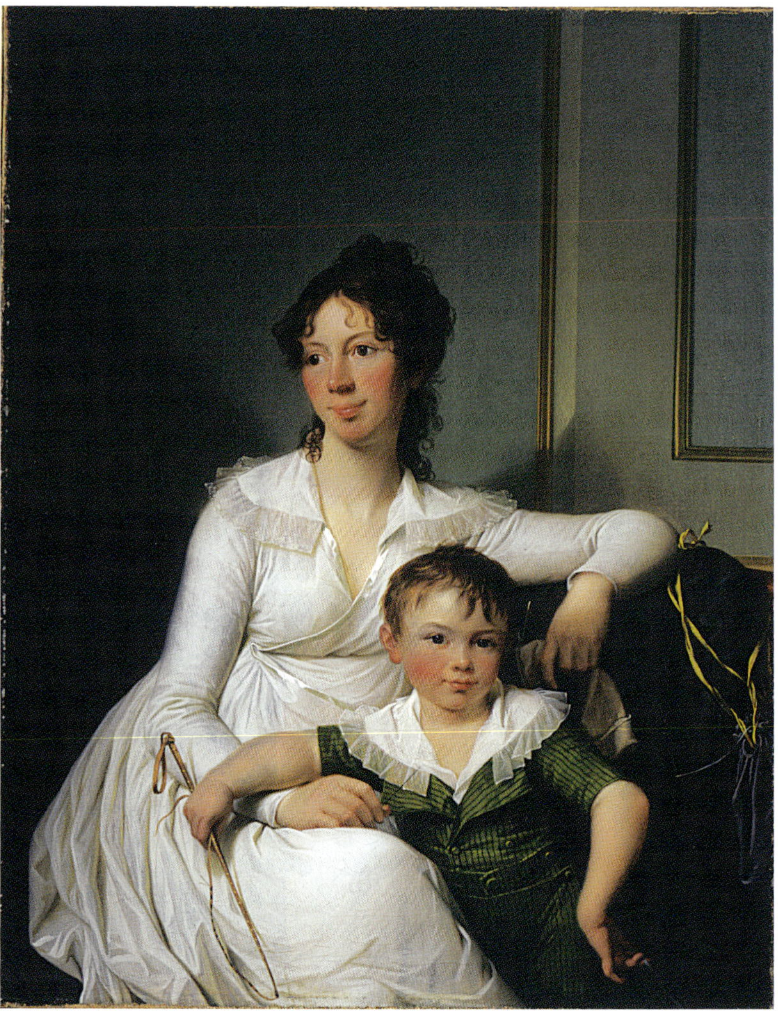

8.
Jens Juel
*Elisabeth Henriette Bruun de Neergaard
(née Baudissin) with her Eldest Son
Henrik*, 1799–1800
Oil on canvas, 25 x 19 in.
(63.5 x 48.5 cm)
Ny Carlsberg Glyptotek, Copenhagen

During his years of travel, Juel had established close connections with some of Europe's leading intellectuals, among them Bonnet and the renowned German poet Gottlieb Klopstock (1724–1803), whom he first met in Hamburg (and who had earlier resided in Copenhagen at Frederik V's invitation). These significant cultural figures in turn made introductions for Juel, helping him to build a wide network of patrons and to establish his reputation in Denmark even before his return in 1780. Art historian Kasper Monrad also notes that it was under the influence of Bonnet's circle of Enlightenment philosophers and scientists that Juel became attentive to the study of nature. Both in his portraiture, in which his sitters are placed in scrupulously observed indoor and outdoor spaces, and in his landscapes, Juel was exceptionally astute at registering light and textural effects. Juel, more importantly, was a keen observer of personality and comportment and he imbued his representations of Danish royalty and nobility with a sense of intimacy and naturalness.

His family portraits also articulated new Enlightenment attitudes toward marriage and child rearing. Juel's portrait *Elisabeth Henriette Brun de Neergaard (née Baudissin, 1777–1864) and Her Eldest Son, Henrik (born 1795)* (1799–1800; fig. 8), representing a young mother and her child, offers a scene of maternal intimacy and protectiveness. Seemingly interrupted from

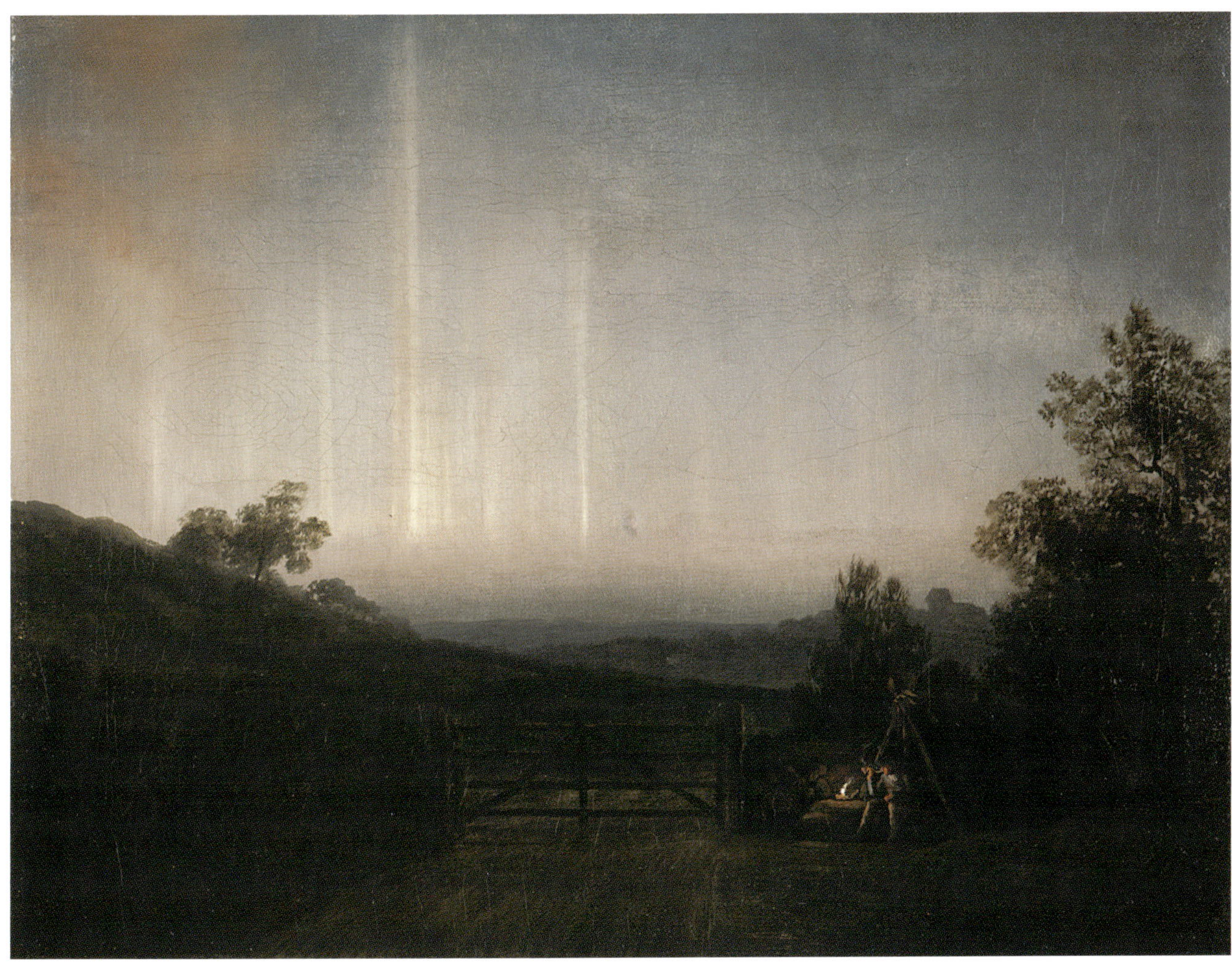

her needlework, the mother, clad in fashionable French Directoire-inspired clothing, serves as a foil for her confident son. The heads of the figures are subtly turned in opposite directions on either side of the central axis of the painting, their arms echo one another in gesture, and the outer flanks of their bodies operate as sides of an acute triangle that converge in the mother's head. In addition to the trajectory of the boy's torso, which exactly corresponds to that of his mother's left leg, these details serve to unify the figures within the framework of the rectilinear pattern of the wall behind them. The bravura surface treatment of lace, silk, velvet, flesh, and hair, all luminously popping out against the darkened background, masks this rigorous geometric orchestration. What is most strongly communicated is the sense of relaxation and comfort shared by the cultivated son and the nurturing mother.

Juel was also noted for his landscape paintings in which he brought the same keen sense of observation to topography and atmospheric effects as he did to human physiognomy and relationships. Juel had begun painting pure landscape compositions "in spare moments and for my own pleasure" in Hamburg, and he was likely encouraged in his interest in classical landscape compositions while living in Rome.[12] But it was in Switzerland that Juel became most strongly engaged in painting the landscape.[13] In this regard, the Swiss naturalist Bonnet's influ-

9.
Jens Juel
Landscape with Aurora Borealis. In the Background Middelfart Church. Attempt to Paint the Aurora Borealis, ca. 1790s
Oil on canvas, 12¼ x 15½ in.
(31.2 x 39.5 cm)
Ny Carlsberg Glyptotek, Copenhagen

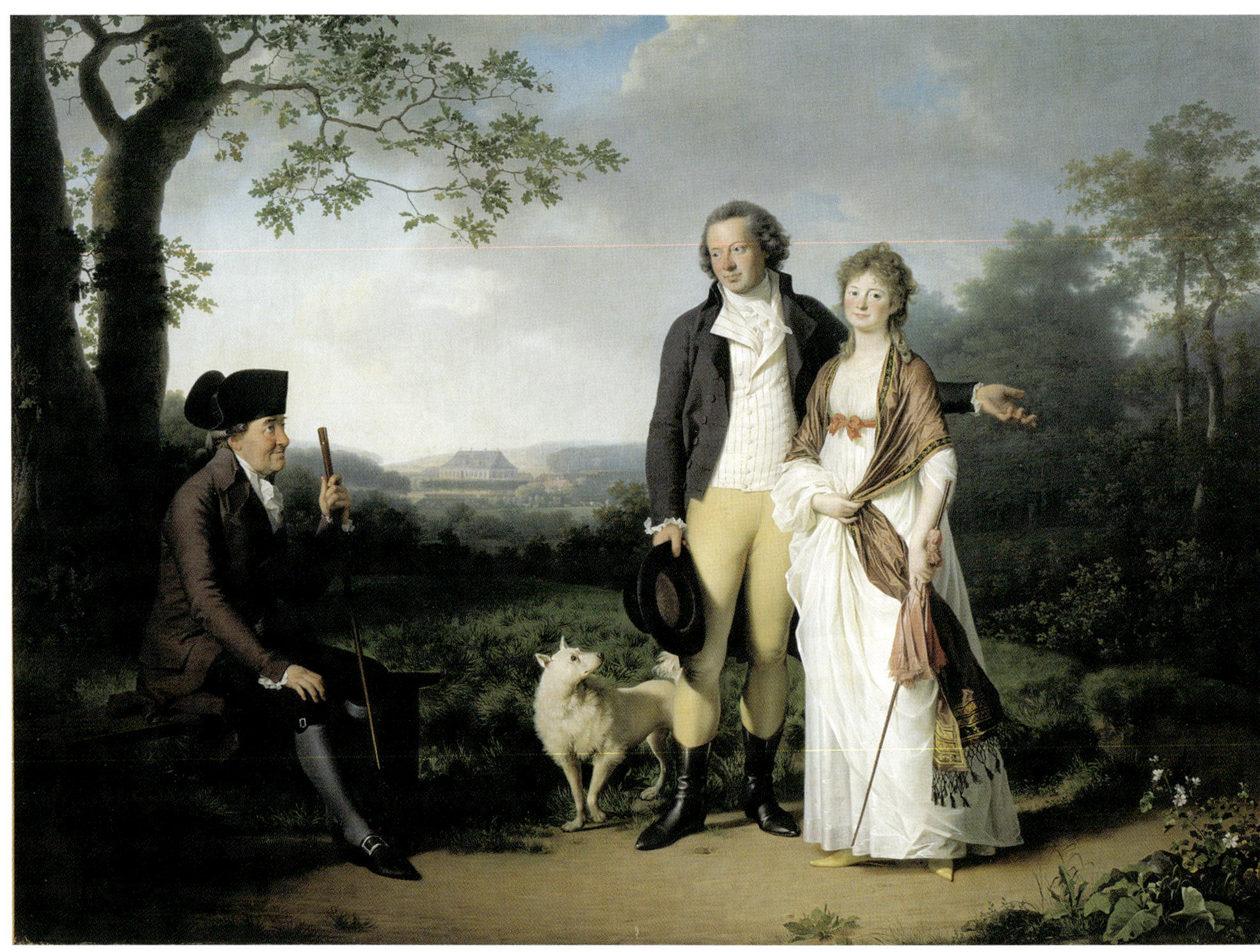

10.
Jens Juel
The Ryberg Family, 1797
Oil on canvas, 99⅝ x 132½ in.
(253 x 336.5 cm)
Statens Museum for Kunst,
Copenhagen

ence on Juel was decisive.[14] From his encounter with Swiss naturalist philosophy as well as his later work as a restorer at the Royal Gallery in close contact with Dutch and other landscape paintings,[15] he created landscape compositions, initiating the genre that would become one of Denmark's greatest pictorial achievements in the nineteenth century.

It was ultimately in landscape painting that Juel's legacy was most strongly felt among artists. His views of Denmark, such as *Landscape with Aurora Borealis. In the Background Middelfart Church. Attempt to Paint the Aurora Borealis* (ca. 1790s; fig. 9), are often marked by an attentiveness to fugitive light and weather conditions, and to an investment of sentiment into the scene by means of a gathering storm, lightning cutting across the sky, or, as here, the northern lights.[16] Sublime and harmonious, such paintings were structured according to Baroque conventions and echoed the works of Jacob van Ruisdael, Peter Paul Rubens, and Meindert Hobbema, which he knew both from his travels and from local collections. At the same time, they were strongly shaped by Juel's own scientific observations and by his strategy of shrouding his foregrounds in shadow so as to emphasize the light, glowing expanse of the sky. Here the low horizon line, dissolving in roseate shadow, emphasizes the spectacular sight of the aurora as witnessed by a solitary property guardian, whose small encampment provides the only lighted area in the foreground. As art historian Joseph Koerner has noted, Juel's meticulous canvases suggested to his student Caspar David Friedrich the possibility that "the sublime

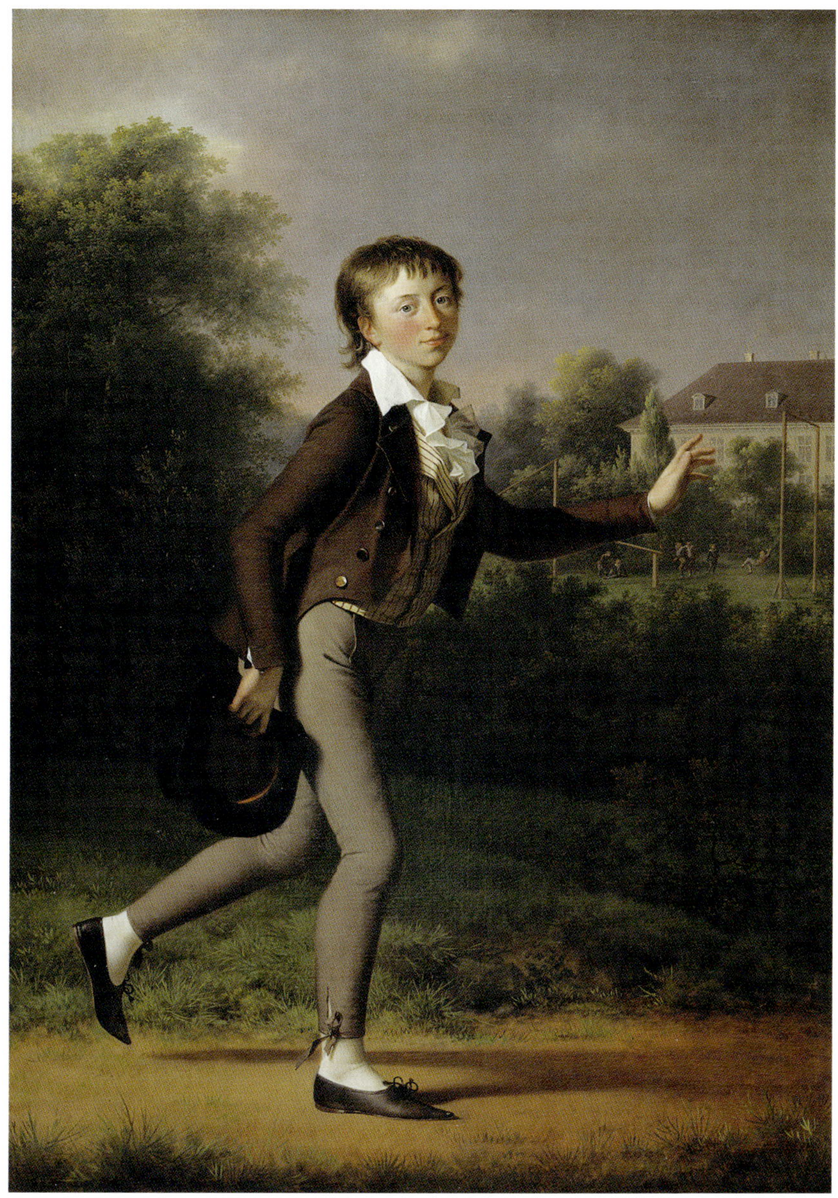

11.
Jens Juel
The Running Boy. Marcus Holst von Schmidten, 1802
Oil on canvas, 71 x 49⅝ in.
(180.5 x 126 cm)
Statens Museum for Kunst,
Copenhagen

can be present in landscapes neither exotic nor Antique, that pathos and sentiment can be expressed without histrionic plots of storms, shipwrecks, avalanches, and erupting volcanoes, and that infinities, everywhere present, must be invoked subjectively, not as attributes of setting or event, but as simply the transformation, through painting, of *how* to see."[17] Such investment of sensibility into recognizable native localities would have enormous resonance with Danish landscape painters of Friedrich's generation.

Landscapes also served as the foil for Juel's portraits, naturalizing both his elite and bourgeois subjects. His ambitious portrait *The Ryberg Family* (1797; fig. 10) is a life-sized work representing the Counselor of State Niels Ryberg resting on a bench near a footpath at Frederiksgave (now Hagenskov), his estate on the island of Funen. Ryberg's son Johan Christian and his daughter-in-law Engelke Charlotte, née Falbe, approach him along the winding

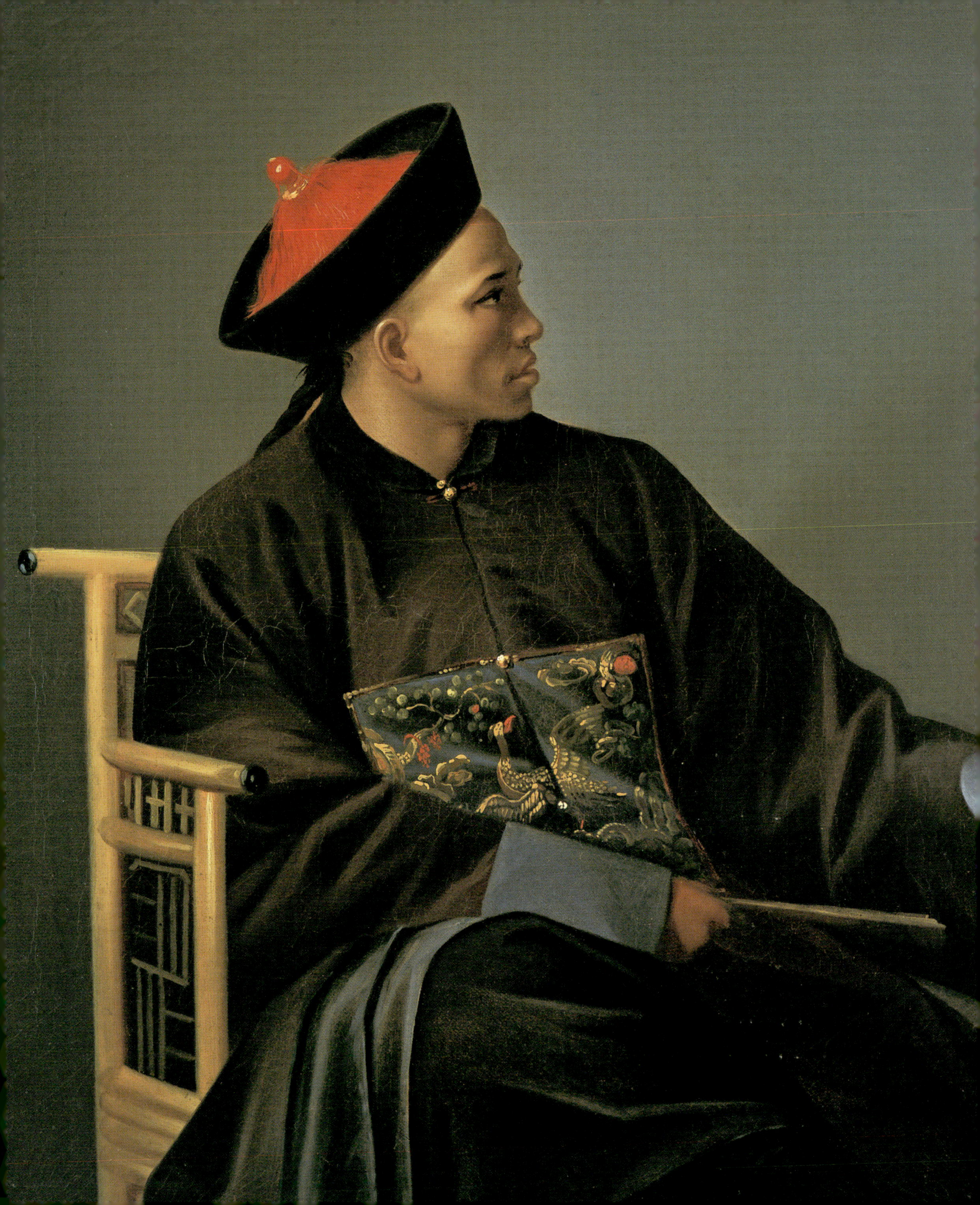

path that cuts diagonally across the immediate foreground. Art historian
Ellen Poulsen describes this painting as a representation of absolute
harmony among the three subjects, the landscape that they inhabit, and
the light. She further notes the elements that will become characteristics of Danish landscape painting of the next generation: the botanical
specificity of the foreground plants in combination with a deeply receding
atmosphere-soaked background. With its affinities to works by Johann
Zoffany and Thomas Gainsborough, this painting seems closely allied
with European aristocratic portraiture of the period as well as the Dutch
prototypes upon which it was based.[18] The sympathetic representation
of his subjects, for which Juel was noted, at his best, animates the aging
features of Counselor Ryberg and the direct gaze of his daughter-in-law.

This painting is also an idealized image of the Danish official
classes as they wished to see themselves at century's end, displaying a
noble earthiness while offering a view of the spectacular manor house.[19] It
is a painting that represents contractual relationships, of property passing
from father to son, and between husband and wife. Its themes of mastery
over the land, material comfort (suggested by the scale and house and
the splendor of Engelke's silks), and *gemütlich* filial relations allude both
to the influence of Jean-Jacques Rousseau's influential writings on nature
and to the idea of the family as the kernel of the nation. A masterwork
of character, sociability, and natural observation, the painting represents
both a depiction of individuals and a portrait of an era.

Another late painting by Juel exploits landscape as a foil for human identity. In the
monumentally scaled *A Running Boy*, painted in 1802, the year of Juel's death, the artist offers
a landscape setting that throws the remarkable action of his subject into relief (fig. 11). The
painting represents Marcus Pauli Holst von Schmidten, a young nobleman, running to school.
The school yard, with pupils at play, can be seen in the background. Ellen Poulsen has suggested that an etching after Gilbert Stuart's *The Skater* (1782, National Gallery of Art, Washington) may have inspired the figure of the boy.[20] The layering of landscape elements in parallel
horizontal bands, from the path in the foreground, to the alternating strips of grass and trees,
creates a stable background against which the boy's body is strongly modeled by an oblique
light. He seems poised between absolute stasis and forward motion, almost, as Poulsen also
suggests, like a figure in a sculptural frieze. Kasper Monrad notes that the children playing in
the background, as well as the action of the subject, reflect Enlightenment attitudes toward
children and their education. The school that is depicted is the Christiani Institute, outside
Copenhagen (now in the Vesterbro District), which pioneered the notion of offering children
the opportunity to engage in open-air exercise, and thus established the first children's play-
ground in Denmark.[21] The boy's long trousers also position him as a modern youth of the
Enlightenment. Such trousers came into vogue after the French revolution, when even members of the aristocracy began to wear long pants in sympathy with new egalitarian principles.

Juel's paintings record the changing ideas of noble Danish life in the late eighteenth century, but they also depict aspects of mercantile life. The fascinating portrait of a *Seated Chinese
Man in Mandarin Dress* (1780s; fig. 12), offers a dignified representation of a non-European
subject and testifies to the internationalism of Copenhagen's commercial trade. Despite Juel's

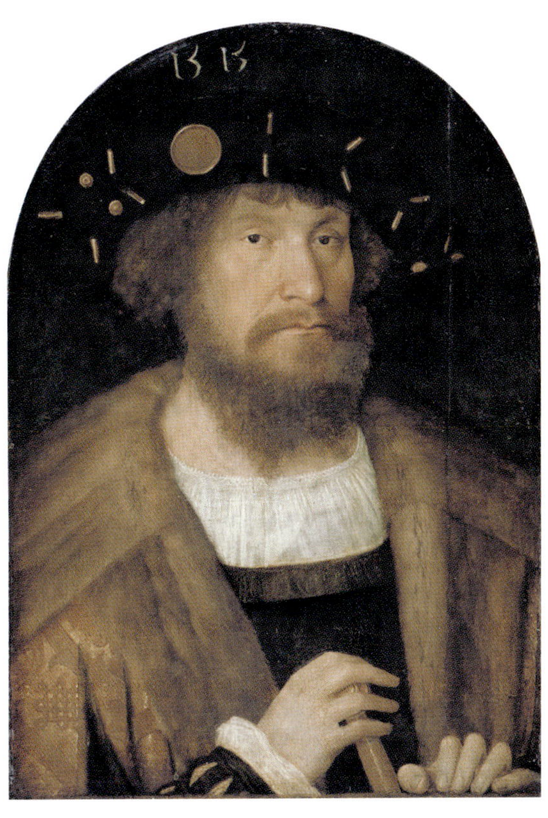

attentiveness to the tactility of brocaded fabric, enameled wood, and silk, the artist also accords the sitter a vivid psychological presence. In another, larger, version of this image, the seated model is seen from a greater distance. On its back is inscribed: "A Chinese second helmsman on a Danish China clipper, which was partly crewed by Chinese. Painted from life (but in Mandarin clothes) by the great portrait painter Jens Juel of Copenhagen."[22] Juel gave the more intimate version of the motif reproduced here to a friend who was an official at the Royal Asiatic Company engaged in the China trade.

Since the middle of the sixteenth century, the Danish monarchy had assumed virtually all patronage of the arts, hiring foreign artists, sometimes of great renown, and portraiture had, of course, been a critical component of that patronage. Michael Sittow's portrait of *Christian II* of 1515 (fig. 13), was the first painting to enter the Royal Art Gallery and is a significant early Danish court portrait.[23] From this Flemish example, Danish kings successively sought court portraitists from abroad, with Christian IV engaging Dutch painters, and then Frederik III, who established absolutism, aligning himself symbolically with the French courts by appointing French artists. The appointment of French sculptor Jacques-François-Joseph Saly (sculptor of the equestrian portrait of Frederik V) as the director of the Royal Danish Academy assured the domination of French artistic taste, enhanced by the Rococo court style of Swedish Carl Gustav Pilo (1711–1793). Juel's intimate, psychologically resonant portrait style, and his subtlety of color and lighting, represented a new court style suggestive of Enlightenment values and articulating the sobriety of a post-Rococo court identity.

Although not well known outside of Denmark, Jens Juel was one of the greatest portraitists of his generation.[24] Noted particularly by his contemporaries for his balance between fidelity and generous idealization, Juel was described in hyperbolic terms: "Never did I see a portrait that did not resemble the person represented," wrote one critic. His colleague, portraitist Hans Hansen, offered even higher praise, "If angels paint, I scarcely think they do it any better."[25] In the over eight hundred works in oil and pastel that have been attributed to him, Juel demonstrated a wide variety of visual and thematic approaches to his subjects, and he left behind an influential and much-emulated body of work. His portraits dominated the Royal Picture Gallery in his and succeeding generations. Juel thus fulfilled King Frederik's desire to enrich his country with native talent.[26] In his late paintings, Juel invested his work with a rigorous classicism, establishing the terms for a bourgeois as well as an aristocratic tradition of portraiture in Denmark.

It was, however, Juel's contemporary, Nicolai Abildgaard (1743–1809), a major figure in European art of the late eighteenth century, who was the leading proponent of Neoclassicism within the academy and the first and foremost history painter in Denmark. A deeply learned man, Abildgaard drew his motifs from classical literature and mythology, and from Norse myths, Shakespeare, and other world literatures, and he developed dramatic and idiosyncratic interpretations of his literary motifs. A frequently commissioned and highly influential architectural painter and designer, he was also critical of absolutism, and he engaged in political critique in his work, even when working on royal commissions.

Abildgaard began his training as a journeyman artist and then enrolled at the academy around 1764, where he won the great Gold Medal three years later. The medal carried with it the academy's top travel grant for six years of study abroad. With it, Abildgaard traveled to Italy in 1772, where he resided principally in Rome. There, he studied first-hand the art of classical antiquity as well as works by Raphael, Michelangelo, and the Carracci. He also

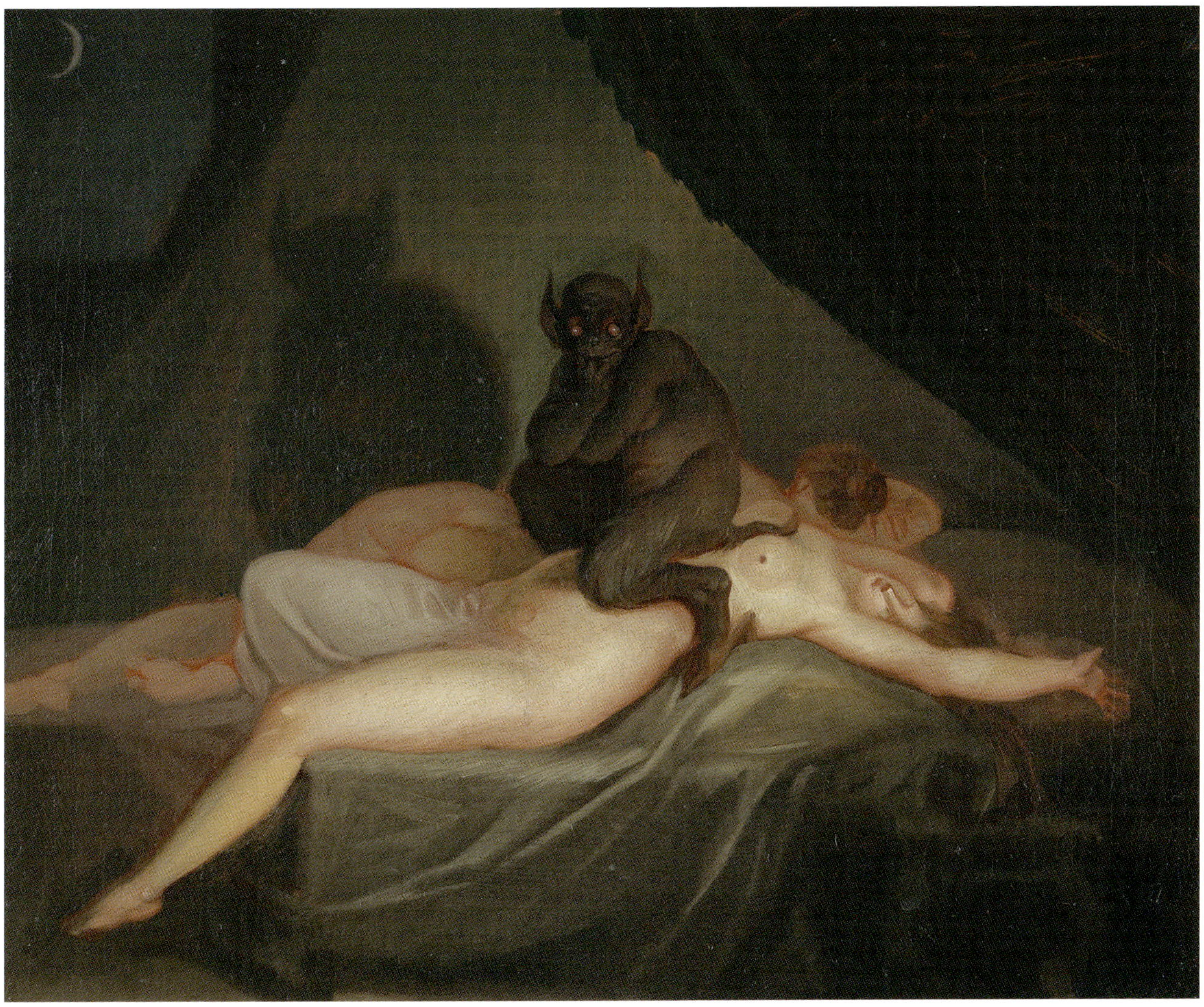

joined an international group of artists, including the Swiss-British painter Henry Fuseli (also
known as Johann Heinrich Füssli, 1741–1825), and the Swedish sculptor Johan Tobias Sergel
(1740–1814), who were engaged in the European-wide Neoclassical movement, replacing
what they regarded as decadent Rococo stylization with a rigorous classicism associated with
republican values. These same artists were also fascinated by the ideas of the Sturm und Drang
movement, the prelude to the German Romantic movement that explored the volatile inner
workings of the mind.

    Fuseli was a particularly influential figure for Abildgaard, and the two artists' work
shared many narrative and painterly characteristics. In fact, in a painting from 1800 (fig. 14),
Abildgaard created a version of Fuseli's acclaimed work, *The Nightmare* (1781, Detroit Institute of Art), justifying Abildgaard's reputation as a painter of the Sublime. In the picture, a
demonic figure crouches on the torso of a sleeping woman, its tail marking the space between
her breasts. Next to the woman's supine semi-nude body lies another woman, seen from
behind. The multiple layers of eroticism and the glowering monster exaggerate the interest in
the irrational that Abildgaard, Fuseli, and their circle had explored in Rome.[27] For a period,

14.
Nicolai Abildgaard
The Nightmare, 1800
Oil on canvas, 13⅞ x 16⅜ in.
(35.3 x 41.7 cm)
Vestsjællands Kunstmuseum, Sorø

this painting hung in the house of the artist and writer Holger Drachmann in Skagen (see chapter 5).[28]

As we shall see, the art collections, architecture, and particularly
the intellectual interchange among expatriate artists and writers in
Rome shaped the vision of Abildgaard's generation and the one that
followed. Abildgaard's years in Rome were marked by political transformation among Europe's liberal intelligentsia. He and his circle encountered the ideas of the European Enlightenment that were questioning
the authority of church and monarchy and investigating all aspects of
individual will and responsibility. Abildgaard's extensive library offers
evidence of the importance of Enlightenment principles to his work, the
depth of his interest in and commitment to literature, and particularly
to the cosmopolitanism of his taste.[29]

Abildgaard's major painting completed in Rome, *The Wounded Philoctetes* (1775 or later; fig. 15), offers an example of his erudition. Indeed,
art historian Patrick Kragelund regards this painting as Abildgaard's
artistic manifesto.[30] Here, Abildgaard reworks the well-known story of
Philoctetes from the play by Sophocles and other sources. The father of
Philoctetes had assisted in the lighting of the funeral pyre of Herakles
and had thus been given the hero's bow, and the son inherited the bow
from his father. Philoctetes embarked with his Greek compatriots to participate in the Trojan War. On the way, however, they abandoned him on
the island of Lemnos after his foot, bitten by a poisonous snake, began
to putrify. Philoctetes remained on Lemnos for ten agonizing years.
Odysseus returned to Lemnos to retrieve the bitter hero after a captured
Trojan seer foretold that the war could not be won without Herakles'
miraculous bow. In the end, Philoctetes helped to overcome the Trojans
and his foot was healed.

Abildgaard represents Philoctetes at a moment of acute horror and
pathos—isolated and abandoned. His heroic body is twisted in pain and
his loose hair is carried outward away from his body. His face, partially
masked by his hunched shoulder, is contorted, his eyes glazed, and his
mouth open as if bellowing. The compression of the body is enhanced
by its scale in relation to the confines of the canvas, and by its light,
heated colors against the shadowy background. Triply imprisoned—by
pain, isolation, and by the canvas itself—his powerfully muscled torso
is exaggerated in its length and torsion, offering the spectacle of a cur-
tailed masculinity. The torso also testifies to Abildgaard's assertion of

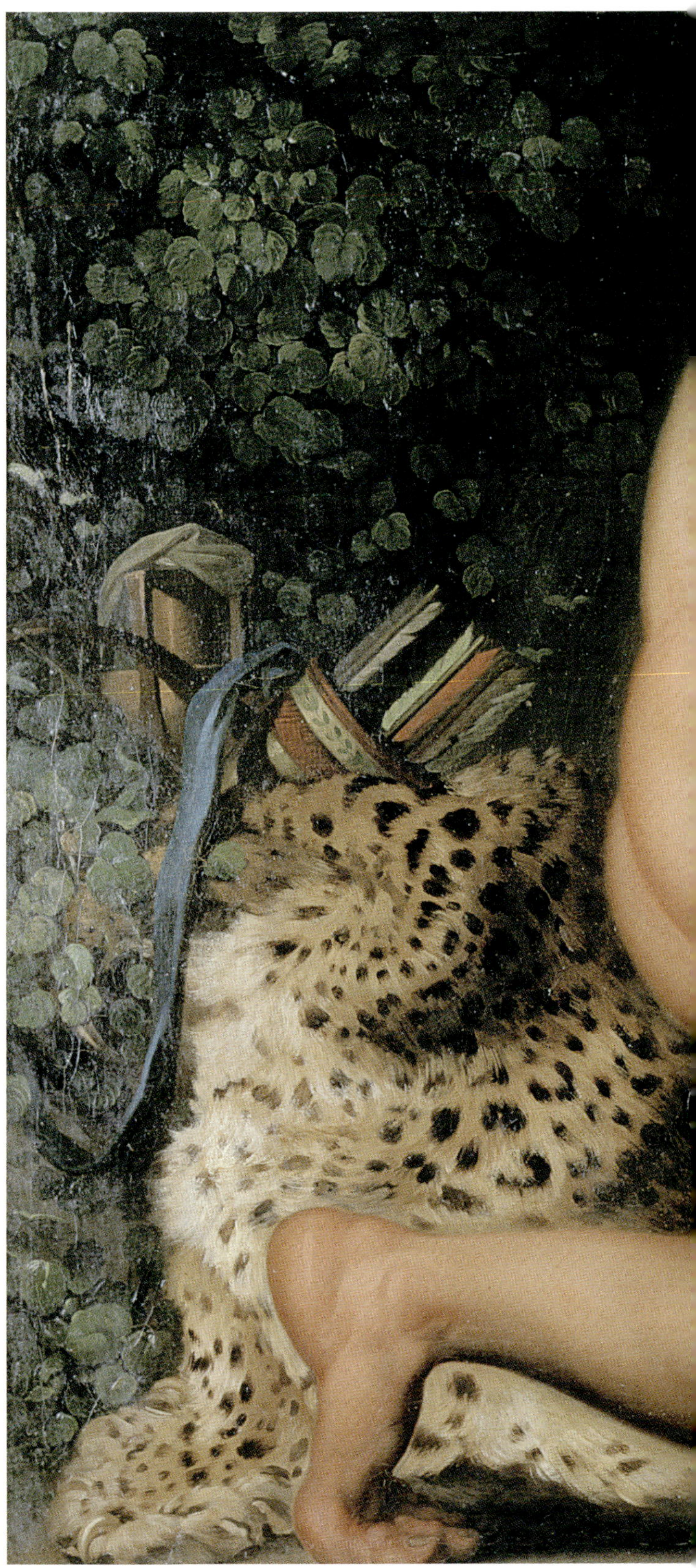

15.
Nicolai Abildgaard
The Wounded Philoctetes, 1775 or later
Oil on canvas, 48½ x 69⅛ in.
(123 x 173.5 cm)
Statens Museum for Kunst, Copenhagen

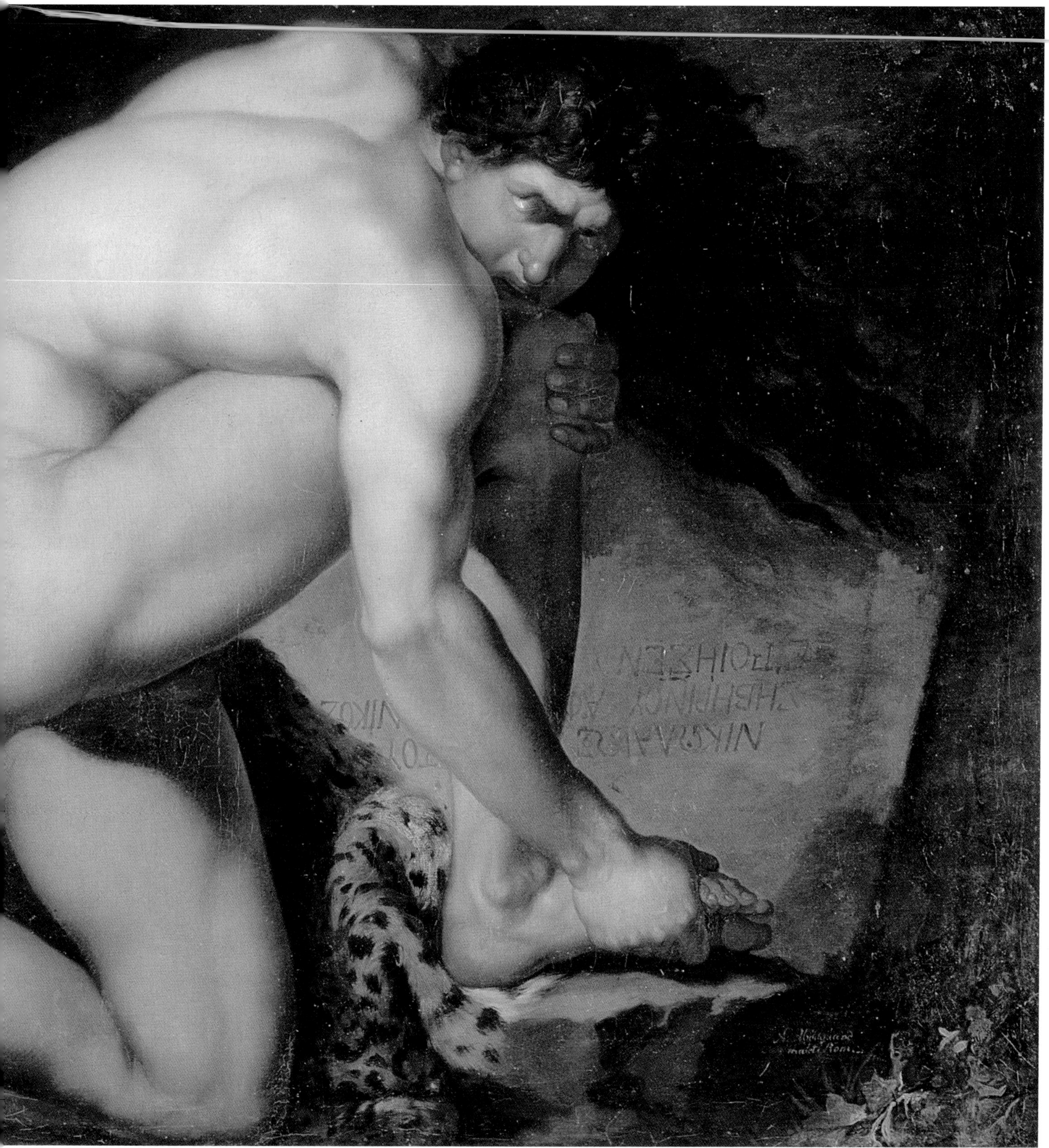

art-historical Roman genealogy, quoting as it does the figures of Michelangelo's *ignudi* on the Sistine Ceiling and particularly the venerated marble fragment, the *Belvedere Torso* (first century B.C.E., Vatican Museums).[31] By inscribing on a stone fragment in the painting the words in Greek: "Nikolai, Søren's son from Copenhagen, painted this,"[32] Abildgaard asserted double filial attachment, to home and to his new identity secured in antique tradition. When he sent the painting to Copenhagen, it was received at the academy as evidence of the artist's sublime imagination and of his philosophical sophistication.

Abildgaard's Philoctetes, the avatar of a terrible agony, offers a radical deviation from many contemporary interpretations of heroic classical stoicism. Its tension between male beauty and physical violence offers an erudite commentary on classical scholarship itself. As his biographers have noted, Abildgaard embodied the charge by German archaeologist and art historian Johann Joachim Winckelmann (1717–1768) that an artist must also be a philosopher and, indeed, he was well versed in Winckelmann's writings.[33] Winckelmann's *Gedanken über die Nachahmung der griechischen Werke in der Malerei und Bildhauerkunst* (1755, *Reflections on the Painting and Sculpture of the Greeks)*, which Henry Fuseli had translated into English in 1765, invoked Greek classicism as a model for contemporary aspiration and defined Greek sculpture as having a "noble simplicity and quiet grandeur." Abildgaard also engaged in the polemics around Winckelmann's work, including Gotthard Lessing's reading of Philoctetes as an avatar of unrestrained suffering.[34] Lessing's assertion of the dramatic grandeur of antiquity, in opposition to its restrained nobility, offered Abildgaard an interpretation of Philoctetes that translated the figure into a theatrically damaged heroism.[35] *The Wounded Philoctetes*, a landmark in European painting of the 1770s that blurred the boundaries between Neoclassicism and Romanticism, offered the Royal Academy a powerful new vision of a native artist and his capacities.

On his return to Copenhagen in 1778, Abildgaard was appointed professor of the Danish Academy, where he served as a temperamental and brilliant teacher and was recognized as Denmark's first important history painter.[36] In addition to directing the academy from 1789 to 1791 and from 1801 to 1809, he was also among its most frequently commissioned architectural painters, creating decorative works for, among other places, the Great Hall of the Christiansborg Palace (1778–1791).[37]

The Christianborg painting cycle, commissioned within a few months of Abildgaard's return from Rome, was the artist's most important project. Christiansborg Palace, the residence of Christian VII, was the center of government and therefore the seat of the absolutist monarchy. Its Great Hall (*Riddersalen*) had been planned as the visual manifestation of royal power. It was said to be the largest hall of its kind in Northern Europe, standing an impressive forty by twenty meters in area and fifteen meters in height.[38] The iconography of the decoration had been predetermined: a national historical homage to the ruling dynasty, the Oldenburgs, who came to power in 1448. Abildgaard produced twenty-five paintings for this dynastic hall and its antechamber. The chief works were ten large panels (a full three meters in height), symbolizing the history of Denmark through the chronological representation of the individual Oldenburg kings.

The paintings were installed in the hall, as art historian Patrick Kragelund notes, as both a chronological and a geographical map of empire, with the central panels allegorizing events taking place in the old royal castle, and the peripheral panels representing events in Denmark's territories.[39] The first of the panels, *Christian I Elevates Holstein to a Duchy in 1474* (fig. 16),

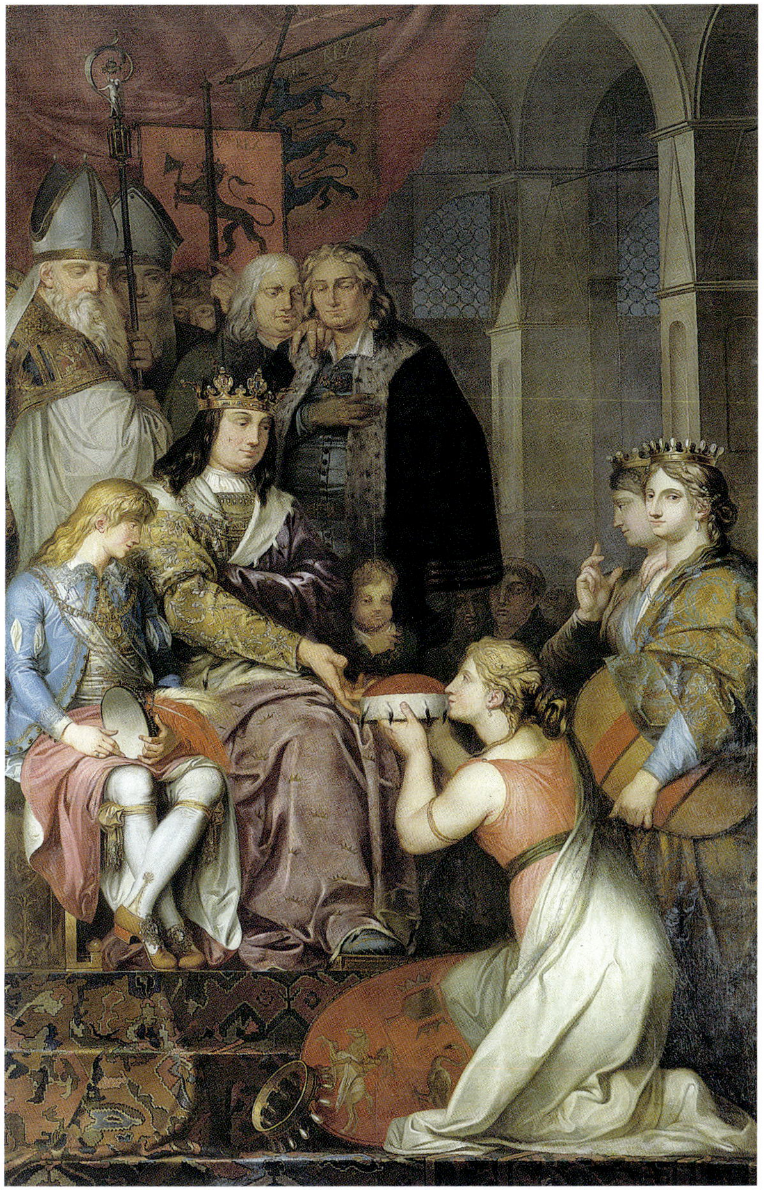

16.
Nicolai Abildgaard
*Christian I Elevates Holstein to a Duchy
in 1474*, 1778–79
Oil on canvas, 121¼ x 77½ in.
(308 x 197 cm)
Statens Museum for Kunst,
Copenhagen

begun by Abildgaard immediately upon receiving the commission in 1778, was formulated
by the king and his advisors.[40] Hearkening back to Baroque conventions and thus supporting
visually the power of the absolutist monarchy, the painting departs markedly from the learned
classicism of Abildgaard's Roman sojourn.[41] Christian I, founder of the Oldenburg dynasty, is
shown seated on a throne, flanked by his sons, the future King Frederik to his left and Prince
Hans to his right, who wears the medallion of the Order of the Elephant. They are clothed
in the most sumptuous satins, brocades, and jewels, suggesting their magisterial wealth.[42]
Holstein, allegorized in the persona of a classically garbed woman, kneels before the king and
receives a ducal crown from him, the old heraldic shield and supplanted crown having fallen to
the floor at her feet. Figures representing the Oldenburg and Delmenhorst lines stand behind
her, and heraldic emblems of Eric VII of Denmark and Haakon V of Norway rise behind the

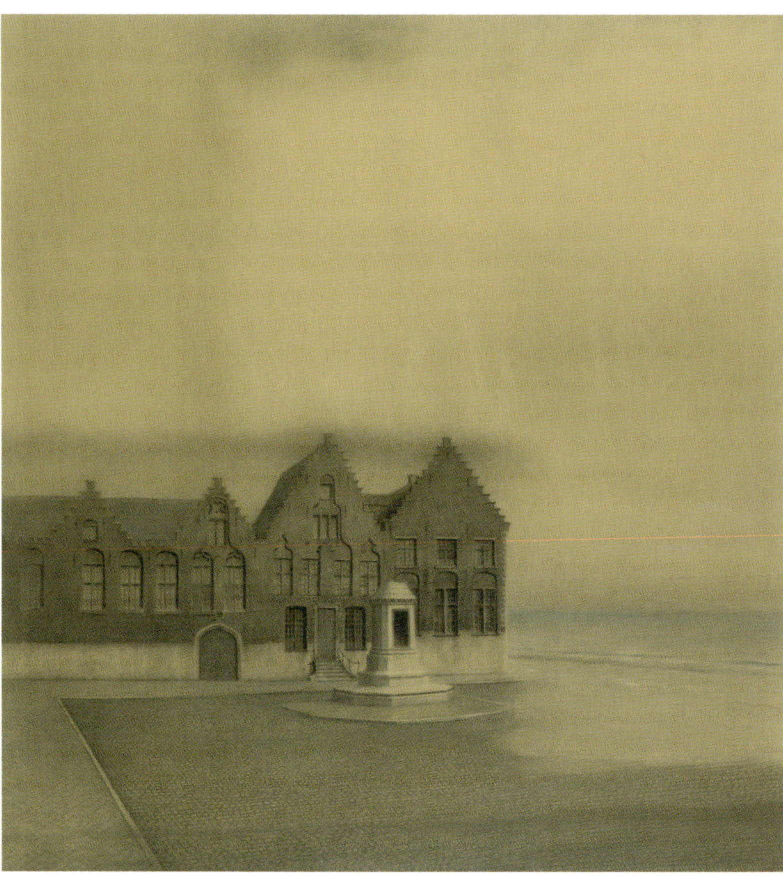

17.
Fernand Khnopff
Abandoned City, 1904
Pastel and crayon on paper mounted
on canvas, 30 x 27⅛ in.
(76 x 69 cm)
Musées royaux des Beaux-Arts
de Belgique, Brussels

king and his advisors. Consolidating the symbols of Norway, Denmark, and the southern territories, and showing the assembly standing on a Persian carpet, itself a token of international
trade, the painting anchors Denmark's history in this one imaginary gesture, securing its genealogy and geography in a massive jewel-toned proclamation of royal origins.

Between 1778 and 1791 Abildgaard produced the ten panels, creating, in effect, a unified
iconography for Denmark's national memory as defined by the monarchy.[43] Art historian Robert
Rosenblum has likened the importance of this cycle to Benjamin West's scenes from British history for the King's Audience Hall at Windsor Castle (1786–1789).[44] However, in 1791, the king
suspended the commission, to Abildgaard's enormous frustration. Then, to make matters worse,
on 26 February 1794, the palace was destroyed by fire. Contemporary witnesses reported the
"awesomely beautiful drama" of the blaze,[45] and the aftermath was described in words that may
be seen in retrospect as premonitory of Denmark's fate in the following decades: "Copenhagen no
longer boasts its proud Christiansborg Palace, whose tremendous dimensions and lavish interior
filled every beholder with amazement. The building, whose rock-solid foundations and sturdy
expanses of brickwork appeared to defy the ravages of time, is no more. It went up in smoke in
fewer hours than it had taken years to build it."[46] Abildgaard is said to have watched the conflagration, lamenting, "My name is going up in flames."[47]

Three of the ten monumental paintings were rescued from the great fire; the other seven
paintings can only be known from oil sketches (Statens Museum for Kunst). The destruction

of this ambitious monument to the monarchy, and of the grandiose palace that framed it, bracketed the expansive eighteenth century. With the Fire of Copenhagen following this conflagration by only two years, and the British assaults on the harbor only a few years after that, in 1801 and 1807, Copenhagen became a city of displacement and rebuilding. Despite the loss of these paintings, Abildgaard's influential Neoclassical work in painting and the functional arts, carried on by his students and colleagues, became the new visual vocabulary for the city as it was rebuilt after the fires.

Abildgaard's literary interests and ambitions were not satisfied by the imperial narrative of the Christiansborg paintings, nor did it appeal to his republican sympathies.[48] Consequently, while working on this royal commission, he also painted private compositions, often dramatic and violent scenes drawn from Shakespeare, Voltaire, Homer, and James MacPherson's Ossian. These works are filled with visual puns and complex literary conceits. He also raised funds and designed and created relief sculptures for the *Freedom Monument* (*Frihedsstøtten*, 1797) in 1791, a sculptural work that celebrated the land reforms of the monarchy under Frederik VI. This was the first monument in Denmark to be created on the initiative of a public body independent of the monarchy, expressing its idea of an enlightened society.[49] In the later 1790s, Abildgaard devoted himself to interior decoration, principally at the Amalienborg Palace, where the young Bertel Thorvaldsen was his assistant (see chapter 3). At his death in 1809, Abildgaard was an institution in Denmark, a native son who, along with Juel, had replaced the previously foreign professoriate at the Royal Academy. Their very internationalism, drawing upon the European-wide Neoclassical movement as well as new Romantic theories of nature and of human emotion, were seen in their own day as the genesis of a national school of art.

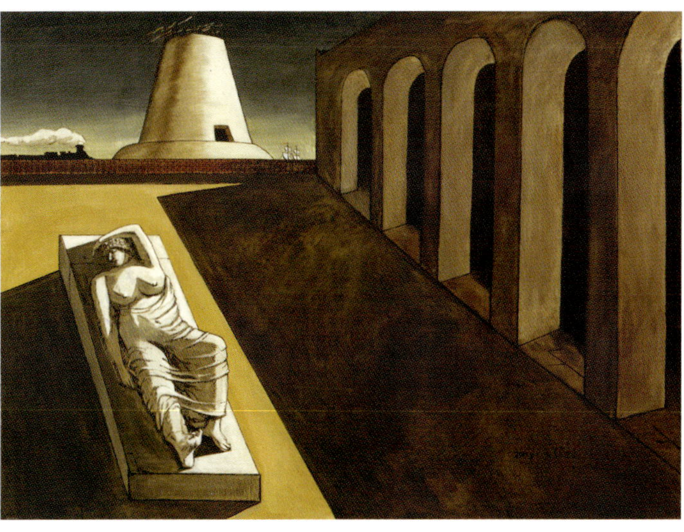

18.
Giorgio de Chirico
Ariadne, 1913
Oil and graphite on canvas, 53⅜ x 71 in.
(135.6 x 180.3 cm)
The Metropolitan Museum of Art, New York
Bequest of Florence M. Schoenborn, 1995

When, nearly nine decades later, Hammershøi painted *Amalienborg Square* (fig. 1), he rendered silent witness to the wavering state of Danish prestige. His painting, close in sensibility to Belgian painter Fernand Khnopff's (1858–1921) quiescent views of a faded, dusky Bruges (fig. 17) and presaging Italian Giorgio de Chirico's (1888–1978) vitiated, uncanny cityscapes (fig. 18), re-imagines Copenhagen, the monarchy, and Danish history. A site of the royal residence, a showplace for the Royal East India Company, the nexus of a dynamic Baroque Copenhagen, and the site of Abildgaard's later achievements, Amalienborg Square as a physical place is a palimpsest of Danish history and heritage. Hammershøi's mysterious, modern, antiquarian view of the site compressed a century of Denmark's complex political and cultural transformation and its artistic legacy.

In its eccentric cropping and rigorously controlled forms, and most particularly in its assertion of light as an agent of meaning, Hammershøi's *Amalienborg Square* embodies and critiques the achievement of the generation of Danish artists—that of Christoffer Wilhelm Eckersberg and his students—that made an indelible impact on the Royal Academy around 1820 and ushered in Denmark's Golden Age.

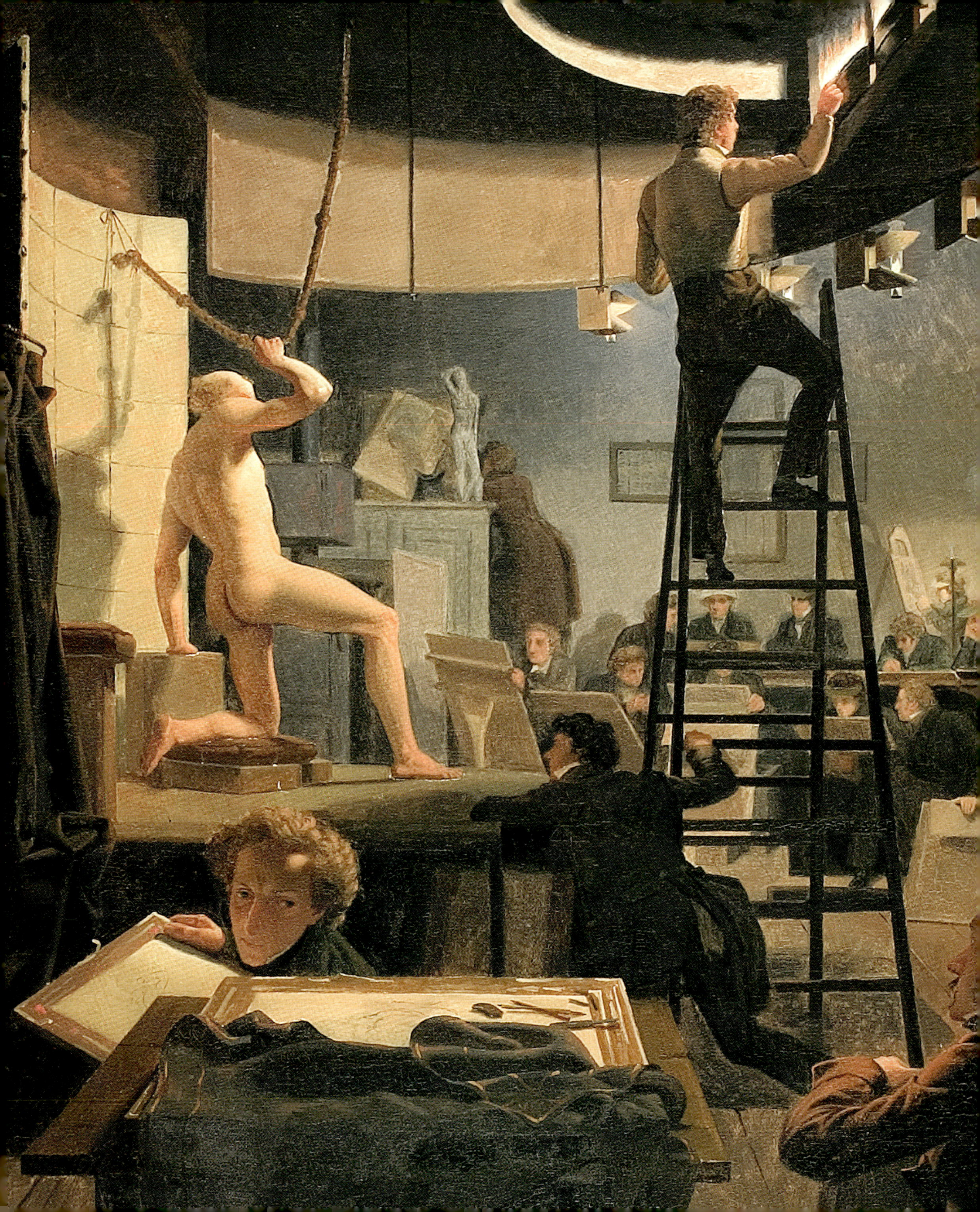

2

The Royal Academy
in the Golden Age

IN 1826, SEVENTY YEARS BEFORE HAMMERSHØI PAINTED *Amalienborg Square*, Wilhelm Bendz (1804–1832) helped to establish a new theme in Danish painting: the representation of artists at work. *Life Class at the Royal Academy of Fine Arts, Copenhagen* (fig. 19) records one of the chief pedagogical disciplines of the academy—figure drawing, the process that enabled students to learn anatomy and internalize classical rhetoric. By drawing the live figure, students prepared for their emergence as practitioners of history painting—that is, scenes from classical mythology, the Bible, and grand historic events, ancient to contemporary— the most elevated of the academic genres. As Bendz illustrates, a male model, located on a raised platform, has been instructed by a professor to assume a heroic posture suitable for historical or mythological narratives, while the students, seated in a semi-circle, observe and "copy." The session takes place in the evening under artificial illumination, which was favored in academic practice for providing consistent lighting and abstracting the model's naked body. Both of these conditions suggested stability and timelessness—desirable goals in rendering the model. Bendz included in the painting such details as the plaster écorché figure by Danish sculptor Andreas Weidenhaupt (1772), in the left background, used as a reference in the study of ideal anatomy.

The painting also suggests the social and ideological dynamics of this pedagogical exercise, alluding to the generation of students, including Bendz (looking over his shoulder in the lower left corner), who increasingly favored the direct observation of everyday life over the classical curriculum. Life sessions such as this were founded on a built-in fiction that is emphasized here by Bendz: the model kneels on a cushion to relieve the tension in his bent left leg; his left arm is braced by a wooden stand and his right by a knotted rope, suspended from the ceiling and the back wall of the stage. The students' drawings, attached to their individual boards, reveal the routine omission of the setting of the figure and reflect the students' training to turn studio props and supports into accoutrements as would befit an antique warrior. Art historian Kasper Monrad has noted that Bendz's painting also alludes to the students' growing disregard of academic bombast: the figure of the servant who stands on the ladder, adjusting the lighting, assumes a more relaxed, natural posture

19.
Wilhelm Bendz,
*Life Class at the Royal Academy of Fine
Arts, Copenhagen*, 1826
(detail)

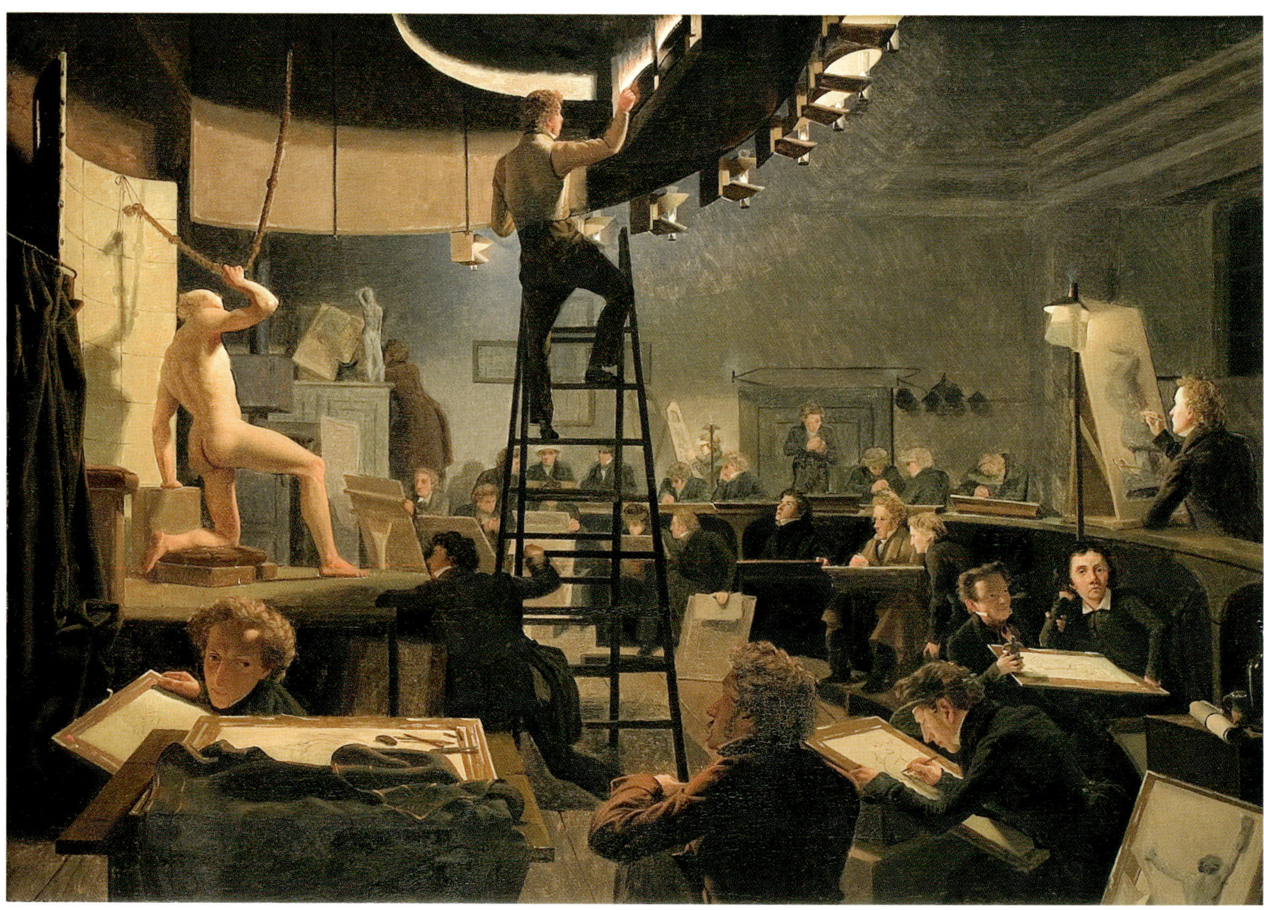

19.
Wilhelm Bendz,
Life Class at the Royal Academy of Fine Arts, Copenhagen, 1826
Oil on canvas, 22¾ x 32½ in.
(57.7 x 82.5 cm)
Statens Museum for Kunst, Copenhagen

than that of the model, but one that nonetheless mirrors its dynamics. At least one of the students seems more intent upon observing this clothed man—from "life"—than the pedagogically determined motif on the stage.[1]

This was a decisive generation at the academy, the one that turned away from the grand tradition—from the elevated, literary subjects of the past that were associated with imperial culture and foreign influence—and which instead embraced tranquil scenes from everyday life to define a new, more "authentic" Danish art. For these artists, scenes representing labor and domesticity symbolized the new Denmark, an increasingly bourgeois country in the post-Napoleonic years. These scenes, in contrast to the timeless idealism of academic classicism, also suggested change, growth, and an attachment to nature.

In fact, the tension between the classical tradition, with its aspirations to history painting, and a growing attachment to quotidian life, to genre painting, marked the culture of the academy during Denmark's Golden Age.[2] In 1818, Christoffer Wilhelm Eckersberg was appointed professor. In the 1820s, he and history painter Johan Ludwig Lund (1777–1867) began to introduce the depiction of people and objects seen in nature within academic study, encouraging students to paint what was familiar to them, rather than distant literary themes and inventions. The basis of Eckersberg's theories and pedagogy was what he called "the fundamental image," a coalescence of Platonic form with transient material reality existing before the artist's eye. He wrote, "The real value of every work of art is for the most part based upon an exact accordance between Form and the Essential Image, and the 'Idea' lets itself not only be united with the external and true shape of the object, but furthermore it would appear that this shape is a necessity in order that the 'Idea' is enhanced and clarified . . . Therefore, let us with assiduity scrutinize Nature's Great Book, let us endeavor to eradicate all kinds of prejudice and seek out the nearest path to the goal—namely Truth!"[3] His innovations—the replacement of stable, idealizing artificial light with the more unstable and sharp characteristics of daylight and the study of color and texture in a living scene—animated the classical tradition with a new naturalism.

His students, who included Bendz, Christen Købke, Constantin Hansen, and Conrad Blunck, developed and extended these ways of seeing throughout the next decades. Bendz, who died at the age of 28, entered the academy in 1820, and took private lessons from Eckersberg in 1822. The two artists became particularly close in 1827 although a notation in Eckersberg's diary suggests that Bendz had lost contact for several intervening years.[4] Bendz's *Life Class at the Royal Academy of Fine Arts*, representing the first generation of students to develop Eckersberg's values and strategies, crystallizes some of the tensions and aspirations of the period.

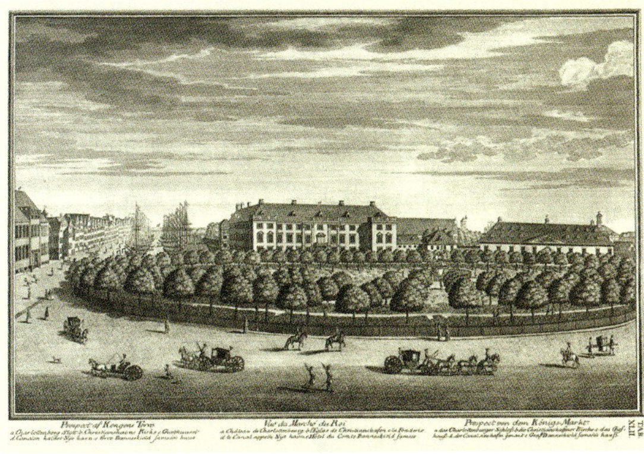

20.
Evert Janssen
Charlottenborg, Copenhagen, 1672–1677, 1683
Thurah, *Den Danske Vitruvius*, Vol. 1, plate 42
Danish National Art Library, Copenhagen

After several attempts to found a state academy of art in the early seventeenth century,[5] "The Royal Danish Painting, Sculpture, and Architecture Academy in Copenhagen" received its charter in 1754, the first of such academies to be established in Northern Europe. It drew students from around the Nordic nations and from northern Germany, including such eventual luminaries as the Romantic painters Caspar David Friedrich and Philipp Otto Runge. The second half of the eighteenth century was, as chronicled by Nikolaus Pevsner, the "age of the academy," with state academies founded throughout Europe based on the French and Italian models.[6] Coinciding with the revival of classicism and the assertion of monarchic power throughout Europe, art academies functioned as statements of imperial authority as well as serving the practical need to train court artists.[7] According to its charter, Frederik V's Danish Academy was founded "to bring the useful and the fine arts into great efflorescence . . . for the betterment of our Realm and Land."[8] Through its painting and sculpture competitions, elevated themes that mirrored national ideals were continually represented by its artists.

The academy's well-being was allied to that of the monarchy and the nation. In addition to having an artist-director, the academy had a *praeses* (protector), a position first awarded to Frederik V's influential advisor, Count Adam von Moltke.[9] In its first significant iteration, the academy was a cosmopolitan, French-inflected, institution. The architect Niels Eigtved (1701–1754), who helped to shape the academy, was the first to assume the role of director. Upon Eigtved's death in June 1754, Frederik V appointed the French sculptor Jacques-François-Joseph Saly (1717–1776), who was already at work on the king's equestrian monument, replacing Eigtved's Rococo-inspired vision with a mode of French art that better embodied the new absolutist regime. Saly staffed the academy with French artists, and founded the academy's library and plaster cast collection. He also specifically modeled the curriculum after that of the Académie Royale de Peinture et de Sculpture in Paris. After the death of Frederik V in 1766, the academy underwent a radical change under Christian VII when his physician, Johann Frie-

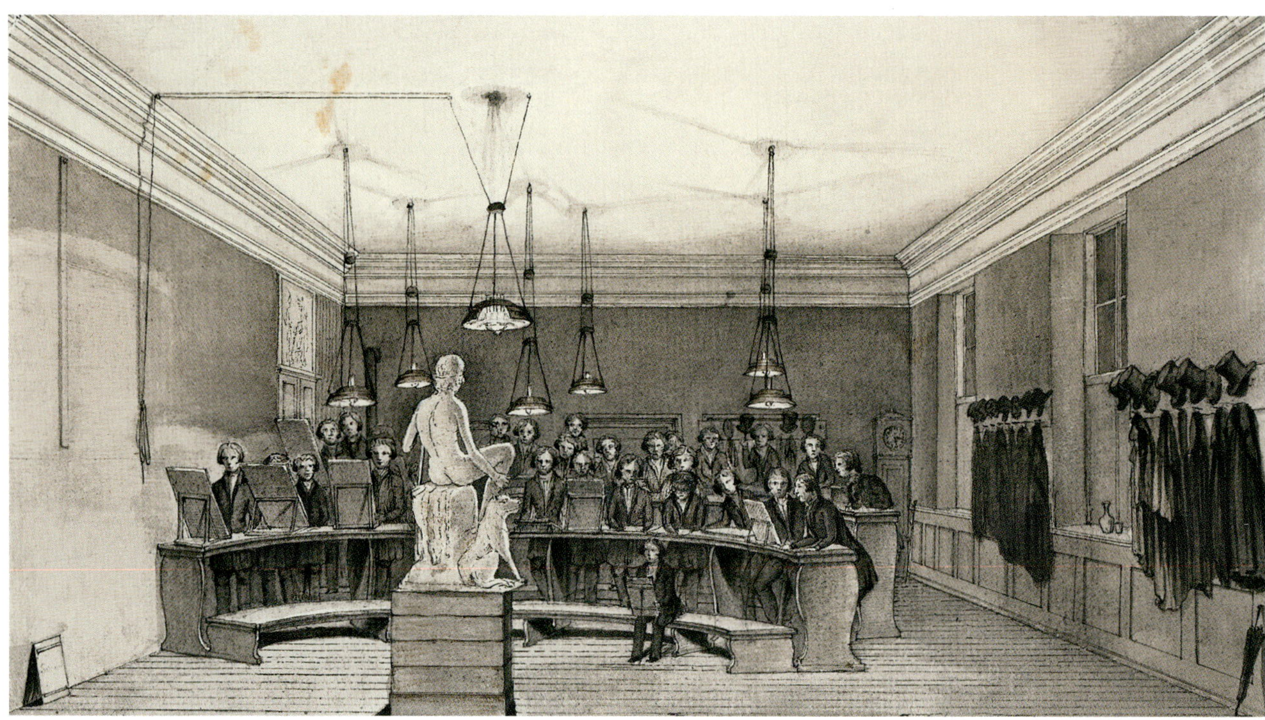

drich Struensee (1737–1772), asserted control over the monarchy. Struensee cleared the court of many of its French members, replacing them with Germans. Saly was dismissed in 1771, and new regulations were established for the academy, ushering in a period of relative isolation. It was also given a new name, emphasizing its centralized location: Painting, Sculpture, and Architecture Academy at Charlottenborg Palace in Copenhagen.

For eight non-consecutive years between 1772 and 1802, the Danish neoclassical sculptor Johannes Wiedewelt (1731–1802) served as the academy's director, amassing a Danish and German professoriate. Wiedewelt, who had been a protégé of Winckelmann's in Rome and had published a treatise based on Winckelmann's theories,[11] was a critical force in anchoring the pedagogy and practice of the academy in a rigorous classicism. This was the era of Juel and Abildgaard, the period of the academy's greatest prestige. By 1784, 138 students were enrolled in the beginning classes,[12] and by the late 1780s, the academy occupied all of the Charlottenborg Palace, with facilities that were, according to one foreign visitor, superior to those at the Louvre.[13]

The Charlottenborg Palace, home of the academy since 1753 (fig. 20), was the center of all art activities. There, artists were trained, competed for travel stipends, attracted patrons, and, if they were lucky enough to receive academic posts, were provided with living quarters. The Charlottenborg contained the academy's great hall and classrooms and the apartments and studios for the professors, and, in the first years of the academy, it also housed the royal lottery, the Institute of Natural History, and other scientific societies.[14] The Charlottenborg was also the site of the academy's exhibitions, which were open to the public. Under Saly, the academy held its initial Salon, the first Danish art exhibition, in 1769, including 137 works by fifteen artists.[15] The second Salon, which opened with much fanfare almost ten years later in 1778, included 212 works, many of them based on literary themes and neoclassical in orientation. One critic marked the occasion with an "Essai historique sur les arts et sur leur progrès en Dannemarc,"[16] a trea-

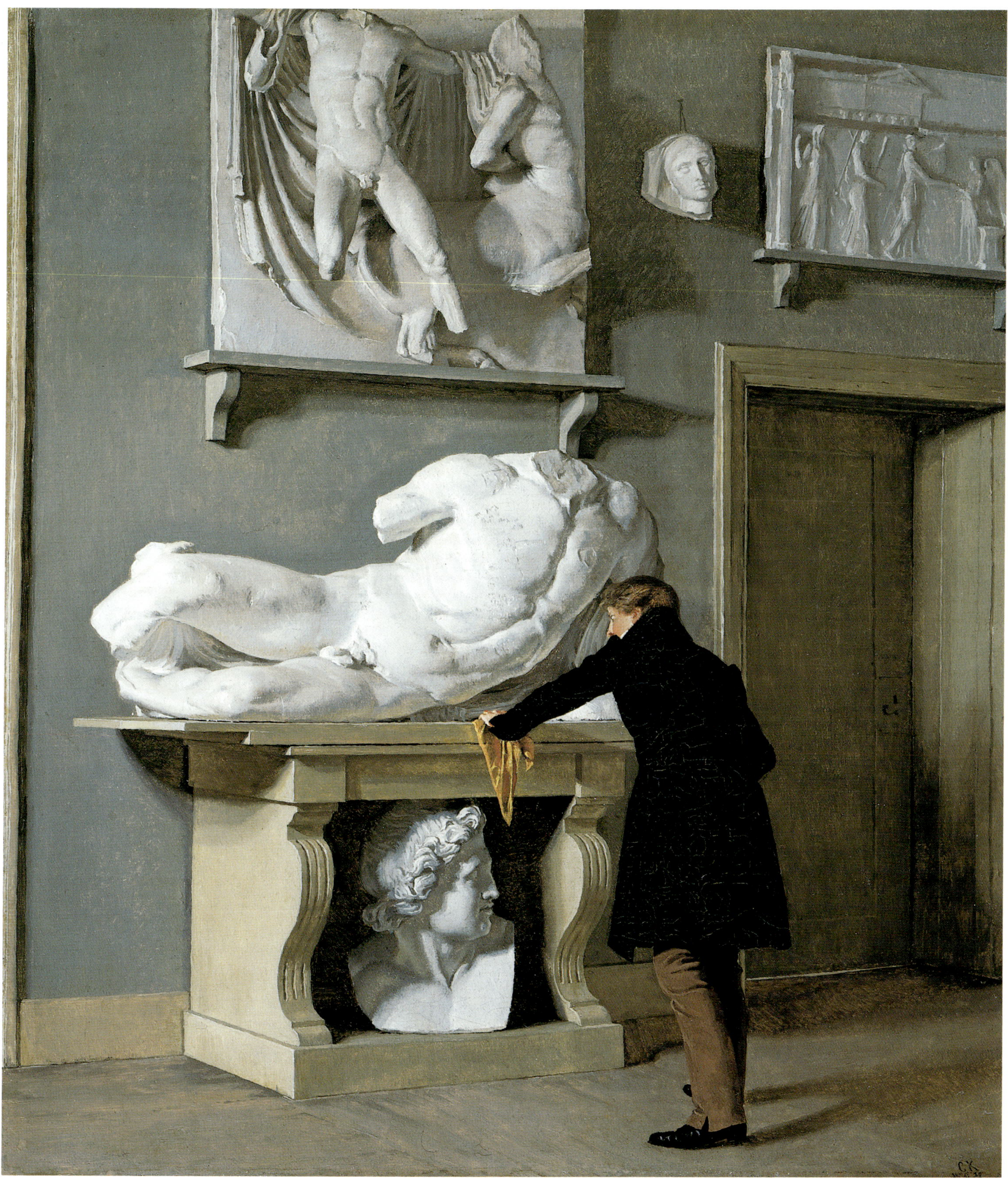

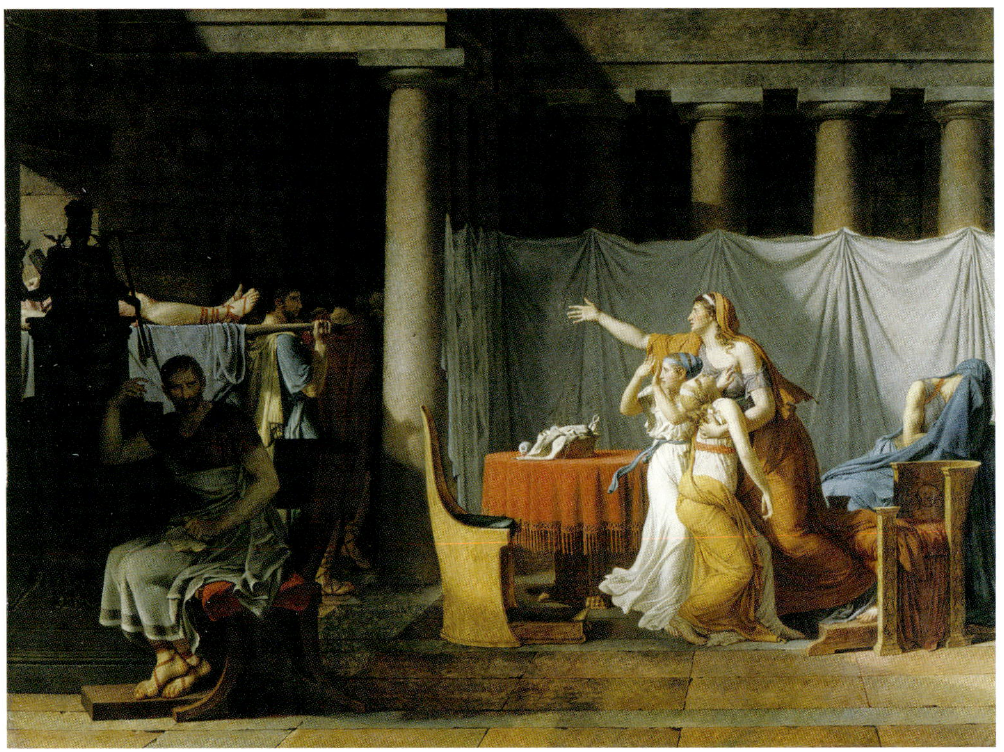

tise equating the maturity of the academy with that of the nation. The third Salon, held in 1794, was an immensely popular success, receiving 25,000 visitors.[17] The nineteenth-century art historian Niels Laurits Høyen (1798–1870) later noted that the exhibitions marked the generation of Danes that attended them, constituting "an absolute epoch in their lives."[18] The academy, founded as a royal institution, was recognized by the end of the century as a national institution, a mark of the nation's stature. In 1807, annual exhibitions began to be held at the Charlottenborg Palace, featuring juried selections of the works of members of the academy and students based on the model of the annual Paris Salon. The Charlottenborg exhibitions (which continue today) replaced the more exclusive and infrequent earlier Danish Salons in order to fully and regularly display the academy's talent to the public and offer aesthetic and social instruction through its art.

The fourth and last salon held under the aegis of the academy's director C. F. Hansen (1756–1845), the influential neoclassical architect, was held in 1815. In the previous year, 1814, new regulations had been established for the academy that expanded the teaching staff and the curriculum and that revised the stipulations for ongoing competitions and travel stipends. In April of that year, Frederik VI also granted funds to expand the plaster cast collection. All this despite Denmark's grave economic position.[19]

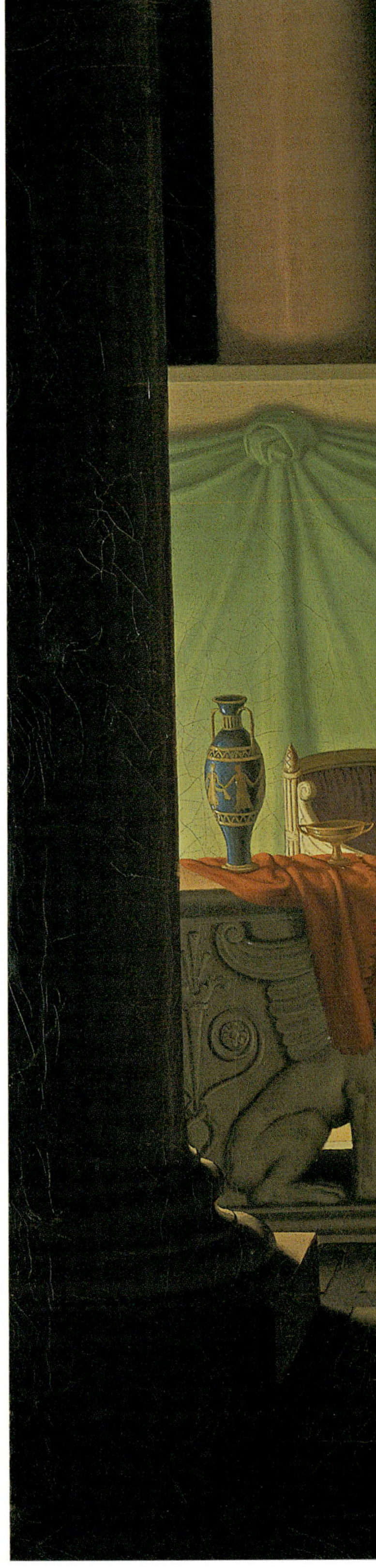

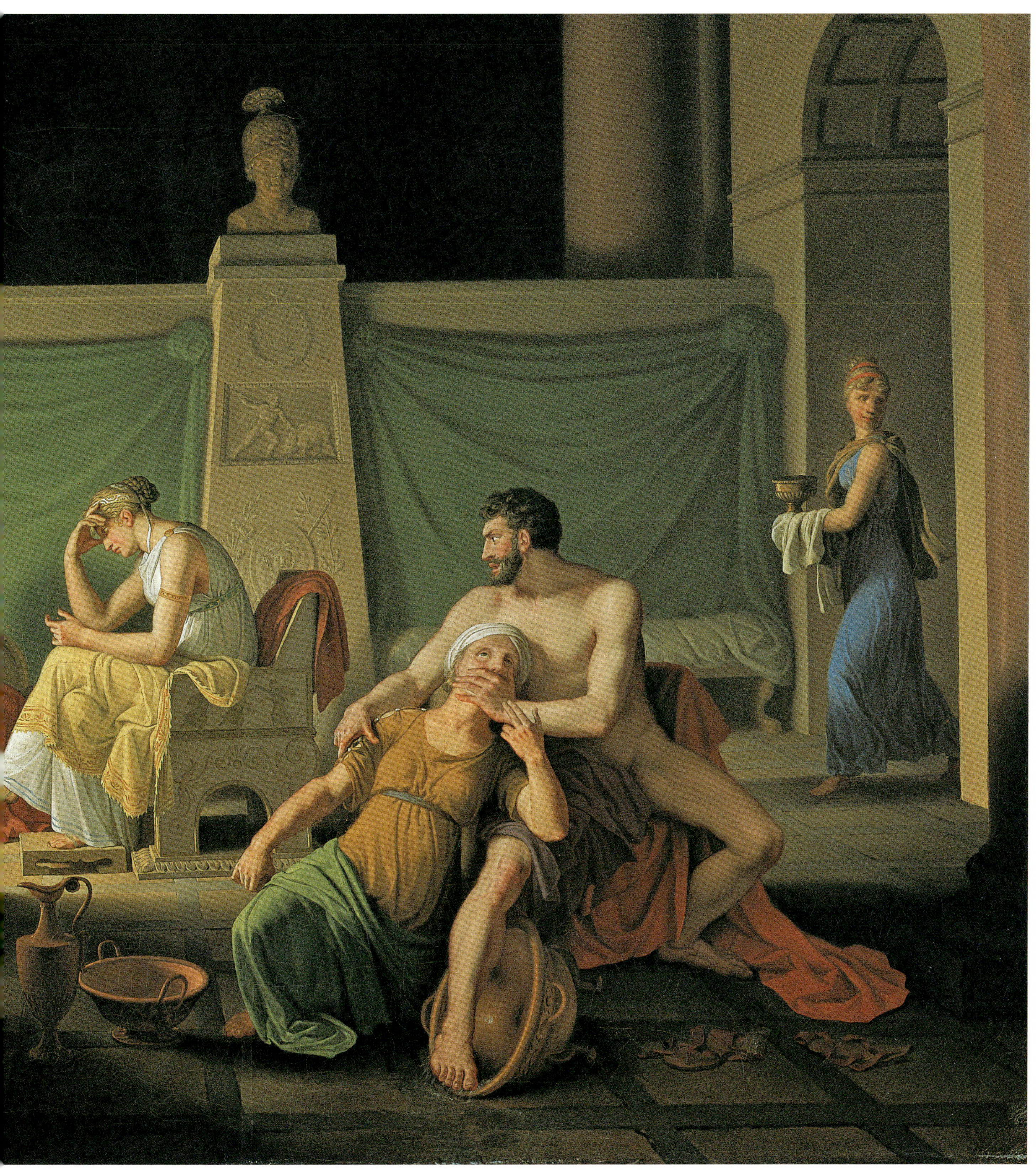

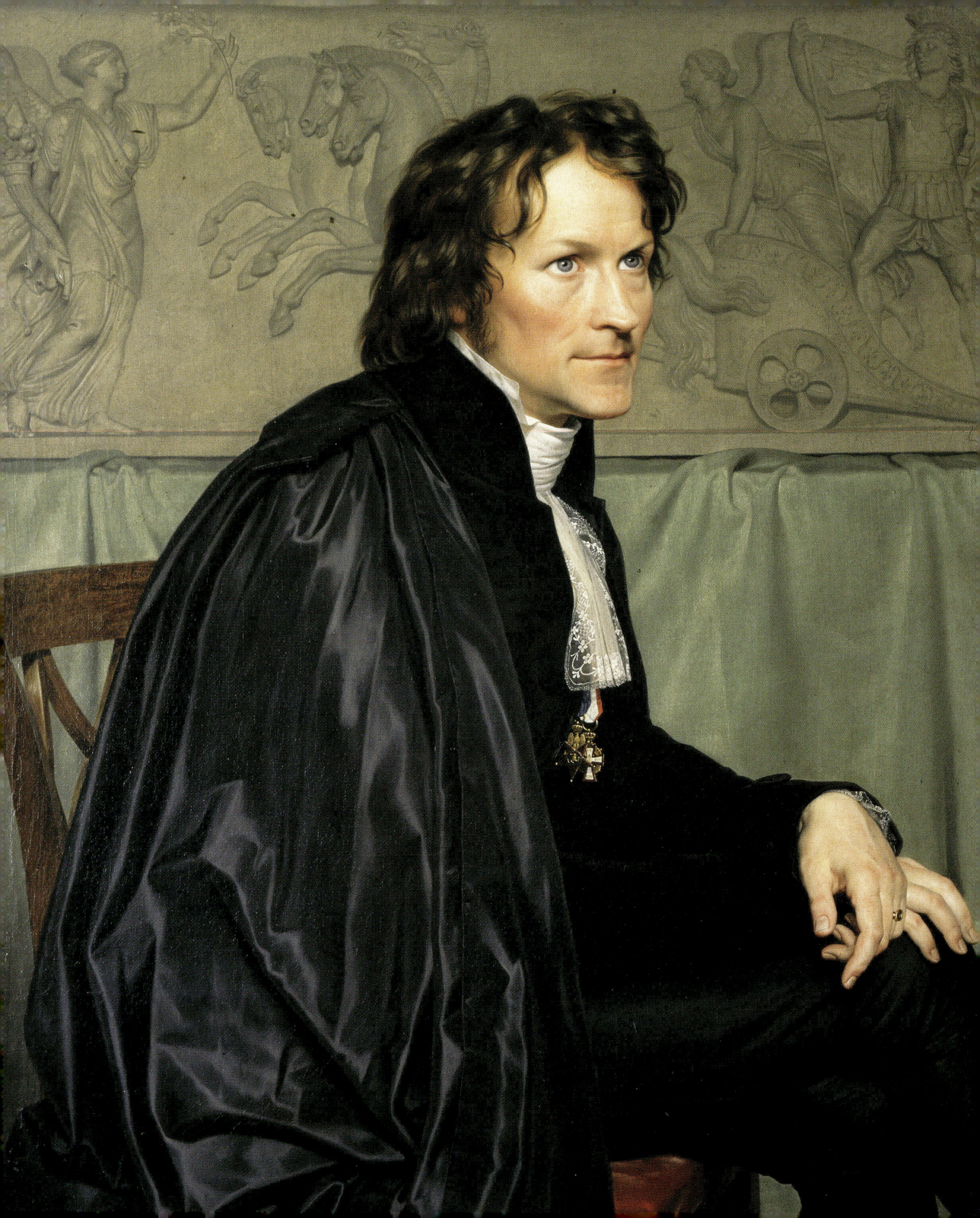

The citywide fires of the late eighteenth century and the English bombardment in 1807 had left Copenhagen gutted and its population displaced, but the year 1814, which saw Denmark's loss of Norway and a financial collapse which left the country impoverished, represented a nadir in Danish history. It was in this period of particular devastation that the academy was reconstituted to instill learned taste,[20] as reflected by its new title, Det kongelige Academie for de skiønne Kunster i København (The Royal Academy of Fine Arts in Copenhagen). Crown Prince Christian Frederik (later Christian VIII) had become the academy's *praeses* in 1808, the same year in which Frederick VI had assumed the throne, and his influence, as well as Hansen's firm commitment to Neoclassicism, redoubled the rigor of the institution. He stated in 1812, "The development of good taste in art is also beneficial for the functional arts, offering an education that assists the individual as well as the nation as a whole."[21] Nonetheless, reflecting the reversal of Denmark's fortunes, the academy was also in a decline. The most influential professors had died, Juel and Wiedewelt in 1802, and Abildgaard in 1809, leaving no immediate successors. When C. W. Eckersberg later became a professor, his new theories and strategies reestablished the academy's relevance and prestige.

Despite the academy's institutional changes and the vagaries of empire, instruction at the academy adhered to its original model. In the lower classes, art students commenced their studies by copying prints then sketching from plaster casts, and architecture students copied the classical orders. Upon advancement to the upper classes, painters, sculptors, and engravers drew from live male models. Within the arena of painting, history painting was supreme, followed, in order of importance, by portraiture, animal painting, landscape, and still life. In an effort to create learned artists, instruction was also offered in the disciplines of geometry, mathematics, perspective, mechanics, building materials, anatomy, history, art history, and mythology.[22]

As they did throughout Europe, students at the academy spent months making drawings after plaster casts of Greek and Roman antiquities. The practice had three-fold significance: it developed a student's dexterity and ability to render form and space, it offered a first critical lesson in human anatomy, and it instilled, at almost a subconscious level, the classical body as the basis of all art—what the sixteenth century theorist Giovanni Battista Armenini called "the good and ancient path."[23] Night classes, in which candlelight softened and added shadows to the contours of the plaster casts, offered the students the opportunity to deepen their impressions of sculptural form, as portrayed by Carl Anton Schmidt's *Evening Class at the Art Academy's Plaster Cast Collection* (fig. 21).

Students also worked individually within the large collection of somewhat capriciously juxtaposed plaster copies of works from different eras and in varying scales. Christen Købke's *View of the Plaster Cast Collection at Charlottenborg Palace*, (fig. 22), although painted as late as 1830, represents a standard practice that hearkened back to the founding of the academy. However, it shows not students assiduously copying from the replicas of antiquities, but a solitary man gazing at the god Cephisus from the Parthenon, or perhaps removing the dust that has gathered around it. The collection of antiquities is rendered in a monochrome gray palette, and the young man is dressed in black and earth tones and wields a yellow cloth, creating a marked distinction between the living and the dead. It has been proposed that this work, which contrasts the heroic figures of antiquity to the modesty of nineteenth-century Copenhagen, suggests the artist's own sense of aspiration and desire in 1830.[24]

The next step in the students' training was drawing from live models. Students competed in the studio for proximity to the model, their position in the room determined by their

25.
C. W. Eckersberg
Portrait of Bertel Thorvaldsen, 1814
Oil on canvas, 35¾ x 29¼ in.
(90.7 x 74.3 cm)
The Royal Academy of Fine Arts,
Copenhagen

status, as measured by honors they had earned. Study at the academy included a succession of examinations and competitions for medals, the so-called "minor" and "great" silver and gold medals. The great Gold Medal, modeled after the French Prix de Rome, was the most sought after, separating the "student" from the "artist,"[25] and bringing with it travel funds for study abroad. The rules established in 1814 specifically stated that history painters were eligible for travel grants and that genre, portrait, and landscape painters were not.[26] The students' interest in the servant, offered in Wilhelm Bendz's 1826 *Life Class at the Royal Academy*, and Bendz's own interest in genre painting, were at variance with their need to compete as history painters in order to win academic awards.

Since Abildgaard's time, the academy's culture of mimesis had been a source of discontent among students committed to the Romantic ideals of invention and individual expression. A number of northern German artists at the turn of the century, several of whom became the leading artists of the Romantic movement, studied at the academy at the turn of the century. As art historian Joseph Koerner notes, they were drawn as much by the romance of the Nordic "Renaissance," the romance of Nordic sagas and stories that emerged in the late eighteenth century, as by the academic curriculum itself.[27] Abildgaard, in particular, was an attraction for the twenty-year-old Caspar David Friedrich (1774–1840), who entered the academy in 1794 and who would later exert a great influence on Danish landscape painting. Asmus Jakob Carstens (1754–1798), who entered the academy in 1776, had found its emphasis on copying to be numbing. After working for a period under Abildgaard, he left for Rome in 1783. Philipp Otto Runge (1777–1810), who attended the academy between 1799 and 1801, noted in his letters to Goethe that he learned composition from Abildgaard and color from Juel,[28] but that overall he responded to the academy's curriculum with an "eternal attack of yawning."[29]

It was into this culture of the "yawning"—the rigidified curriculum and lack of inspired teaching in the wake of Juel's and Abildgaard's deaths—that the brilliant polymath Christoffer Wilhelm Eckersberg (1783–1853) entered as professor in 1818. As the teacher of two generations of Danish painters, Bendz and Købke among them, Eckersberg helped to establish artistic nationalism in Denmark, the terms of a native school of painting, through his synthesis of classical formulae and scientific observation. Born in Schleswig, Eckersberg was among the north German artists who studied at the academy. Enrolling in 1803 with the hope of studying with Abildgaard, he trained to be a history painter. In 1809, he received the great Gold Medal after several failed attempts (Abildgaard had refused him the medal in 1805). However, because the funds were not available at that time from the academy, he sought private patronage, traveling to Paris in 1810 with the well-connected amateur artist and royal officer Tønnes Christian Bruun Neergaard (1776–1824).

In 1811, Eckersberg began to frequent the studio of the French neoclassical master Jacques-Louis David (1748–1825), whom he described as one of "the modern era's greatest artists,"[30] and whose teaching shaped and inspired the young painter. David's studio practice in Paris was similar to that of the Royal Academy's model school in Copenhagen, but, according to Eckersberg, from David's emphasis on his students' individual perceptions and the acuity of their observations, "I have gained much, and afterwards have seen more clearly then before, that there is scarcely a better way than that which he has shown."[31] Eckersberg's *The Return of Odysseus* (1812; fig. 23) demonstrates most directly David's influence on his art. The scene from Homer's *Odyssey*, represents Odysseus as he returns to Ithaca after an absence of some twenty years. He places his hand over the mouth of Euryklea, his old wet nurse, so that she

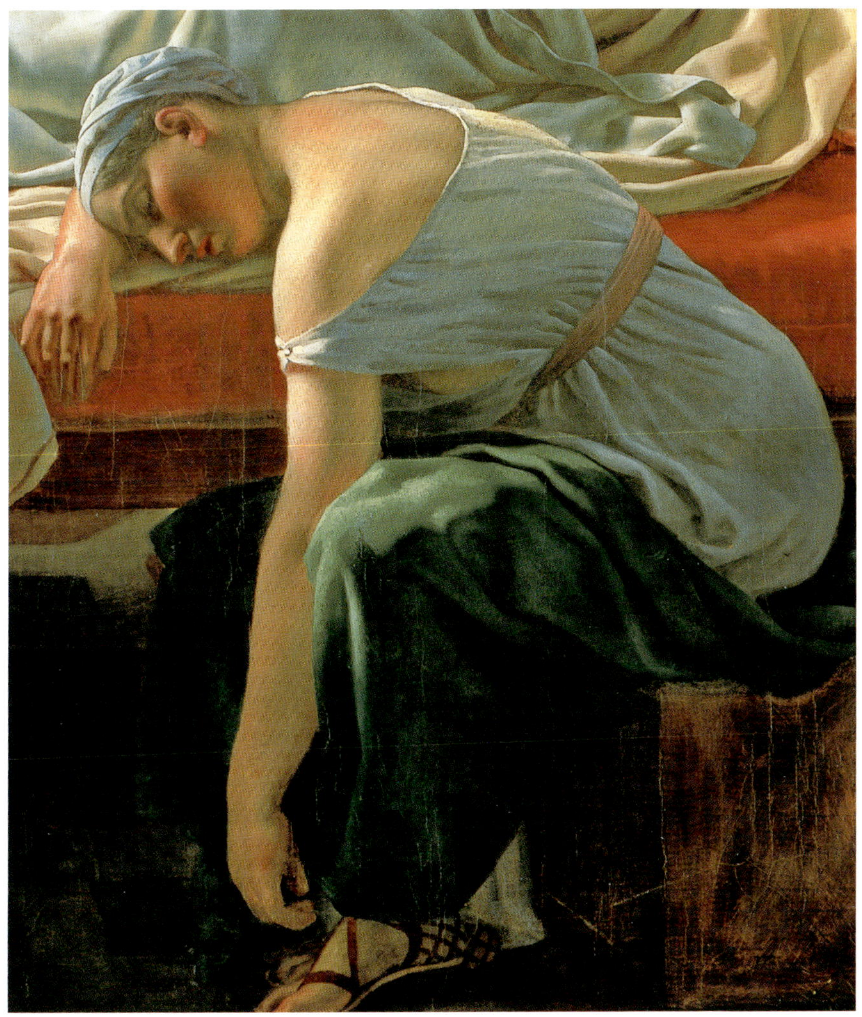

26.
C. W. Eckersberg
Sleeping Woman in Antique Garb
(fragment of Dream of Alcyone), 1813
Oil on canvas, 17½ x 15⅜ in.
(44.5 x 39.2 cm)
Thorvaldsens Museum, Copenhagen

will not reveal his identity to his wife Penelope, who sits as if spot-lit to the left. The structure of the antique room, the differential lighting, and the postures and figural types are strongly reminiscent of David's *The Lictors Returning to Brutus the Bodies of His Sons* (1789; fig. 24), which Eckersberg likely knew either through the original painting, via engravings produced after the painting, or through an ink study by David (Getty Museum) owned by his friend and patron Bruun Neergaard.[32] Kasper Monrad also notes that the painting represents a kind of pastiche of Davidian motifs. Penelope's posture, for example, echoes that of one of the grieving women represented in David's *Oath of the Horatii* (1784, Louvre). Eckersberg's painting is one of a series of works that he created around the theme of Odysseus around 1812.[33] Nevertheless, unlike David, Eckersberg's goals were not political.[34] Eckersberg reported in his diaries that David offered him exceptional praise and opportunity to earn further recognition for Danish art: "Denmark is now also beginning to count its good artists; there is a sculptor in Rome who does his country honor, and now as you go forth, you will do the same, and I advise you, if possible, to remain here next year and enter the concourse, because you will be able to win a prize, although as a foreigner you cannot accept the stipend connected with it, but it would be an honor for you and your country."[35] In addition to his paintings of nude models in

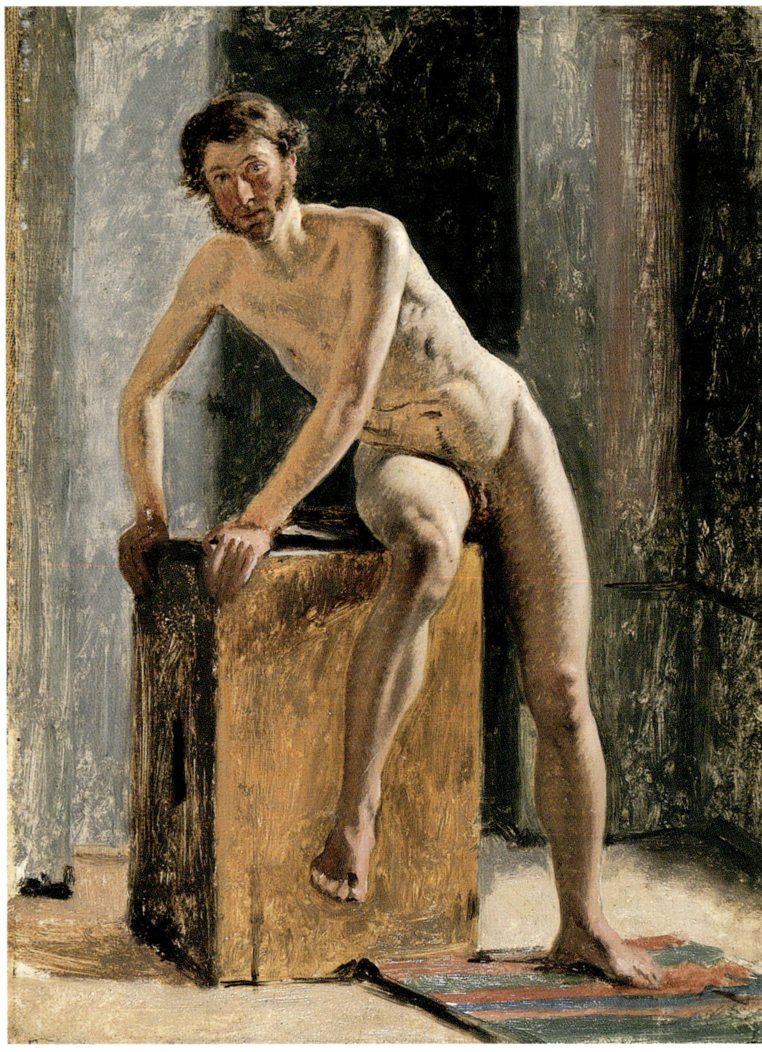

David's atelier, Eckersberg began to create landscape compositions. It has even been suggested that while in Paris he began to paint outdoors directly before his motifs, then an uncommon practice and one that he would continue to explore in Rome.[36] He also began to develop a keen interest in meteorology and in perspective, in part inspired by the practice and writings of landscape painter Pierre-Henri de Valenciennes (1750–1819).[37] Valenciennes argued that a landscape painter must be, in the first instance, a keen observer of nature and should become proficient in recording natural details in studies made out of doors. These disciplines would become central to Eckersberg's painting and to his teaching later in his career.

In the summer of 1813, Eckersberg finally traveled on to Rome. There he became part of the Danish-German expatriate community gathered around the Danish sculptor Bertel Thorvaldsen (1770–1844)—one the foremost Neoclassical sculptors in Europe and the famous "sculptor in Rome" to which David referred. When Eckersberg had first arrived in Rome in 1813, he sought out Thorvaldsen, but the latter left almost immediately for a visit to Copenhagen. By the following year, however, Eckersberg had painted Thorvaldsen's portrait, and it is one of the acknowledged masterpieces of Danish art (fig. 25). Seated casually,

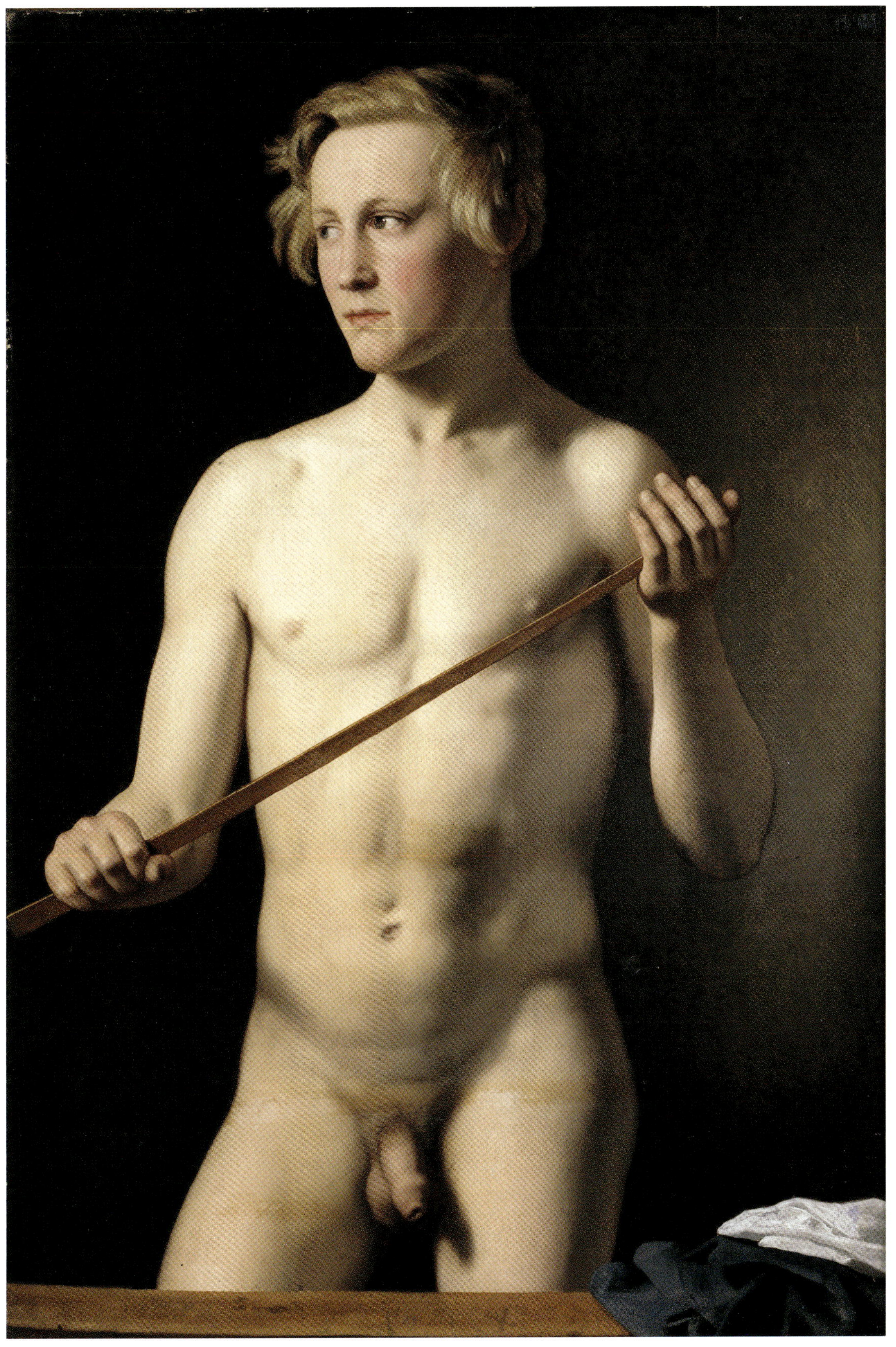

his elegantly manicured hands resting on his crossed knees, Thorvaldsen wears the cloak and medal of the Accademia di San Luca, to which he had been elected a member in 1808. He poses before a section of his monumental stucco frieze for the Palazzo del Quirinale (created in 1812 in anticipation of Napoleon's arrival in Rome). The frieze is situated in the painting so that Thorvaldsen's head is flanked by two winged figures, and so its representation of Alexander the Great's triumphal entry into Babylon becomes a celebratory tribute to the artist himself.[38] Framed by his unruly hair, his ice-blue eyes gaze upward and his facial muscles are compressed as though in inspired concentration. This portrait, much copied by Eckersberg's students and later by the artist himself, became a talisman of Thorvaldsen's genius and also that of Eckersberg.[39]

Shortly after his arrival in Rome, Eckersberg also began to work with a female model, creating two paintings which he described in a letter to a colleague, the master engraver Johann Friderich Clemens: "I am working on two paintings whose themes are taken from Ovid's beautiful tale about Ceyx and Alcyone. The one is Alcyone after she has taken leave of her beloved husband on a beach. . . . In the companion piece she is shown sleeping at night as Ceyx's ghost appears before her in a dream to explain the manner of his death, and in order to explain her troubled dream I have placed her maid by the bedside—she has fallen asleep and sleeps tranquilly. The figures have Pousin's [sic] dimensions."[40] A small fragment of the latter painting, *Sleeping Woman in Antique Garb* (fig. 26), is a painting of exceptional jewel-like clarity and color, reflecting the assimilation of the anatomical lessons and attentiveness to light, color, and texture, that he gleaned from David's studio.[41] A masterwork of light effects, the painting depicts a diffuse light descending from the upper left, falling directly onto the figure's back, rendering it smoothly opalescent, and reflecting off her flesh and clothing, illuminating her nose, chin, ear, and especially lips with a heated glow. In Rome, Eckersberg also created a series of crystalline views of the city, increasingly replacing his interest in history painting with genre scenes, unexceptional in theme but grand in observation and execution (see chapter 3).

Eckersberg's reputation had preceded him when he returned to Copenhagen in 1816. He submitted *The Death of Baldur* (1817), a history painting drawn from Johannes Ewald's 1775 literary classic, as his official application to the academy, and he was elected a member in 1817. It was around that time that mythological Nordic themes—those drawn from what were seen as indigenous sources, such as the Norse Sagas and Eddas—began to supplant Greek and Roman themes within academic competitions. The poet Adam Oehlenschläger's important collection *Nordiske Digt* (1807) and Rasmus Nyerup's 1808 publication of *Edda* (1808), offered new or revised sources of non-classical literature for increasingly nationally-oriented intellectuals.[42]

Eckersberg received his professorship in 1818 and quickly distinguished himself as an innovator of academic practice. Within his first decade of teaching, he revolutionized the study of the nude and the relationship between art and science through his insistent study of perspective. Among his other achievements, he welcomed women artists to train in his studio long before they were allowed admittance to the academy (this only occurred officially in 1888, and then to a special school within the academy). Among his female students was his daughter Julie, whose brief biographical sketch of her father offers personal insight into his private atelier.[43]

In the 1820s, Eckersberg and the history painter Johan Ludwig Lund, also installed as professor at the academy in 1818, instituted courses in painting in their private studios in Char-

29.
Heinrich Eddelien
The Origin of Painting, 1830
Oil on canvas, 50¾ x 29⅜ in.
(129 x 100 cm)
Statens Museum for Kunst,
Copenhagen

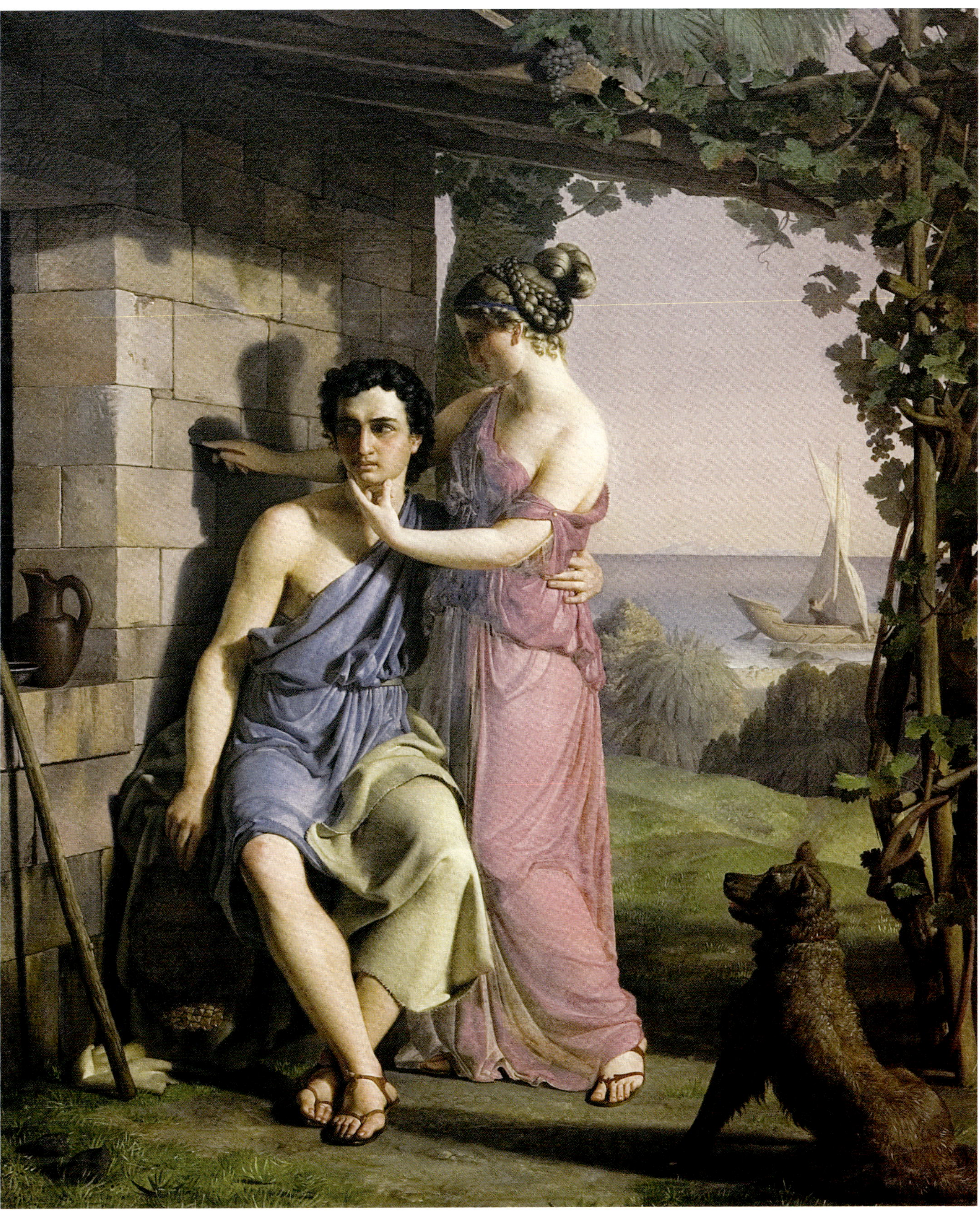

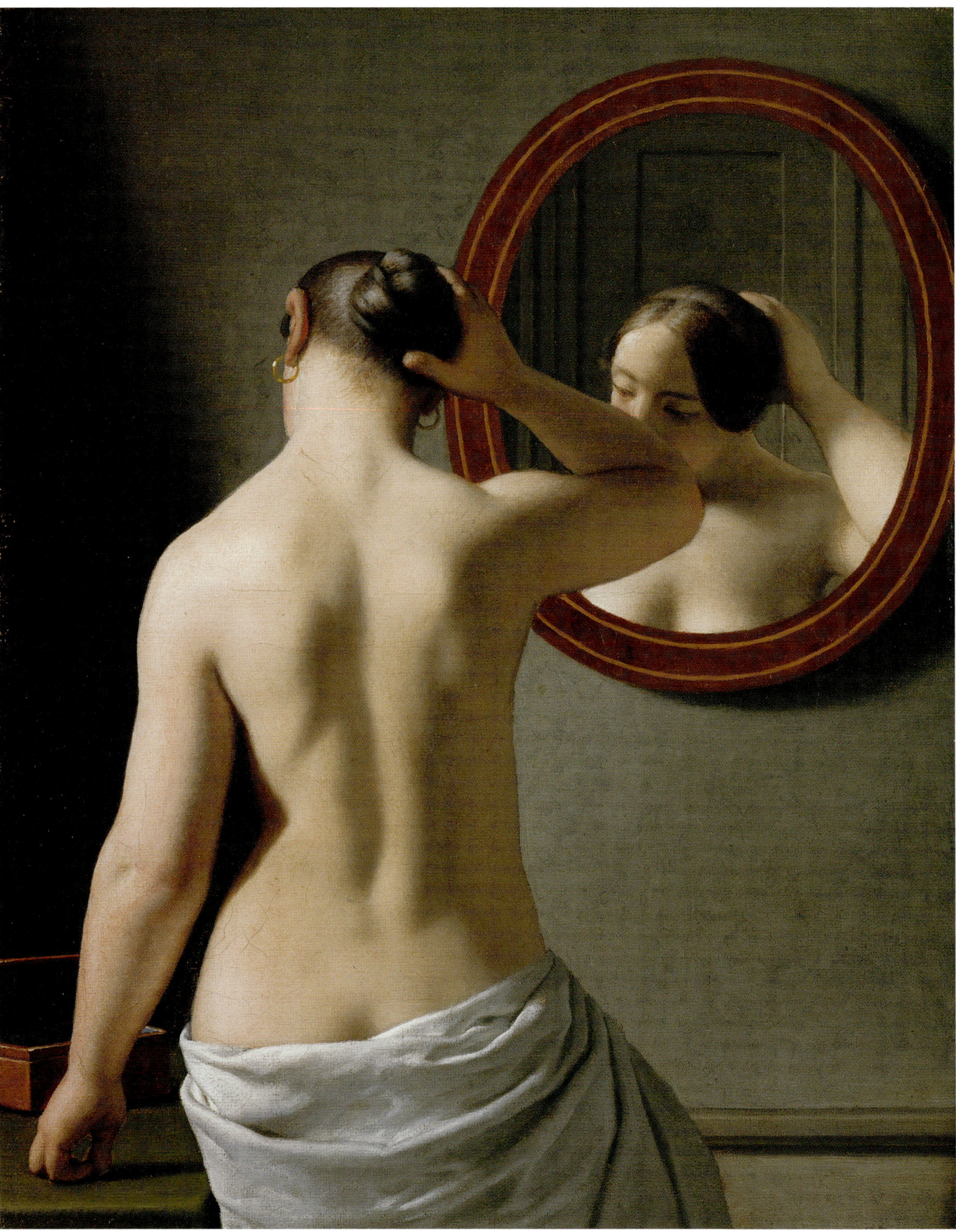

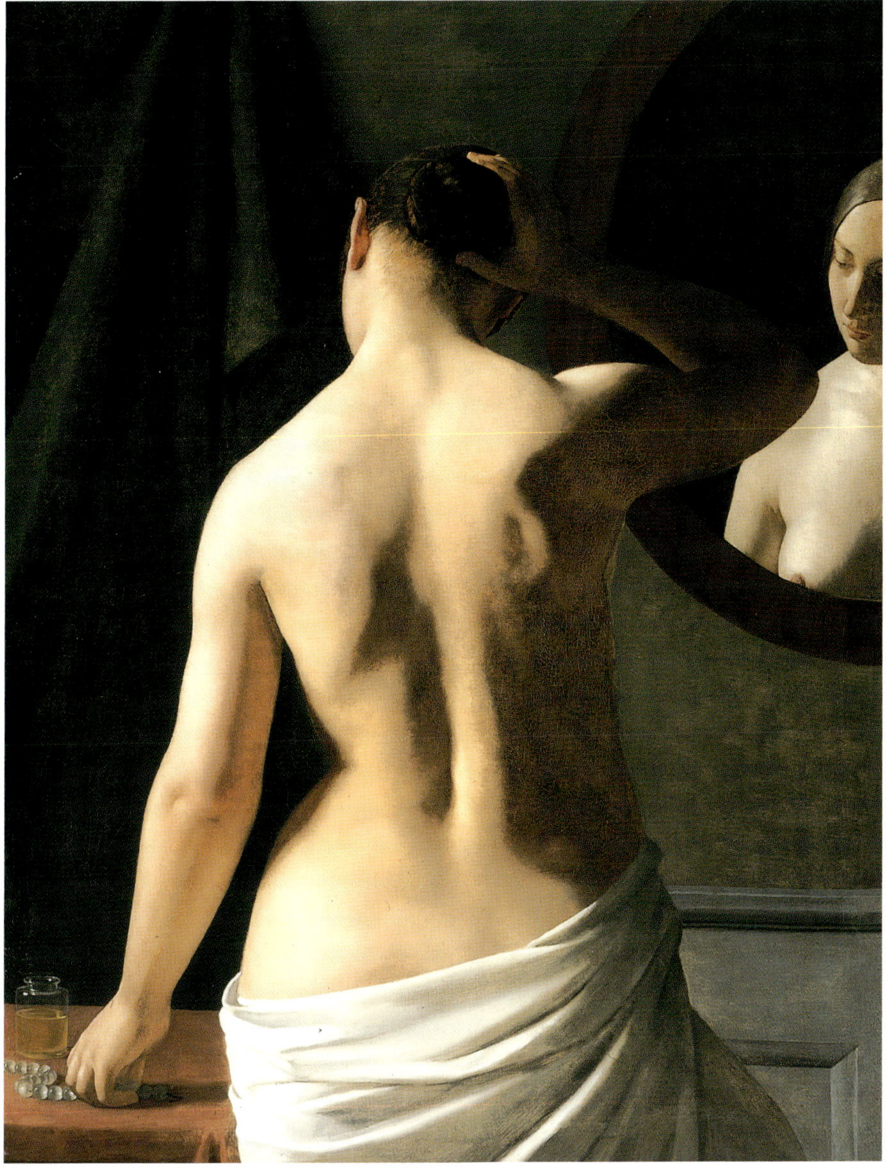

lottenborg.[44] Prior to this time, figure painting per se was not officially taught at the academy, only drawing from prints, casts, and models. In the summer of 1822, during the official academic break, Lund began to offer four hours of figure painting from a live model. This practice was so popular that in October of that year, he and Eckersberg sought a permanent room within the academy for this instruction. Permission was granted in 1824. Around the same time, the academy established prizes for landscape, animal, and flower painting, suggesting a major revision of the regulations that had previously favored history painting.[45] These reforms bear witness to Eckersberg's commitment to the direct study of nature, and of his obligation to offer his students objective study.

Eckersberg's student Constantin Hansen painted *Male Model Sitting on a Box* (fig. 27) during such a session in 1833. Rendered in Eckersberg's studio at the Charlottenborg, the painting presents not a generalized, heroic nude, familiar from the works routinely produced in the model school (as suggested by Bendz), but a painting of a model at work. It is a carefully observed study of anatomy, and particularly of the effects of natural light animating the body's surface without the idealizing generalities of the traditional academic approach. One major innovation in this painting is that it was rendered directly in front of the model, rather than created selectively by synthesizing a number of sketches. Typically in such works, flaccid skin, body hair, irregular pigmentation, and eye contact with the model would be glossed over to suggest the figure's timelessness. Here, however, Hansen offers the vision of a living man, his imperfections evidence of his human presence. It was this set of innovations—the acknowledgement and scrutiny of unstable natural light and color, the incorporation of the material setting into the picture, and finally, the un-glamorized view of the model as a living, breathing person and not as a classical avatar—that Eckersberg ushered in with his live-model painting sessions.

All of these changes represent a significant revitalization of academic pedagogy. Eckersberg's painting, teaching, and pedagogical writings were dedicated to creating a fusion of the scrupulous observation of material reality with the embodiment of a higher order of sentiment, one that imbues matter with structure and meaning. Eckersberg's observations were strongly supported by his interest in natural science. Julie Eckersberg reports on her father's preoccupation with the natural sciences, and in particular with meteorology and perspective. Eckersberg's interest in perspective led to the institution of formal classes on the subject, replacing his previously informal instruction,[46] and to his publication of two treatises on perspective in 1833 and 1841.[47]

Such tensions between material observation and idealized form characterize Eckersberg's own nude studies from the 1830s such as his *Standing Male Model* (1837; fig. 28). Eckersberg referred to this as a "portrait figure," and inscribed it with the model's name and age, "Carl Frørup 18 years." In this way, he blended the otherwise distinct genres of portraiture and academic nude.[48] Dramatic in the scale of the model in relation to the frame, and highly charged in the model's scrupulously observed body, this is one of several large-scale nudes painted by Eckersberg in that year.[49] Rather than assuming a conventional antique posture preferred in the academy, Frørup stands in a curiously ambivalent pose, his diagonally aligned hips suggesting a contrapposto position but his back and shoulders are held rigidly. The subtle collision of these conflicting angles creates an abstract geometry of the body, an idealized figure of unusual dignity. At the same time, the specificity of the model's features, including the youthful blush of his cheeks and the articulation of his groin area, anchors this painting in direct observation. It is this practice to which Wilhelm Bendz alludes in his painting of the Royal Academy's life drawing class.

At the academy, however, the idealized figure continued to serve as the basis for history painting. Heinrich Eddelien (1802–1852), who entered the academy in 1821 and was one of the few students to receive the great Gold Medal in the 1830s, practiced history painting throughout his career and became an expert in Pompeian decoration. His *Origin of Painting* (1830; fig. 29) both relies on the academic observation of the body and eroticizes the act of making art. The painting depicts the Greek legend of the genesis of painting, as recounted by Pliny the Elder (d. 79 C.E.), in which the Corinthian woman Dibutade traces the shadow of her departing lover on the wall of her father's pottery studio. A subject at once bearing the erudition of an admired classical text and the articulation of romantic desire, this was a popular motif among Neoclassical artists.[50] It is also self-referential in its rendering of the act of drawing itself, and programmatic in its statement of an image as projected reality.

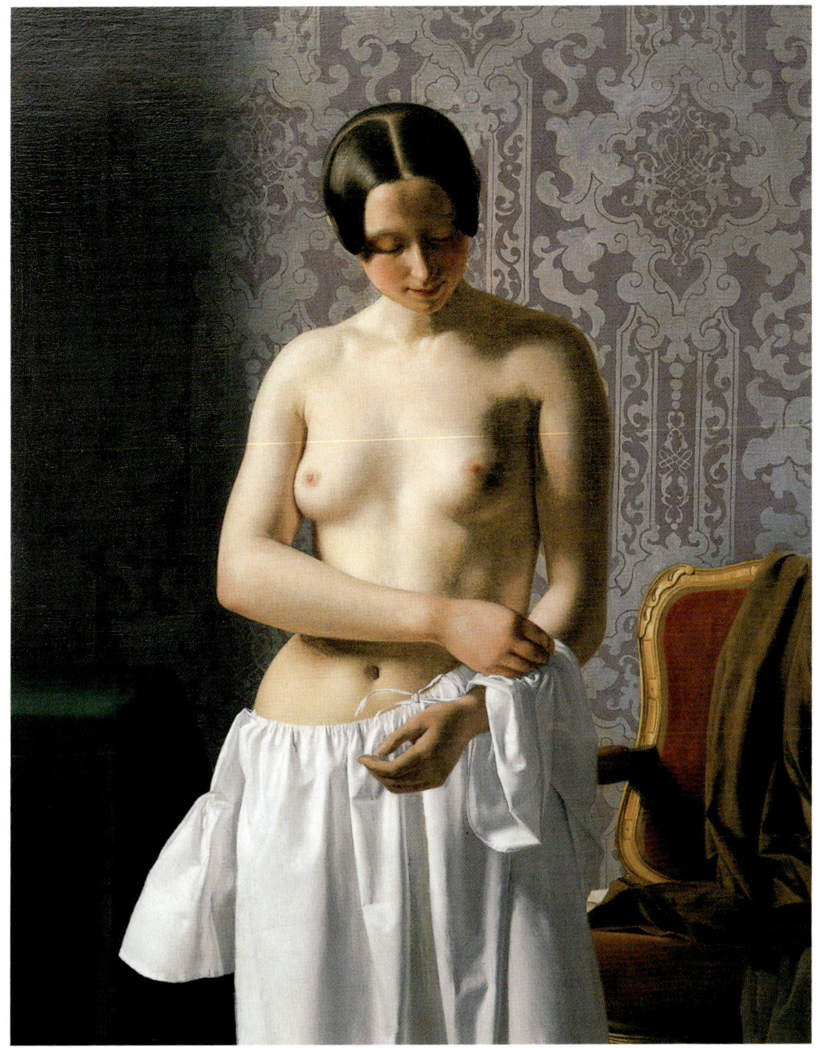

32.
Joel Ballin
Study of a Model, Young Girl Undressing, 1844
Oil on canvas, 46 x 36¼ in.
(117 x 92 cm)
Collection of Ambassador John L. Loeb Jr.,
New York

Through such rhetoric, the human figure was ennobled and made remote as a physical entity. Eckersberg's paintings depart from this practice. His landmark painting *Female Model Standing in Front of a Mirror* (1841; fig. 30), while referring tangentially to classical figures of Venus,[51] is rendered as a genre painting. Like *Standing Male Model*, it represents a model positioned close to the picture plane, creating a sense of intimacy and immediate availability. Moreover, it positions a nude model in a domestic setting. This in itself was extraordinary in Danish art at the time. Eckersberg views the model from behind, the reflection of her face and shoulders in the mirror before her masked by her raised right arm. A gently filtered natural light, flowing from the left, both heightens the contours of the model's silhouette and blurs the muscle transitions within her back. The model rests her left hand on a table upon which sits a small, open chest. The drapery wrapped around her hips falls just below the swelling of her buttocks, offering an eroticized glimpse of her otherwise concealed backside. The austerity of the setting and cool palette, offset by the smooth tactility of the model's flesh, creates a coy circuit of desire. The restraint of this rendering is thrown into relief by *Female Model Before a Mirror*, (1841; fig. 31), a painting by Eckersberg's student Ludvig August Smith (1820–1906), created during the same modeling session. Smith was seemingly stationed just to the left and slightly above Eckersberg, his different angle of view most notable in the mirror's reflection (offering the model's face and left breast), and by the room's wainscoting raised to hip level. The light is exploited by Smith to create crisper shadows across the model's body, offering a stronger sense of her muscled presence than Eckersberg's marmoreal smoothness. Smith also drapes the table to the model's left with a red cloth, placing on it a glass jar and a set of beads. In contrast, the consistently cooler tones and reduced detailing of Eckersberg's painting create a sense of abstract harmony, poised between the limpid worlds of Vermeer and Hammershøi.

The model has been identified as a woman named Florentine, who posed for Eckersberg and his students during the summers of 1840 and 1841.[52] Such modeling sessions, relying on female models, were practices that Eckersberg had initiated in the summer of 1833. For reasons of propriety, female models were not included in life drawing sessions at the academy before that time. Beginning in that year, however, female nudes, bathed in diffused opalescent light, became common in Danish academic painting.[53] Eckersberg was a master of the genre. Among his students was Joel Ballin (1822–1885), who studied both in his academic classes and privately between 1837 and 1844. [54] Ballin's painting of a seminude woman (1844; fig. 32) provides a fusion of the artistic modes of academic model study and informal genre scene, a specialty of Eckersberg's later career. Ballin's study is closely allied with Eckersberg's paintings of the same model from the summer of 1844, and with those of his other students.[55] The smooth idealization and eroticization of the model's body typifies the academic approach to the nude in this period. The nudes painted by Eckersberg and his students were largely private paintings, and not intended for public exhibition. However, painting these works helped the students develop the skills that they needed to strengthen their genre or history paintings. But they did occasionally find private patronage for such nudes.[56]

Arts patronage was, of course, critical for the academicians' survival. With the bankruptcy of Denmark and the decline of the power of the court, artists were scarcely assured of monetary support. Eckersberg noted that the situation of the court artist was "the same as a cab driver."[57] Artists, who largely had middle-class origins,[58] needed to attract patrons through such official channels as the annual Charlottenborg exhibitions and the Fine Arts Society (Kunstforeningen), a private organization established in 1825 to support artists by encouraging the commission, purchase, and appreciation of works of art.

The Fine Arts Society, which was founded in part through the efforts of Eckersberg, Lund, and art historian N. L. Høyen, was an important institution during the Golden Age for attempting to integrate art into the daily lives of middle-class citizens.[59] It held thematic painting competitions, such as those invoking Nordic history and national monuments (see chapter 4), which were fundamentally different in subject from the academy's emphasis on the grand tradition of history painting. In this way, the Fine Arts Society directed the attention of both artists and patrons to nationalistic subjects. The Fine Arts Society also held annual lotteries of paintings that it had purchased, with the proceeds to be distributed to its members, and it offered an arena for emerging artists. In this way, the Fine Arts Society was critical to the rise of landscape, portrait, and genre painting, which had a broad appeal to a middle-class buying public, supplanting the primacy of history painting.[60] Kasper Monrad has demonstrated that upwards of two-thirds of Eckersberg's portraits were commissioned by members of the middle class, as the bureaucratic classes gained power in Denmark.[61]

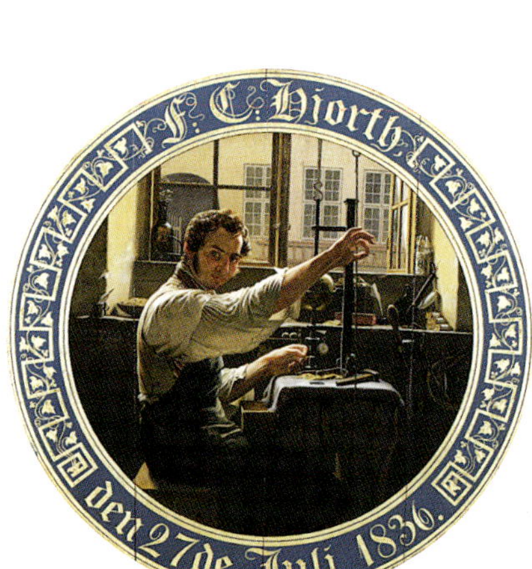

33.
Heinrich Eddelien
Shield for Frants Christian Hjorth, 1836
Oil on wood, diameter 24⅝ in. (62 cm)
Royal Shooting Society,
Copenhagen City Museum

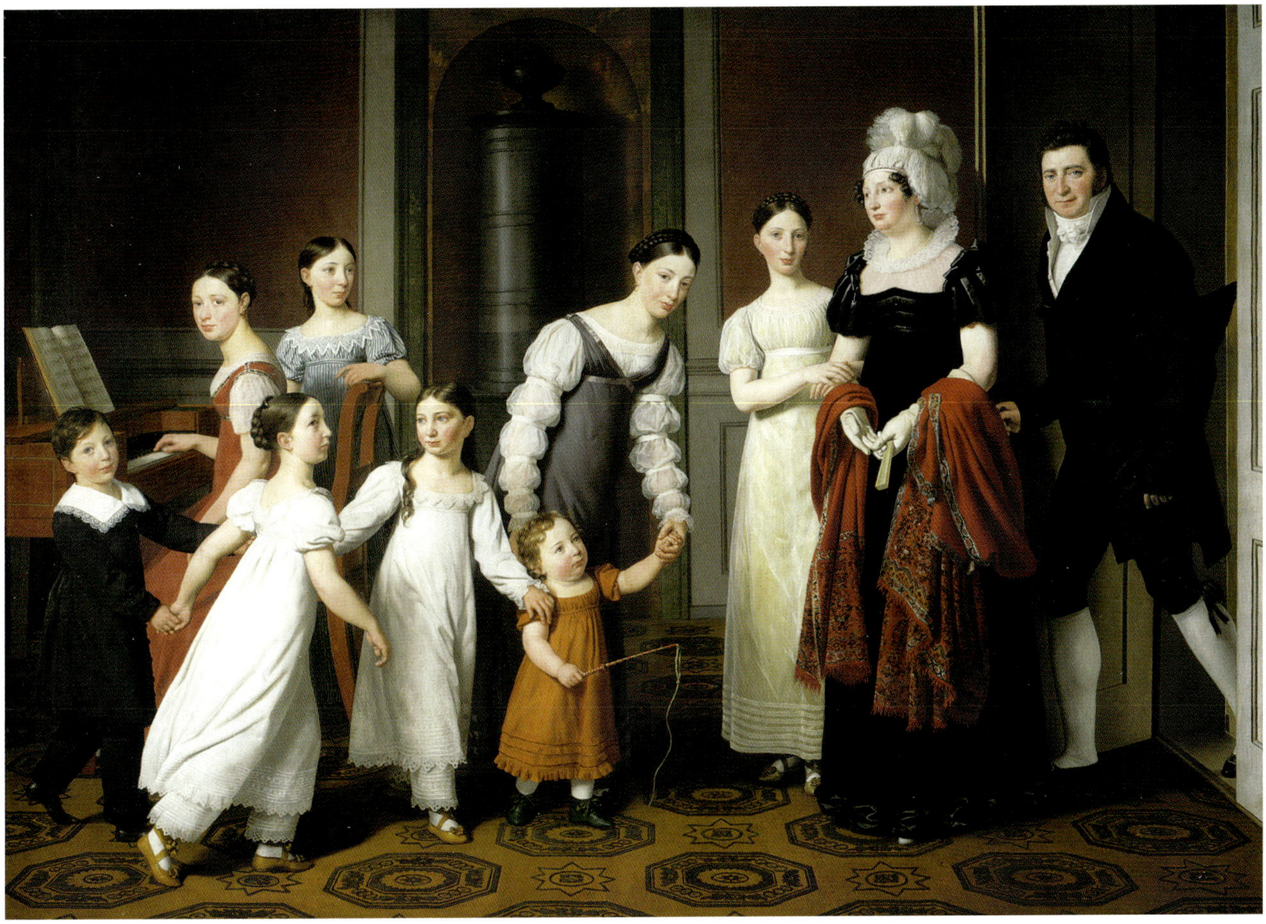

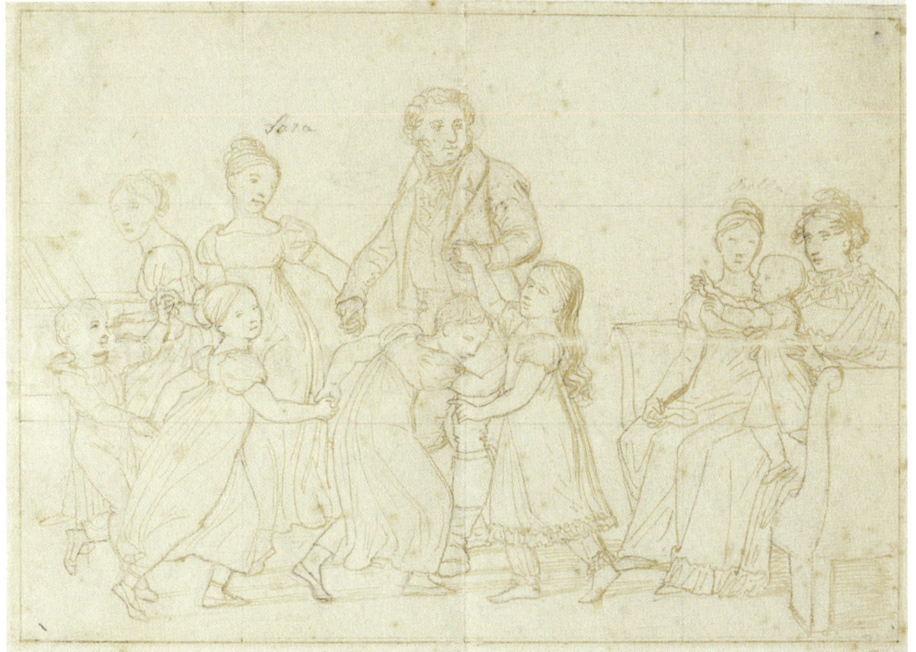

ABOVE
34.
C. W. Eckersberg
The Nathanson Family, 1818
Oil on canvas, 49⅝ x 67⅞ in.
(126 x 172.5 cm)
Statens Museum for Kunst,
Copenhagen

LEFT
35.
C. W. Eckersberg
*Sketch for the Nathanson Family
Portrait*, 1818
Ink on paper, 5½ x 7½ in.
(13.8 x 19 cm)
The Hirschsprung Collection,
Copenhagen

One path toward recognition by patrons and the public represents a peculiarly Danish tradition. The Royal Shooting Society (Det Kongelige Kjøbenhavnske Skydeselskab og Danske Broderskab), Denmark's oldest membership organization (established in the fifteenth century), required of new members the submission to the society of a painted target. Aspiring members, increasingly from the bourgeoisie, commissioned artists to prepare their targets for admission. Great prestige was attached to the quality of the targets, which were retained as property of the society. In his 1836 target for the Copenhagen needle-maker Frants Christian Hjorth (1782–1865), Heinrich Eddelien represented the patron diligently at work in his shop (fig. 33), fusing portraiture with highly particularized renderings of the machines and paraphernalia of his successful trade. Admired paintings such as this, which typically represented men at work or depicted the sources of their wealth (ships, business locations, estates, allegories of their home regions), were like calling-cards to potential patrons.[62]

Some patrons of the arts believed that support of the arts was in itself a civic virtue. One such patron was Mendel Levin Nathanson (1780–1868), an influential Copenhagen publisher and merchant. Nathanson had helped to finance Eckersberg's travel to Paris and had commissioned several history paintings from him in Rome, including the mythological paintings of Alcyone and Ceyx. He also developed a plan to commission artists to paint scenes from the works of Ludvig Holberg's (1684–1754) plays, emulating the literary and national aspirations of Boydell's Shakespeare Gallery in England.[63] Among his commissions were portraits of his family, of which the *Nathanson Family* (fig. 34) represents a landmark in Danish portraiture. Combining portraiture and genre painting, it offers a new kind of bourgeois self-presentation. As we shall see in the following chapters, such gemütlich representations, which form part of the Biedermeyer culture of the post-Napoleonic War years, came to furnish the imaginations and reinforce the social position of the middle class as the emerging leadership of Denmark.

The Nathanson family is represented at the moment that the parents have arrived home from an audience with the queen,[64] their movement through the door posing them between public and private life. A sketch for the painting represents Mendel Nathanson dancing in a circle with his daughters, and his wife Ester (née Herfort) seated on a sofa with a child on her lap (fig. 35). The final painting focuses less on informal family intimacy than the couple's social position. The Nathansons' wealth is evidenced by their fashionable clothing and by the cultivated activities of their elegantly clad and coiffed children. At the same time, the clean lines and austerity of their Empire-style room testify to their sobriety in taste, in keeping with the general frugality of the period. The painting also asserts a new representation of motherhood: Ester Nathanson, the anchor of the family, is statuesque in relation to the figure of her husband and children who are mobile and lively.[65] The painting is a programmatic representation of a new social order, the rising middle class asserting its identity through domesticity.

Nathanson was a leading member of Copenhagen's business community, noted for his publications on economic history (and later his editorship of Copenhagen's leading newspaper, *Berlingske Tidende*), his patronage of the arts and sciences, and also his attention to the social position of Jews. In 1814, he had been instrumental in shaping the royal decree extending full civil rights to Denmark's small Jewish population.[66] He also helped to establish Reform Judaism in Denmark and to found a school for Jewish boys in 1805, and one for girls in 1810, thereby enabling them to seek formal education outside of the home. The Nathanson family portrait, extolling the virtues of domesticity, which became one of the central motifs of the

36.
C. W. Eckersberg
Mendel Levin Nathanson's Elder Daughters, Bella and Hanna, 1820
Oil on canvas, 49¼ x 33⅝ in.
(125 x 85.5 cm)
Statens Museum for Kunst, Copenhagen

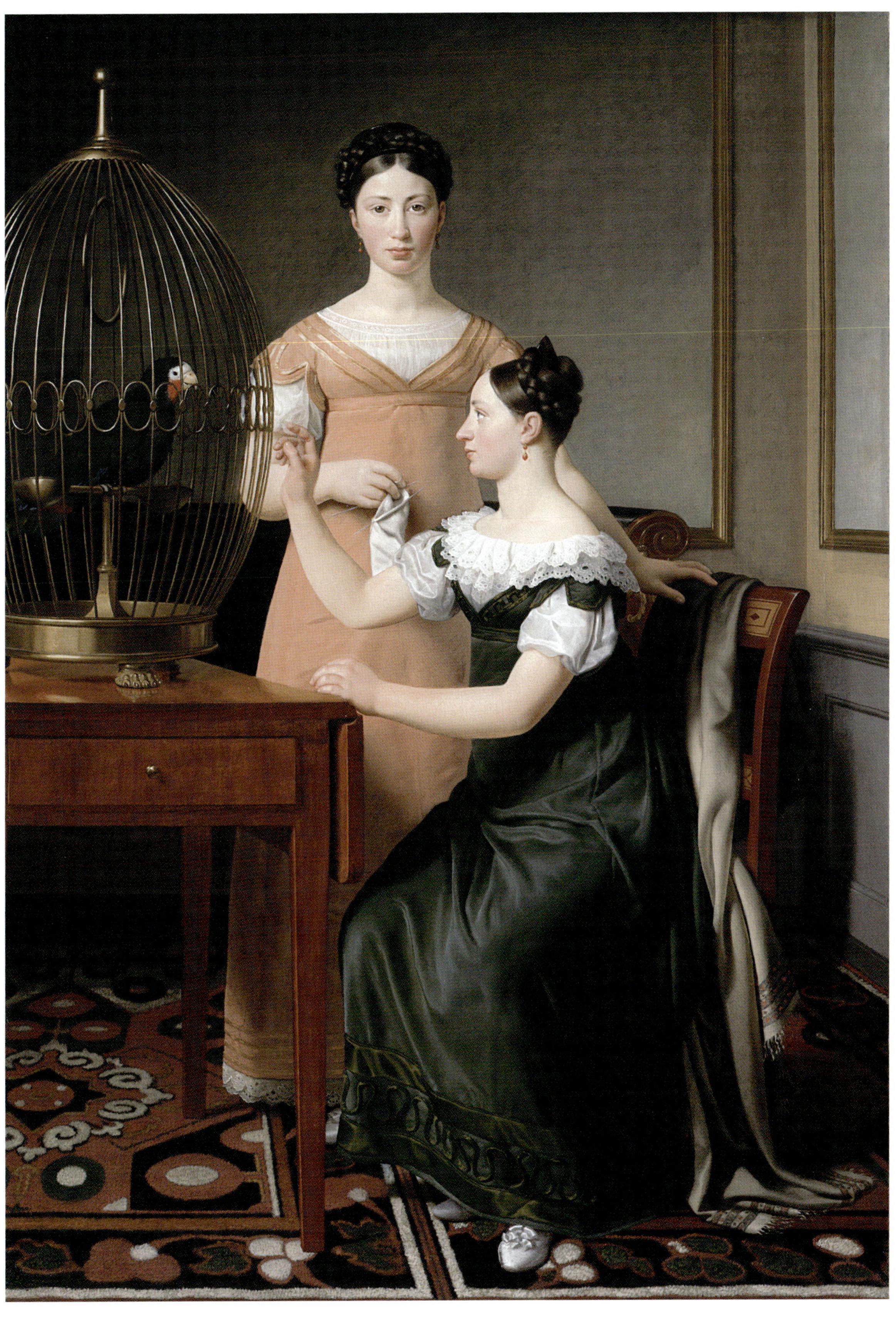

period,[67] also articulates the literal arrival of a social group. This was particularly important for such Jewish families as the Nathansons, with their newly gained citizenship in Denmark.

In 1820, Eckersberg portrayed two of the Nathanson children in *Mendel Levin Nathanson's Elder Daughters, Bella and Hanna* (fig. 36), cementing a language of domesticity and simplicity that would help to shape the Copenhagen bourgeoisie's image of itself. The two girls, portrayed as active, creative, and industrious in the family portrait (in which Hanna plays the piano and Bella, at the compositional center, minds her baby brother) are here rendered as static and nearly timeless, echoing Raphael's representations of the Virgin Mary.[68] In the back, just to the left of the compositional center, stands the frontal, symmetrical Bella, her direct gaze and oval face suggesting a deep complacency. Hanna, seated before her, is shown from the neck up in strict formal profile, but from the neck down in a seemingly active position, her legs awkwardly spread beneath her green dress, and her arms raised as she gestures toward a large brightly colored parrot in a golden cage.[69] The girls are unified both in appearance— tightly coifed hair, matching earrings, and harmonized dresses—and in their gestures of domesticity, knitting a stocking and addressing a household pet. The contrast between the idealized geometry of these figures and the emphasis on the ordinariness of their activities—austere formality wed to keen physical observation, the lessons of Paris and Rome transported home for domestic consumption—characterizes Eckersberg's portraits in this period at the same time that it stabilizes middle-class identity.

In the years just after the Napoleonic Wars, and following Denmark's bankruptcy, new modes of portraiture such as the Nathanson paintings, began to flourish. Among Eckersberg's students at the academy, *freundschaftbilder*, testimonies of friendship, but also of artistic labor, became a notable genre.

Christen Købke's sunny, seemingly straightforward *Portrait of Frederik Sødring* (1832; fig. 37) is such a record of artistic alliance.[70] The painting is signed and dated 26 May 1832 on the lower right, and on its back Sødring inscribed: "Given to me by my friend Chr. Købke on my birthday 31 May 1832."[71] Even without that privileged knowledge, the spectator can glean the relaxed intimacy of the portrayal. Sødring seems to have been captured on the verge of speech, his eyes twinkling in the bright sunlight that enlivens the room, and his shirt and collar indecorously pushed up as he leans back in his chair. Købke represents the landscape painter holding a palette and a palette knife as an affirmation of his identity, sitting in the studio that he and Købke shared for a time in Copenhagen. Dabs of oil paint, largely earth tones, are tidily arrayed on Sødring's palette, the reflexive organization of academic teaching.[72] The dot of red stands out amidst the darker hues, just as the small red box propped against the flowerpot behind Sødring is a focal point for the overall composition. The corner of a landscape painting (fig. 69) appears in the mirror that hangs over his head (see chapter 4).

This is also a didactic painting. Prints, pinned to the wall and bracketing the mirror, map the curious tension between the scrupulous observation of the material world and the high idealism of which Eckersberg wrote. To the right are views of Roman ruins, evidence of the artists' devotion to Roman antiquity. To the left is an image of a cow. Poised between the humble cow and the historically-resonant archaeological views, Sødring occupies a position located in national self-definition.[73] Such artists as Købke and Sødring were dedicated both to antiquity and to the present, to the authority of past imperial might and to the security and familiar pleasures of the local farm. These tensions—between the indigenous and the international, nature and imagination, history and the present—shaped the academy in this period.

37.
Christian Købke
Portrait of Frederik Sødring, 1832
Oil on canvas, 16⅝ x 15 in.
(42.2 x 37.9 cm)
The Hirschsprung Collection,
Copenhagen

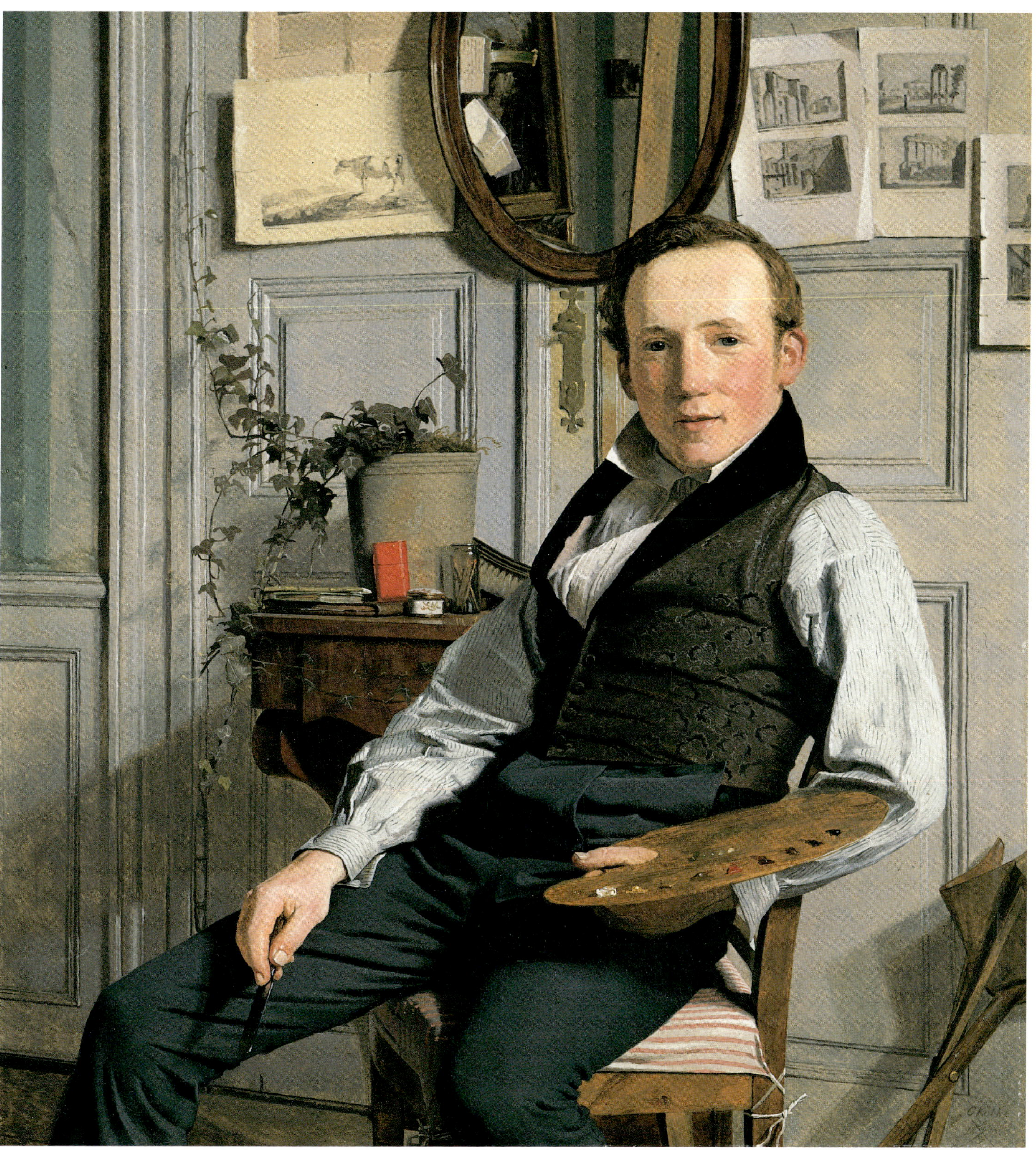

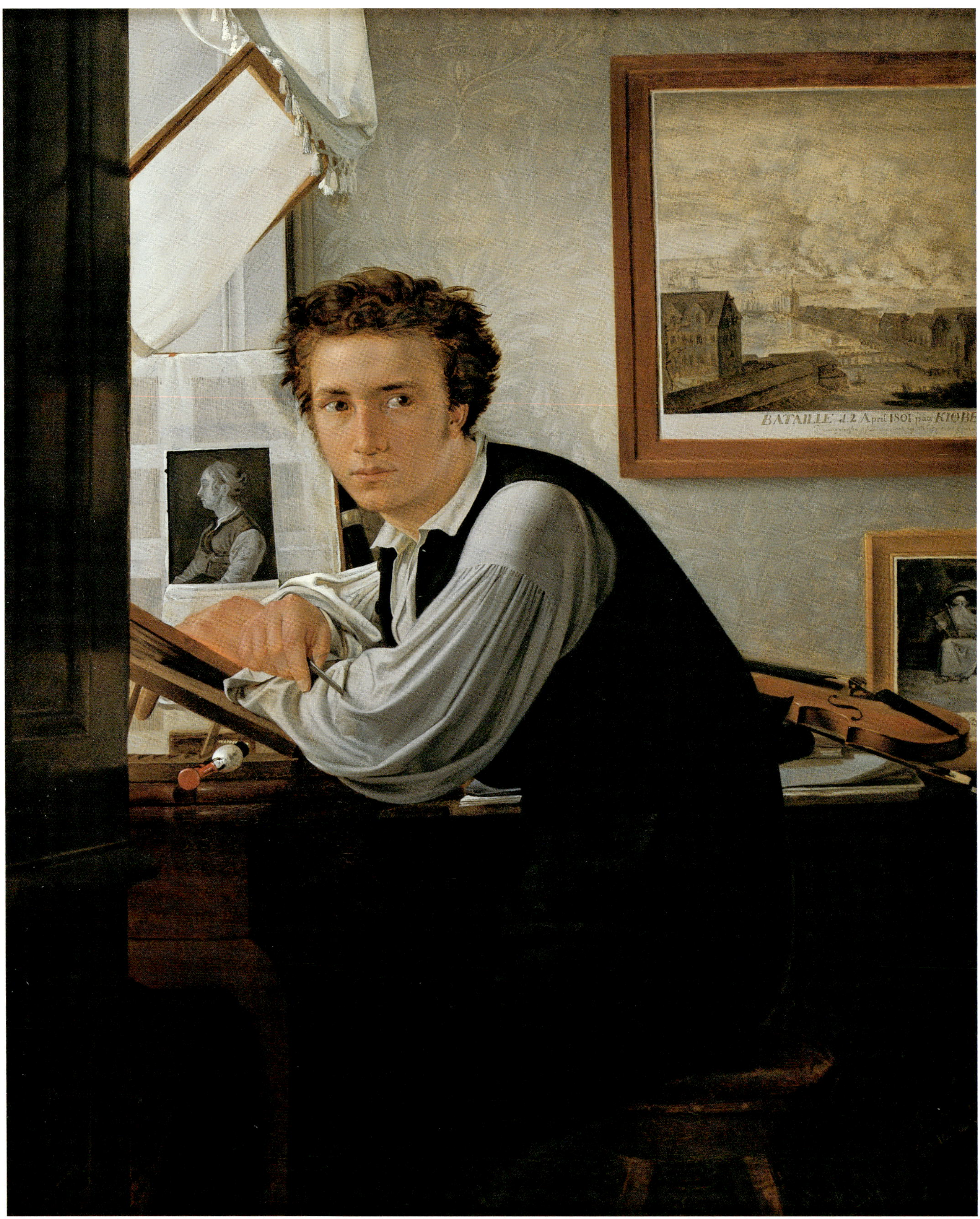

BATAILLE d. 2 April 1801 paa KIOBE

Such artists' portraits suggest how small and interrelated the academic student circles were. Ditlev Conrad Blunck's (1798–1854) *Portrait of the Copperplate Engraver Carl Edvard Sonne* (ca. 1826; fig. 38) represents Sonne (1804–1878) resting at his work table, the light reflected from a copper plate illuminating his motionless left hand. In his right, he holds a burin, and on the wall behind him are engravings by Johann Friderich Clemens, the acknowledged master in his field.[74] These prints are engraved versions of works by Abildgaard and Christian August Lorentzen, including the latter's representation of the *Battle of Copenhagen, 1801*, furnishing the background with emblems of Denmark's history. Sonne's austere clothing, in the black and white of his craft, is cooled by the light that filters through a white scrim attached to the artist's window. Other assertions of identity also appear, including a Turkish pipe resting under Sonne's elevated worktable and the violin and bow behind him, allusions to his pleasures and aspirations.

In turn, Wilhelm Bendz portrayed Blunck in *A Young Artist (Ditlev Blunck) Examining a Sketch in a Mirror* (1826; fig. 39). Here, Blunck regards the reflection of a small oil sketch for his version of an artist's portrait, *Military Painter (Jørgen Sonne) in His Studio* (ca. 1826, Statens Museum for Kunst), portraying the engraver Carl Edvard Sonne's brother.[75] Behind the artist, pinned to his easel, is a black-and-white portrait sketch on paper. Each of these representations is doubled in the mirror's reflection. The painting is also a virtuoso study of spatial, iconographic, and cultural complexity. Spatially, the painting seems to embrace the spectator, displaying not only what is putatively within the frame of the painting, but also the reflection of the room in which the viewer would stand, the far walls and ceiling. We do not see directly the painting on which Blunck works, but only its reflection in the mirror. Recording a standard studio practice in which a painter uses a mirror to gain distance and objectivity from a motif, the painting is also perhaps a complex philosophical commentary on the dualism of nature and art.[76]

As noted by art historian Jens Peter Munk, such representations of shared artistic values were a particular feature of Denmark's Golden Age, a period of camaraderie within the academy, and of aesthetic and cultural self-consciousness among student artists.[77] Taken together, they represent an effort on the part of younger Danish artists to assert themselves as a cultural presence. Bendz's *A Sculptor in His Studio*, (1827; fig. 40), painted in the following year, announces the artist's ambition for artists as modern day heros. The sculptor, Christen Christensen (1806–1845), who received the great Gold Medal in that year, stands well back from the picture plane, gesticulating toward a male model striking a pugilist's pose. The model's jacket is draped in the immediate foreground and his white shirt unceremoniously unbuttoned and tucked into the waist of his uniform trousers. The many plaster casts that line the studio, including the Medici Venus and figures from the Niobe group, offer idealized anatomies that contrast with the soldier's rough, hypermasculine physique. On the sculpture stand is the classicized anatomy that the more delicately shaped artist has created from the working class model. The gestures that echo one another throughout the plaster collection, the strong orthogonal lines of the shelves and cabinets to the left, and the low angle of vision unify the space; a tiny dog which has clamped its diminutive mouth onto a piece of cloth, domesticates it.

Wilhem Bendz's *Interior from Amaliegade with the Artist's Brothers* (ca. 1830; fig. 41) offers both a view into his family's home and the secure world of the Copenhagen middle class. Within it, two brothers are engaged in study, surrounded by books, a skull and an écorché figure (a copy of the one Bendz rendered in *Life Class at the Royal Academy*), and other objects

38.
Ditlev Conrad Blunck
Portrait of the Copperplate Engraver Carl Edvard Sonne, ca. 1826
Oil on canvas, 27⅜ x 22 in.
(69.5 x 56 cm)
Statens Museum for Kunst,
Copenhagen

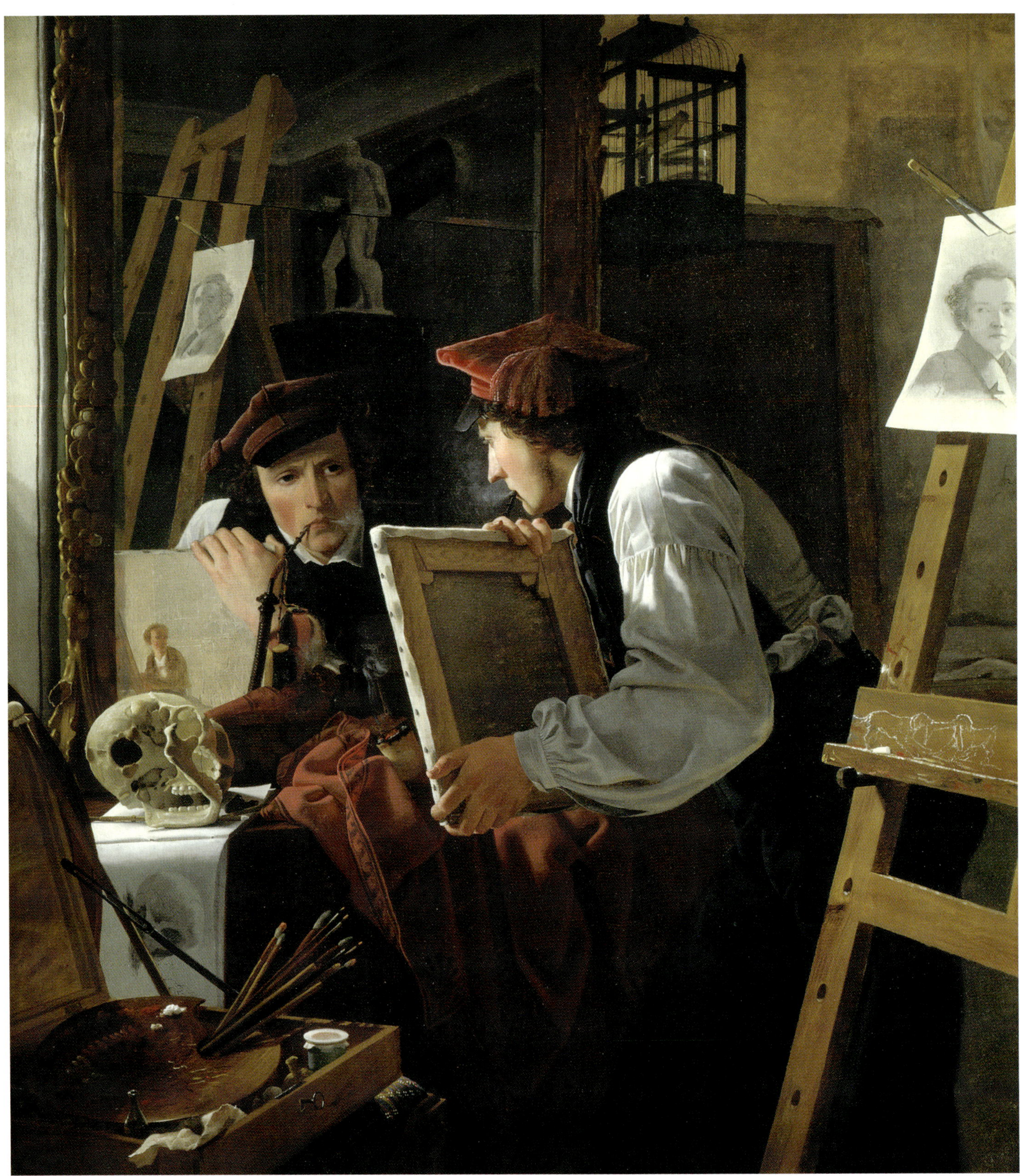

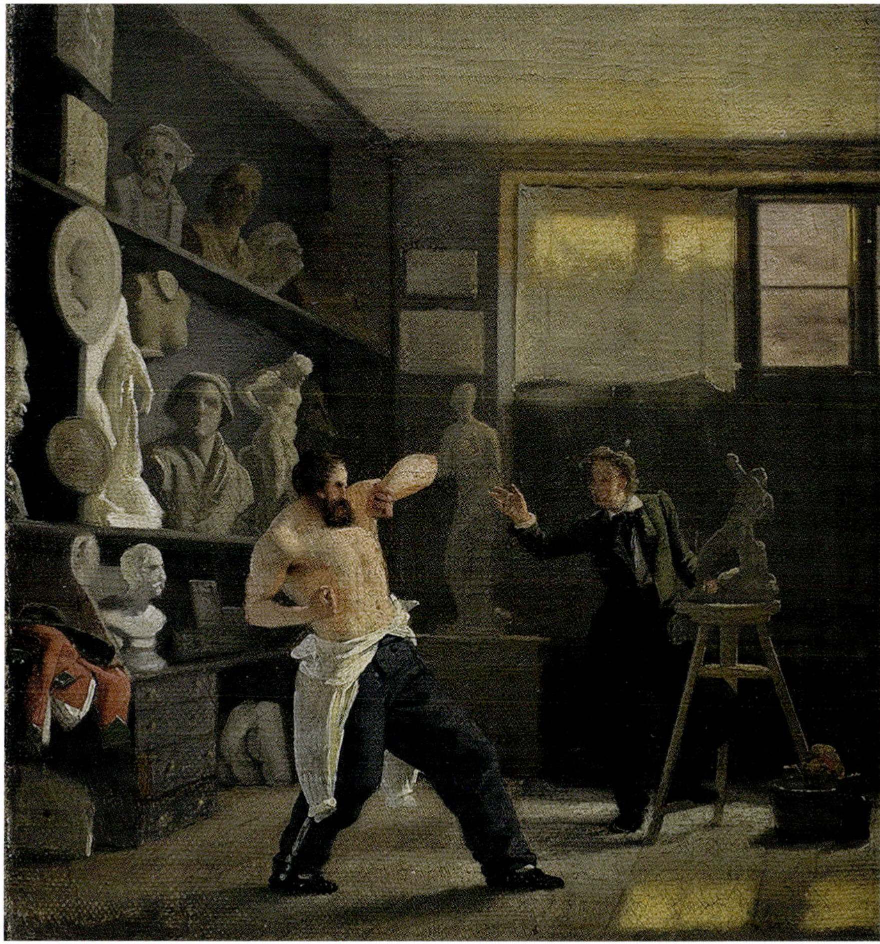

of scientific study. Even the scrubbed wood floor and its scant detritus, the result of the brothers' researches, allude to tidiness and diligence. The proscenium-like space offers a compressed
view of ceiling and floor, perhaps rendered with the aid of an optical device advocated by his
teacher Eckersberg (see chapter 4). Bathed in cool filtered daylight, the room is an austere
space of calm.

Bendz's work reflects Eckersberg's clarity of form and analysis of light effects and geometry, but it also suggests strong affinities with German art of the period. So similar is his
ambitious painting *A Smoking Party* (1827–28; fig. 42) to Johann Erdmann Hummel's *Chess
Party* (1818–19, Nationalgalerie Berlin),[78] that Kasper Monrad theorizes that Bendz made an
undocumented trip to Germany. In the smoke-filled room of the law student Christian Jürgensen, later a mathematician at the University of Copenhagen, a circle of young friends smoke
pipes and play music on a Sunday evening. As Monrad notes, all of the youths represented in
the painting are sons of the bourgeoisie, and all approach the completion of their education.
Among the other members of the group is Bendz, seen in profile, who half stands behind the
table to the left.[79] Relying on Baroque compositional devices, Bendz has organized two of
his figures along sharp diagonal lines that converge at the center, their arms both inviting the
viewer into the painting and gesticulating toward the concentrated fraternity at the table. The
sense of staging is underscored by the swags of fabric on the bed to the right, and the military

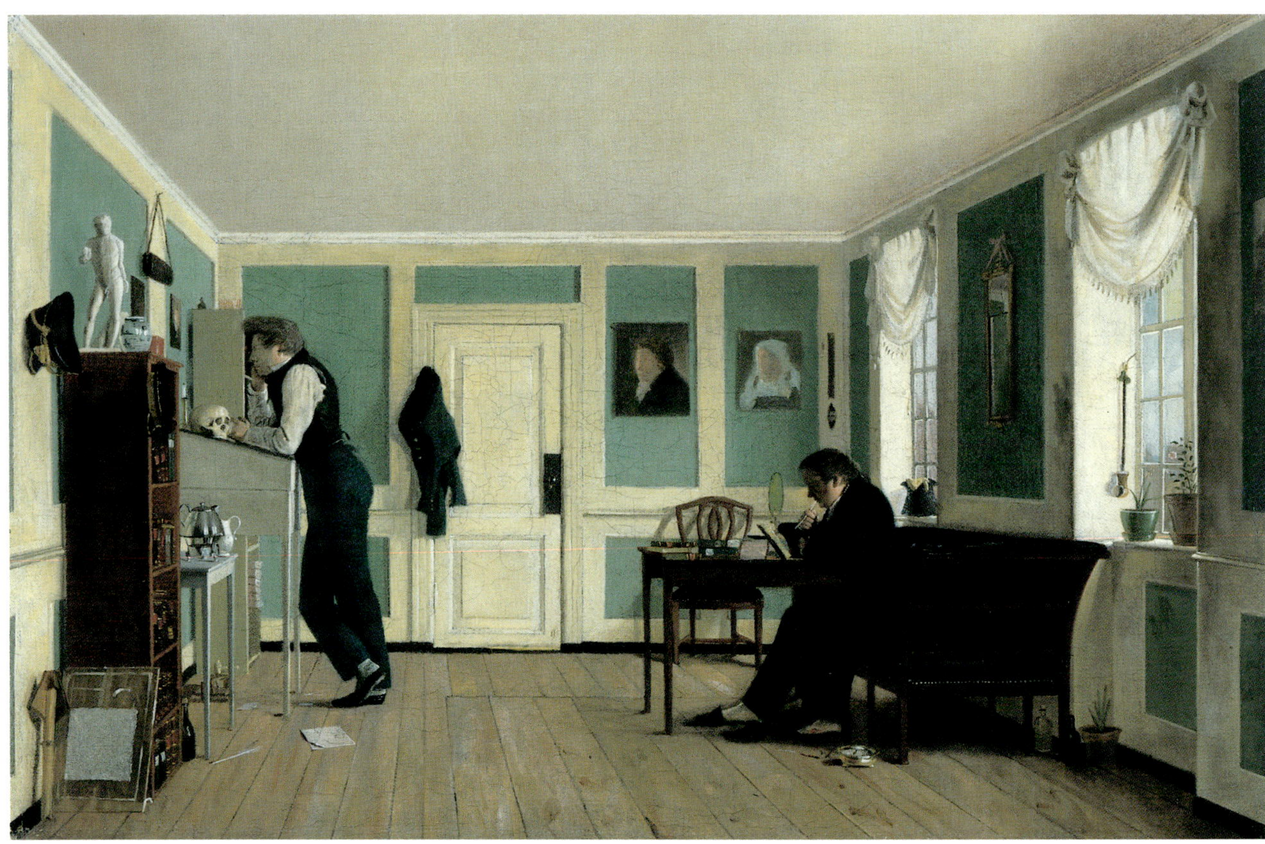

overcoat hanging from the doors at left, the latter detail objected to by Jürgensen's mother as being inaccurate.[80]

This painting is a tour de force, punching up the drama of lighting, perspective, the interplay of figures, atmosphere, and every other formal means at the young artist's disposal. Bendz used the opportunity of the smoke haloing two unseen sources of illumination to create uncanny light effects, from the elegantly softened contours of some of the figures seated at the table, the backlit and linear faces of others, and the exaggeratedly crisp, extravagant shadows that rise up the wall. The room, rendered in rigorously telescoping perspective, forms a stage-like setting. The geometric ordering of the figures suspends their gestures, creating a crystalline stasis that is both reminiscent of Piero della Francesca's compositions and anticipates such modern figurative artists as Balthus. Celebrating smoking, music, and male camaraderie, themes that emerged during the Dutch Golden Age, this painting speaks of leisure, wealth, and privilege and offers a view of the social milieu of Copenhagen's burgeoning cultural scene.

Such a painting underscores the fundamental shift that had taken place within the academy in the first three decades of the nineteenth century, from royal to bourgeois patronage, and from Abildgaard's literary aspirations to Eckersberg's emphasis on the everyday. Like Bendz's nocturnal view of the Royal Academy from 1826, his *Smoking Party* articulates the private ambitions of Danish artists in the classroom and increasingly out in the world. Many of Bendz's colleagues began to realize their ambitions during their study sojourns in Rome, which became for them a second, informal academy.

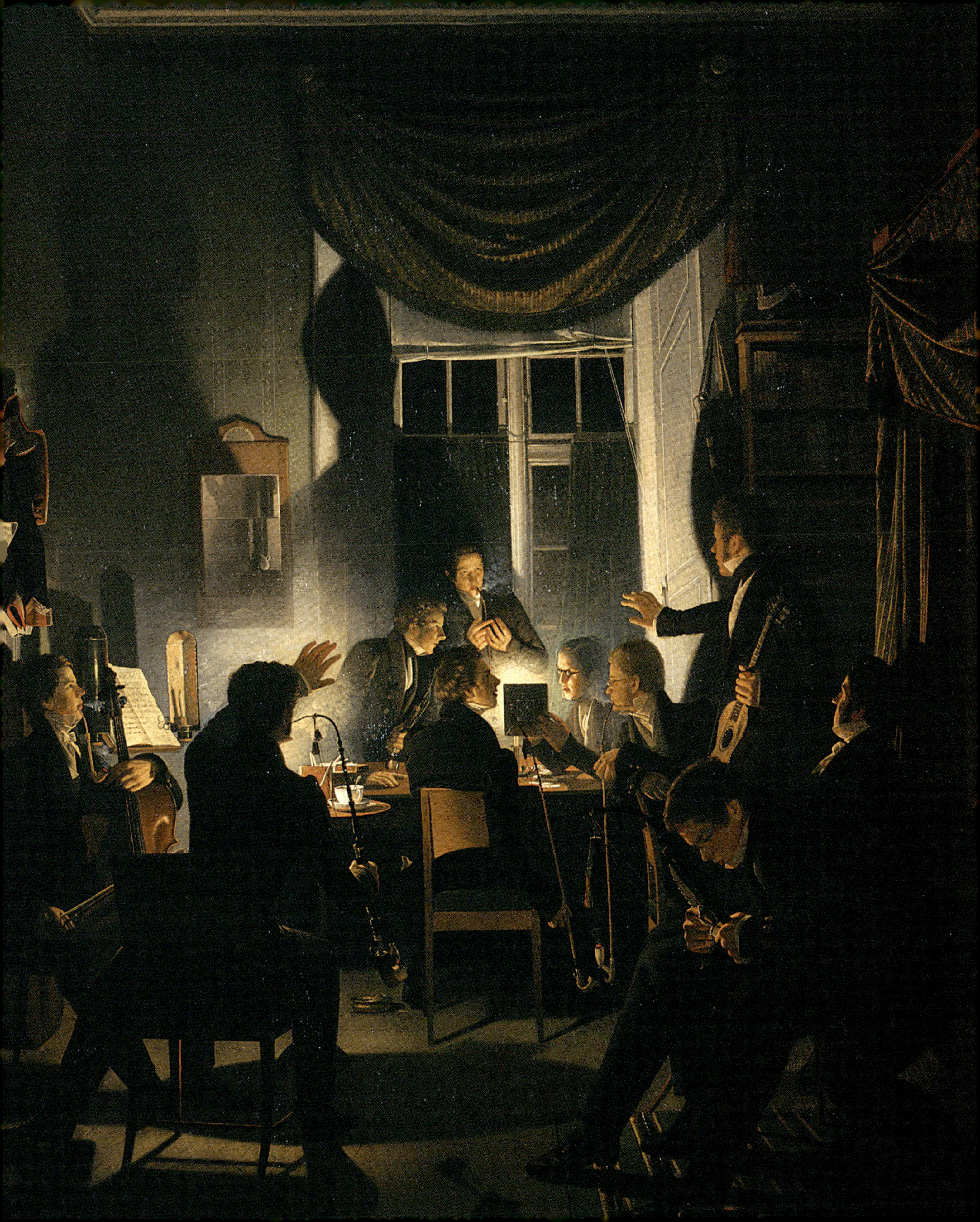

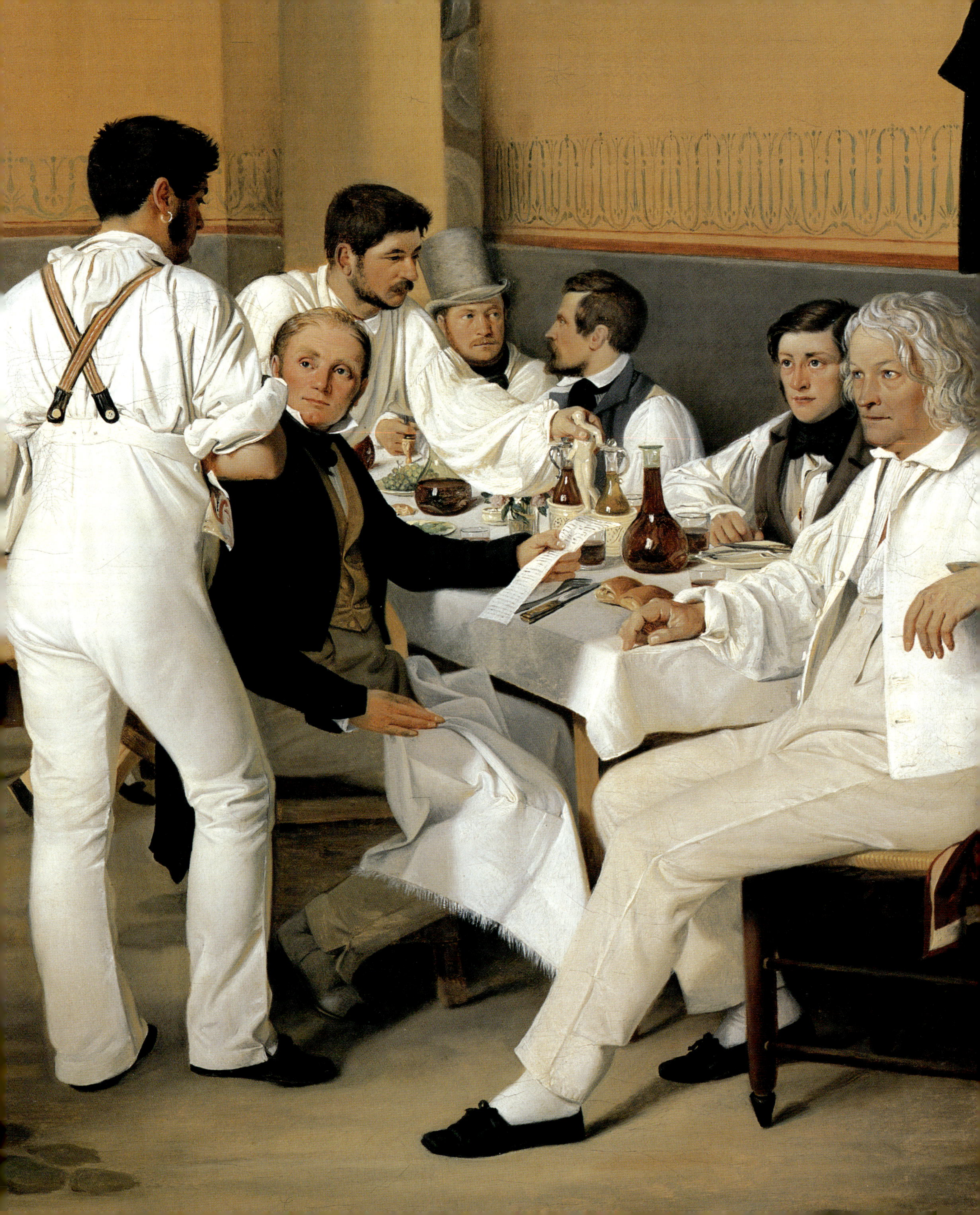

3

Rome as an International Academy

I am growing here into the very ruins, I live with the petrified gods, and the
roses are always blooming, and the church bells ringing—and yet Rome is not
the Rome it was thirteen years ago when I first was here. It is as if everything
were modernized, the ruins even, grass and bushes are cleared away. Everything
is made so neat; the very life of the people seems to have retired; I no longer
hear the tambourines in the streets, no longer see the young girls dancing their
Saltarella, even in the Campagna intelligence has entered by invisible railroads;
the peasant no longer believes as he used to do. . . . But in all that happens,
everything is for the best; one always must love Rome; it is like a storybook, one
is always discovering new wonders, and one lives in imagination and reality.

—Hans Christian Andersen[1]

ALTHOUGH THE AUTHOR HANS CHRISTIAN ANDERSEN'S (1805–
1875) sojourns in Rome were occasionally marked by illness and strife, his memories of the
Eternal City were ultimately colored by the rhetoric of renewal.[2] His romantic desire for exotic
topography, ethnography, and sociability articulates the European-wide preoccupation with
Rome as a fulcrum for the imagination, as a site of transformation and otherness.[3] Andersen's
first experiences of Rome were to a large extent shaped by his friendship with the sculptor Bertel Thorvaldsen, whom he first met in 1833 and who introduced him to the grand tradition.
For Danish artists and intellectuals in Rome, no one was a greater model or mentor than Thorvaldsen, one of the foremost Neoclassical sculptors in Europe. Thorvaldsen's studio on the Via
Sistina was the Alpha and Omega of the Danish artists in Rome, and the nearby Caffè Greco
their collective sitting room. Many Danish artists arrived in Rome fresh from their studies at
the Danish Royal Academy, and some, such as Christoffer Wilhelm Eckersberg, had received
the great Gold Medal and were supported by official stipends.[4] These artists, like Andersen,
eagerly anticipated Rome's influence upon them and were receptive both to antiquity and to
the modern aspects of international urban life.[5]

Rome offered these artists a kind of second, informal "academy" whose greatest lessons lay
not in its classical legacy but in the artistic milieu of the city. Typical of tourist culture, members
of the Danish community experienced a sense of displacement in a foreign landscape as well as
freedom from the strictures and social norms of home.[6] Engulfed by the exoticism of Catholic

43.
Ditlev Conrad Blunck
*Danish Artists in the Osteria
La Gensola in Rome*, ca. 1836
(detail)

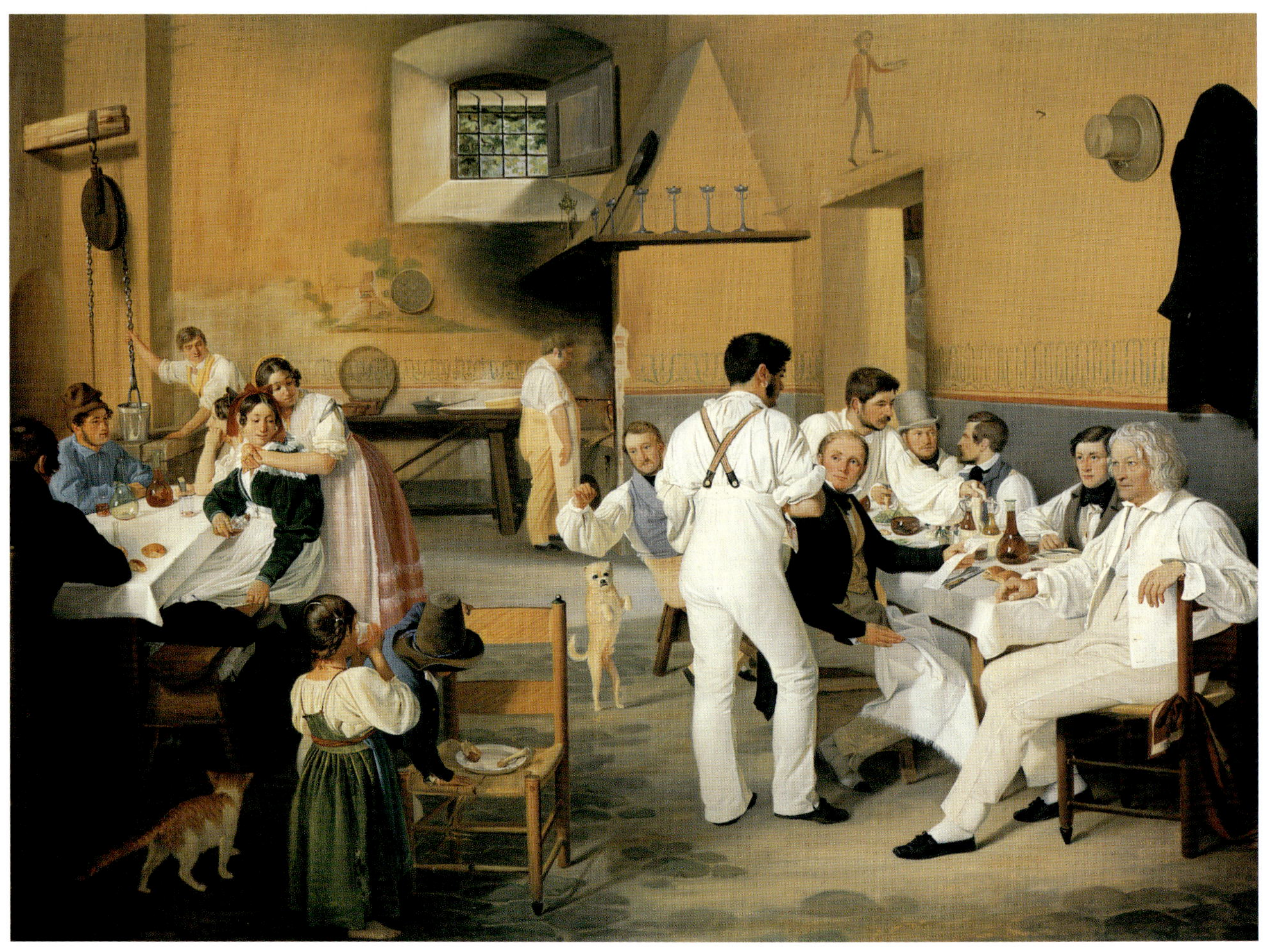

43.
Ditlev Conrad Blunck
*Danish Artists in the Osteria La Gensola
in Rome*, ca. 1836
Oil on canvas, 28 x 37⅞ in. (71 x 94.5 cm)
The Museum of National History
at Frederiksborg Castle, Hillerød

culture and often enamored of the city's romanticized history, Danish artists began to stretch the tethers of their academic training. The most radical innovation of Eckersberg, and later his students, was the synthesis of neoclassical academicism and the keen scrutiny of nature, and the assertion of landscape painting as equal in status to history painting. Rome offered Eckersberg the stage for a new kind of unheroic view painting, invested with the rigorous ordering of David and Thorvaldsen's classicism, and embodying the subjectivity of German Romantic theory. For his students from the academy, including Ditlev Blunck, Christen Købke, Constantin Hansen, and Martinus Rørbye, the artist community in Rome provided a new cosmopolitanism. Their new approaches to art emerged in Rome, both the storybook Rome of Andersen's imagination and the one of reality. Bertel Thorvaldsen was central to both.

The storybook Rome is illustrated in Ditlev Blunck's *Danish Artists in the Osteria La Gensola in Rome* (ca. 1836; fig. 43). This painting of artistic camaraderie echoes Blunck's interest in artistic culture and life as alluded to in his *Portrait of Copperplate Engraver Carl Edvard Sonne* (chapter 2). Here, however, the setting is not an artist's studio, but a restaurant in which a group of Danish artists, gathered around the table to the right with Thorvaldsen seated at the head of the table, are engaged in the life of modern Rome. A group of locals, some exoticized by their costuming, sit at the table to the left of the composition while others are shown at work in the restaurant. The genre painter Albert Küchler (1803–1886), seated furthest to the left at the artists' table, engages playfully with the group of children and animals in the foreground. Also included are Just Henrik Mundt (1782–1859, later the mayor of Copenhagen), and the architect Michael Gottlieb Bindesbøll (1800–1856). The motif, commissioned in 1835 by Mundt, and produced in two variations by Blunck, was exhibited at Charlottenborg Palace as a tableau of artistic life in Rome.[7] Thorvaldsen is seated at the head of the table in what amounts to the figure of a latter-day Jesus, the composition reminiscent of Tintoretto's *Last Supper* (1592–94) in San Giorgio Maggiore in Venice.[8]

Thorvaldsen was the most famous Danish artist in Europe and the stuff of myth for Danes by the time this painting was created. Born into the most modest of circumstances, Thorvaldsen had entered the Royal Academy at the age of 11 in 1781, where he studied under Johannes Wiedewelt and Nicolai Abildgaard and won a succession of academic prizes. During his years of study, he worked with Abildgaard on the sculptural decoration of the Amalienborg Palace, among other projects. Awarded the great Gold Medal in 1793, Thorvaldsen arrived in Rome in 1797. There, he quickly found support from the well-connected Danish archaeologist Georg Zoëga (1755–1809), one of Rome's leading authorities on antiquity.[9] Thorvaldsen remained in Rome on and off for the next forty years. His early work was influenced decisively by his friend Asmus Jakob Carstens (1754–1798), the northern German history painter whom he had first met at the academy in 1782, and by the Swedish sculptor Johan Tobias Sergel (1740–1814). Just after the turn of the century, Thorvaldsen began to receive significant commissions from all over Europe, beginning with his first acknowledged masterpiece, *Jason and the Golden Fleece* (1802–03; fig. 44). First modeled in clay in 1800, *Jason* was created in plaster at the request of the influential poet and travel writer Friederike Brun (1765–1835), and then in marble for the renowned British connoisseur and author Thomas Hope (1769–1831). *Jason* displayed the grand scale, heroic theme, and severe anatomy of Thorvaldsen's immensely influential early style, an interpretation of antiquity that was perceived as "northern" in comparison to the slightly older Italian master Antonio Canova's (1757–1822) "southern" sensibility.[10] Other commissions quickly followed, particularly portrait busts, which constituted a major part of his production. In 1812, Thorvaldsen created the Alexander Frieze for the Palazzo del Quirinale in a matter of a few months. The frieze was commissioned in anticipation of Napoleon's arrival in Rome, and the work cemented Thorvaldsen's reputation as a genius (see fig. 25). Four years later, the artist began his restoration of the so-called Aegina Marbles, the sculpture from the Temple of Aphaia at Aegina, later housed in the Munich Glyptotek (fig. 45), which was seen at the time as the most important restoration of an antique monument.[11] Thorvaldsen also became the restoration advisor to the Vatican. Such important and remunerative work enabled the artist to establish large studios in which he employed other artists to size up and cast his work, to carve the marbles after his clay and plaster originals, and to finish all but the most important commissions.[12] By

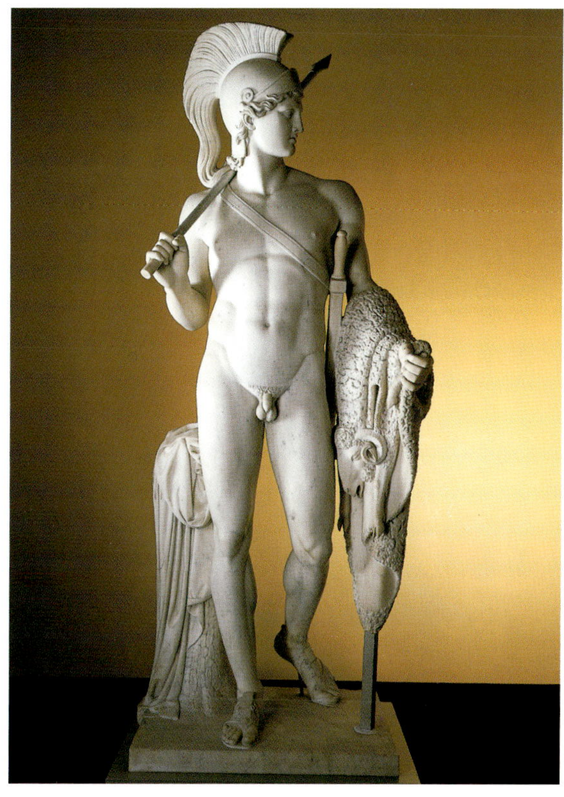

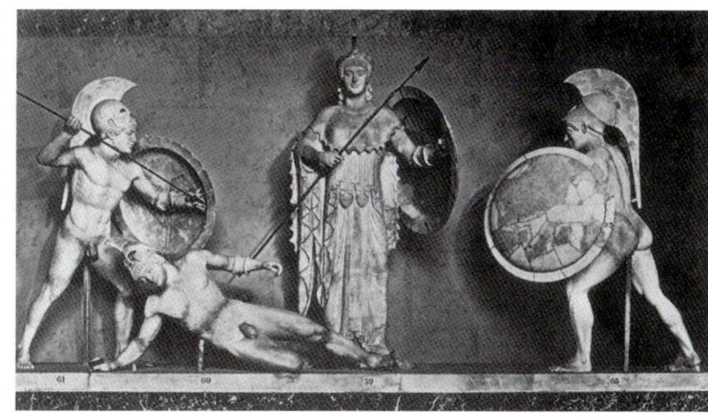

44.
Bertel Thorvaldsen
Jason and the Golden Fleece, 1802–1803
Plaster, height 96¾ in. (245.5 cm)
Thorvaldsens Museum, Copenhagen

45.
Athena Flanked by Warriors, central group
(as restored by Thorvaldsen, late 1810s)
from west pediment, Temple of Aphaia,
Aegina, ca. 500–490 B.C.E.
Staatliche Antikensammlungen
und Glyptothek, Munich

the later 1830s he had achieved among the mightiest reputations of any artist in Europe, and the example of his career operated as part of the "dream of Rome" for aspiring Danish artists.[13]

For Danes, Thorvaldsen embodied a new Danish nobility, born of inspiration and diligence rather than bloodlines in the unstable post-Napoleonic years. A painting from 1830 dramatizes his unique cultural position. Thorvaldsen had received the commission to create a tomb for Pope Pius VII (1824–1831) in St. Peter's basilica, an unprecedented honor for a non-Catholic artist. In 1826, Pope Leo XII made a formal visit to inspect the artist's progress on the sculptures. Hans Ditlev Martens (1795–1864), one of Eckersberg's first students in Copenhagen and a protégé of Thorvaldsen in Rome, recorded the event in *Pope Leo XII on the Feast Day of St. Luke (October 18) 1826, Visiting Thorvaldsen's Studio on the Piazza Barberini in Rome* (fig. 46). Trained in part as an architectural painter, Martens portrays Thorvaldsen's studio (one of several) as cavernous. Within its sublime monumentality, the northern artist greets the Catholic father amid a virtual survey of the former's life's work.[14] Thorvaldsen's figures, including those commissioned for St. Peter's, render all human presence, even that of the pope at the center of the composition, diminutive.

Hans Christian Andersen offered a view of Thorvaldsen's own stature in his diary: "During the previous papacy, His Holiness visited Thorvaldsen's workshop on the day of St. Luke. Because it was a holiday, there was no one there to meet him, and he had to wait by the main door until the keys could be found. Thorvaldsen himself was not to be found. Finally, one of the artists located him. Dressed in his old blue coat, with leather patches, and over-sized shoes, Thorvaldsen insisted on being true to the Italian custom of kneeling in front of the pope. But the pope would have none of it, and as the pope stepped into his carriage at the end of the visit, he continued an earnest conversation with Thorvaldsen while the entire square beyond were full of people kneeling in deference to the pope's presence. As the pope took his leave, he blessed Thorvaldsen, who, by then, was bowing deeply."[15] This modern history painting served as a token of individual and national prestige for the Copenhagen art audience.

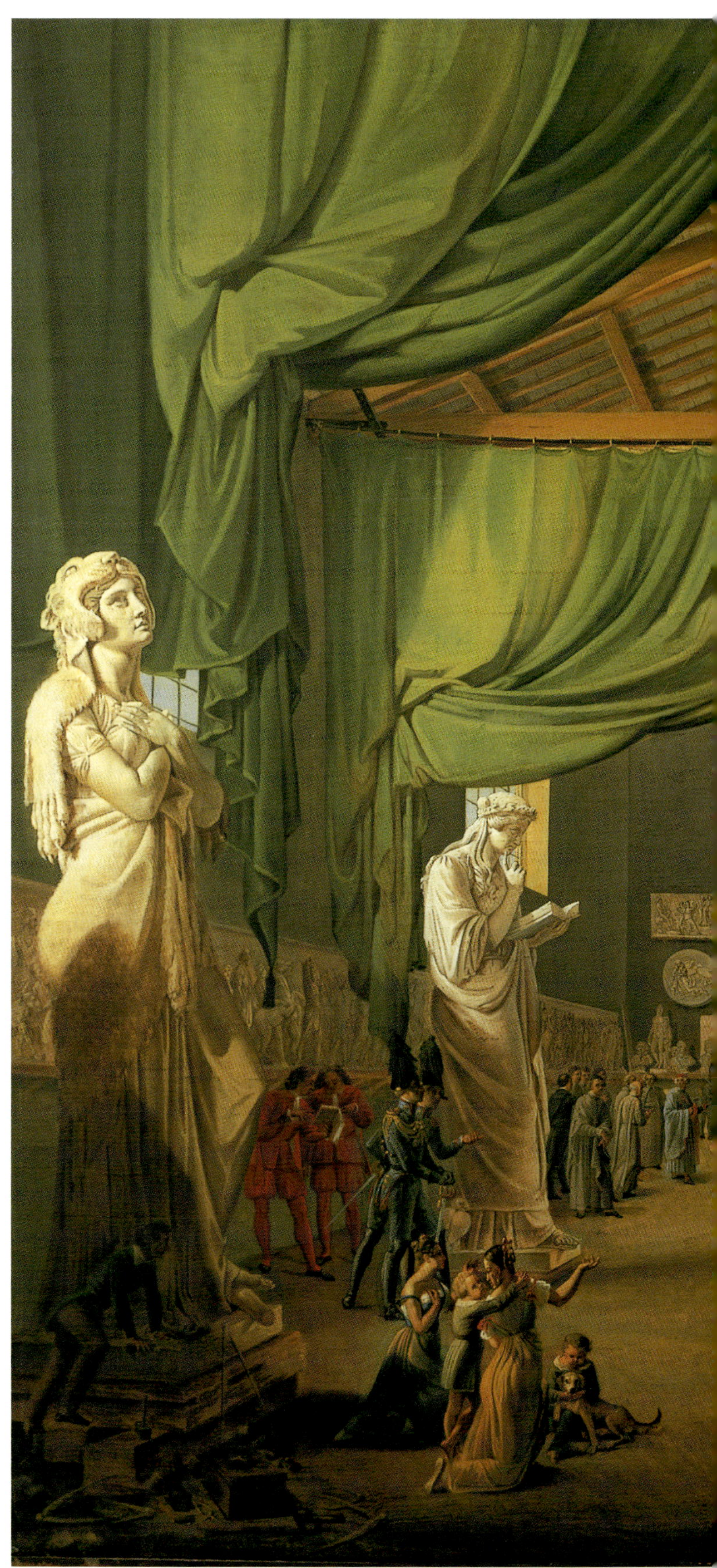

46.
Hans Ditlev Martens
Pope Leo XII on the Feast Day of St. Luke (October 18) 1826, Visiting Thorvaldsen's Studio on the Piazza Barberini in Rome, 1830
Oil on canvas, 39⅜ x 54⅜ in.
(100 x 138 cm)
Thorvaldsens Museum, Copenhagen

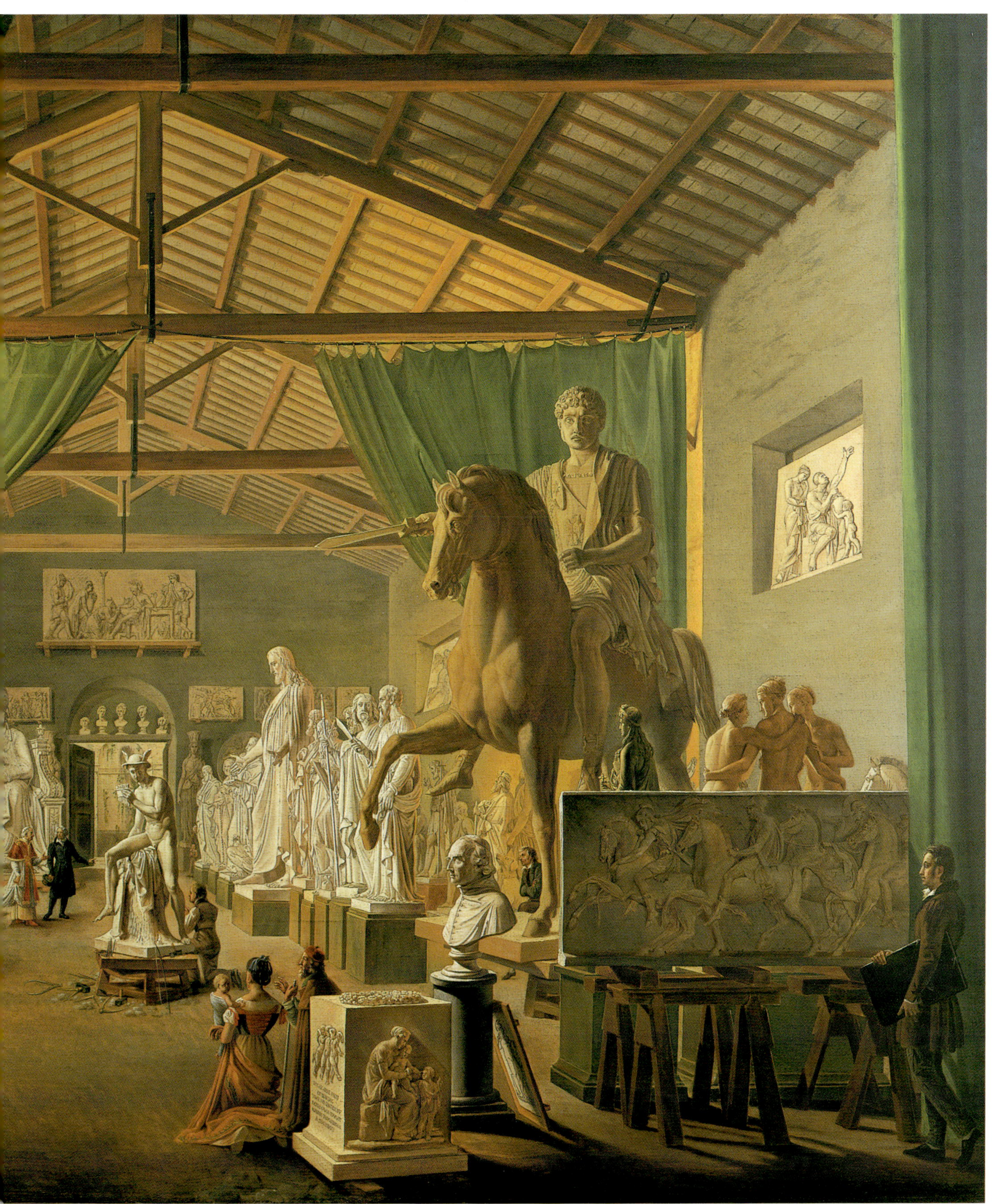

In 1838 Thorvaldsen returned to settle in Copenhagen. Staged as a triumphal procession as for a conquering hero, the homecoming was recorded by Hans Christian Andersen:

> Thorwaldsen [sic] . . . was expected in Denmark in the autumn of 1838, and great festive preparations were made in consequence. A flag was to wave upon one of the towers of Copenhagen as soon as the vessel which brought him should come in sight. It was a national festival. Boats decorated with flowers and flags filled the Rhede; painters, sculptors, all had their flags with emblems; the students bore a Minerva, the poets a Pegasus. It was misty weather, and the ship was first seen when it was already close by the city, and all poured out to meet him. . . . In honor of Thorwaldsen . . . I wrote of Jason who fetched the golden fleece—that is to say, Jason-Thorwaldsen, who went forth to win golden art.[16]

Like Thorvaldsen's homecoming, his funeral in 1844 was organized as a remarkable spectacle, and an extensive set of rituals that bound the artist to the nation.

While establishing for Denmark international stature and significance in the arts and being a kind of icon for aspiring artists, Thorvaldsen also gave Copenhagen a living legacy. Prior to his return to Copenhagen, the artist offered the nation his sizeable art collection; his will drawn up in 1830 first formalized this intention.[17] In addition to his own vast corpus of original works in clay and plaster, and the works of antiquity that he collected, Thorvaldsen had also amassed the largest collection of modern art in Rome,[18] much of it purchased from within his immediate circle. Plans were put in place, after much debate, for a museum dedicated to the artist and his collection in the center of Copenhagen, next to the rebuilt Christiansborg Palace on the site of the old Royal Coach House. Designed by architect Michael Gottlieb Bindesbøll, the Thorvaldsen Museum (1839–1847) is a radically abstracted building—in the words of Robert Rosenblum, a "monument of wilful archaism."[19] Synthesizing elements from Egyptian and Greek architecture—Western architecture's "earliest" roots—Bindesbøll intended the museum as a rhetorical new democratic "beginning" for the Danish public.[20]

This was the first building to be constructed as a museum in Denmark, and it was created for the broad public. Constantin Hansen's sun-soaked 1858 painting of the *Thorvaldsen Museum* (fig. 47) depicts the museum as part of an accessible urban landscape, asserting the Thorvaldsen Museum as the people's museum, its former imperial location now the site of both labor and leisure, and as a locus of family life. Hansen also emphasizes its geometric form and strong golden coloration. Bindesbøll, enamored of the traces of ancient architectural polychromy, determined that the museum would be rendered in a style and in colors befitting Thorvaldsen's archeological passions. Painted friezes by military painter Jørgen Sonne (brother of Edvard Sonne) on the building's north and south façades, one barely visible in Hansen's painting, elaborate the scene of Thorvaldsen's triumphal return to Denmark in 1838. On one wall, Thorvaldsen is welcomed by Denmark's intellectual and cultural elite, and on the other, his works are shown being transported from his studio in Rome to the new, as yet unbuilt, museum (fig. 48).[21] During Denmark's period of emerging democratization, the museum and its archaizing architecture embodied the values of freedom and coherence.[22]

Both Constantin Hansen and Jørgen Sonne had been members of Thorvaldsen's circle in Rome. While in Rome in the 1830s, Bindesbøll was already at work on Thorvaldsen's museum. Hansen's *A Party of the Danish Artists in Rome* (1837; fig. 49), set in Bindesbøll's

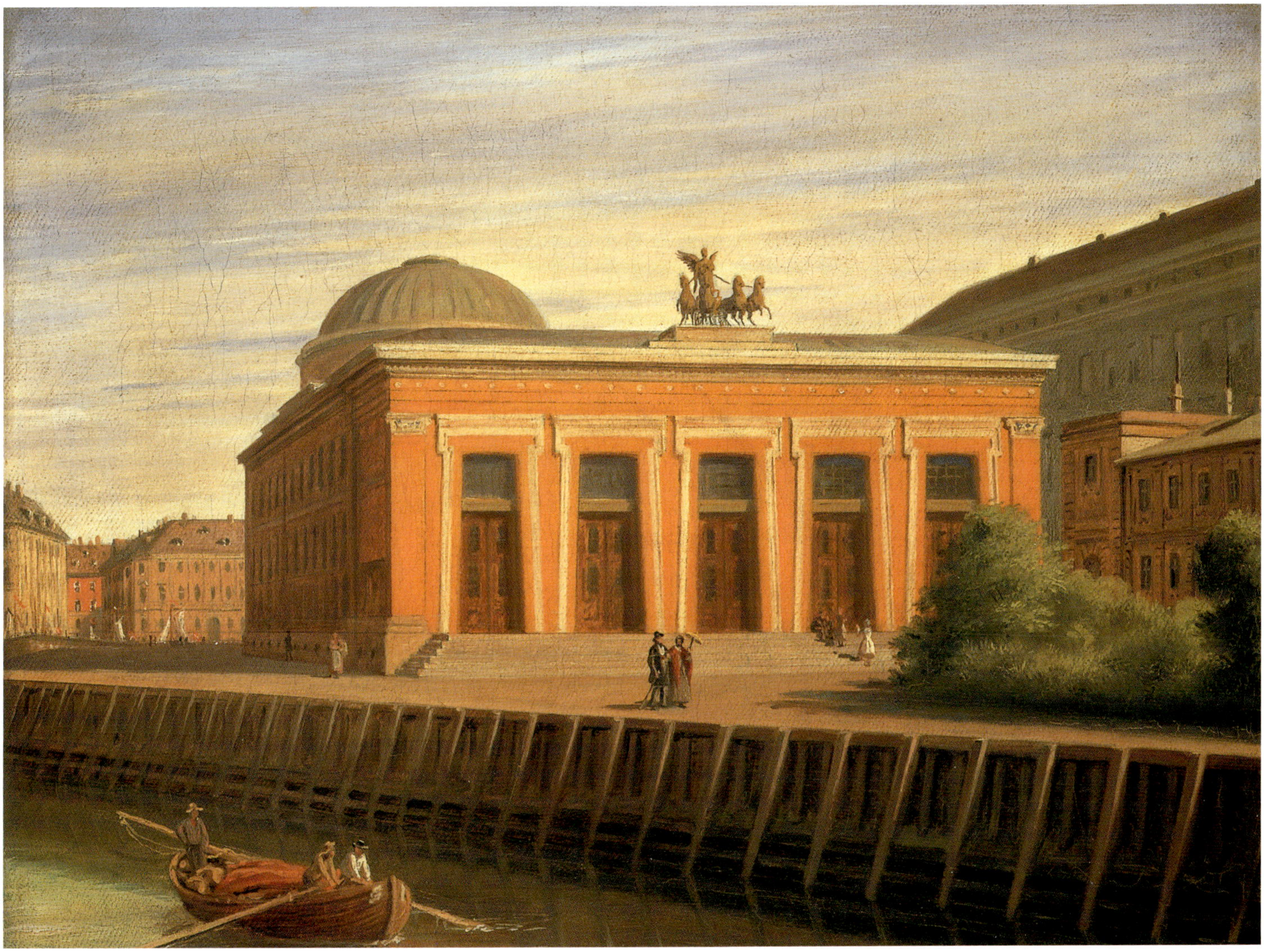

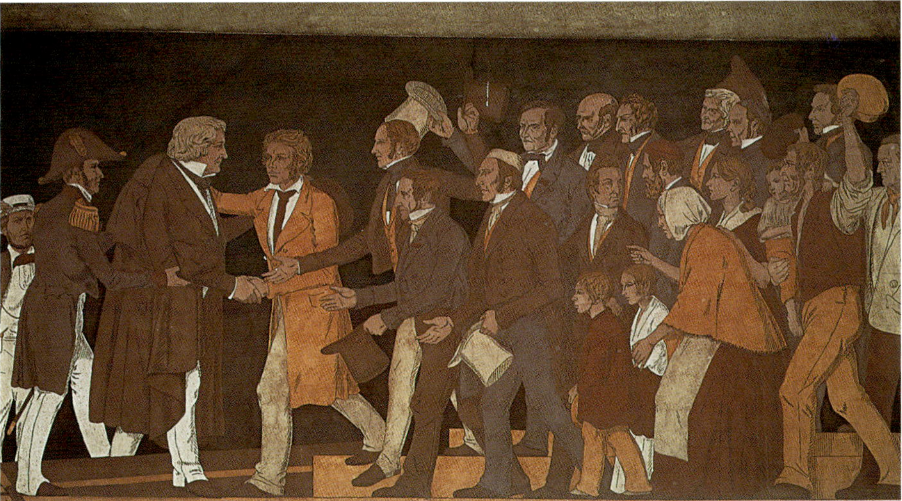

47.
Constantin Hansen
Thorvaldsens Museum, 1858
Oil on canvas, 14⅜ x 17¼ in.
(36.3 x 43.8 cm)
Thorvaldsens Museum, Copenhagen

48.
Jørgen Sonne
Thorvaldsens Frieze, Section 1
(*Thorvaldsen's Homecoming*), 1850
Painted plaster
Thorvaldsens Museum, Copenhagen

room on the Via Sistina, includes a sketch for the museum on the table at the right. The limned museum acts as a stand-in for Thorvaldsen, who is absent from the painting but who was central to the experience of these artists. Hansen included in this painting seven Danes, all of whom had studied at the academy and received subsidies to study in Rome (some had appeared in Blunck's painting of the previous year)—Hansen at left, the reclining Bindesbøll, painter Martinus Rørbye (1803–1848), Wilhelm Marstrand (1810–1873), Albert Küchler, Ditlev Conrad Blunck, and Jørgen Sonne. The artists are surrounded by their work, including Bindesbøll's drawing of the Thorvaldsen Museum, a portrait by Hansen and his view of the Vesta Temple above it on the wall, and additional sketches and a small sculpture by Hermann Wilhelm Bissen (1798–1868) at the left.

As noted by art historian Søren Kaspersen, Hansen's modest genre painting emulates Raphael's *School of Athens* (ca. 1510–11) in the Vatican's Stanza della Segnatura by highlighting a difference of philosophical views: Hansen depicts Marstrand pointing to the landscape in contrast to his peers' regard for the interior (a pun on the opposing gestures of Plato and Socrates in Raphael's fresco). In this way, he translates ancient philosophical debates into the growing contemporary artistic question of whether artistic truth arises from nature or the imagination.[23] Painted on commission for the Fine Arts Society of Copenhagen, which had moreover specifically named the participants in the scene, the painting is a demonstration piece of the Dano-Romans' seriousness and collectivity of purpose.[24] The collective, or gemeinschaft, was a central concern for the Danish artists in Rome.

One of the critical experiences for the Dano-Roman community was the cosmopolitanism both of the city and of Thorvaldsen's social and artistic circles. There was a large community of northern Europeans living in Rome, among them some 1,200 German artists, between the years 1814–1848. As Torsten Gunnarsson notes, the Danes' close cultural and linguistic links to the Germans played a critical role in shaping the Danish artists' responses to both the antiquities they encountered in Rome and to the surrounding landscape, enriching the formal training they had received at home with emotive approaches to landscape drawn from German Romantic philosophy.[25]

Thorvaldsen was closely connected with scholars, collectors, and patrons of the arts within this community who were advocates of German Romantic philosophy. One of the earliest was the poet, travel writer, and saloniste Friederike Brun, who brought together Danish, British, and German artists and intellectuals.[26] Her immense erudition contributed to her circle's discussions of the authors of the Sturm und Drang movement as well as classical literature,[27] in particular the mystical ideas of Wilhelm Heinrich Wackenroder (1773–1798) and Johan Ludwig Tieck (1773–1853).

Thorvaldsen's circle also included members of the Nazarene movement, the German artists who rejected the tenets of academic neoclassicism in favor of medieval and early Renaissance Catholic-inspired art. They shared a commitment to communal art and ideals, and to the assertion of emotion over intellect as the creative force of art. They also helped to revive contemporary interest in narrative fresco painting through their cycle for the Casa Bartholdy Palazzo Zuccari (1816–1817, now the Biblioteca Herziana), an important source of inspiration for northern artists in Rome and greatly praised by Thorvaldsen.[28]

Through his circle of affiliates, Thorvaldsen, one of the greatest proponents of Neoclassicism, helped to influence the younger Danish artists' move away from academic classicism.

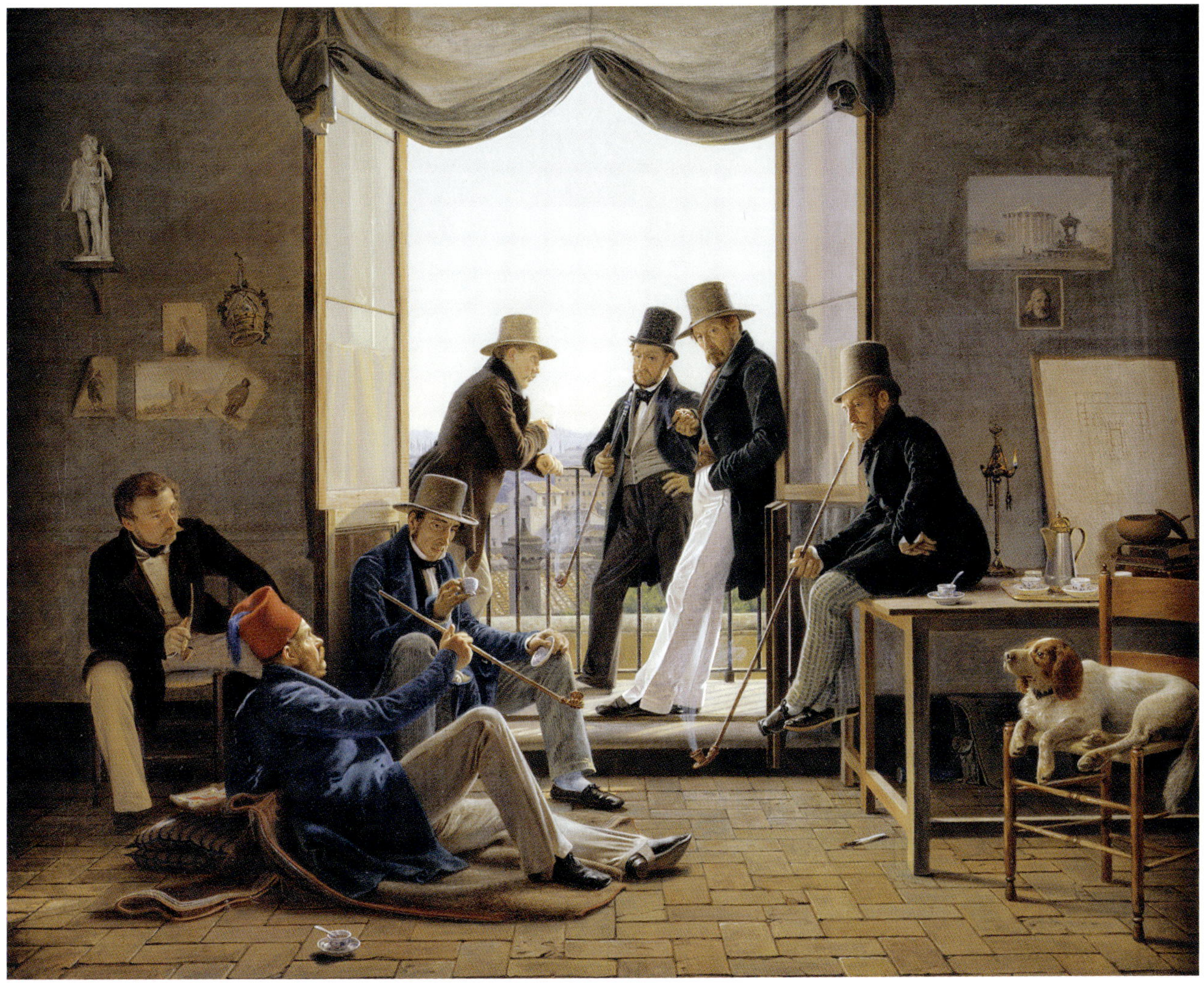

49.
Constantin Hansen
A Party of the Danish Artists in Rome, 1837
Oil on canvas, 24⅜ x 29⅛ in. (62 x 74 cm)
Statens Museum for Kunst,
Copenhagen

Among the German artists in Thorvaldsen's circle, Joseph Anton Koch (1768–1839) provided a fresh approach to landscape by defining it as a manifestation of heroic, monumental forces. Koch helped to fuel the popularity of landscape painting among the northerners through his commitment to the artist's creative vision and subjectivity, that one's instincts and spiritual yearnings could be realized through the direct study of nature. He also helped to redirect the Dano-Romans away from their youthful adherence to academic training by disparaging the practices of classical pedagogy. As Koch wrote: "Like a swarm of maggots, crawling from a rotting cheese, a countless mob of artists crawls from the Academies. . . . In these Academies, or Schools of Beauty, reigns a despotism which permits only what can be seen every day to enter the students' brains. Mindless drawing after plaster casts and models goes on for years; the goal is not to teach truth to nature but an abstract aesthetic mannerism which kills all character."[29] Instead, he and his generation proposed "nature" as a school for character through its monumentality and sense of immanence. Idealizing nature—investing it with meaning and poetic ideas—represented the cultivation of the self, a release from institutional rationalization.

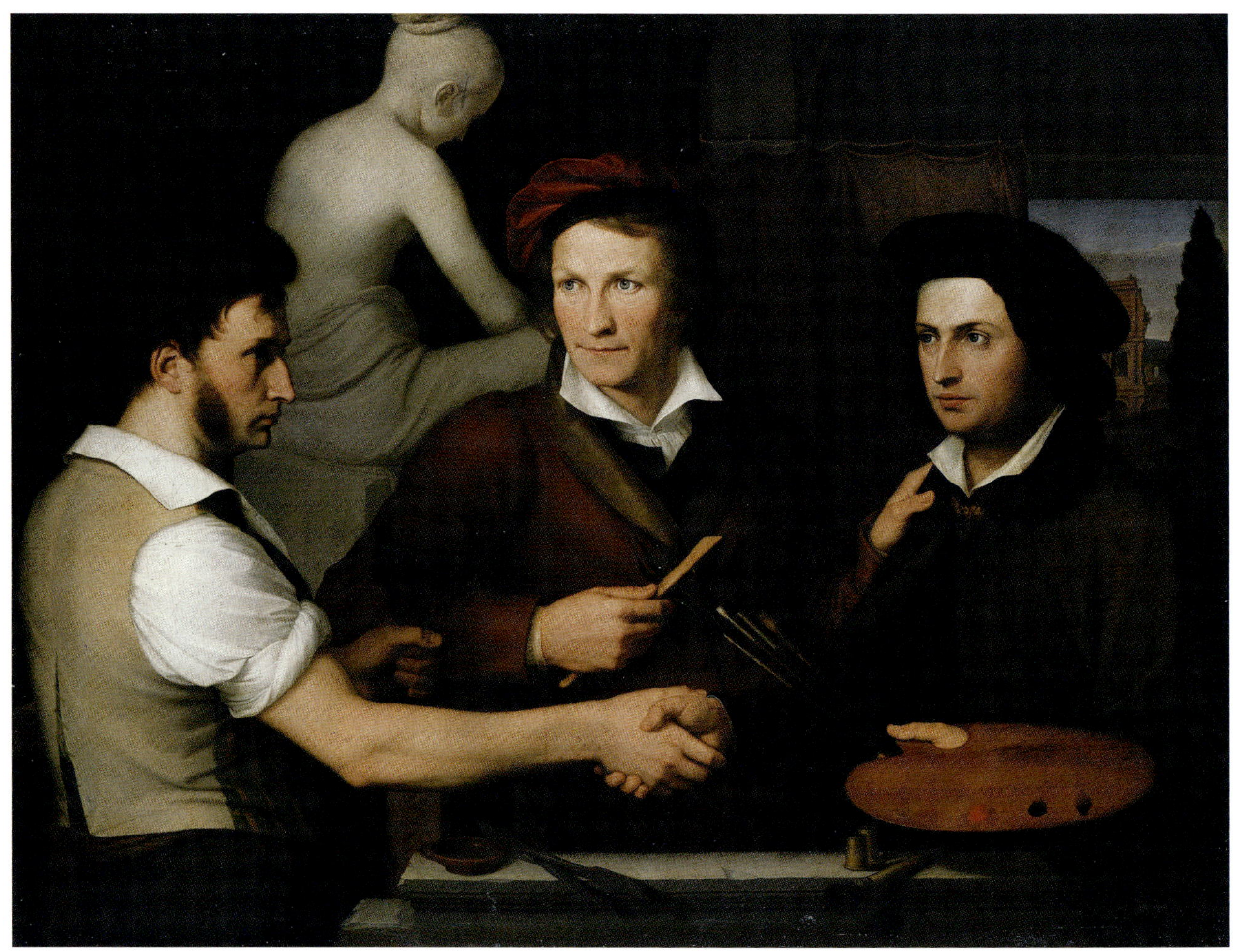

The notion of an intimate artists' community formed outside of an academy was itself important within Thorvaldsen's circle. Friedrich Wilhelm Schadow (1788–1862), a member of the Nazarene circle, painted *Self-Portrait with his Brother Ridolfo and Bertel Thorvaldsen* (ca. 1815–16; fig. 50), a *freundschaft* (committed friendship), painting marking Thorvaldsen's mentorship of the sculptor Ridolfo (Rudolph Schadow, 1786–1822), and an ode to shared ideals. This painting by Schadow as well as those by Blunck (*Danish Artists in the Osteria La Gensola in Rome*) and Hansen (*Party of the Danish Artists in Rome*) testify to the Dano-German community's Romantic emphasis on gemeinschaft, adapted from Friedrich Schlegel (1772–1829)—the importance not of isolated effort, but of collective values and philosophies.[30] Schadow's painting is overtly didactic, uniting the media of painting and sculpture, as embodied by the Schadow brothers, with a handshake, a resolution of the Renaissance *paragone*. Joining the two German artist-brothers is Thorvaldsen, whose stark linear work was venerated by the members of the Nazarene group.[31] Thorvaldsen's stature among German artists living in Rome is also commented upon in a satirical work by Hieronymus Hess (1799–1850). *A Party of German Artists in Rome* (1823; fig. 51) shows Thorvaldsen's portrait along with those of Hans Holbein, William Hogarth, David Teniers, and Joseph Anton Koch flanking the initials of Albrecht Dürer on the back wall of the studio of the inebriated Bohemian students. In these

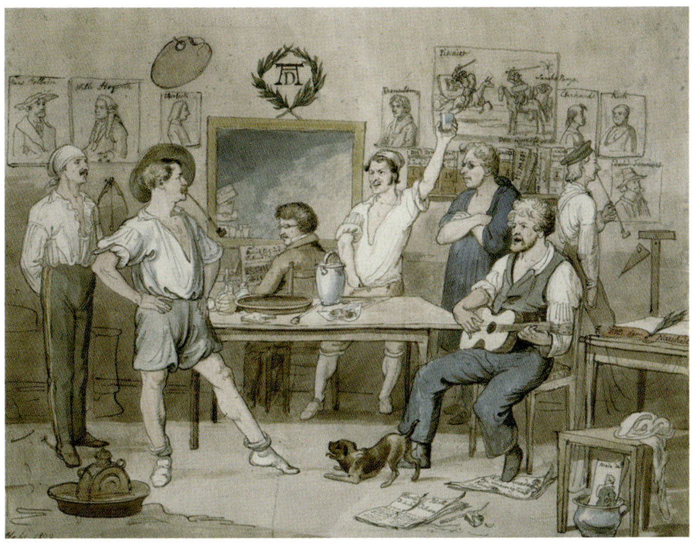

51.
Hieronymous Hess
A Party of German Artists in Rome, 1823
Watercolor and ink on paper, 12½ x 15¾ in.
(31.8 x 40 cm)
Stadtmuseum, Munich

paintings, Rome provides the setting for the endless party, for eating, drinking, camaraderie, and theorizing. This was the Danes' special storybook Rome.

When Christoffer Eckersberg first arrived in Rome in 1812, it was as a history painter fresh from Jacques-Louis David's atelier in Paris where he produced such works as *The Return of Odysseus* (chapter 2). While in Paris, Eckersberg had wandered through the city, sketching its parks and architecture. His period in Rome, which extended to 1816, provided him with the opportunity to digest the lessons of David and apply his teacher's rigorous observation of form to the study of landscape outside of the framework of the master's studio. Eckersberg immediately began to produce intimate and refined city views, paintings that articulate the viewer's specific position in space and suggest, through their enhancement of color and specificity of detail, a kind of perceptual immediacy. He had rendered informal views of Paris in his wanderings of that city, perhaps even directly on the spot. In Rome, informal *vedute* (views) became his most innovative work.

Eckersberg's *Marble Steps Leading Up to Santa Maria in Aracoeli in Rome* (1813–16; fig. 52), shows the church from the Piazza d'Aracoeli, a somewhat conventional tourist motif of the Aracoeli steps, the severe church façade, and the steps at the right leading to the Capitoline Hill. Rome's many layers of history are suggested by the ghosted remains of changes to the church façade, the urban tissue at the base of the stairs, and the soiled and patched stucco and stone throughout. What is wholly unconventional is the complexity of the view and the exaggeratedly warm light. Eckersberg chose as his perspective the point at which the two sets of stairs rise up from the pavement at different angles, establishing a strongly rushing convergence of diagonal lines in the composition's lower left corner. The colorfully-clad women going about their daily chores, and the men, some of whom seem to be tourists, accentuate the angles of incline and the monumental scale of the steps while also providing a sense of everyday street life. Bathed in rich honeyed light, the scene is unusually palpable and warm. In contrast to the views of Rome by Hubert Robert (1733–1808) or Giovanni Battista Piranesi (1720–1778; fig. 53) made popular throughout Europe by cognoscenti on the Grand Tour, Eckersberg did not image Roman architecture as a marker of an age gone by, but as integrated into the fabric of a living city.[32]

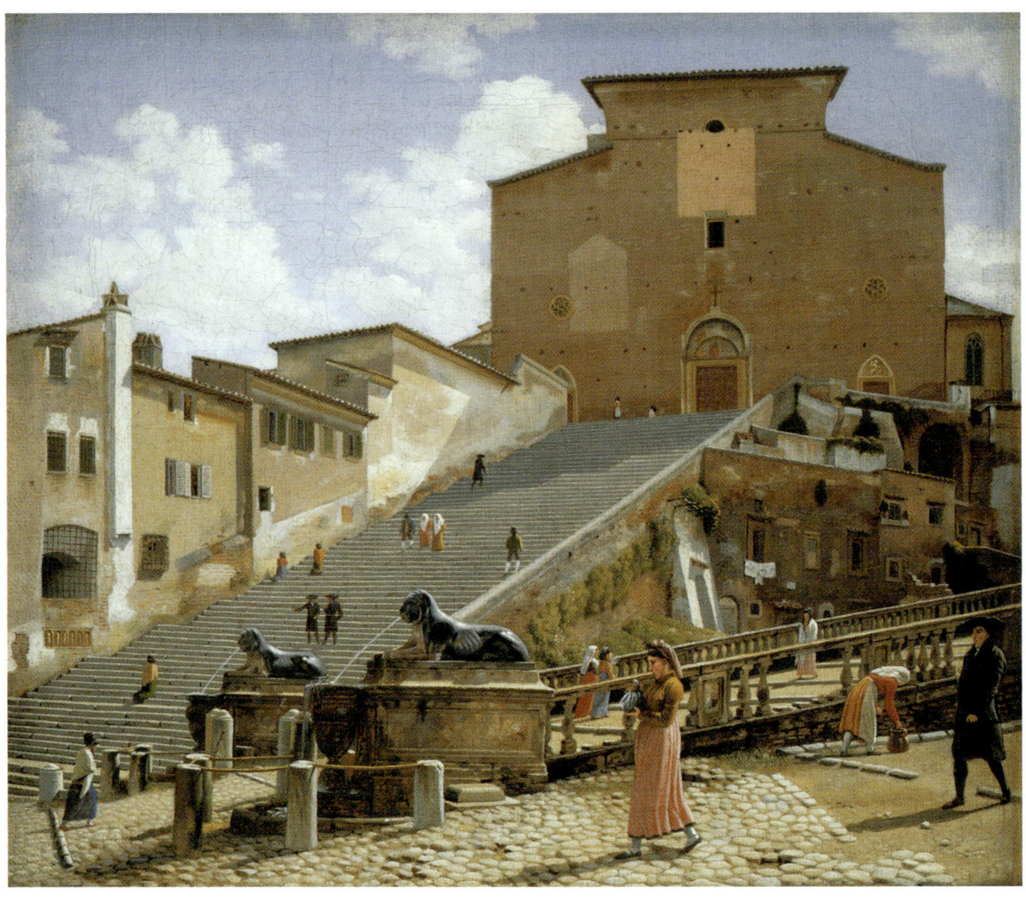

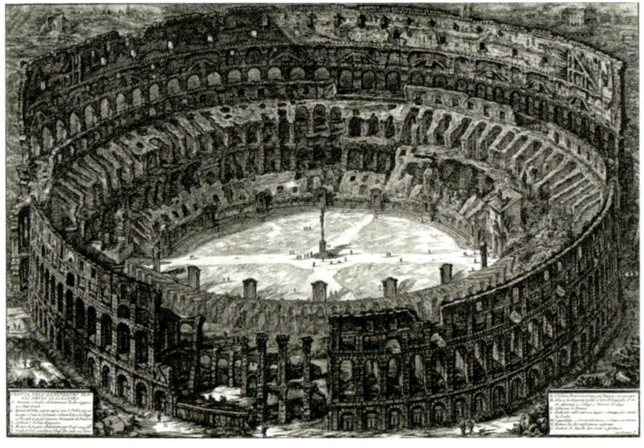

52.
C. W. Eckersberg
The Marble Steps Leading Up to Santa Maria in Aracoeli in Rome, 1813–16
Oil on canvas, 12¾ x 14⅜ in. (32.4 x 36.5 cm)
Statens Museum for Kunst, Copenhagen

53.
Giovanni Battista Piranesi
View of the Flavian Amphitheater Known as the Colosseum
From *Vedute di Roma*, 1776
Etching, first state, 16 x 27 in. (40.5 x 68.5 cm)
The Metropolitan Museum of Art, New York
The Elisha Whittelsey Collection, The Elisha Whittlesey Fund, 1959

54.
C. W. Eckersberg
The Piazza of St. Peter's in Rome in the Sunshine, 1813–16
Oil on canvas, 12⅜ x 10½ in. (31.4 x 26.8 cm)
Thorvaldsens Museum, Copenhagen

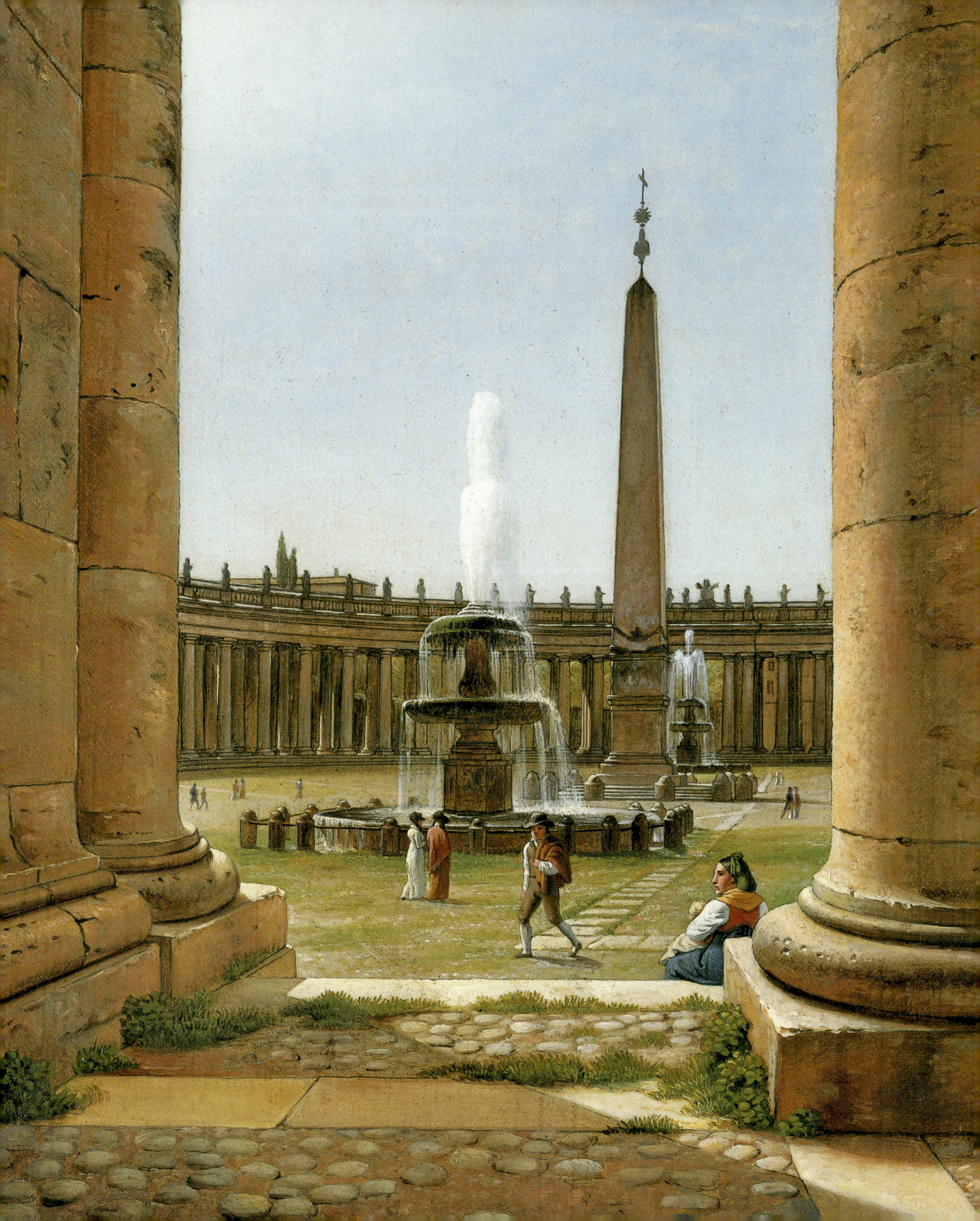

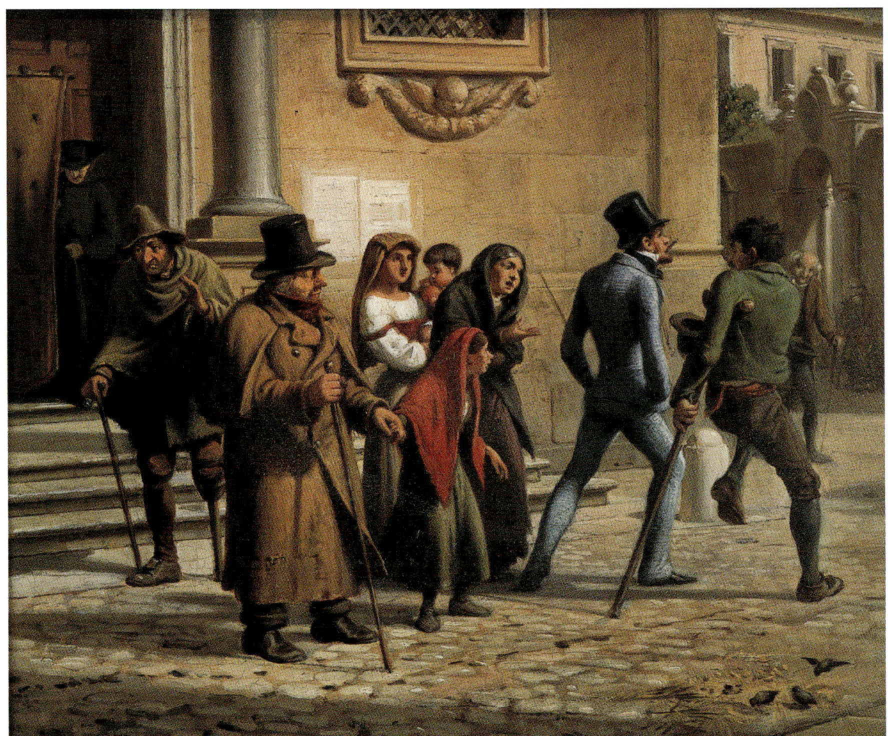

55.
Wilhelm Marstrand
*An Englishman Pursued by Beggars
in Rome*, 1848
Oil on canvas, 11 x 12⅝ in.
(28 x 32 cm)
Collection of Ambassador John L. Loeb Jr.,
New York

Eckersberg's *Piazza of St. Peter's in Rome in the Sunshine* (1813–16; fig. 54) presents a Roman monument as a more defined stage for daily life. Here, however, he has eschewed the monumentality of Bernini's piazza and colonnade for a truncated glimpse through two of its columns.[33] Its scale is nonetheless articulated by the vast leap in size between the massive foreground columns and their counterparts across the piazza. The columns, two on the left and one on the right, frame a solitary seated woman and serve as an irregular opening onto a stage in which tourists stroll and fountains release their cascades of water. Poised between an architectural view and a genre scene, this painting, organized as though viewed through an aperture, records Baroque Rome as a site of tourism and spectatorship.

A quite different street view of tourist Rome is offered in Wilhelm Marstrand's *An Englishman Pursued by Beggars in Rome* (1848; fig. 55), a painting echoing William Hogarth's social satire and particularly Bartolomeo Pinelli's (1781–1835) graphic commentary on foreign visitors to Rome.[34] A prolific and admired genre painter and portraitist, and one of Eckersberg's prized pupils, Marstrand (1810–1873) created a large body of social commentary, including published illustrations. Here, a foppish English gentleman, in his spotless suit and glossy top hat, aggressively ignores a group of beggars outside a church. The tourist is so intent upon pursuing H. C. Andersen's storybook Rome—the ancient and the scenic—that he will not acknowledge and is discomfited by the Eternal City's dispossessed, unemployed, and physically handicapped. As art historian Emil Hannover wrote, the small girl at the center of the painting, guiding a blind man, gapes in disbelief at the Englishman.[35] Such familiar moments of guilt, desperation, and disregard marked the tourist experience, but were often erased or minimized in the street views and the travel narratives of Rome in the Neoclassical and Romantic age.[36] Despite its vaudevillian overtones, Marstrand's view may have been closer to the artists' daily social encounters than the

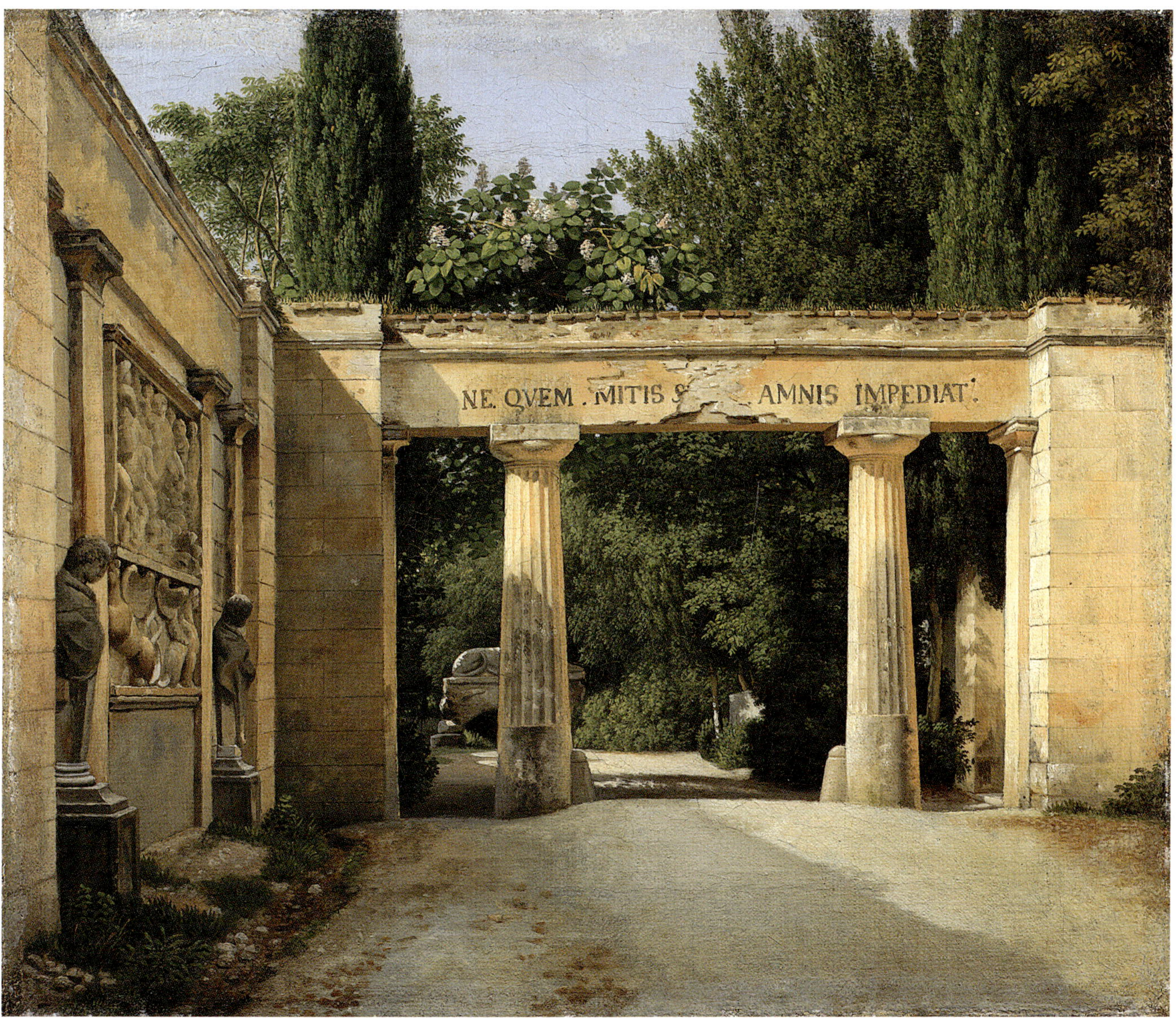

café scenes. There was an exceptionally high unemployment and illiteracy rate among the Roman population of the early nineteenth century, as well as poor sanitary and hygienic conditions.[37]

Eckersberg's celebrated and influential views of Rome depict a different city. Eckersberg's *View of the Garden of the Villa Borghese in Rome* (ca. 1814; fig. 56) reflects his desire, as stated in a letter to the engraver Johann Friderich Clemens, to paint "a collection of the most beautiful and picturesque views (Maleriske Partier) of Rome and its environs"[38] With his emphasis on the term *maleriske* or picturesque, Eckersberg evoked the aesthetic category of the Picturesque, connoting intimacy and irregularity, as opposed to the beautiful or the sublime.[39] The notion of the picturesque, stated most prominently in works by the English theorist William Gilpin (1724–1804), accommodated one's intimate experience in nature. Nature was a motif to be seen subjectively rather than formalized according to classical academic formulae or invested with the overwhelming power of the Sublime. The painting's orientation is eccen-

56.
C. W. Eckersberg
View of the Garden of the Villa Borghese in Rome, 1814
Oil on canvas, 11¼ x 12¾ in.
(28.5 x 32.5 cm)
Statens Museum for Kunst,
Copenhagen

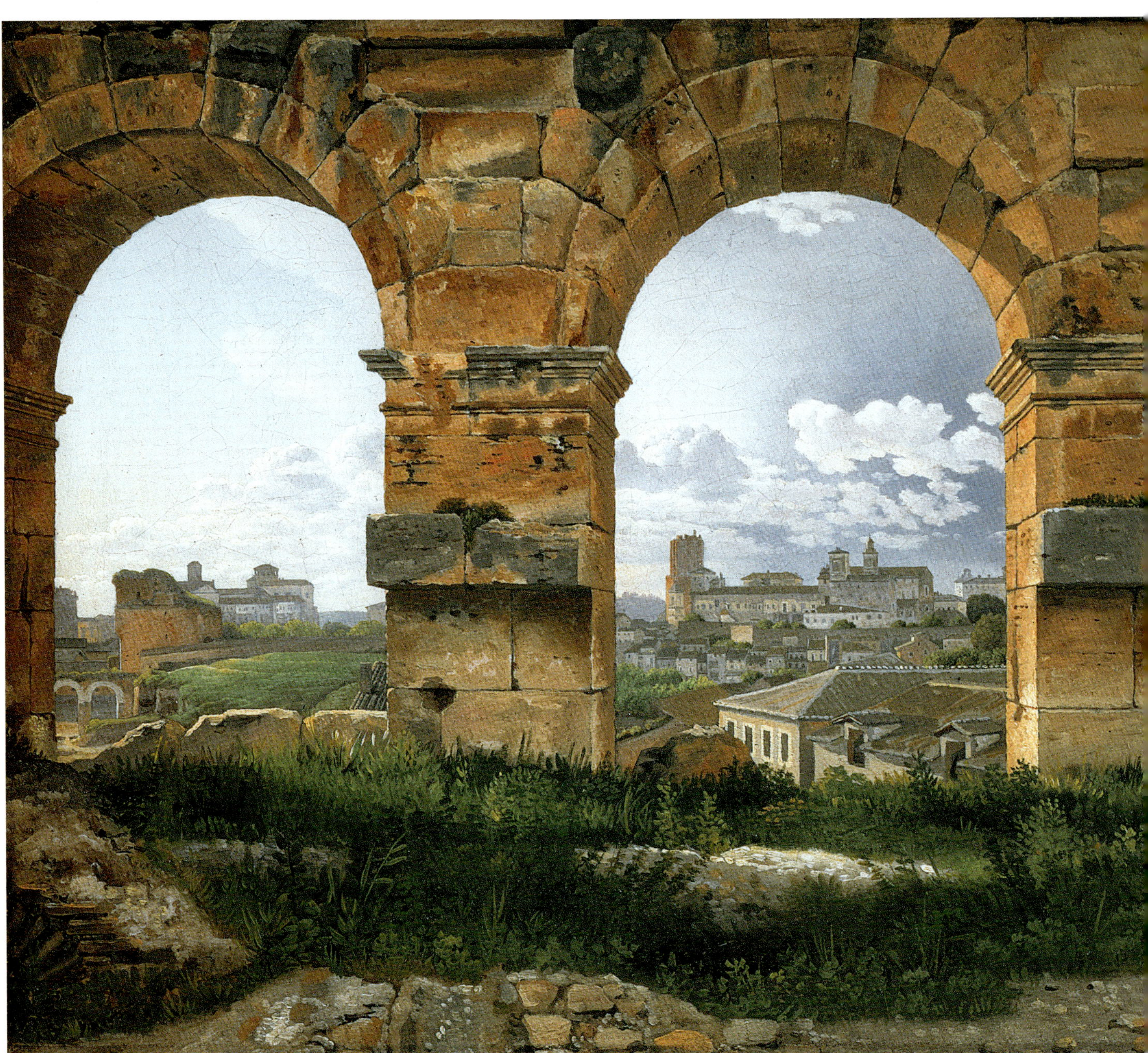

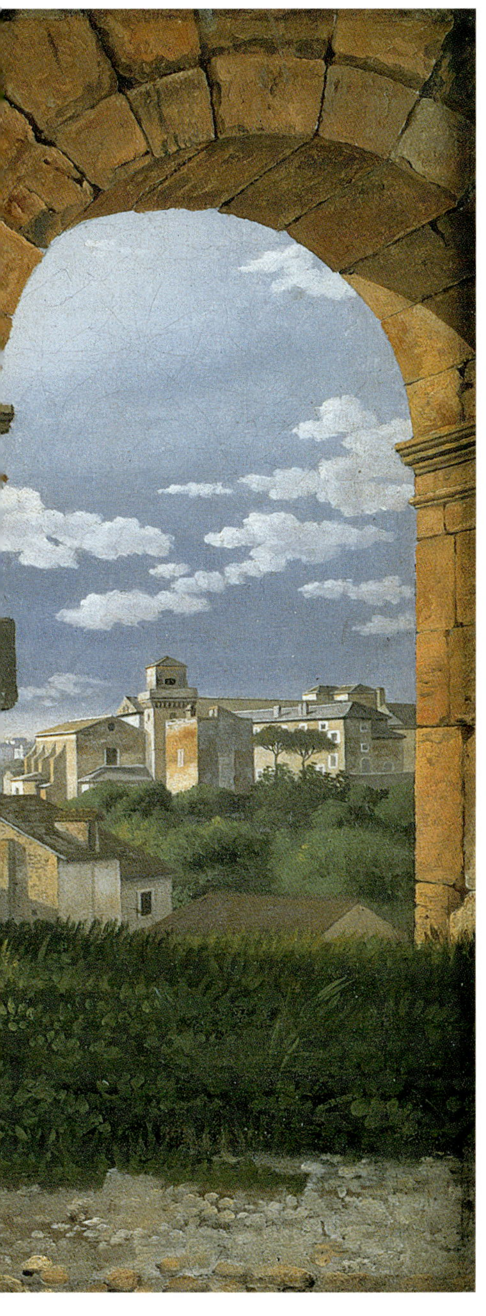

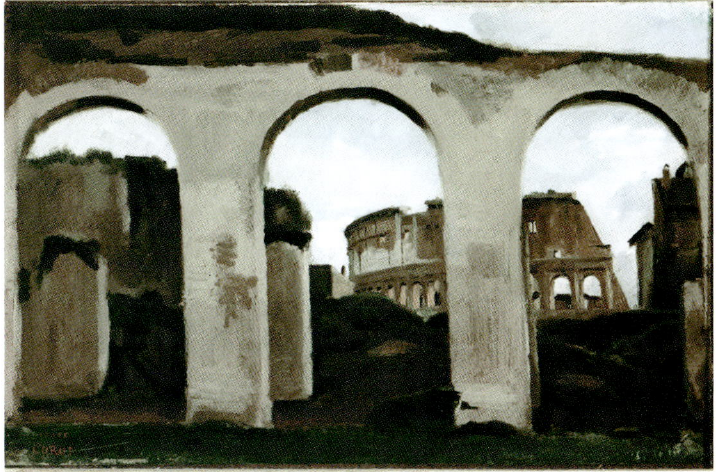

tric, organized through an empty foreground, a middle ground in which a spare tripartite Doric portal frames an unremarkable section of the garden while cutting off visual access on the periphery, and framed on the left by a telescoping wall embedded with antiquities. As Monrad has pointed out, it is a view that seems resolutely opposed to grander tourist-oriented views of such famous sites.[40] Here he paints not the lush meandering gardens or imitation antiquities noted in the proliferating tourist guides to Rome, but a section of the aqueduct built in 1776–78 to carry water from the Aqua Felice aqueduct into the park.[41]

Eckersberg's subject seems to be intimacy itself, the artist's bodily experience of standing in a semienclosed place, finding an immediate and unexpected connection with a notable site on the European Grand Tour. Within this small realm, Eckersberg has orchestrated the elements into a carefully wrought geometry, noting with great precision foliage, the effects of weathering on the stone and stucco surfaces, and above all, the warmth of the sunlight bathing the right side of the courtyard. Editing or correcting distracting details, and at the same time making even the smallest detail seem exaggeratedly present, Eckersberg suspends the painting between high idealization and natural observation.

Eckersberg's *A View Through Three of the Northwestern Arches of the Third Story of the Colosseum* (1815–16; fig. 57) provides an even more eccentric view of Roman architecture. A painting of astonishing spatial complexity, it uses western Europe's most familiar ancient ruin as a kind of triple aperture to frame the city. A small section of the Colosseum's arcade acts as a visual barrier to the background, alternately occluding and miniaturizing the landscape beyond. The meticulously detailed and shadowy foreground anchors the shimmering, soaring city and sky beyond. The Colosseum as a monument itself, however, is deemphasized, even more so than in Jean-Baptiste Camille Corot's (1796–1875) allied *View of the Colosseum through the Arches of the Basilica of Constantine in Rome* from a decade later (1825; fig. 58). Instead, the painting's title and the visual inventory that Eckersberg offered when it was exhibited in 1828, anchor the location: "Through the arch on the left can be seen the splendid ruins of the Temple of Peace and behind it the Church of Santa Maria in Ara Celi [Aracoeli] in the distance. Through the middle arch can be seen the so-called Tower of Nero (Torre delle Milizie, erected in the 13th century) at the foot of Mount Quirinale, and even further back can be discerned the palace on Monte Cavallo. Just in front of the arch on the right lies the Church of San Pietro in Vincoli in the vicinity of the baths of Titus."[42] Through such oddly vectored views, Eckersberg transformed Rome's most monumental structures into scenes of attentive intimacy. He reinvestigated its ruins neither as antique monuments of veneration nor as avatars of Romantic voids—"tragic visions of the ultimate physical expiration of a dead civilization." [43] Moreover, as Monrad notes, the view as offered by Eckersberg is physically impossible. One must walk several paces in each direction from the central opening to encompass the three separate views of the distant city that Eckersberg has created as an idealized composite.[44]

With these views and others like them, Eckersberg helped to initiate the important practice of open-air painting in Rome. More than a decade before Corot began to paint his direct views of Rome in the 1820s, Eckersberg had begun to render oil sketches outdoors in the presence of his motifs.[45] Following the work and teachings of Pierre-Henri de Valenciennes in Paris (see chapter 2), and likely with knowledge of the eighteenth-century open-air studies of Rome created by such artists as Richard Wilson (1713–1782), Eckersberg was among the vanguard of artists creating oil renderings in the 1810s, including François-Marius Granet (1775–1849) and, in England, J. M. W. Turner (1775–1851). Such informal studies were traditionally created as sketches for more finished works, completed in the studio. But the practice of rendering such detailed, complete and yet informal views, in part directly before the motif, was an important departure from academic practice, and it was fostered in Rome by an international coterie of artists in the 1810s through the 1840s.[46]

Eckersberg stated in a letter to Johann Friderich Clemens, dated July 23, 1814, that his Roman pictures were "finished on the spot, from Nature."[47] A few months earlier, he had noted in his diaries the purchase of a portable painting box and other equipment for outdoor painting,[48] suggesting that it was around this time that he began the regular practice of painting on site: "As an artist and a foreigner here you have all the possible advantages, because you live in the greatest freedom and can do or leave what you will. . . . my happiest hours have been when I run into the open air to paint a little, with my paint box and stool under my arm, to paint after nature."[49] Gunnarsson has determined that several of his paintings, such as *A View Through Three of the Northwestern Arches in the Third Story of the Colosseum in Rome* were begun en plein air and completed in the studio.[50] Nonetheless, the freshness with which the paintings were rendered, and especially their attentiveness to the changing conditions of light and weather, initiated a new aesthetic among the Dano-Germans in Rome, and they must be seen as innovative within the broader European context.

Eckersberg's small, intensely observed renderings of Rome's architectural legacy were not immediately well received in Copenhagen, but they helped to cultivate a school of intimate landscape painting among Danish artists in the 1820s and 1830s. Conrad Blunck had written to Eckersberg from Rome, "many times have I enjoyed seeking out the very places where you have

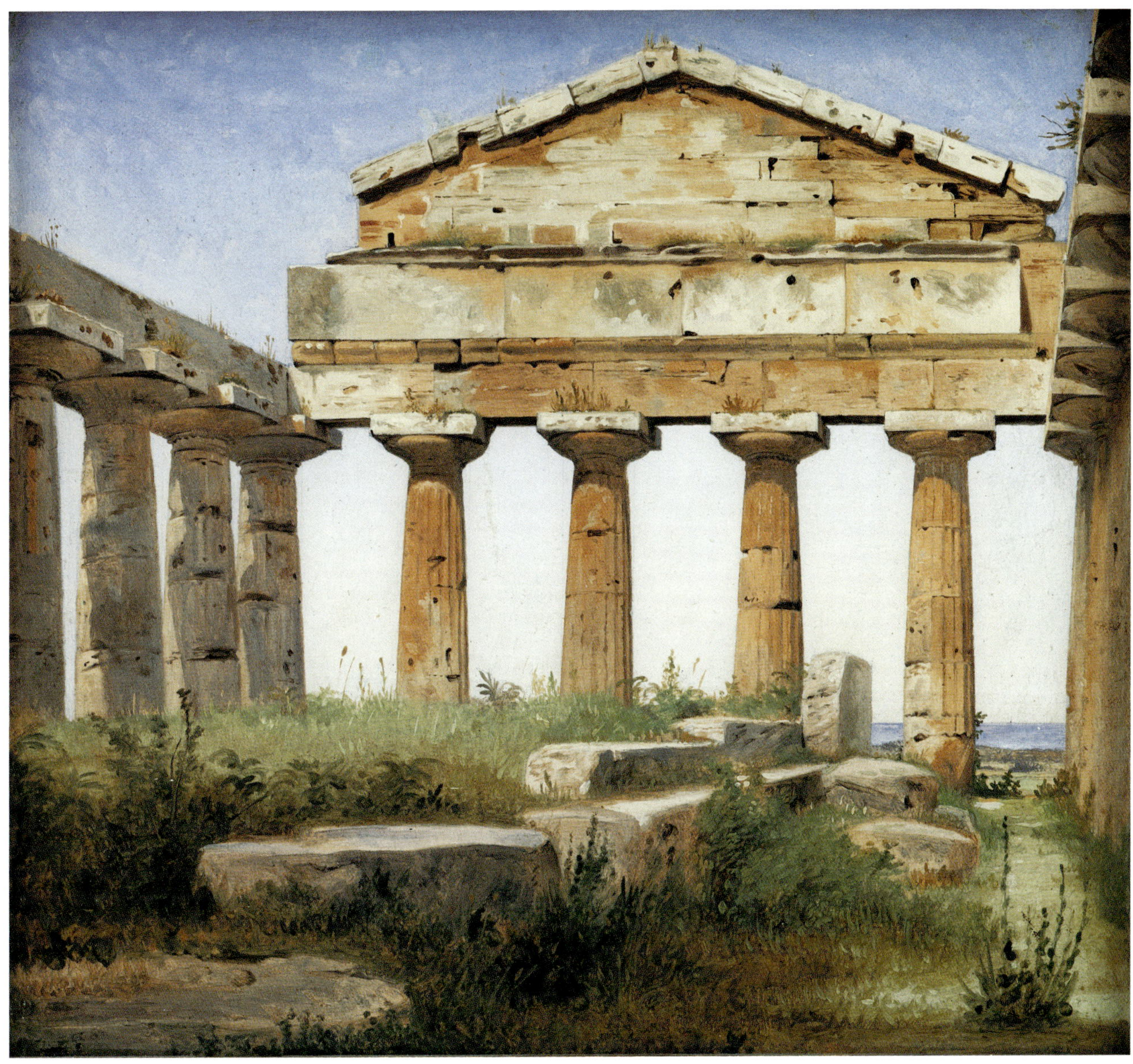

sat during your work. . . . Rome often seems to me as though everything has been built for the sake of painters."[51] In 1838, Constantin Hansen reprised Eckersberg's procedure of selecting and rendering intimately a monumental historical structure. In that year he traveled from Rome to Paestum where he painted *The Temple of Athena at Paestum* (fig. 59), a modest view of one of the earliest extant Doric temples in the Mediterranean. The ruined condition of the Temple of Athena (500 B.C.E.), thought in the nineteenth century to be consecrated to Ceres, is emphasized by the structure's isolation from its setting. Hansen emphasized one of the features of the temple most admired in tourist accounts, and he resisted a second.

One of the notable aspects of the temple was its great age and perceived primitive simplicity. The temple fragments, which speak of the ravages of time, weather, and war are invested with a sense of melancholy in works by Piranesi and British painter Alexander Cozens. Here Han-

59.
Constantin Hansen
The Temple of Athena at Paestum, 1838
Oil on paper on canvas, 11⅜ x 11¾ in.
(29 x 30 cm)
Statens Museum for Kunst,
Copenhagen

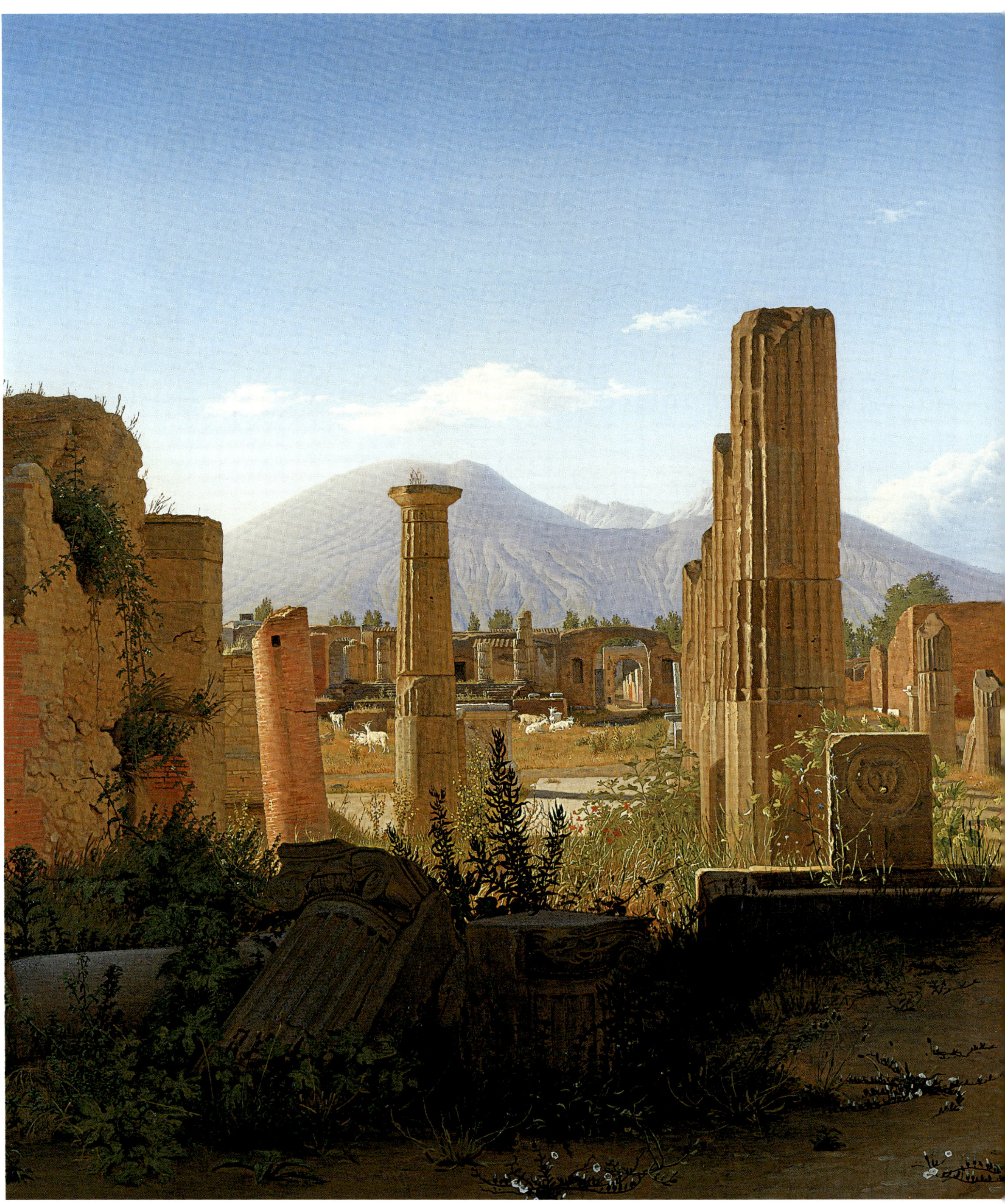

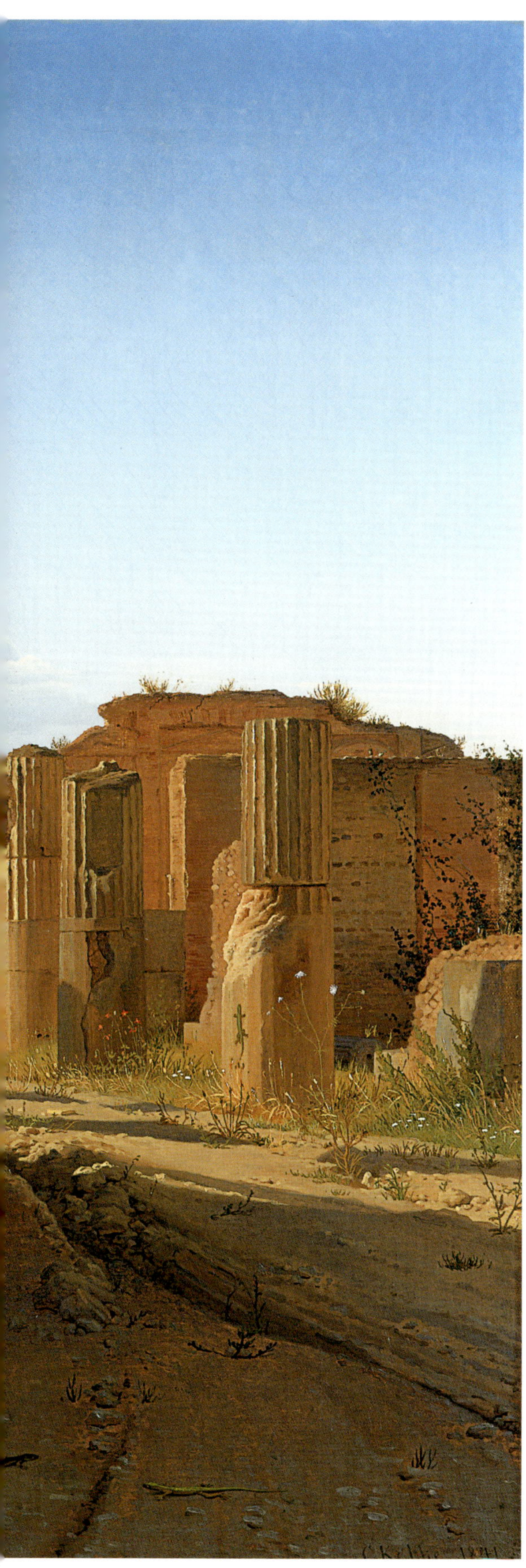

sen offers the pockmarked surface of the great stones, the open roof, and the vegetation that grows in the crevices of the ruins. The other notable feature of the temples at Paestum was their resolutely stark simplicity and symmetry. But by locating his angle of view inside the temple, almost at ground level, and far to the right, Hansen ruptured the axis of the structure, rendering it as an enclosure for the viewer. Its swelling ground line and irregularly damaged columns transform their geometric forms into moldering nature. As Robert Rosenblum noted, images such as these, of Roman ruins understood as metaphors of organic cultural growth and degeneration, offered a romantic meditation on human folly.[52] The thin line of luminous sea in the distant background heightens the sense that the temple is isolated from the present. This careful and highly personalized view of the temple served as a model for later paintings by Hansen through the 1870s.[53]

Eckersberg's limpid views of historical monuments continued to inspire innovation among Danish artists at mid-century. Christen Købke, who had painted the luminous and convivial portrait of Frederik Sødring in 1832 (chapter 2), first traveled to Italy in 1838. In such views as *The Forum in Pompeii with Mt. Vesuvius in the Background* (1841; fig. 60), he created a sense of majesty and melancholy through the orchestration of what appears to be a meticulously rendered view of nature. Pompeii had been a site of both scientific and popular fascination since excavations had begun there in 1748. The terrible romance of the site, in which one of the wealthiest cities in the Roman Empire was destroyed by the cataclysmic force of Mount Vesuvius, is only subtly invested in the painting. Købke offers a view of massive, partially destroyed columns aligned to orchestrate a deep and direct movement into the background where Mount Vesuvius rises under a vivid blue sky. Yet in contrast to J. C. C. Dahl's sublime views of Vesuvius erupting in 1820 (see chapter 4), or the powerful ways in which Vesuvius's destructive presence shaped tourist experiences of Naples (even down to the "lava" fragment dealers),[54] Købke invests the scene with intimacy. The hot yellow and ocher ruins in the middle ground are rendered in miniaturized particularity, visually and tactilely accessible and yet barricaded by the shadowed foreground. The cooler, darker values that define the foreground, combined with precise renderings of weeds that have overtaken the ruins and the lizards that dart across the path to the right, add a sense of pathos to the scene. As described by art historian Joseph Koerner, such a strategic use of a visual barrier causes the landscape to plunge suddenly from the "world of murky boundaries into the boundless and insubstantial sky." Such alignments and unexpected physical barriers "articulate not just the physical attributes of the setting, but the very act of seeing."[55] It is a work that summarizes the interests of Eckersberg's students in Italy, suggesting both their vestigial attachment to classicism, and their commitment to informal, personalized views of nature. Købke's paintings, with their nuanced balance between physical particularity and abstract pictorial order, and largely

60.
Christen Købke
The Forum in Pompeii with Vesuvius in the Distance, 1841
Oil on canvas, 28 x 34⅝ in.
(71 x 88 cm)
J. Paul Getty Museum, Los Angeles

focused on architectural subjects back home in Denmark, have been acknowledged to be among the greatest achievements of Denmark's Golden Age.

The strategy of making the spectator aware of one's angle of view and specific physical location in relation to a motif was, in fact, a hallmark of the landscape scenes created by Eckersberg and later by his students in Italy. The depiction of a floating, ungraspable background anchored by a shadowed foreground was perhaps most sentimentally deployed by Martinus Rørbye in his *View of the Roman Campagna with the Tiber and Monte Soracte in the Background* (1835; fig. 61). His work, like that of Købke and Hansen, was characterized by an exceptional precision in touch, scientific observation of light and meteorological effects, odd angles of view, and by an uncanny sense of living presence in even the most inert objects. Here he opens up the landscape view, representing the fertile plain of the Campagna, and the mountains in the background, with a miniaturist's precision. Houses, sheep, and a few isolated human figures are miniscule within a vast, nearly ungraspable panorama, viewed in the foreground by a traveler with a pile of dry sticks at his feet and a wooden cross to his left. The body of the traveler is oriented toward the spectator, but his face is turned back towards the great flat plain and winding river. The sense of melancholy that pervades the painting is heightened by the contrast in scale and in color between the weary traveler's immediate realm in the foreground and the golden distance. The sky, vast and marked only by a few isolated birds, offers a glimpse of the infinite, utterly unattainable by the seated, earthbound traveler. This *Rüchenfigur*, familiar by the 1830s from the influential paintings of German Caspar David Friedrich, in turn provides a double for the spectator. Faraway from the landscape for which he seems to yearn, his presence redoubles the spectator's own distance from and desire for unity with the motif. This statement of enraptured isolation and yearning could not be more different from the collective camaraderie of Bindesbøll's studio, as depicted by Constantin Hansen. The two taken together, however—the gemeinschaft of Thorvaldsen's cosmopolitan society and the small acts of revelation in nature— demarcate the emotional and artistic territory of the Danish artists in Rome.

As H. C. Andersen recounted, Rome itself was a place of yearning and of storybook revelations embedded in everyday life for the Danish artists of the early and mid-nineteenth century. Their mastery of anatomy, light effects, and pictorial geometry, first shaped by the terms of their academic training, incubated within this Roman community, and freed from the constraints of home, enabled the artists to return to Denmark with fresh eyes for the tiny revelations in their own landscape and material culture. Thorvaldsen, as a mentor and ideal, was crucial to this process, offering a glimpse of Denmark's international prestige in the arts while also supporting younger artists through his patronage. When he, and they, returned to Denmark, their works, and their Roman experiences, shaped nation building efforts in the mid-nineteenth century.

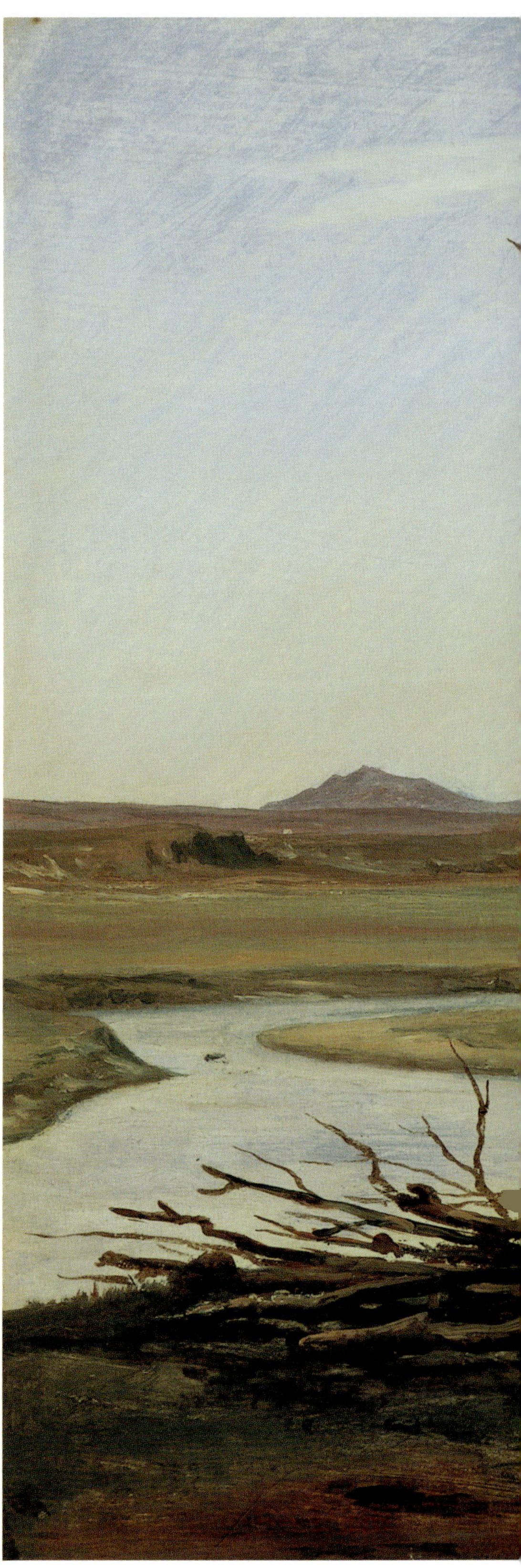

61.
Martinus Rørbye
*View of the Roman Campagna with the Tiber
and Monte Soracte in the Background*, 1835
Oil on paper on canvas, 12⅝ x 16⅛ in.
(32 x 41 cm)
Göteborgs Konstmuseum, Göteborg

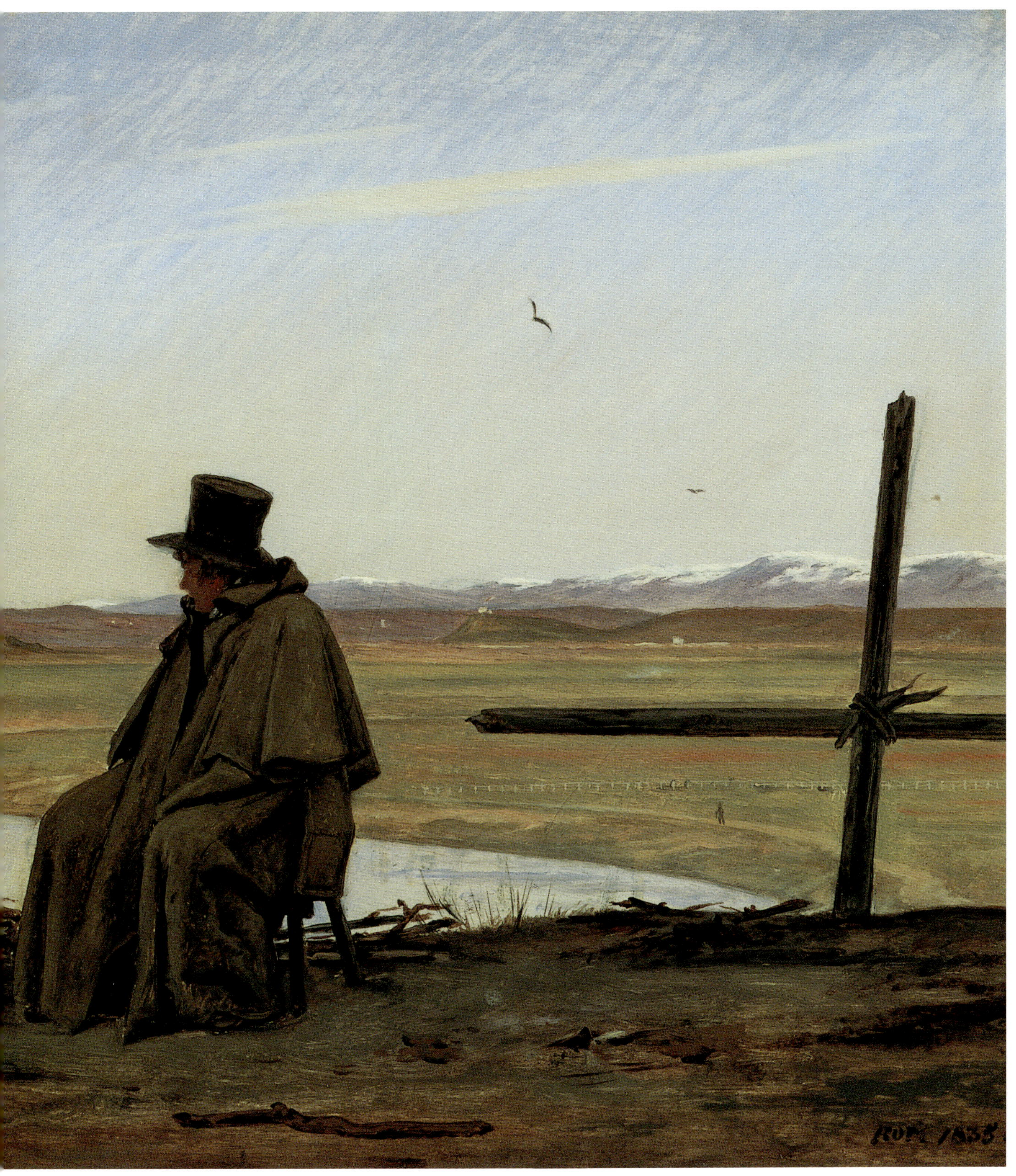

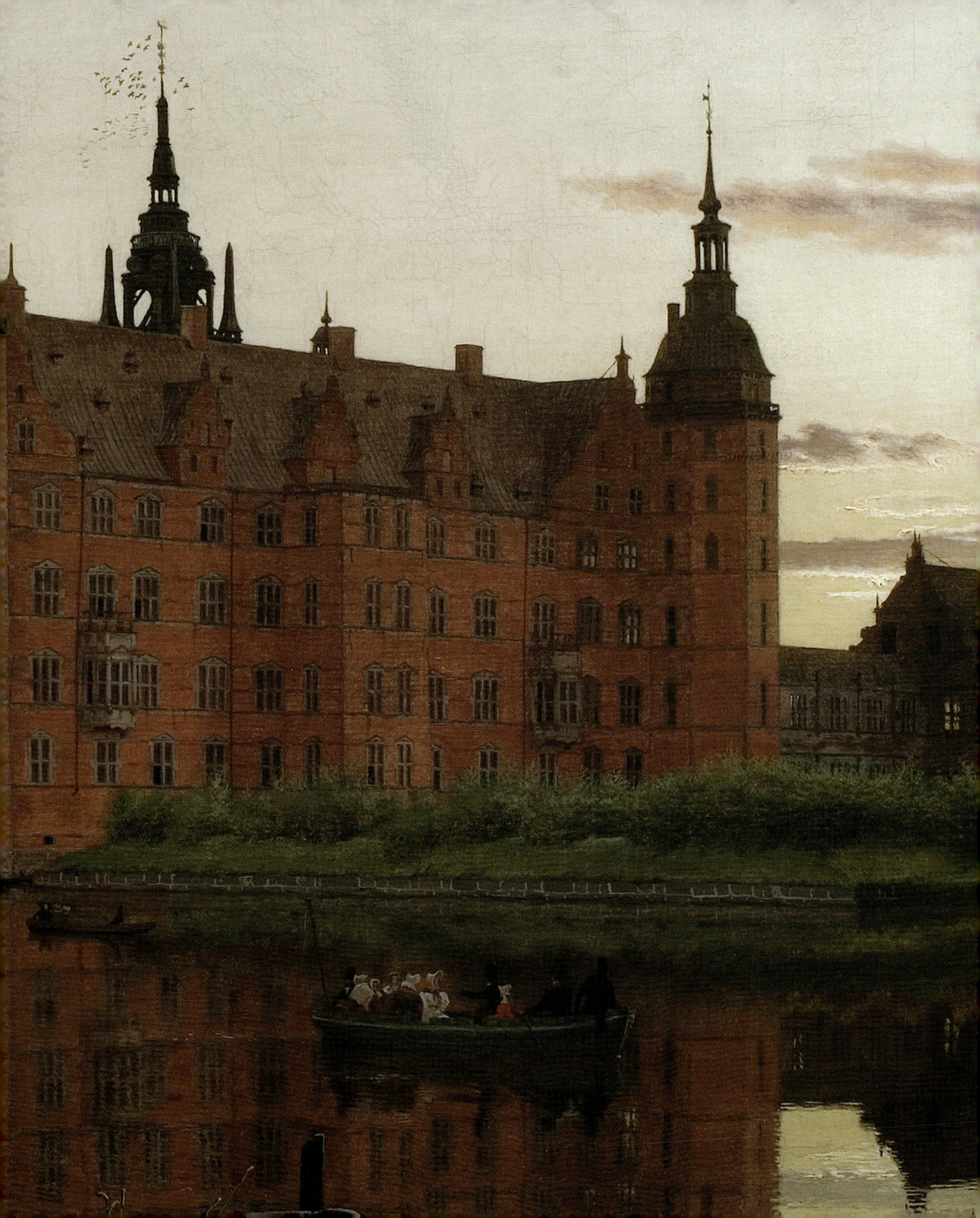

4

Picturing Denmark in the Golden Age

THE YEARS BETWEEN ECKERSBERG'S RETURN FROM ITALY in 1816 and the German-Danish wars of the late 1840s constitute Denmark's Golden Age, the period in which imperial traditions dissolved and modern Denmark emerged as a constitutional democracy. The period began in literal bankruptcy and concluded in emerging prosperity, and in the visual arts with a burgeoning self-identified national school of painting. In this period, artists from within the Royal Academy traveled to Rome and to other foreign capitals for both artistic and pecuniary enrichment (see chapters 2 and 3). However, their experiences in Rome had a paradoxical effect on their work back in Denmark. Rather than focusing on formal views and grand narratives, the artists increasingly engaged rural themes, reinterpreting the classical tradition to ennoble local topography and cultural life. The art of this period both reflected and shaped middle-class identity, stripped as it was of overt metaphor or embellishment while retaining and amplifying a sense of spiritual belonging.

Many of the aspirations of this generation are embodied by Christen Købke's *Frederiksborg Castle in the Evening Light* (1835; fig. 62), a painting that simultaneously honors Denmark's architectural and cultural heritage, renders nature as majestic and spiritualized, and celebrates middle-class stability. This painting helped to initiate a period of national Romanticism—the veneration of the nation as a unified, spiritual entity—that arose in the wake of the political and economic chaos of the Napoleonic Wars. In the years between the 1810s and 1850s, the authority of the absolutist monarchy declined and then collapsed, and Denmark underwent a rapid democratization in all realms. A group of intellectuals, including Denmark's foremost authors, scientists, philologists, theologians, and art historians assisted in this effort. The visual arts, including this painting, were crucial to its permeation into daily life.

Købke painted *Frederiksborg Castle in the Evening Light* prior to his own trip to Italy (see chapter 3), but it was based in part on Christoffer Wilhelm Eckersberg's intimate, oblique views of Rome. Købke had first visited Frederiksborg Castle in 1831 when he cared for his ailing sister in Hillerød, a short distance north of Copenhagen.[1] Over the following years, he rendered a number of views of this national monument. One of the most radically reductive is *One of the Small Towers of Frederiksborg Castle* (ca. 1834–35; fig. 63), in which one small

62.
Christian Købke
Frederiksborg Castle in the Evening Light, 1835
(detail)

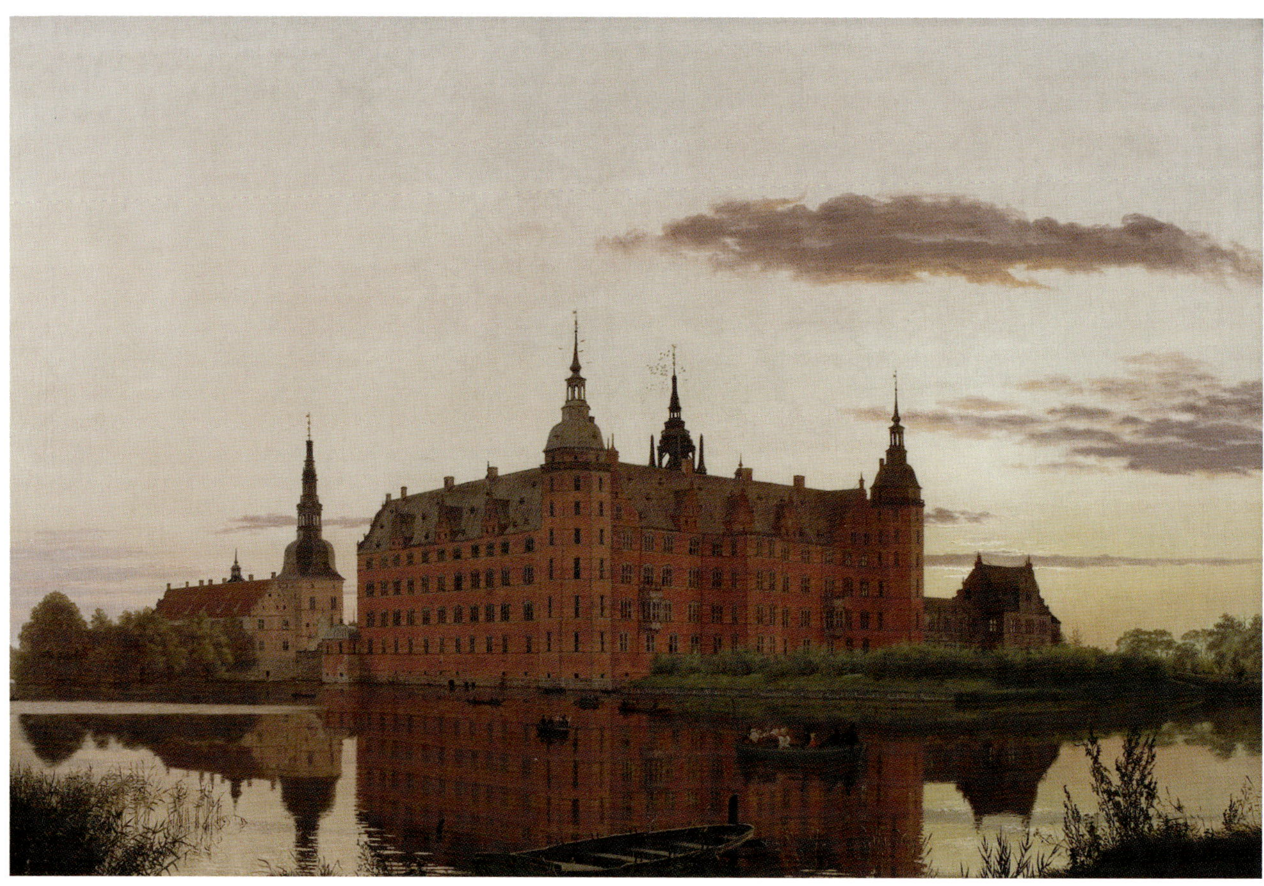

element of the massive Baroque building has been isolated and poeticized. Købke painted this view as one of four large decorations for the dining room of his parents' new home near Sortedamssøen, then just outside of Copenhagen.[2] The image of the tower is coextensive with the height of this large painting, its base occluded by the roofline, chimneys, and a smaller tower, and its lacelike weathervane is barely touching the painting's top edge. This slim form is located just to the right of center, animating the static composition through its deformation of what first appears to be a bilaterally symmetrical arrangement. The tower structure, bathed in the midday sun, is hypnotically linear and crisp in its rendering in comparison to the gently blurred, undulating agricultural land beyond. Incidental details, such as the stork perched atop a chimney and its mate that floats over the fields, and the miniature people who walk the meandering paths, imbue the painting with a transitory sense.

This work fragments the palace, the largest in all of Scandinavia. First begun under Frederik II in 1560 and then built for Christian IV in the 1620s (see chapter 1), Frederiksborg housed the Royal Painting Collection, including portraits of the Danish monarchy, and the chapel where the absolutist kings were crowned. Its formal Baroque garden is among the largest in northern Europe. In an 1831 essay, art historian Niels Laurits Høyen (1798–1870) emphasized the collective importance of the palace and located its succession of additions and styles within Denmark's national and cultural history. Høyen, one of Denmark's increasingly prominent cultural figures, also argued for the preservation of Frederiksborg, concluding: "Its youth has faded, and it is rapidly aging. Yet, given love and care, it will retain sufficient vitality to live on for genera-

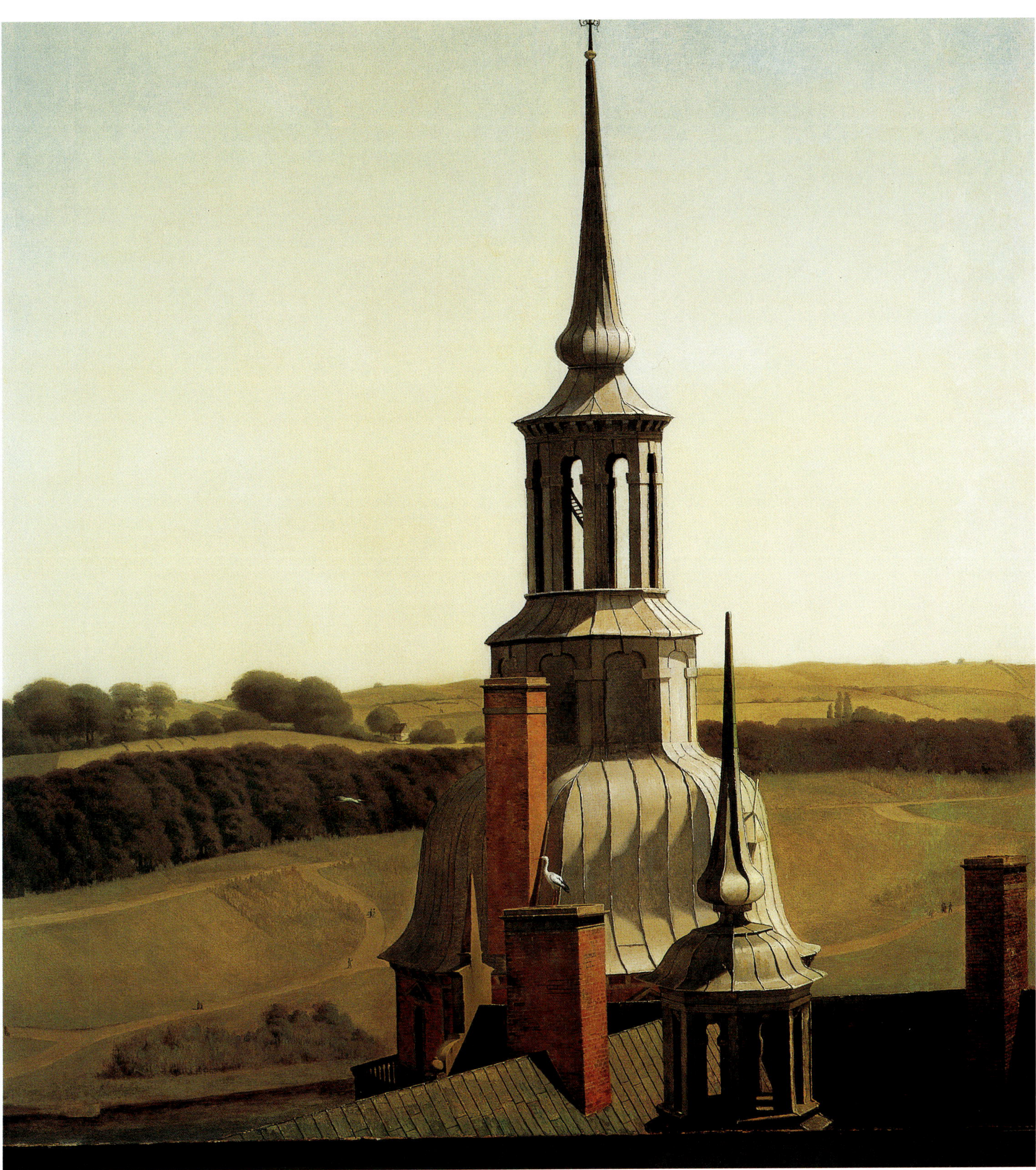

tions. It would be a sad day when the reputation of the loveliest castle in northern Europe would rest only on the excitement generated among artists searching for beautiful ruins."[3]

In *Frederiksborg Castle in the Evening Light*, the castle and its allied structures are doubled as reflections on the lake in the foreground. Although the fenestration is detailed with great accuracy, the gray stonework on the palace façade is suppressed to unify the red brick exterior, itself increasingly identified as a native Danish phenomenon.[4] Købke expresses the monumentality of the palace, and he also offers it as a kind of natural structure nestled into the land. Such a naturalization of Frederiksborg had been previously offered by the historian, philologist, and folk collector Christian Molbech (1783–1857) in his 1811 publication *Ungdomsvandringer i mit Fødeland* (*Youthful Travels in the Land of My Birth*): "The lovely old castle stands before me, in all its splendor. Like a sheer rock it rises out of the ocean, solidly anchored at the bottom. It is an eternal monument, by Denmark's great king Christian."[5] Molbech further romanticized the palace by shrouding it in mystery: "But as we regard the old castle from different angles during daylight, we must not forget that this is essentially a Romantic building. Thus, in the evening and after dusk, we notice many aspects of the building that are not readily apparent during the day. It is actually at its grandest and most beautiful in the evening."[6] Similarly, with flocks of birds circling its towers and silhouetted against the vast sky, Købke's Frederiksborg seems mountain-like, its crepuscular mood as significant to the artist as the rendering of architecture itself.

Købke created this painting for a competition arranged by the Fine Arts Society in Copenhagen to depict "a public place or building in Denmark."[7] By the 1830s, architectural painting emerged in Denmark as a serious practice, no longer subordinated to history painting as a minor genre. Niels Laurits Høyen, one of the founders of the Fine Arts Society, and a driving force behind Denmark's fledgling architectural preservation movement, had helped to inspire such competitions. These, in turn, suggested to artists and to the art buying public that Denmark's architecture was worthy of study and commemoration. Architectural painting had become a serious genre among Eckersberg's students in Rome who, like artists throughout Europe, venerated Rome's romanticized architectural legacy. Eckersberg's Roman studies and those of his students had been valued in part because of their evocation of classical antiquity and were thus tangentially related to history painting.

Høyen was one of Denmark's most influential advocates of national identity as represented by the land and the material culture of the country. Denmark's first professional art historian, Høyen began to teach at the academy in the mid-1820s, became a professor there in 1829, and then in 1856 he was appointed the first professor of art history at the University of Copenhagen. He was also one of Denmark's most energetic arts institution builders, helping to found the Fine Arts Society in 1825. In 1829, he edited the first three issues of *Maanedsskrift for Litteratur*, an academic journal that he founded with Molbech and J. L. Heiberg, among others, and which brought together the works of such important contemporary Danish writers as H. C. Andersen and poet Adam Gottlob Oehlenschläger. Appointed as Inspector of the Royal Painting Collection in 1836, he and renowned archaeologist Christian Jürgensen Thomsen (1788–1865) directed the collection in the 1840s and 1850s, transforming it into the National Museum (he became director following Thomsen's death). Høyen also established the Nordic Art Society (Selskabet for nordisk Kunst) in 1847 and, beginning in 1852, he lectured widely on ecclesiastical architecture for the Society for the History of the Danish Church (Selskabet for Danmarks Kirkehistorie). Much of his work was dedicated to the belief that art embodies individual vision

64.
Christen Købke
The Transept of Aarhus Cathedral, 1830
Oil on canvas, 19⅛ x 13⅜ in.
(48.5 x 34 cm)
Statens Museum for Kunst,
Copenhagen

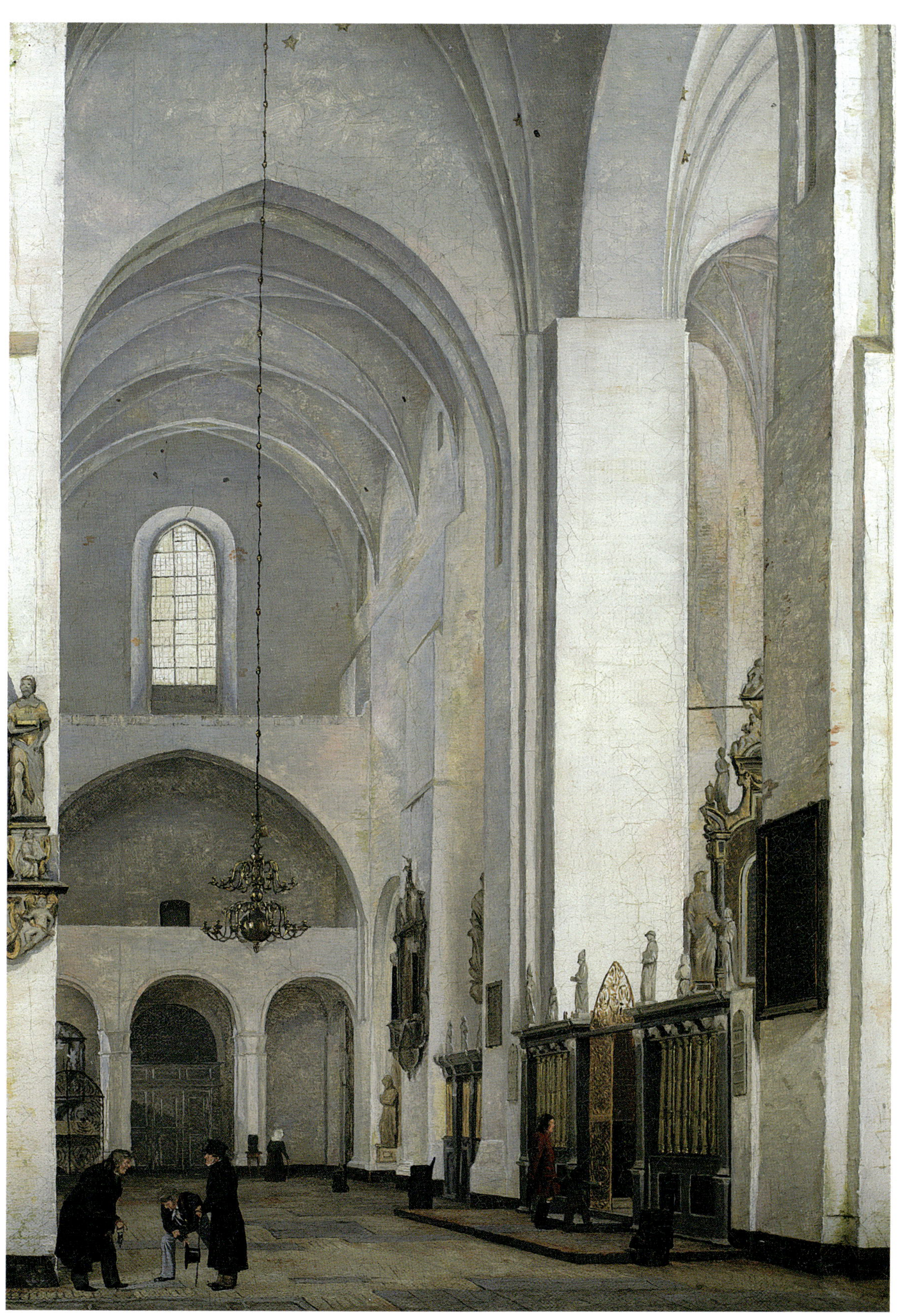

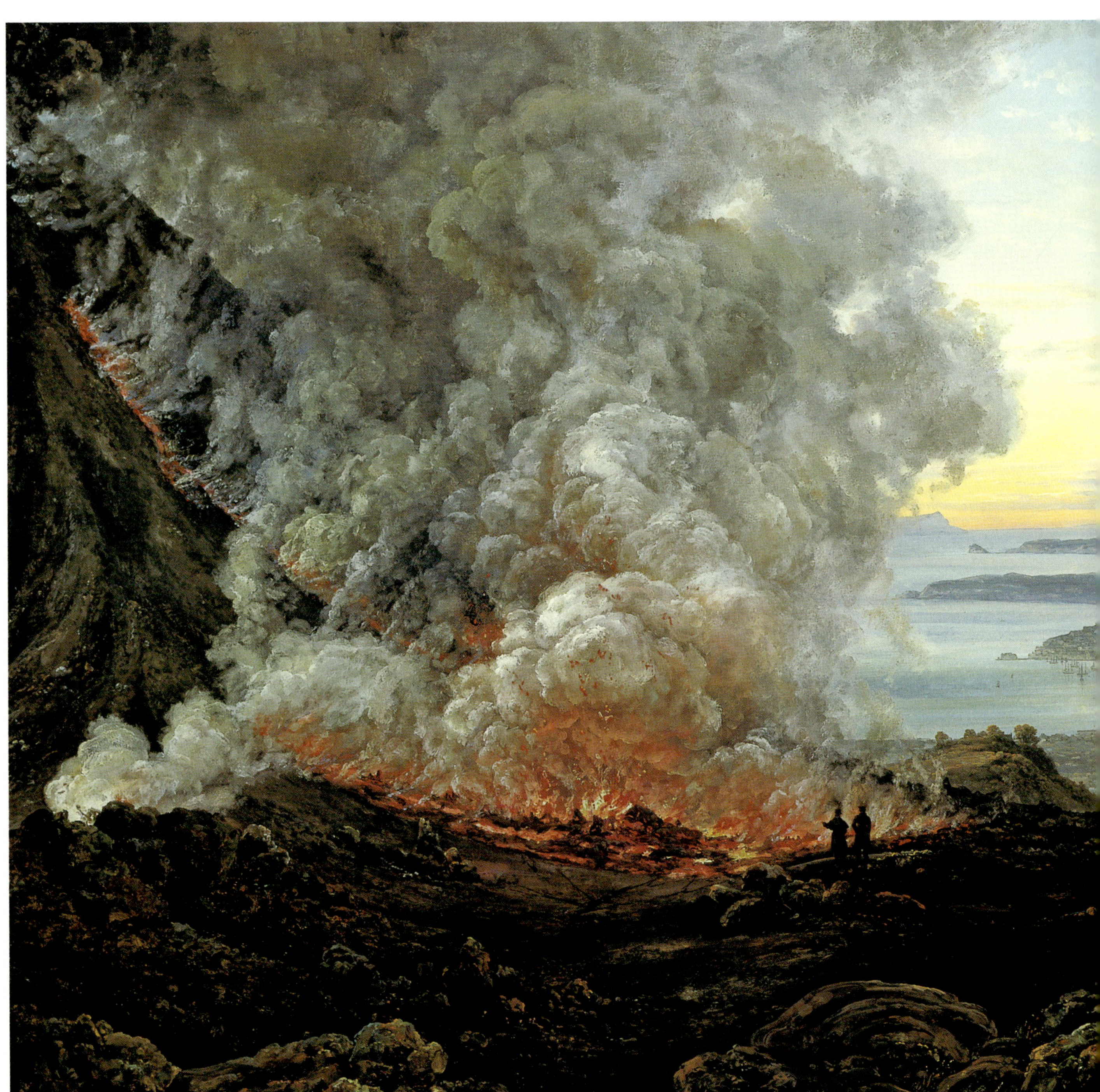

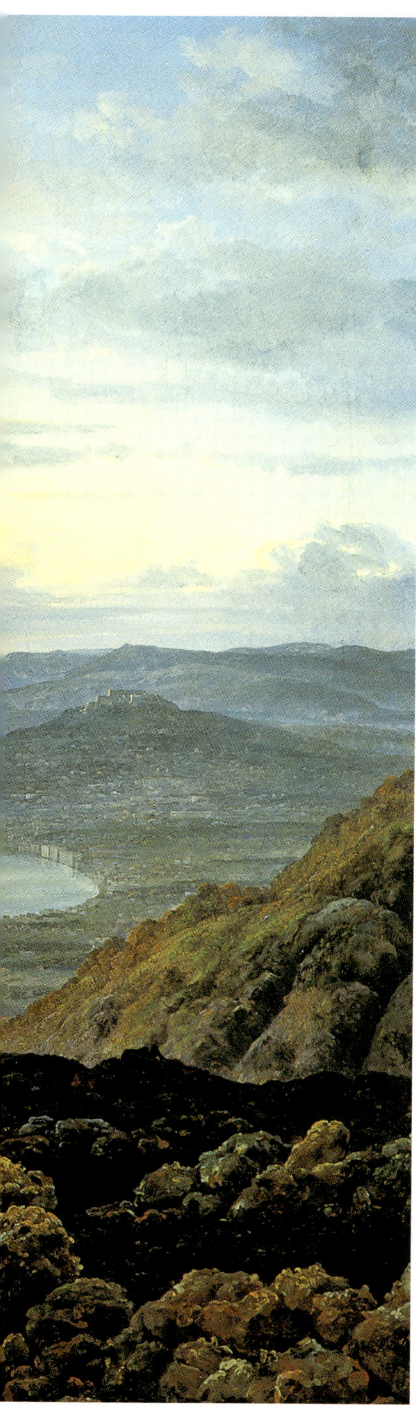

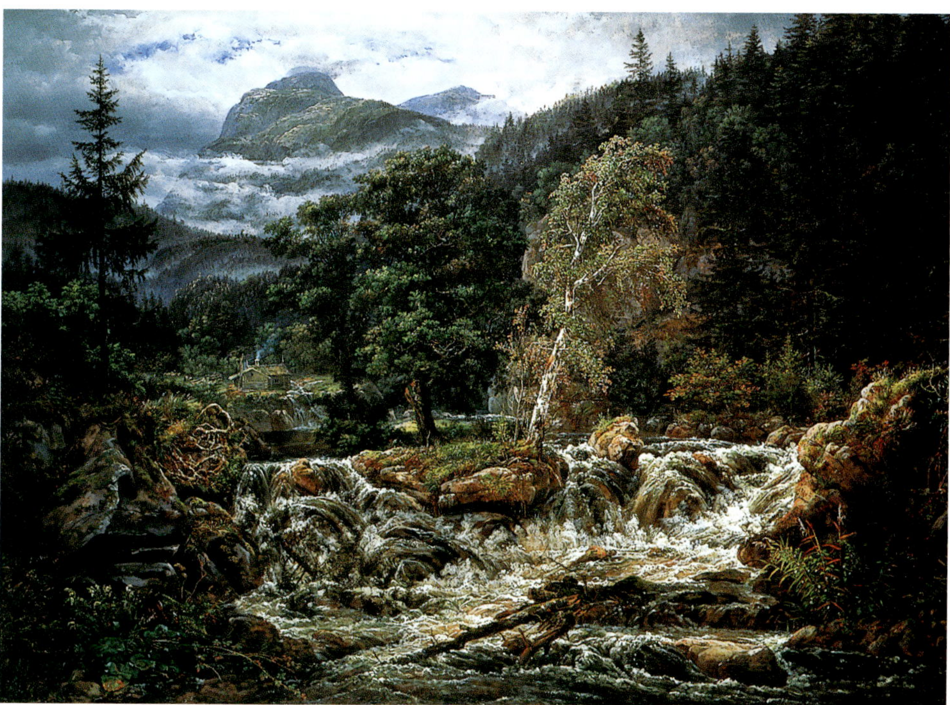

and collective identity. Moreover, in his view, art served an ethical purpose by magnifying and shaping patriotism.

With early training in theology, history, and law, Høyen studied at the Royal Academy's drawing school before leaving on a three-year trip to Germany, Austria, and Italy in 1822, in part inspired by the writings of Goethe. During his travels, he became especially interested in medieval art and architecture, and he observed a number of important restoration projects. As a student, he had been exposed to emerging romantic philosophies of nationhood, including those formulated by German philosophers Johann Gottfried von Herder and Johann Gottlieb Fichte (1762–1814). Fichte's *Reden an die deutsche Nation* (1807–08)[8] mobilized the notion that unique inherited cultural patrimony and the education of common rituals assured the spiritual flowering of a people: "Only when each people, left to itself, develops and forms itself in accordance with its own peculiar quality, and only when in every people each individual develops himself in accordance with that common quality . . . then and only then does the manifestation of divinity appear."[9] Høyen shared with theorists of his generation the belief in the spiritual value of local customs, rituals, and material culture, and he endeavored through his scholarship, lectures, institutional work, and his friendship with artists and intellectuals, to render coherent a sense of Denmark's history. Architectural preservation was one critical branch of that endeavor.

OPPOSITE
65.
J. C. C. Dahl
The Eruption of Vesuvius, 1820
Oil on canvas, 16⅞ x 26½ in.
(43 x 67.5 cm)
Statens Museum for Kunst,
Copenhagen

ABOVE
66.
J. C. C. Dahl
Norwegian Mountain Landscape with Waterfall, 1821
Oil on canvas, 38⅞ x 54 in.
(98.8 x 137.3 cm)
Thorvaldsens Museum, Copenhagen

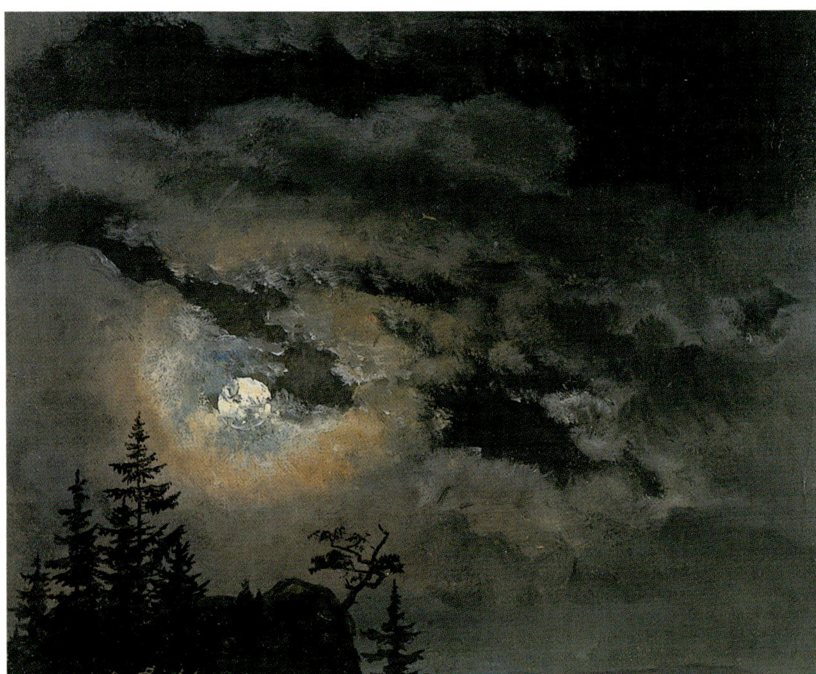

67.
J. C. C. Dahl
Study of Clouds at Full Moon, 1822
Oil on paper on canvas, 6¼ x 7⅜ in.
(15.8 x 18.6 cm)
Fine Arts Museums of San Francisco,
Magnin Income Fund

In the later 1820s Høyen applied to the state for, and received, funds to travel throughout Denmark, southern Sweden, and northern Germany to study the material remains of Denmark's expansive past. Beginning in 1829 he chronicled Danish architecture and argued for the restoration of buildings of historical significance. This study trip fostered a movement to preserve public and vernacular architecture.[10] Restoration work on cathedral exteriors and the uncovering of interior wall paintings, such as at Aarhus (Aarhus Cathedral / St. Clemens Church, begun 1197), became common activities for archaeologists by mid-century, based in part on Høyen's art-historical analyses of the buildings and their decoration.[11] Høyen also helped to stimulate a broad interest among artists in Denmark's architectural treasures, such as Aarhus Cathedral, which Købke rendered in 1830 in *The Transept of Aarhus Cathedral*, subsequently considered his first mature work (fig. 64). By the end of the century, the establishment of folk museums—encyclopedic open-air collections of houses, stables, and other vernacular forms from throughout the country—had become common. Within the folk museum, modern urban dwellers could visit the spaces and view the artifacts of past generations of Danes or of far-flung fellow countrymen, effecting a sense of national connectedness, what historian Benedict Anderson calls an "imagined community."[12] Finally, Høyen assembled one of the first systematic histories of Danish art, establishing for younger artists and scholars the critical model of artistic genealogy.[13] As different as these projects were one from another—encouraging the depiction of historical monuments, architectural restoration, and folk collecting—they had at their root Høyen's determination to identify, consolidate, and celebrate a sense of the native.

With archaeologist Christian Jürgensen Thomsen, best known for establishing the tripartite designation of prehistoric artifacts (Stone, Bronze, and Iron Ages), Høyen helped to articulate a Danish folk soul embedded in both topography and archaeological remains. These were described as atavistic cultural survivals: "From our pre-Christian forebears we have inherited no art," began an important lecture entitled "Om Betingelserne for en skandinavisk

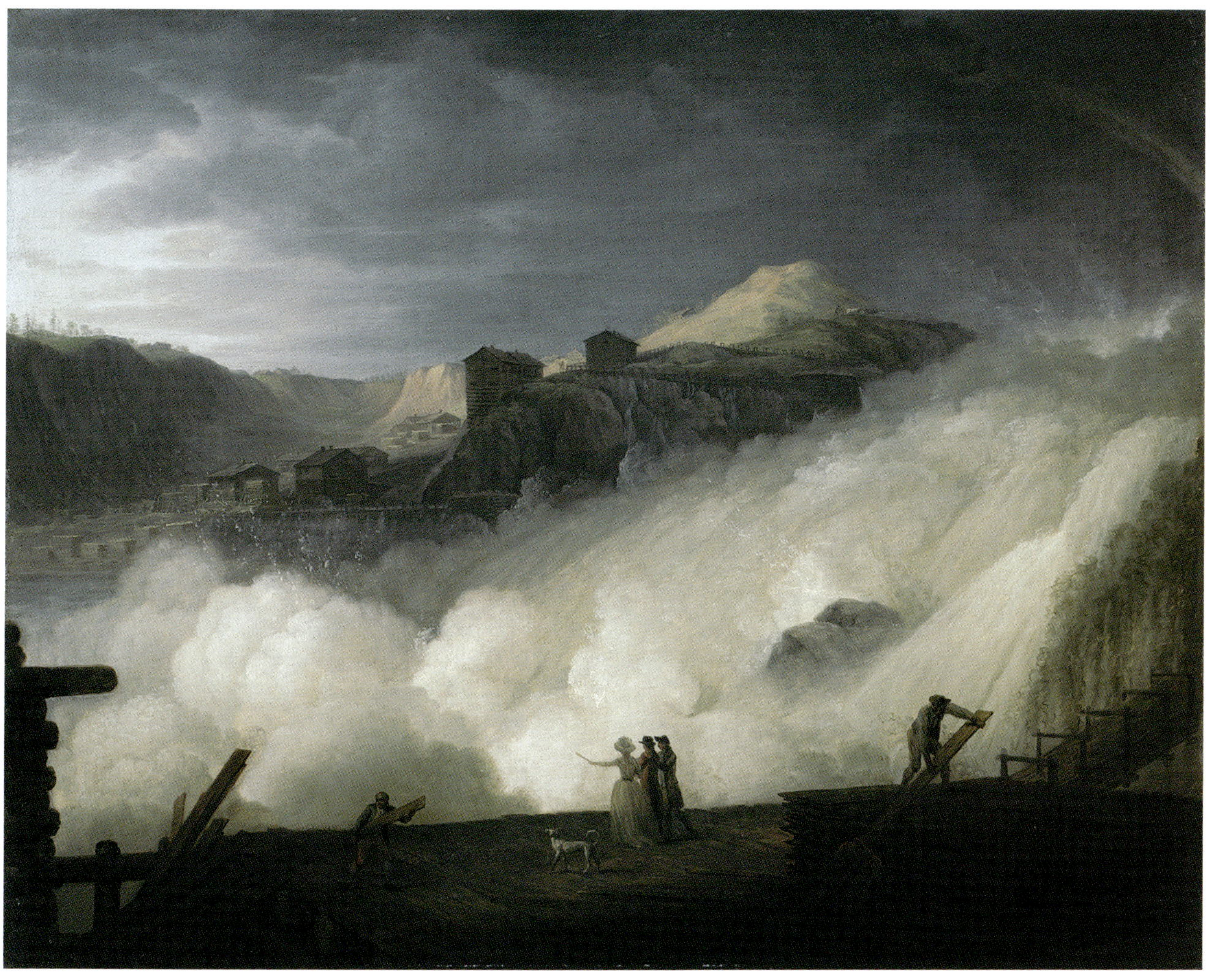

68.
Erik Pauelsen
Sarpfossen, 1789
Oil on canvas, 25 x 31⅛ in.
(63.5 x 79 cm)
Statens Museum for Kunst,
Copenhagen

Nationalkonsts Udvikling" (On the Conditions Required for the Development of a Scandinavian National Art), delivered in March 1844. But he continued by asserting that it was precisely through folk traditions, collective rituals, and a concerted effort to engage with Danish material culture (and to eschew foreign and elite influence) that "we can hope to create a *folkelig* historical art."[14] Cultural leaders, including chemist and physicist Hans Christian Ørstad (1777–1851), who offered a bridge between science and spirituality, and the botanist Joakim Frederik Schouw (1789–1852), who promulgated the notion that national identities were shaped by the relationship between a people and their topography, contributed to the growing nationalist discourse by asserting that archaeological traces tied the Danish people inexorably to the land.[15] This view was strongly shaped by German philosopher Friedrich Wilhelm Joseph von Schelling's *Naturphilosophie*, in which he views God as manifest in nature through the workings of the mind, and consequently each corner of nature is immanent. It was in turn popularized in Denmark by Norwegian-born Henrik Steffens (1773–1845), whose lectures on natural philosophy in 1802 (published in 1803 as *Indledning til philosophiske Forelæsninger*) were widely attended by, among others, the poet Adam Oehlenschläger and theologist and poet Nikolai Grundtvig (1783–1872; see chapter 6).

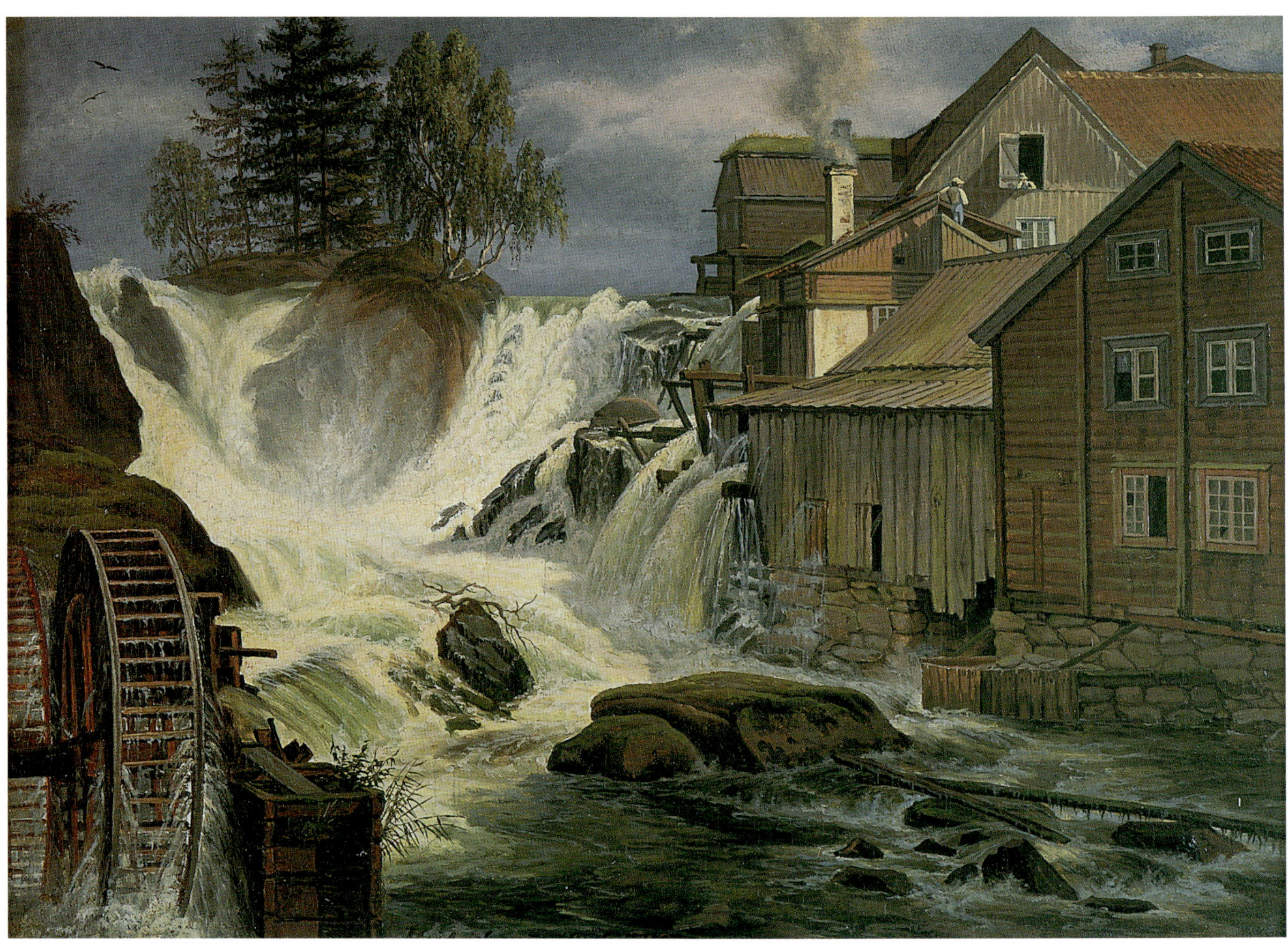

69.
Frederik Sødring
*Rønneby Waterfall at Blekinge,
Sweden*, 1836
Oil on canvas, 12 x 16 in.
(30.5 x 40.5 cm)
Collection of Ambassador John L. Loeb Jr.,
New York

Art historian Michelle Facos identifies this rhetoric with sociologist Pierre Bordieu's notion of *habitus*, a term describing the process of cultural coalescence, the active role played by memory to affect identity.[16] In this regard, Høyen was also instrumental in shaping a Danish artistic geography. He lectured and published widely on the need for Danish artists to dispense with any taint of foreign influence in their work and paint their native landscape. Høyen was an impetus behind the Royal Academy's reassessment of its travel stipend in March 1857, at which time it became possible for artists to use the funds to remain in Denmark rather than relocate, for example, to Rome.[17] In his lecture "On the Conditions Required for the Development of a Scandinavian National Art," Høyen summarized many of these impulses and offered a powerful impetus for the emerging generation of artists to imagine their country as a repository for a folk soul. He offered that a collective and fundamental identity, rooted in the land and "folk," was a sacred cultural inheritance. The new art produced from such a legacy communicates a feeling of spirituality.[18] In addition to his other arenas of influence, Høyen also helped to influence the perception of Danish landscape painting as descriptive of a new native Eden.

By the mid-century, the result of these efforts was a growing recognition by artists, patrons, and the middle class public of a coherent national school. Clearly, efforts such as those

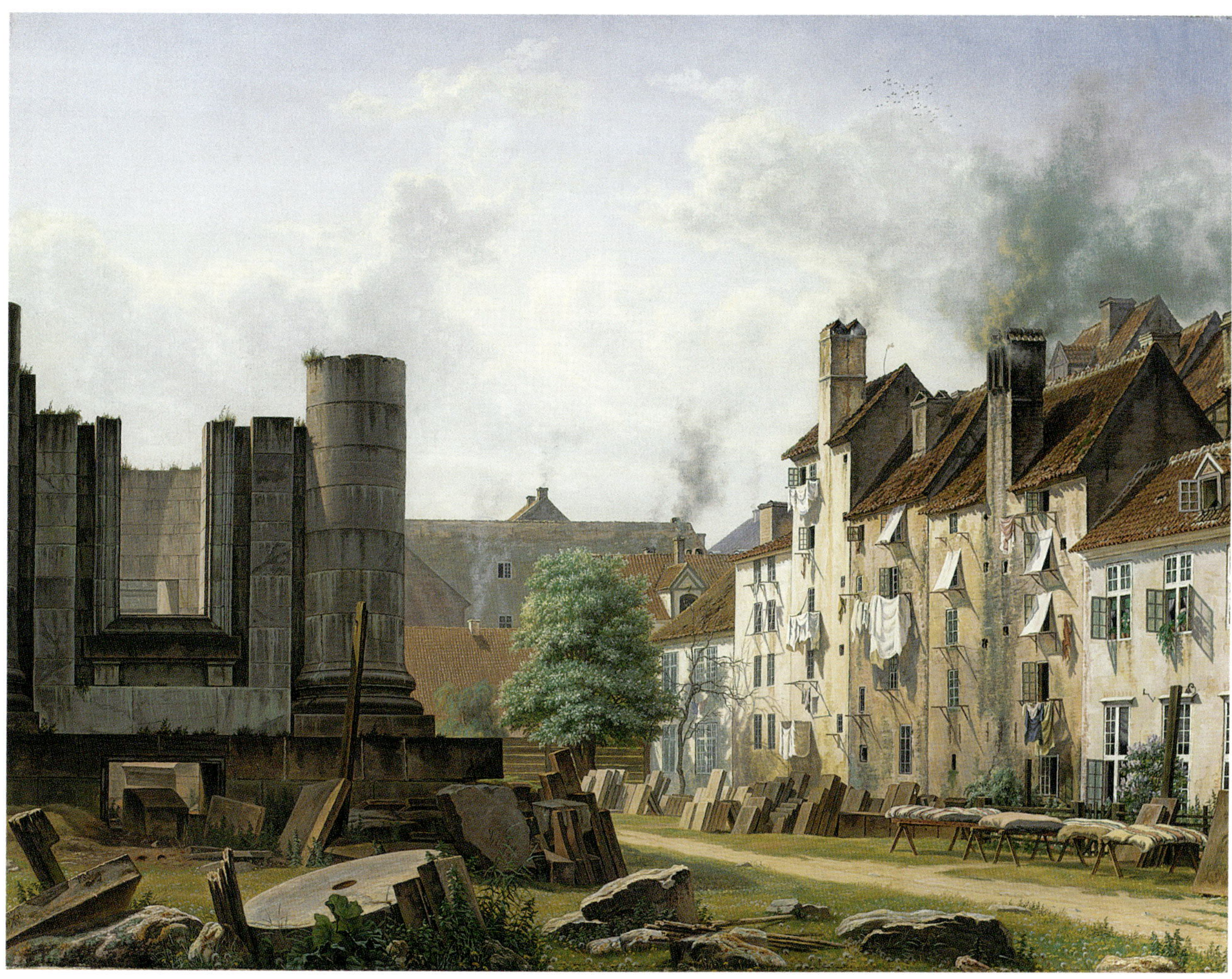

of Høyen and Thomsen reflected the larger political agenda of nationalist historians dedicated to the narration of Denmark as a land of rural folk living simple lives which, especially in the wake of the 1864 loss of Schleswig and Holstein, eclipsed the public's identification with Denmark's absolutist past.[19] In a review of the 1828 Charlottenborg exhibition, Høyen had offered an ethos that marked the period: "History painting, when applied to scenes of daily life in works of modest dimension, have recently been identified as 'genre' paintings. The better the artist is at choosing images from his environment that will arouse the viewers' sympathy, the greater the effect."[20] Through such important statements, Høyen helped to effect the ascendance of vernacular culture as a theme in Danish art. Exhortations to paint one's immediate experience, to immerse oneself in nature, and to seek genuine motifs specific to the nation— down to the tiniest details—shaped landscape painting in the mid- and late-nineteenth century. Høyen was, in addition, a strong proponent of Caspar David Friedrich's landscape painting. Høyen was in residence at Frederiksborg Castle chronicling the painting collection at the time that Købke worked on *Frederiksborg Castle in the Evening Light*. It was likely through Høyen that Købke first came to know Friedrich's work.[21] In Købke's painting, the nearness of a wooden boat and of particularized foliage physically locate the viewer in the immediate fore-

70.
Frederik Sødring
View of the Marble Square with the Uncompleted Frederik's Church, 1835
Oil on canvas, 30½ x 38⅝ in.
(77.5 x 98 cm)
Statens Museum for Kunst,
Copenhagen

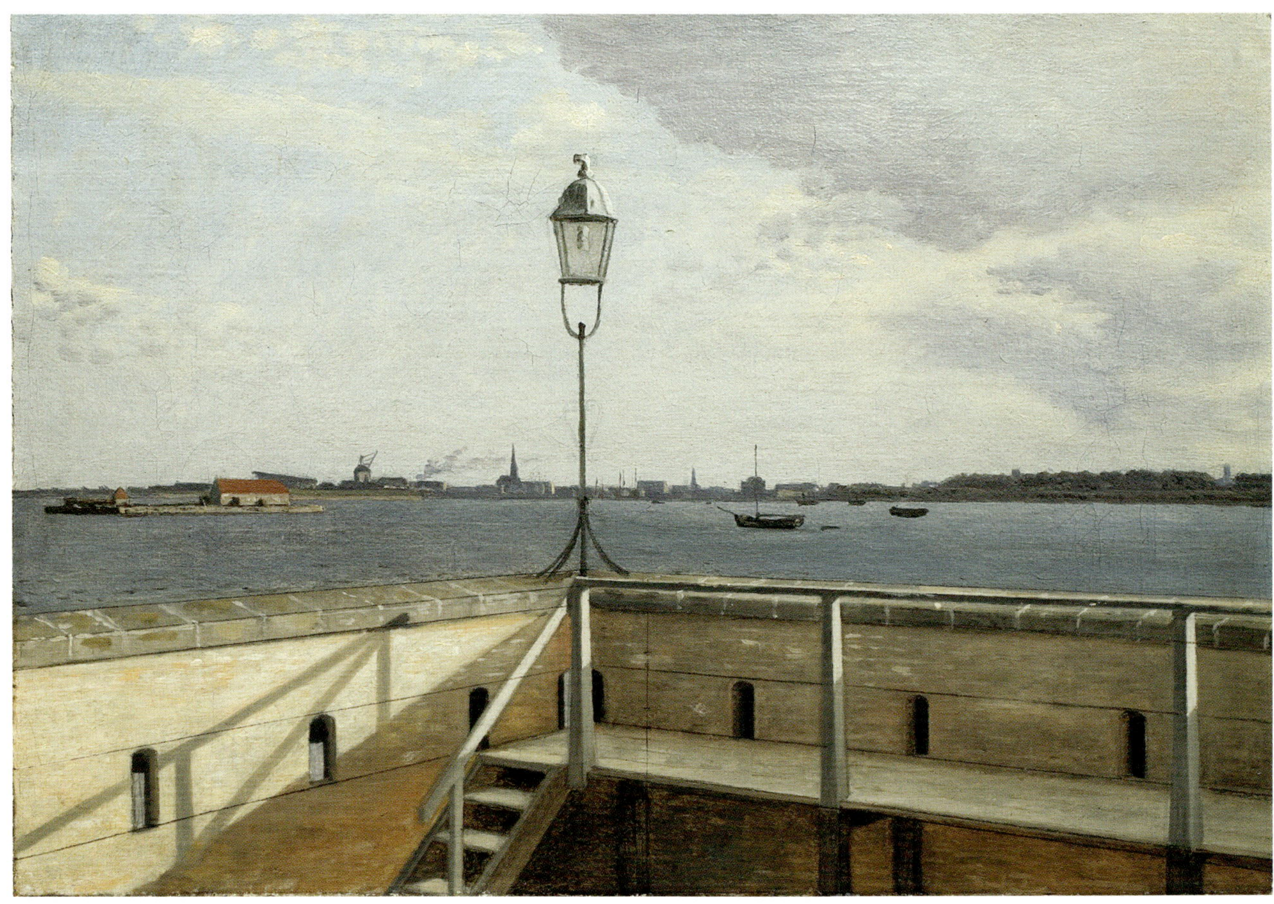

ground, on the edge of Jægerbakken and the formal gardens to the north. Separated from the background by a clearly demarcated middle ground, we understand ourselves to be physically and emotionally distant from the palace, a strategy evoking emotional yearning familiar from Friedrich's work. Indeed, the painting's structure, anchored by the darkened foreground and culminating in the glowing sky, represents the first strong echoes of Friedrich's work. A former student at Denmark's Royal Academy, Friedrich was one of the most famous teachers at the Dresden Academy in the 1820s and 1830s. His work became enormously influential within Denmark via Høyen, who had met and befriended the artist in Dresden in the mid-1820s. According to Kasper Monrad, Høyen had offered many of Friedrich's artistic principles in his lectures and writings, particularly his exhortations to "express your heart's fullest and deepest feelings," as the assertion of "truth."[22] In the works of Friedrich, landscape functions as analogy, as the articulation of inner sentiment.

The painter Johan Christian Clausen Dahl (1788–1857), who was closely associated with Friedrich and Romantic landscape painting in Dresden, had already been promoted by Høyen in the 1810s as an important emerging voice. He later stated: "In landscape painting, the Norwegian painter Dahl, who died far too early, provided us with the impetus for moving forward ... he succeeded at demonstrating that it was possible for a talented artist to forge new paths entirely independently."[23] Dahl became one of the most influential painters in Denmark of emotive, sublime landscapes. The perspective that Købke offered in *Frederiksborg*

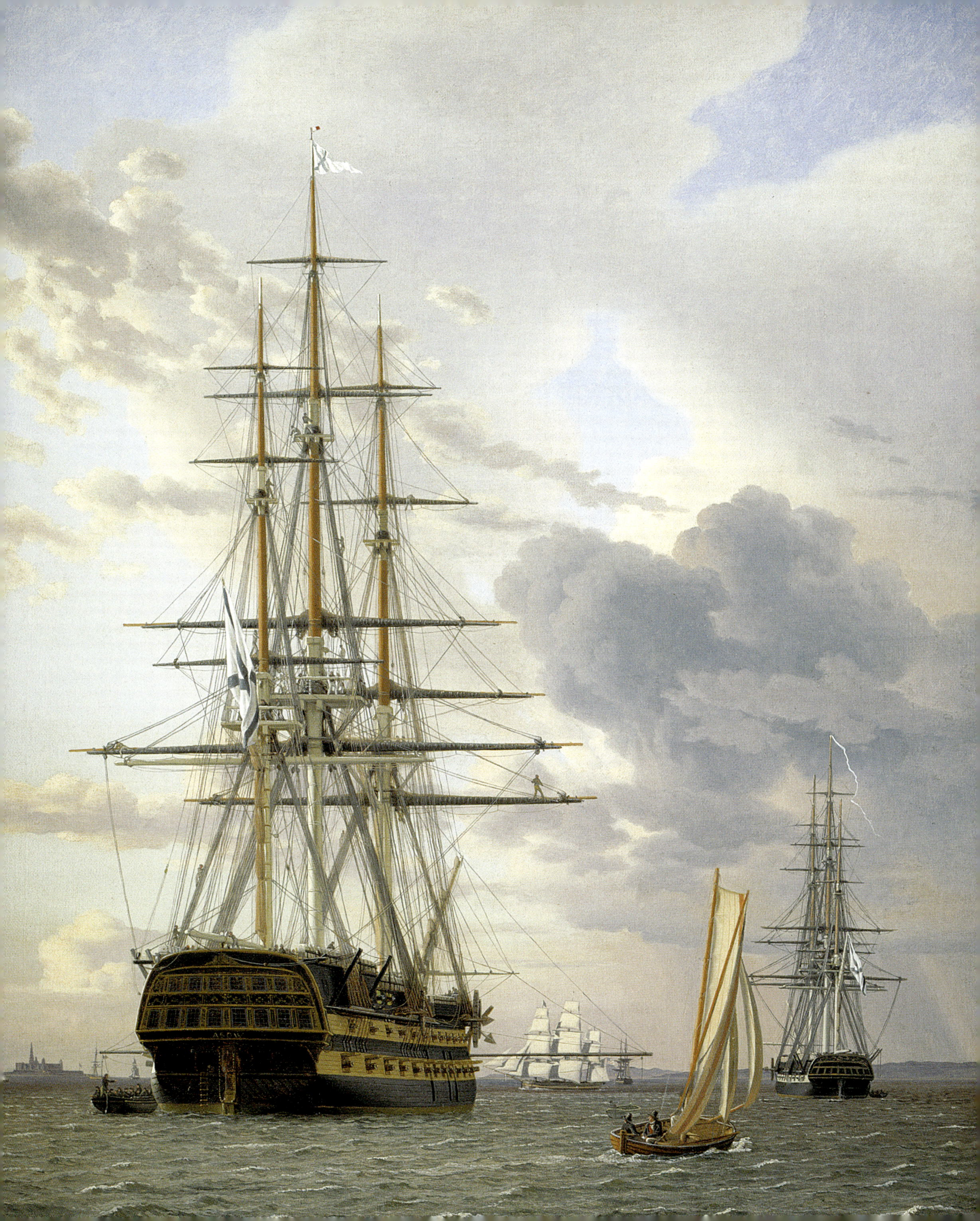

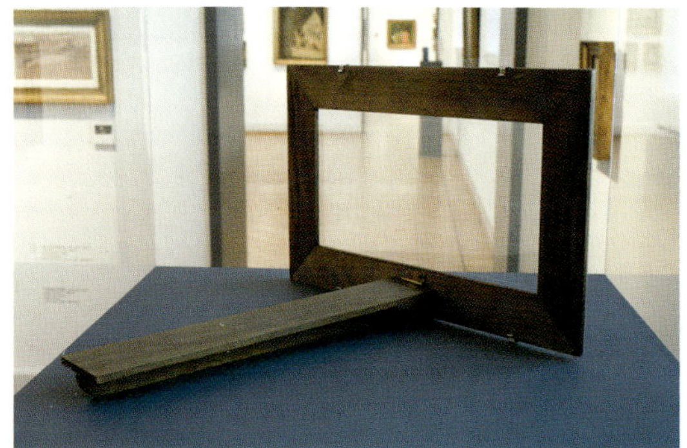

Castle in the Evening Light repeated views rendered by Dahl of Frederiksborg in 1814 and 1817 (fig. 5).[24] Born in Bergen, Norway, then part of Denmark, Dahl studied at the Royal Academy beginning in 1811 and remained in Copenhagen even after Denmark ceded Norway to Sweden in 1814. In 1818, Dahl moved to Dresden where he first encountered Friedrich. Dahl had begun to make open-air studies in Denmark in 1814[25] and then extended this practice in Italy, rendering small works on paper *alla prima*—before the subject.

Living in Italy in 1820–21, Dahl painted dramatic, seemingly journalistic views of Mount Vesuvius erupting, an event that he witnessed and sketched in December 1820, and that he had subsequently formalized in his studio (fig. 65). While living in Rome, Dahl also produced large paintings of Norwegian landscapes, including *Norwegian Mountain Landscape with Waterfall* (1821; fig. 66), commissioned by Thorvaldsen. Rendered from memory and fantasy rather than direct observation (he did not visit inland Norway until 1826), the painting dramatizes nature's majesty. The dizzying perspective of the mountains in the background and the rough, snaking waterfall subjugate the tiny rustic cabin in the foreground, investing in the canvas a sublimity of scale, enhanced by the shadowed foreground and the veiled, foggy background.

Dahl also produced a prodigious number of small, exquisite oil depictions of clouds. In such informal works as *Study of Clouds at Full Moon* (1822; fig. 67), Dahl registered the fugitive light effects of the night sky. Paralleling Eckersberg's interest in meteorology, Dahl studied the ephemeral atmospheric textures and luminosity of the clouds. The British meteorologist Luke Howard's *Essay on the Modification of Clouds*, published in 1802, offered for Dahl's generation a way of interpreting the sky in physical terms. More influential for the Dano-Germans, however, were the ways in which Howard's research was poeticized by Goethe in his 1820 essay *Wolkengestalt nach Howard* and in his collection of poems entitled *Howards Ehrengedächtnis* (1822), which invested sentiment in cloud typologies.[26] Dahl's studies offer the sky as a site of both positivist study and ineffable emotionalism.

A mode of landscape painting in Denmark that may be characterized as emotive or "sublime" had begun with Erik Pauelsen (1749–1790), who was supported by the king to travel to Norway in 1788. His painting *Sarpfossen* (1789; fig. 68) was among those that provided a Nordic framework for an emerging interest in dramatic mountain landscapes in the period.[27] In addition to the raging falls and turbulent sky, Pauelsen catalogued local ethnography in the form of wooden architecture as well as a display of harvested trees. The themes of nature's violence, persistence, and seemingly endless resources marked Norway's identity in turn-of-the-century Denmark, and they were repeated in Dahl's views of Norway in the 1820s.

In the 1770s, landscape painting had been a distant cousin to history painting within the academy, but by the 1820s it had arrived as an important vehicle for collective sentiment. Views of violent, emotive nature were rendered in that generation by Dahl and by Frederik Sødring, whom Købke had painted on the artist's birthday in 1832 (chapter 2). Raised in North Jutland and Norway, Sødring rendered mountain landscapes in the manner of Dahl and Friedrich. Sødring first debuted at the Charlottenborg Palace with two copies of paintings by Dahl, and in 1833 he traveled with Dahl in coastal Norway. He also traveled to southern Sweden in the early 1830s, where he first painted motifs in the region of Blekinge. *Rønneby Waterfall at Blekinge, Sweden* (1836; fig. 69) repeats the artist's composition from 1831, which he exhibited in that

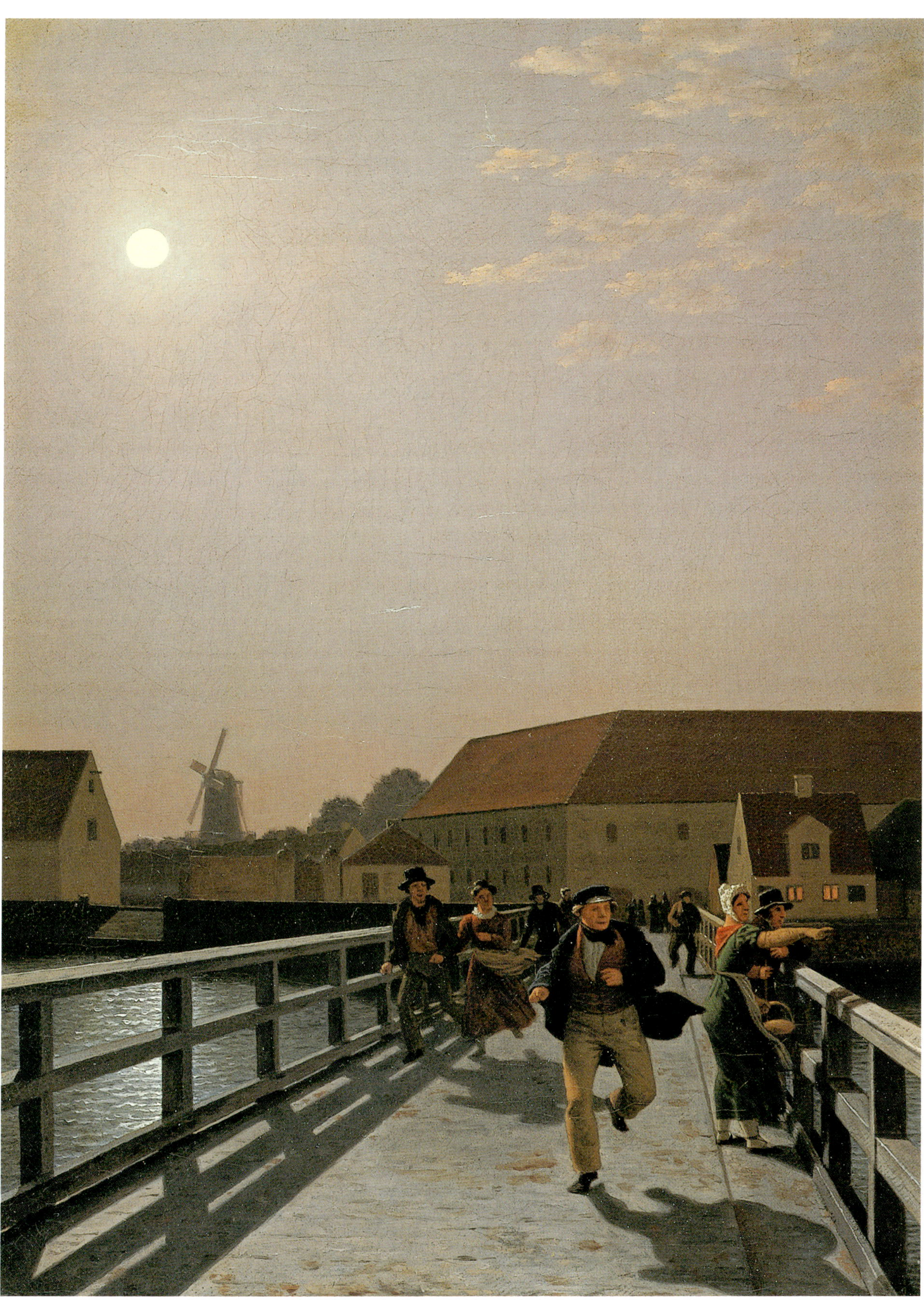

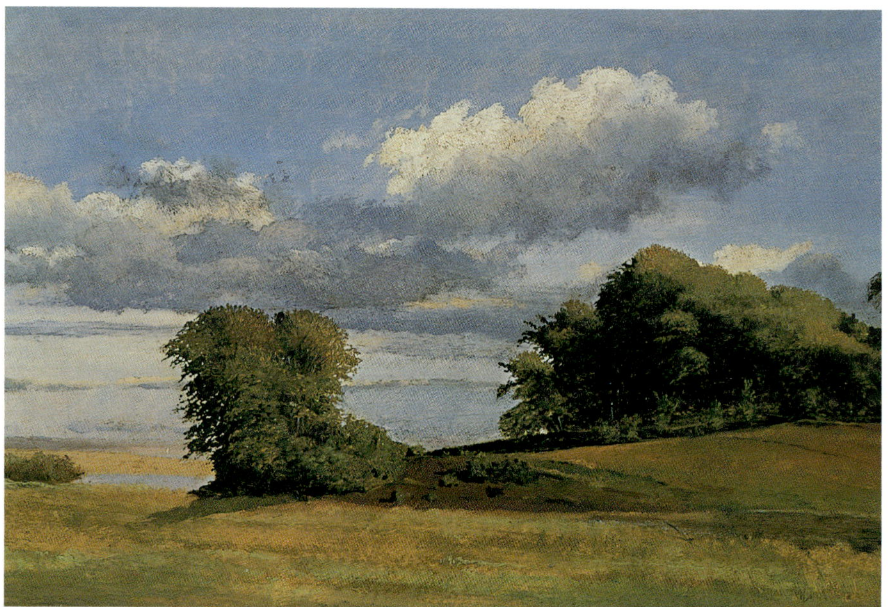

75.
Johan Thomas Lundbye
*Landscape Near Lake Arresø,
Frederiksværk*, 1838
Oil on cardboard mounted on canvas,
8⅜ x 12⅜ in.
(21.2 x 31.5 cm)
Collection of Ambassador
John L. Loeb Jr., New York

year as having been painted directly before the motif.[28] The original painting was purchased by
the Fine Arts Society and offered by lottery to one of its members. Its current whereabouts are
unknown. However, the motif seems to be the painting reflected in the mirror in Købke's portrait of Sødring (fig. 37), the waterfall seen in reverse peeking out from behind a few letters that
have been pushed into the frame.[29] Like Pauelsen's mountain view, Sødring's painting describes
the Nordic landscape as both sublime and productive—human engineering, in the form of a
mill and a factory, may have harnessed the crashing waterfall, but the presence of dead limbs and
waterlogged wooden planks serve as talismans of the river's destructive force.

Sødring's *View of the Marble Square with the Uncompleted Frederik's Church* (1835; fig. 70)
represents another side of this artist's work, a view of Copenhagen's urban fabric. On the left side
of the painting, the abandonment of the partially built Frederick's Church has been emphasized.
The church, known as the Marble Church, had been planned in the 1740s by Nikolai Eigtved,
along with the Amalienborg complex, as the centerpiece of Copenhagen's Frederiksstad district in
celebration of the 300th anniversary of the House of Oldenburg (see chapter 1). The project had
been interrupted by Eigtved's death, and then abandoned in the later eighteenth century because
of its enormous expense. In Sødring's painting, soot, weather, and weeds have taken their toll on
the interrupted monument to the king, while stone cladding and tools, once rallied for use, sit
abandoned in the middle of the surrounding residential neighborhood.

Completed in 1894 by architect Ferdinand Meldahl, the Marble Church was throughout
the earlier nineteenth-century a marker of an ambitious past. These outsized ruins, poignant in
their interjection of monumental classicism into the working city, had attracted artists such as
Eckersberg, who painted a view of them upon his return from Rome (ca. 1817, Hirschsprung
Collection), and Wilhelm Bendz (1824, National Museum at Frederiksborg).[30] Sødring
employs Eckerberg's clarity of light and perspectival geometry in his version, emphasizing the
sunny domestic apartment life facing the broken and shadowed monument. In close proximity
to the Amalienborg Palace complex (later rendered by Vilhelm Hammershøi), the houses and
apartments that Sødring depicts are modest. With laundry hanging from the windows, the air

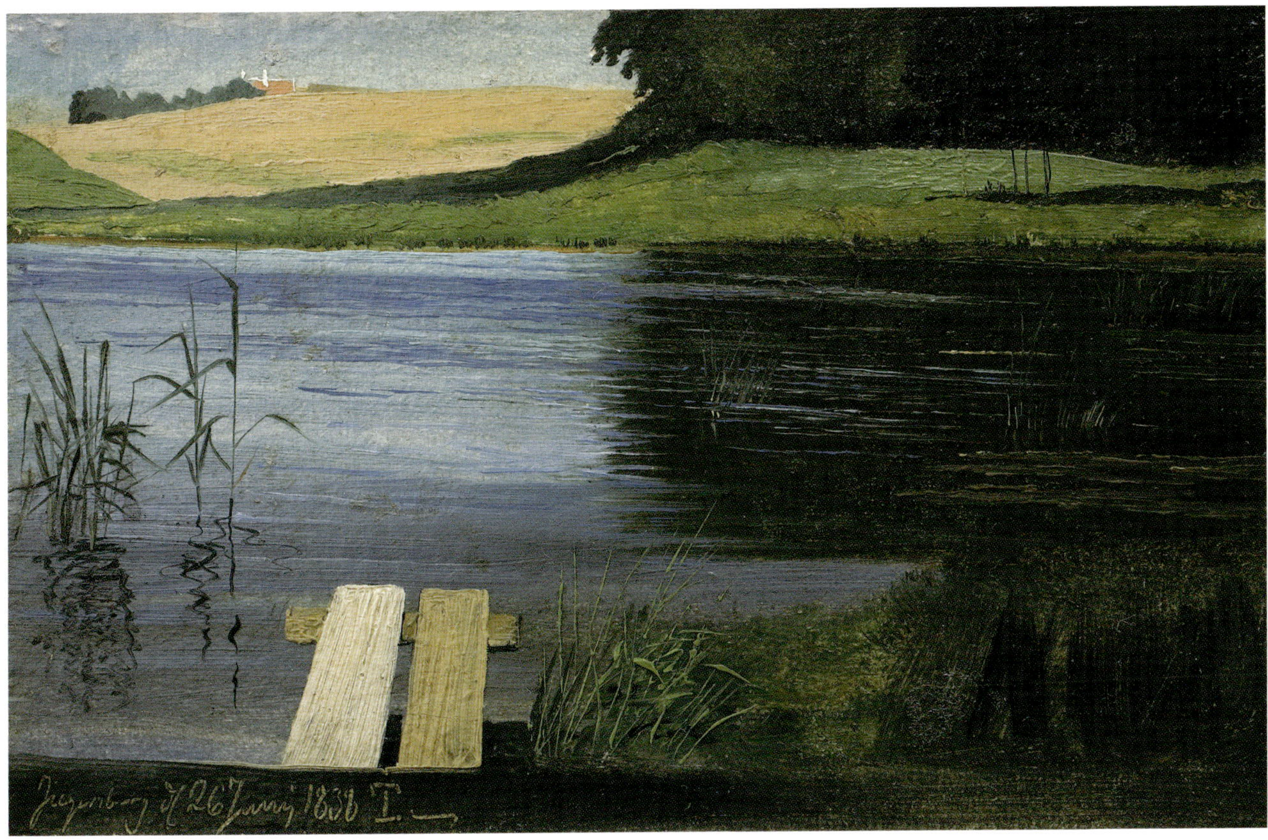

76.
Johan Thomas Lundbye
View of a Pond, 1838
Oil on paper on canvas, 6⅛ x 8⅞ in.
(15.4 x 22.4 cm)
The Hirschsprung Collection,
Copenhagen

sullied by smoke rising from the chimneys, and mattresses airing in the sun, these urban homes contrast in every regard to the grandiose ruins. Sødring's inclusion of such details, and indeed his insistence on visual acuity, was anchored in the teaching of Eckersberg.

The landscape and view painters working in Denmark from the 1820s onward were indebted to the pedagogy of Christoffer Wilhelm Eckersberg, as well as to his paintings produced in Italy (see chapter 3) and in Denmark. One of Eckersberg's commitments as an artist and as a teacher was to the study of the natural sciences. His ability to register the most ephemeral light conditions fused with a material stasis born of geometrical control—what he termed the "fundamental image"—shaped the landscape painting of the Golden Age. An example of this approach is his *View from the Three Crowns Fort toward Copenhagen* (1836; fig. 71), which melds the rigor of scientific perspective with an eccentrically vectored, seemingly informal view. In the lower half, the view of Copenhagen harbor is linear and mathematical in its precise network of architectural elements and shadow. In the large upper register, a series of cloud formations, subtly harnessed into diagonal forms, provide softened counterpoints to the abstract architecture beneath.

Eckersberg reported in his diary on 25 April 1836 that he had recorded the site using a perspective octant, "a sketch of one of the many painterly points found on the battery." [31] As previously noted, he was a committed student of linear perspective, the mathematical system of creating the illusion of depth on a flat surface. In 1841, when Eckersberg published his second, large-format handbook on perspective entitled *Linearperspectiven, anvendt paa Malerkunsten* (Linear Perspective in Painting), he included a precise diagram for what he termed a "Perspec-

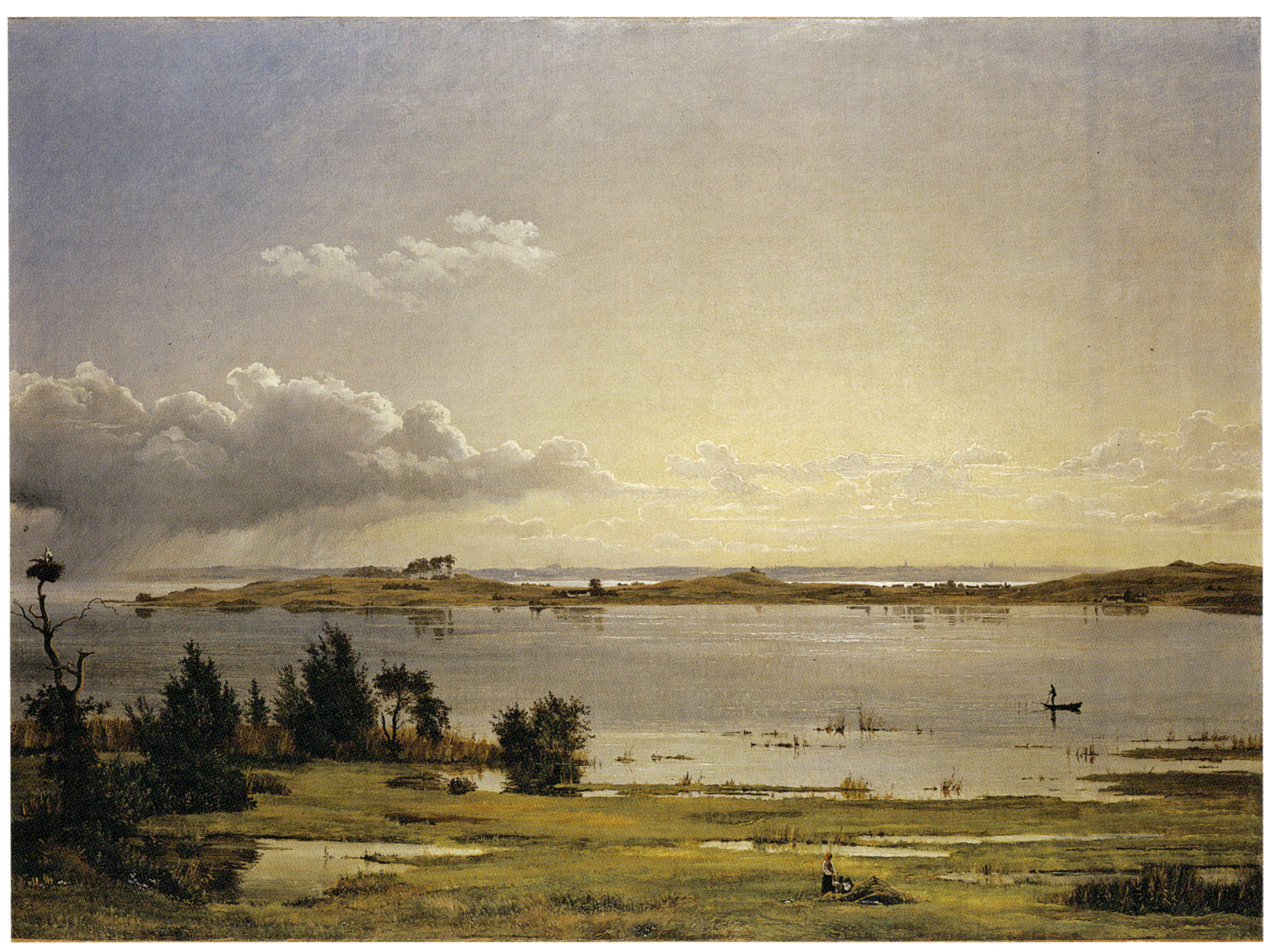

77.
Johan Thomas Lundbye
Landscape at Arresø (Lake Arre), 1838
Oil on canvas, 25⅛ x 34 in.
(64 x 86.5 cm)
Ny Carlsberg Glyptotek, Copenhagen

tive Octant" in 1/3 size.[32] Eckersberg's perspective octant (fig. 73), reminiscent of Albrecht Dürer's drawing machines from the early sixteenth century, offered what the artist termed "mechanical assistance" like the camera obscura, "but simpler," to rationalize the dimensions of objects in nature that are otherwise fugitive, such as "the breadth of the moon or the width of a rainbow."[33] Proposing such a tool to "correct" the view before an artist's eye, Eckersberg fused representations of the everyday with mathematical correctness and precision. Such a means of rationalizing and perfecting nature in turn shaped Christen Købke's views of Frederiksborg Castle. In *Frederiksborg Castle in the Evening Light*, Købke invests a gentle sublimity extracted from Friedrich and Dahl's views of nature into the rigorous pictorial geometry that he had garnered from Eckersberg's teaching. The motif itself also echoed Eckersberg's views of official Copenhagen.

From the Three Crowns Fort, in 1824, Eckersberg had first seen the Russian naval fleet that he would depict four years later in *'Asow,' A Russian Ship of the Line, Together with a Frigate, Riding at Anchor at Elsinore* (1828; fig. 72), a brilliant demonstration of perspective and atmosphere. In addition to the artist's avowed interest in marine painting as a subject,[34] such a view offered him an opportunity to engage the natural and abstract sciences within the practice of his art. This painting represents, in the foreground, a "ship of the line," a warship powerful enough to stand up to enemy lines, with cannons on two decks. It is a mesmerizingly precise rendering

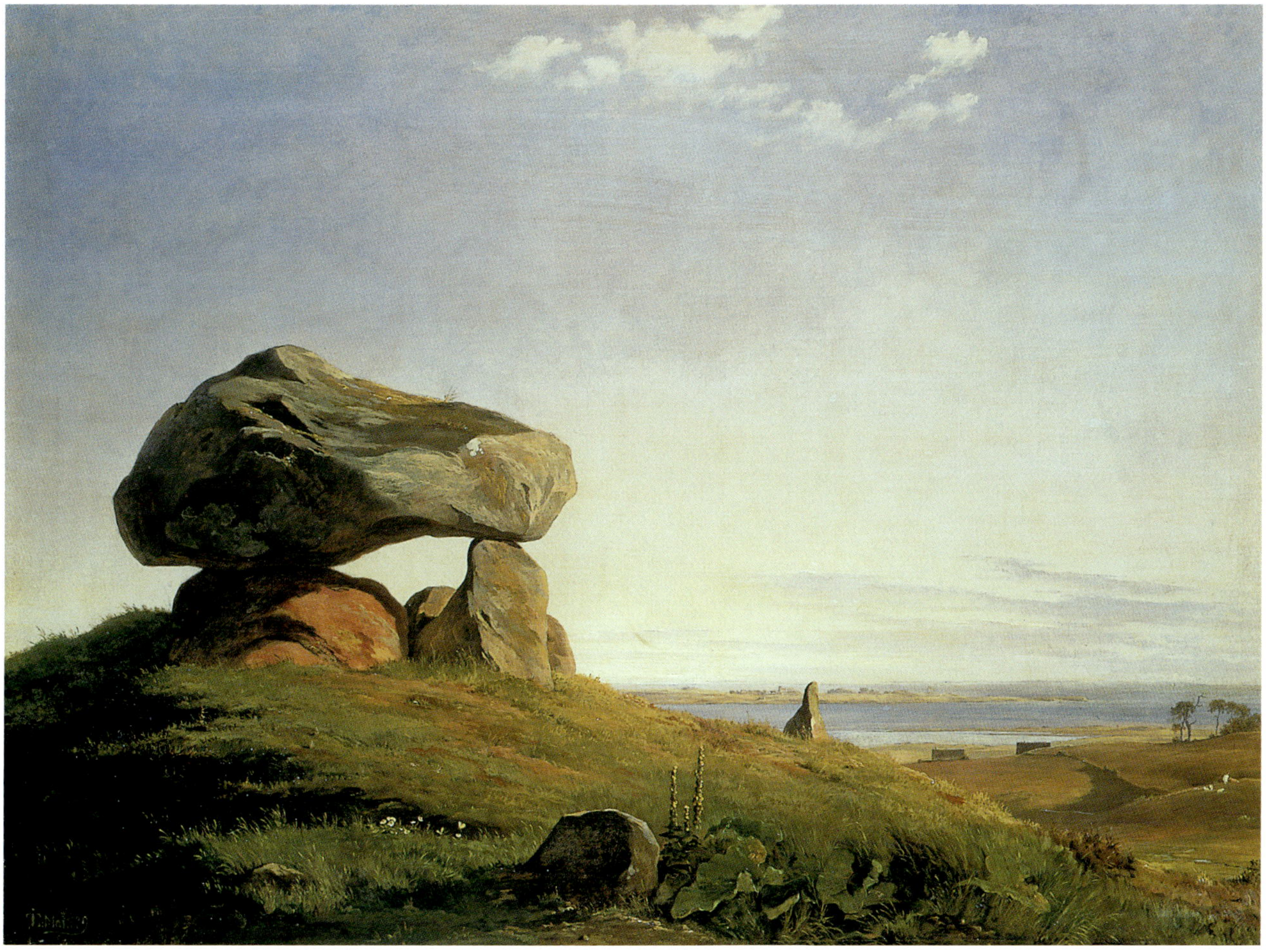

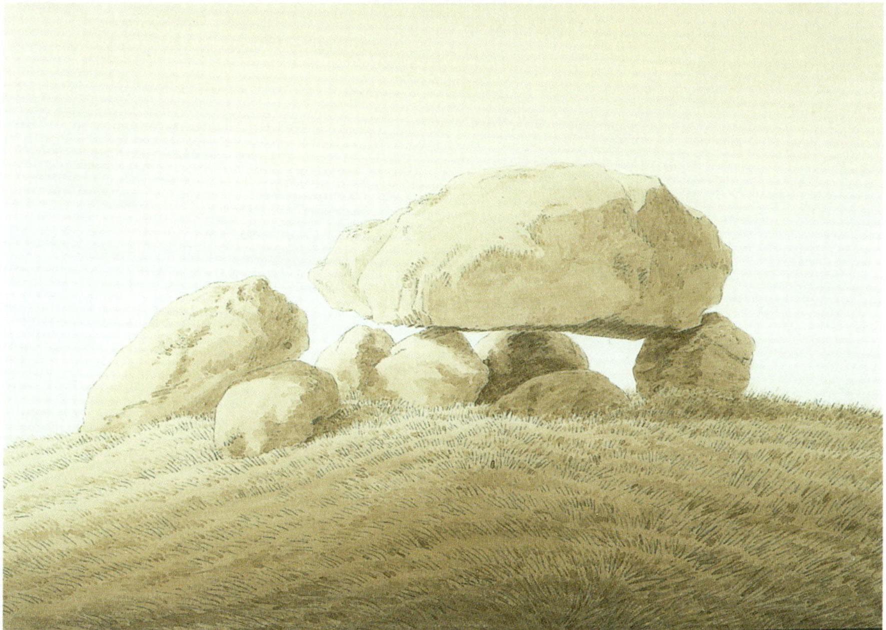

ABOVE
78.
Johan Thomas Lundbye
Dolmen at Raklev, 1839
Oil on canvas, 26¼ x 35 in.
(66.7 x 88.9 cm)
Thorvaldsens Museum, Copenhagen

LEFT
79.
Caspar David Friedrich
Burial Mound on Rügen, ca. 1837–38
Pen and sepia on paper, 9 x 12⅛ in.
(23 x 30.8 cm)
The Queen's Reference
Library, Copenhagen

of naval engineering, of complex ropes and rigging, offering a water-level view upward toward the majestic Russian ship and across to its smaller companions. Helsingør Harbor is shown in miniature on the left, and to the right, under storm clouds and a cascade of rain, is the nearby coast of Sweden.

Although the painting appears journalistic, *'Asow,' A Russian Ship of the Line* was poetically constructed from studies based on perspectival diagrams that Eckersberg produced, ships' plans that he borrowed from the naval dockyard, his experiences on board ship, meteorological studies, and his own sense of nature's drama.[35] In his 1841 treatise on perspective, Eckersberg advised his students that it is pleasant to stand by the harbor on a calm day, but that drama comes with turbulent weather and with waves.[36] Further, the painting was based on several years' worth of Eckersberg's observations of the Russian navy. He reports that he had viewed the Russian ships first at Helsingør in 1826, and then in Copenhagen in 1827, when he boarded "the beautiful ship."[37] In July 1828, he noted that he had again seen a Russian ship of the line and a frigate anchored in Copenhagen.[38]

Eckersberg had an intimate knowledge of ships, both from his observations and from concerted study in Holmen, the Royal Shipyard, in the center of Copenhagen. Eckersberg not only painted representations of ships, but beginning in the 1820s, he also participated in their decoration.[39] In 1824, Eckersberg collaborated with chief naval engineer Andreas Schifter (1779–1852), who had attended the drawing school at the Royal Academy, on the decoration of Dronning Marie, one of the last great Danish ships of the line produced by the Copenhagen naval yard. As precise as *'Asow,' A Russian Ship of the Line* appears to be, its zigzag pattern of ships receding into the background and its stormy sea and sky to the right, are shaped by Eckersberg's romance with maritime drama and his sense of renewal as the great navies and merchant fleets ply the coastal waters.

Eckersberg's investment of narrative drama into underlying pictorial geometry creates a sense of the uncanny in *Long Bridge, Copenhagen, in the Moonlight* (1836; fig. 74). The telescoping structure of the painting is closely allied with plates from the artist's studies of perspective,[40] and the nighttime setting and emphasis on lunar effects are reminiscent of Jens Juel's nocturne *Landscape with Aurora Borealis* (fig. 9) as well as the romantic landscapes of Friedrich and Dahl. *Long Bridge, Copenhagen, in the Moonlight* seems to have begun with direct observation during one of the artist's evening strolls around Copenhagen[41] and was then, like *'Asow,' A Russian Ship of the Line*, elaborated by narrative fantasy. The painting recalls Eckersberg's theatricality during his period as a history painter, although rather than invoking classical or biblical

80.
Johan Thomas Lundbye
A Danish Coast: Motif from Kitnæs by the Isefjord, 1843
Oil on canvas, 74¼ x 100⅝ in.
(188.5 x 255.5 cm)
Statens Museum for Kunst, Copenhagen

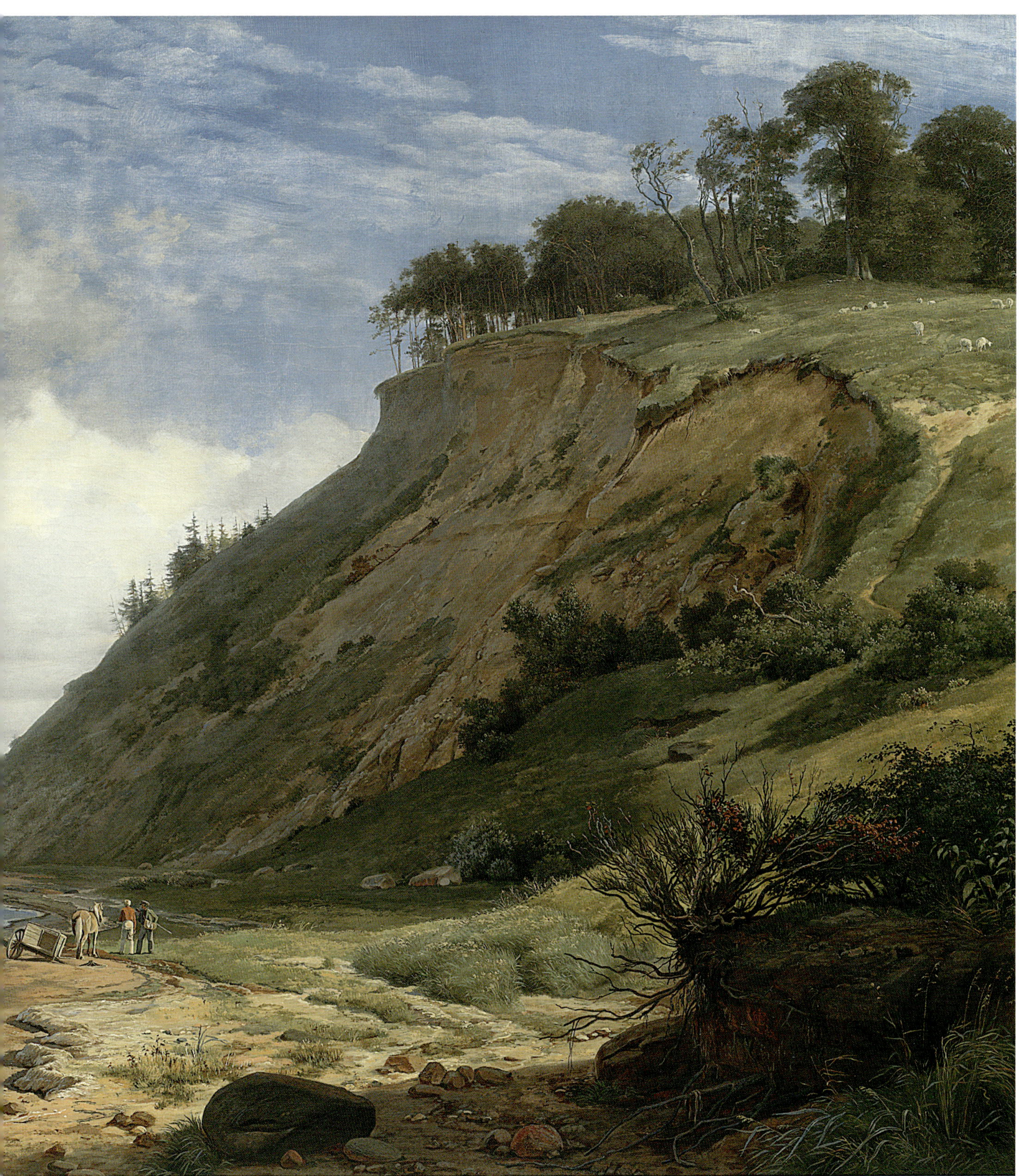

literature, his figures in the foreground enact an unintelligible narrative. A man is shown rushing toward the painting's extreme foreground, followed by other people who likewise run toward the viewer. Their attention, like that of the woman standing and pointing on the right, is drawn to the right, outside of our viewing range. It has been suggested that the painting both alludes to the chaos of the 1807 British bombardment of Copenhagen (which Eckersberg chronicled in a much reproduced painting of that year)[42] and engages contemporary popular fiction: a short story by author Carl Bernhardt entitled "The Day Coach," published in 1836, recounts the story of a woman, betrayed by her lover, who attempts suicide by throwing herself (and her child) from Long Bridge. She is rescued by her future husband, who had been strolling across the bridge.[43] The curiously dramatic and ambiguous narrative makes the painting unique in Eckersberg's work.

Eckersberg's influence on landscape painting of the post-Napoleonic years was incalculable. Creating an echo effect with his friend N. L. Høyen's mandate to celebrate native culture, Eckersberg had advocated that his students paint what they could observe directly, regardless of how humble their subjects might be.

By the middle of the century, humility itself resonated with the notion of otherworldliness, interpolated through native topography. Johan Thomas Lundbye (1818–1848) was the master of this genre. Lundbye's career was profoundly shaped by Høyen's desire to erase foreign influence from Danish painting and by J. C. C. Dahl's assertions of landscape as a site of emotion. In Lundbye's work, Danish topography became both formally dignified and intimately raw. About a decade younger than Købke, Sødring, and Marstrand, Lundbye had entered the Royal Academy in 1832, where he studied under J. L. Lund and received support from the archaeologist and museum director Thomsen. Lundbye's paintings seemed to put into effect Høyen, Thomsen, and Schouw's rhetorical mapping of ethnicity and nationhood onto physical place: "I have made it the goal of my life as a painter to paint my beloved Denmark, but with all the simplicity and modesty which are so characteristic of it. What beauty there is in these fine lines of our hills, which are so gracefully wave-formed that they seem to have risen from the sea, from the mighty sea along whose shores the steep yellow cliffs stand among our forests, acres, and heaths. But only a Dane can paint it."[44]

Originally from northwest Zealand, Lundbye's family had moved to the Citadel in Copenhagen where his father, a colonel in the army, was stationed, and where Købke's family was also located. In 1836, Lundbye's parents moved to Frederiksværk, north of Copenhagen, when his father was made commander of the Rocket Corps. Visiting his parents there, Lundbye created numerous views of this area between the Roskilde Fjord and Arresø Lake, many of them riveting in their immediacy. *Landscape Near Lake Arresø, Frederiksværk* (1838; fig. 75) is an informal view of the area painted on cardboard, likely in the open air, a practice that had been encouraged by Eckersberg and Lund to a generation of Royal Academy students. Lundbye stationed himself before a small hillock to take advantage of the undulating landscape, opening at left in a serpentine pattern to reveal layers of water and turf, a classic picturesque landscape strategy. His *View of a Pond* (fig. 76), dated 26 June 1838, is astonishing in its freshness and the intimacy of its angle of view. Reminiscent of Eckersberg and Hansen's paintings from Rome, the scene has been summarized into a few telling details and rendered from a high-angled viewpoint, perhaps even deriving from perspective studies as practiced by Eckersberg's students.[45] The brightness of his palette and fluidity of his paint, combined with

81.
Vilhelm Kyhn
The Parsonage at Greve, 1877
Oil on canvas, 37 x 29½ in. (94 x 75 cm)
Collection of Ambassador John L. Loeb Jr.,
New York

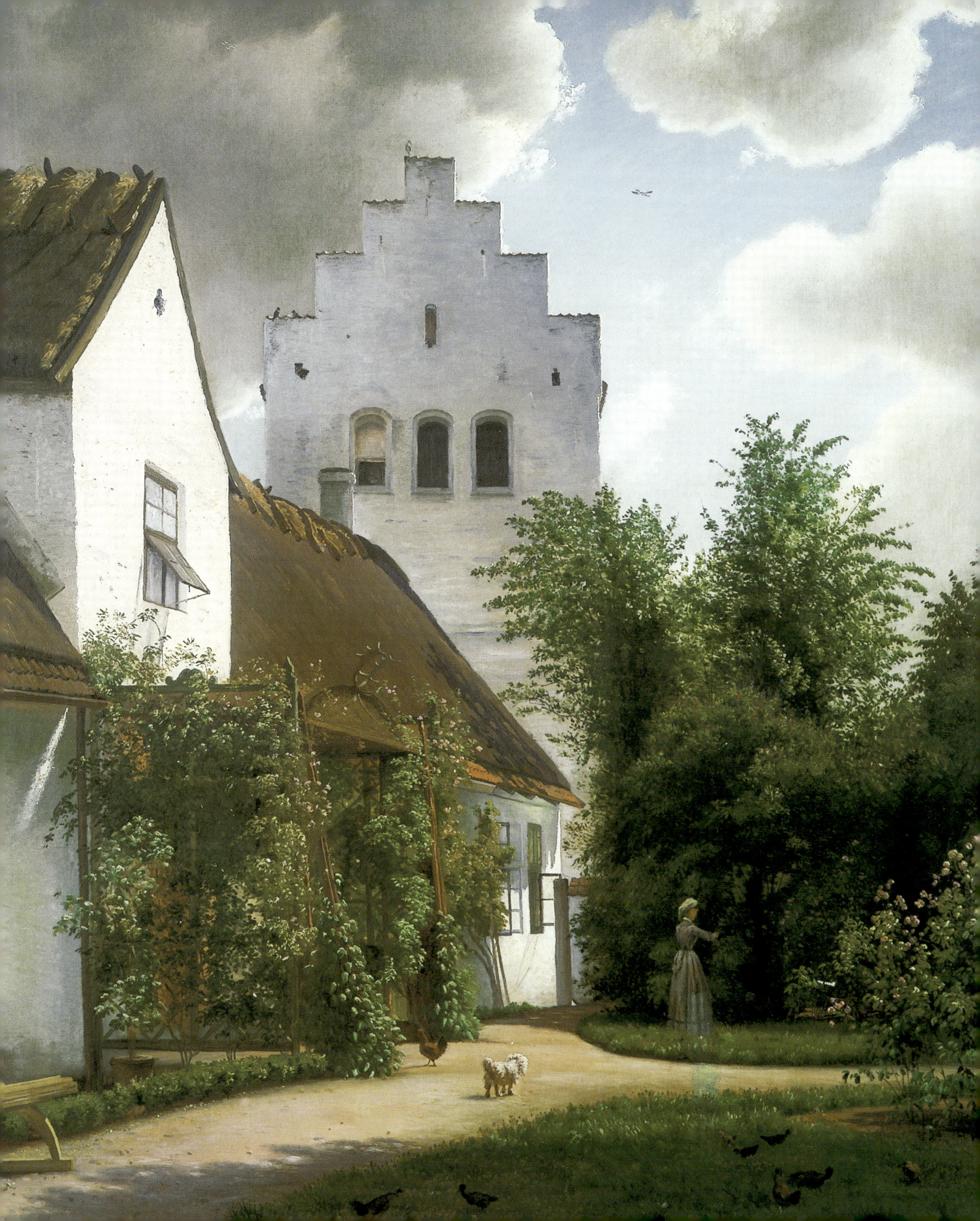

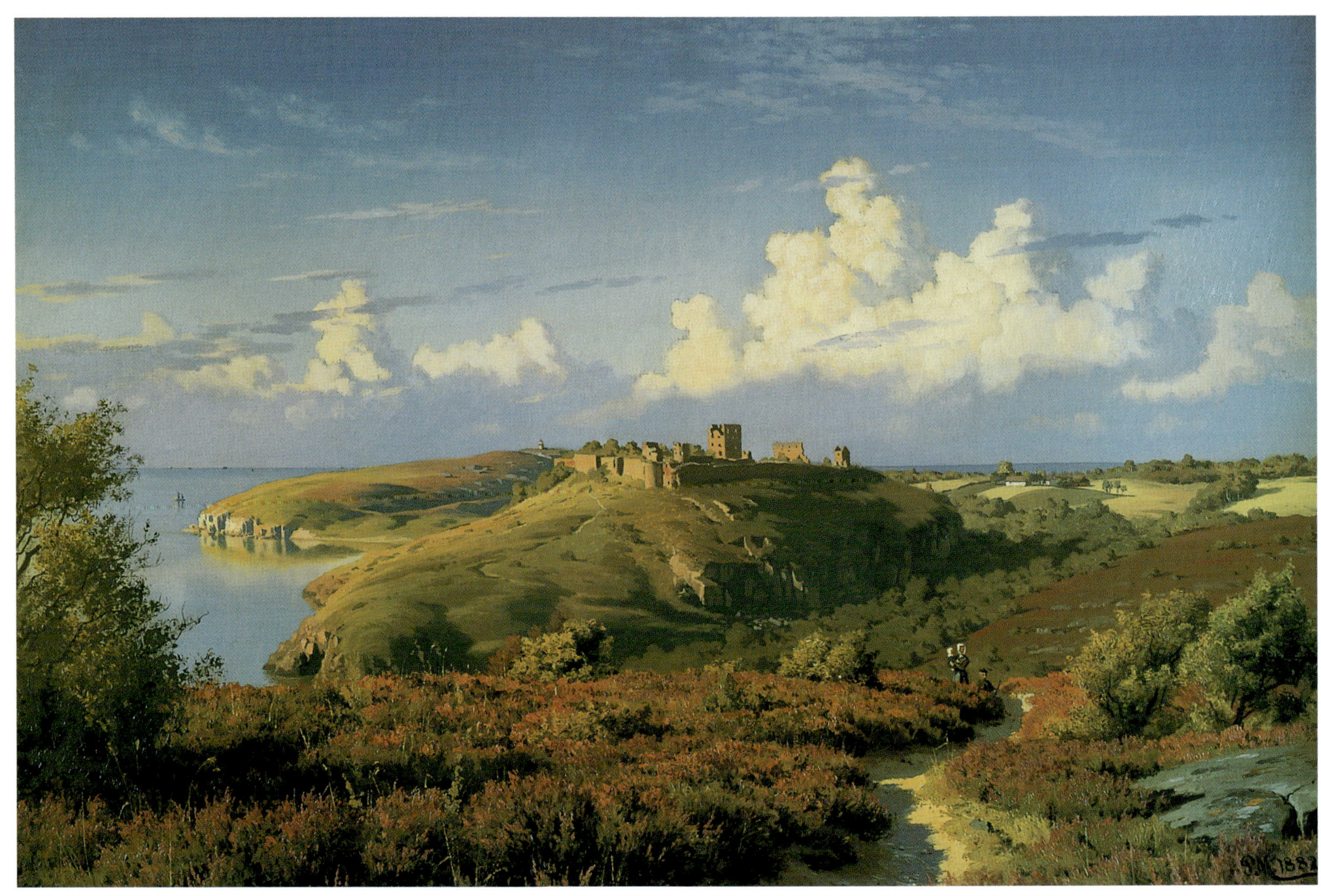

82.
Peder Mønsted
*Summer's Day Opposite Hammeren,
Bornholm*, 1882
Oil on canvas, 24⅜ x 37⅜ in.
(62 x 95 cm)
Collection of Ambassador John L. Loeb Jr.,
New York

the fragmentary, cropped view of the rural scene, suggest an experimental use of paint more
familiar from the late nineteenth century than from the 1830s.

Such informal sketches offered the building blocks for larger, more ambitious views of the
area, such as *Landscape at Arresø (Lake Arre)* from the same year (fig. 77). This composition
transforms Denmark's flat landscape as a vast monumental fantasy. Storm clouds bathe the left
side of the composition in a dusky light, which warms toward the right into the golden glow of
a placid sunny day. Lundbye layered his landscape from front to back by sandwiching layers of
bright, reflective water between green fingers of land, offering not one but two horizon lines in
the background. These minute distant shores offer a summary of Danish history, including the
towers of Frederiksborg Palace, prehistoric burial mounds, and rural architecture—the persistence of the past into the present. A fisherman gathering nets and figures raking the fields in the
foreground suggest the harmony between marine and agricultural labor, and the stork, seated in
her treetop nest, offers the reassurance of rebirth and renewal within this idealized landscape.

Lundbye offered the allied notion of a continuity in his views of ancient monuments. In
Dolmen at Raklev (1839; fig. 78) Lundbye examines a prehistoric burial mound at close range.
Such traces of primal Denmark were increasingly hailed as national symbols. The Royal Commission for the Preservation of Ancient Monuments (*Kommissionen for Oldsagers Opbevaring*) had
been founded in 1807 to preserve rune stones and other portable finds. These were assembled in

Copenhagen and, in 1819, the Oldsagssamlingen and other state collections were opened to the public by Christian Jürgensen Thomsen, newly appointed as the first director. This commission was also committed to the preservation of burial mounds and other finds in situ as land use patterns changed with the breakup of old manor farms and village collectives toward mid-century. As the Danish countryside became more intensively developed and farmed, burial mounds were destroyed by plowing. In 1843, the archaeologist J. J. A. Worsaae (1821–1885) published an influential book entitled *Ancient Denmark* (*Danmarks Oldtid*) that regarded such fragile finds as telluric traces of Danish traditions, markers of national affiliation. With its vast sky and close-up focus on local flora, and its view upward toward the looming structure and downward into the distant verdant farmland, Lundbye's painting offers the visualization of cultural continuity. Here, the romantic taste for the ruins of Rome and Paestum are focused on the Danish landscape, familiar and unremarkable yet yielding constant anchors in the ancient past. In theme, Lundbye's painting reprises the views of prehistoric burial sites by Caspar David Friedrich, including his *Burial mound on Rügen* (ca. 1837–38; fig. 79), which entered the collection of Danish crown prince Christian Frederik (later Christian VIII) in 1838–39. Such views engage notions advanced in Ørstad's, Worsaae's, and Schouw's invocations of biological and psychic belonging.

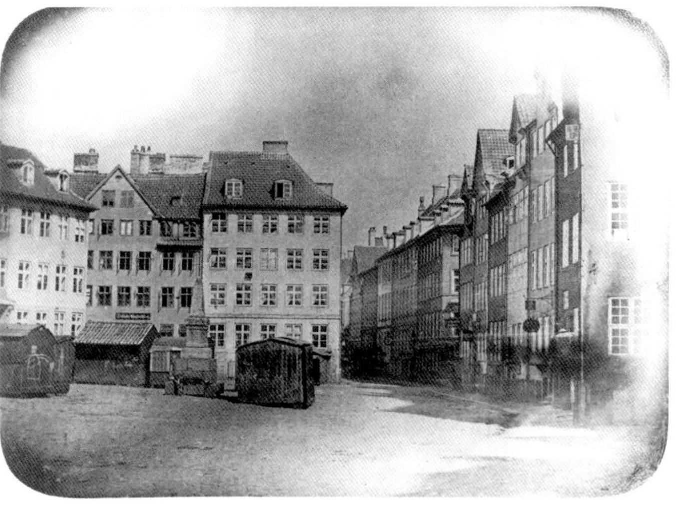

83.
Peter Faber
Ulfeldts Plads with the Monument of Infamy, 1840
Daguerreotype, 5⅝ x 7⅝ in.
(14.5 x 19.37 cm)
(Rephotographed by Frederik Riise, 1900)
Copenhagen City Museum

Lundbye's most ambitious painting was *A Danish Coast* (1843; fig. 80), which invests the gentle Danish topography with a sense of the sublime, the "mighty sea and steep yellow cliffs" of which he wrote. He struggled with the execution of the painting, over six feet in height and eight feet in width. Having made numerous direct outdoor sketches, he was faced with the task of retaining the spontaneity of the sketches while also registering the exact landscape elements.[46] In a diary entry from 2 June 1838, he noted the beautiful weather and quality of light and air: "[I hope] to remember something of what I have seen today, when I paint the atmosphere.... Oh, I have so much in my head, I only hope that I can make good on canvas."[47] This is a programmatic painting, created on a grand scale and with a strong consciousness about Denmark's international reputation. Indebted in structural drama to the works of Dahl and Friedrich, it may even be seen as a painting created using Denmark's own native topography to rival mountain landscapes painted by Friedrich.

By mid-century, Lundbye's model of a Danish painter traveling throughout Denmark to poeticize its national culture was emulated and practiced widely.[48] One of the most well traveled painters in Denmark was Vilhelm Kyhn (1819–1903), a former student of Eckerberg's, who pursued a nearly encyclopedic representation of all regions in Denmark. As in his painting *The Parsonage at Greve* (1877; fig. 81), his works record seemingly unremarkable settings, articulating the local architecture and topographic elements of rural landscapes. His observation of the bowed roofline of the thatch-roofed house to the left, the roof support beams extending beyond the thatching, and the weather-worn stucco just below the roofline reflect a general ethnographic interest in Danish indigenous forms that began to shape the politics of the period.[49] The loving attention that Kyhn and Lundbye paid to their native topography, almost always basking in sunlight and swelling with plant growth, generated a nostalgic form of landscape painting that lasted into the early twentieth century, as in, for example, Peder Mønsted's *Summer's Day Opposite Hammeren, Bornholm*, (1882; fig. 82). It also helped to inspire a more socially tendentious form of rural representation with the emergence of such artists as L. A. Ring in the next decades (see chapter 6).

The picturing of Danish landscape expanded in this period with the advent of photography. Louis-Jacques-Mandé Daguerre's (1787–1851) method for creating daguerreotypes, first announced in France in January 1839, had been published in a Danish journal later that year.[50] Christian Frederik, who that same year ascended the throne as Christian VIII, commissioned Christian Falbe, Denmark's war commissary-general, to purchase daguerreotype equipment in Paris. There Falbe took two views of the city that were shown in Copenhagen at the Society for the Expression of Physics in October and then at the Royal Academy of Fine Arts, the Royal Danish Academy of Science and Letters, the Industrial Association, and at the Fine Arts Society.[51] One of the first photographs made in Denmark was Peter Faber and Jørgen Albert Bech's daguerreotype *Ulfeldts Plads with the Monument of Infamy* (1840; fig. 83). Taken on a Sunday morning in June 1840, the image required an exposure time of fifteen minutes. Toward the left of Ulfeldts Plads (now Gråbrødretorv) is the monument (the so-called Monument of Infamy) to Corfitz Ulfeldt (1604–64), who had tried to undermine the absolute monarchy and was sentenced to death in absentia. At the base of the monument, Faber's partner has lain down as if asleep, offering a rare view of an exterior street scene and a static city inhabitant.

Portrait and view photographs soon became popular middle-class collectibles, and portrait photography flowered in Denmark, as elsewhere in Europe.[52] Bertel Thorvaldsen was the first person in Denmark to sit for a portrait photograph. In a daguerreotype from 1840, the artist assumes a posture reminiscent of Eckersberg's portrait of him (chapter 3) and his own proposed monument to Goethe, asserting the convergence of the man, his art, and his myth.[53]

By the later part of the century, there were between 80 and 120 independent photographers working in Copenhagen.[54] Photography was also enlisted to record national treasures. The Danish Photographic Society (Selskabet for Dansk Fotografi), founded in 1879, put forward proposals to record old Copenhagen, in the manner of the French *Monuments historiques*, and to create an archive of Danish historical materials.[55] An article entitled "Fotografiens Betydning for Historien" (Photography's Importance for History) in the society's journal offered "One is exposed to a snapshot of the nation in its present form—from the lowest form of life to the flower of society."[56] Commercially produced photographs dispersed images resonating with Lundbye's chosen motifs to a broad public.

Regardless of the subject or location of Golden Age landscape painting rendered by Købke or Lundbye, local topography, architecture, and flora are articulated as though they have been cleansed and structured in the crystalline light of a perfect day. This act of making everyday scenery extraordinary, even revelatory, was the achievement of the Golden Age topographic painters. In the 1830s, Christen Købke helped to embed this mode of painting into Danish critical consciousness through such works as *Frederiksborg Castle in the Evening Light*. The power of his work was often, in fact, derived from the common settings that he ennobled. For a time in the 1830s, these derived from his family's home at Blegdamen (the bleaching grounds), near the man-made lake, Sortedam, then on the outskirts of Copenhagen. Købke made numerous views of the lake, several of which include the distant towers of the city.[57]

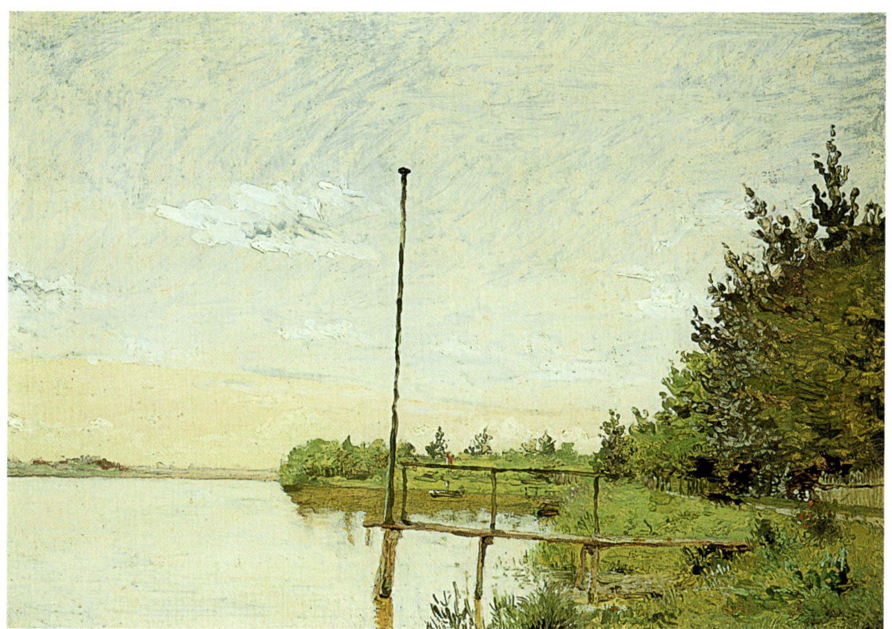

84.
Christen Købke
*View from Dosseringen at Lake Sortedam
toward Nørrebro. Study*, ca. 1838
Oil on canvas, 8½ x 11⅞ in.
(21.5 x 30 cm)
Statens Museum for Kunst,
Copenhagen

An oil sketch on paper, *View from Dosseringen at Lake Sortedam towards Nørrebro* (ca. 1838; fig. 84), offers an entirely unremarkable view of the lake, a dock and flagpole, a tiny boat seen through the railings, foliage on the right, and the distant shore at left. Brushy and calligraphic in its details, the painting is a sketch made en plein air, an unofficial study rendered to capture light and atmospheric effects. In *View from Dosseringen at Lake Sortedam towards Nørrebro* (1838; fig. 85), a painting intended for exhibition,[58] the motif has been reformulated in a crisp, linear view in which the boat has become a narrative element, its distance from two women standing on the jetty creating a sense of separation and anticipation. The foliage has been disciplined and the overall coloration transformed to communicate a twilight mood. The flag that has been added to the composition offers it as a paean to the nation, anchoring the composition in Høyen's entreaties to represent the local.[59] As Gunnarsson notes, the spontaneity of the sketches for this painting were replaced by classically well-defined forms, and the sense of transitoriness with that of timelessness.[60] Similarly, Købke invested his painting *Frederiksborg Castle in the Evening Light* with a lapidary sense of temporal arrest.

When Købke painted *Frederiksborg Castle in the Evening Light*, he included in it pleasure boats on the surface of the lake. According to the artist, these broke up the palace's reflection and interrupted a direct view into the background, offering instead "a slow winding view" to the castle.[61] In addition to this formal function, the boats operate on an ideological level. With their large and small parties of tourists, they domesticate the scene, presenting the castle as both an organic part of Danish landscape and as the scenic backdrop to a leisurely summer night, a painting of everyday life. In this regard, the castle, transformed from a royal edifice to a pleasurable national monument, narrated the ascendency of the middle class into all areas of the Danish government and economy in Denmark's Golden Age.

Such a move toward domestication and the incorporation of architectural painting into the canon of Danish identity formation is also reflected in portraiture of these years. Indeed, the notion of the land as Denmark's "home" was reinforced by intimate and often innovative paintings of Danish homes themselves.

Ideals of domesticity were most directly communicated through portraiture. As noted earlier (chapter 2), portraiture became a mainstay of artists
working in the early nineteenth century as members of the rising middle
class increasingly desired images of themselves. The themes and styles
of Copenhagen-based portraiture derived initially from the prolific and
influential Jens Juel (see chapter 1) and from the works of C. W. Eckersberg. In July 1817, Eckersberg had painted *Portrait of Julie Eckersberg, The
Artist's Second Wife* (fig. 86), after the artist's return from Rome and five
months after their marriage. Seated near a window, Julie Juel Eckersberg,
Jens Juel's daughter, is bathed in cool daylight, making her blushing cheeks,
steady gray eyes, and pearl earrings nearly iridescent. The swirl of her dress,
echoing the small rolls of flesh at the base of her neck, animate the static
composition. They also frame Julie's subtly swollen belly, an indication of
her pregnancy.[62] Homely details, such as her ruddy cheeks, her dimpled
hands, and swollen ring finger, suggest an unedited observation of the sitter. At the same time, isolated within a corner, the lines of her body echoing and eliding the molding on the walls behind her, Julie is situated in a
precisely wrought geometric composition.[63] Eckersberg's leading students,
who had followed his landscape practices in Rome, likewise extended his
portraiture typology. The hallmarks of Eckersberg's portraits, public and
private, established a type that dominated Danish painting through the
later nineteenth century—the seeming realism of details coupled with a
rigorous clarity of composition, embedded in everyday ritual. Eckersberg
also sought and received numerous portrait commissions, including those
for the Nathanson family pictures (figs. 35, 36) which, when exhibited,
helped to shape the domestic period style.

Within Golden Age portraiture, like landscape painting, small domestic settings and habits, the private habitats of the everyday, attain great stature. Wilhelm Marstrand's portrait *The Waagepetersen Family* (1836; fig.
87) crystallizes the aspirations for much portraiture at this time. Christian
Waagepetersen (1787–1840), a successful wine merchant and patron of
the arts, had commissioned a portrait of himself, his wife, and their first
two children from Wilhelm Bendz in 1830. Marstrand represents the
family six years later, with Waagepetersen absent, but his wife securing the
household. Albertine Emerentze Schmidt Waagepetersen, the daughter of
wealthy business people (copies of their portraits by Eckersberg hang on the
back wall), sits with four of her children at a table as a nurse presents the

85.
Christen Købke
*View from Dosseringen at Lake Sortedam
toward Nørrebro*, 1838
Oil on canvas, 20⅞ x 28⅛ in.
(53 x 71.5 cm)
Statens Museum for Kunst, Copenhagen

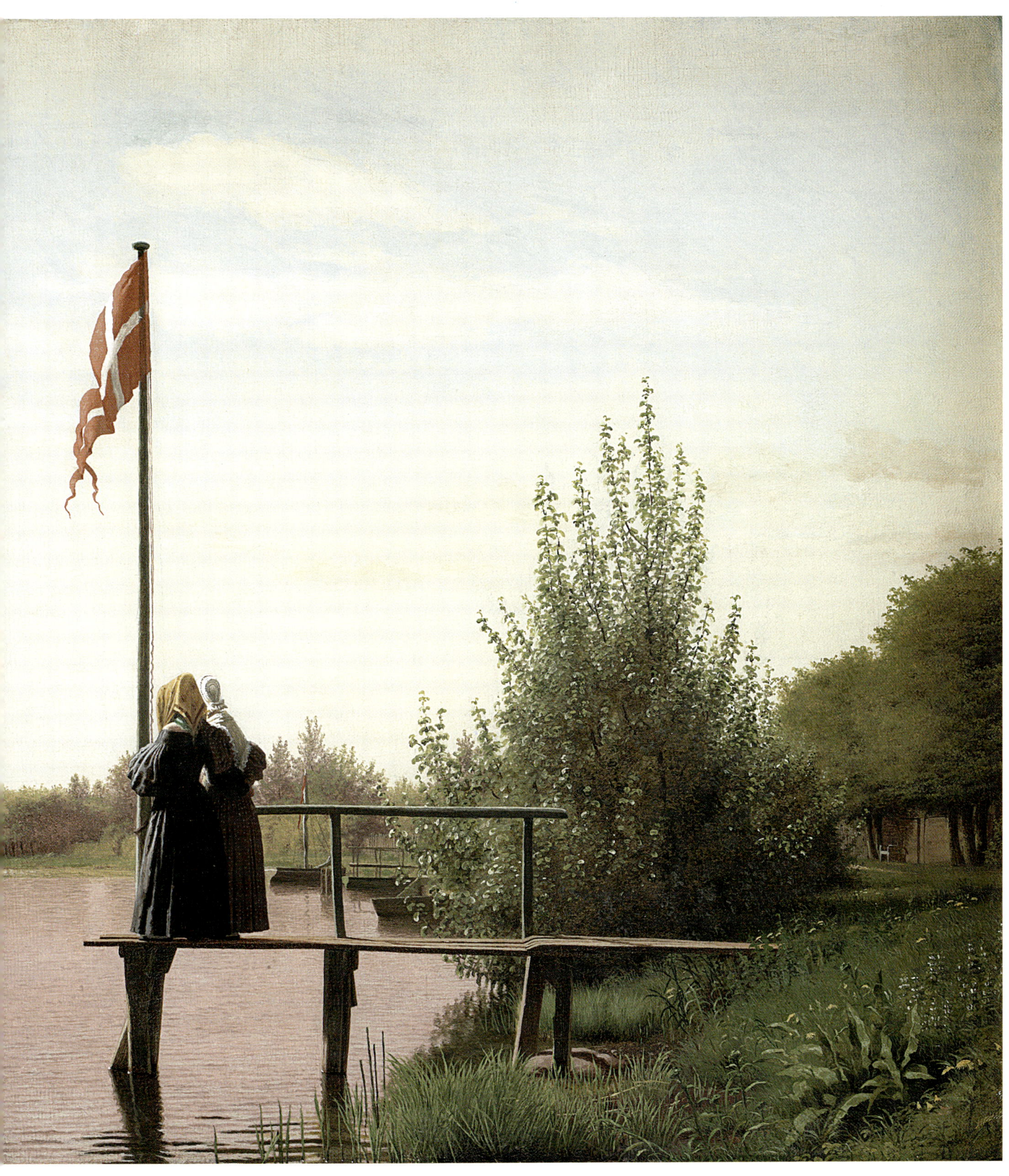

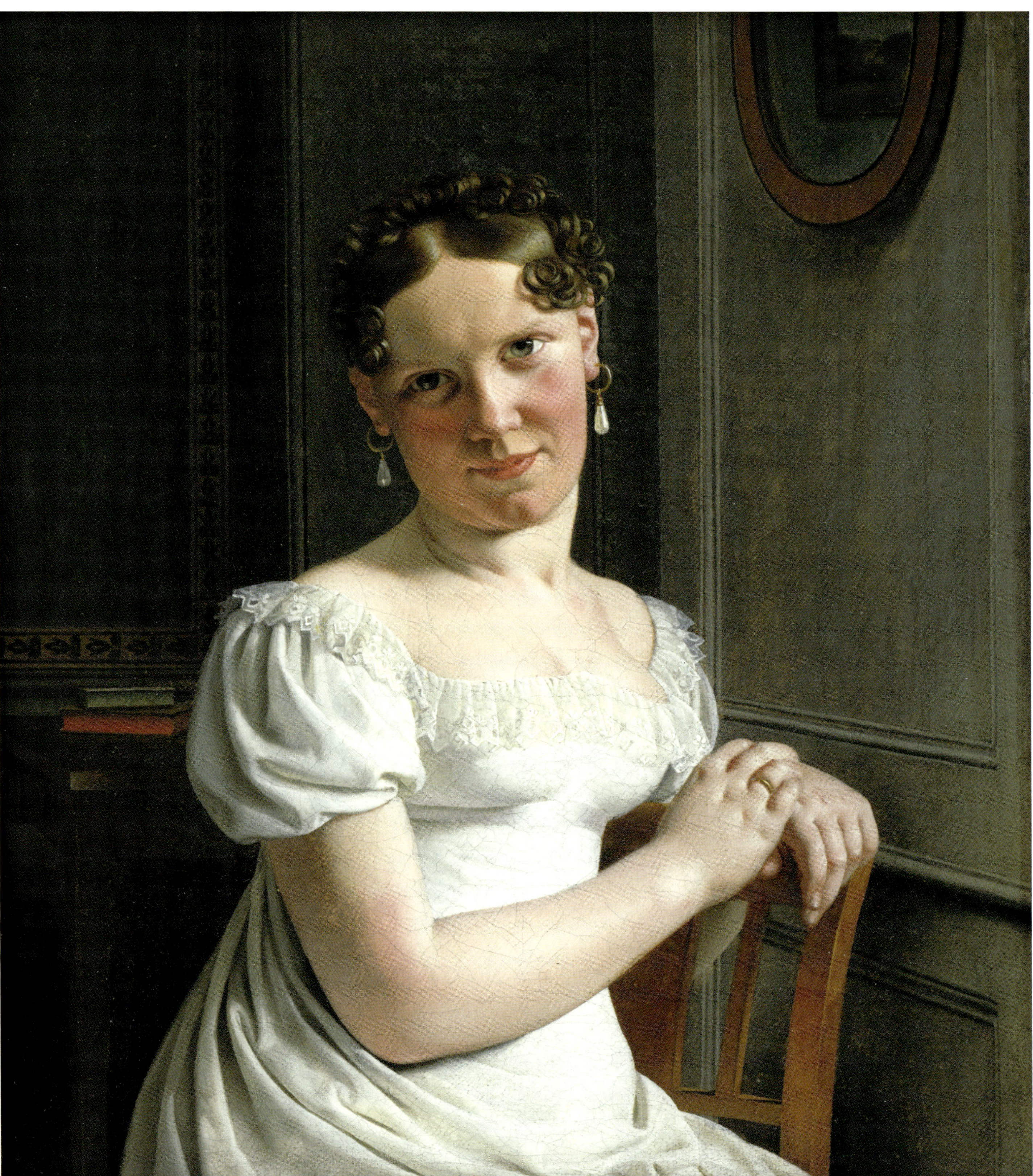

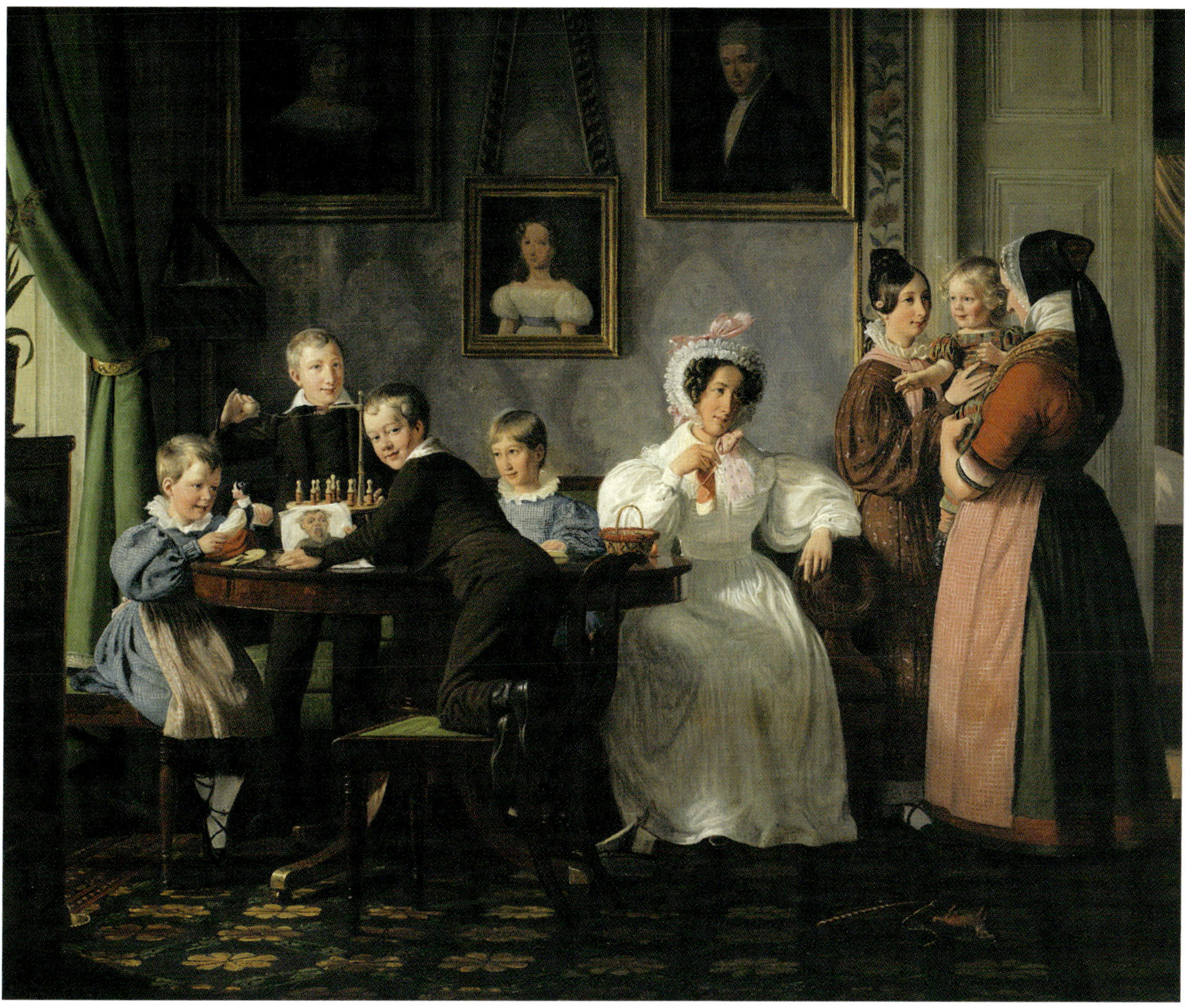

baby of the family to the eldest daughter. Mrs. Waagepetersen is engaged in knitting, an activity performed by bourgeois women throughout Golden Age portraiture. Christian Waagepetersen's very absence, as Kasper Monrad notes, also signifies his industriousness as the public and economic anchor of the family.[64]

The painting renders the grand family home, the setting for elegant musical events (as depicted by Marstrand in *Et Musicalsk Aftenselskab*, 1834, Frederiksborg Castle), as well as the intimate and ordinary events of daily life. The height of the door to the right and a glimmer of gilded moldings suggest the scale and luxury of the family's sitting room, but those details are subordinated to the room's simple mahogany furniture and the glimpse, through the door at right, of the bedchamber. When exhibited at the Fine Arts Society in 1837, the painting was described as symbol of stability: "... one is immediately delighted by the humor and brilliance with which the artist has given us a true picture of cheerful, informal life in a happy family circle. Look at these four happy children, who in the most natural manner are grouped around the table!"[65] Like Eckersberg's portrait of the Nathanson family, this painting offers a performance of domesticity.

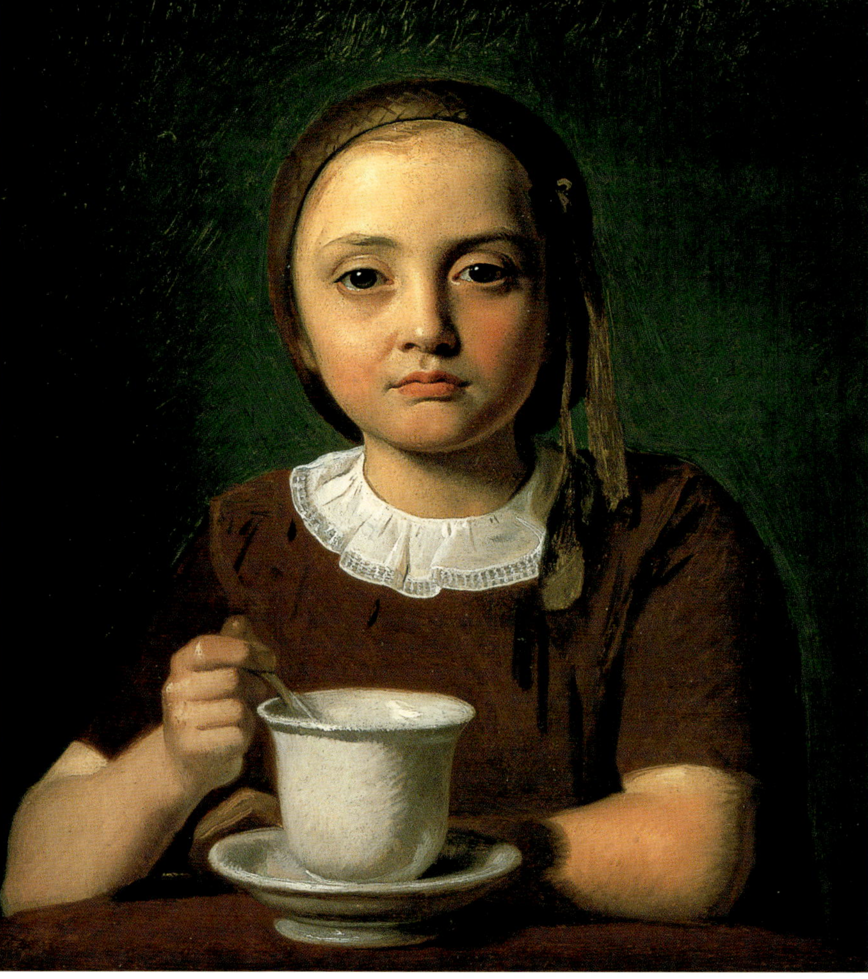

In this period, middle-class cultural life was invested in the home. New apartment buildings, designed for the middle class, began to replace the structures that had been destroyed in the fires at the turn of the century, their interiors light and well ordered.[66] The comfort and orderliness of the interior world became a paradigm and a dream for this immensely disordered period, in which the ideals of domestic comfort were expressed as a kernel of the nation itself. A cult of domesticity, which in Germany and Austria came to be designated Biedermeier, inflected both the way in which architecture and the functional arts were designed for the urban bourgeoisie, but also how this class pictured itself. Eckersberg and Marstrand's paintings embody these values.

Just as artists explored the theme of gemeinschaft within their circles in Copenhagen and Rome (chapters 2 and 3), painting portraits of one another, they also portrayed the rituals of their own home lives in support of this notion. In some painters' work, the smallest details become vehicles for studies of intimacy. A young child stirring a cup in Constantin Hansen's *Portrait of a Little Girl, Elise Købke, with a Cup in Front of Her* (1850; fig. 88) assumes a hieratic expression. Elise, the sister of Hansen's wife, is pictured against a dark background, her face and upper body and particularly the porcelain cup and saucer in front of her are given startling plasticity by the warm light that illuminates them. The direct gaze of the child, intensified by

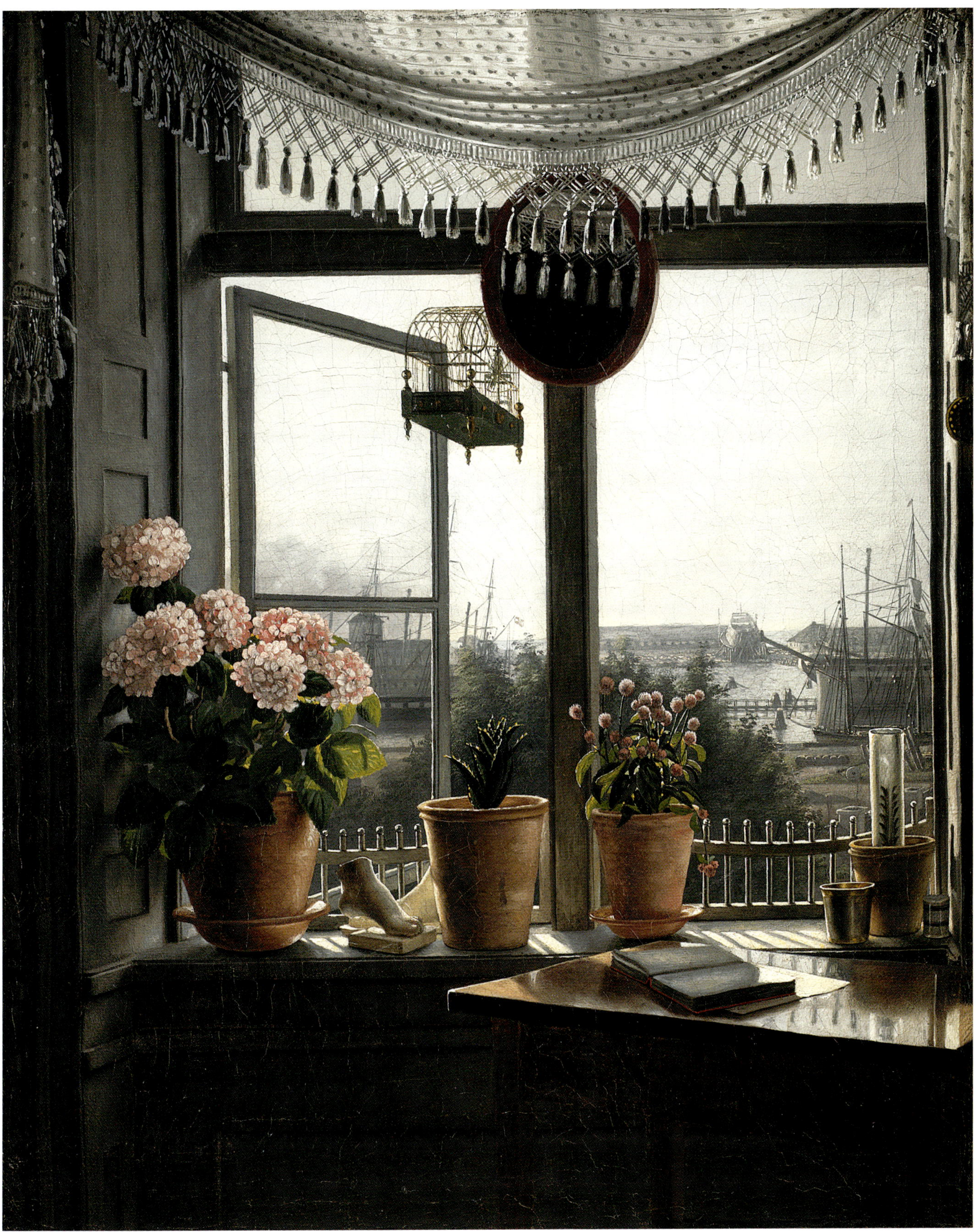

the almost imperceptible difference in the shapes of her eyes, gives a sense of near uncanny gravitas to the simple act of drinking chocolate.

In such images, the family home is a space of both common activity and, like the landscape of the period, of uncommon sublimity and sublimation. A decade before Martinus Rørbye painted his melancholic *View of the Roman Campagna with the Tiber and Monte Soracte in the Background* (fig. 61), he used the very terms of interior comfort to create a view of longing. His *View from the Artist's Window* (ca. 1825; fig. 89), created when he was 22, locates the viewer at a window in his parents' home on Amaliegade, overlooking Copenhagen's harbor. Anne-Birgitte Fonsmark has suggested that this is an allegorical painting, narrating the young man's desire to break free from the coddled interior. In this view, the plaster cast of a child's foot, juxtaposed against that of an adult on the windowsill, suggest a parallel development to the artist's own. This shelf offers further elaboration: plants at successive stages of growth, from the seedling pot and the protected cutting in a glass tube at right through the flowering hydrangea to the left, articulate both growth and captivity. The caged canary, suspended just outside of the window and basking in sunlight, reinforces the romantic symbol of the open window as a site of both invitation and physical barrier.[67]

By mid-century, the bourgeois parlor was a mainstay in family portraiture and genre painting. Carl Bloch (1824–1890), a student of Marstrand's, and one of the few committed history painters of his generation, had painted *The Artist's Parents, Mr. and Mrs. J. P. Bloch in Their Sitting Room* in 1855 (fig. 90). Bloch represents his parents in a fashion reflecting the continuity of values from the early nineteenth century in his mother's knitting. Here, however, his father is shown at leisure. The décor of their home is represented as slightly grandiose yet still embodying the Biedermeier aesthetic—a printed linoleum floor covered by a rug, mahogany furniture, and a saturated interior color palette. His father, a clothing merchant, and his mother, are also shown here to be arbiters of taste, displaying in their sitting room a small-scale reproduction of Thorvaldsen's figure of Jesus from Our Lady's Church in Copenhagen (1821), a fjord landscape, and family portraits.[68]

Such interiors picture the artistic tastes of Denmark's middle classes. In the early nineteenth century, one of the means of forging a sense of a renewed Danish identity had been by reaching back to symbols of past eras of power and prestige, initially to Greece and Rome via the French academic model, and then to Baroque Holland. The admiration of Danish Golden Age artists for Dutch and Flemish art (such as landscapes by Ruisdael) had, in turn, mirrored and encouraged their growing interest in local landscape and genre painting. One branch of painting that had flourished in the Golden Age was flower painting, a genre popular among the Danish bourgeoisie, and of which J. L. Jensen (1800–1856) was the master. In his *Still Life of Fruits with Pineapple* (fig. 91), he applied a formal geometric structure and jewel-like touch of the Golden Age to an array of riches, a fantasy arrangement of precious, exotic fruits. Like his student Sophie Henck (1822–1893), Jensen drew inspiration from the rich holdings of Dutch and Flemish art found in the Royal Collection and the collection of Count Adam Gottlob Moltke, both of which had been established in the eighteenth century and were available for artists to study. Henck (fig. 92) was particularly attentive to the floral paintings in these collections, copying, among others, *Vase with Flowers* (fig. 93) by the Dutch master still-life painter Jan van Huysum (1682–1749). Works such as these provided artists from the Danish Golden Age through the Symbolist period at the end of the nineteenth century with the opportunity for contact with a body of work that could be understood to be simultaneously international and domestic. Such works were avidly

90.
Carl Bloch
The Artist's Parents,
Mr. and Mrs. J. P. Bloch
in Their Sitting Room, 1855
Oil on canvas, 21⅞ x 18⅞ in.
(55 x 48 cm)
Collection of Ambassador John L. Loeb Jr.,
New York

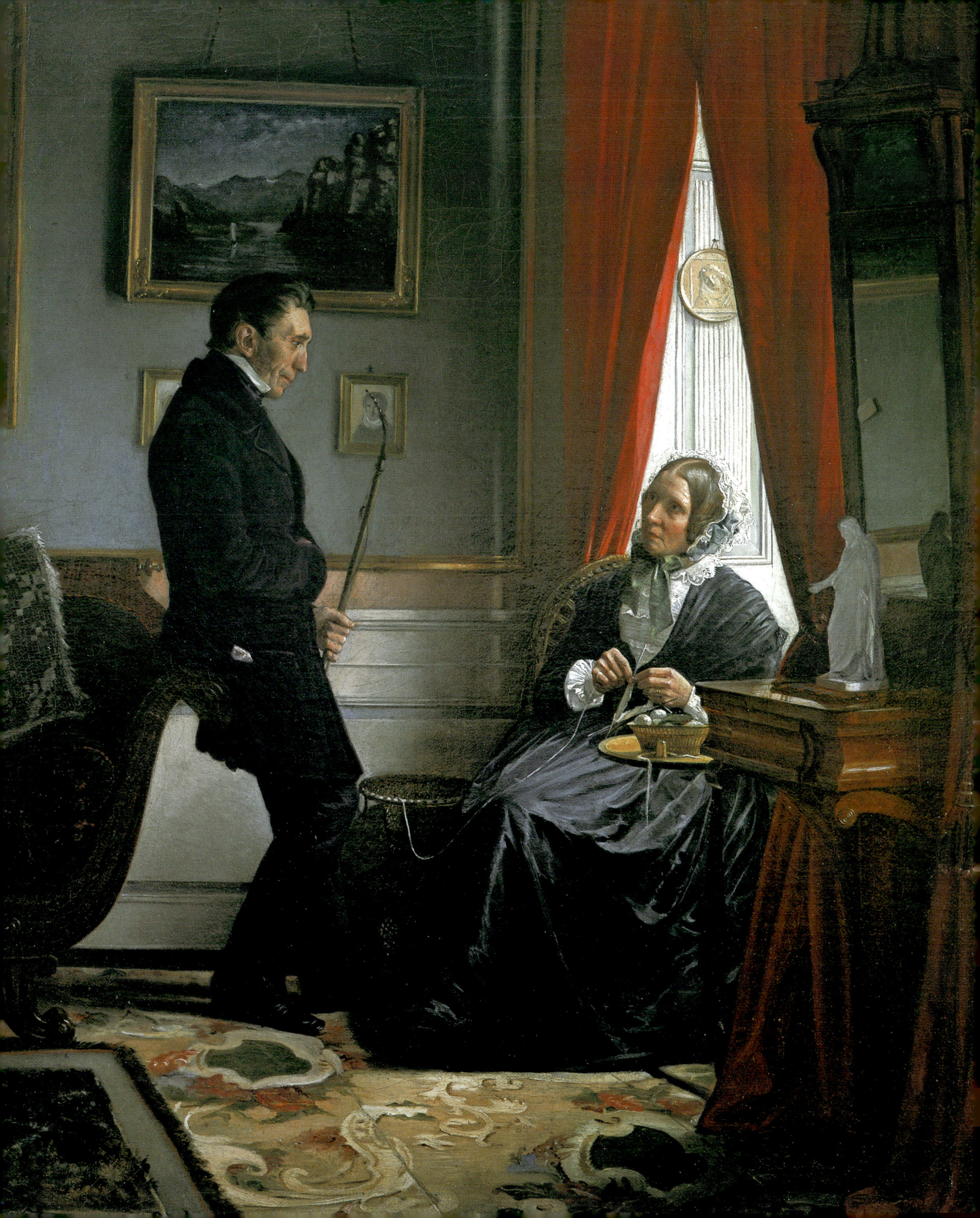

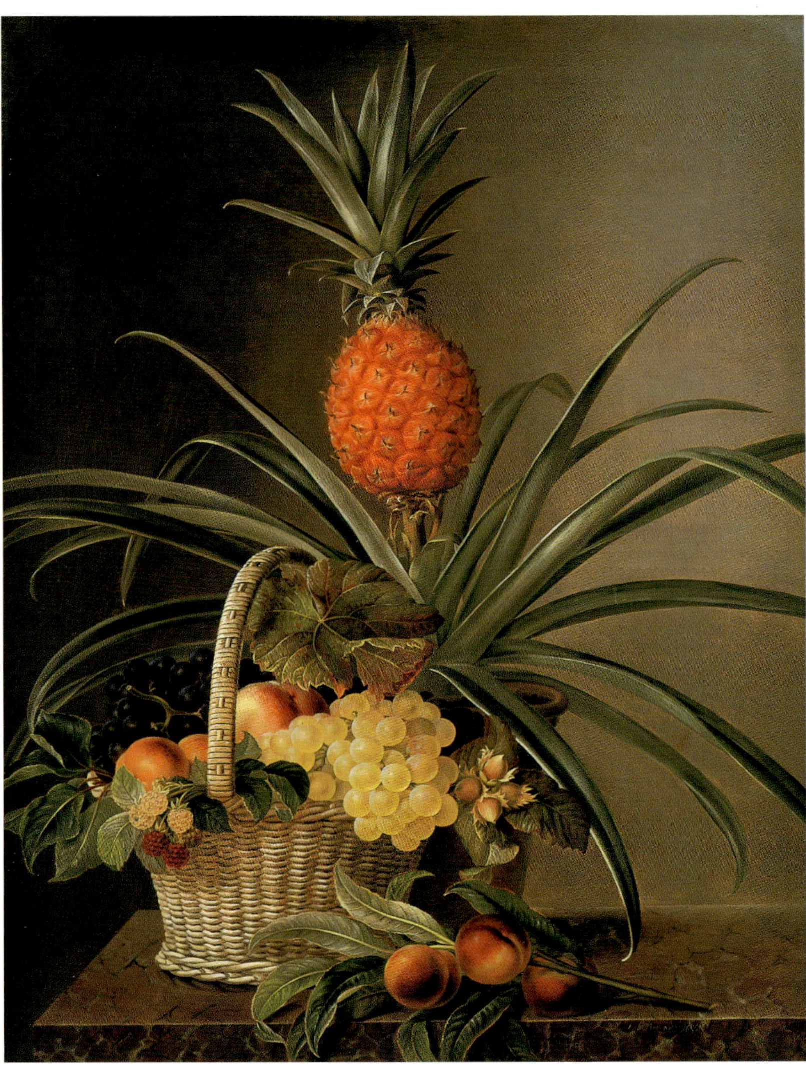

91.
J. L. Jensen
Still Life of Fruits with Pineapple, 1833
Oil on canvas, 27½ x 21⅝ in.
(70 x 55 cm)
Collection of Ambassador John L. Loeb Jr.,
New York

collected by the public.[69] Flower painting was also among the only avenues open to talented and ambitious women painters at mid-century.

The domestic ideal was also widely deployed as a way of picturing rural Denmark in the later nineteenth century. Through paintings such as Christen Dalsgaard's *Young Girl Writing* (1871; fig. 94), a version of which was exhibited at the 1878 World's Exhibition in Paris, Høyen's exhortations to represent the rural and local bore fruit. Born into an elite family from Northern Jutland, Dalsgaard (1824–1907) grew up in a manor house embellished with Rococo decorations. He sought training at the Royal Academy, and became inspired by Høyen. Returning to his home region each summer, he sketched and painted local rural people at work and in their home environments. He even collected local regional dress to preserve material culture and to bring authenticity to his paintings. Fusing the rigorous visual training of Eckersberg with the national romantic dictum to build culture through the celebration of the vernacular, Dalsgaard embodied the ethos of the era. Diligent, literate, tidy, ethnographically specific, and coupled with a rural landscape permeated with sunlight, the girl represents the *folkelig*—the transcendent, collective, stable essence of the people.

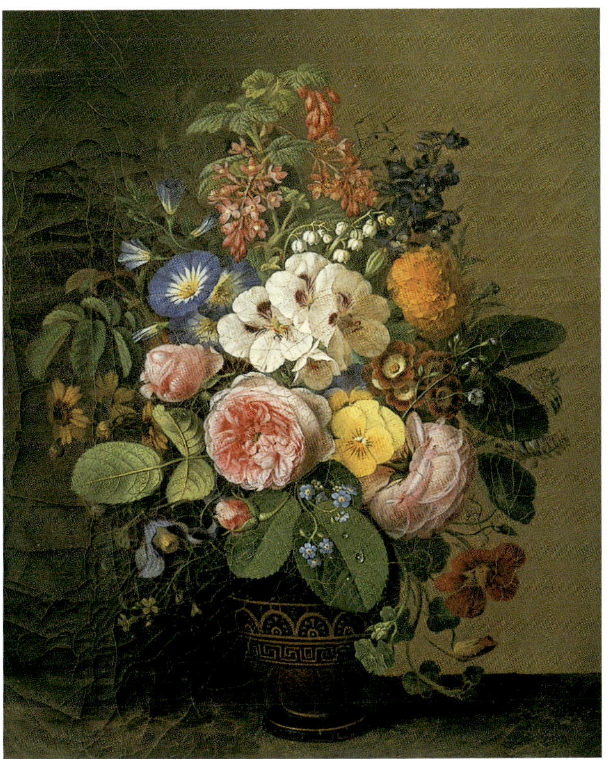

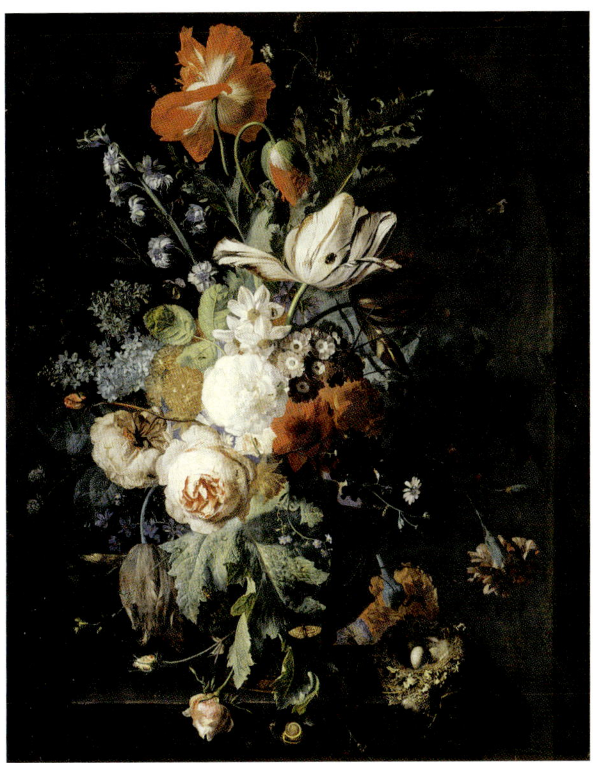

The reassurances of the interior world extended into the twentieth century in the work of some artists. Julius Exner (1825–1910) offered an almost elegiac view of his domestic world, mapped onto the Royal Academy itself, in his 1910 *Self-Portrait, the Artist's Last Work* (fig. 95) painted in the year of his death. Having trained under Lund and Eckersberg between 1839 and 1845, Exner became a protégé of Høyen's, painting both national history paintings and adulatory views of rural people and material culture. Several of these images flank Exner's self-portrait. Revising an earlier self-portrait (1906, location unknown), Exner locates himself in the corner of his studio in the Charlottenborg Palace (he was appointed professor at the academy in 1876), bracketed by the small survey of his life's work and by a refulgent fig tree, illuminated by the studio's large skylight.[70] The elegance and dignity of artist and studio, and the display of the tools of the artist's trade (the studio easel, the collapsible traveling easel at which he works, his smock in the foreground, palette, brushes, bottles of oil, and painting stretchers) offer a retrospective view of a life's work and a way of life at the academy that by 1910 had already been eclipsed by the emergence of a young modernist generation. In the work of Vilhelm Hammershøi (see chapter 7), the Golden Age world of domesticity and the construct of *habitus* came under a very different scrutiny.

Denmark's Golden Age was understood by its historians to come to a conclusion in the late 1840s with the wars over Schleswig and Holstein, and with the establishment of Denmark's parliamentary democracy in 1849. Lundbye, Købke, and Rørbye all died in 1848. Six years later, Eckersberg passed away just as the Royal Academy observed its centennial. Their careers coincided with the effort among intellectuals and politicians to forge a durable Danish identity,

92.
Sophie Henck
Bouquet of Flowers in Greek Vase, n.d.
Oil on canvas, 16¼ x 12⅝ in.
(41 x 32 cm)
Collection of Ambassador John L. Loeb Jr.,
New York

93.
Jan van Huysum
Vase with Flowers, n.d.
Oil on panel, 31⅛ x 23⅞ in.
(79 x 60.5 cm)
Statens Museum for Kunst, Copenhagen

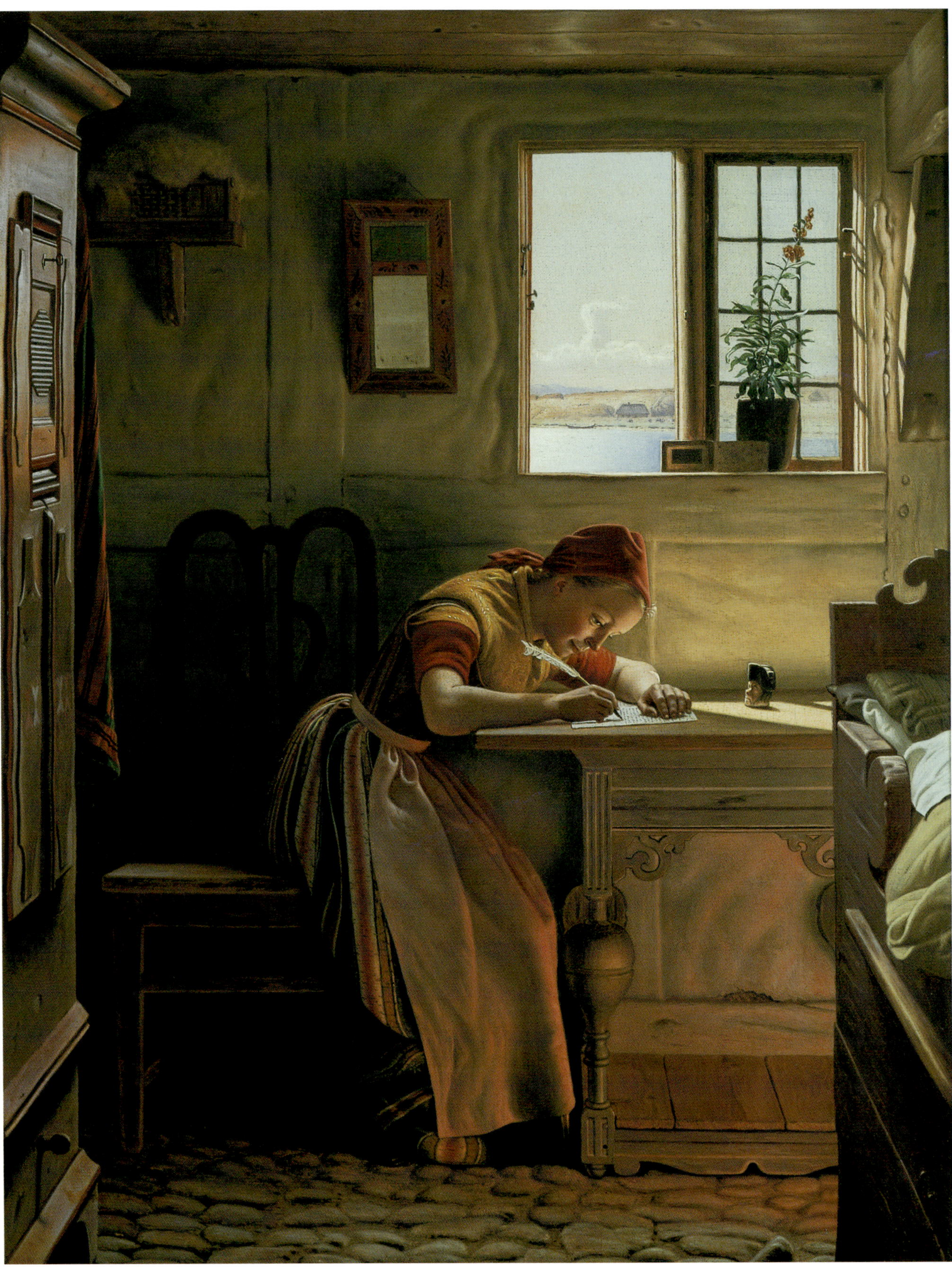

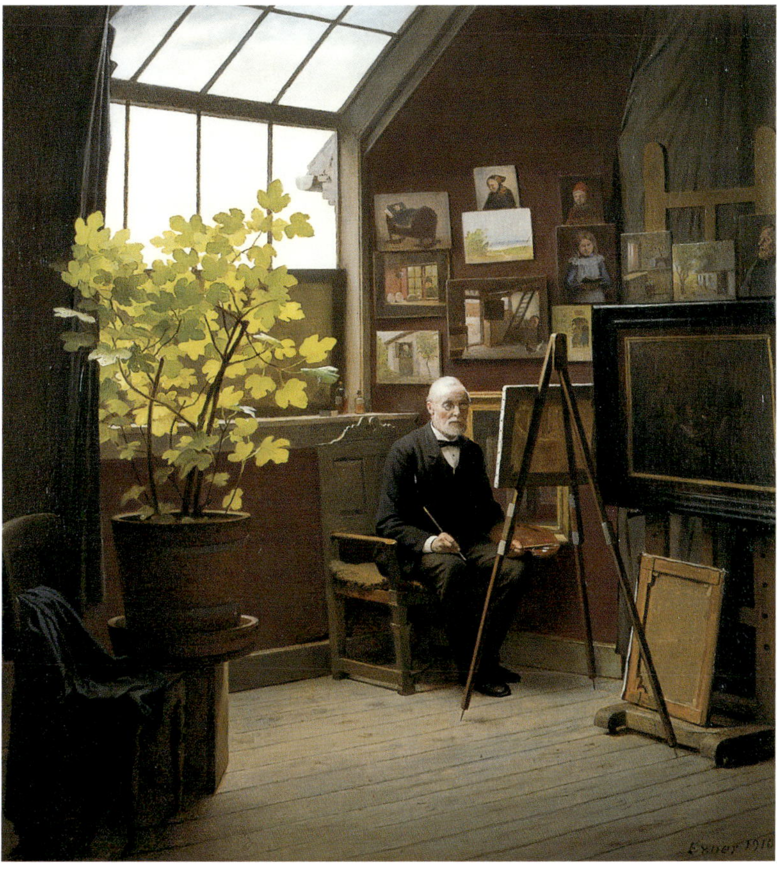

founded in its sustaining soil and continuous culture. Adam Gottlob Oehlenschläger's verse
"There is a Lovely Land," adapted as Denmark's second national anthem in 1844 (in addition
to the royal anthem), poeticizes the period's yearning for home and place:[71]

> I know a lovely land
> With spreading, shady beaches
> Near Baltic's salty strand,
> Near Baltic's salty strand.
> Its hills and valleys gently fall,
> Its ancient name is Denmark,
> And it is Freya's hall
> And it is Freya's hall.

This rhetoric of ancient history entering the present, of the gentle and nurturing land,
and of the nation as a home, persisted throughout the rest of the nineteenth century. However, by the late 1870s, new, anti-romantic and resolutely internationalist tendencies began to
reshape the art world. The Golden Age's emphasis on cultural isolation came under criticism
in the work of art historian Julius Lange, literary critic Georg Brandes, and particularly artists
who began to become established in that decade and the next—and for whom as we shall see,
advanced Parisian painting had as much resonance as Frederiksborg Castle.

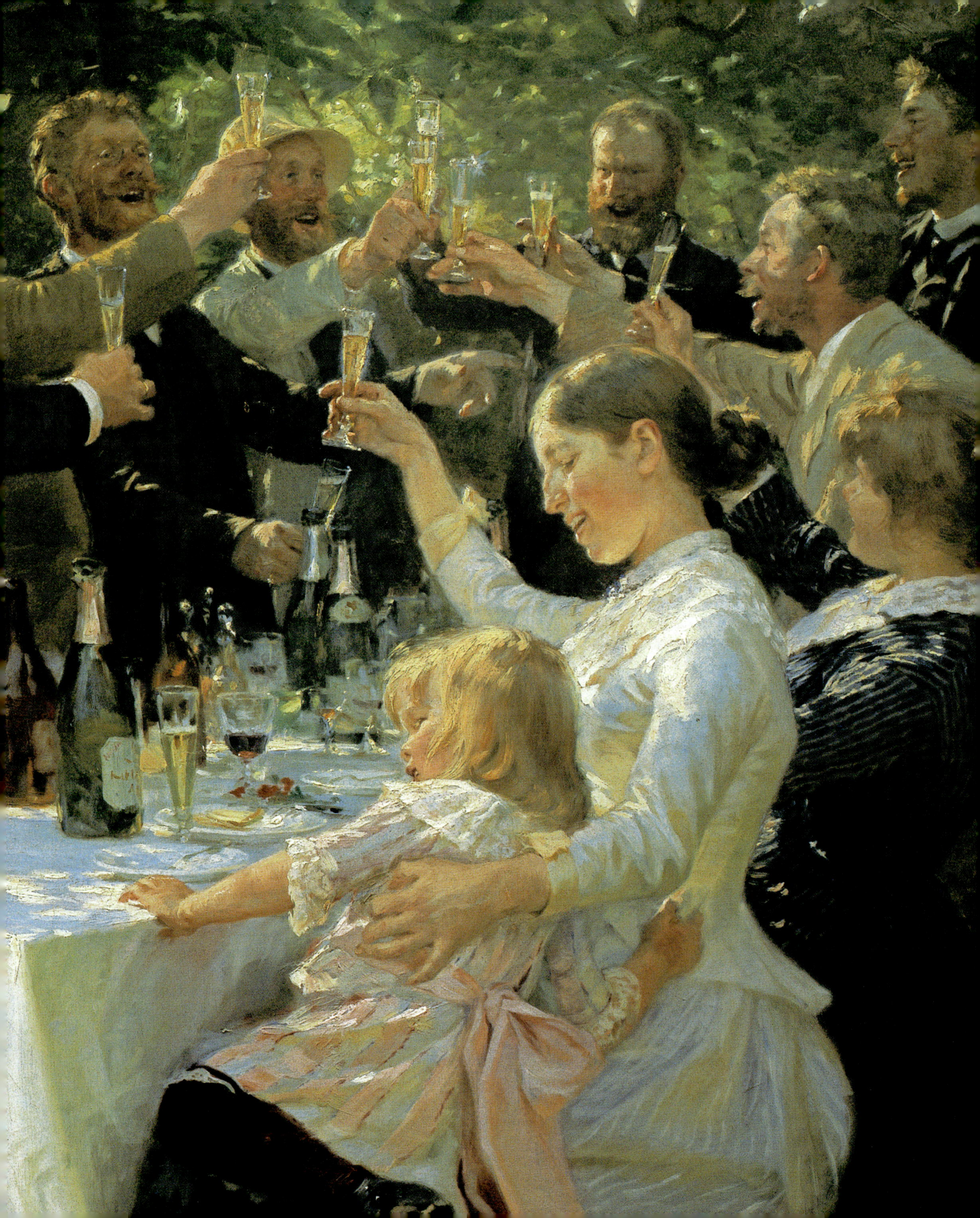

5

Skagen and the
Modern Breakthrough

The history of Skagen is a history of gales, and sand-drifts, and shipwrecks . . .
It is one of the wildest and most desolate spots in the world, yet within a couple
hours' journey from fertile, peaceful, and idyllic rustic landscapes. To the long
straggling town of Skagen the railway will never penetrate.
—*Murray's Handbook for Travelers in Denmark*, 1875[1]

SUCH DESCRIPTIONS BECKONED ARTISTS AND OTHERS SEEKING
inspiration in an uncorrupted countryside to the fishing town of Skagen in the later nineteenth
century. Skagen occupies an extraordinary position at the northern-most tip of Jutland at the
convergence of the Skagerrak and Kattegat straits (leading to the North and Baltic seas) (fig. 2).
The churning waters, assisted by a triple reef system, grind everything that comes within reach
of this spit of land into powder, producing the largest fine sandy beach in Scandinavia. Before
the late nineteenth century, the town was only accessible by small boat or by the horse-drawn
mail cart. Even Skagen's fishermen, who harvested some of the most prolific fishing grounds in
Denmark, had to ply their trade from specially designed vessels, or from the beach.

However, by the 1880s, Skagen had become one of Scandinavia's most famous artist colonies, attracting painters, writers, and musicians from throughout the Nordic countries. In the
1830s and 1840s, Golden Age painters such as Martinus Rørbye traveled to Skagen to record
its seas and its fishing population, extending N. L. Høyen's notion of Danish national tourism
from the more familiar landscapes of Zealand and Bornholm to North Jutland. By mid-century, and particularly following the German annexation of Schleswig and Holstein in 1864,
a rising sense of nationalism impelled some intellectuals to seek what they considered to be
people and places so untouched by foreign influence that they might be identified as symbols
of an essential Denmark. Skagen's fishermen provided romantic nationalists with such figures.
By the 1870s, a core group of these painters had attracted others to Skagen each summer and
by the 1880s an art colony had coalesced.

Within the Skagen colony, the artists shared a common ethos, regardless of their styles
or other affiliations. The painting that has come to symbolize the ethos in that place at that
time is *Hip, Hip, Hurrah!* (fig. 96), completed in 1888 by Peder Severin Krøyer (1851–1909).
In a sun-dappled outdoor setting, ten artists raise their glasses in a toast as effervescent as the

96.
P. S. Krøyer
Hip, Hip, Hurrah!, 1888
(detail)

133

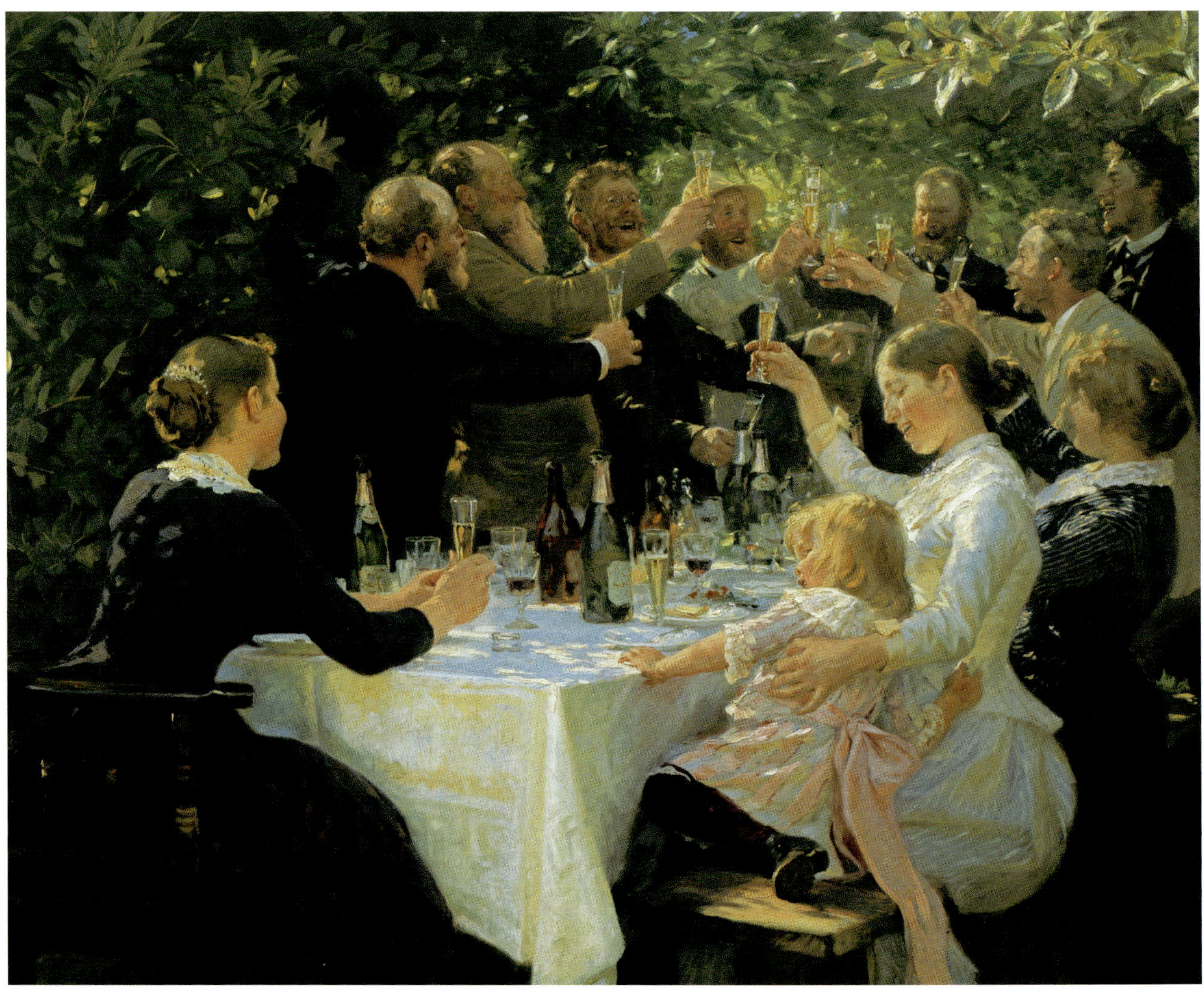

96.
P. S. Krøyer
Hip, Hip, Hurrah!, 1888
Oil on canvas, 53 x 65⅛ in.
(134.5 x 165.5 cm)
Göteborgs Konstmuseum

bubbles of their champagne. They surround a table that is covered with a creamy white cloth and placed strategically on a diagonal to draw us into the scene. With its network of convivial gazes and gestures that unite the gathering, *Hip, Hip, Hurrah!* is a *freundschaftbild* (friendship picture) in the tradition of Blunck, Bendz, Hansen, and other earlier nineteenth-century Danish artists who intended to demonstrate artistic communality.[2] However, by including artists from Norway, Sweden, and Denmark in the painting, Krøyer here emphasizes a pan-Nordic community. Further, women artists also participate within this congenial group, reflecting a transformation in the institutional practices of the Danish art world in the 1880s.

Krøyer also demonstrates an international affiliation through his technique. His dazzling colors, fleeting light effects, and wet, spontaneous-seeming paint application announce his connection to French Naturalism and Impressionism. With its formal affinities to advanced continental painting, *Hip, Hip, Hurrah!* marks a profound shift that took place in later nineteenth-century Danish painting. Artists of Krøyer's generation saw themselves as part of an international, cosmopolitan circuit of ideas and production—as the "breakthrough generation" in the words of critic Georg Brandes—rather than as carriers of N. L. Høyen's

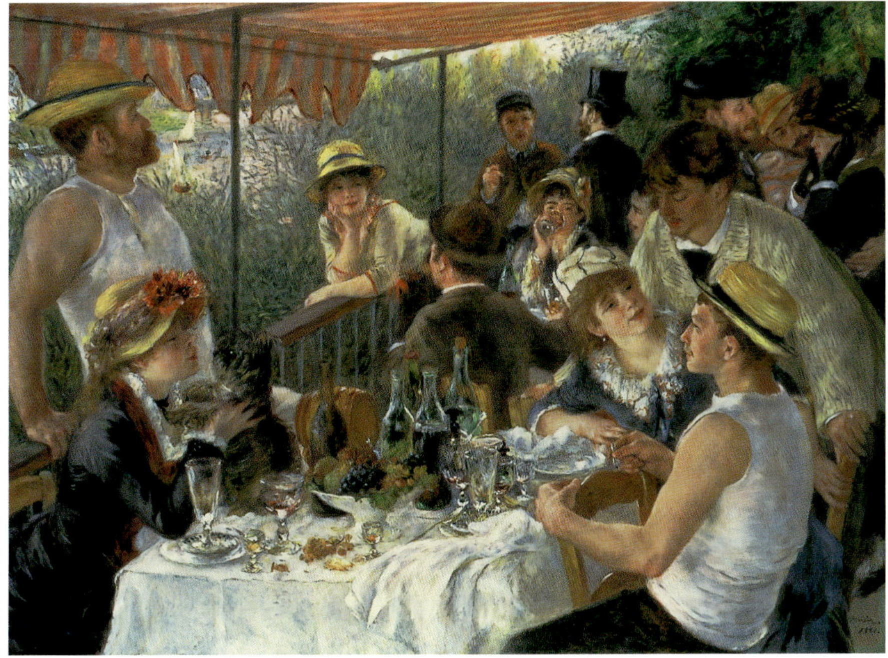

97.
Pierre-Auguste Renoir
Luncheon of the Boating Party,
1880–81
Oil on Canvas, 51⅛ x 68⅛ in.
(130 x 173 cm)
The Phillips Collection, Washington

isolated nationalism. The town of Skagen, and its commodious beaches, became a laboratory for the artists' new identities and ideas.

Exhibited in 1888 at the Charlottenborg, *Hip, Hip, Hurrah!* is a picture of modern leisure akin to Pierre-Auguste Renoir's *Luncheon of the Boating Party* (1880–81; fig. 97). This gathering, and these artists in it, who will be identified later in the chapter, came to solidify Skagen as a Danish "place-myth,"[3] a primitive rural setting—"one of the wildest and most desolate spots in the world"—that gave rise to some of Denmark's most cosmopolitan artists. Embedded in this painting is a network of complex stories—of a new internationalism in Danish painting, of the growth and decline of the art colony, of the women who are represented, and of the social identity of the town.[4]

Founded in the twelfth century, Skagen evolved into two villages, the old and the new. Located one-half mile apart, they were surrounded by large, shifting sand dunes. Over the years, the dunes had thwarted most attempts at agriculture (old fields were buried under the sand and only barley was grown between gales), obscured parts of the village, and, in the latter eighteenth century, buried the St. Laurentius Church, leaving only the tower visible (the so-called Buried Church). The mail cart, which traveled from Fredrikshavn, provided the only land transportation to the town. Finnish painter Hanna Rönnberg (1862–1946) described the journey by land:

> At the end of the eighties Skagen had as yet neither railway nor harbor, the
> means of communication were, if not exactly temporary, then so primitive and
> old-fashioned, that the pampered travelers of our own days would suffer if they
> were forced to travel as we did at that time. . . . we came out into the dunes and
> the speed decreased greatly, it was like riding in flour, up dune and down dune,

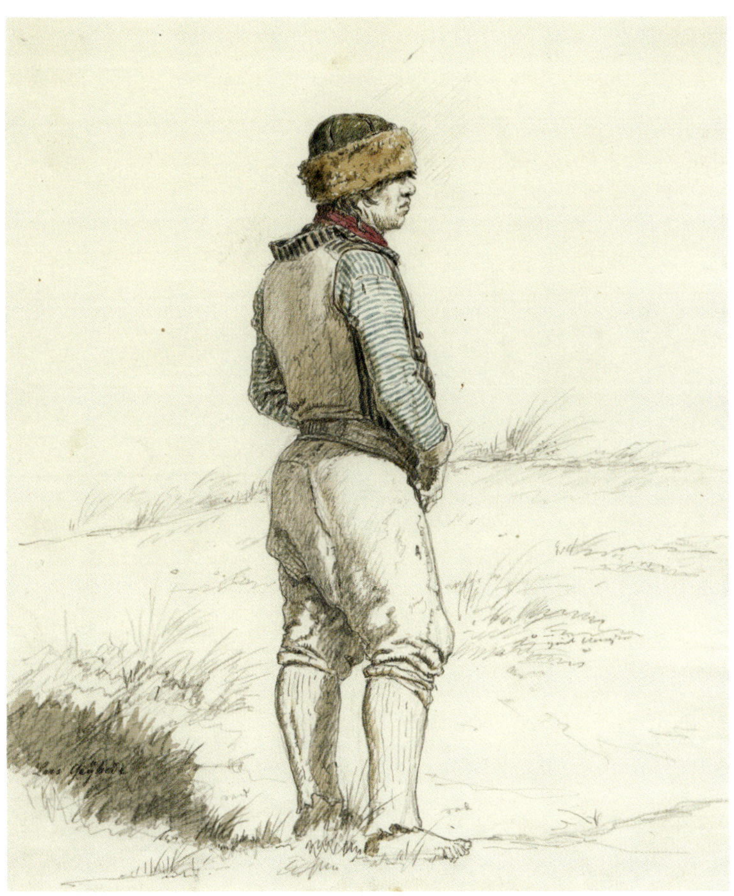

98.
Martinus Rørbye
The Fisherman Lars Gaihede, 1847
Pencil and India ink on paper, 11⅝ x 9½ in.
(29.5 x 24 cm)
Skagens Museum

foot by foot. Amongst other things we left our carriage and walked in the soft
sand, until we became so tired that we had to return to our coach, and from it
look upon magnificent nature in all its abundance . . . and one understood that
here was the home of all the old stories and fairytales, this was where Andersen
was inspired to write his tale of the "Dunes." . . . Yes, it was a land of sagas, and
now we drove straight into it, forgetting weariness and tiredness, the mind was
open and receptive to new impressions and experiences.[5]

Norwegian painter Christian Krohg (1852–1925), who first traveled to Skagen in 1879,
described the journey by boat in an essay written in 1894:

I sailed there one lovely summer's day with a pilot boat, for the steamships cannot
dock there, as there is nothing which even appears to be a harbor, and the pilot
boat had to remain several hundred feet outside. But we raised the flag, and then a
rowing boat came. Even that could not go all the way in [to the coast]. For the last
stretch we had to be carried on the back of the fisherman and then finally we stood
on the beach of Skagen. I have never stepped on anything like it.[6]

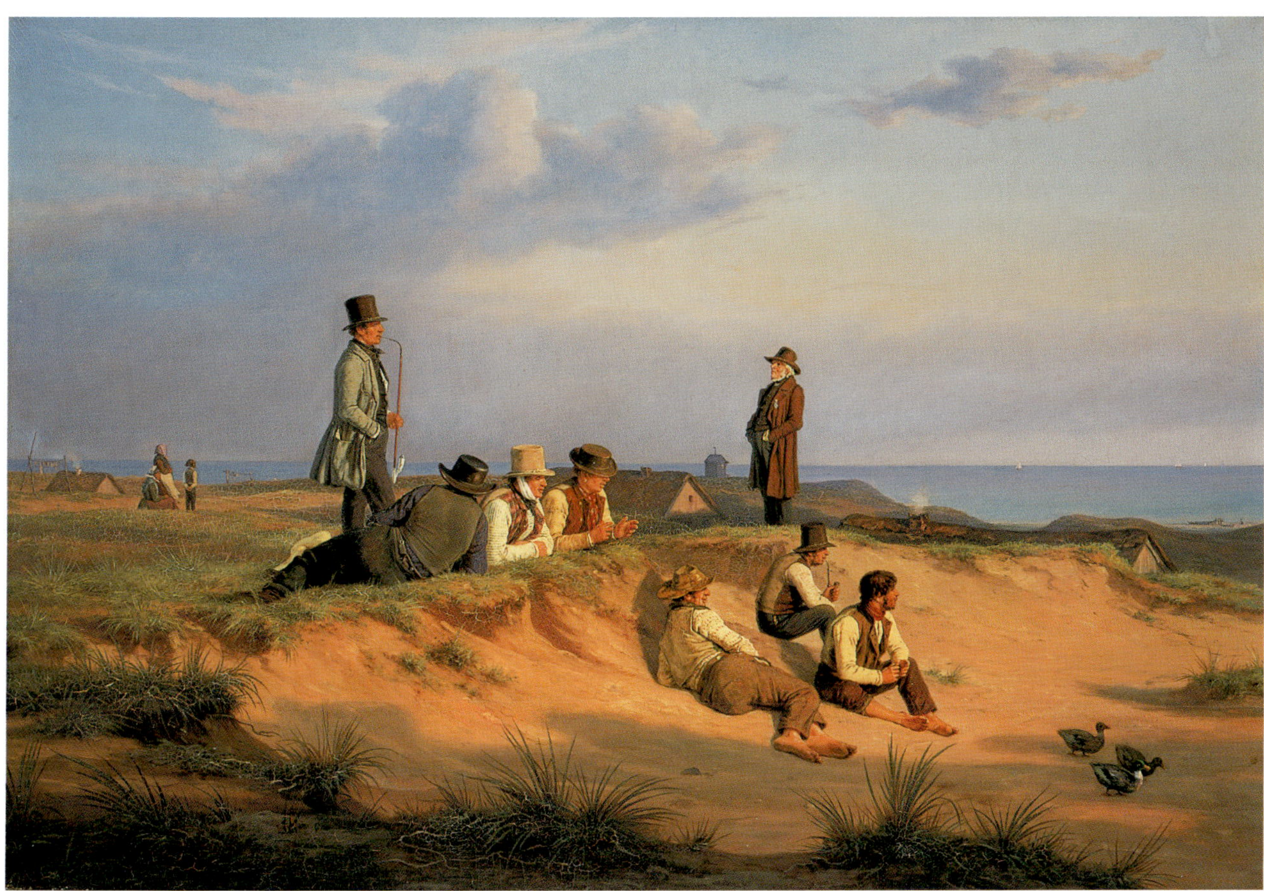

99.
Martinus Rørbye
*Men of Skagen on a Summer Evening
in Good Weather*, 1848
Oil on canvas, 34¼ x 48⅞ in.
(87 x 124 cm)
Statens Museum for Kunst,
Copenhagen

The slowing down and then suspension of time that Rönnberg describes, and the exoticism of Krohg's transport, echo the expectations of the earliest urban travelers of Skagen as a threshold experience. Hans Christian Andersen recalled his first visit to northern Jutland as a turning point in his work:

> Until now I had only seen a small part of my native land, that is to say, a few points in [the islands of] Funen and Zealand, as well as Moen's Klint, which last is truly one of our most beautiful places. . . . I wished, therefore, in the summer of 1830, to devote my first literary proceeds to seeing Jutland, and making myself more thoroughly acquainted with my own Funen. I had no idea how much solidity of mind I should derive from this summer excursion, or what a change was about to take place in my inner life. Jutland, which stretches between the German Ocean and the Baltic, until it ends at Skagen in a reef of quicksands, possesses a peculiar character. Towards the Baltic extend immense woods and hills; towards the North Sea, mountains and quicksands, scenery of a grand and solitary character; and between the two, infinite expanses of brown heath, with their wandering gipsies, wailing birds, and their deep solitude, which the Danish poet, Steen Blicher, has described in his novels.[7]

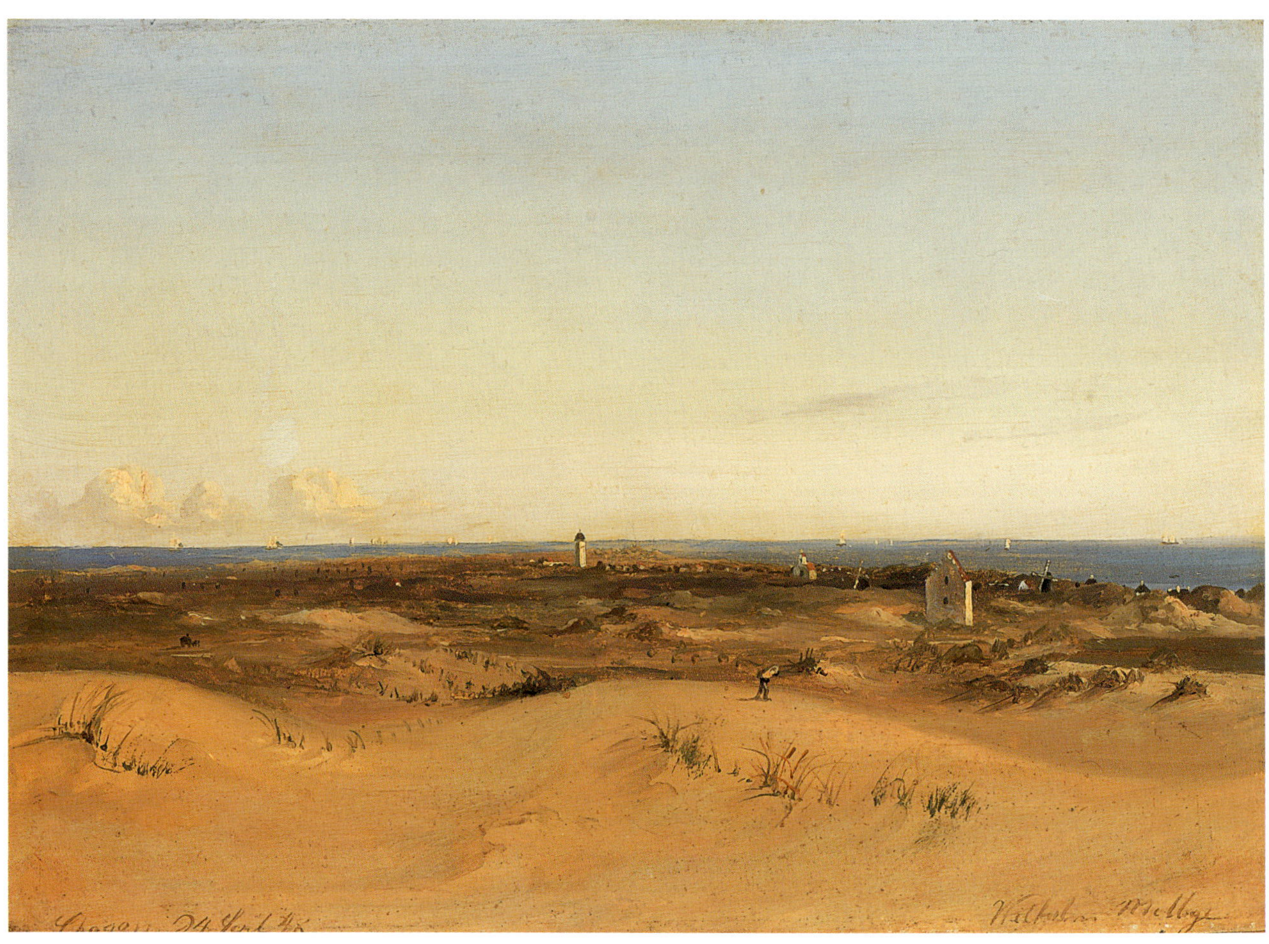

100.
Vilhelm Melbye
View Over Skagen from the Dunes Northwest of the Old Church, 1848
Oil on canvas, 10⅜ x 14⅝ in. (26.5 x 37 cm)
Skagens Museum

After a summer spent in Skagen in 1859, Andersen wrote a travel account entitled "Skagen," and a short story, "Tale of the Dunes," based on the Buried Church, both published in December 1859. He also published his poem, "Jylland" (Jutland) in 1860 in Copenhagen's *Illustreret Tidende*.[8] All combine the picturesque and the brutal, aesthetic delight and physical danger. In "Skagen," he described an unspoiled, primitive Denmark, as exotic and "distant" for urbanites as North Africa or Southern Italy, offering the following advice to artists and poets:

> We wanted to visit this far away place . . . this desert between two foaming
> oceans, the town with neither streets nor alleys . . . If you are a painter, follow us
> here, because you will find a profusion of subjects to paint. Here are scenes to
> inspire poetry. Here in the Danish environment you will find images reminiscent
> of Africa´s deserts, of Pompeii´s ashes . . . Skagen is indeed worth a visit."[9]

Andersen's visit also coincided with (and in his memoirs, precipitated) the birth of painter Anna Brøndum Ancher (1859–1935), daughter of the proprietors of Brøndum's Hotel, where the writer stayed, and the woman seated in the foreground of *Hip, Hip, Hurrah!* whose golden-haired daughter wriggles against her.[10]

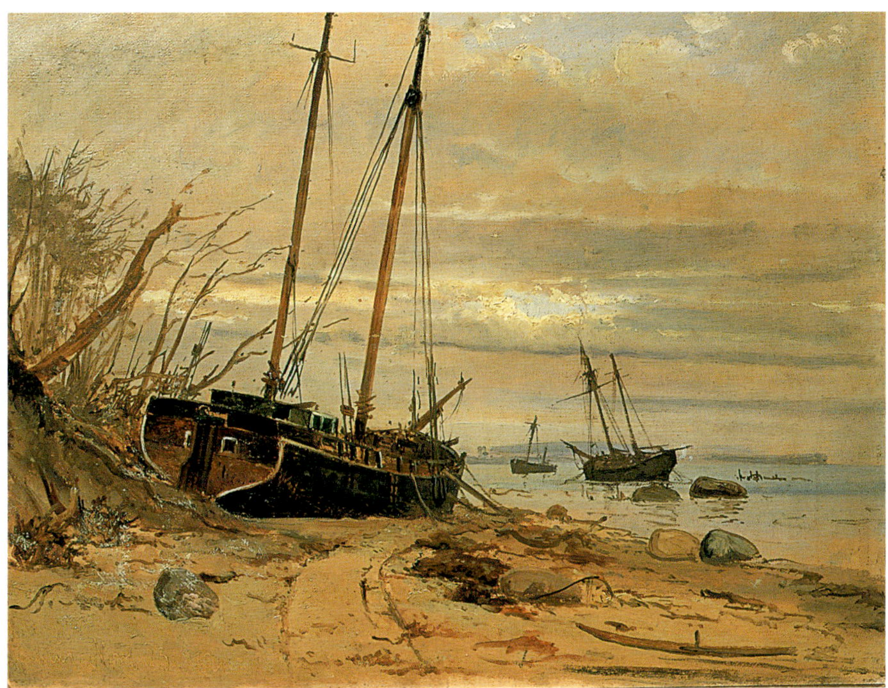

101.
Holger Drachmann
Storm Surge, Falster, 1872
Oil on canvas, 12¼ x 15¾ in.
(31 x 40 cm)
Ribe Kunstmuseum

Such tantalizing descriptions, and the visual appeal of Skagen as depicted in the work of an increasing number of artists, drew other artists to the town. Each, in turn, recommended Skagen to others. The first major artist to work in north Jutland was Martinus Rørbye, who first visited in 1830, accompanying H. C. Andersen. His motifs from that trip are largely sketches of folk life set in the market towns or landscape. He traveled to Skagen in 1833, producing a series of small genre scenes of fishermen (Skagens Museum and the Royal Print Collection). At the time, the town consisted of a few hundred homes and 1,200 inhabitants.[11] There was as yet no hotel.

Rørbye again traveled to Skagen in 1847, escaping a particularly hot summer season in Copenhagen.[12] During his two-week visit, he sketched in pencil and in oil, recording the maritime life of the town. One of these drawings is a near-ethnographic portrait entitled *The Fisherman Lars Gaihede* (1847; fig. 98), representing Gaihede (1805–1887), who would later become one of the most popular models in the town. Rørbye had to pay for his services.[13] With its emphasis on Gaihede's bare feet, patched knee breeches, leather hat, and rounded facial features, the drawing suggests a primitive Rousseauian hero, an effect enhanced by the model's upright posture and stable contrapposto position. Rørbye's most ambitious motif from that town, *Men of Skagen on a Summer Evening in Good Weather* (1848; fig. 99), encapsulated the artistic objectives of the period as they had been shaped by N. L. Høyen. It represents a group of picturesque figures embedded in their local landscape, a scene from daily life.[14] Bathed in low-angled summer light, and bracketed by shadows that extend across the foregound, the painting appears to represent working men (and in the background, women) at leisure, in contemplation at the end of the day. However, to the right stands the businessman and salvage operator Jakob Andersen, representing the constant vigilance that the town maintained for ships in distress.

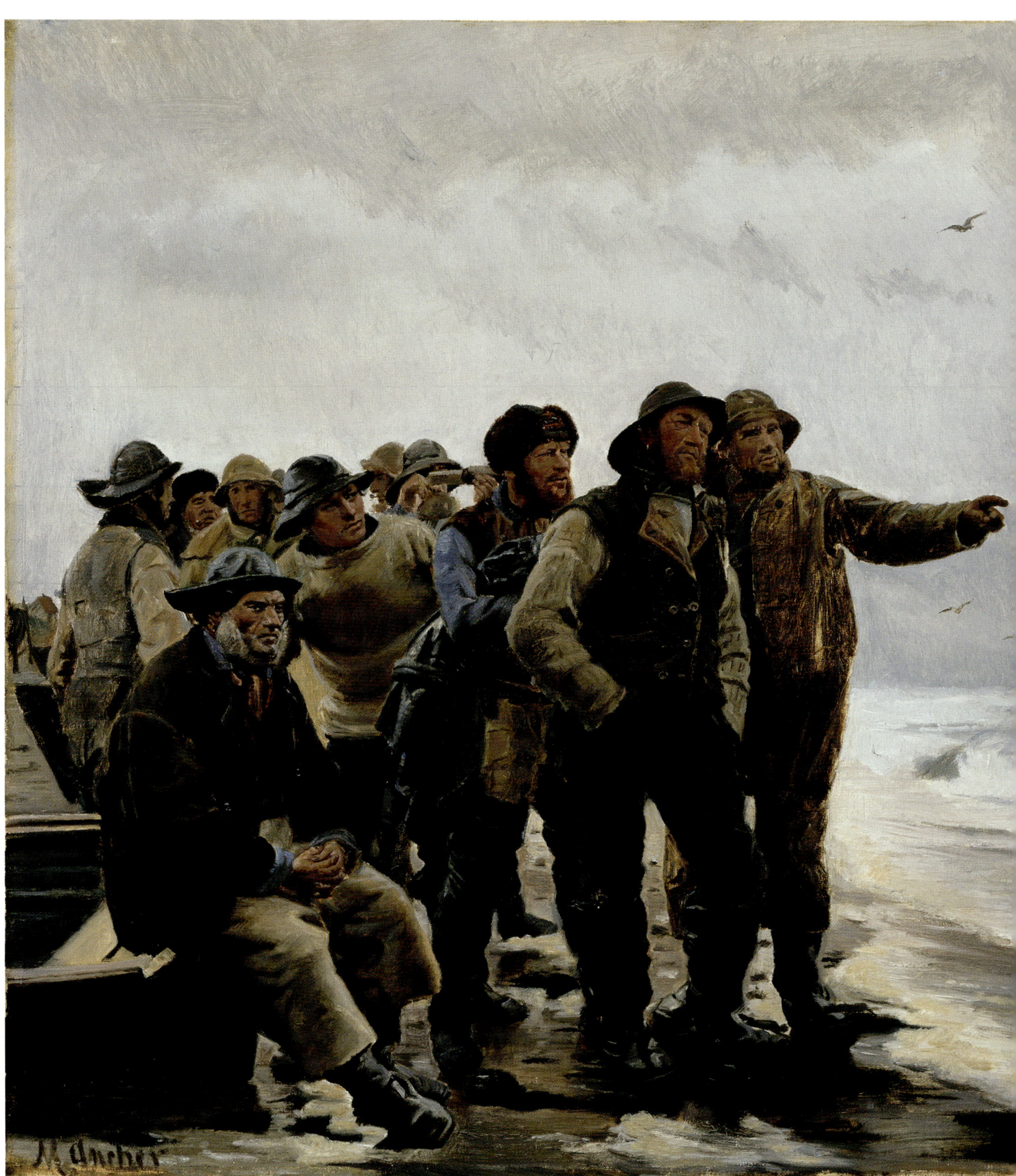

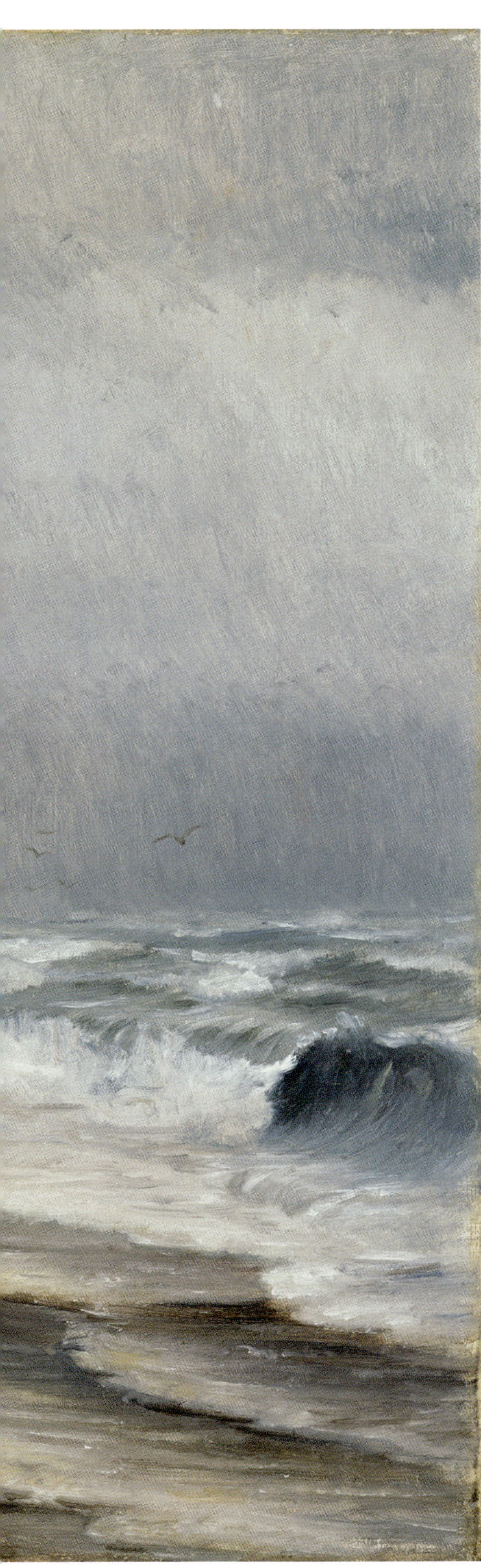

The painting was purchased by Frederik VII after it was exhibited at the Charlottenborg in 1848, the same year as Rørbye's death, calling attention to the motif and to the town as a setting. In September of that year, marine painter Vilhelm Melbye (1824–1882) endured the rugged trip to Skagen in search of motifs. The youngest of three brothers, all marine painters, Melbye had traveled to Iceland in the previous year and was on his way to France. His *View over Skagen from the Dunes Northwest of the Old Church* (1848; fig. 100) is a small painting rendered on site that captures the saturated blond light, shimmering sky, and sense of openness that characterizes the town's dune landscapes. The view northeast toward the new town is punctuated by three churches, windmills, and the roofs of domestic dwellings. All are dwarfed by the windswept dunes and distant horizon. In the foreground is the Buried Church, which Hans Christian Andersen had likened to a motif from Pompeii.[15]

In the 1870s, Skagen began to gain status as an attractive site for artists. In fact, in 1871 the poet and painter Holger Drachmann published an article announcing Skagen as "an eldorado for artists."[16] Drachmann (1846–1908), who first visited Skagen in that year, would later become a resident, one of its most important interpreters in prose and poetry and a fixture of its art colony until his death (he is buried near Grenen, the tip of the peninsula where the seas meet). Drawn by the desire to live with "fishermen and salvage commissioners," he returned in 1872 with Carl Locher (1851–1915), who likewise built a home in Skagen. In that year, he also brought Norwegian painter Frits Thaulow (1847–1906), who would become an important conduit of French Impressionism and help to establish a Parisian network for Nordic artists. Drachmann's early Danish coastal scenes, like his poems and essays, suggest the romance of the violent sea and the devastation left in its wake (fig. 101).

In 1872 and 1873, Norwegian painter Christian Skredsvig (1854–1937), who had studied at the Royal Academy, and Danish painter and art historian Karl Madsen (1855–1938) visited Skagen on their way to Norway. Over the next several years, Madsen returned to Skagen, becoming one of the town's notable chroniclers. Madsen stimulated painter Michael Ancher's interest in visiting Skagen, which he did for the first time in July 1874. Ancher (the man standing at the end of the table in *Hip, Hip, Hurrah!*) returned annually, married artist Anna Brøndum, daughter of the innkeepers, and settled permanently in the town.

Michael Ancher (1849–1927), who had studied at the Royal Academy with ambitions to be a figure painter, began to produce and exhibit massive, densely populated narrative paintings of Skagen's fishermen in the late 1870s. Ancher's *Will He Round the Point?* (1879; fig. 102 is a later replica) is one of his most famous works. It was based on sketches created over the summer and completed during the winter of 1879.[17] The painting presents coastal laborers, typically treated anonymously or as types, with the specificity of portraiture and on the scale of history painting. The gathering of men directs their attention to the right, where, as the title informs us, a ship is attempting to maneuver the reefs. Exhibited at the Charlottenborg spring exhibition in 1880, the painting was purchased three times in rapid succession, initially by the Fine Arts Society in Copenhagen, then by the National Gallery at Christiansborg, and finally by Christian

102.
Michael Ancher
Will He Round the Point?, 1879
Oil on canvas, 36⅝ x 43 in.
(93 x 109 cm)
Skagens Museum

IX.[18] Reproduced in the Copenhagen newspaper *Illlustreret Tidende* and subsequently in popular prints that were diffused throughout Denmark, it was Ancher's breakthrough painting.[19]

The exhibition of the painting corresponded to the publication of Holger Drachmann's story of Lars Kruse, a Skagen fisherman and lifeboat operator, entitled *Lars Kruse—en Skildring fra Virkelighedens og Sandets Regioner (A Story from the Regions of Reality and Sand)*. Given the treacherous waters around Skagen, large, stable, fully equipped life boats had been stationed up and down the coast since the 1840s. When a ship foundered (as did over two hundred in the 1870s), fishermen who also worked on lifeboat crews set out to rescue the sailors. Lars Kruse (1828–1894), who had been among Skagen's first organized lifesavers, took part, most famously, in the rescue of the Swedish brig *Daphne*, which had run aground just after Christmas in 1862. Eight Skagen fishermen drowned attempting to save the crew, but Kruse had set out in his own boat to rescue them. Kruse received no award for his bravery because in his younger days he had salvaged some driftwood, sold it, and kept the money, which was then considered a crime. Drachmann, "fired by social indignation and righteous anger" at Kruse's mistreatment by the authorities, wrote the story, using notes that Michael Ancher had persuaded Kruse to record of the rescue operation.[20] Drachmann recounts Kruse's extraordinary career as a lifesaver, sometimes in the fisherman's own simple words, chronicling some of his efforts, ship by wrecked ship, and culminating in the rescue operation in 1862. Kruse, a "man of the people," deserved, according to Drachmann, to be decorated for bravery and not punished for an old and unfairly identified crime.[21] Drachmann's story was an immense success, drawing attention to Skagen and to Kruse, whom the author depicted as a national hero.[22]

Drachmann's epic story, written in prose and verse, also described Skagen as a dangerous natural paradise, further investing in the place enormous romantic appeal: "In the evening— on a late June night—after the sun has set . . . the shimmer of mid-summer has faded like a distant piece of classical music." This harmony, however, is often disturbed: "Skagen's South Beach lies exposed to gales blowing from the Southeast. These seas can be mighty, and if you look carefully up and down the coastline between here and Aalbæk, you might well discover half-buried, now almost vanished, wreckage giving eloquent witness to perils and foundering ships. . . . on this ferocious reef, which extends from Skagen´s beaches, the eyes of numerous sailors have been forever closed."[23] Such a confluence of the picturesque and the savage were, as art historian Nina Lübbren notes, part of the matrix of meaning for romantic tourism during this period.[24]

The reception of Ancher's and Drachmann's work reverberated in both the public regard for the Skagen fishermen and the Skagen community's reception of the artists. Ancher produced numerous other paintings of rescue operations throughout the 1890s, such as his 1883 *Taking the Lifeboat Through the Dunes* (fig. 103). Such large Naturalist compositions, placing equal emphasis on portraiture and action, offered the art audience the vicarious experience of the rescuers' drama and resolve. Small oil sketches, such as one created to capture the effects of a swirling snowstorm (fig. 104), assisted Ancher in his effort to make the large studio works vital and convincing. In these works, Ancher reanimated the figurative tradition of Eckersberg and his generation and advertised Skagen's inhabitants as a population of handsome, stalwart mariners.[25]

In 1879, Christian Krohg visited Skagen for the first time, and he would return several times in the 1880s and into the 1890s. He was there in 1888, accompanied by his new wife, the painter Oda Lasson Krohg (1860–1935), and Krøyer included him, third from the left, in *Hip, Hip, Hurrah!* Krohg's residences in Skagen had a galvanizing effect on his fellow artists.[26]

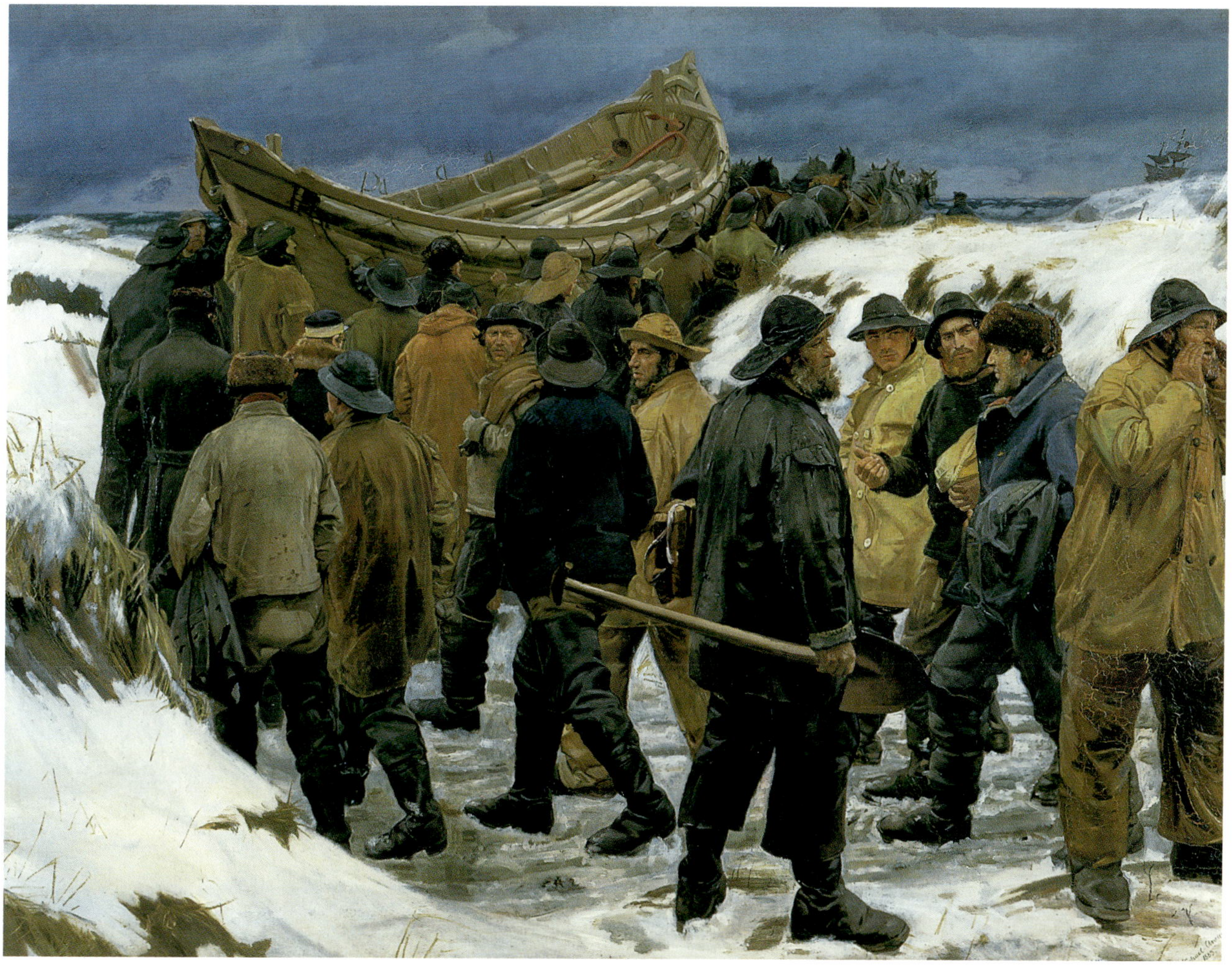

ABOVE
103.
Michael Ancher
Taking the Lifeboat Through the Dunes, 1883
Oil on canvas, 67⅜ x 87 in.
(171 x 221 cm)
Statens Museum for Kunst,
Copenhagen

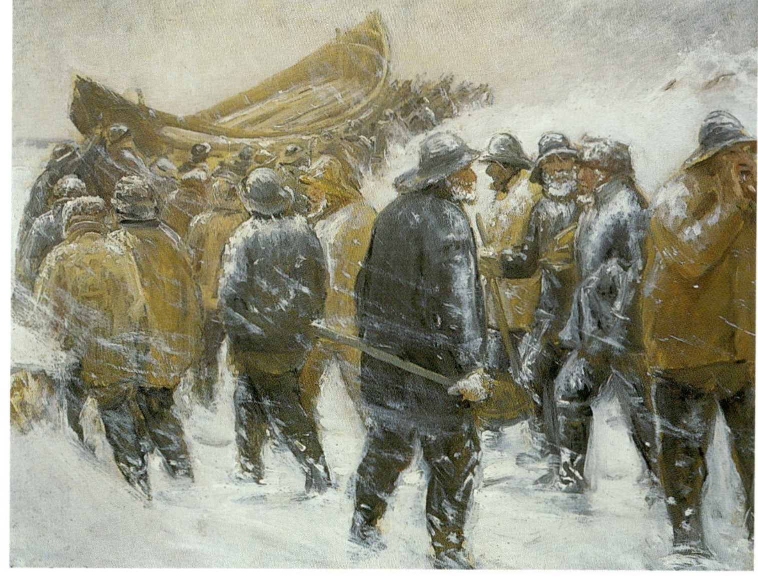

RIGHT
104.
Michael Ancher
Sketch for Taking the Lifeboat through the Dunes, 1883
Oil on canvas, 18⅛ x 22⅞ in.
(46 x 58 cm)
Collection of Ambassador John L. Loeb Jr.,
New York

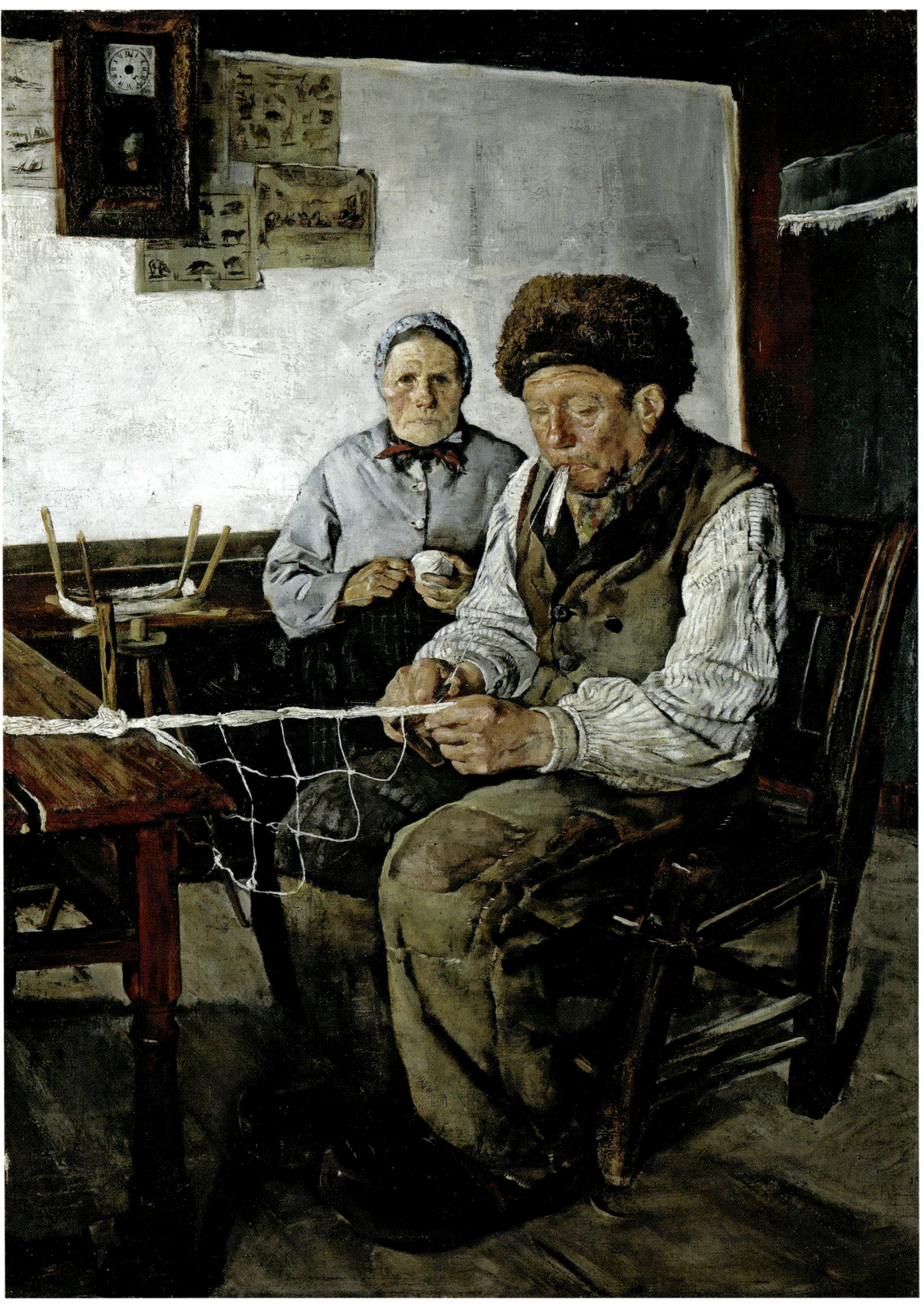

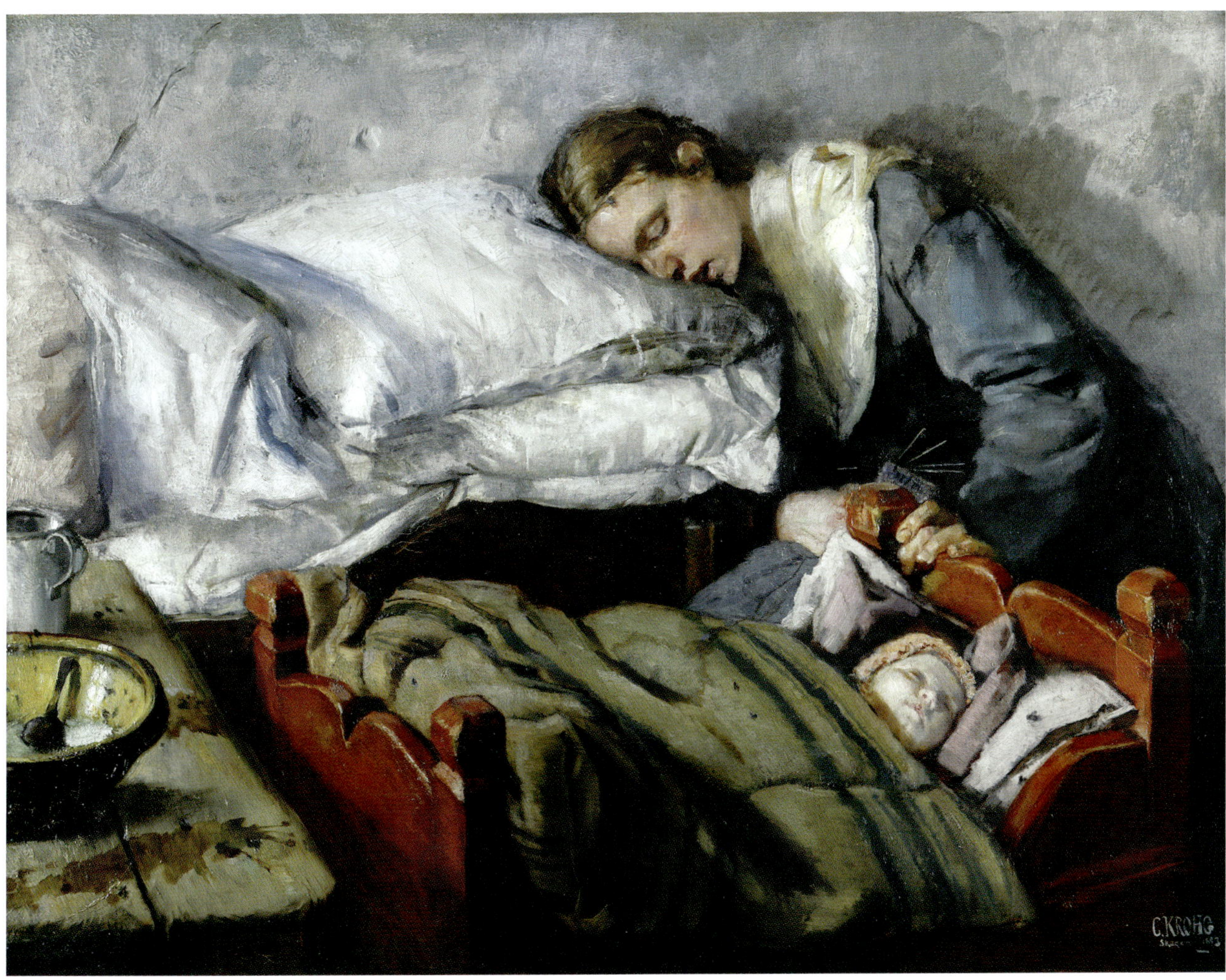

Krohg took his initial training in Kristiania (the nineteenth century name for Oslo), and then studied and worked in Karlsruhe and Berlin from 1874–1879. He then lived in Paris from autumn 1881 to spring 1882, traveled to Belgium in 1883 and 1885, and lived in Copenhagen in the late 1880s. By the time he arrived in Skagen, Krohg had begun to formulate a social theory of art in which painting should address contemporary political questions and should offer realistic, unembellished representations of its subjects. A writer as well as a painter, Krohg published his impressions of Skagen in the 1890s, focusing on the complex ways in which the town's inhabitants scratched out a living under difficult circumstances. Earlier writers and artists had offered romantic commentary on Skagen, while Krohg described a community doing what was necessary for survival. One of the things he wrote about was the importance of salvage operations to the local economy. He reports stumbling over the detritus from multiple wrecks during his first stroll along the beach, and that he himself had witnessed no fewer than seven shipwrecks during his two-month visit. He was therefore initially perplexed by the local fishermen's slow reactions upon seeing a ship foundering near the shore until he realized that "they were most anxious to try to guess what the cargo was. The reward depended on it."[27]

When a ship was rescued, there was an "intense" competition among the salvaging agents to secure contracts with the desperate captains.[28]

His paintings from his first summer in Skagen are likewise anchored in the unassuming, and often intimate, rituals of maritime work. *The Net Mender* (1879; fig. 105) represents a radical formal and thematic departure from Ancher's paintings of the town's fishermen. The models are the aging Ane Gaihede (1812–1904) and her husband Niels (1816–1890), the brother of Lars Gaihede who had modeled for Rørbye in 1847 (fig. 98). The extended Gaihede family served as models for Krohg throughout the years he visited Skagen. Seated in their austere home, Niels mends a fishing net and Ane balls yarn. Krohg noted:

> The people of Skagen are unlike other Danes, both in looks and temperament. When the fishermen are not at sea, or busy around the harbor, they repair their nets. It looks like the kind of work one would expect women to do, but women are not permitted to work with the nets. The old and retired fishermen, who can no longer go out fishing, spend all day sitting by the window, mending nets. From here they can command a splendid view of the ocean and witness the winds changing and the movements of the ships.[29]

The multiple layers of patches on Niels's clothing, his soiled shirt, heavy wooden shoes, and the bulging knuckles of his hands offer a deadpan view of rural labor, not as picturesque as in Christen Dalsgaard's views (fig. 94), but as hard scrabbling. Ane's arthritic hands and weather-beaten face speak of hardship and endurance, as does the spartan room and its well-used furniture. Cheap prints are tacked to the wall behind them flanking the clock (offered as the couple's only elegant possession), including a reproduction of Leonardo da Vinci's *Last Supper*. (Another version [Private Collection] of the scene, emphasizing the room's starkness, shows a maritime painting on the wall behind Niels's head.) The dignity of the couple's labor in these bare environs, animated by light entering the room from two directions, offers a commentary on the tight economy of the fishing community. The spavined perspective, in which the foreground seems to rise and jut forward (in contrast to the rapidly telescoping background), suggest the use of a camera lucida, an optical device with which both Krohg and Thaulow experimented in that summer.[30]

Krohg's painting *Sleeping Mother* (1883; fig. 106) likewise goes against the grain of sentimentalized images of maternal devotion that had been initiated by Jens Juel's portraiture (fig. 8) and which was a mainstay in bourgeois Golden Age painting. The model is Tine Gaihede (1859–1937) with her baby Sophus—daughter-in-law and granddaughter of Lars and Ane. Collapsed in exhaustion, Tine's mouth is open indecorously and her hands have gone limp, her knitting in her lap and the fingers of her left hand resting on the cradle, while the child's tiny head is viewed obliquely—the baby layered in grubby fabric. The scene is thus a reversal of the sweetness and clarity that usually characterizes such representations. Flies dotting the stained tabletop and dirty bowl and the baby's bedding in the foreground, and the compression of the composition, give emphasis to the room's close quarters and squalor. Begun during Krohg's third visit to Skagen, the painting is radically cropped like *The Net Menders*, but far more experimental in color and touch, reflecting Krohg's indebtedness to Impressionist painting from his study in Paris in 1881–82.[31]

107.
Anna Ancher
Lars Gaihede Whittling a Stick, 1880
Oil on panel, 15⅜ x 11⅜ in.
(39 x 29 cm)
Skagens Museum

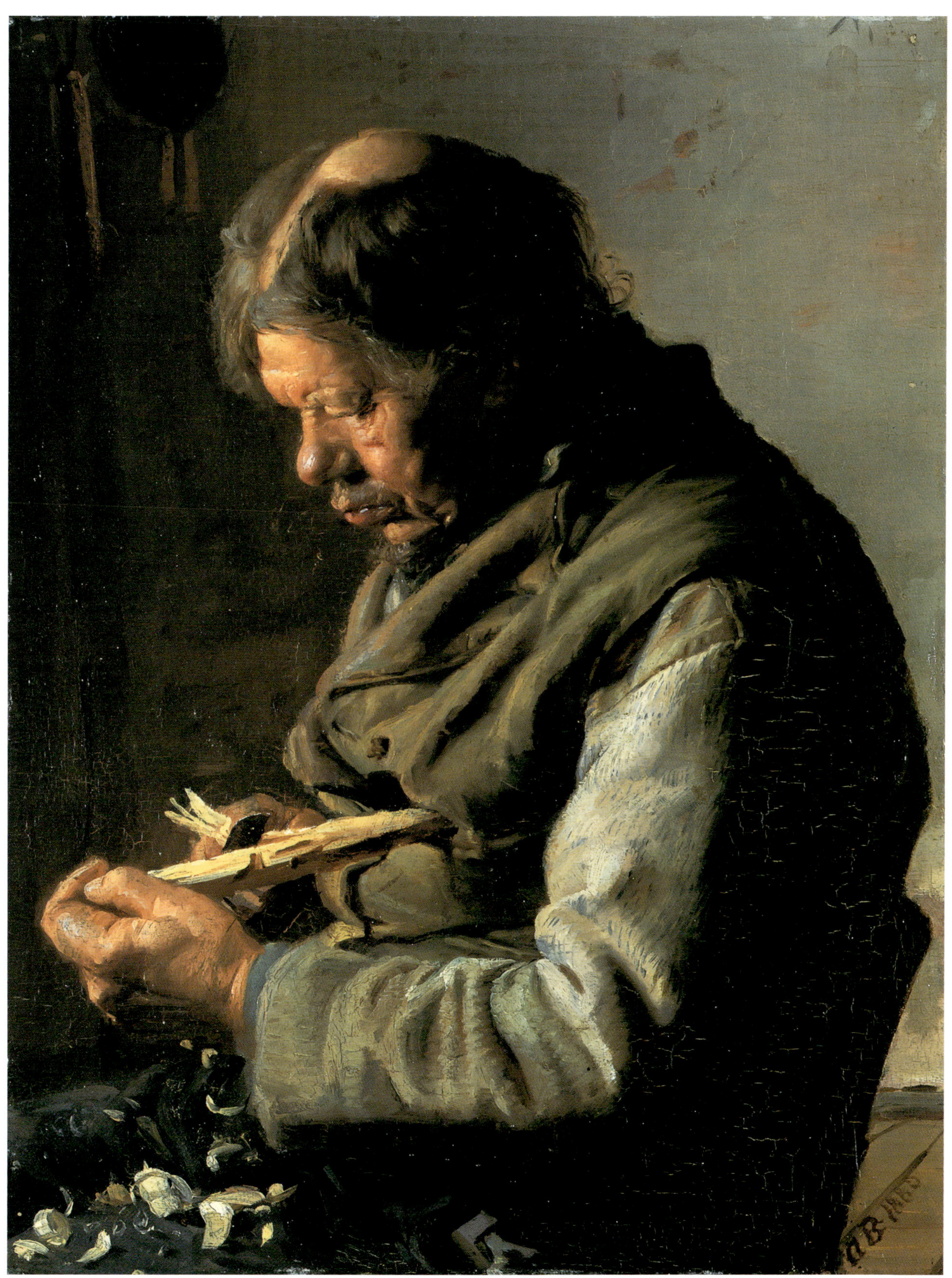

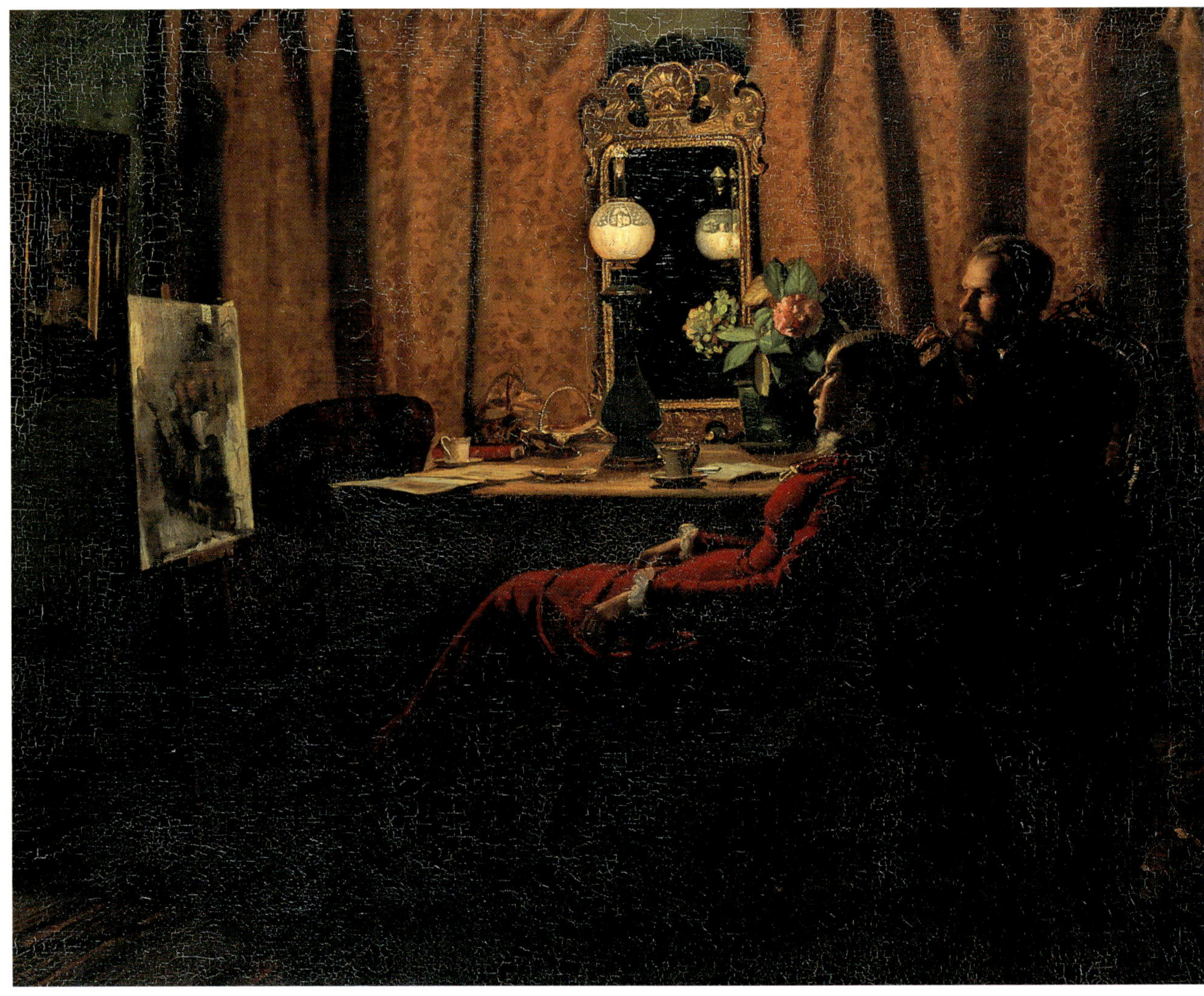

Krohg's unconventional cropping techniques, keyed up color palette, and social vision shaped the direction of the Skagen artists from 1879 onward. In 1880, Anna Brøndum Ancher (1859–1935) painted *Lars Gaihede Whittling a Stick* (fig. 107), a portrait of Niels's brother—and Rørbye's model from three decades earlier, represented in a dignified, intimate manner reminiscent of Krohg's work. Pushed close to the picture plane, Gaihede's massive form is tempered by the delicacy of his facial expression and concentration on his work. Despite the dark earth tones that dominate the composition, Ancher employs a glowing back-light as well as bounced light to suggest a sacred quality to Gaihede's gestures. In this and Krohg's work the private lives of laborers and not their heroicized or picturesque public actions are made visible.

Anna Brøndum Ancher, the most astute colorist among the Skagen artists, was the daughter of the proprietors of the Brøndum Hotel and shop. The hotel had welcomed visitors to Skagen since 1859 when it was a small, informal inn, but it had expanded over the years to accommodate the growing summer clientele. As the only hotel in town for several decades and as an institution operated by a family sympathetic to the arts, it was the heart of Skagen's artist

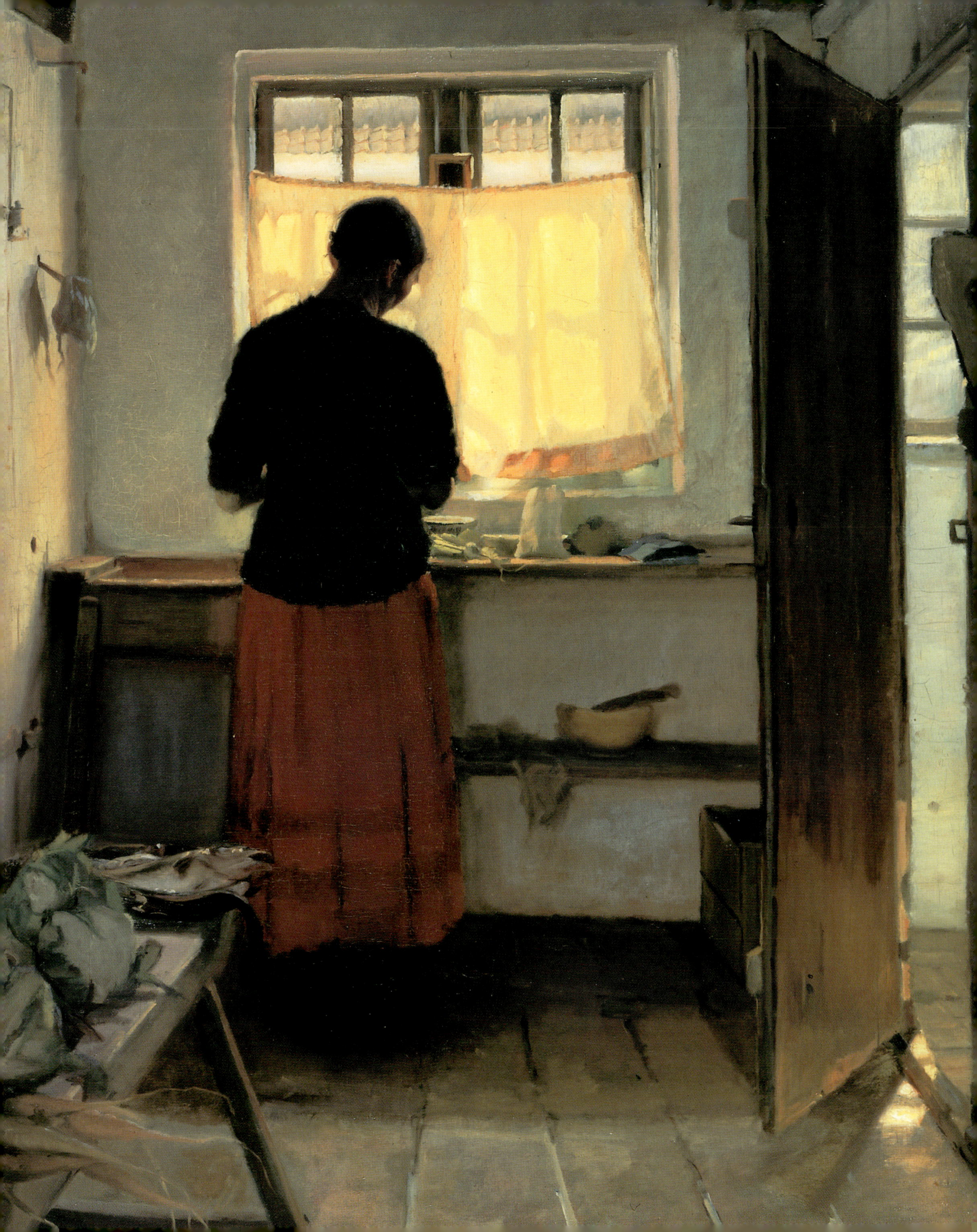

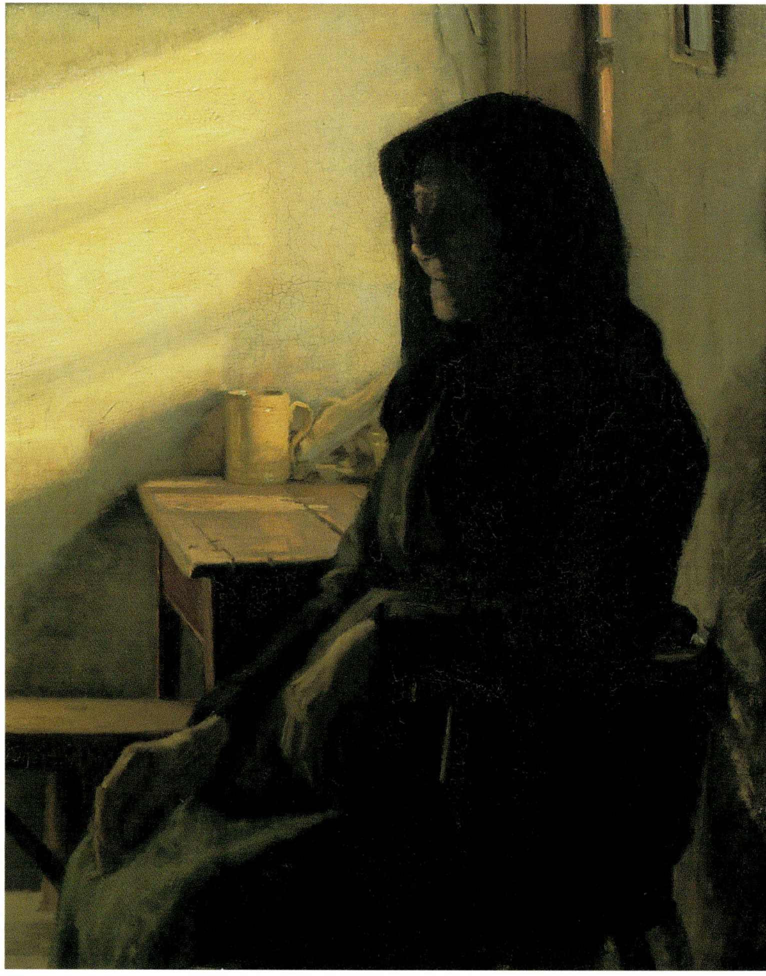

community. [32] Anna Brøndum's talent was evident from her childhood, and she was encouraged to seek professional training by Karl Madsen and the other painters who stayed at her parents' hotel. She was sent by her family to study in Copenhagen with Vilhelm Kyhn (see chapter 4) who ran one of the few private schools for women. She married Michael Ancher in 1880, at which time Kyhn had advised her to throw her palette and paints into the ocean, telling her that her duty was to her marriage. [33] Instead, the Anchers established a highly unusual partnership, eschewing the usual assumption that if an artist couple married, the husband's career was naturally more important than the wife's career. In 1883, the year of their daughter Helga's birth, they completed a joint painting entitled *Contemplating the Day's Work* (1883; fig. 108). In a letter of 1882, Michael Ancher recounted how much they enjoyed working together, a feeling that is borne out in the painting's sense of gravity and intimacy. [34] As a painting of artistic gender parity in the early 1880s, it is also one of the most unusual *freundschaft* paintings in Danish art.

The Anchers settled in Skagen and became important members of the artistic community who bridged the cultural divide between the locals and the visiting artists. [35] Anna Ancher's work was focused primarily on women in domestic settings, in which she experimented with a variety of light effects linked to the art of the Parisian Impressionists and to the

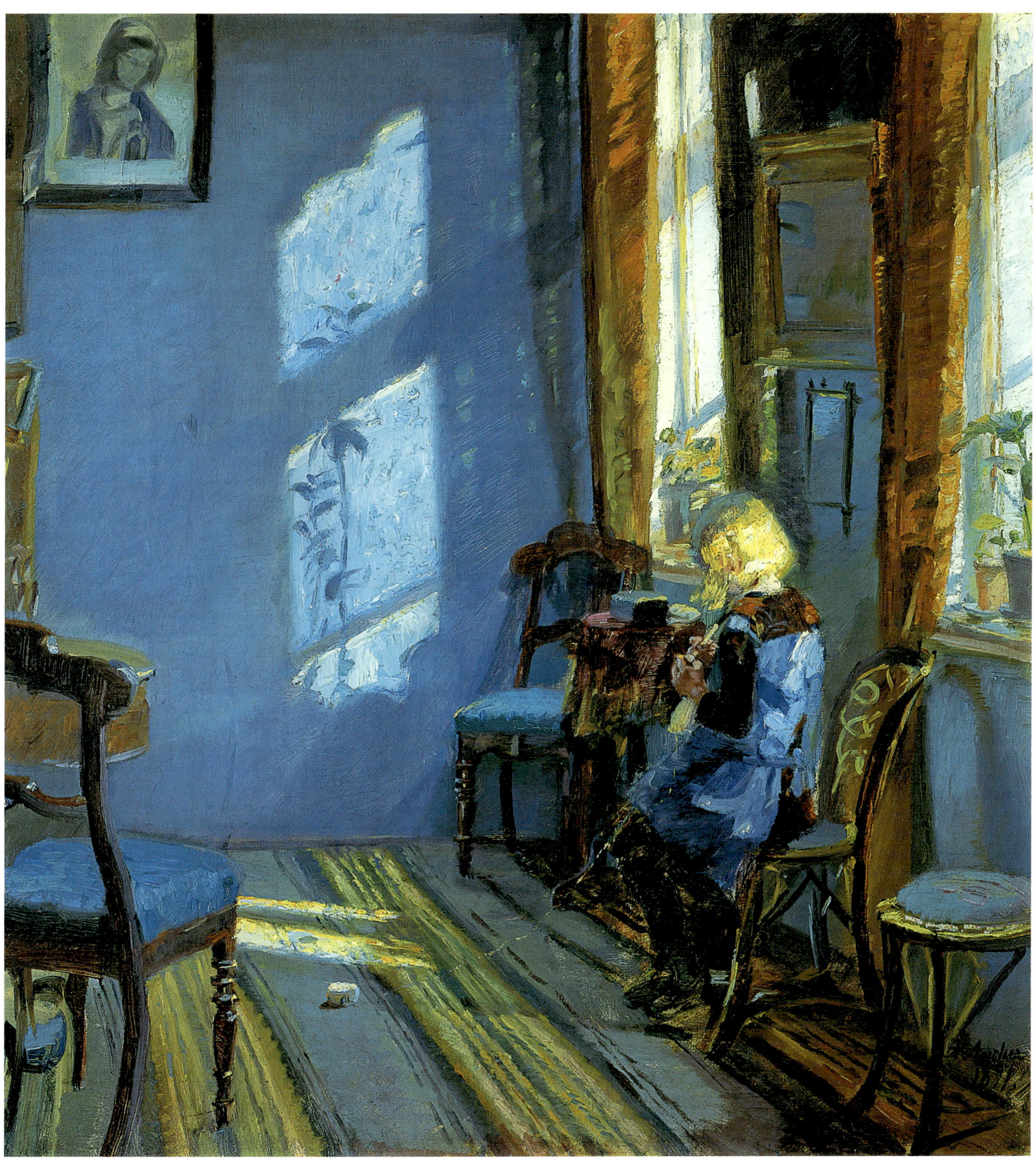

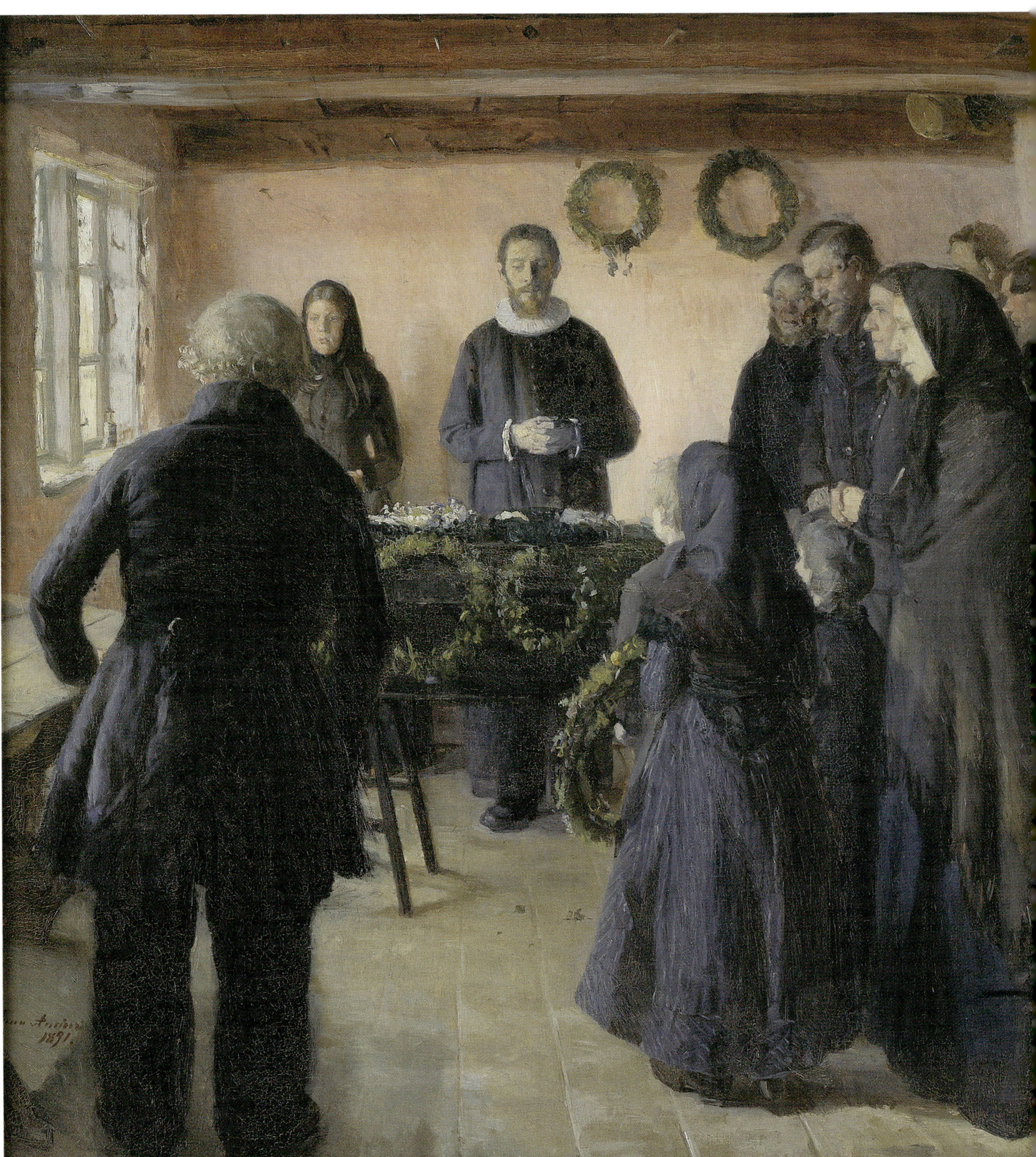

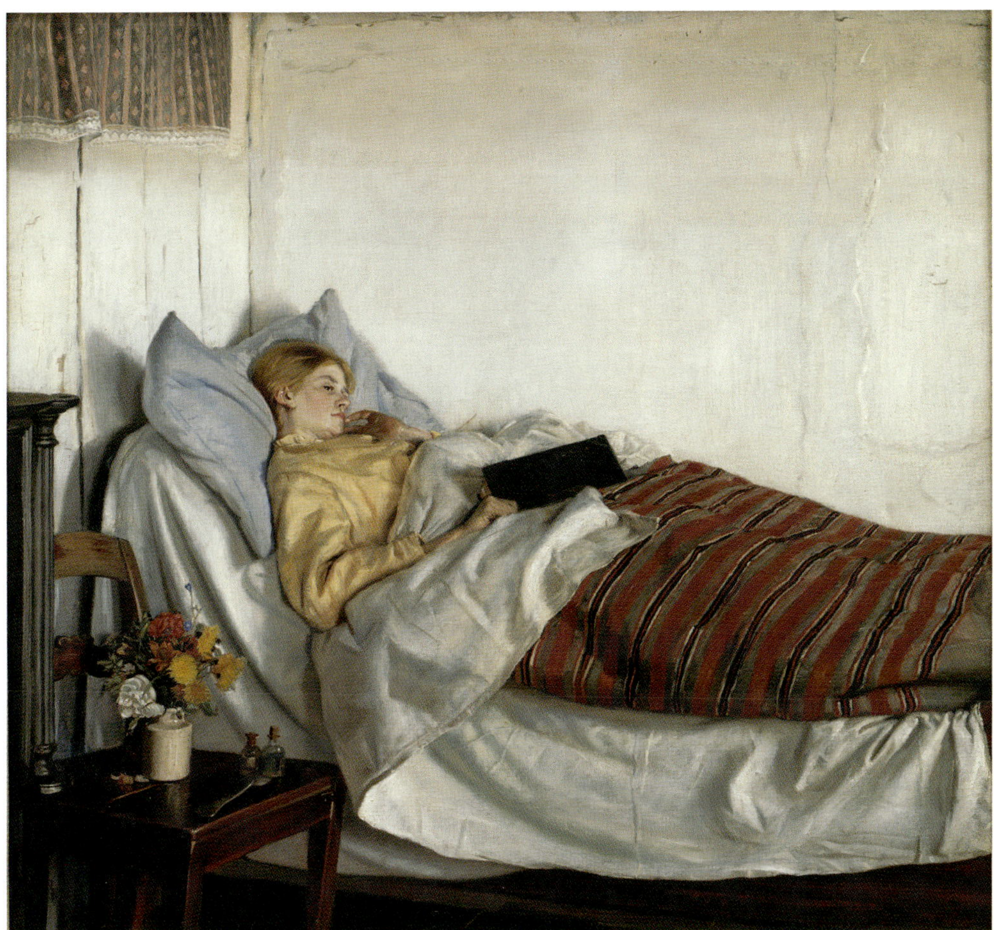

Dutch seventeenth-century painter Johannes Vermeer. *The Girl in the Kitchen* (fig. 109), several versions of which were painted between 1883 and 1886, represents a women, seen from behind, going about her daily chores. Her quiet, static form is embedded in the quiet pyrotechnics of sunlight—strong rays of the sun that bleach out local color, indirect light that glows from the next room, golden filtered light through the window, bounced light, and ambient light, each transmitting a different range of colors. Here, too, Ancher exaggerates the intensity of local color, creating among the most highly saturated color harmonies of any artist working in Denmark at the time.

A *Blind Woman in Her Room* (1883; fig. 110), a portrait of a Skagen woman called Blue Ane (1804–1886), likewise offers both a stunning display of color and light and an astute portrayal of a woman in her accustomed physical space. Seated in the foreground, Blue Ane is backlit, her darkened features chiseled and molded by the room's radiant glow. Unable to see and with her

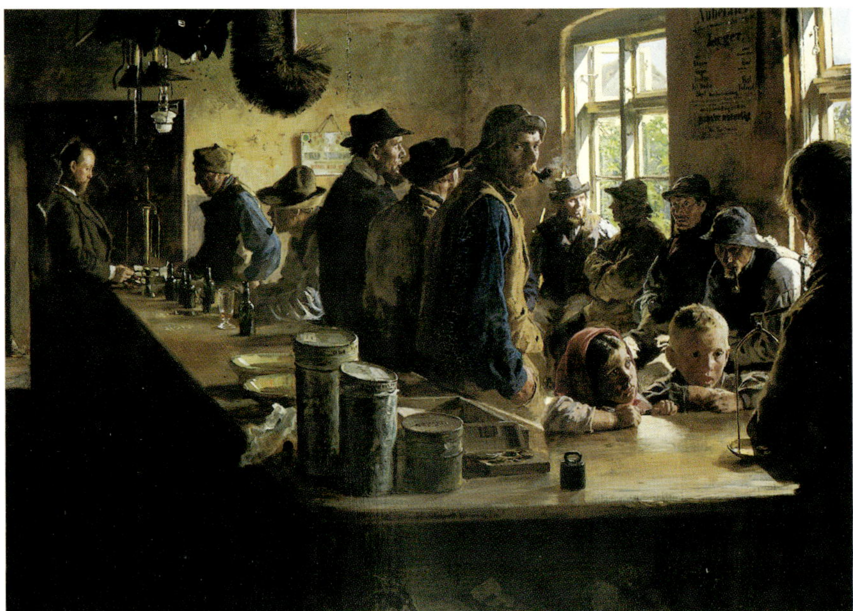

114.
P. S. Krøyer
In the Store During a Pause from Fishing,
1882
Oil on canvas, 31¼ x 43¼ in.
(79.5 x 109.8 cm)
The Hirschsprung Collection,
Copanhagen

back to the window, she is nonetheless warmed by the sunlight, experiencing it tactilely. The shimmering sunlight on the back wall reveals subtle swirls and variations of color and form. Within this rich visual realm sits the aging woman whose quiet suspension of activity is itself an important state of being.[36]

Following a six-month study trip that she and her husband made to Paris in 1888–89, Anna Ancher depicted her grandmother using pastel which she had been inspired to explore after seeing examples of French Impressionist work in that medium. Cropping her grandmother's figure and representing it from a dynamic, oblique perspective, Ancher experimented with the visual formulae of Edgar Degas applied to the closest people in her life.[37] A few years later, following the death of her grandmother and her father, Anna Ancher painted *Sunshine in the Blue Room, Helga Ancher Crocheting in Her Grandmother's Room* (1891; fig. 111), a representation of her eight-year-old daughter Helga (1883–1964) seated in a room that signified family privacy and continuity. This was the room in which Anna's own mother sought solitude when she wasn't attending to her hotel guests. She applied fresh color, unmixed on the palette, side by side in a technique that Ole Wivel describes as pastel application translated into oils, a breakthrough into Impressionism.[38] In the same year, Ancher painted her most ambitious figure painting, *The Funeral* (1891; fig. 112), in which fifteen people are assembled in an interior space, their environment compressed by the low ceiling, raking floor, and deep pink walls. This, like Ancher's other interiors, is a space redolent of psychological presence. What began as Anna's experience of the funeral for Stine Bollerhus (1811–1885), a neighbor who also had served as Anna's model,[39] became an austere and yet coloristically charged rendering of loss, individual and collective. Stine's husband Per stands alone on the left, separated from the rest of the assembly. With the subtlest manipulations of anatomy and gesture, Anna communicates both the religious rituals of a small town and the vacuum left behind in a neighbor's passing.

Anna Ancher's emphasis on scenes from her intimate emotional life and on light as a constructive element in painting in turn shaped her husband Michael's vision. In addition to grand heroic representations of labor and of sublime nature, Michael Ancher began to create

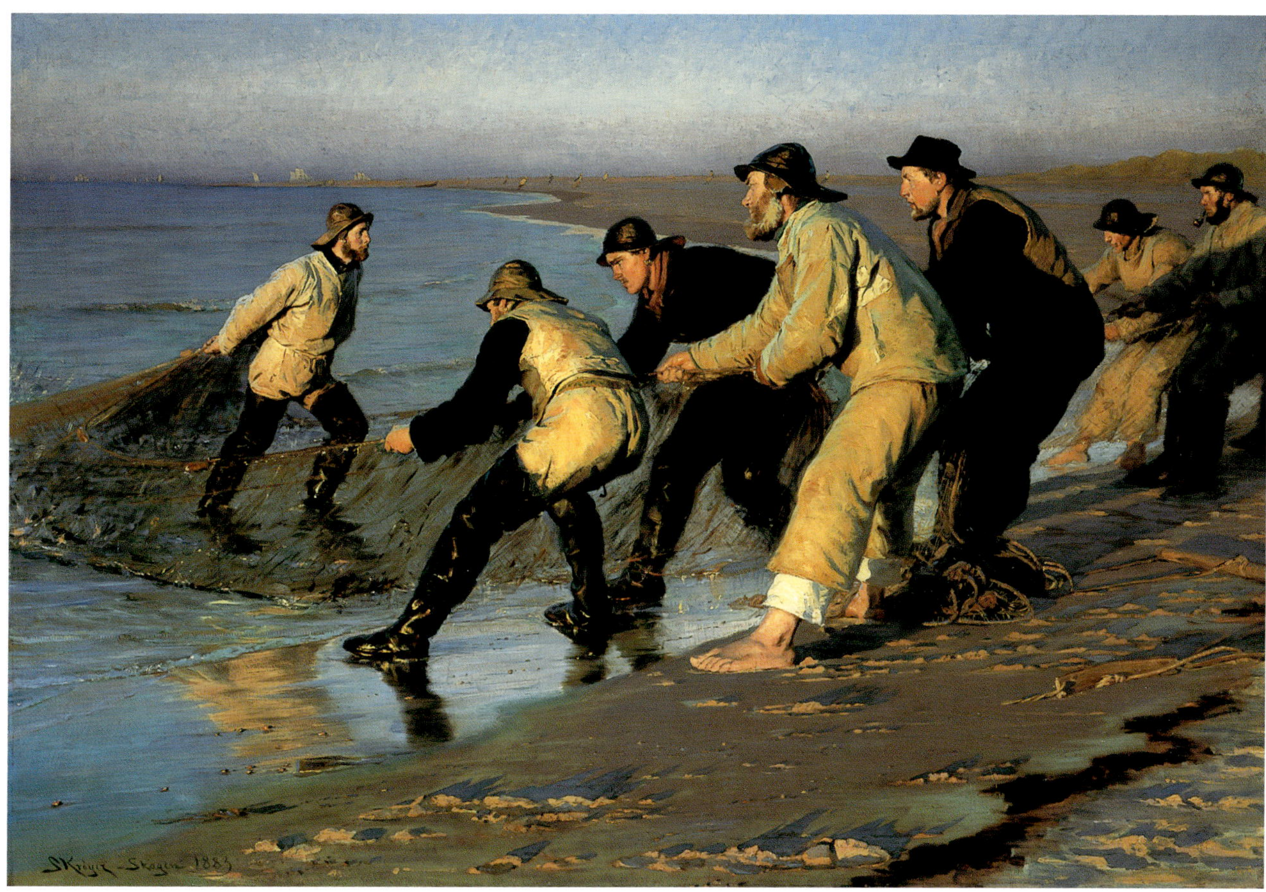

intimate scenes of family and friends, including *The Sick Girl* (1882; fig. 113). The model is Tine Normand, the daughter of a local fisherman and his widow who, bored by illness and convalescence, turns aside her book. The softening of form and intensification of color in this composition also suggest the impact of a trip that the Anchers took to the continent in 1882, where they studied paintings by Johannes Vermeer and the work of French and German Naturalist and Impressionist painters.

They also traveled to Vienna where Michael was exhibiting *Will He Round the Point?* There they met Peter Severin Krøyer who was already well-known as a figure painter. Krøyer became the most internationally admired Danish artist of this generation. Born in Norway to an impoverished mother, Krøyer had been raised by an aunt and uncle in Copenhagen. He attended the Technical High School and the Royal Academy, and he traveled to Holland and then to Paris where he studied in the studio of Léon Bonnat. In 1878, he traveled to Spain where he studied the works of Velázquez. He also traveled to and participated in the artist colonies in Saint-Malo, Pont Aven, and Concarneau in Brittany. Beginning in 1879 Krøyer exhibited in the annual Paris Salon, winning a series of medals throughout the 1880s. He was named a Chevalier in the Legion of Honor in 1887, and he was awarded a gold medal at the World's Fair in Paris in 1900. He first visited Skagen in 1882, where by all accounts he became the life of the artist community, the sunny, extroverted organizer of parties and artists' spectacles. He later settled in Skagen.

115.
P. S. Krøyer
Fishermen Hauling the Net on Skagen's North Beach, 1883
Oil on canvas, 53⅛ x 75 in.
(135 x 190.5 cm)
Skagens Museum

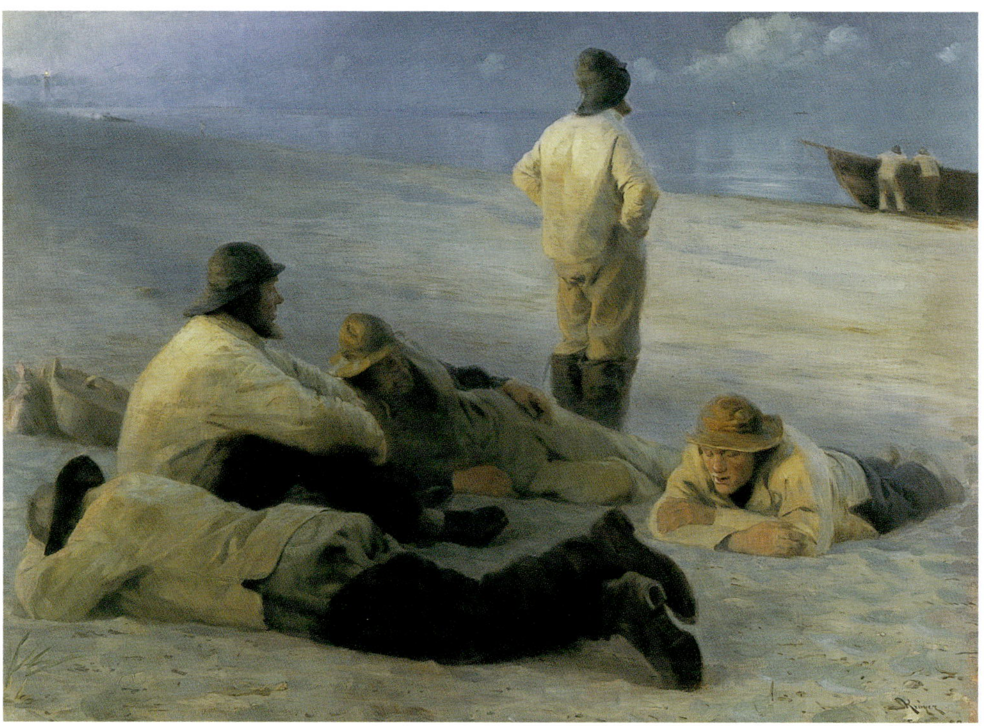

During his first summer in town, Krøyer had sought out both the local fishermen and the large expanse of dazzling white beach as his motifs. His first important painting from Skagen was *In the Store During a Pause from Fishing* (1882; fig. 114), which represents the provisions shop run by the Brøndum family. The darkened interior space is divided by a dynamic L-shaped counter that separates Anna's brother Degn Brøndum, on the left, and their father, on the right, from the fishermen and their families who congregate at the center. All of the figures in the composition are identified.[40] By representing the fishermen and their families idle or engaged in commerce, rather than battling the elements or in their homes, Krøyer violated the heroic or folkish tenor of much of the painting created in Skagen.[41] He also caused Michael Ancher some consternation by having represented the Ancher family's world.[42]

In the following year, Krøyer revisited some of Michael Ancher's favored motifs, producing dynamic views of the fishermen engaged in their labor. These included *Fishermen Hauling the Net on Skagen's North Beach* (1883; fig. 115), which enhances the physical drama of the fishermen's action by using diagonal lines and keyed up color, and *Fishermen on Skagens Beach* (1883; fig. 116), which shows the fisherman at rest, exhausted from their labor. When Krøyer's Skagen paintings were exhibited throughout Europe, they drew increasing numbers of artists to Skagen.[43] In later years, Krøyer represented the beach as a gentle site for the men, women, and children of the fishing community, whom he often represented in the warm mid-summer light to communicate tranquility. In the later paintings, such as *A White Boat at Shoreline. Late Summer Evening* (1895; fig. 117), the artist focused more on formal values—color and the effects of nocturnal light—than on the narratives of labor. Such work in turn shaped Michael Ancher's later paintings of Skagen's beach (fig. 118), in which women's labor and the glowing effects of light and atmosphere became the focal points. Krøyer's *Self-Portrait, Sitting by His Easel at Skagen Beach* (1902; fig. 119) offers a view of the artist as a successful plein-air painter, embellished with jewels

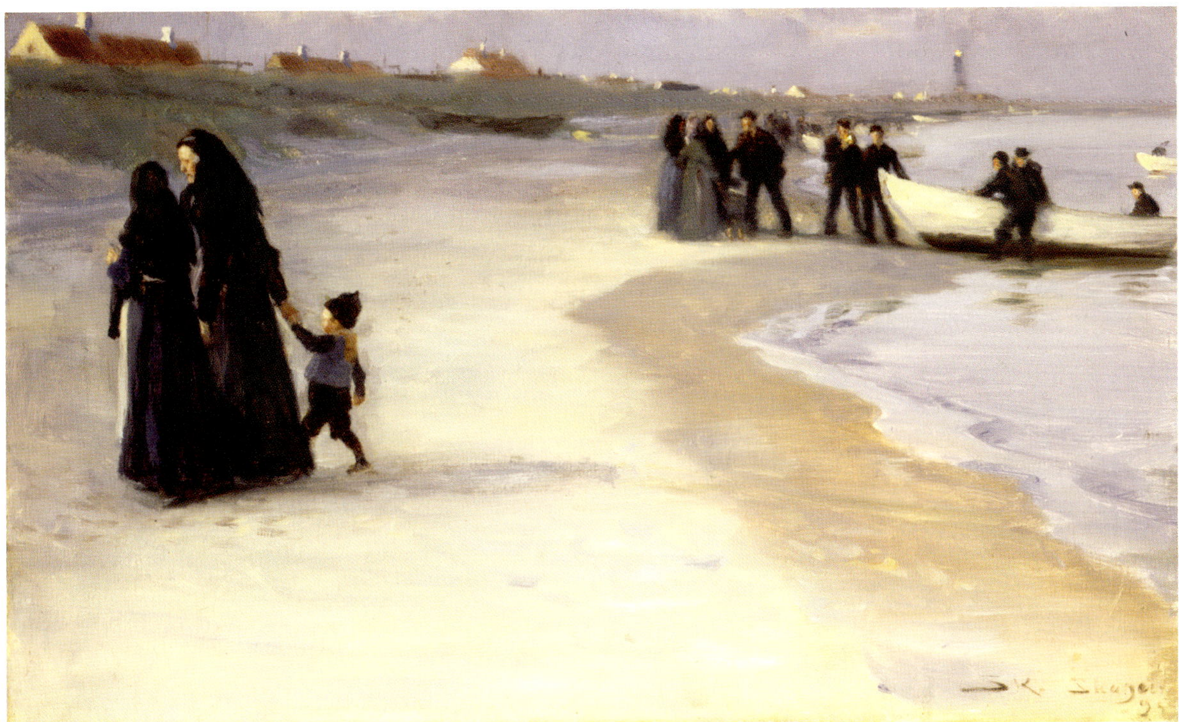

and wearing the white clothing associated with the Life Reform movement. The self-representation demonstrates not only his bravura technique, his commitment to painting out of doors, and his professional success, but also his identification with the location.

By 1883, Krøyer's second summer in Skagen, the artists who summered there had coalesced into a true colony with its own rituals, rhythms, and norms distinct from the town. The author and critic Georg Brandes, who arrived for a visit to Skagen on 19 August 1883, described their milieu: "A group of artists lived or congregated daily at the Brøndum's Hotel, a group in which one felt extremely at ease. . . . The entire company sat from morning to evening around the table at Brøndum's, constantly eating, drinking, debating, discussing, contradicting, damning. A couple of times a day they got up from the table and went for a swim."[44] Krøyer's *Artists' Luncheon in Skagen* (fig. 120), painted in 1883, affirms the camaraderie and shared aesthetic of the group of artists in the Brøndum dining room. Painted with a rapid, ribbon-like touch in diluted oil paint, it suggests a freshness and spontaneity that is allied with Parisian Impressionism. Its vibrant colors and emphasis on the enlivening effects of sunlight on an interior space also suggest the influence of Anna Ancher on Krøyer's work. The painting pictures a pan-Scandinavian gathering of artists, including (clockwise from front left to right), Norwegian painters Charles Lundh (1856–1908), Eilif Peterssen (1852–1928), and Wilhelm Peters (1851–1935), Michael Ancher (standing), Degn Brøndum, the Swedes Johan Krouthén (1858–1938) and Oscar Björck (1860–1929), and Christian Krohg. Several of them would also appear in *Hip, Hip, Hurrah!*[45]

Artists' Luncheon at Skagen was soon installed as a permanent feature in Brøndum's dining room. Throughout the summers, the artists gathered in the Brøndum hotel dining room for nightly parties, which they dubbed their "Evening Academy." That summer, the dining room was transformed by the artists into a gallery to which each artist contributed a self-

117.
P. S. Krøyer
*A White Boat at the Shoreline.
Late Summer Evening*, 1895
Oil on canvas, 16¼ x 26⅛ in.
(41.2 x 66.3 cm)
Skagens Museum

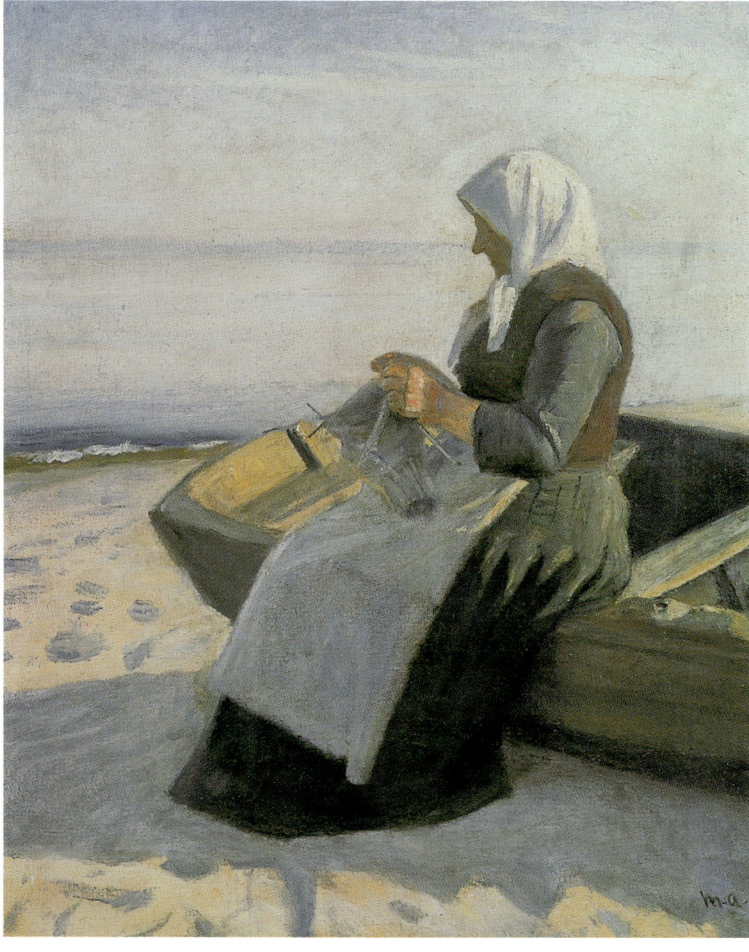

portrait or portraits of each other. During one of the hotel's renovations, Thorvald Bindes-bøll (1846–1908), Denmark's leading Art Nouveau architect (and son of the architect of the Thorvaldsen Museum), redesigned the room as an aesthetic frame for the growing collection of artist portraits. By the 1890s, Bindesbøll had himself joined the Skagen painters' circle, just as his father had done with the Danish painters in Rome (chapter 3).

Krøyer's *Artists on the South Beach at Skagen* (1882, Private Collection), records the sense of shared artistic enterprise during the artist's first years there. South Beach, which Michael Ancher had represented as a site of rural labor and which was described as the staging ground for trag-edy in Holger Drachmann's *Lars Kruse*, is now viewed as an open-air studio. Krohg, Krøyer, and others of their generation practiced open-air painting, insisting upon painting outdoors directly in front of their motifs in order to achieve the freshest impressions of their models and subjects. Open-air painting had been practiced by Eckersberg's generation to create scientific representa-tions of nature and to record a landscape site's atmosphere and mood. Often such works were employed to create more formal paintings later, back in the artists' studios (see chapter 4). In Krøyer's generation, open-air painting, using pigments that approached the clarity of colors in sunlight, offered an immediacy and empathy with the landscape and communicated the artists' own sensory responses to their environment. Open-air painting at Skagen itself became a kind

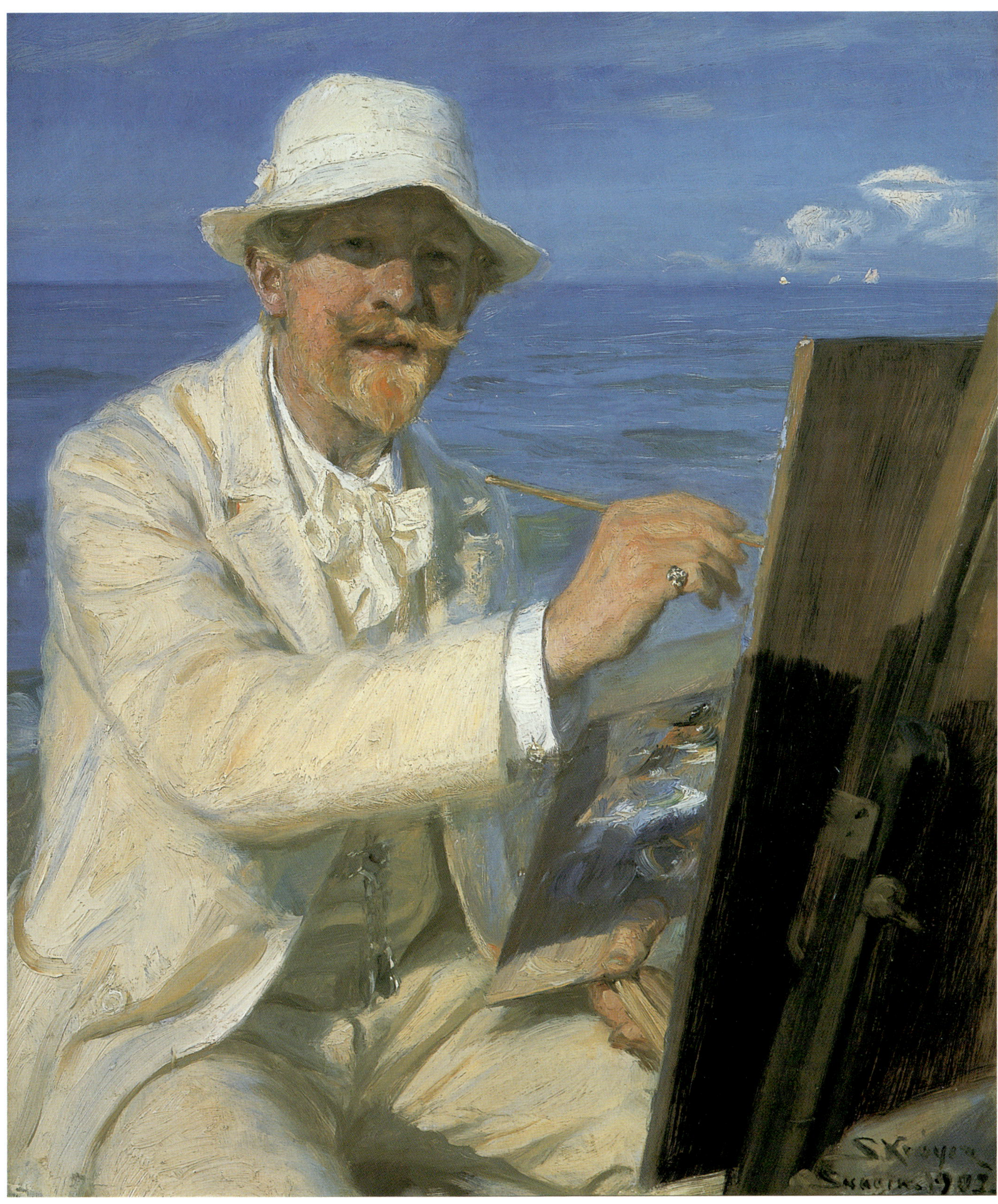

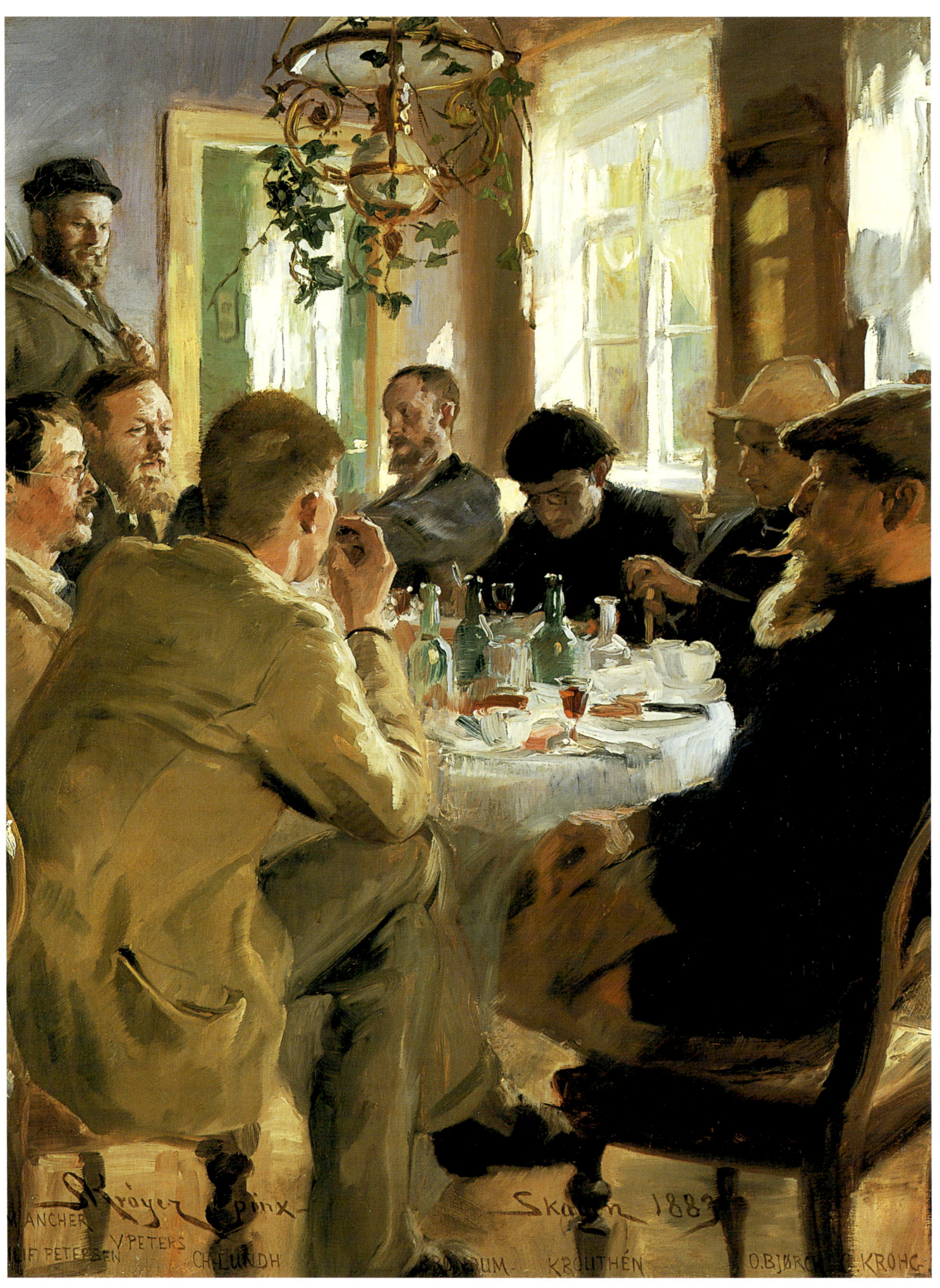

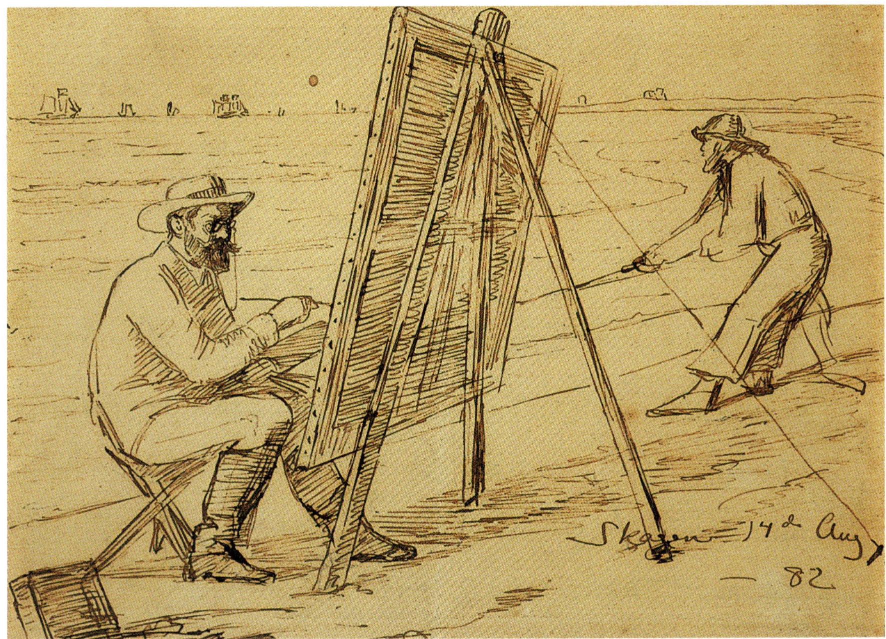

OPPOSITE
120.
P. S. Krøyer
Artists' Luncheon in Skagen, 1883
Oil on canvas, 32¼ x 24 in.
(82 x 61cm)
Skagens Museum

LEFT
121.
P. S. Krøyer
The Artist Painting on the Beach, 1882
Pen and ink on paper, 3⅞ x 5⅜ in.
(9.8 x 13.5 cm)
Skagens Museum

of artistic labor, and the beach became an accustomed arena of both the fishermen and the artists who painted them (fig. 121).

The town provided the opportunity for artists (often newly arrived from study trips to metropolitan centers) to digest new ideas. There, they cultivated their interests in Japanese *ukiyo-e* prints, collected by the Krøyers and analyzed by Madsen,[46] and they explored the potential of photography as an aide-mémoire and as an independent medium with a unique tactile and pictorial idiom.[47] Many of Krøyer's paintings were based on photographs that he took himself, having purchased his first camera in 1885.[48] *Hip, Hip, Hurrah!* was itself modeled in part on photographs of the Skagen artists (but not all of the same characters portrayed in the painting) taken in 1884 by Fritz Stoltenberg, a German marine painter.

The core of this community was represented by Krøyer in *Hip, Hip, Hurrah!*, which he began in 1884, shortly after he, Oscar Björck, and Eilif Peterssen returned to Skagen from a visit to the art colony in Grèz, France. One of the high points of that summer was a house-warming party for the Anchers, who had just moved into the home that they would share for the rest of their lives and that would eventually become their museum. Fritz Stoltenberg (1855–1921) took several photographs of the occasion, inspiring Krøyer to memorialize the party in a painting. Krøyer set up his easel in the Anchers' garden the very next day, but was asked by Michael Ancher to move to a different location to give the Anchers privacy.[49] The setting is consequently not the original party locale, but the Anchers' old garden. Indeed, the painting, which seems to be spontaneous, is an entirely constructed composition, created from numerous studies as Krøyer's models came and went, and as new models appeared that were not part of the original party. The painting represents, from left to right, Martha Møller Johansen, Viggo Johansen, Christian Krohg, Krøyer, Degn Brøndum, Michael Ancher, Oscar Björck, Thorvald Niss, Helene Christensen (at the time Krøyer's girlfriend), Anna Ancher, and Helga Ancher.[50] Helga had been one year old when the party took place and when Krøyer made his initial oil sketches, including the first figure painting of Anna and Helga together

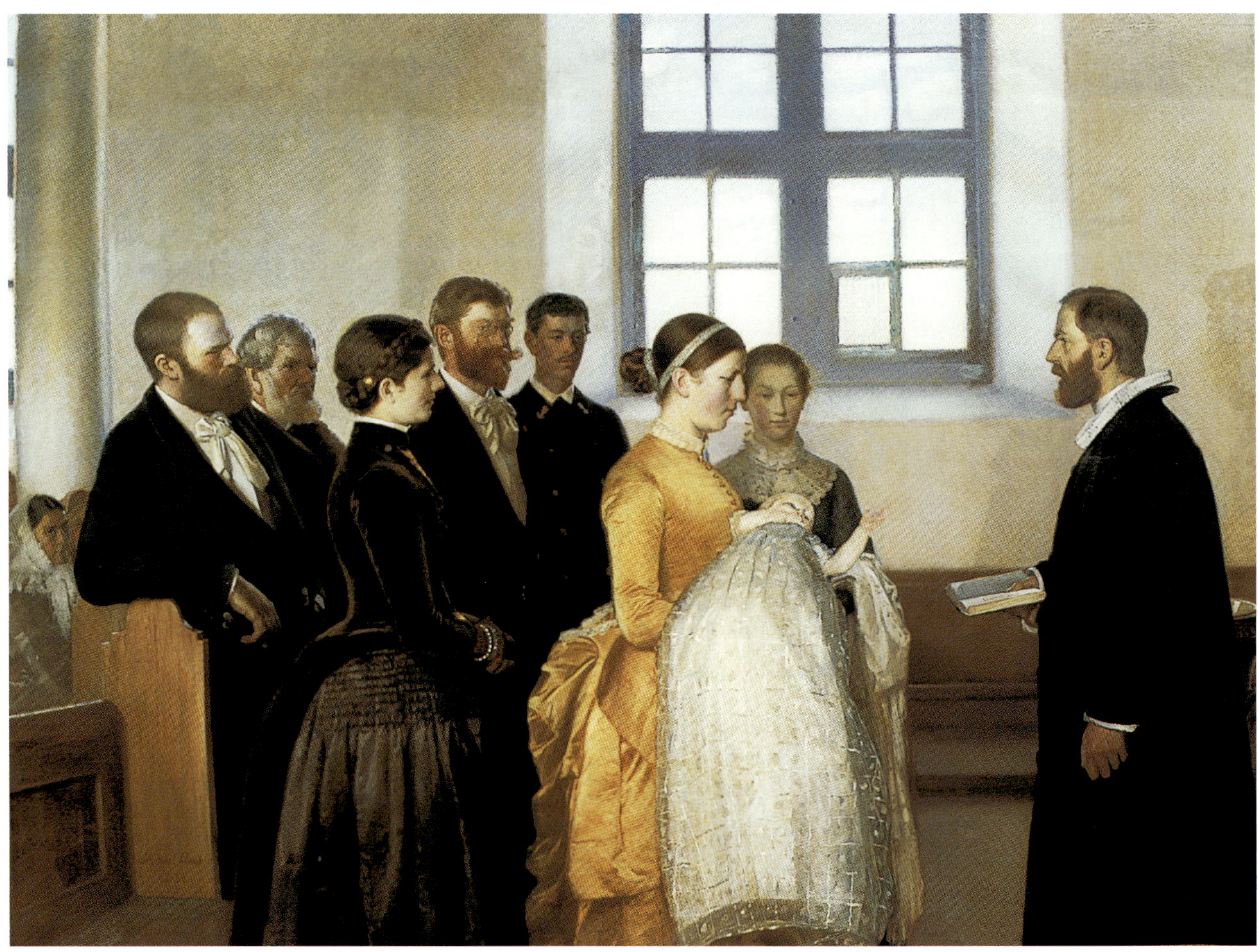

122.
Michael Ancher
A Christening, 1888
Oil on canvas, 73¼ x 98⅜ in.
(186 x 250 cm)
Ribe Kunstmuseum

(Michael and Anna Anchers Hus). Krøyer's four-year struggle to work from live models and to reconstruct and gild the original event, speaks to both the commitment of the painters to paint from nature and to the romance of their community.

At the same time that Krøyer struggled with *Hip, Hip, Hurrah!* Michael Ancher began painting *A Christening*, begun in 1884 and completed in 1888 (fig. 122). The painting is a parallel representation of the art colony, but one inflected with religious ritual and a solemnity reminiscent of old master works. The painting was based on Helga Ancher's christening on 21 October 1883. Anna Ancher holds the infant against her golden dress, her face and body silhouetted in the formal manner of a quattrocento Florentine portrait. Behind Anna Ancher stand Krøyer, Krohg, and Eilif Peterssen, the godfathers. Over the next several years Ancher had to substitute models for the godparents, who were unable to return to Skagen. The British painter Marianne Stokes (1855–1927), who first visited Skagen two years after the christening, is represented as one of the godmothers, standing behind Anna Ancher in the dark dress. Both paintings, exhibited in Denmark and internationally, helped to solidify the modern identity of the Skagen art colony. With young Helga present in both compositions, the artists coalesce as a family.

The growth of the Skagen artist community was part of a larger and new cultural phenomenon in the nineteenth century, the rural art colony, the most famous of which were Barbizon in

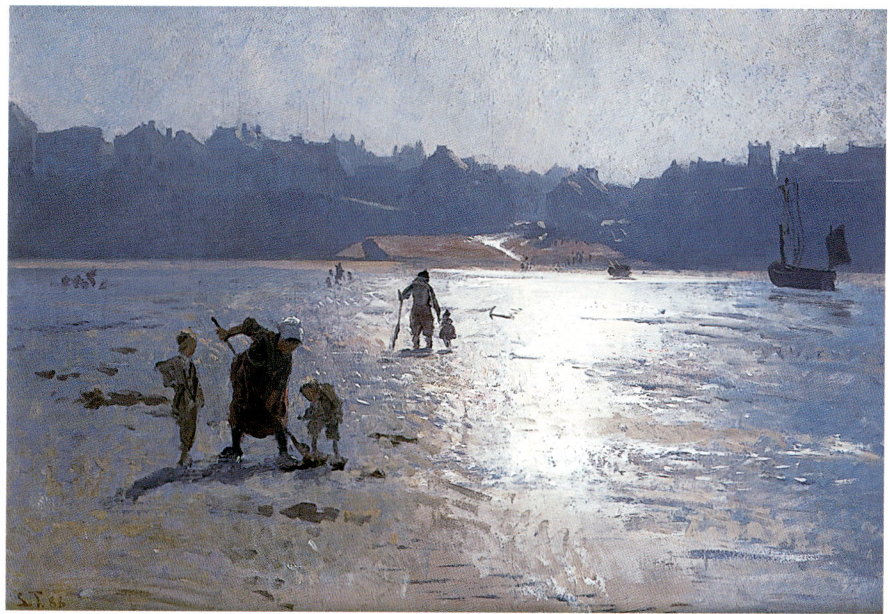

123.
Laurits Tuxen
*Collecting Mussels at Low Tide
at Le Portel, France*, 1888
Oil on canvas on wood, 20⅞ x 29⅛ in.
(53 x 74 cm)
Collection of Ambassador John L. Loeb Jr.,
New York

the mid-nineteenth century and Paul Gauguin's circle at Pont-Aven in the 1880s. Nina Lübbren notes that such communities "hatched some of the most exciting innovations of late nineteenth-century painting and interacted with the concerns of the canonical modernists in unexpected ways."[51] She further observes that nearly 3000 European artists chose to leave urban places, the conventional site of artistic production—with their academies, markets, audiences, material availability, and career opportunities—to participate in rural colonies between 1870 and 1900. Nearly fifteen percent of these artists were women, representing a far greater female participation in professionally acknowledged art-making practices than in cities.[52] Art historian Erik Mørstad observes that such communities also operated as networking opportunities, offering aspiring artists contact with more established artists and critics and their collectors and dealers.[53] There was a strong Nordic presence at the artist communities formed at Grèz-sur-Loing in the 1880s, which Christian Krohg, for example, visited for the first time in 1881. Several of the artists who summered in Skagen also participated in or worked in concert with artist communities in France. Laurits Tuxen (1853–1927), who first visited Skagen in the 1870s, resided in Paris in the 1880s, and traveled to coastal communities to register both the special light and the local fishing populations. His painting *Collecting Mussels at Low Tide at Le Portel, France* (1888; fig. 123) captures the reflection of nocturnal light on wet sand and represents residents of the northern coastal town harvesting the beach. Within these colonies, like Skagen, the formal strategies of various avant-garde groups were aligned with Impressionism. These included a brightened palette, radically cropped forms, and wet paint application, all of which were imbued with a nostalgic or social view of the local population.

The Skagen artists were, in fact, among the first and most influential "Impressionist" painters in Scandinavia. Each summer the artists returned to Skagen fresh from their cosmopolitan sojourns in Paris, Berlin, or London, or time spent in Copenhagen. In the midst of this era of nation building and with a growing sense of the prestige of Denmark's contribution to the arts, a significant group of artists sent their work to the Exposition Universelle in Paris in 1878. The French critics devastated them, criticizing their work as retrograde, provincial, and

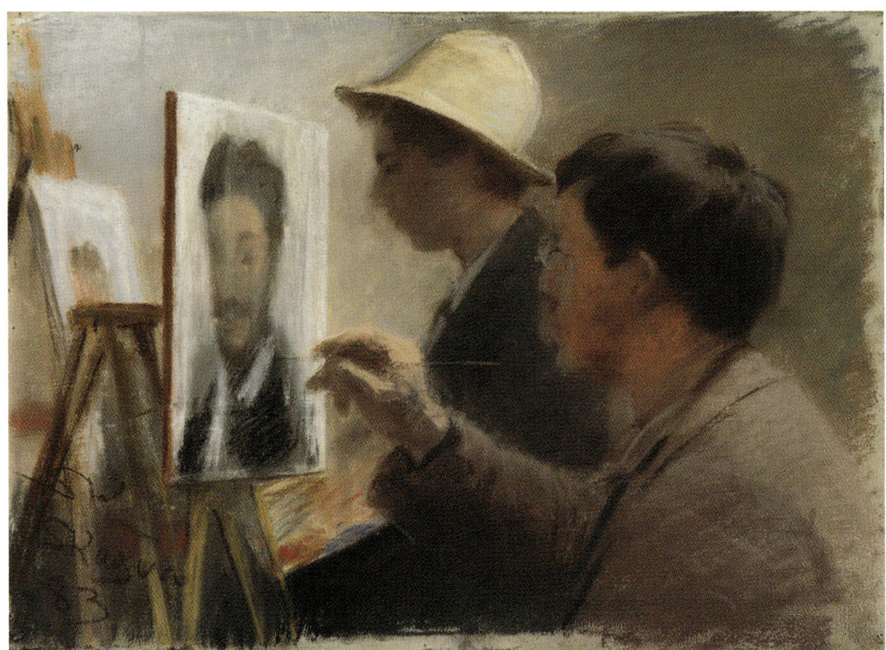

124.
P. S. Krøyer
Oscar Björck and Eilif Peterssen Painting Portraits of Georg Brandes, 1883
Pastel on paper, 12⅝ x 17½ in. (32 x 44.4 cm)
Randers Kunstmuseum

lacking in "motifs." As one critic put it, "Art vegetates in Denmark, lives slightly in Sweden, and doesn't exist at all in Norway."[54] The art historian and critic Julius Lange (1838–1896), who had been N. L. Høyen's student, in turn published an essay in 1879 that helped to reshape a national ethos in the arts. In a lecture entitled "Vor Kunst og Udlandets" (Art in Denmark and Abroad), Lange stated that Danish artists needed to expand beyond the exclusive nationalism of the previous generations, to engage with modern technologies, and to embody modern modes of thought: "What Høyen taught about the relationship between nationality and art is no longer applicable for our time."[55]

Karl Madsen also played a major role in encouraging an international orientation in Danish art. Trained as an art historian as well as a painter in Paris, Madsen had also begun writing professionally in 1881, publishing his writing in the influential Danish newspapers *Dagsavisen*, *Morgenbladet*, *Den ny Tid*, and *Politiken* with the goal of broadening artistic and literary cosmopolitanism. A series of polemical articles published in 1882 helped to encourage a broad interest in the art of the French Impressionists and to identify an Impressionist school in Denmark.[56] His first published book, on Japanese art (1885), had an enormous impact on the Danish artistic community. Moreover, his scholarship on Dutch and Flemish art and on contemporary Danish art shaped a new internationalism in the 1890s.[57]

Perhaps the most influential critical voice for the Skagen artists was that of philosopher and critic Georg Brandes (1842–1927), who was briefly a member of their circle. He was Denmark's strongest advocate for Realism and internationalism in the arts, and for the overthrowing of older romantic formulas. Brandes already knew Christian Krohg and P. S. Krøyer when he first visited Skagen in the summer of 1883. There he became acquainted with the other artists in the circle, posing for several of them (fig. 124).[58] Brandes was one of Denmark's most influential writers and later one of Europe's most complex interpreters of Realist literature and the philosophical writings of Friedrich Nietzsche and Søren Kierkegaard.[59] Brandes's controversial lectures at the University of Copenhagen, delivered in the 1870s, had formed the

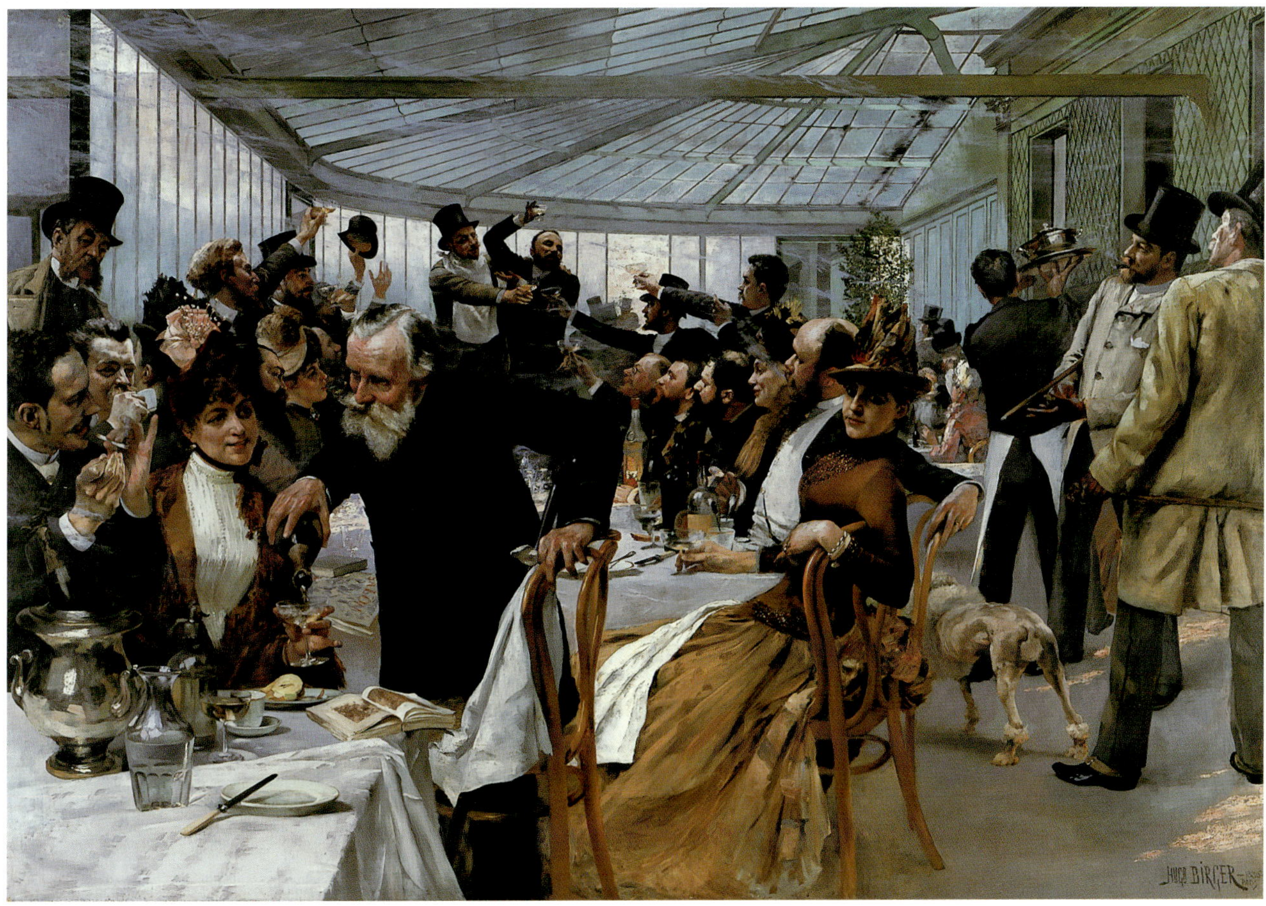

core of his most influential publication, the multi-volume *Main Currents in Nineteenth-Century Literature*. He is credited with both stimulating and identifying "the modern breakthrough" in Scandinavian literature, the Naturalist movement of the 1870s to 1890s that included Henrik Ibsen, August Strindberg, Hermann Bang, and, for a time, Holger Drachmann. A social progressive, he translated John Stuart Mill's *On the Subjection of Women* (1869) into Danish within a year of its publication.[60] Through his writing, Brandes helped to transform the term "modern" from a chronological designation to one indicative of ideology, suggesting a fusion of advanced thought and literary activity throughout Europe into a generational "breakthrough."[61] His subjectivist interpretation of nature and Naturalism mirrored and shaped the Skagen artists' approach to landscape and genre painting. In turn, Brandes promoted the modernism of the Skagen artists, writing in 1899, "We note that in the last generation, Denmark has produced, among others, an original and significant school of painting. It is no less significant than the German school and in the opinion of some, it towers above it. Indeed, show me German painters of this generation who are better than Krøyer, [Kristian] Zahrtmann, Viggo Johansen, [Michael] Ancher, Hammershøi, Joakim Skovgaard, or woman painters with the gift of color such as Anna Ancher or the poetic originality of Agnes Slott-Møller?"[62]

In the 1880s, reacting both to the harsh criticism of the Parisian critics in 1879, and inspired by advocates of modern international artistic currents, many of the Skagen artists, among them the Anchers, began to seek advanced training in Paris. Through their study in

125.
Hugo Birger
Scandinavian Artists' Luncheon at Café Ledoyen, on Varnishing Day 1886, 1886
Oil on canvas, 72¼ x 103 in. (183.5 x 261.5 cm)
Göteborgs Konstmuseum

academic and avant-garde studios (Anna studied under Pierre Puvis de Chavannes [see chapter 6] in association with Alfred-Philippe Roll's studio in 1888–89), their literary contacts, and participation and attendance in exhibitions, the Scandinavians gained valuable knowledge of French and international avant-garde art and ideas. Regardless of the success of their work with critics and patrons, the Scandinavian artists in Paris recorded their experience as a romanticized vie bohème. The Swedish painter Hugo Birger (1854–1887) captured the community's esprit de corps in his 1886 *Scandinavian Artists' Luncheon at Café Ledoyen, on Varnishing Day 1886* (fig. 125) on the eve of the Salon of that year. Hanna Rönnberg, who accompanied the Anchers to Paris in 1888, reports that the Scandinavians, including the Anchers, Krøyer, J. F. Willumsen, Anna Petersen, and Norwegians Kitty Kielland and Erik Werenskiold, met every Thursday at the Café de la Regence. It was here that Krøyer first noticed his future wife, the painter Marie Triepcke (1867–1940).[63]

Triepcke was a member of Copenhagen's upper bourgeoisie, born of German parents. A highly educated and ambitious woman, her greatest desire was to become an artist. As represented in a portrait by Bertha Wegmann (1847–1926), a mentor to Triepcke in the mid-1880s, the young artist appears in a garden setting, holding not the tools of her desired profession, but the accoutrements of an elegant young bourgeois woman (fig. 126). Wegmann was an accomplished and sought-after portraitist and genre painter who mentored younger artists, especially women. Because the Danish Academy was closed to women in the 1860s, Wegmann had studied in Munich, debuted in the Charlottenborg in 1875, and then traveled to Paris in 1881.[64] She began to exhibit at the Paris Salon, receiving a gold medal in 1882. At a time when it was difficult for women to receive academic training on a par with men, Wegmann, Krøyer, Kyhn, and several other Danish artists opened classes to female students in Copenhagen (see chapter 6). They also encouraged these women to study art in Paris. A pioneer in both technique and in institution building, she served on the governing body of the Drawing School for Women from 1887 to 1907.[65] Marie Triepcke later recalled modeling for this painting—whose loose, staccato touch reflects Wegmann's interest in advanced French art—and confessing to Wegmann her desire to become a professional artist.[66]

Marie Triepcke was herself an institution builder. She studied first in Copenhagen at Carl Thomsen's private school for women. In early 1885, she, Agnes Rambusch (later Slott-Møller), and several other women founded "Den Lille Malerskole" (The Little Painting School) in Copenhagen, where Tuxen and Krøyer briefly visited to make "corrections." This was the forerunner to the Danish Academy's "School of Art for Women," which opened in 1888.[67] In addition to her career as a painter, Marie participated in a circle of progressive and emancipated women in Copenhagen, including those who organized the first pan-Nordic Women's Conference in 1888. Among Triepcke's closest friends and colleagues was the painter Agnes Slott-Møller (see chapter 6). Marie and Agnes are pictured by Agnes's new husband, Harald Slott-Møller in 1888 in *Summer Day* (fig. 127), when the artists spent part of a summer together on southeastern Jutland. Triepcke then traveled to Paris where she entered the studios of Gustave Courtois and Alfred-Philippe Roll, and then worked with Pierre Puvis de Chavannes who was popular with Scandinavian women artists, including Anna Ancher. She represented herself in a dramatically lit, brooding image whose touch is indebted to Édouard Manet and his circle (fig. 128). The strength of her ambition and her historical self-consciousness may be gleaned from her diary on her first day of classes in Paris:

126.
Bertha Wegmann
A Young Woman, Marie Triepcke, Sitting in a Boat, ca. 1884
Oil on canvas, 50x 42⅛ in.
(127 x 107 cm)
Collection of Ambassador John L. Loeb Jr.,
New York

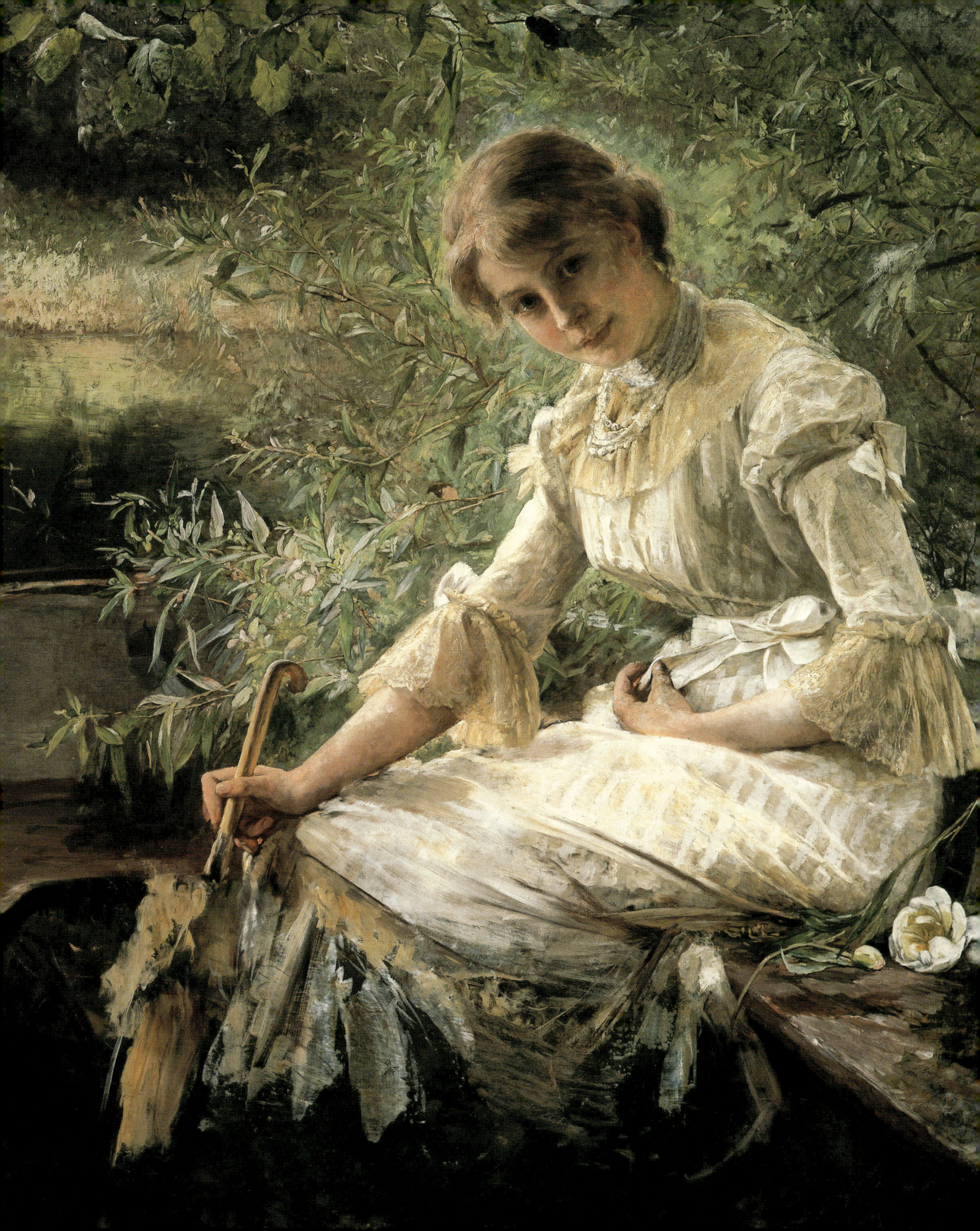

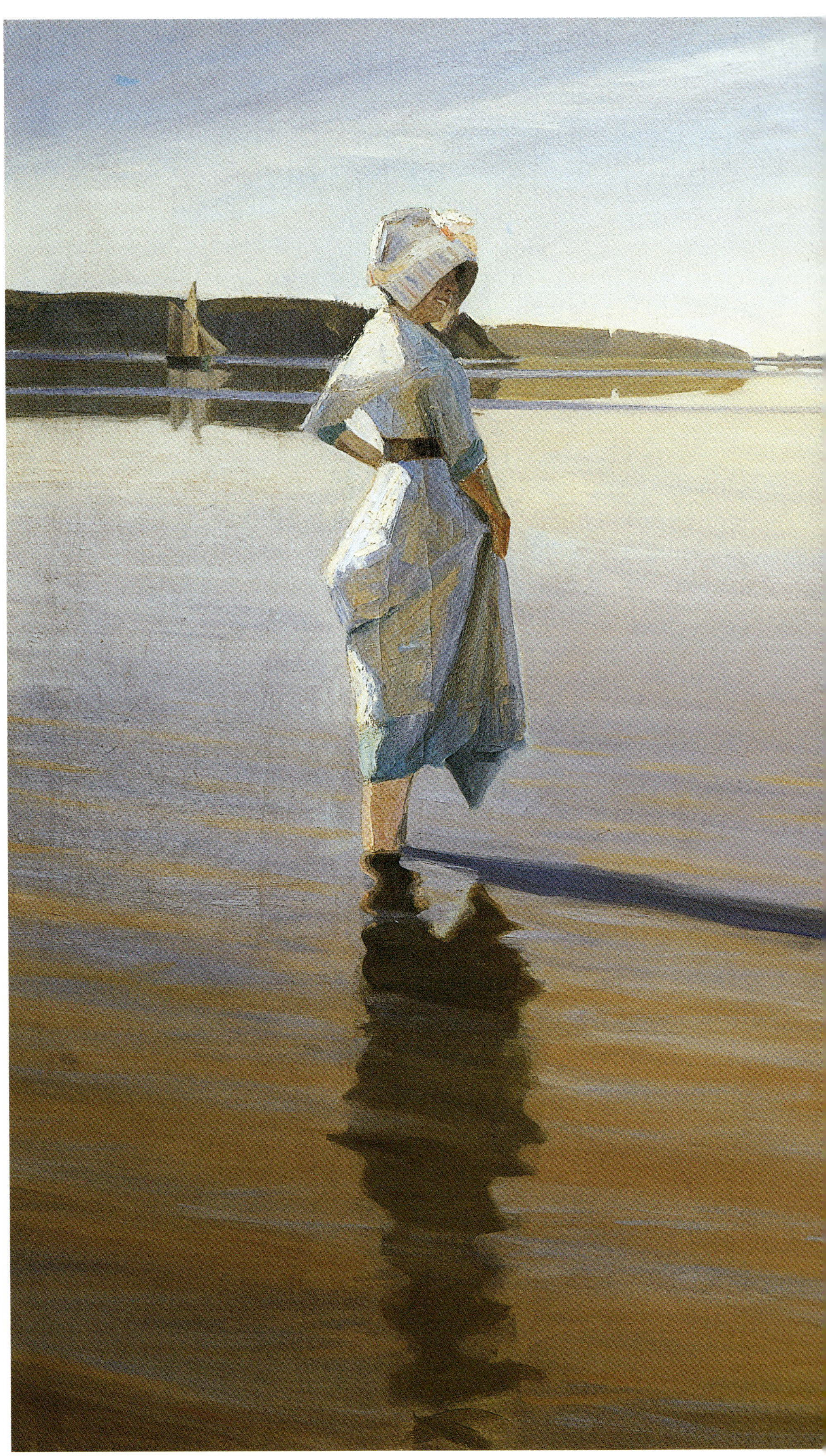

127.
Harald Slott-Møller
Summer Day, 1888
Oil on canvas, 48⅜ x 70⅛ in.
(123 x 178 cm)
Collection of Ambassador John L. Loeb Jr.,
New York

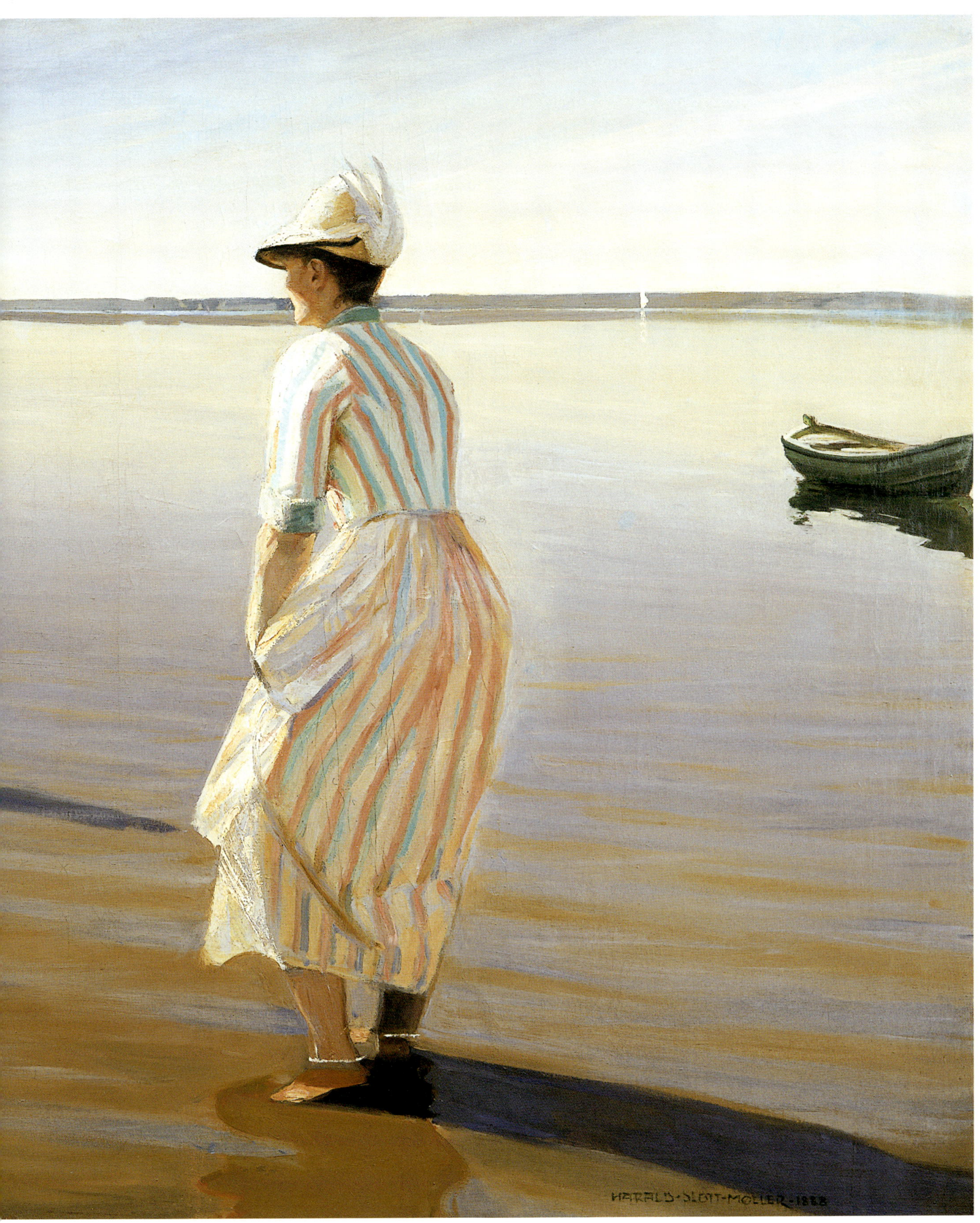

HARALD·SLOTT-MØLLER·1888

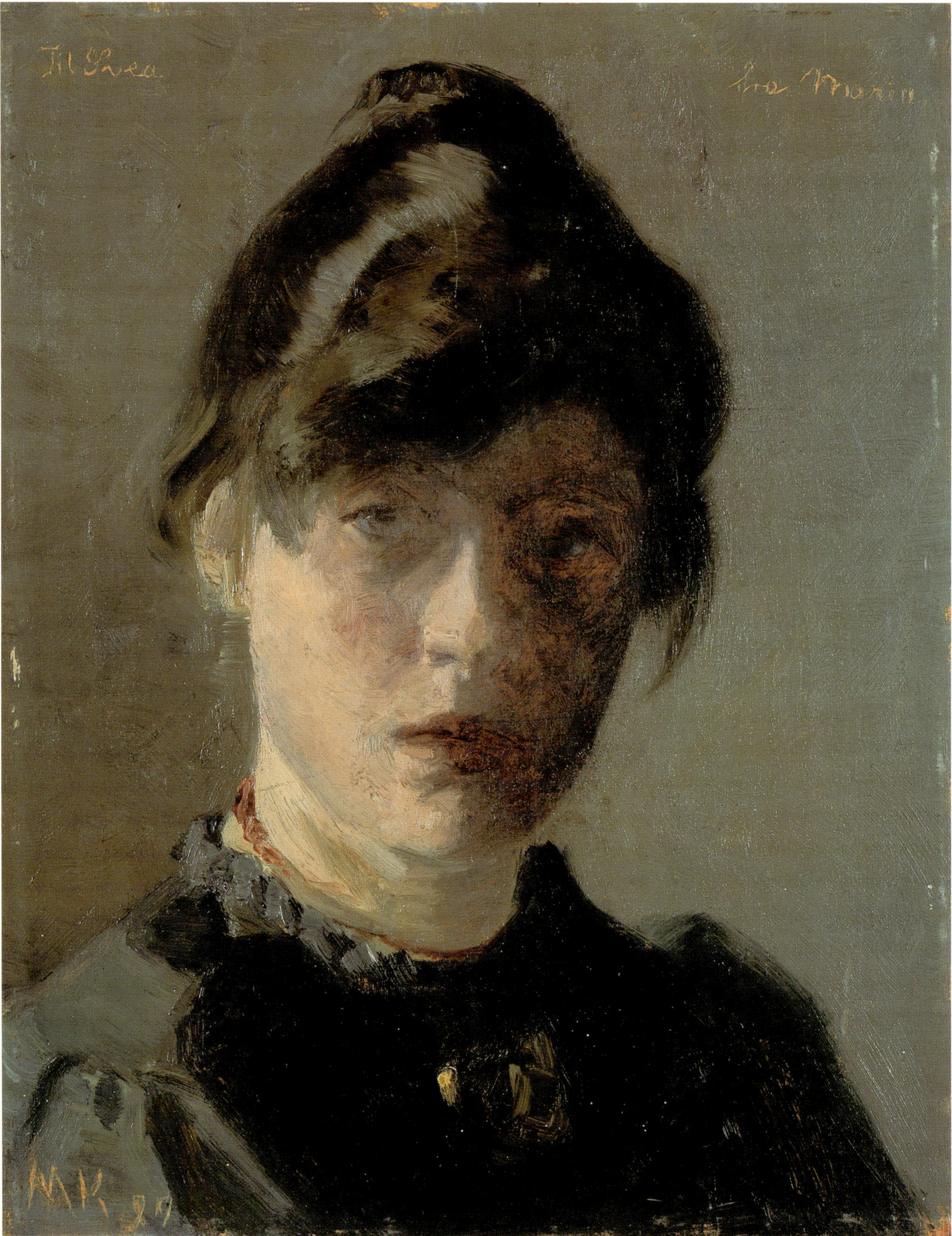
Til Svea.
Ira. Marie
MK 84

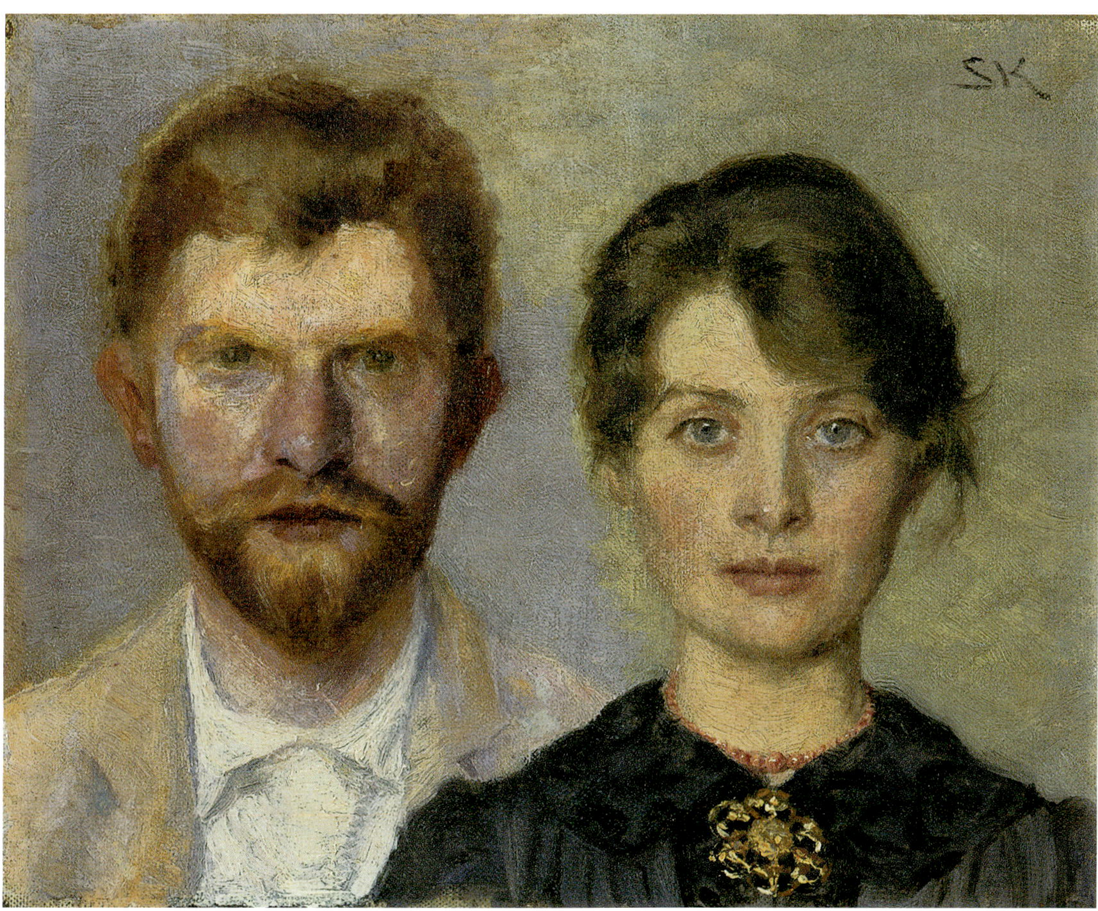

I become melancholy when I think [of woman painters] . . . I sometimes think everything is so futile, I have far too much to overcome, too much to struggle with, so much inherited misery . . . What would it really matter if I paint, what use. I will never, ever attain anything great, unfortunately it only becomes more and more apparent that we and our generation are destined to be nothing but cannon fodder to make a breach, we must hope that all our sufferings and struggles may really weigh down the scales and facilitate the way for the next to come. I am not naive enough to believe that we will reach the goal and reach the level of men, but it must come. . . . I will believe in our cause, even if it sometimes will be dreadfully hard. [68]

The Scandinavian women studying in Paris lived as a subculture within a subculture.[69] Women often lived together, accompanied each other to class, and traveled in groups to copy paintings at the Louvre. Regardless of the studio in which they were studying, women were not allowed to be alone with their painting masters, and therefore often painted side-by-side, in closer contact with one another than their male counterparts were. The working conditions in Paris were reported by Scandinavian women to be inferior—over-crowding, marginal working hours, and often irregular appearances by their teachers characterized their days. In 1889, when Marie began her studies, the progressive Académie Julian had 600 students enrolled in

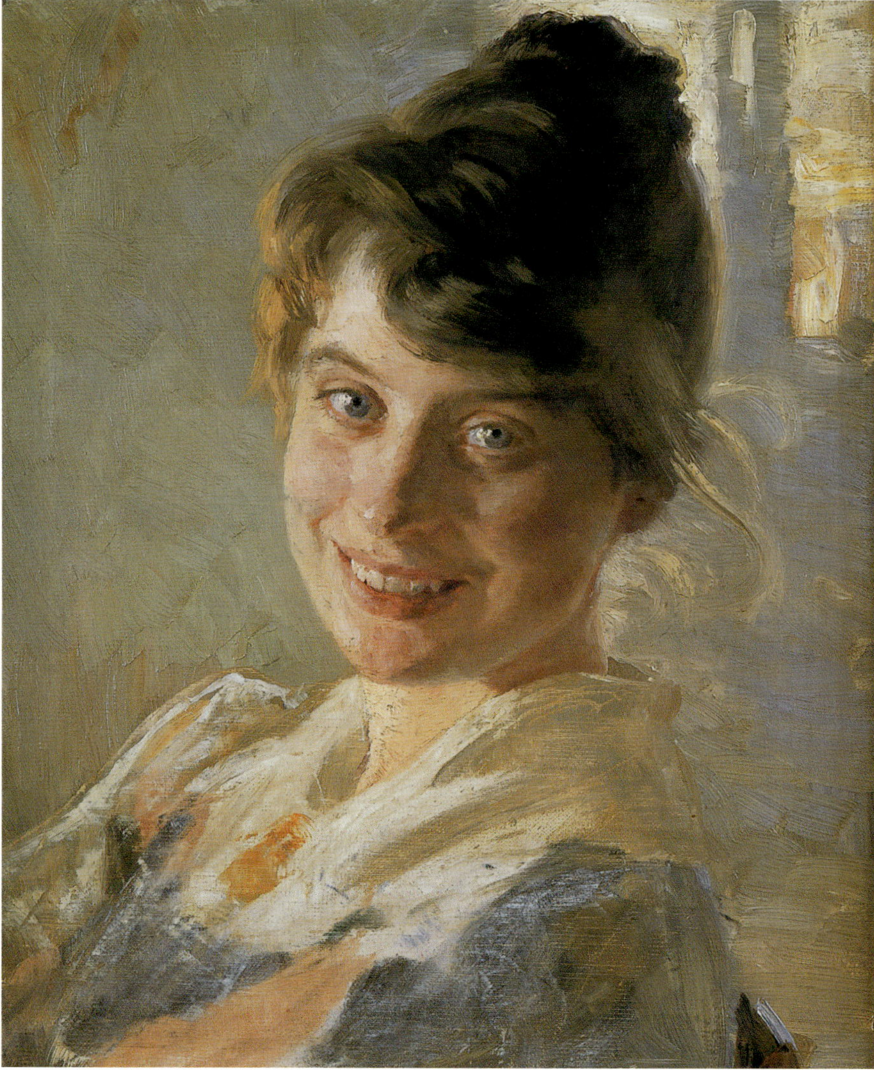

many locations around Paris; only three of those ateliers were reserved for the large population of women students.[70] Moreover, the women students paid higher fees for enrollment than their male colleagues. Many were treated as amateurs who would disappear into marriage and motherhood, as Vilhelm Kyhn had advised Anna Ancher to do. Comparing their experiences with those of their male colleagues, the Nordic women in Paris recognized that the institutional biases militating against their success in Paris were equal to their homelands, but that the opportunities were far greater.[71]

Marie married P. S. Krøyer later in 1889.[72] In a double portrait from 1890 (fig. 129), the two artists painted one another, Marie Krøyer representing her husband with a feathery touch, brooding like her own self-portrait from the previous year. By this time her work had fallen under the influence of French Symbolist painter Eugène Carrière, noted for his nocturnes and indistinct touch. In contrast, Krøyer represented Marie with great clarity and facility, illuminating her even, symmetrical features as fully as possible to emphasize her beauty. The distance between Marie Triepcke's vision of herself and Krøyer's vision of her was wide, and premoni-

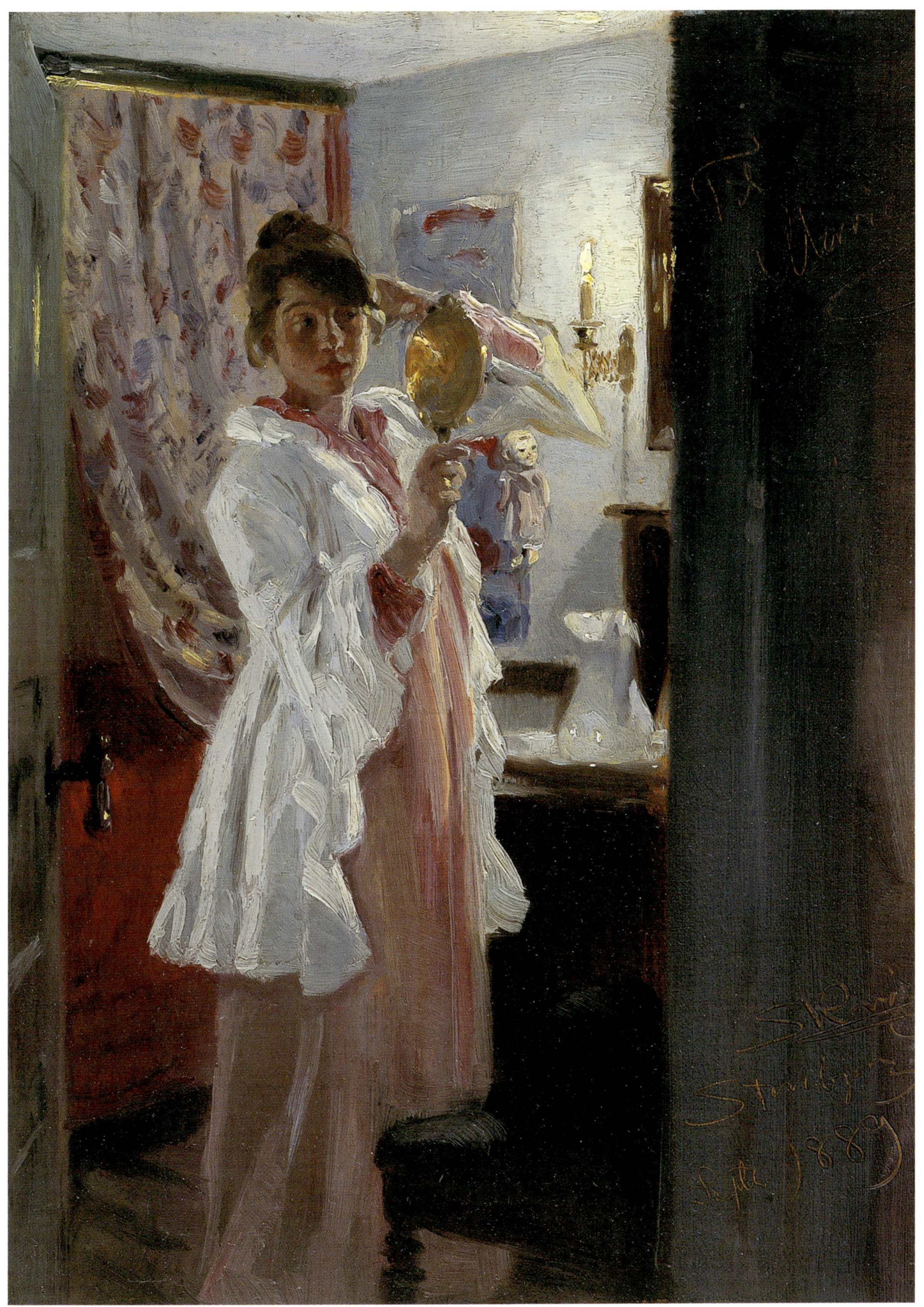

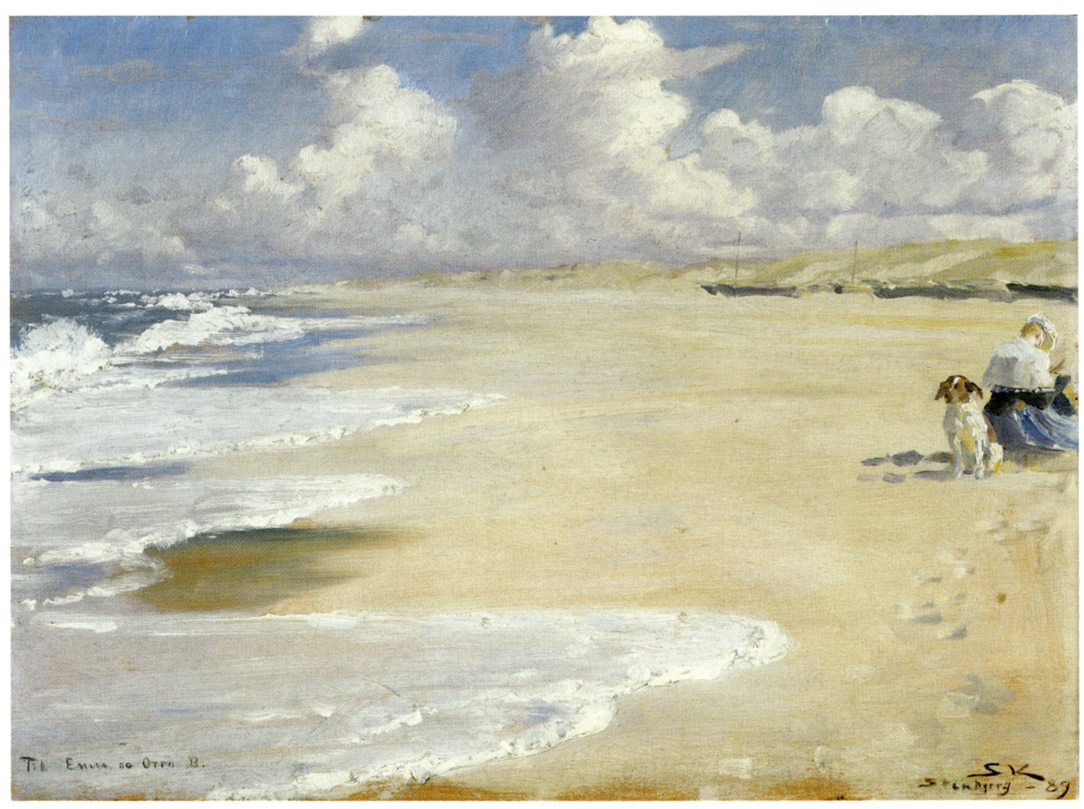

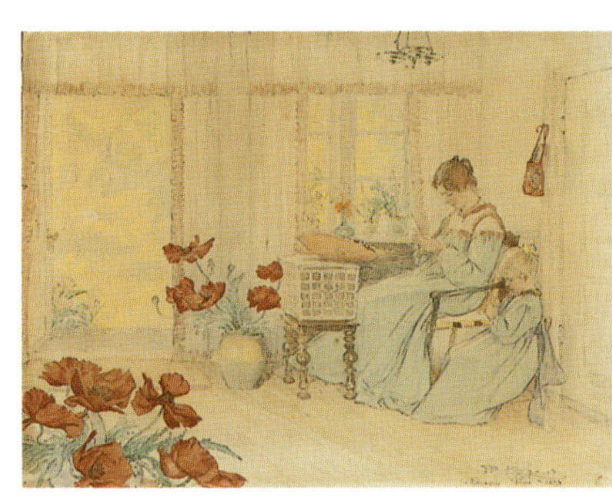

tory. From the beginning of their marriage, one of P. S. Krøyer's chief motifs was Maria (fig. 130)—Marie in the privacy of their boudoir (fig. 131) and at work behind her easel on the beach at Skagen (fig. 132). In a pattern true of many women artists of her generation, Marie Krøyer's output as an artist dwindled following her marriage, and there are fewer than two dozen canvases that can be attributed to her as she became his model and muse.

However, she was one of the pioneers of the Danish arts-and-crafts movement. In 1895, she gave birth to the couple's only child, a daughter, and for the next decade Triepcke, the youthful emancipated woman, pursued a different brand of feminism, closer to the maternalist feminism of the Swedish progressive and educator Ellen Key (1849–1926).[73] In a letter to Agnes Slott-Møller, she quoted from John Keats's "Ode on a Grecian Urn" (a rallying point for the British Aesthetic Movement): "Beauty is truth (sic) —that is all ye know on earth and all ye need to know."[74] She decorated the interiors of the Krøyers' homes in Skagen and Copenhagen in a manner echoing that of the English arts-and-crafts theorist William Morris,[75] wore Reform clothing, designed furniture for her friends, and funneled her energies into domestic design (fig. 133). In this way, she helped to establish a partnership between painting and the functional arts, and between art and daily life, which became significant movements in 1890s Denmark (see chapter 6).[76] After the turn of the century, she divorced her husband and married the Swedish composer Hugo Alfvén (1872–1960).[77]

Anna Brøndum Ancher and Marie Triepcke Krøyer had become close friends and artistic colleagues in Paris before Marie married, and the two remained intimate friends throughout their many summers in Skagen. In 1893, P. S. Krøyer painted them strolling together in

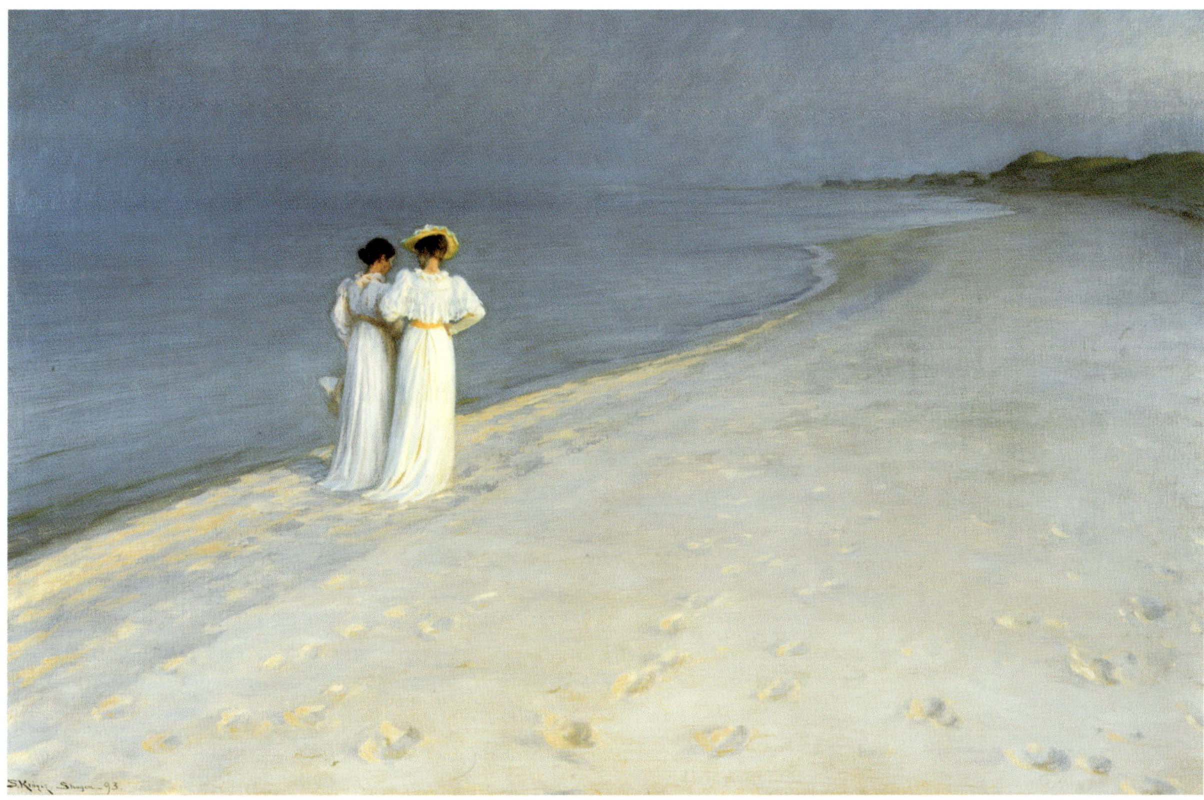

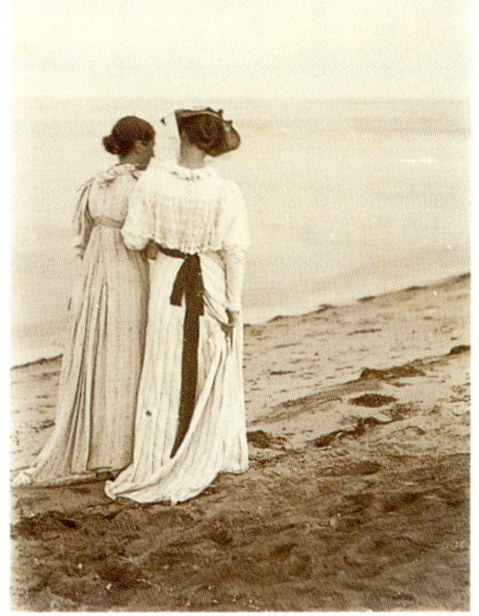

Summer Night on the South Beach at Skagen (fig. 134), one of the most famous images from the Skagen colony. As Krøyer and others report, the Krøyers, the Anchers, and several friends had moved the remnants of a celebratory dinner to the beach. The two women broke away from the group to stroll on the beach and P. S. Krøyer was inspired to paint them. He subsequently posed the women and took at least two photographic studies of them (fig. 135), which he used as the basis of the painting. Throughout the summer of 1893, as he reported, he struggled with the motif, experimenting with the placement of the two women on the shore and with the key of the color palette. Rather than work directly on the beach, Krøyer remained in his studio until he arrived at the final, large version of the painting. This he painted quickly late in the summer.

Far from the untamable environment described in tourist literature, the painting represents the beach becalmed in the blue light of a summer night. The last warm rays of the sun pool in the footprints dotting the sand and gild the women's pale dresses. To the left, sea and sky dissolve into a continuous medium, and to the right, the elliptical shoreline encloses the women. The artist's decision to paint the scene in the unstable blue light of a midsummer evening is in part due to his exposure to the work of American artist James McNeill Whistler (1834–1903), one of the most influential figures among Scandinavians in the late nineteenth century. Critical

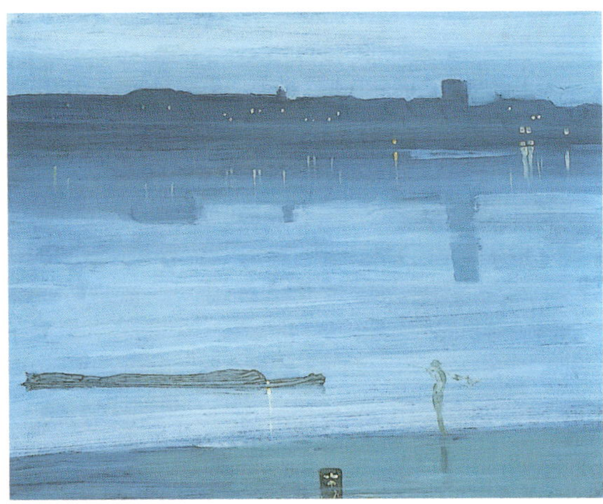

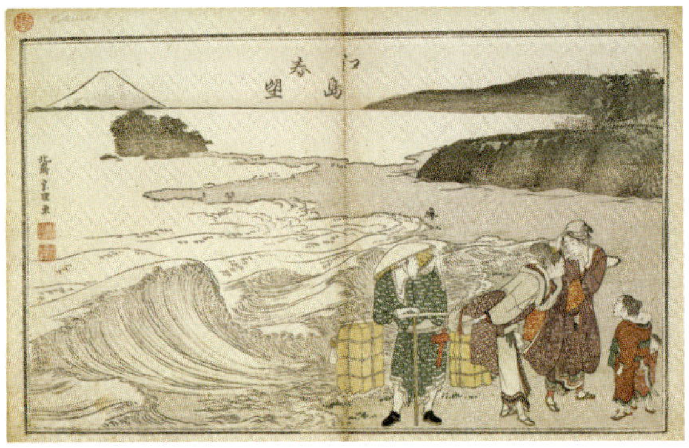

to the development of Krøyer's and many Scandinavian artists' visions were Whistler's nocturnes, such as *Nocturne: Blue and Silver—Chelsea* (1871; fig. 136), in which the tight tonal and value structure representing an evening atmosphere obscures local detail and operates as the abstract equivalent of music.[78] Here, even the density of working London dissolves in the evening light, as the air itself becomes more palpable as the light fades (see chapter 6).

All of these artists had in turn studied and extracted ideas from Japanese *ukiyo-e* prints, woodcut prints on paper that had begun to enter, and then flood, the French market with the opening of Yokohama in 1868. Krøyer's oblique view of Skagen's South Beach, with its sand dunes curving into the water, even reflects Katshushika Hokusai's (1760–1849) landscape formulae (fig. 137), suggesting the multiple dynamic points where the land and water meet as their partition zigzags across the surface, and the point at which land, water, and sky dissolve on the elevated horizon.[79] As collectors of Japanese art and memorabilia, the Krøyers maintained a home and studio in Skagen that held within it examples of advanced artistic culture in urban Europe, including Japanese prints.[80]

This painting registers a transformation in Krøyer's work in the 1890s, when he began to practice a more emotive and abstracted form of painting allied with Symbolism (see chapter 6). The profoundly reduced, decorative character of the painting, and the presence of the elegantly clad women, transform Skagen's South Beach from its daily utilitarian character into a realm of languid desire and nostalgia—for summer, for the artists' community, and for the quiet of the beach. Indeed, in the summer of 1893 the beach was anything but silent.

Between Hans Christian Andersen's call for artists to visit Skagen in the 1850s and the summer evening in 1893 that Marie and Anna strolled the beach, Skagen had become a tourist destination. In the mid-1870s, when Michael Ancher first arrived, guidebooks listed the Brøndum Hotel as the town's sole hostelry. By the turn of the century, Karl Baedeker's handbook of Scandinavia listed several hotels, including a bathing hotel. Indeed, Baedeker refers to Skagen both as Denmark's "chief fishing port" and as "a favorite sea-bathing place."[81] In the summer of 1890, the first railway had opened, replacing the charming but unreliable mail cart described by Hanna Rönnberg, and had become the conveyance of choice for summer pleasure seekers. Michael Ancher had played a key public role in promoting the railroad. The opening celebration of the Skagen line was reported throughout Denmark, including descriptions of the picturesque quality of the train (the little "doll train").[82] Within a short time, Skagen began to attract members of the bourgeoisie from all over Denmark. After noting that tourists were drawn to the shores for therapeutic bathing in the early and mid-1890s, some savvy local investors built and opened Skagen's first bathing hotel in 1898. A second bathing hotel opened in 1905. Both were geared to the wealthy tourists who had followed the painters to Skagen. Articles published in Denmark and Germany in the 1880s and early 1890s promoting Skagen's "unspoiled, primitive" town, beaches, and waters that had first attracted sea bathers. By the turn of the century, the bathhouses could offer: "Denmark's most international bathing. The water has a 2.5% salt concentration, strong wave action, and warm sea baths."[83]

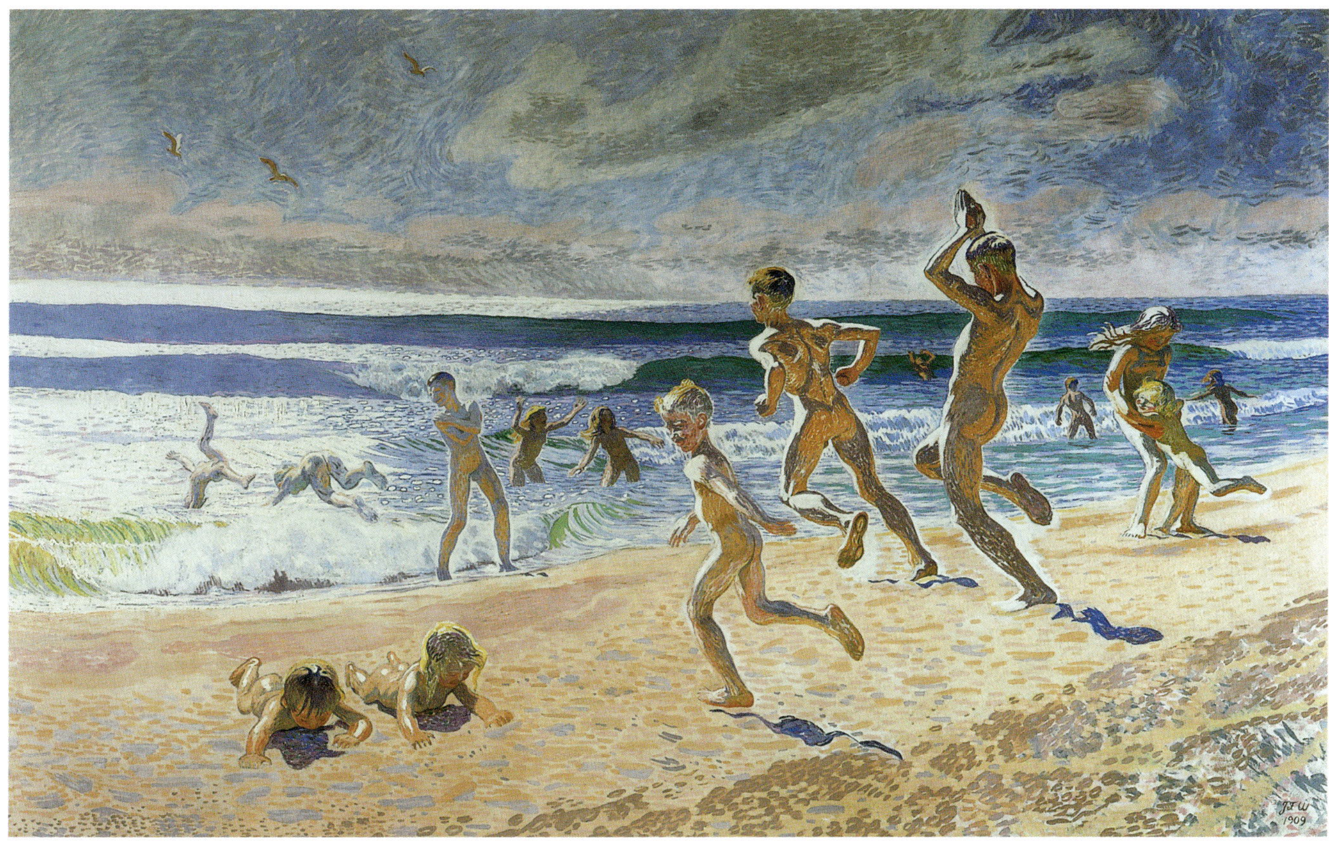

When the bathing hotels opened in Skagen, they became part of a tourist infrastructure that is now the economic base of the town. The deepwater port was excavated in 1907, and warehouses to prepare and package fish were designed and built by Thorvald Bindesbøll. Within a few years of the hotels' establishment, the first museum had opened, displaying detritus from shipwrecks. Later, the homes of the Skagen artists would become museums themselves. As Krøyer struggled with his motif in the summer of 1893, Skagen's South Beach was moving from a site of labor to one of leisure and sybaritic pleasures. This emerging culture in Skagen is recorded in J. F. Willumsen's *Sun and Youth* from 1909 (fig. 138), painted in part on South Beach. As we shall see, in the 1890s and after Danish artists of the avant-garde, such as Willumsen, began to conceive of nature in a fundamentally different manner from their predecessors, as a site of exaltation and mystery.

Summer Night on the South Beach at Skagen is a scene of evanescence, representing a place in uneasy transformation, the artist whose toil with his motif would presage larger struggles, and, finally, the two women artists, walking arm in arm, whose paths were already diverging. In turn, it was the painters, their images such as this and *Hip, Hip, Hurrah!* and their homes preserved as museums, that transformed the remote fishing village—"one of the wildest and most desolate on earth"—into one of the most significant sites of artistic production and mythologizing in late nineteenth-century Scandinavia.

138.
J. F. Willumsen
Sun and Youth, 1909
Oil on canvas, 104⅜ x 167⅜ in.
(265 x 425 cm)
Skagens Museum

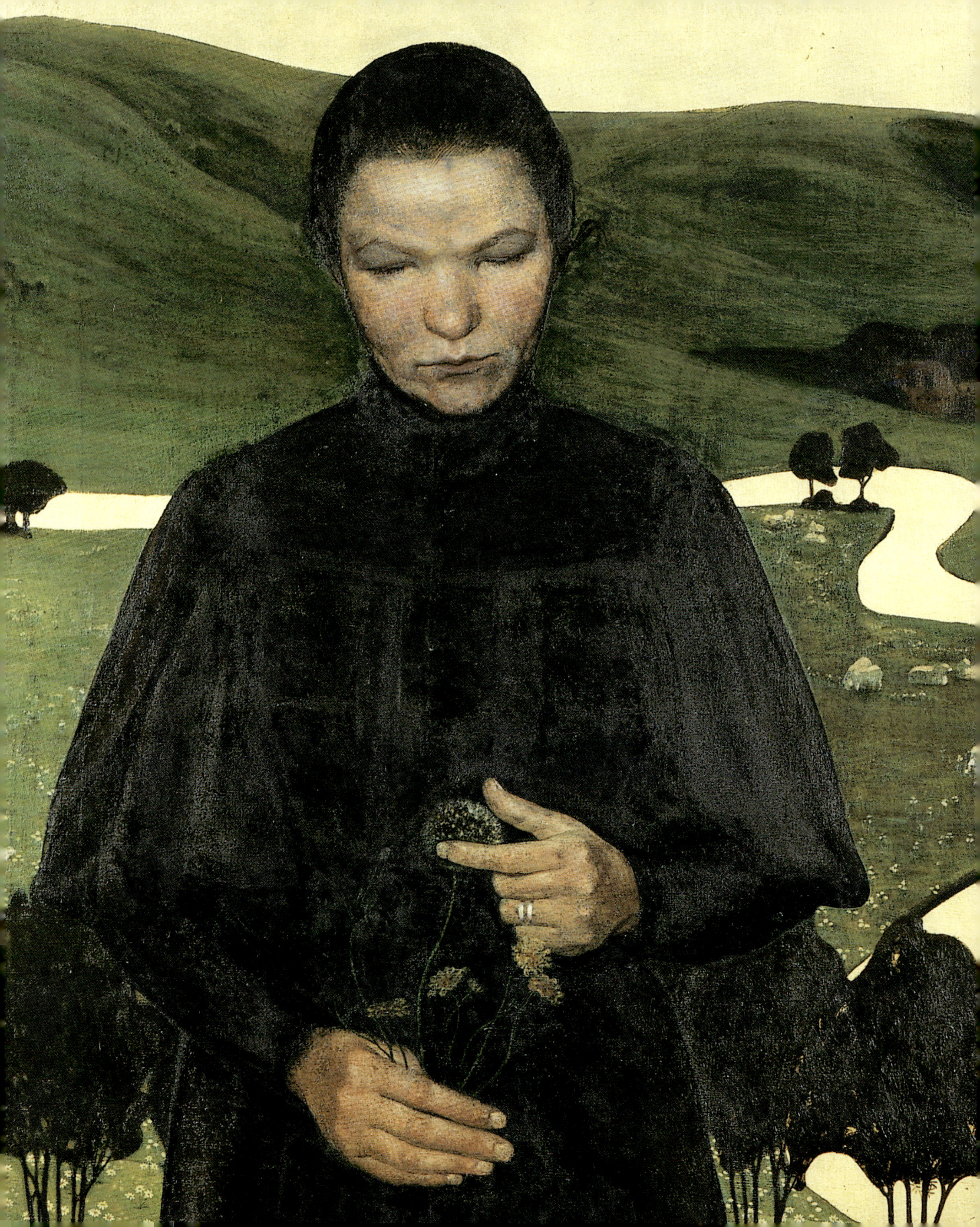

6

The Free Exhibition and the Psychological Breakthrough

IN THE 1880s AND 1890s, A NEW GENERATION OF DANISH
artists emerged that challenged the Royal Academy's status as the privileged site of training
and exhibition. By founding such artist-run institutions as the Free Exhibition (Den Frie
Udstilling), they reshaped Denmark's artistic culture. For these artists, who included Vilhelm
Hammershøi, J. F. Willumsen, Harald and Agnes Slott-Møller, L. A. Ring, and Ejnar Nielsen,
the question of representation itself was at stake in this period. They infused what they saw as
an obsolete artistic attachment to empiricism with new techniques and themes suggestive of
inner subjectivity. Although variously engaged in social, political, spiritual, and aesthetic causes,
these artists shared a commitment to communicate the individual's emotional and visual sen-
sations. In the later 1880s, critic Karl Madsen termed the new work "emotional realism,"[1] the
dual articulation of the outer world and inner states of being. In the 1890s, these emerging
subjectivist tendencies were termed Symbolist.

Ejnar Nielsen's *The Blind Girl. Gjern* (1896–98; fig. 139), painted in oil and gold and
representing a sightless rural peasant girl, summarizes many of these tendencies. In the foreground of this large composition, a girl dressed in black, her hair pulled back against her austere oval head, tentatively fingers a modest nosegay of daisies and dandelions. Standing so close
to the picture plane that her skirt has been cropped at knee-level, she seems to tower over the
viewer. Her closed eyes and compressed mouth communicate her tactile, rather than visual,
experience of the flowers. Nielsen represents her as a kind of visionary—in the manner of the
French Symbolist poet Maurice Maeterlinck (1862–1949) who romanticized blindness as a
condition of poetic vision.[2] A common metaphor in Symbolist writing and painting, blindness
represented an esoteric relationship between the self and the universe without recourse to the
material world, a "second sight" offering a connection to the soul.[3] As in French artist Paul
Gauguin's stoneware *Self-Portrait Jug* (1889; fig. 140), it announces an artistic credo that offers
the imagination, rather than nature, as the source for art.[4] Behind the girl, a rolling landscape
dotted with sheep, flowering fields, and a farm is transformed from the familiar undulating Jutland terrain of Johan Thomas Lundbye's generation to a golden, decorative fantasy. The Gjern

139.
Ejnar Nielsen
The Blind Girl. Gjern, 1896–98
(detail)

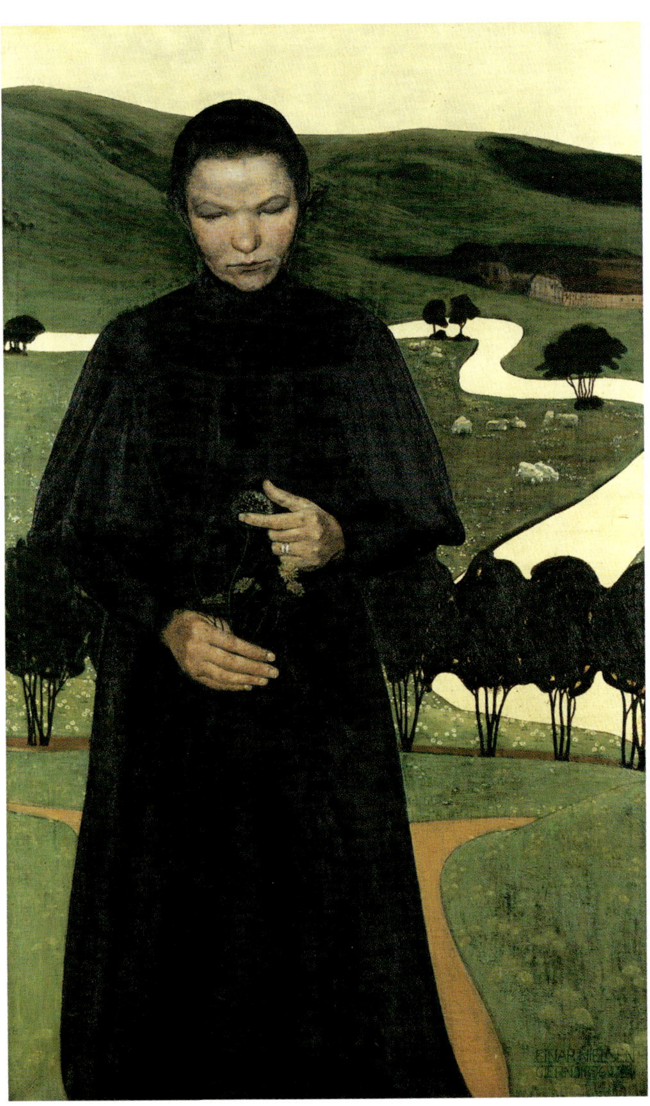

139.
Ejnar Nielsen
The Blind Girl. Gjern, 1896–98
Oil and gold on panel, 51¾ x 31¼ in.
(131.5 x 79.2 cm)
The Hirschsprung Collection,
Copenhagen

River meandering through the background is gilded, as is the sky, its reflected light flattening and darkening the hieroglyph-like trees that demarcate the middle ground. In Nielsen's painting, nature is a backdrop for and shaped by the creative imagination. The precisely delineated peasant, surrounded by the decorative symbols of her empathic response to nature, mirrors the larger tensions within Danish avant-garde art.

    This chapter traces some of the transformations in Danish art of the 1880s and 1890s that conditioned such an image. Examining the social movements that impelled institutional rebellions, the founding of independent artists' schools and exhibition societies, and the emergence of a new generation of art patrons and collectors committed to the internationalization of Danish art, this chapter maps the rise of a modern arts infrastructure in Copenhagen. Within this new network, artists developed increasingly international contacts and vocabularies, offering a renewed vision of Denmark, like Nielsen's *Blind Girl*, as both physical place and psychic realm.

TRANSITIONS

The last two decades of the nineteenth century were marked by a continued national malaise in the wake of Denmark's loss of Schleswig and Holstein in 1864, and by political tensions as the liberal middle class, urban underclass, and rural poor were increasingly marginalized by the conservative (Høyre) government under J. B. S. Estrup (1825–1913; prime minister 1875–1894). With the growing strength of the Left Party (Venstre) and the founding of the Socialist Democratic Party (Socialdemokratiet) in 1871, notions of what it meant to be Danish and how Denmark could find strength and stability were increasingly polarized. In general, Høyre, vigilant against Germany and other foreign threats, argued for the defense of the country, while the left promoted popular parliamentarianism and the "self-determination of the People" as Denmark's greatest obligation.[5] Høyre supported king and flag as the symbols of nationhood, while branches of the left looked to the peasants and small landholders as the nation's core. However, Denmark's rural peasants were not just imagined by intellectuals to be romantic embodiments of the nation, they were also increasingly collectivizing themselves to steer the nation's future.

This political orientation had in part been shaped by Nikolaj Frederik Severin Grundtvig (1783–1872), the poet, writer, philosopher, historian, and pastor whose influence on Danish national consciousness and on issues of social justice was almost without peer. Throughout his life, Grundtvig focused on the economic, spiritual, and educational conditions of rural Danes, and he is credited with, among other things, founding the Folk High School movement. In the early and mid-nineteenth century, when formal education was generally the privilege of the urban upper classes, Grundtvig believed that all Danes should have access to education according to their needs. The spread of the folk school system was an integral part of nation building after mid-century and it helped to strengthen the cultural position of farmers and small landholders and, later, urban industrial workers.[6] His followers, the Grundtvigians, shaped the terms of the more centrist left.

The ideology of the far left, which eschewed the religious, romantic, and isolationist components of Grundtvigianism, was informed by critic Georg Brandes's ideas concerning a "modern breakthrough" (see chapter 5). These ideas were in turn disseminated in the left-wing Copenhagen newspaper *Politikken*, founded in 1884 by Brandes's brother Edvard (1847–1931). *Politikken* became an important platform for social debates about class conflicts, suffrage, religion, and contemporary morality.[7]

One of *Politikken's* early faithful readers was the painter Laurits Andersen Ring (1854–1933).[8] Ring himself described the mid-1880s as "the years of political agitation when I firmly believed in the revolution against Estrup."[9] And in his work of this period, he engaged socially tendentious themes. Ring started out as a rural house painter, but he enrolled in the Danish Academy in the 1870s. He then debuted at the Charlottenborg in 1882 and studied with P. S. Krøyer in 1886. In *The Lineman*, painted in 1884 (fig. 141), Ring symbolized the physical and social transformations of rural Denmark. A railroad man stands in the foreground of the painting, hand dangling by his side, facing a distant oncoming train. He is turned away

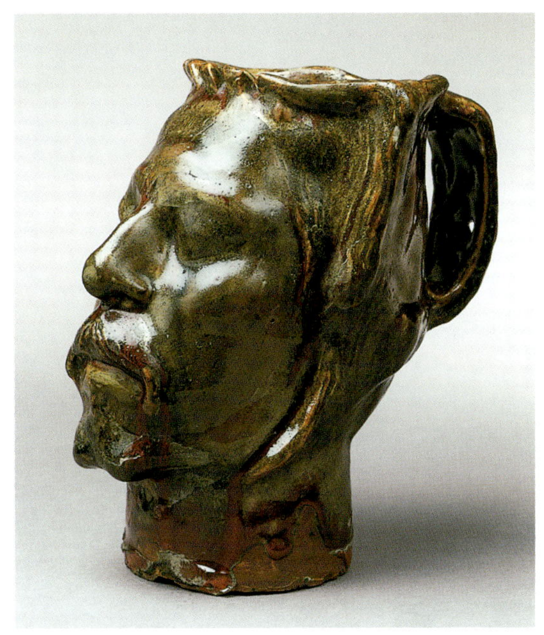

140.
Paul Gauguin
Self-Portrait Jug, 1889
Stoneware, height: 7⅝ in.
(19.3 cm)
Danish Museum of Decorative Art,
Copenhagen

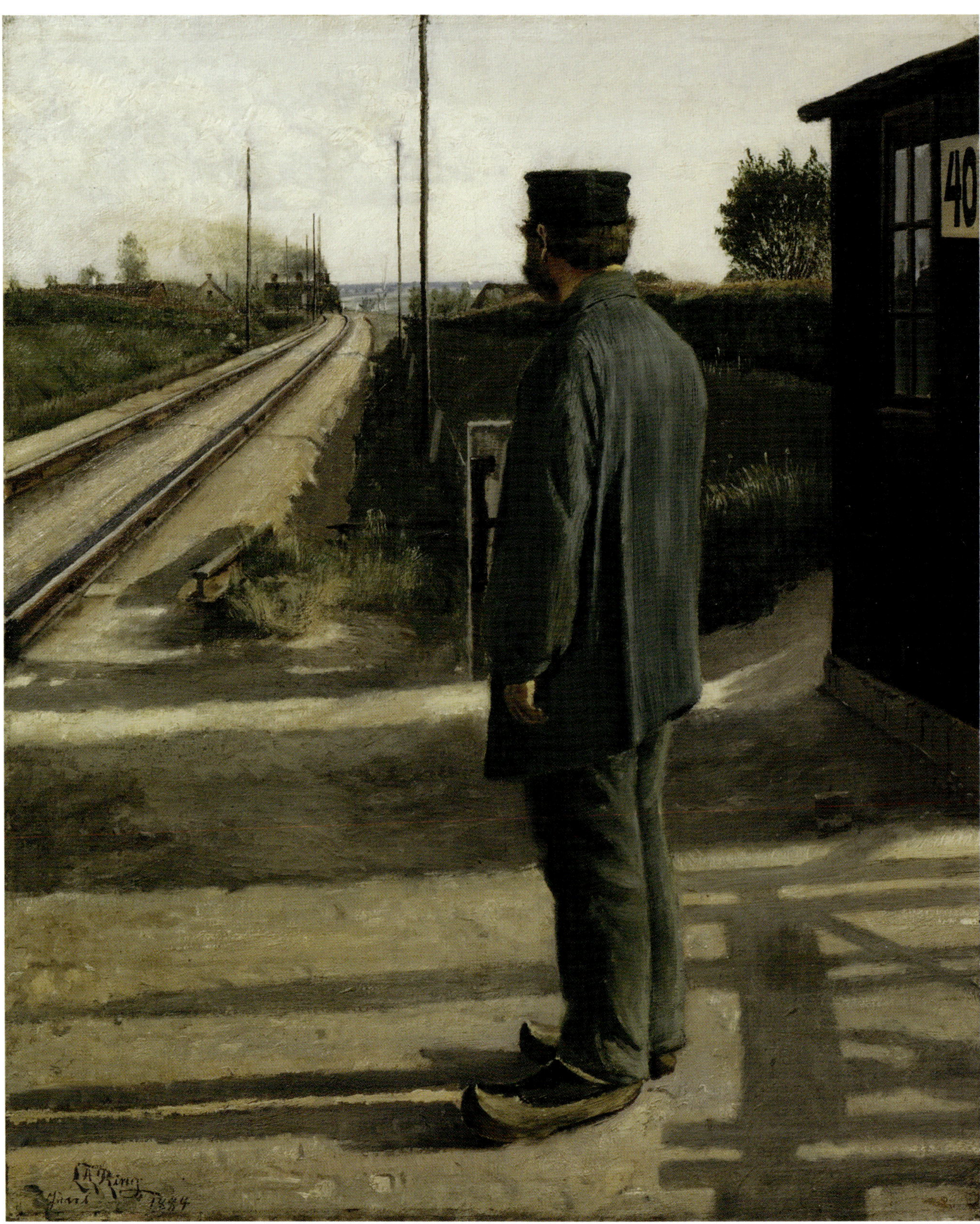

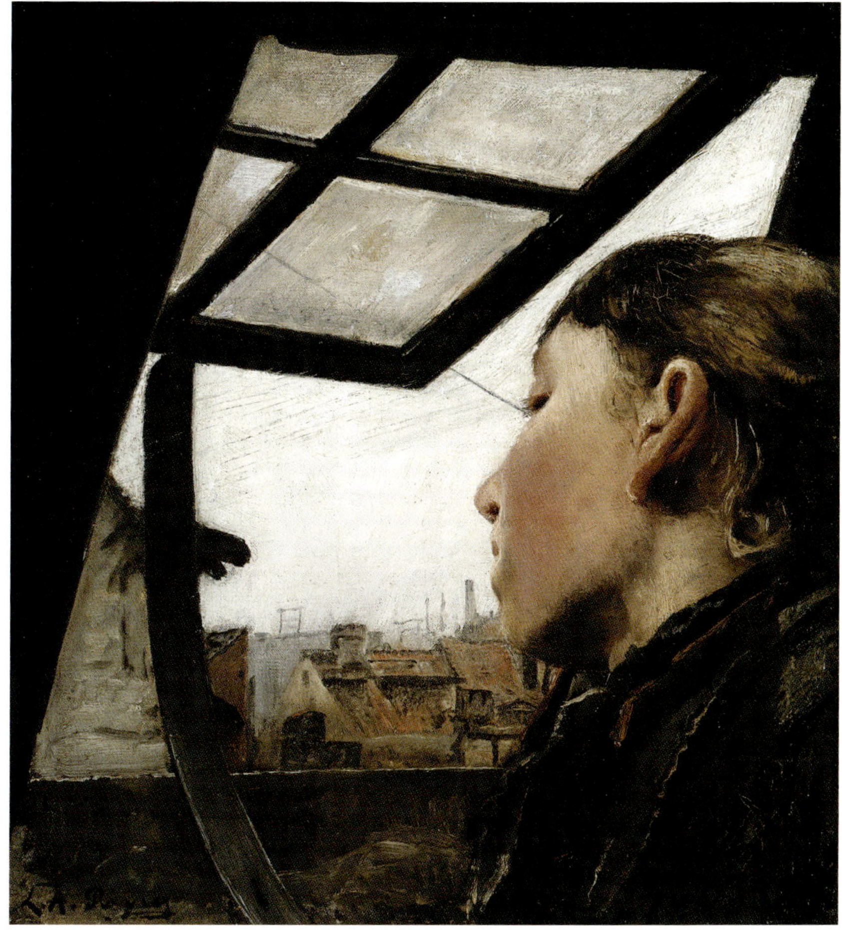

from the spectator and wears wooden clogs and a blue smock, his anonymity and slightly hunched posture suggest a confrontation between old local patterns and the new technologies transforming the countryside.[10] Although he at first appears solitary, the shadows of the crossing gate and of two unseen figures also impart a sense of expectation to the scene, this effect heightened by the strong diagonal element of the train tracks that bisect the left side of the painting. With its unusual angle of view, its strong differentiation in scale and detail between foreground and background, and its heroization of the human subject, the painting reflects Ring's indebtedness to the immensely popular work of the French Naturalist painter Jules Bastien-Lepage (1848–1884), which was first introduced to Denmark by, among others, P. S. Krøyer.[11] Painted in Ring's home town, the work resonates with both the artist's intimate understanding of his rural community and his larger concerns about the economic plight of rural Denmark in the face of industrial modernity.[12]

Ring spent the winter of that year in Copenhagen where, in his rented attic room, he painted *Young Girl Looking Out of a Window* (1885; fig. 142), another view of an isolated individual confronting modernity. Despite the model's extreme proximity to the picture plane, suggestive of the pictorial strategies of Edgar Degas (1834–1917), her features are barely visible. She is turned away from us and seems to strain to look out of the darkened room's skylight onto the city below. As noted by art historian Peter Nørgaard Larsen, her gaze, the artist's gaze,

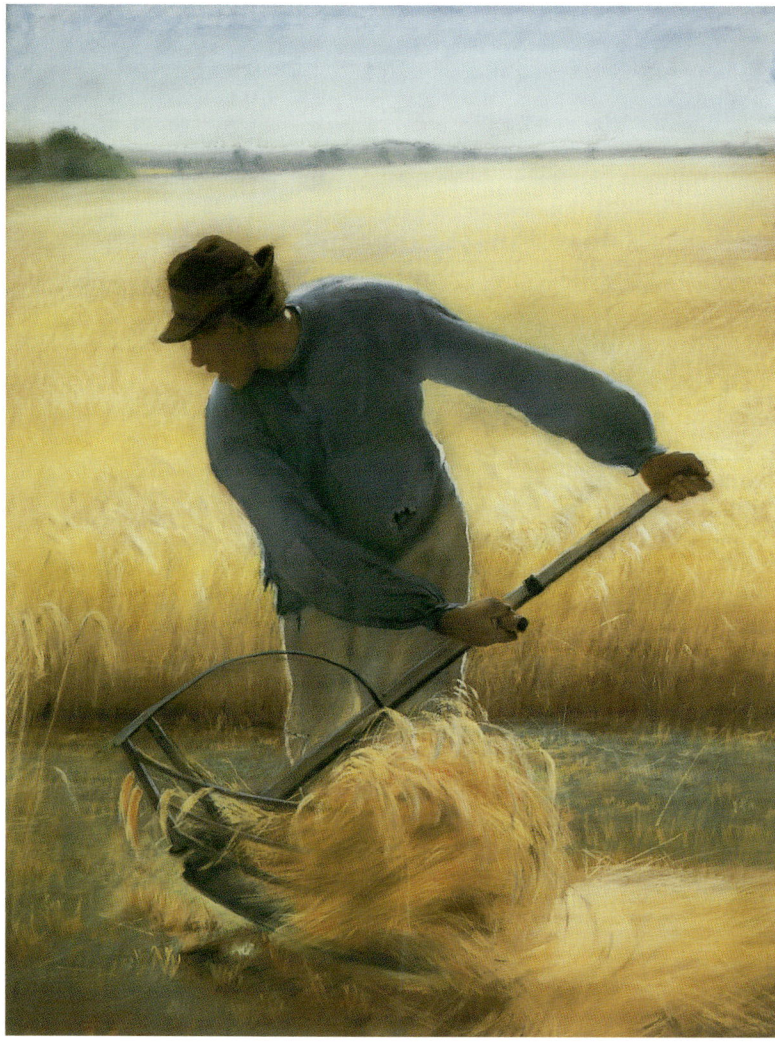

and our own angle of view coalesce as we observe her watching the city. Her act of seeing is reinforced by the diagonal wire that bisects the window and is aligned exactly with her eye.[13] The cityscape beyond the window is composed of rooftops and scaffolding, a negation of the historic, royal, monumental city.

In the summer of 1885, Ring likewise turned his brother into an archetypal figure in order to create "a monument to the Danish peasant."[14] The monumentally-scaled canvas, *Harvest* (1885, Statens Museum for Kunst), to which this small, glowing pastel is related (1886; fig. 143), represents Ole Peter Ring working on his farm near Fakse, on Zealand. The seemingly endless horizon of wheat rises up to engulf the laborer's elongated figure which is, moreover, distorted—his arms too long for his torso, his right shoulder impossibly rounded and his left shoulder exaggerated in its extension. Such anatomical distortions communicate the physical stress of the labor, a sensation reinforced by the vast scale of the field that the solitary farmer must harvest.

Ring's brother died in the following year, after which time the artist's work increasingly embraced uncanny elements that may be related to late Romantic or Symbolist painting. In

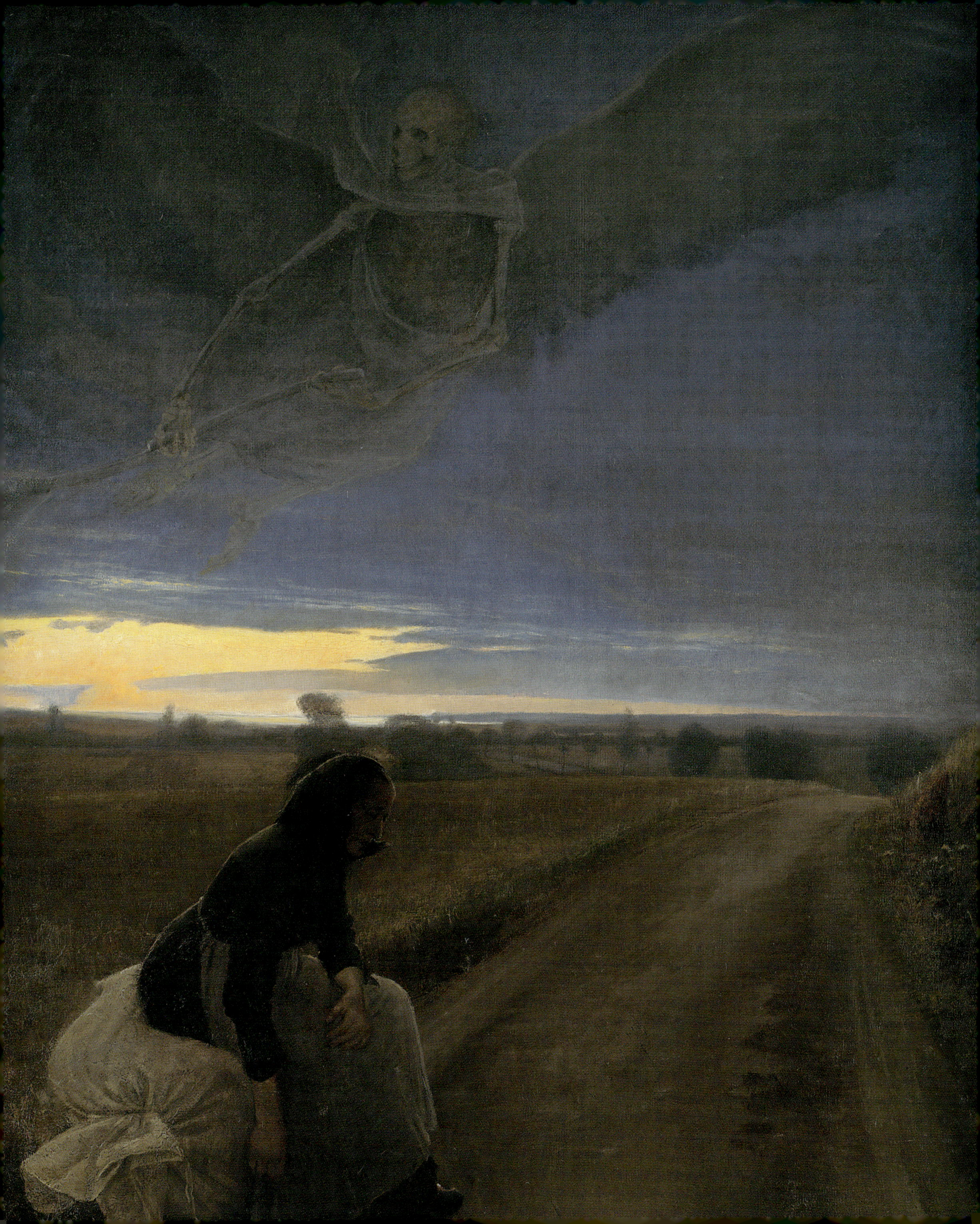

1887, one year after his brother's death, Ring painted *Evening. The Old Woman and Death* (1887; fig. 144) in which the supernatural figure of the Grim Reaper dominates the sky of an otherwise naturalistic scene. The peasant woman, whose every line and gesture communicates exhaustion, sits by the side of a winding road on a large sack, a burden too great for even her strong back. Ring makes death palpable in every element of the painting by marshaling traditional symbols of evanescence—the path, dandelions, the brown grass of autumn, the setting sun, and the winged skeleton with the scythe—to communicate the inevitability of the peasant woman's lonely end.[15] Certainly, there were examples of such expressive and symbolic landscapes throughout Danish art of the nineteenth century, from Jens Juel's views of celestial events (fig. 9) to Vilhelm Kyhn's *Evening Atmosphere* (1861; fig. 145). However, it is the very intimacy of Ring's view and the unromanticized representation of the human inhabitant of the landscape that separate his work from that of his predecessors. Like Jean-Francois Millet's (1814–1875) *Death and the Woodcutter* (1858–59, Ny Carlsberg Glyptotek), which Ring may have known from Carl Jacobsen's collection—soon to become a public museum (see below), this painting suggests an empathy with the subject so strong that it tends to mysticism.[16] Poised between a socially based Realism, examining the specific burdens of the contemporary Danish peasantry, and Symbolism, which universalizes and poeticizes the scene, *Evening. The Old Woman and Death* represents the transition from description to poetic evocation that characterized socially engaged art of this generation.

A Naturalist representation of death invested with a Symbolist eeriness is most pronounced in *Three Skeletons in the Capuchin Monastery Near Palermo* (1894; fig. 146), which Ring painted while visiting Italy from 1893 to 1895. He represented two skeletons and a mummified corpse in the catacombs of the Convento dei Cappuccini in preparation for an ambitious painting (never realized) on the theme of the medieval Dance of Death. Ring records the seemingly animated postures and clothing of the dead members of the order down

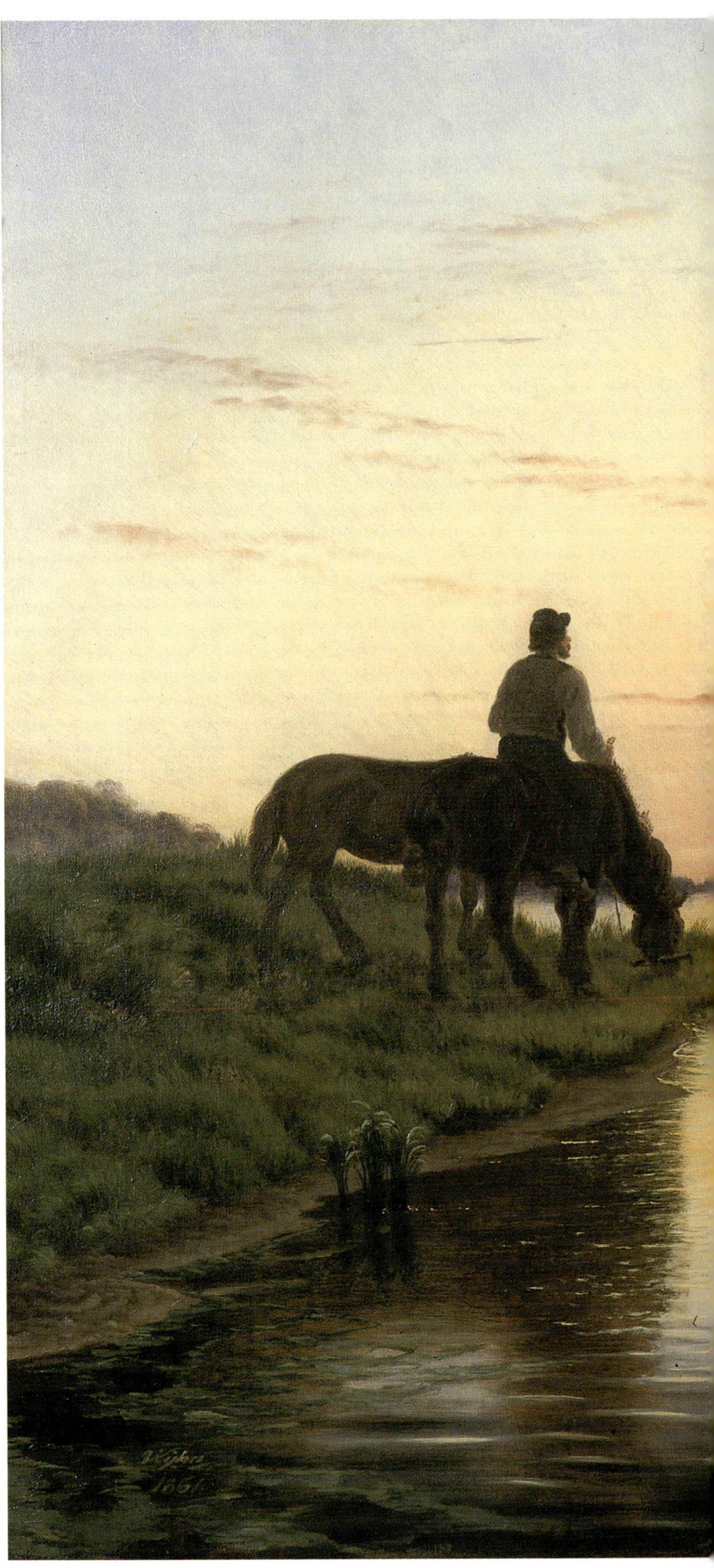

145.
Vilhelm Kyhn
Evening Atmosphere, 1861
Oil on canvas, 27⅛ x 37 in.
(69 x 94 cm)
Collection of Ambassador John L. Loeb Jr.,
New York

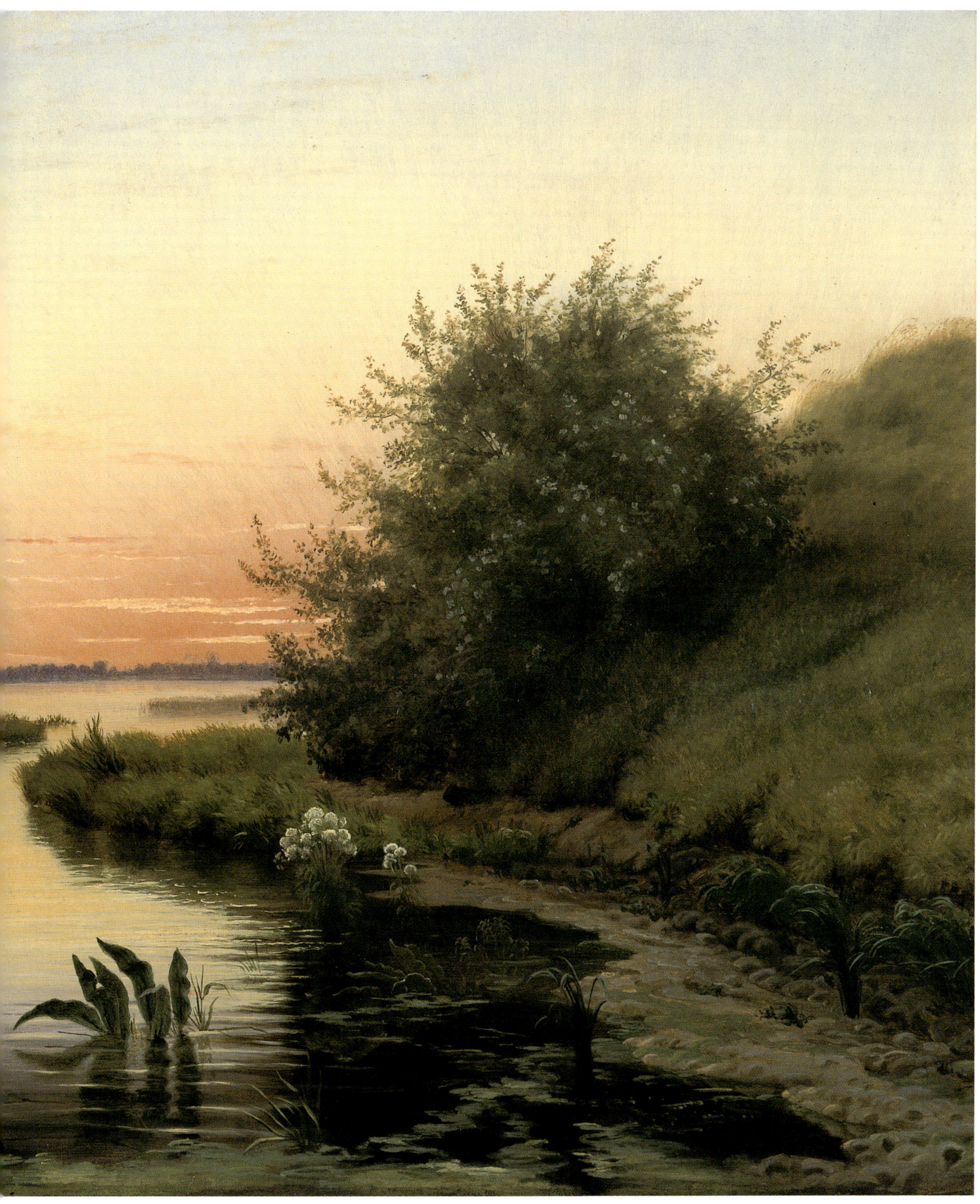

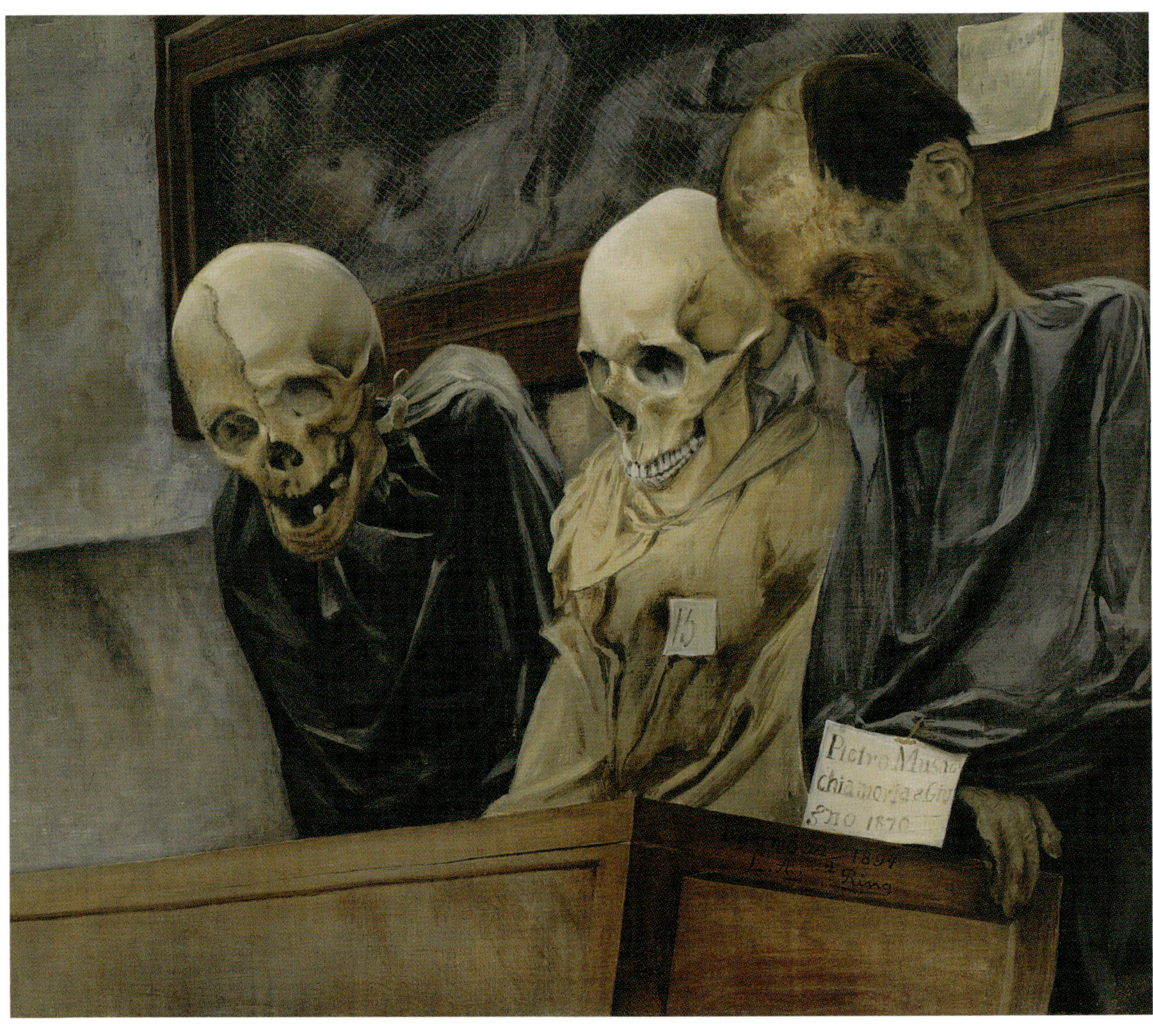

146.
L. A. Ring
Three Skeletons in the Capuchin Monastery near Palermo, 1894
Oil on canvas, 21⅝ x 24⅜ in.
(55 x 62 cm)
Statens Museum for Kunst,
Copenhagen

to the detail of the name tags and, in a macabre gesture, he signed his name on the wooden structure against which they rest. In a letter to a friend, he expressed something of this droll humor: "I am painting prominent Palermo citizens right now, three to a painting, but they are very easy to get along with as they utter not a word. They are dead, you see, the latest having died in 1870."[17] In its representation of the dead mimicking the postures of the living, this painting conjures associations with the parodic skeletons that inhabit Belgian painter James Ensor's compositions of the 1880s and thereafter, such as *Skeletons Warming Themselves* (1889; fig. 147). Offering a strange foray into the world of the dead and at the same time pictorial fidelity to the visual facts, Ring's painting defies easy categorization.

In these years, Ring was among a very few artists who created socially based representations of rural laborers with psychological insight and advanced artistic means. Niels Bjerre (1864–1942), whose central preoccupation was the landscape and rural inhabitants of his native West Jutland, also worked in this tradition. Having studied at the Royal Academy and the Artists' Study School in the 1880s, Bjerre was invited by Harald Slott-Møller (see below) to exhibit with the radical Free Exhibition in 1892.[18] *A Prayer Meeting. Harboøre (Children of God)* (1897; fig. 148), his best-known work, represents a meeting of the Home Mission evangelical movement, which was strong in his native region, and to which members of his family belonged. Adapting compositional devices from the work of Christian Krohg (chapter 5), such as the vast jumps in scale between the figures in the fore- and background, and a neutralized palette indebted to Vilhelm Hammershøi, whose work he admired,[19] Bjerre communicates bleakness and isolation. The Home Mission (Indremissionen) was a pietistic revival movement that emerged in the mid-nineteenth century renouncing the institution of the church and offering instead small evangelical enclaves. The converted, or "Children of God," practiced individual Bible study and eschewed frivolity such as dance and other "sins," separating themselves from the "Children of the Earth." In small rural communities like Harboøre, the Home Mission's prohibitions divided families and neighbors, increasing the hardship during what was an economically depressed period.[20] A writer as well as a painter, Bjerre also wrote short stories describing the effects of the Home Mission movement on his town that resonate strongly with the painting.[21] Bjerre was himself a free thinker, raised within the collectivist traditions of Grundtvig. His painting *From the Lecture Hall of a Folk High School at Sorø* (1890; Hirschsprung Collection) refers to that significant phenomenon.

Ring's and Bjerre's social subjects, rendered using new pictorial formulae adapted from advanced French painting, had in turn been indebted to the pioneering work of some members of the Skagen circle (chapter 5), among them, Christian Krohg and P. S. Krøyer. In 1882, Krøyer exhibited a Realist painting, *Italian Village Hatters* (1880; fig. 149), that was considered a breakthrough in Danish painting on the order of the literary breakthrough about which Georg Brandes had written. The painting offered, in the words of art historian Emil Hannover (1864–1923), "a turning point in the history of Danish art."[22] Rendered in a flowing style reminiscent of advanced continental painting, *Italian Village Hatters* provides an intimate view of laborers, a man and two pre-adolescent boys, sweating and toiling in a darkened interior. The specificity of the environment and the broader implications of their labor, particularly at a time when the far left advocated child labor laws, had galvanized a few other artists to offer their work as a social platform as well.

In addition to paintings by Ring and Bjerre, Harald Slott-Møller's *The Poor: The Waiting Room of Death* (1888; fig. 150) allegorized the plight of Copenhagen's dispossessed so as to invest contemporary art with a moral imperative. Copenhagen grew dramatically in the late nineteenth century. From a population of around 100,000 in 1801, Copenhagen quadrupled in size, particularly in the late nineteenth century. Its inhabitants representing nearly twenty percent of Denmark's overall population.[23] The structural density and physical boundaries of Copenhagen likewise grew during this period, explosively so in the years after 1870.[24] Much of its building activity was focused on new bourgeois sections of the city. However, some real estate speculators also developed increasingly cramped and airless apartments to accommodate the rural workers streaming into the city to seek industrial work but instead finding illness and unemployment. In Slott-Møller's painting, a group of the urban poor, assembled in a room reminiscent of contemporary public health clinics for indigents, passively awaits death. When the painting was first created, an allegorical figure of Death appeared in the blackened doorway in the form of a skeleton, but the skeleton was painted out and death is now symbolized simply by the central, black void of the doorway itself. The physiognomies of the figures

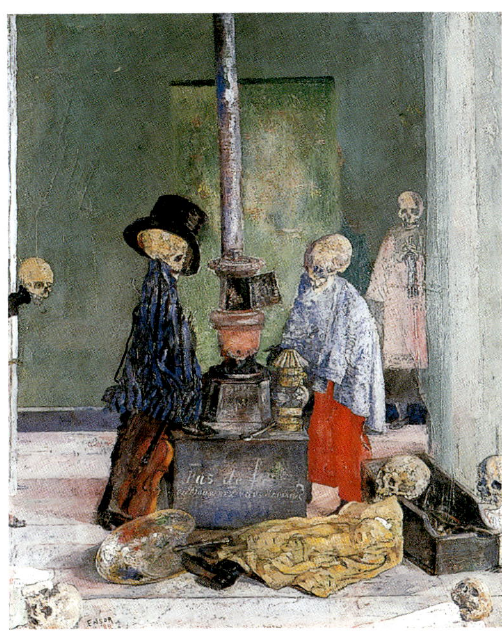

147.
James Ensor
Skeletons Warming Themselves, 1889
Oil on canvas, 29½ x 23⅝ in.
(74.8 x 60 cm)
Kimbell Art Museum, Fort Worth

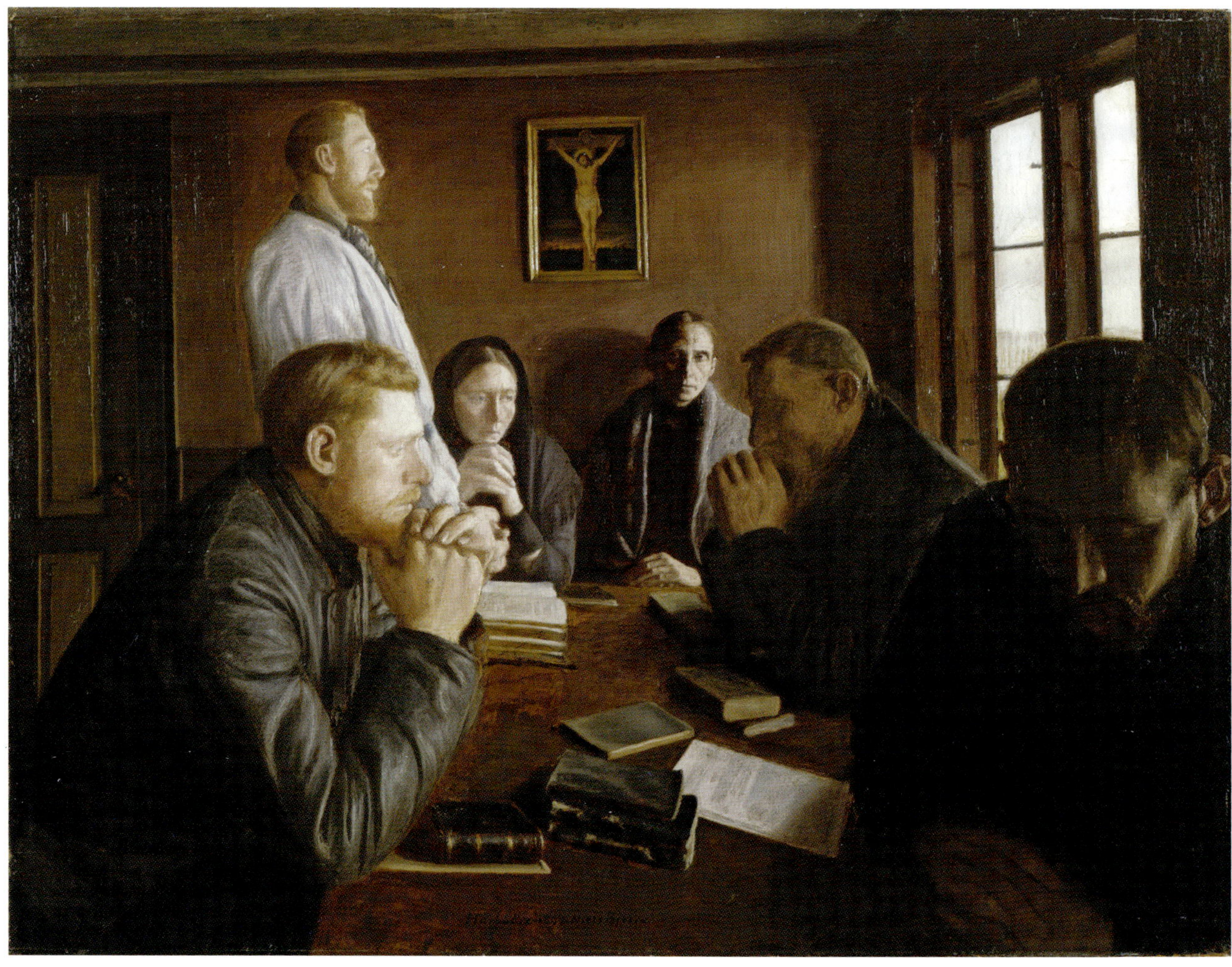

are carefully articulated to suggest brutality, toil, and exhaustion, including the stooped child in the frayed coat who stands in the center of the composition, already responding to what would have been the skeleton's call.[25] This was one of a small group of paintings in Denmark to picture urban poverty.

In *Georg Brandes Lecturing in the University of Copenhagen* (1890; fig. 151), Slott-Møller also created a sympathetic representation of one of the inspiring voices behind *The Poor: The Waiting Room of Death*. Brandes, by then an international literary celebrity, is shown as vulnerable, the podium in front of him, the high blank wall behind him and the large overhead lights above him dwarfing his body. In comparison to the optimistic portraits rendered in 1884 by the Skagen artists (fig. 124), Slott-Møller's painting hints at the morality campaigns and anti-Semitism that had barred Brandes from assuming a chair in aesthetics at the University of Copenhagen. Brandes's pulpit as the site of his famous lectures (see chapter 5) is invested with irony and pathos. Slott-Møller had been P. S. Krøyer's student at the Artists' Study School, initiating his career with such reformist works in the mid-1880s.

It was precisely this blend of social concern (or commitment to the collective) and a conscious desire to articulate empathy (or individual internal sensation) that opened a path

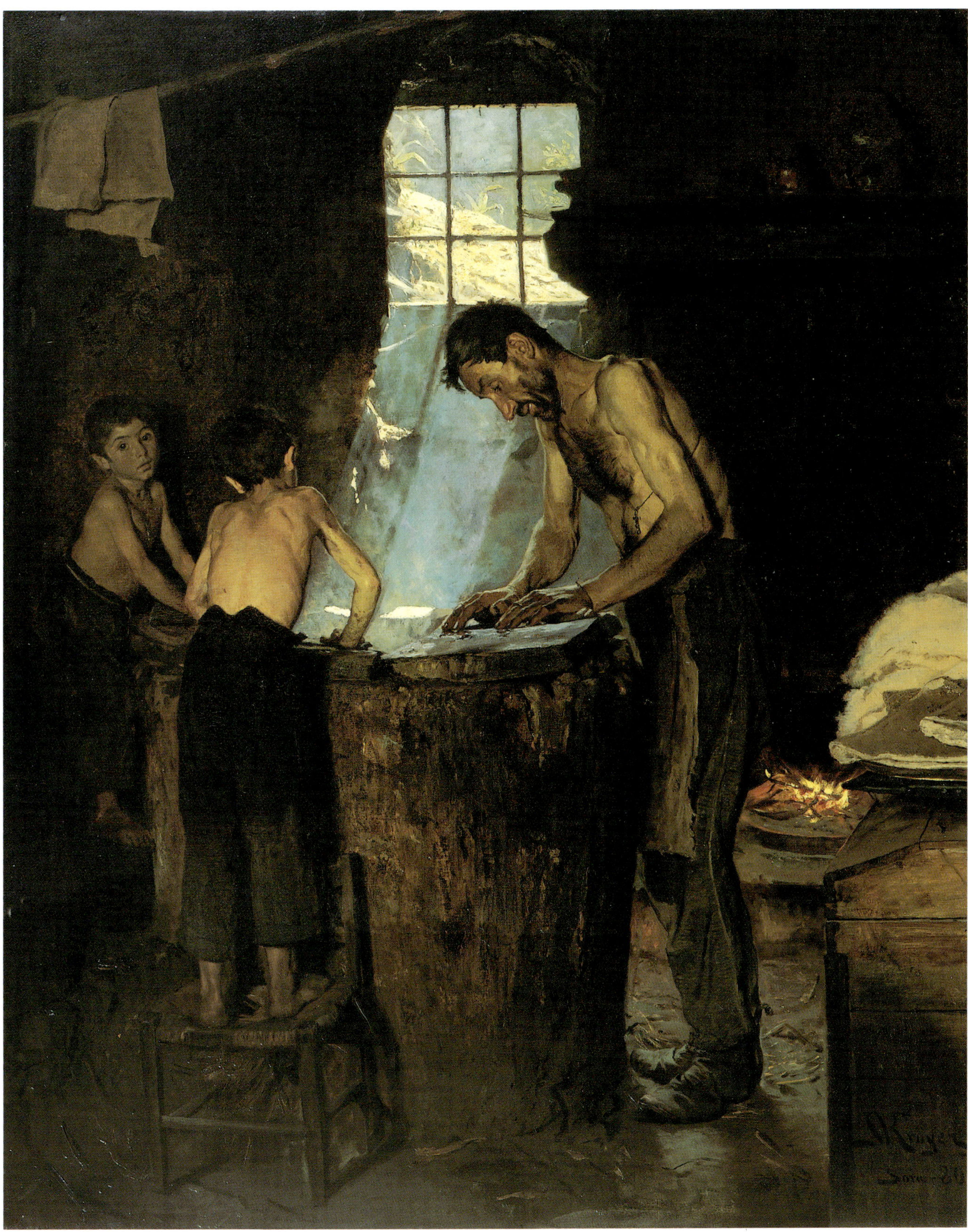

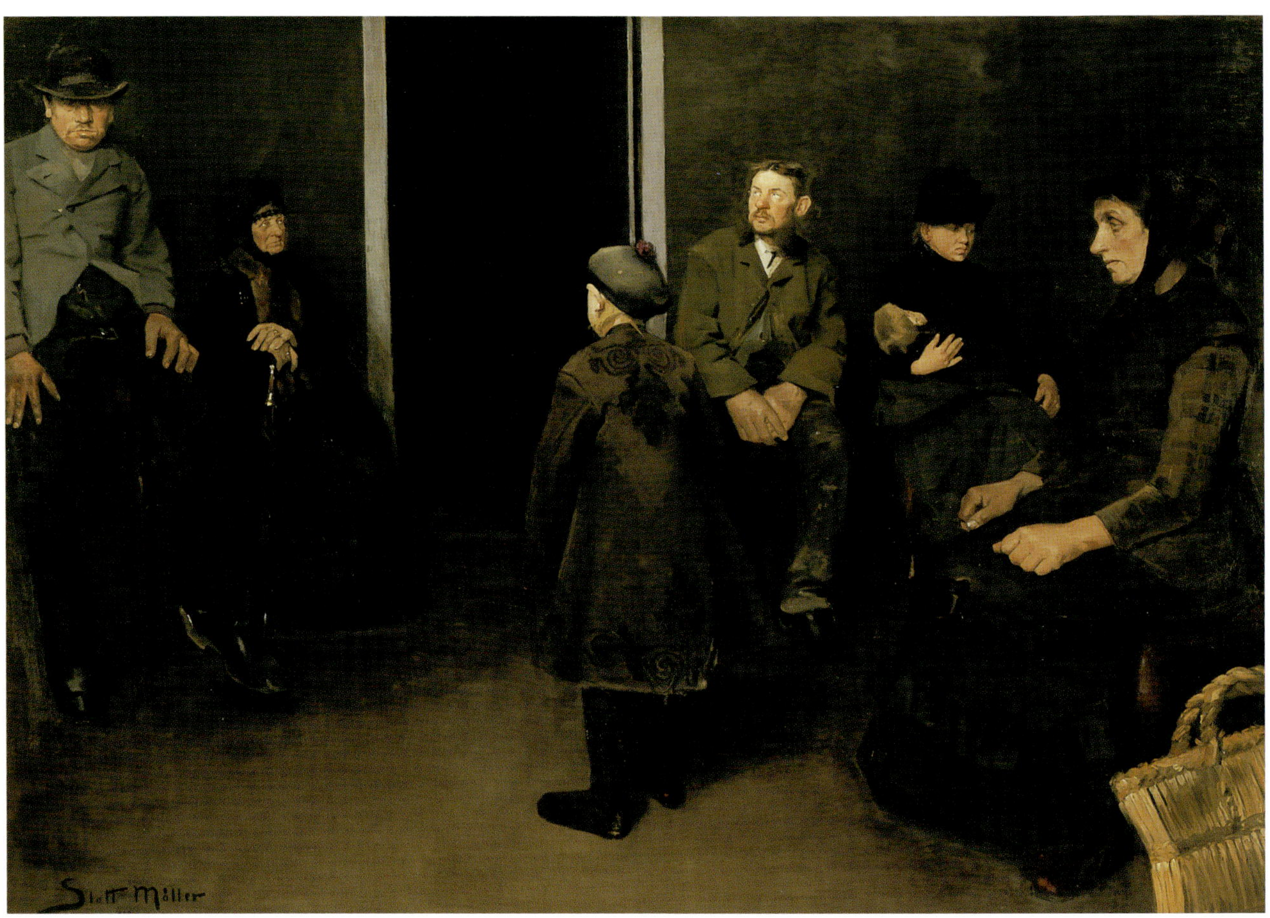

150.
Harald Slott-Møller
The Poor: The Waiting Room of Death,
1888
Oil on canvas, 51⅝ x 72⅝ in.
(131 x 184.5 cm)
Statens Museum for Kunst,
Copenhagen

toward new and often phantasmal modes of painting in 1890s Denmark. In 1888, poet Valdemar Vedel had published a polemical essay, calling for a new soulful art that transcended material particularities and instead would:

> . . . create new forms of beauty, suited to our nerves and our taste. The mature, complicated spiritual life of our age does not move in simple, great waves as did that of former ages; it is not the great, uncomplicated emotions of hatred, love, sorrow, anger, rejoicing, that alternate in us, but predominantly the strange, mixed moods that outwardly seem grey and homogeneous, but for more receptive nerves are infinitely richer, more heterogeneous and refined. The same applies to our eyes: They shun bright, garish single colors to seek gentler and mixed intermediate shades. But therefore, art, too, will choose colors—both those of the external world and those from the spiritual life—with a different taste from the art of earlier times. It will not sketch life with the unrelenting black of tragedy or the bitter green of satire or the traditional color scale of lyric poetry, but it will paint life in a rich range of nuances, in the same strange mixtures of mood that our nerves live and of which our taste approves.[26]

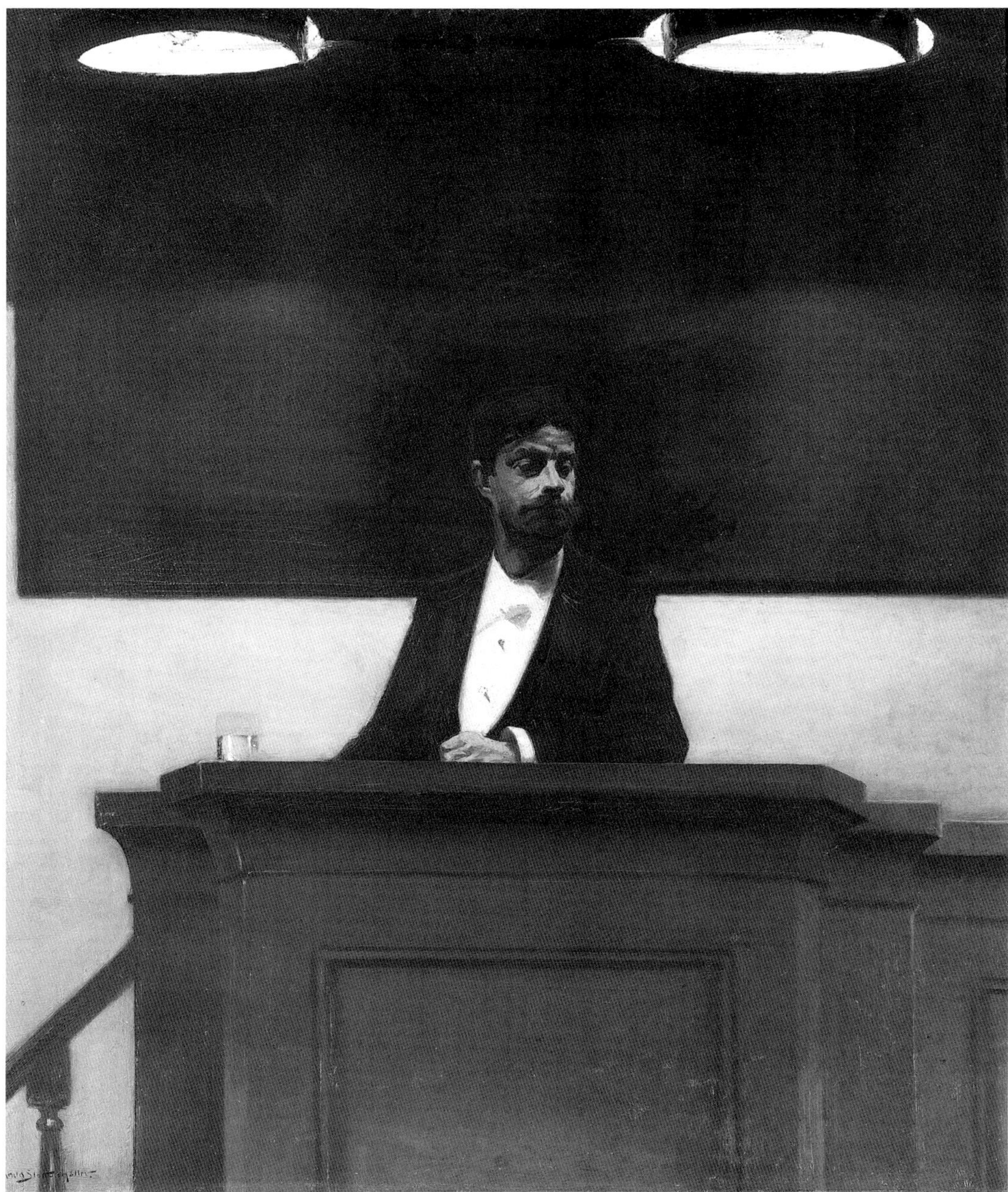

In other words, he claimed that modernity gave rise to a kind of aberrancy, a hypersensitivity or receptivity to sense stimuli, and he called for poets to expand the known territory of consciousness by expressing this receptivity.

L. A. Ring's work, too, began to resonate with such rhetoric. In his landscape painting such as *Alder Stumps, Næstved* (1893, H. M. The Queen), the artist invested what appears to be a clearly rendered, "objective" view of nature with such "strange mixtures of mood." Observing alder trees growing from a bog in Næstved, in the southwest of Zealand, Ring offers the still, dark surface of the water as a mirror of the darkened sky and denuded trees. The haunting strangeness of the trees has attracted such descriptions as "skeletal joints"[27] and "psychological

151.
Harald Slott-Møller
Georg Brandes Lecturing in the University of Copenhagen, 1890
Oil on canvas, 37¼ x 32¼ in.
(94.5 x 82 cm)
The Royal Library, Copenhagen

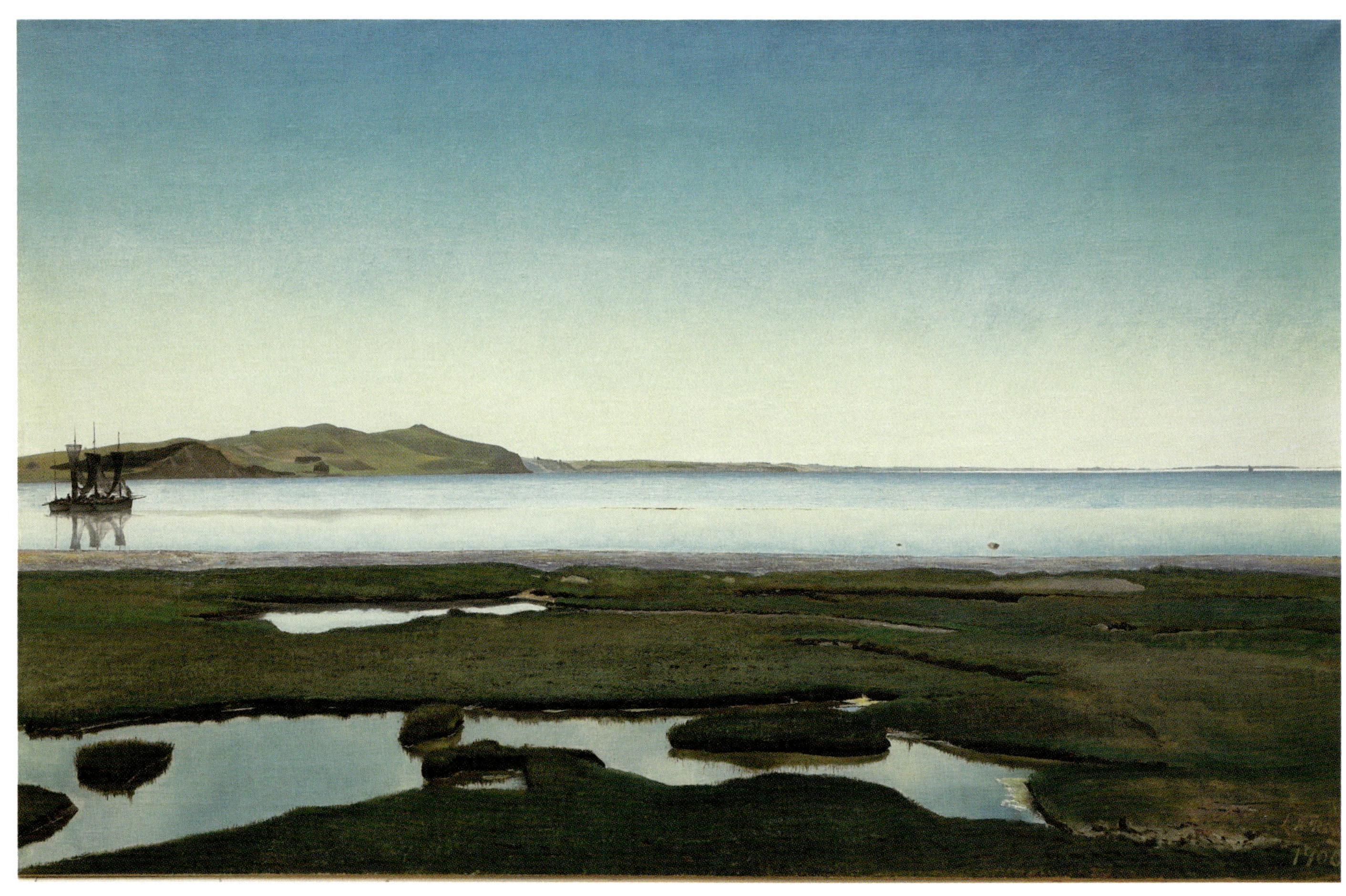

152.
L. A. Ring
Summer Day by Roskilde Fjord, 1900
Oil on canvas, 37⅞ x 56⅞ in.
(95.5 x 144.5 cm)
Randers Kunstmuseum

tentacles,"[28] and it has been likened to the watery death described in H. C. Andersen's *The Marsh King's Daughter*.[29]

Ring's *Summer Day by Roskilde Fjord*, painted in 1900 (fig. 152), likewise cannot be easily understood to be either Naturalist or Symbolist, but it occupies a space between, as did much advanced Danish painting at the turn of the century. It is a view of the Roskilde Fjord, just south of Frederiksværk, in which Ring registered the finest nuances of topography, light, and atmosphere. It records the period just before sunrise, when the surface of the fjord and atmospheric moisture amplify the first light of the day, and every detail of the land is particularized. The watery middle ground and the small channels cut from the peat in the foreground therefore shine a smooth silvery blue, and the horizon glows against the darker areas of land. The landscape seems uninhabited and denuded, with the exception of the small house on the distant hillock to the left and three dark boats tied together, their nets drying, at the left edge of the painting.[30] Art historians Henrik Wivel and Poul Erik Tøjner have read into the expansive emptiness of the painting a fixation with death,[31] but Finn Terman Frederiksen sees the picture in contrast, as an "inner landscape."[32] This grand, ambitious canvas in fact seems to oscillate between the commonplace and the uncanny. In its stasis, crystalline clarity, harmonious palette, and hyperacute detailing, it is both believable as a physical recording and as elusive as a dream.

SYMBOLISM AND THE FREE EXHIBITION

In the 1890s, the art of Ring, Bjerre, and Slott-Møller was poised on the cusp of representation where the marvelous and the mundane intersected. In this regard, the artists have been associated by recent scholars with Symbolism, the movement that was identified in Paris as a literary phenomenon in 1886 by the poet and critic Jean Moréas (1856–1910), and then as a new development in the visual arts by Gabriel-Albert Aurier (1865–1892), who identified Paul Gauguin as the harbinger of this subjective, anti-naturalist art.[33] Symbolism arose as a sensibility in dialogue with new studies of human subjectivity offered by the burgeoning field of psychology.[34] The term spread throughout Europe and began to characterize artists who reacted against the material and optical bases of Realism and Impressionism by asserting some sense of a greater transcendent reality and the deployment of symbols as the equivalents of inner sensation.

Symbolism was first introduced to the Danish public, and then championed, by poet and critic Johannes Jørgensen (1866–1956) in his journal *Taarnet* (The Tower), published from October 1893 to September 1894.[35] In the December 1893 issue of *Taarnet*, Jørgensen published an article entitled "Symbolism." In it, he asserted the superiority of that movement to positivism because of its mission to see beyond mere appearances and its assertion of the artist's individual poetic and spiritual temperament: "All true art is and will always be symbolic. With all of the great masters you will find a perception of nature as an exterior sign of an inner spiritual life. . . . It is furthermore my firm belief that any true view of the world must necessarily be mystical. The world is deep."[36] One of the characteristics of this sensibility is its eclecticism: an anti-positivist sensibility was expressed in a wide range of media, styles, and techniques. It is consequently as difficult to characterize the Symbolist movement now as it was in the 1890s.[37]

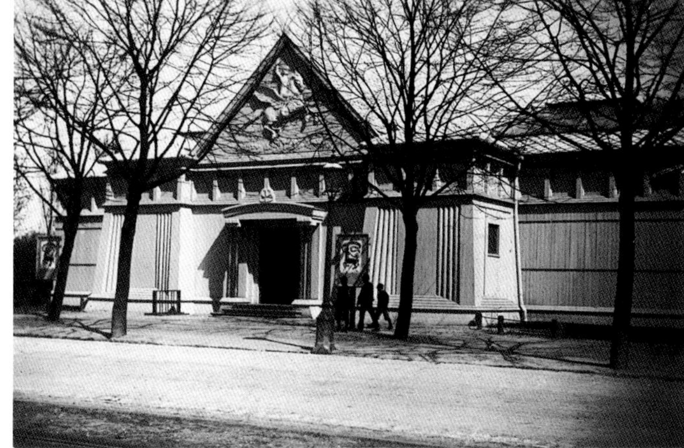

153.
J. F. Willumsen
Den Frie Udstilling, Copenhagen, 1898–1913
(Photograph by Frederik Riise)
J. F. Willumsens Museum, Frederikssund

Such imperatives as Jørgensen's and Vedel's, for sensitive modern visionaries to liberate late nineteenth-century culture from its materialism, were intimately tied to the artists who had begun to rebel against the teaching and exhibition practices of the Royal Academy in the 1880s. In a period when, as Jørgensen asserted in *Taarnet*, "the body of the Danish nation had suffered a terrible mutilation and now lay with wound fever after the amputation of southern Jutland" (referring to Denmark's 1864 loss of Schleswig and Holstein to Prussia), visionary artists who could grasp the deeper roots of consciousness, identity, and sacred meaning would cure the body politic.[38] The artists most powerfully allied with that sentiment were those who exhibited with the Free Exhibition (Den Frie Udstilling), a breakaway organization that formed in 1891 on the model of the French Salon des Refusés (1873), and that paralleled other artist-driven organizations such as Les XX in Belgium (established in 1884). The Free Exhibition immediately became Denmark's most influential artistic group and exhibition society.

Until 1891, the Royal Academy's annual Charlottenborg exhibitions, and the Fine Arts Society, were the only important venues for Danish artists, and these were viewed by many younger artists as restrictive and censorious in regard to new ideas and styles.[39] Even though the Charlottenborg exhibition had become more loosely affiliated with the academy in 1857

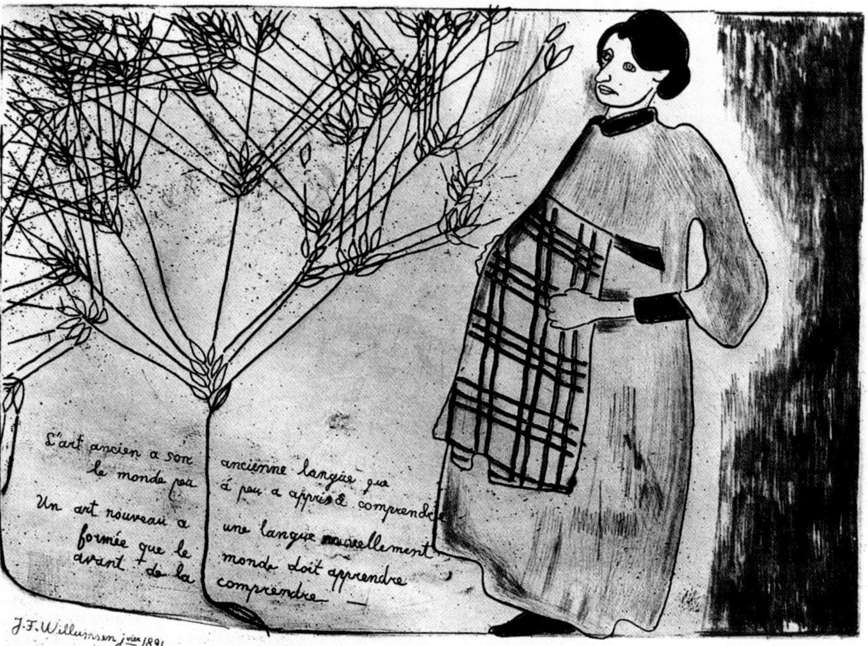

and was open to all artists who wished to submit works, the selection committee continued to privilege the Danish artists who painted history and genre scenes in the manner of the Golden Age masters.[40] Such traditional taste was anathema to emerging artists who were already adapting continental Realism, Naturalism, and Impressionism in the light of their experiences in Paris and elsewhere, and who were intent upon communicating their intimate responses to modernity.

The history of the Free Exhibition was connected to other new artists' institutions, particularly the Artists' Study School, a network of individual artists' studios, modeled after the atelier system in Paris, that had been established in Copenhagen in 1882–83. Among the participants were P.S. Krøyer, Vilhelm Kyhn, and Kristian Zahrtmann.[41] The Artists' Study School provided an alternative education to the Royal Academy, which held a "monopoly" on art education in Copenhagen,[42] and which was perceived to use its hegemony to bury new tendencies.[43] Importantly, these studios also accepted women, who were not yet able to enroll at the academy. Zahrtmann's school was the most popular, described by one of his students as "a Forum where students could experiment, question, and find themselves."[44]

In 1887, when canvases by most of Zahrtmann's students and others from the Artists' Study School had been refused from the Charlottenborg's spring exhibition, the artists paraded their work up the street in protest and, in 1888, they held a Salon des Refusés in the studio of painters Johan Rohde (1856–1935) and Rasmus Christiansen. Among these works was Vilhelm Hammershøi's *Young Girl, Sewing. Portrait of the Artist's Sister Anna* (1887, Ordrupgaard; see chapter 7). A second protest exhibition took place in Valdemar Kleis's gallery in 1890.[45]

In 1891, Johan Rohde was instrumental in starting the Free Exhibition, assembling Vilhelm Hammershøi, Christian Mourier-Petersen, Agnes and Harald Slott-Møller, and J. F. Willumsen to endorse the founding document (also signed by Malthe Engelsted) in January 1891:

"The undersigned hereby join a society consisting of Danish artists whose purpose it is to arrange yearly, independent, and for members of their society, uncensored exhibitions" including "works of art of any nature."[46] Shortly thereafter, the young artists were joined by more established artists, including P. S. and Marie Krøyer, the siblings Joakim, Niels, and Suzette Skovgaard, Viggo Pedersen, Theodor Philipsen, Julius Paulsen, Edma Frølich, and Johanne Krebs.[47] The first members therefore included a relatively large delegation of women, many of whom had been working toward the establishment of a women's school within the Royal Academy.[48] Holding its exhibitions in Valdemar Kleis's gallery during its first two years, the Free Exhibition opened in 1893 in its own temporary wooden building, designed by Thorvald Bindesbøll. In 1898 it moved to a building by Jens Ferdinand Willumsen (1863–1958; fig. 153).[49] With its prominent location and influential backing, thanks to the progressive critical writings of Karl Madsen and Emil Hannover, the Free Exhibition became the premier site for new cosmopolitan work in Copenhagen.

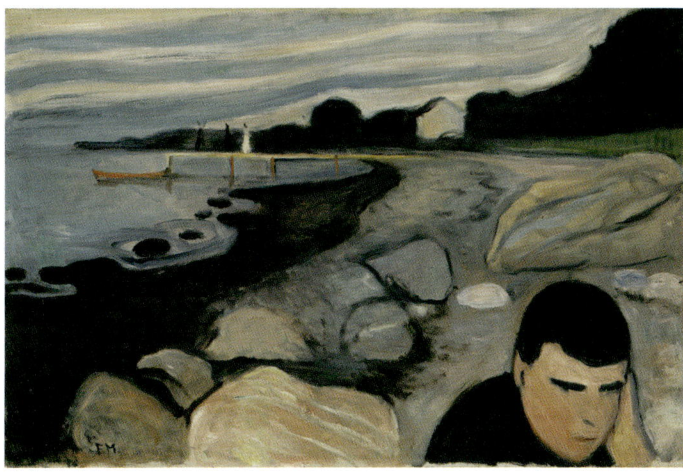

At the opening of the Free Exhibition in 1891, an etching by J. F. Willumsen entitled *Fertility* (1891; fig. 154) sparked controversy, reinforcing the oppositional profile of the organization. *Fertility* represents a pregnant woman, juxtaposed against a stalk of wheat, rendered in a reduced, linear style indebted to the work of Paul Gauguin. The etching includes a French text that translates as: "New art has a new language which one must learn in order to be understood."[50] Both the caricatural quality of the image and the polemical text caused a sensation and Willumsen was attacked in print, accused, among other things, of being derivative of Gauguin.[51]

Despite his later attempts to claim that his work was not indebted to the French master, Willumsen's early vision was profoundly shaped by Gauguin, whom he had met in Pont-Aven in 1890.[52] Willumsen also exchanged work with Gauguin and, along with artist Mogens Ballin (1871–1914; see below), he was among the celebrants at Gauguin's farewell party in Paris before the artist's second trip to Tahiti. By 1891, Gauguin was already well known in Copenhagen. In 1873, he had married Mette Gad (1850–1920) and had settled in Copenhagen in the winter of 1884–1885, exhibiting some of his works, as well as later contributing to an exhibition of Impressionist works organized by the Fine Arts Society in 1889.[53] The latter exhibition, *Nordiske og franske Impressionister*, had been initiated by Karl Madsen. Intended to stimulate fresh directions in Danish painting, the exhibition incorporated work by Oda and Christian Krohg, Viggo Johansen, and Theodor Philipsen as well as French paintings held in private collections, including that of Mette Gad Gauguin.[54]

With the advent of the Free Exhibition, Copenhagen became a venue for some of the most radical exhibitions in Europe in 1893.[55] In January of that year, Johan Rohde helped to arrange for the exhibition of fifty-four paintings by the Norwegian Edvard Munch (1863–1944). Munch's painting had just caused a sensation in Berlin.[56] Munch's work, including a version of *Melancholy* (1892; fig. 155), was identified by Emil Hannover and others as conveying a *stimmung* or mood, an expression of ineffable inner sensation conveyed by the unity of color, composition, and theme as in music.[57] Like Nielsen's *Blind Girl*, the figure in the extreme foreground of

155.
Edvard Munch
Melancholy, 1892
Oil on canvas, 25¼ x 37¾ in.
(64 x 96 cm)
The National Museum of Art,
Architecture, and Design, Oslo

Melancholy seems both isolated and embedded in the landscape setting, his linear flattened head perhaps generating the scene behind it as a fantasy.

In March 1893, the Free Exhibition displayed a major group of works by Gauguin and van Gogh. The exhibition, initiated by painters Johan Rohde and Theodor Philipsen (1840–1920), included twenty-eight works by van Gogh and fifty-one by Gauguin, among them ten of the latter artist's new paintings from Tahiti and his self-portrait stoneware vase. Several of the works were sold and remained in Denmark. As noted below, these works had a tremendous impact on local artists, writers, and collectors and they were the subject of great press attention. Identified by one critic as harbingers of the new Symbolist art,[58] they were described by various reviewers as pioneering, strange, and profound, and, as Karl Madsen contended: a "pleasing contrast with the weak wills of our own domestic sheep."[59]

Theodor Philipsen was the Danish artist who was closest to Gauguin, having befriended him in the mid-1880s and maintained a close relationship. Along with Anna Ancher (chapter 5), Philipsen was also the most important practitioner of Impressionist-derived painting in Denmark and his influence was wide-ranging. Impressionism did not cohere as a movement in Denmark, but the Parisian Impressionists' technique of conveying bright light and atmosphere, their loosening of painterly touch, unusual angles of view, and commitment to contemporary themes were adapted, along with Post-Impressionist currents, into the larger generational anti-naturalist sensibility.[60] Philipsen's *Cattle Seen Against the Sun on the Island of Saltholm. A Color Study* (1892; fig. 156) suggests the degree to which Danish Impressionism deviated from the Paris model. The rural subject, cattle grazing in a vast green field, is strongly allied with both earlier Golden Age landscape traditions and the artist's background in agriculture. However, the spectacular light effects, intense colors, and emphatically visible brush strokes of wet paint convey the optical sensation of sunlight silhouetting objects as it enters the painter's eyes, an emphasis on perception itself.

Johan Rohde, Philipsen's co-organizer of the van Gogh and Gauguin exhibition, is credited as the Danish artist who first "discovered" the art of van Gogh in France, and who approached Theo van Gogh's widow, Johanna van Gogh-Bonger, about organizing the exhibition. In his own work, such as *Quiet Evening in the Harbor at Hoorn* (1893; fig. 157), Rohde translated scenes from Holland and North Germany into moody nocturnes that synthesize the European works he encountered during a lengthy journey he made in 1892 throughout France, Holland, and Belgium. He had visited a Whistler exhibition in Paris two months prior to his trip to the Dutch town of Hoorn, where he painted this canvas, and the tight tonal and value range in this work, as well as the static quality to the generalized forms, reflect this encounter.[61] In his art, as in his commitment to the Copenhagen community, Rohde was ambitious. While visiting an exhibition of modern Dutch and Flemish art in Hoorn, Rohde mused, "Impossible not to walk through the exhibition without thinking about … how stagnant Denmark is.[62] Through his work, his contacts, and the fact of his increasing cosmopolitanism, he hoped to expand the vocabulary and opportunities of Danish artists.

Concurrent with the display of works by van Gogh and Gauguin at the Free Exhibition, Valdemar Kleis exhibited works by a group of younger French Symbolists, including those of Paul Sérusier, Edouard Vuillard, Pierre Bonnard, and Émile Bernard—the Nabi circle in France. The Nabis, who took their collective name from the Hebrew word for prophet, were students who rebelled against the Académie Julian in 1888 and exhibited at the Café Volpini in Paris as *Groupe Impressioniste et Synthétique*. In the early 1890s, Mogens Ballin and Gad F. Clement

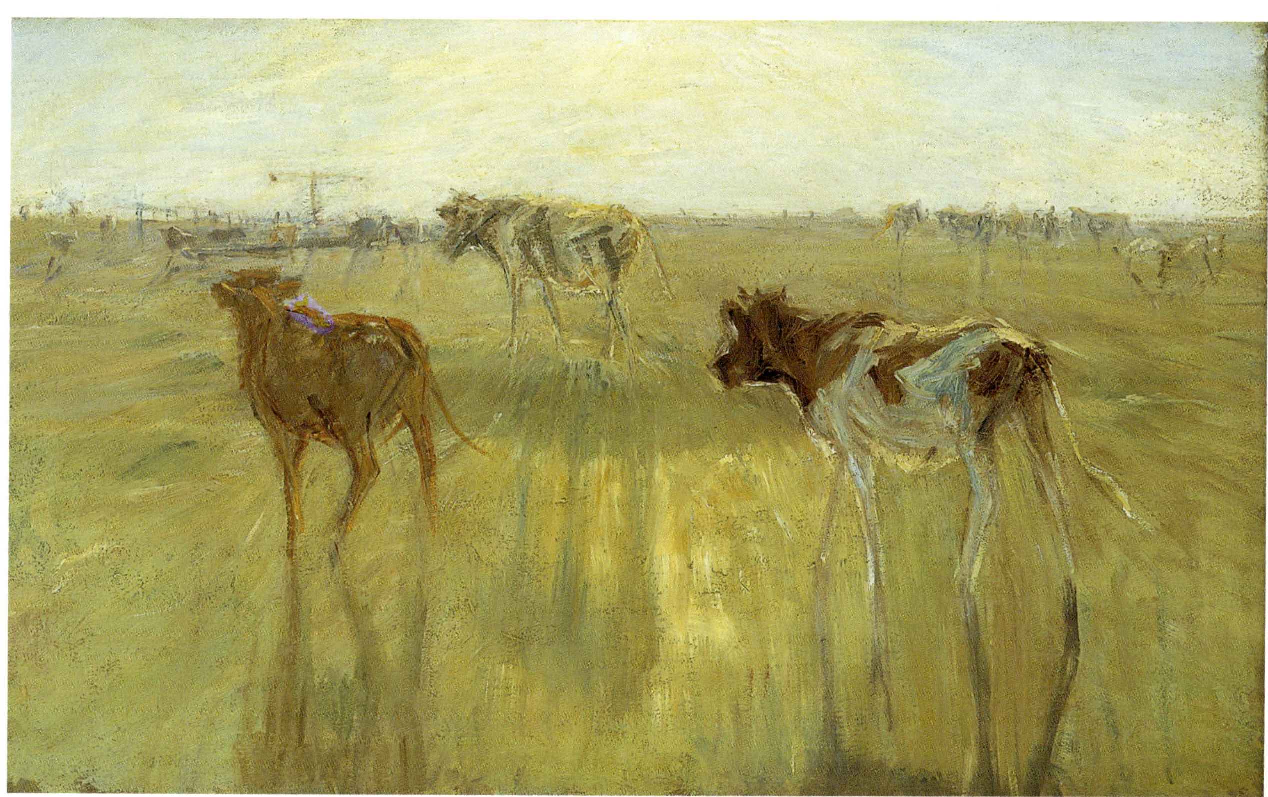

(1867–1933) were their disciples. [63] According to Emil Hannover, Clement was "the prophet of the new art . . . There is not a painter in Copenhagen for whom Clement has not been compelled to explain Synthetism [the term used to describe Gauguin and the Nabis' abstracted art]." [64] The two artists also converted to Catholicism, investing their art with a religious mysticism that appealed to the deeply spiritual Johannes Jørgensen.

During his first trip to Paris, Ballin met Gauguin and became close to Émile Bernard, Paul Sérusier, Paul Ranson, and Maurice Denis. Ballin accompanied Sérusier to Brittany in 1889, writing to Jørgensen in Copenhagen, "We dream of a new, extremely decorative art with powerful colors and simple, strong lines—to a slight extent: a renaissance of the great art there once was—and to a great extent: something quite new and characteristic of *our* century—that is what is coming; we are no longer fin de siècle." [65] In 1890 he returned to Brittany with Gad Clement, and in the following year with the Dutch painter Jan Verkade (1868–1946), when they worked closely with Sérusier, producing paintings like Ballin's *Landscape, Brittany* (1891–92, Private Collection). In its reduced forms, rhythmical brushwork, and heightened colors, the painting reflects Maurice Denis's dictum that "a painting is essentially a flat surface covered with colors assembled in a certain order," [66] and shares the quality of stained glass or cloisonné with Sérusier's work.

Gad F. Clement's *Decorative Picture. The Vision of St. Francis with the Three White Virgins* (1892–93; fig. 158) absorbed the works of the Nabis, dispensing with traditional perspective and constructing a painting through rhythmic, decorative lines and masses that echo one another, thus unifying the painting. Its title, calling attention to the painting's "decorative" identity, offers the notion that internal organizing principles are the hidden forces that structure

156.
Theodor Philipsen
*Cattle Seen Against the Sun
on the Island of Saltholm.
A Color Study*, 1892
Oil on canvas, 24⅞ x 40⅛ in.
(63 x 102 cm)
Statens Museum for Kunst,
Copenhagen

the painting, and all experience. The term "decorative," in this regard, resonated with notions of spirituality, and it is inextricably bound up with the theme of the Catholic saint and his vision.

Shortly after the 1893 exhibition in Kleis's Gallery and of the Gauguin and van Gogh works at the Free Exhibition, Johannes Jørgensen produced the first issue of *Taarnet*, which included an article by critic Simon Koch about painter Ludvig Find (1869–1945; see chapter 7) in whom he recognized a crystallization of new idealist tendencies.[67] Koch began his article combatively, quoting French critic Remy de Gourmont: "The time has surely come now to say quite honestly and openly: There are at the moment two classes of artists: those who have talent—the Symbolists, and those who do not—the others."[68]

The works of these artists and the popularity of the works of the Nabis shaped collecting patterns in 1890s Copenhagen. Mrs. Alice Faber (née Rubin, later Bloch), for example, purchased *Madonna with the Apple* by Maurice Denis and van Gogh's *Dr. Gachet* from Ambroise Vollard in Paris in the spring of 1897 (fig. 159).[69] Through such collections, younger artists had direct access to local and international vanguard painting. These collections were therefore, in turn, didactic, offering and legitimizing new works for the artists that encountered them.

The Danish Nabis represented only one of several eclectic manifestations of Symbolism in the 1890s. Indeed, the Free Exhibition was founded on the very notion of eclecticism, the freedom of expression. In 1894, The Free Exhibition included two ambitious works that came to shape the public reception of Symbolism: Joakim Skovgaard's *Christ in the Realm of the Dead* (1891–94; fig. 160) and Vilhelm Hammershøi's *Artemis* (1893–94; fig. 161). As observed by Peter Nørgaard Larsen, these paintings raised "questions of existence instead of everyday trivialities," in their assertion of strange articulations of older mythologies. Hammershøi's painting represents four life-size nude figures, one of them identified as Artemis by her attribute of the moon. Their androgyny, the isocephalic arrangement, columnar forms, and lack of tactility render them static and otherworldly.[70] In its suppression of pictorial detail and clear narrative, its subdued palette, and its undifferentiated space, Hammershøi's *Artemis* embodied many of the formal definitions of Symbolism as visual art that offers the contents of intellect through pictorial signs.[71] Mogens Ballin delineated these characteristics in a review in *Taarnet*: "How wondrously beautiful are these four naked beings, salutarily removed from the model's simple body, they are not cowed by the weaknesses and battles of a wretched life, they move about freely in the pure world of ideas, without words and almost without movement, they communicate their lofty thought to each other, soul speaks to soul on the deepest mysteries of life, on supreme beauty and the purest harmony."[72]

Hammershøi's painting was strongly indebted to the work of the French painter Pierre Puvis de Chavannes, one of the most admired artists in late nineteenth-century Denmark and also one of the most popular teachers of the Scandinavian women artists in Paris (see chapter 5). The work of Puvis was first exhibited in Copenhagen in 1888, and then again at the Ny Carlsberg Glyptotek's Internationale Kunstudstilling in 1897.[73] In works such as *The Poor Fisherman*,

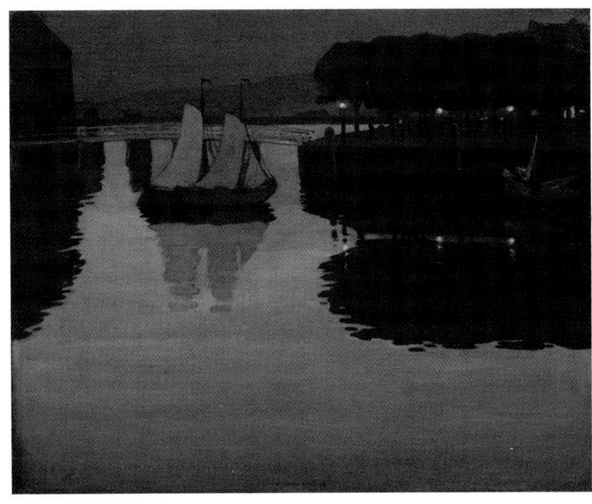

ABOVE

157.
Johan Rohde
Quiet Evening in the Harbor at Hoorn, 1893
Oil on canvas, 20⅞ x 24⅞ in.
(53 x 63 cm)
The Hirschsprung Collection, Copenhagen

OPPOSITE

158.
Gad F. Clement
Decorative Picture. The Vision of St. Francis with the Three White Virgins, 1892–93
Oil on canvas, 63⅜ x 43¼ in.
(161 x 110 cm)
Collection John Hunov, Copenhagen

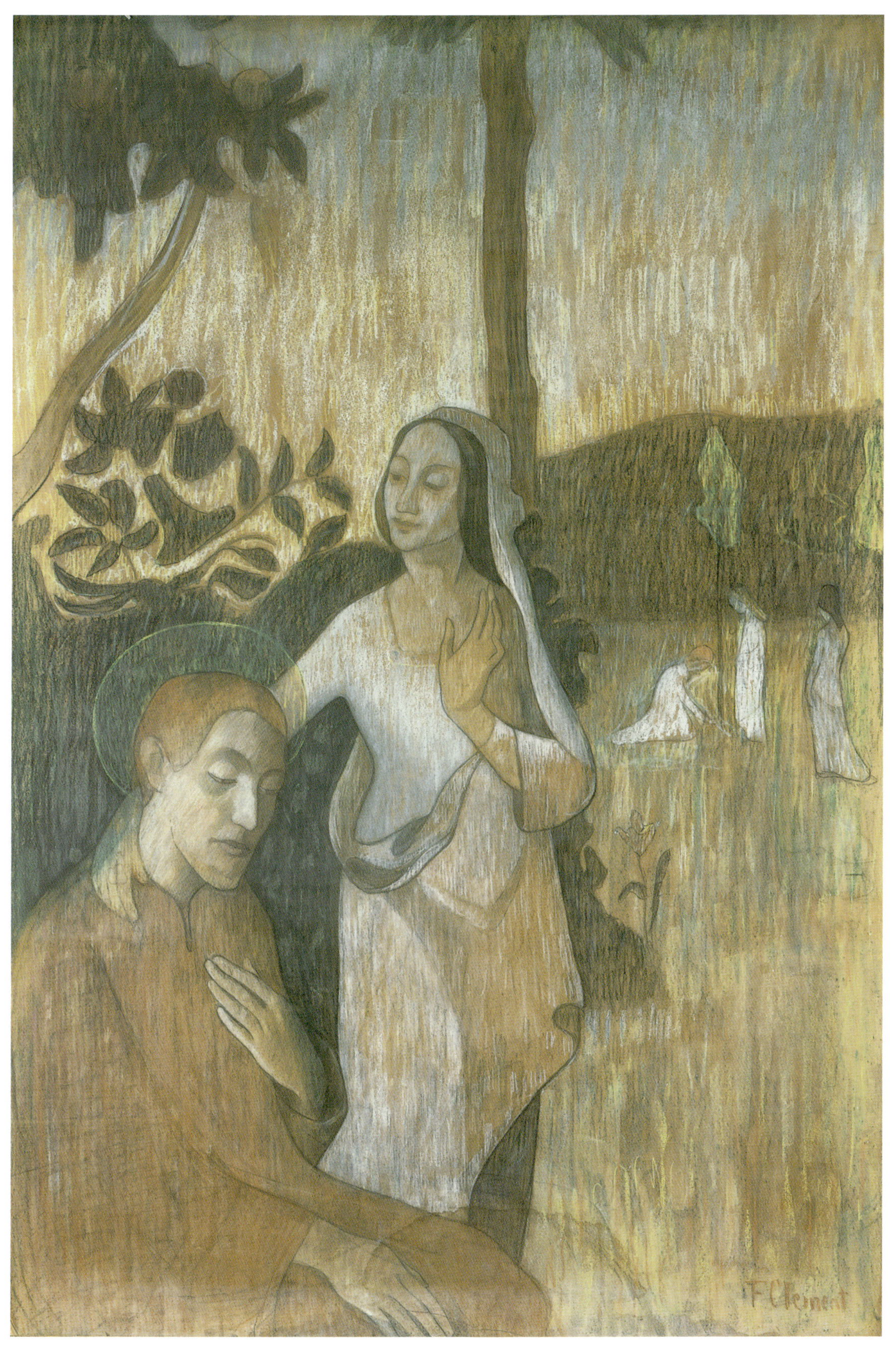

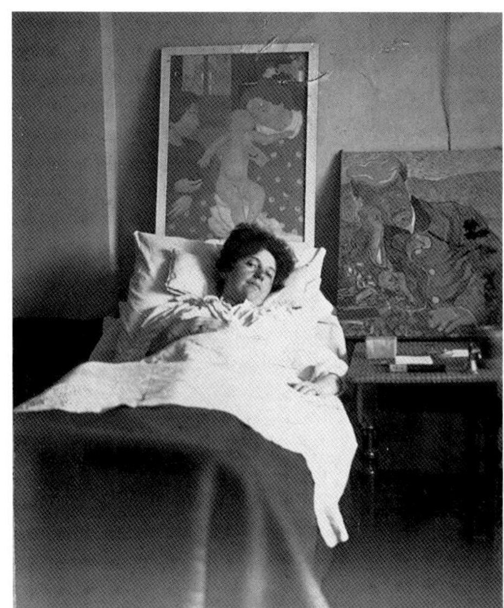

159.
Photographer unknown
Alice Bloch in childbed with Van Gogh's Portrait of Dr. Gachet and Maurice Denis' Madonna with the Apple, n.d.
photograph
Collection John Hunov, Copenhagen

from 1881 (fig. 162), Puvis enhanced the linearity of his forms, drained away sculptural modeling, and created large patches of paint to create flattened, veil-like, and entirely static compositions, suggesting a path toward a highly personal, emotionally laden form of naturalist painting.[74] The pictorial strategies of Puvis, including high horizon lines, meandering contours of land and sky, and a concentration on pockets of isolated, local color shaped the visions of Danish artists as different as Krøyer and Hammershøi.[75] In this regard Hammershøi's painting at the 1894 Free Exhibition represented a new disembodied, static aesthetic, a suggestion of painting as a realm of artifice and internal logic.

In contrast, Skovgaard's *Christ in the Realm of the Dead*, which measures 11.5 x 16 feet, was a watershed in Danish religious art, its "operatic" content offering a revitalization of sacred painting through complex visual spectacle and its grand scale employed to elicit awe.[76] In it, Jesus is greeted by an ecstatic figure of Eve and behind her, as described by Swedish poet Verner von Heidenstam (1859–1940), "hosts of the dead . . . seeking to force their way towards the light like fish against the glass in an aquarium."[77] The painting illustrates Jesus' descent into Hell to succor the souls of the just, a theme repeated from the gospels in thirteenth-century England and adapted by N. F. S. Grundtvig in a poem entitled "This night there was a knocking on the gates of Hell" (1837). A lengthy extract from Grundtvig's poem was exhibited with the painting at the Free Exhibition.[78] The Catholic convert Ballin saw the painting—and the artist—as redemptive forces: "The glowing faith of a great man resonates from this work, the outer beauty and inner truth of which tower above anything our art has produced hitherto, miles above the barren shambles of this unfortunate age."[79]

Taken together, as Peter Nørgaard Larsen states, Skovgaard and Hammershøi's paintings cemented the idealist tendencies that had begun to emerge in the early 1890s, offering oppositional models of production—a secular, decorative, and anti-narrative painting and a sacred work in the form of a metaphysical history painting—for the Danish public. Within this formal and ideological range, other eclectic expressions of anti-naturalism flowered within Danish art, from L. A. Ring's enigmatic landscapes to the Danish Nabi works.

Further enriching the Free Exhibition and wider circles within Denmark was a growing commitment to the decorative and functional arts, in which L. A. Ring played a role. Ring's *Six Portraits in Profile. Herman Kähler's Children* (1898; fig. 163) is a radical departure from his earlier socially engaged paintings and his intensely observed landscapes. Ring painted this composition on the occasion of the anniversary of his parents-in-law, Herman and Jansine Kähler. Herman Kähler (1857–1942), whom Ring first met in 1885, was one of Denmark's leading ceramicists. His studio in Næstved attracted, among others, Thorvald Bindesbøll and Svend Hammershøi (chapter 7). It was one of the centers of the new art ceramics produced in Denmark, where the expressive ceramicists of the 1890s developed their technical abilities.[80] Ring had married the Kählers' oldest daughter, Sigrid (who appears on the far left), in 1896. The background, textured, incised, and over-painted in oil in the manner of a trecento altarpiece, is bracketed by trees whose branches and canopy arch upward and toward the compositional center, creating a frame for the portraits. There is a curious disjunction between the flat gilded background and the compressed portraits of Sigrid and her siblings that, although linear and stylized, have a sculptural plasticity. Peter Nørgaard Larsen believes that Ludvig Find, Ring's closest friend, and Thorvald Bindesbøll,

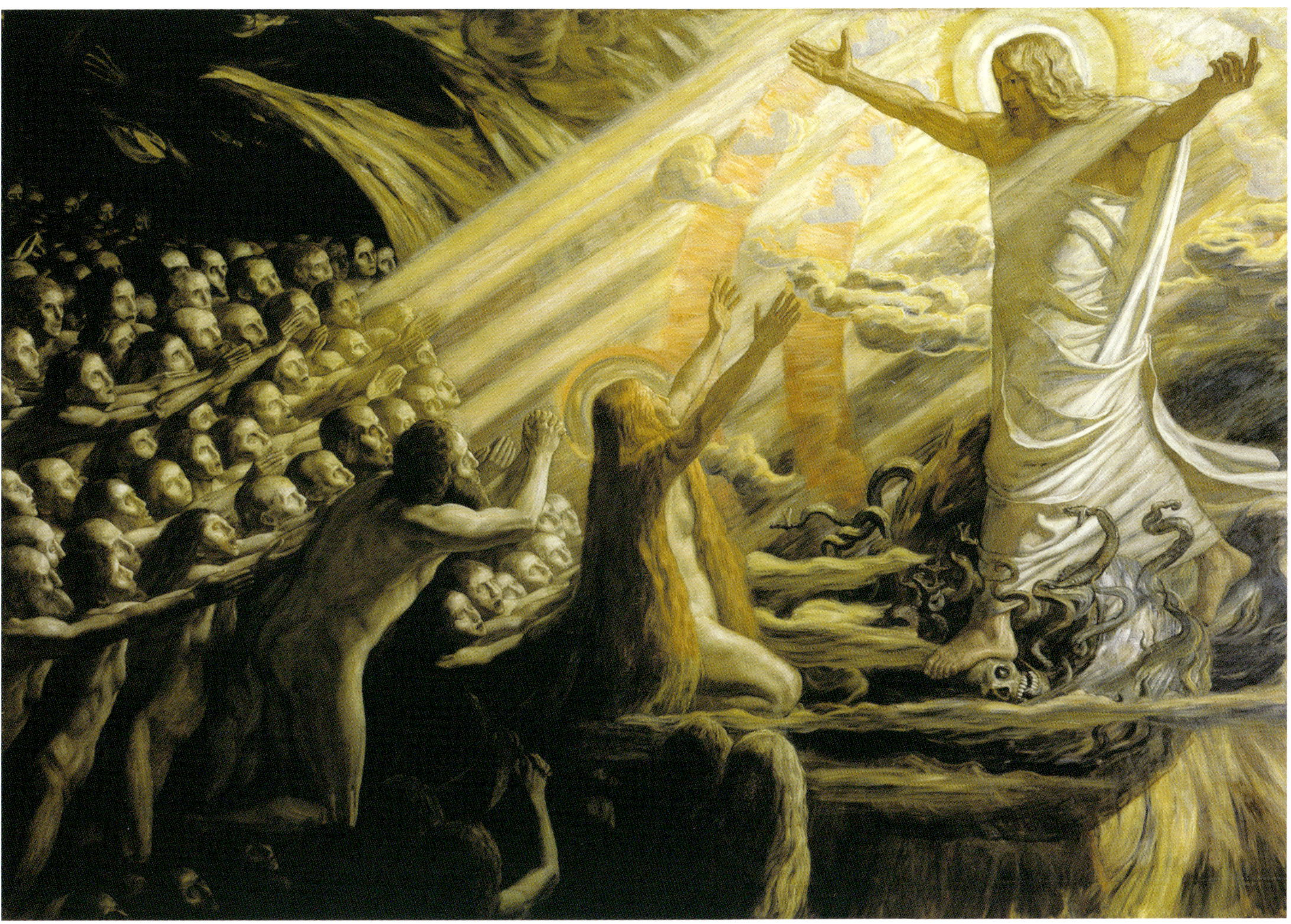

whom Ring encountered at Kähler's studio, were responsible for encouraging the artist to explore this decorative idiom.[81]

Kähler's Workshop had gained great prominence after the 1888 Nordic Exhibition for Industry, Agriculture, and Art (see below), at which it exhibited its wares, and then received a silver medal at the Paris Universal Exposition in the following year. Architect and designer Thorvald Bindesbøll, who designed the Brøndum Hotel dining room, the fish-packing houses at Skagen, and the first temporary building for the Free Exhibition, was also among Denmark's leading ceramicists, and a regular participant in Kähler's Workshop. Bindesbøll's thick, expressionist glazeware (fig. 164) re presented a shared aesthetic with Kähler, Svend Hammershøi, and, briefly, L. A. Ring. Decorated with abstract designs and inscribed in a manner exaggerating Italian sgraffito techniques, Bindesbøll's ceramics bridge Paul Gauguin's figurative stoneware of the 1880s and Expressionist and abstract works in the years before the Great War.[82] For the international audience, Bindesbøll's most enduring decorative work is his label for Carlsberg Pilsner (1904; fig. 165). The streamlined design with the art nouveau script, was commissioned by the brewer Carl Jacobsen, one of Copenhagen's leading patrons of the arts.[83]

160.
Joakim Skovgaard
Christ in the Realm of the Dead, 1891–94
Oil on canvas, 138⅜ x 192½ in.
(351.5 x 489 cm)
Statens Museum for Kunst,
Copenhagen

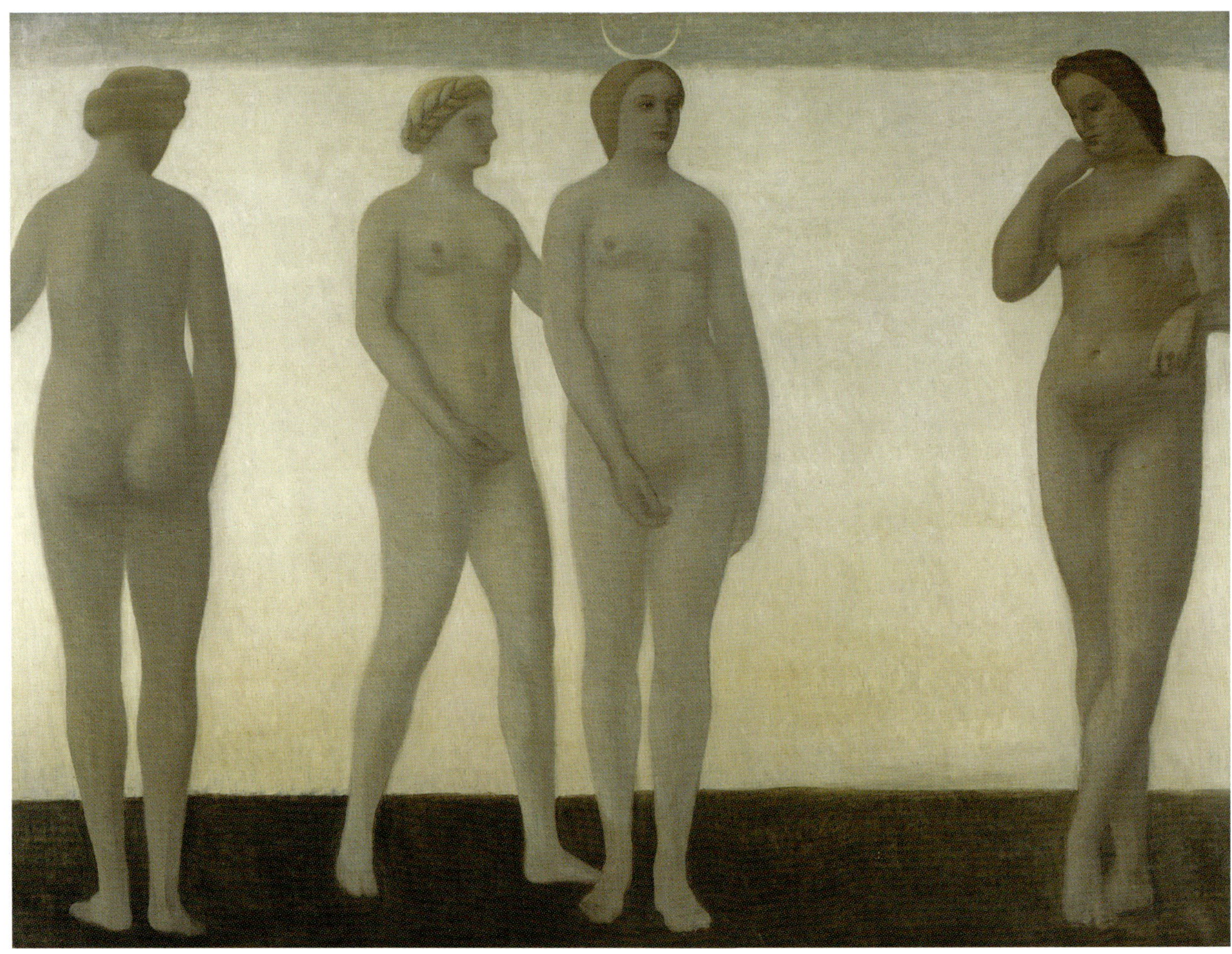

A new generation of art patrons in Denmark had been crucial to the emergence of such institutions as the Kähler Workshop, the Free Exhibition, the Artists Study School, and the circulation of advanced continental art in Denmark. Carl and Otillia Jacobsen had, for example, built the Ny Carlsberg Glyptotek museum in 1892, having donated their collection to the state in 1888 for the benefit of the public. The collection included both antique sculpture and contemporary Danish and French art.[84] It was here that Niels Bjerre and L. A. Ring likely saw the work of Millet, for example. At about the same time, the tobacco manufacturer Heinrich Hirschsprung (1836–1908) and his wife Pauline were also important patrons of the arts, commissioning and collecting works by contemporary Danish artists and then, at the turn of the century, systematically collecting the works of Golden Age painters. Represented in a painting by P. S. Krøyer (fig. 166), whom they had supported in his travels, the Hirschsprung family embodies the cultivated, artistically inclined, civic-minded generation of patrons who modernized Copenhagen's art scene. Through the building of their museum in 1911, the Hirschsprungs joined Mette Gad Gauguin, the Free Exhibition, the Artist Study School, and Carl Jacobsen in establishing institutional structures for the assimilation of new and international art into Danish cultural life.

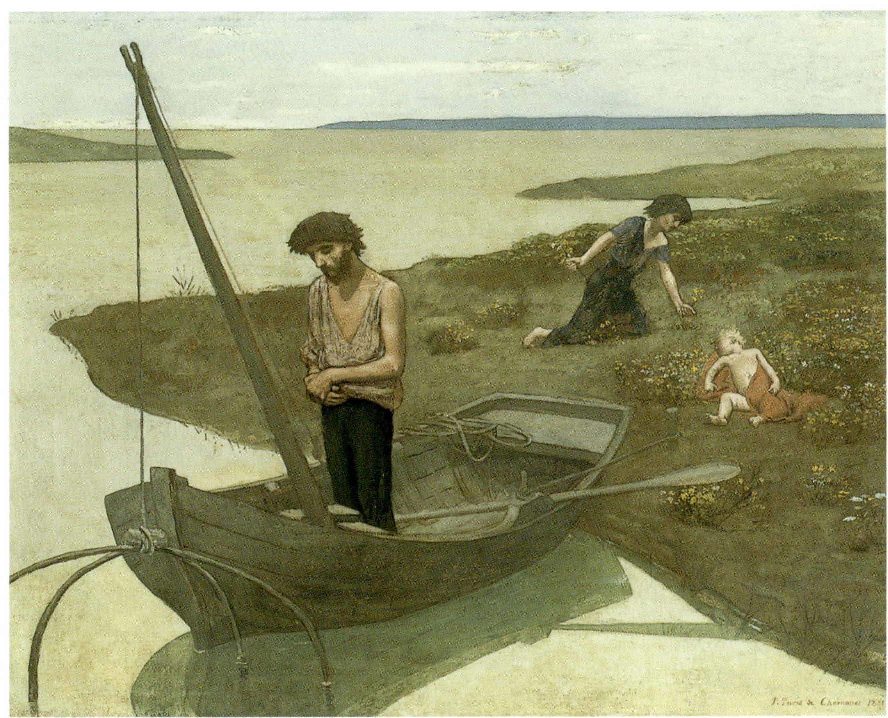

162.
Pierre Puvis de Chavannes
The Poor Fisherman, 1881
Oil on canvas, 61 x 75¾ in.
(155 x 192.5 cm)
Musée d'Orsay, Paris

Such artistic experimentation with pottery and other forms of handwork had been a focus of the Nordic Exhibition of Industry, Agriculture, and Art (Den Nordiske Industri-, Landbrugs- og Kunstudstilling), a vast pan-Nordic industrial exposition that took place in Copenhagen in 1888. In what many historians have noted as a precursor to the Paris Universal Exposition in 1889, the Nordic Exposition offered Copenhagen as a tourist destination and a leader in technology and creativity. Because of the initiative that many collectors had taken to integrate art into the lives of Copenhagen citizens, from Bertel Thorvaldsen to Carl Jacobsen, the guidebook to the fair could proclaim that Copenhagen could take its place as a "city of museums."[85]

The artistic assimilation of handicraft was also promoted by the Free Exhibition. In 1894, Agnes Slott-Møller (1862–1937), Harald Slott-Møller's wife, exhibited *Niels Ebbesen* (1893–94; fig. 167), its vast scale, hand-carved frame, and literary ambitions offering a third dimension, an overt invocation of nationalism, to the monumental pictures exhibited there. Niels Ebbesen (d. 1340), one of Denmark's national heroes, was a nobleman from Jutland who, according to tradition, helped to wrest Western Denmark from the control of the Dukes of Holstein, especially the despotic Duke Gerhard, who exploited the already impoverished peasants. In the years after 1864, Ebbesen was a potent symbol of Danish resistance against German domination.[86] Ebbesen was the subject of ballads, edifying children's stories, scholarly treatises, and national romantic poetry, most influentially in N. F. S. Grundtvig's 1840 poem whose refrain, "Tyskerne reves om Danmark" (The Germans are fighting in Denmark), became a common expression in the years after the Schleswig-Holstein Wars.[87] Ebbesen appears in Slott-Møller's painting as a knight astride an over-scaled horse, walking through the flat wintry landscape of Jutland, facing a darkened gray sky and bringing sunlight in his wake. A series of overlapping compositional triangles converge at the top of his helmet, unifying the composition and suggesting the protagonist's

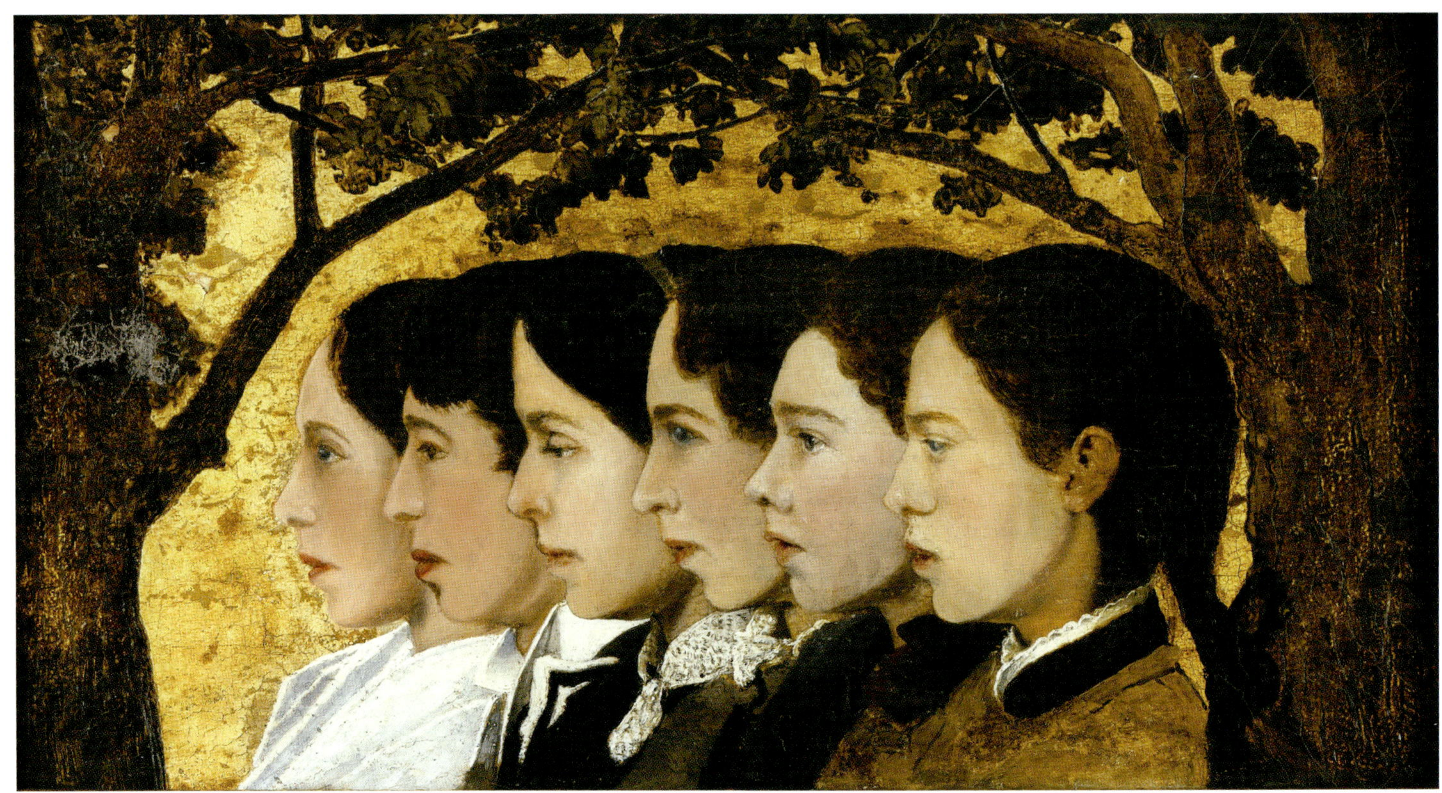

163.
L. A. Ring
Six Portraits in profile. Herman Kähler's Children, 1898
Oil on wood with gold background,
12 x 20⅞ in.
(30.5 x 53 cm)
Private Collection

resolve. Slott-Møller's intention, as described in her memoirs, was to render him both specially Danish and as a universal archetype, but also to provide an offering: "I wanted to paint the picture in order to pay off some of the debt of gratitude which I felt to this giant Dane for having saved the country at one of its darkest moments."[88] With this work, Slott-Møller contributed a new type of image to Denmark's repertory of national representations, a large history painting stripped of incidental anecdote and articulating affinities with Medieval and Renaissance piety through its style and decorative frame.[89]

In 1899, Agnes Slott-Møller painted *The Maiden Blidelil* (fig. 168), representing a scene from one of Denmark's medieval ballads (*folkeviser*).[90] Slott-Møller reports that she had wished to paint this theme from her early years at the Women's Drawing School in 1884, and she pursued the theme on and off through the 1910s.[91] In 1899, she was inspired by a landscape that resonated with the story for her; "There is . . . a high slope falling steeply to the shore, if you stand up there, you will have a large expanse of the bluest water in all Denmark . . . And so the Maiden Blidelil must have seen the blue water below her when she 'put on her suit of feathers and flew until she reached the ships.'"[92] In the painting, Blidelil is suspended high over the water. Only a tiny jetty emerging from the painting's right edge offers a sense of her vertiginous height. Her feathered cloak just grazes the upper edge of the canvas and her body, almost parallel with the exceptionally high horizon line, evokes visual associations with the fall of Icarus.

The ballad of "Blidelil and Tidemand" was one of a large body of medieval Danish *folkeviser* that had been collected and published throughout the eighteenth and nineteenth centuries, but which were most earnestly issued in the years after mid-century. Viewed as survivals of a period of national expansion, they were most systematically collected by Svend Grundtvig

(1824–1883), son of the poet and theologian, who issued the first of his many volumes of *Danmarks Gamle Folkeviser* in 1853.[93] In her commitment to the illustration of such literature, Slott-Møller pursued the notion articulated by the historian and linguist Christian Molbech (see chapter 4) that folk tales were the product of the "folk," and not individual creativity, and that they therefore transmitted the collective imagination of the people: "The folk song is a poem of nature. It does not have one identifiable author. Instead its poet has been lost in the past, leaving his song to move among his people from generation to generation."[94] Further, the publications of ballads and children's songbooks were a critical venture within the project of nation building after 1864, in which the Danish language, history, and collective activity merged.[95] In her memoirs, Slott-Møller stated that she knew the old ballads before she could even read, that they, in a sense, were educated into her as an organic part of her identity.[96]

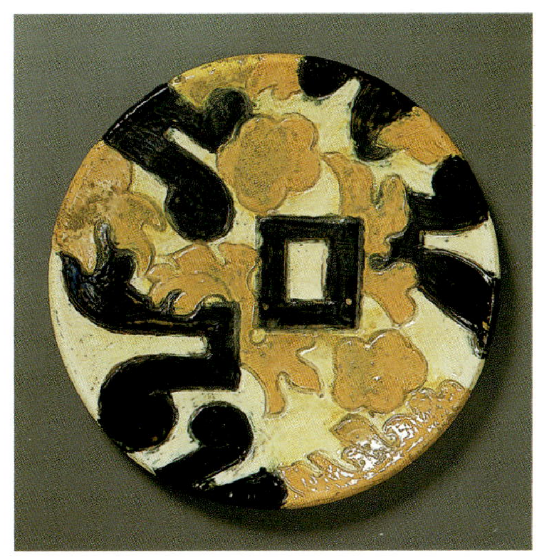

In 1913, Slott-Møller painted three moments from the ballad of "Blide-lil and Tidemand," incorporating them into a triptych embedded in a heavy carved frame decorated with the ballad's text (Hotel Dagmar, Ribe). In so doing, she translated the ballad, a token of Denmark's folk history, into a religious icon.[97]

As noted previously, Agnes and Harald Slott-Møller were among the founding members of the Free Exhibition, and were, for a time, closely allied with Johan Rohde, Johannes Jørgensen, and Emil Hannover. They were also among Denmark's leading advocates of William Morris's Arts and Crafts aesthetic. The need for a return to medieval purity in the face of industrialization, and the redemptive qualities of hand-wrought items, as articulated in John Ruskin's seminal book *The Stones of Venice* (1851–1853), resonated with the Slott-Møllers' own increasing spirituality and with their commitment to national efflorescence.[98]

In the early 1890s, Harald Slott-Møller's earlier commitment to urban social themes, as represented by such works as *The Poor. The Waiting Room of Death* gave way to a symbolic, decorative idiom similar to his wife's nationalist Arts and Crafts aesthetic. In *Danish Landscape* (1891; fig. 169), a hybrid between a painting and a relief sculpture, a field of wheat is transformed into literal gold. When the artist exhibited it at the Free Exhibition in 1891, he announced his new Symbolist orientation. The painting consists of an iron sheet with a chased, gilded decorative relief on which the artist painted the placid sky and a stork hovering over the grain. The composition is surrounded by an oak frame on which waves appear below and bulbous patterns, like budding wheat, are carved above. The experimental work literally sacralizes the Danish landscape, its gilding operating at once as optical decoration, a sign of fertility, and a symbol of divinity.

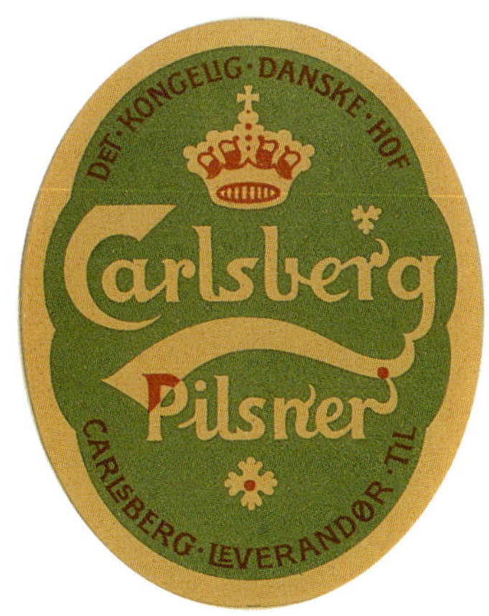

Under the influence of the art of the Italian quattrocento, which the Slott-Møllers encountered during a trip to Italy in 1888–1889, Harald Slott-Møller simplified and regularized his forms in the 1890s, producing such works as *Three Women, Summer Evening* (1895; fig. 170). In it, Agnes Slott-Møller holding the couple's first child, Agnes's sister Agathe Rambusch, and another woman in their circle promenade before a profusion of stylized flowering bushes. By combining painted, gilded, and carved surfaces, Slott-Møller offers this procession, a theme shared with P. S. Krøyer (see fig. 134), as a ritualized and rigorously harmonious event. As noted by art historian Hanne Honnens de Lichtenberg, these portraits also operate as personifications of Spring, Summer, and Autumn, the first holding a blossom-festooned child, the

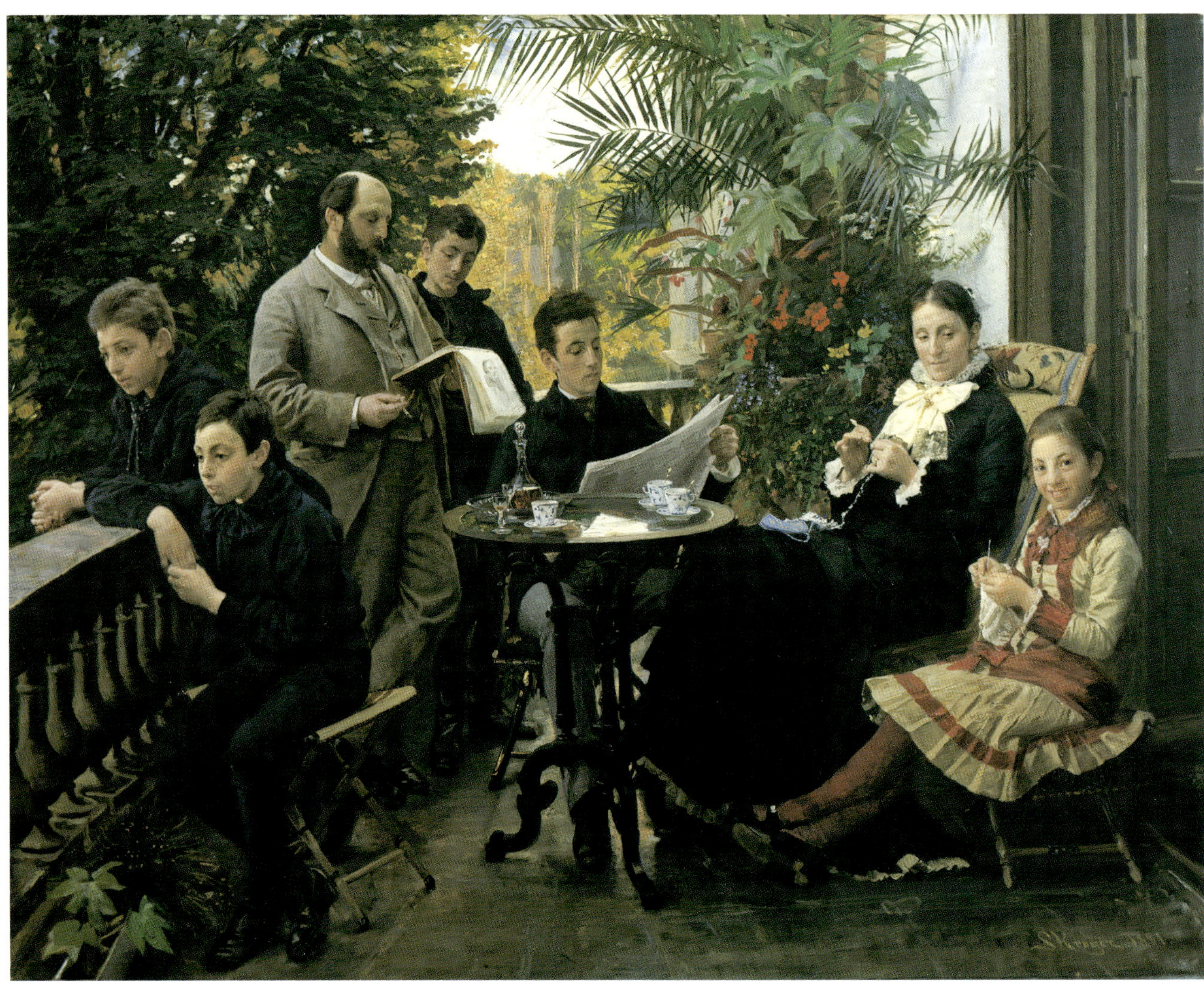

166.
P. S. Krøyer
Portrait of the Hirschsprung Family, 1881
Oil on canvas, 42½ x 50⅜ in.
(108 x 128 cm)
The Hirschsprung Collection,
Copenhagen

second bearing flowering honeysuckle, and the third holding harvested berries.[99] The repetition of forms and high degree of decoration and finish imbue the work with a static quality. Like *Danish Landscape*, this painting symbolizes sacred fertility.

Both Slott-Møllers worked in a range of media, moving among painting and the functional arts. Harald Slott-Møller's medievalized painted wood *Cradle* (1893; fig. 171), exhibited at the Free Exhibition in 1894, funnels aesthetics, domesticity, and didactic historicism into an art form that was intended to revitalize contemporary society. In that year, when Hammershøi, Skovgaard, and Agnes Slott-Møller exhibited their large compositions that shaped the terms of Danish Symbolism, the decorative arts also made a strong showing at the Free Exhibition.[100]

After the turn of the century, the Slott-Møllers became fully engaged with old master art and estranged from other members of the Free Exhibition. Their increasing religiosity and polemical adherence to a medievalizing aesthetic, and a progressively conservative understanding of nationalism, resulted in negative critical responses to their work by their old colleagues. In turn, Harald Slott-Møller wrote a series of essays criticising contemporary Danish art: "The

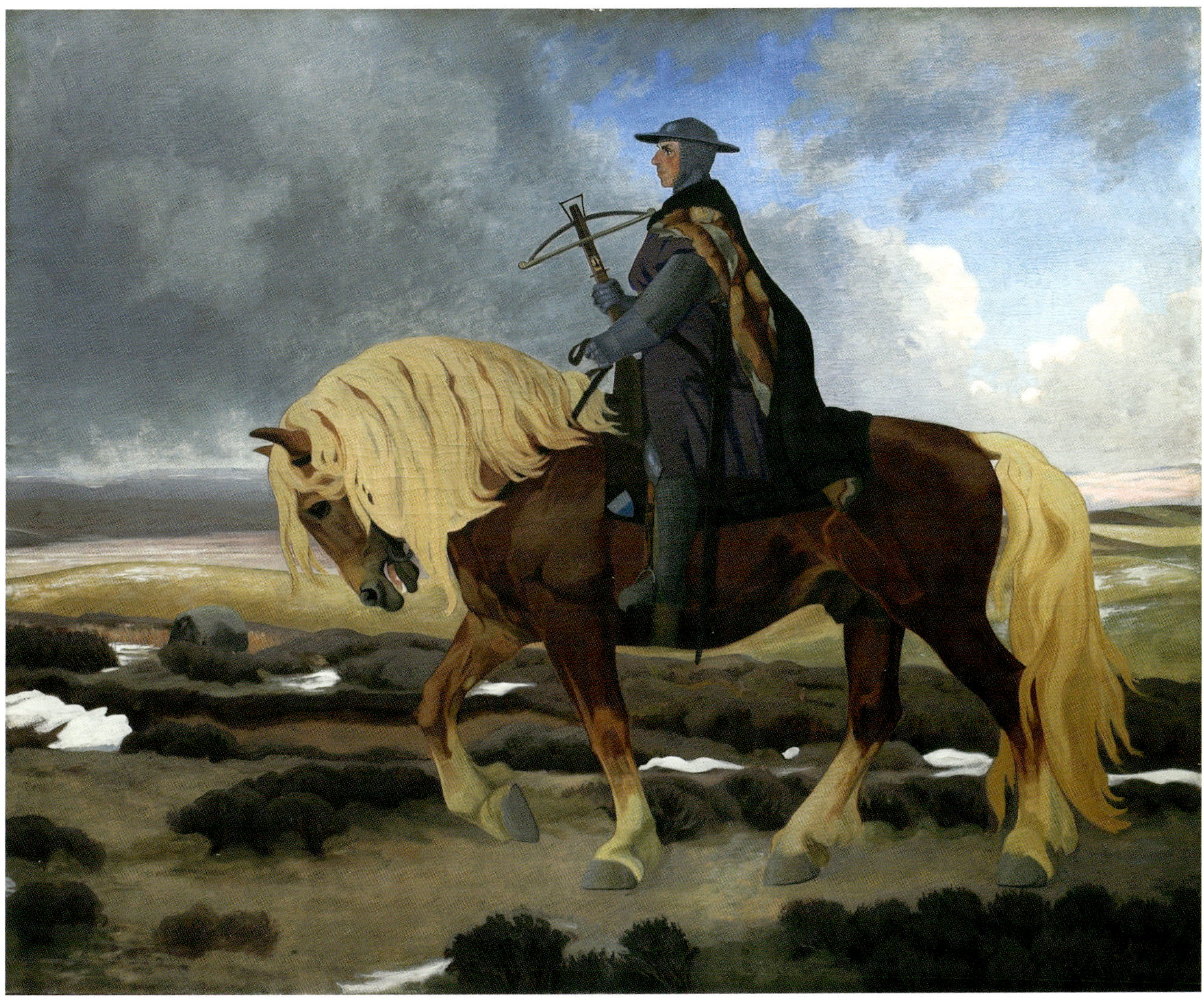

Free Exhibition ought to replace its beautiful symbol over the entrance [to the new building], the rider ascending on his winged horse, with the pitiful work which a young sculptor exhibits in one of the halls and which rightly bears the title 'Decadence.'"[101]

The Slott-Møllers' criticism of many of their former colleagues turned superficially on the question of style. The deeper issues, however, engaged fundamental questions of religion and patriotism. Harald Slott-Møller considered the works of many of his contemporaries to lack the deep engagement of "soul" and belief found in the works of the old masters.[102] Agnes was a historicist, believing that it was the artist's responsibility to tap the nation's well of past historical treasures to enrich contemporary cultural identity: "Everything that is Danish is passed on to us by our fatherland, as if poured from a precious piece of china. Its liquid contains memories which serve to give us strength and make us better."[103] In this regard, she carried on the work of Grundtvig, Molbech, Oehlenschläger, and Høyen, understanding national identity as an ethical position. In her writings and lectures, she criticized those who were blind to such an imperative, and in her art, she cleaved to a crafts-oriented aesthetic that expressed and resonated with historical models.

167.
Agnes Slott-Møller
Niels Ebbesen, 1893–94
Oil on canvas with decorative frame,
122½ x 147⅝ in. (311 x 375 cm)
Randers Kunstmuseum

Their contemporary Jens Ferdinand Willumsen, perhaps the most internationally engaged artist in Denmark, could not have been farther from their orientation. With close affiliations with both French and German art, as art historian Loa Haagen Pictet notes, Willumsen exhibited throughout Europe. He was deemed progressive enough after the turn of the century to be invited by Emil Nolde (1867–1956) to join the expanded circle of the German Expressionist group Die Brücke.[104] The author of the Gauguin-influenced etching *Fertility* that had affected the critical reception of the Free Exhibition, Willumsen was profoundly shaped by notions of spirituality. However, his understanding of religion was decisively different from that of the Slott-Møllers, Jørgensen, Ballin, or Skovgaard.

Willumsen had begun his studies as an aspiring architect in the late 1870s, then entering the Royal Academy in 1881 as a painter. Dissatisfied with the training he received there, he studied at the Free Artist's Study School in 1885. He lived in Paris between 1890 and 1894, at which time he met and befriended Paul Gauguin.[105] Willumsen produced work in painting, architecture, ceramics, and other functional arts. From 1897 to 1900, he served as artistic director of Bing & Grøndal, one of Denmark's foremost porcelain manufacturers. In this regard, he joined Bindesbøll and Kähler as one of Denmark's preeminent fine arts ceramicists.

Willumsen's most ambitious works experimented with the ways in which painting, sculpture, the functional arts, and writing interact. His life-long project was *The Great Relief* (1893–1928, Statens Museum for Kunst, J. F. Willumsen Museum, Frederikssund), a monumental complex of marble and other stones, gilded bronze, and ceramic, offering a grandiose synthesis of human endeavor.[106] In 1893, he also produced *Jotunheimen* (1892–93; fig. 172), a massive composition of oil on canvas, framed by mahogany, painted zinc, and enamel on copper. He began work on this conception during his first trip to Norway, in the summer of 1892, when he had an exhibition in Kristiania. He traveled up the coast to the far north and into the mountains of central Norway. He completed the work in his studio in Paris. In the center of the painting is a view of the Jotunheimen mountain range, containing Norway's tallest mountains, rising from a frozen lake. A second representation of the mountains, in painted metal relief, surmounts the frame, which is itself composed of decorative filigree and nude human figures. In the painting, the mountain peaks, glaciers, and snow fields are described in broad, crisply linear organic forms which stand in contrast to the mosaic-like effect of their reflection on the water's still surface. A string of ochre granite islands interrupts the water's surface in the foreground, offering a second set of reflections composed of floating planes of color. Art historian Troels Branth Pedersen has examined the genesis and sources of *Jotunheimen* and the extent to which the painting drew upon contemporary Norwegian visual culture, including national romantic landscape painting, view photography, maps, and ephemera.[107] When he exhibited it at the Free Exhibition in 1895, he included an explanatory text:

> The clouds drifted away, and I found myself on the edge of a precipice looking out
> across the mountainous landscape in the far north, serious and brutally covered
> with eternal ice and snow, a world uninhabitable for human beings. The images
> in the relief were fashioned under the impression of this serious atmosphere. The
> figures in the relief on the left represent those who determinedly seek through
> learning and the intellect to find the connection between the infinitely great and the
> infinitely small. The infinitely great is represented by a stellar nebula, the infinitely

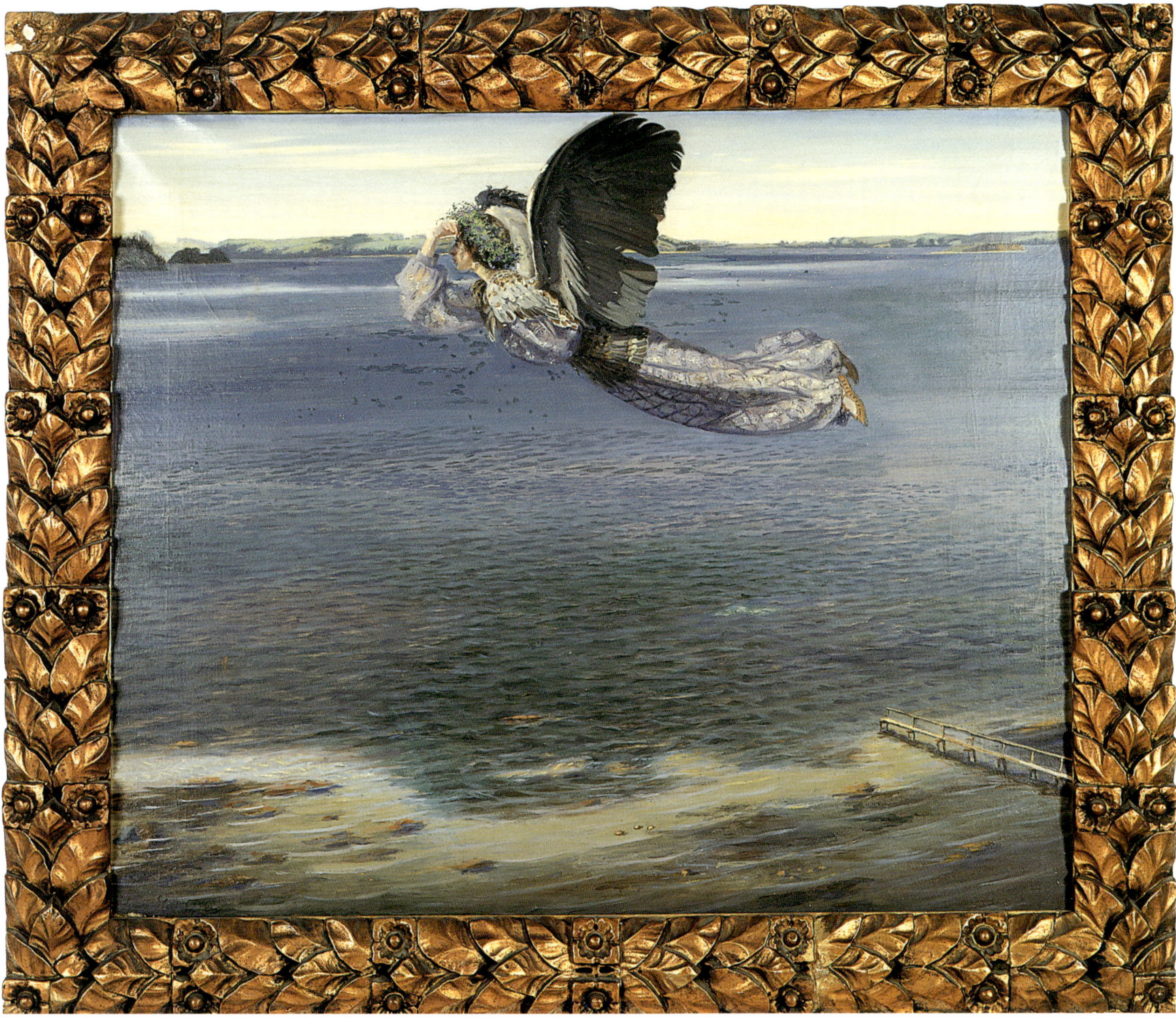

168.
Agnes Slott-Møller
The Maiden Blidelil, 1899
Oil on panel with decorative frame,
31⅛ x 37 in. (79 x 94 cm)
Collection John Hunov, Copenhagen

small by some microbes. The figure at the bottom is expecting inspiration; the figure at the top feels convinced of the correct result of his research. The relief on the right represents a contrast to the relief on the left: pointlessness; at the bottom two men, one of whom is weaving a piece of wickerwork which the other is just as quickly unraveling; in the middle a group of indifferent figures; at the top a figure representing a chimeric dream. The frame at the top contains a decorative picture of a mountain range made in enamel on copper.[108]

This text unfolds from a description of the most ineffable state of being (clouds/precipice) to that of the crassest human materialism (the figures of folly), literally moving from the sublime to the ridiculous. Within it, the eternal, resistant landscape is a realm of purity.

Art historian Merete Bodelsen has linked this programmatic painting to a source in romantic literature, the Scottish essayist and historian Thomas Carlyle's transcendentalist *Sar-*

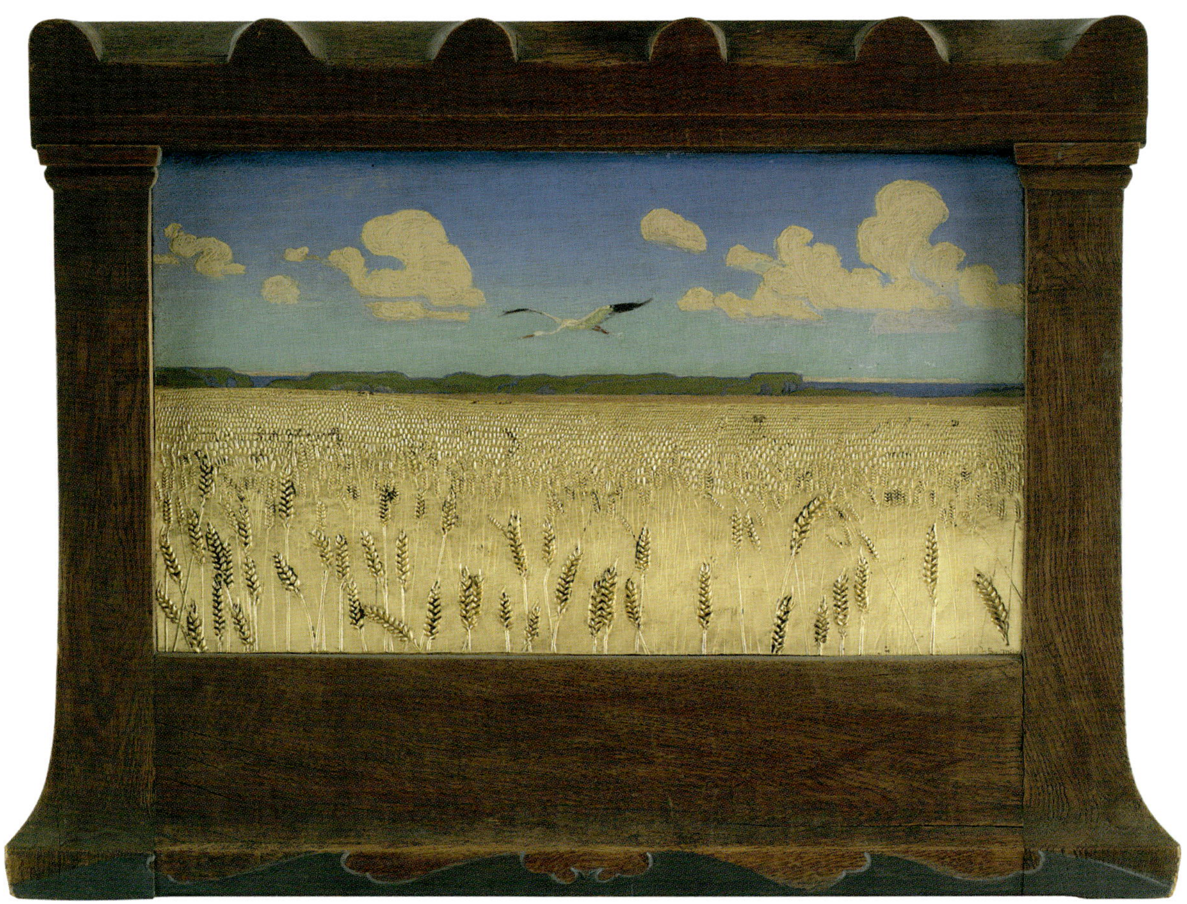

169.
Harald Slott-Møller
Danish Landscape, 1891
Oil on panel, 16⅛ x 27½ in.
(41 x 70 cm)
Private Collection. Long-term
loan to Statens Museum for Kunst,
Copenhagen

tor Resartus (1833–34), in which spirituality, divested from materialism and organized religion, anchors human meaning.[109] In its critique of material striving and its testimony to the supra-human experience of nature, Willumsen's work resonated with Jørgensen's definition of Symbolism in *Taarnet*: "The modern lack of a moral sense is the modern lack of a metaphysics." The artist "feels his soul's union with the soul of Nature and behind the apparent indifference of phenomena intuits the eternity from which his soul has sprung."[110]

The painting's lack of shadows and traditional perspective emphasize the forbidding desolation of the mountains and the clarity of the high altitude, offering them as a realm of purity in contrast to the dissipated activity of the figures on the right side of the relief. Such dualities are embedded throughout this composition, between the rational scientists on the left and the figure of folly on the right, the serpentine mountains and tesserated water, city and wilderness, the two-dimensional and the three-dimensional.

At the turn of the century, Willumsen produced a number of other views of nature as rugged realms of suprahuman force including *Sun Over the Southern Mountains* (1902; fig. 173). In it, the upper half exaggerates a swelling, forbidding, uninhabitable alpine landscape seen in crystalline light, which is separated from the earth below by a layer of clouds. A small village, isolated from the rest of the world, clings to the base of the mountains at the edge of the sea, bathed in a rich golden orange light that issues from above. Layers of water, ground

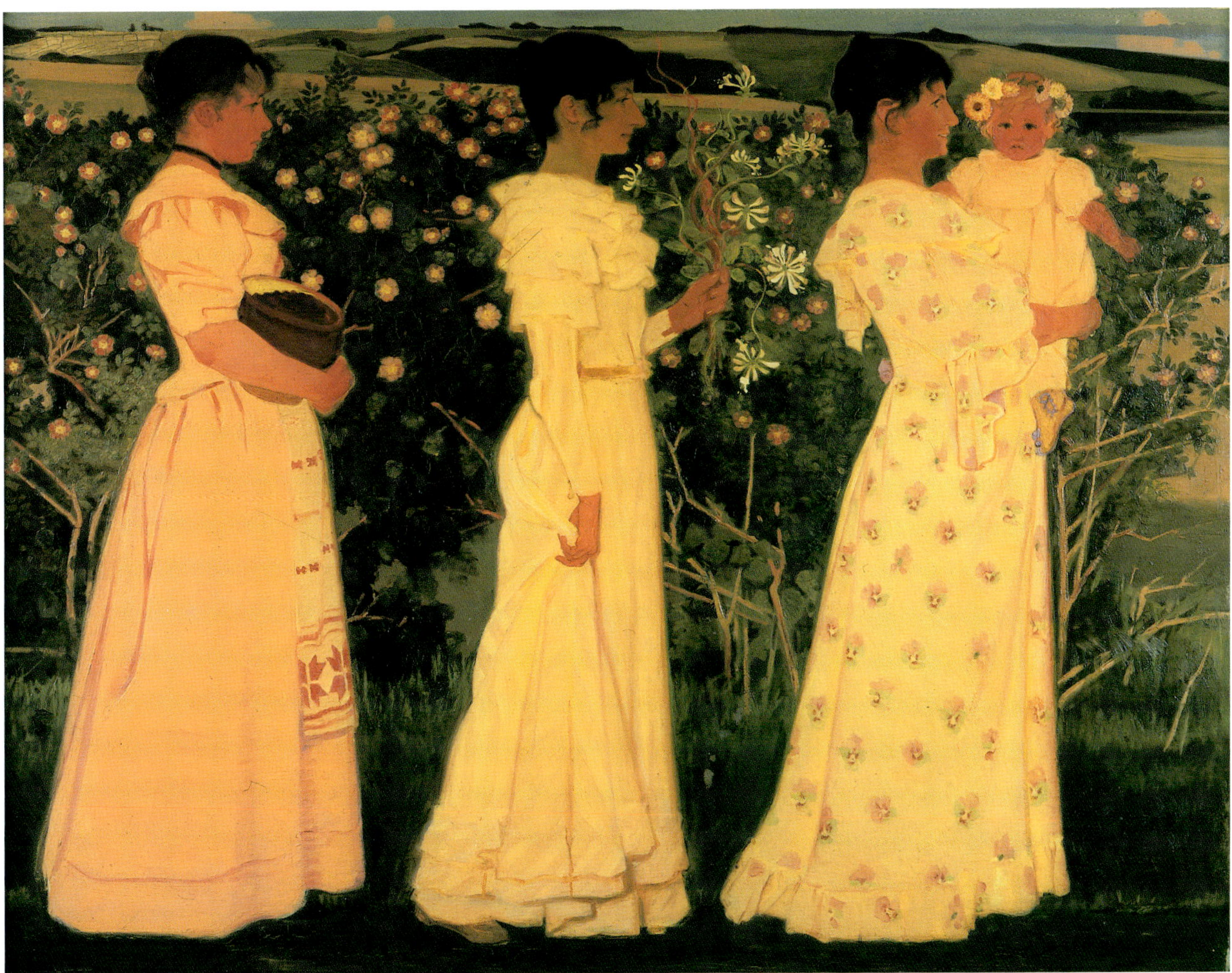

fog, mountain mists, clouds, glaciers, and the nimbus of light in the upper right corner of the canvas invest layer after layer of operatic sublimity to the scene. The smallness and vulnerability of human habitation in the majestic landscape offers both a glimpse of nature's powerful majesty and of inconsequential human existence.[111]

In its evocation of an overwhelming nature and its assertion of flat, planar representation and serpentine, prismatic brush strokes, the painting resonates with a large body of work that began to appear in Germany and the Nordic countries after the turn of the century. This phenomenon has been likened to the Vitalist movement, a philosophical system that proposed a life force that unified all realms of nature. Vitalism offered a point of agreement between positivist Darwinian and traditional Christian belief, a mediating system popularized by the zoologist Ernst Haeckel (1834–1919) at the University of Jena in Germany, and which exerted an exceptional influence over intellectuals throughout the North.[112]

In addition to its sense of the sublime, *Sun Over the Southern Mountains* also evokes the value of natural purity as related to the body. Views of high mountain landscapes were, by the turn of the century, associated throughout Europe with the fashionable culture of Switzerland

170.
Harald Slott-Møller
Three Women, Summer Evening, 1895
Oil on panel, 15⅜ x 24¾ in.
(39 x 62.7 cm)
The Hirschsprung Collection,
Copenhagen

171.

Harald Slott-Møller

Cradle, 1893

Painted wood, 41⅜ x 38⅝ in.
(105 x 98 cm)

Danish Museum of Decorative Art,
Copenhagen

172.

J. F. Willumsen

Jotunheimen, 1892–93

Oil, painted zinc, and enameled copper,
59 x 109⅞ in. (150 x 279 cm)

J. F. Willumsens Museum,
Frederikssund

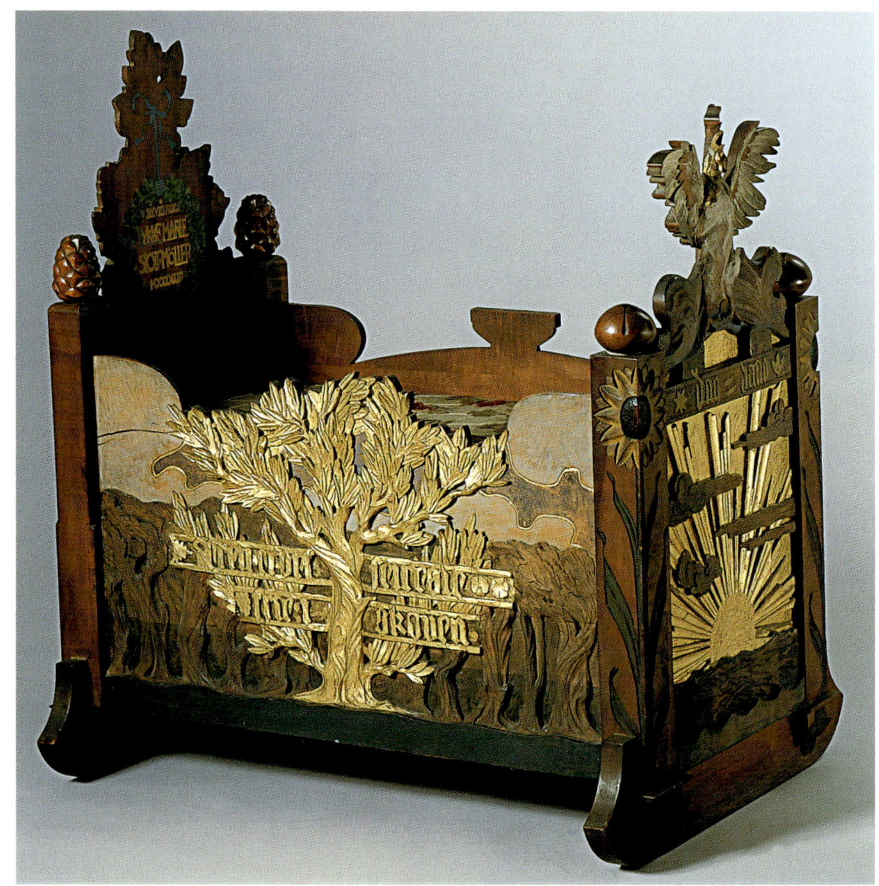

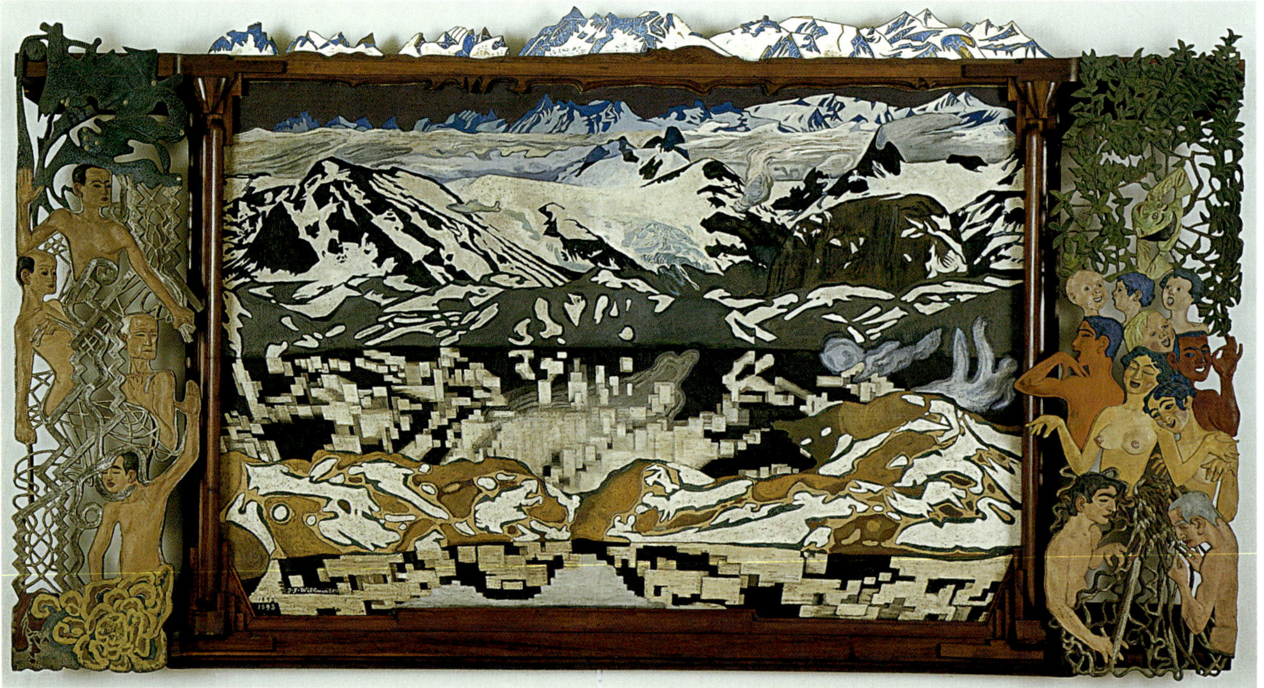

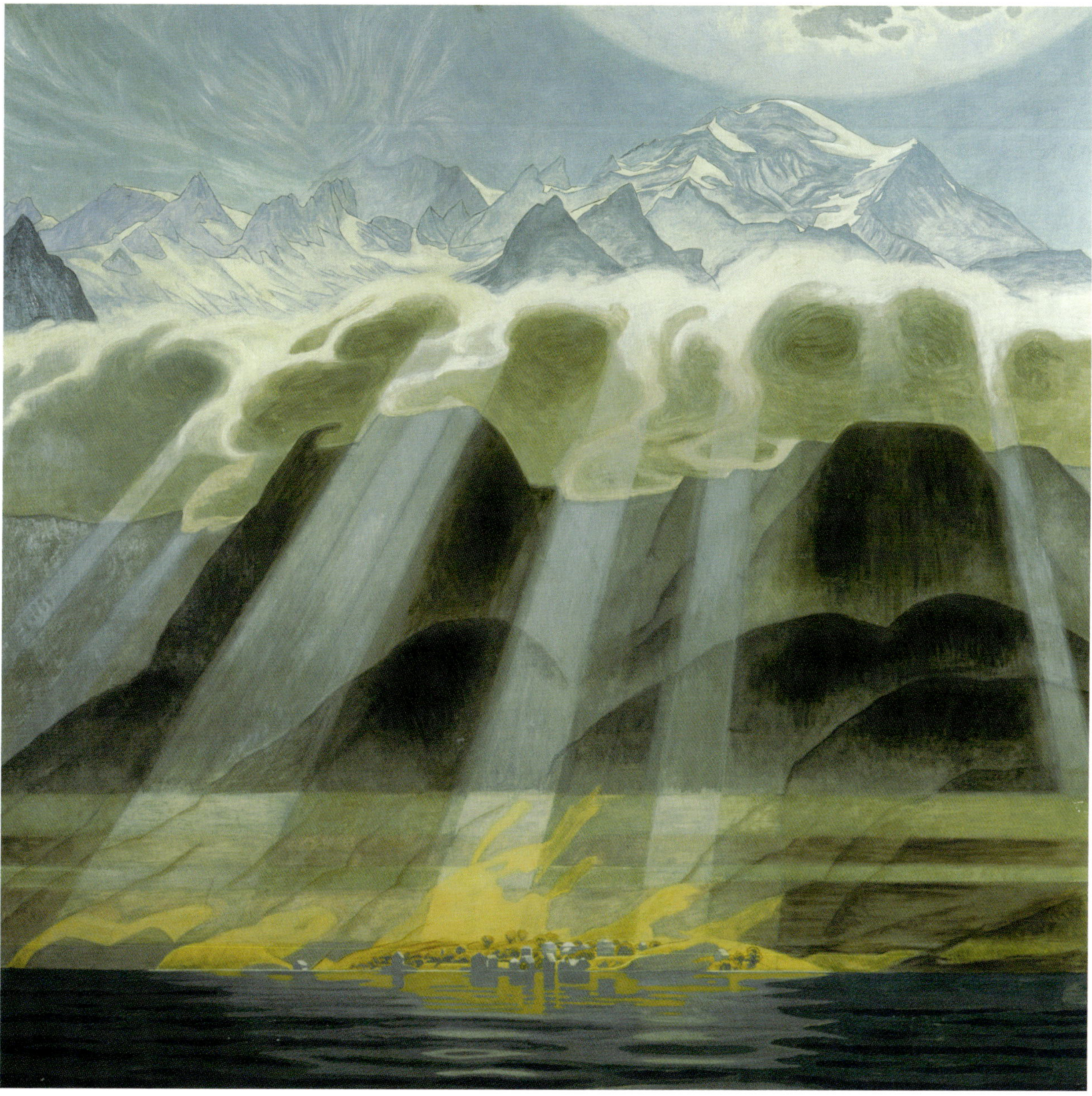

and its high-altitude sanitoriums offering the restoration of health and virility, a symbol of revitalization that counteracted the stultifying effects of the city.[113] Willumsen's *Sun and Youth* (fig. 138), which preoccupied the artist during travels to France and Italy and was finally resolved on the beach at Skagen, offers the sun and the water as ecstatic sites of bodily freedom, nature worship, and health.[114]

Such work, verging on twentieth-century Expressionism, represented another aspect of Danish Symbolist painting. It was profoundly different from Hammershøi's seeming disembodiment yet shared his search for parity between emotional responses to the body and the formal means to communicate them. Willumsen's theme of vitalization of the body also crystallized in the work of Johannes Holbek (1873–1903). Holbek's extraordinarily rhythmical representation

173.
J. F. Willumsen
Sun over the Southern Mountains, 1902
Oil on canvas, 82¼ x 82 in.
(209 x 208 cm)
Thielska Galleriet, Stockholm

of a male model in the *The Plant* (1894; fig. 174) offers an enigmatic view of a nude male figure whose meandering lines and radiating waves of color extend into the background, suggesting both dissolution as well as energy and growth. With his back to the viewer, the model's arms are held in front of his body, away from our view, and the gesture expands the ribcage, creating a strained torsion in his spine. His heavily muscled back and buttocks communicate physical potency, and yet his armlessness and serpentine spine, reminiscent of Auguste Rodin's *Walking Man* (ca. 1900, Musée d'Orsay, Paris), suggest mutilation. The title suggests the transformation of animal body into vegetation.[115]

The relationship between the body and its physical setting was also at the heart of the works of Ejnar Nielsen during the 1890s, among them *The Blind Girl*. In 1894, Nielsen first visited the central Jutland community of Gjern, where he would live for several years, painting bleak views of the gently rising fields, including *Landscape. Gjern* (1896–97; fig. 175). Writing to his fiancée from Gjern in 1896, he stated, "There is something potent here everywhere you go, sometimes intimidating and menacing, sometimes enigmatic, so you never really believe what you are seeing. . . . And the seriousness and sense of unease of the atmosphere, as we can call it, will inevitably get its claws into us when we stand on the great 'Troll's Mound' and the evening is lowering its twilight over the ocean of its hills lying out there bluish and violet like frozen waves or breakers."[116] His response to the topography was filtered through his veneration for the work of German painter Arnold Böcklin (1827–1901), who was popular in Denmark at the time. Nielsen described "a Böcklin-like silent garden is this we are walking in, with its threatening black elements to glimpses of the whiteness of the marble."[117]

The residents of the Gjern, whom Nielsen understood to be inextricably bound to the land, became his most important subjects, describing them as "people who harmonize completely with the nature that produces them."[118] Many of Nielsen's paintings depict illness and death, particularly of young people, including *The Sick Girl* (1896; fig. 176), his breakthrough painting. For a time, Nielsen had made daily visits to the subject, Anna Dorthea Kristensen, who was dying of tuberculosis. He made detailed studies of her, observing the minute and specific ways in which her young body wasted and the flesh faded.[119] In the painting, the girl's fine features are skeletal and her red hair lustreless and pulled away to emphasize her large forehead. She is as sunken into her austere sickbed as fully as possible, lying parallel to the picture plane at the very base of the painting. Every element of the painting, from its large, empty upper section to its gray- and green-tinged palette and middle values, enervates the room and the girl. In the late nineteenth century, tuberculosis was a particular scourge of youth, an image conveyed by Edvard Munch in his own *Sick Child* (1884–85, National Museum, Oslo).[120] In contrast to the heroic, romantic, or otherwise reassuring depictions of death that appeared throughout Danish art, death is here inscribed in every aspect of the girl's physiognomy and setting as a quiet inevitability.[121]

Similarly, Nielsen's *And in His Eyes I Saw Death* (1897; fig. 177) is a strikingly austere composition, composed of an empty room in which a tubercular young man is seated upon a black coffin. The man sits upright in the an apparently windowless, low-ceilinged room with cracked plaster walls and rough-hewn wooden beams stained at the edges. The head and oversized hands of the man are represented with a miniaturist's attention to linear detailing. The artist's closely nuanced palette, similar to the reduced harmonies of Puvis de Chavannes and Vilhelm Hammershøi, resonates with Valdemar Vedel's notions of a "modern, soulful way of seeing."[122] When

174.
Johannes Holbek
The Plant, 1894
Oil on canvas, 31¼ x 25¼ in.
(79.5 x 64 cm)
Silkeborg Kunstmuseum

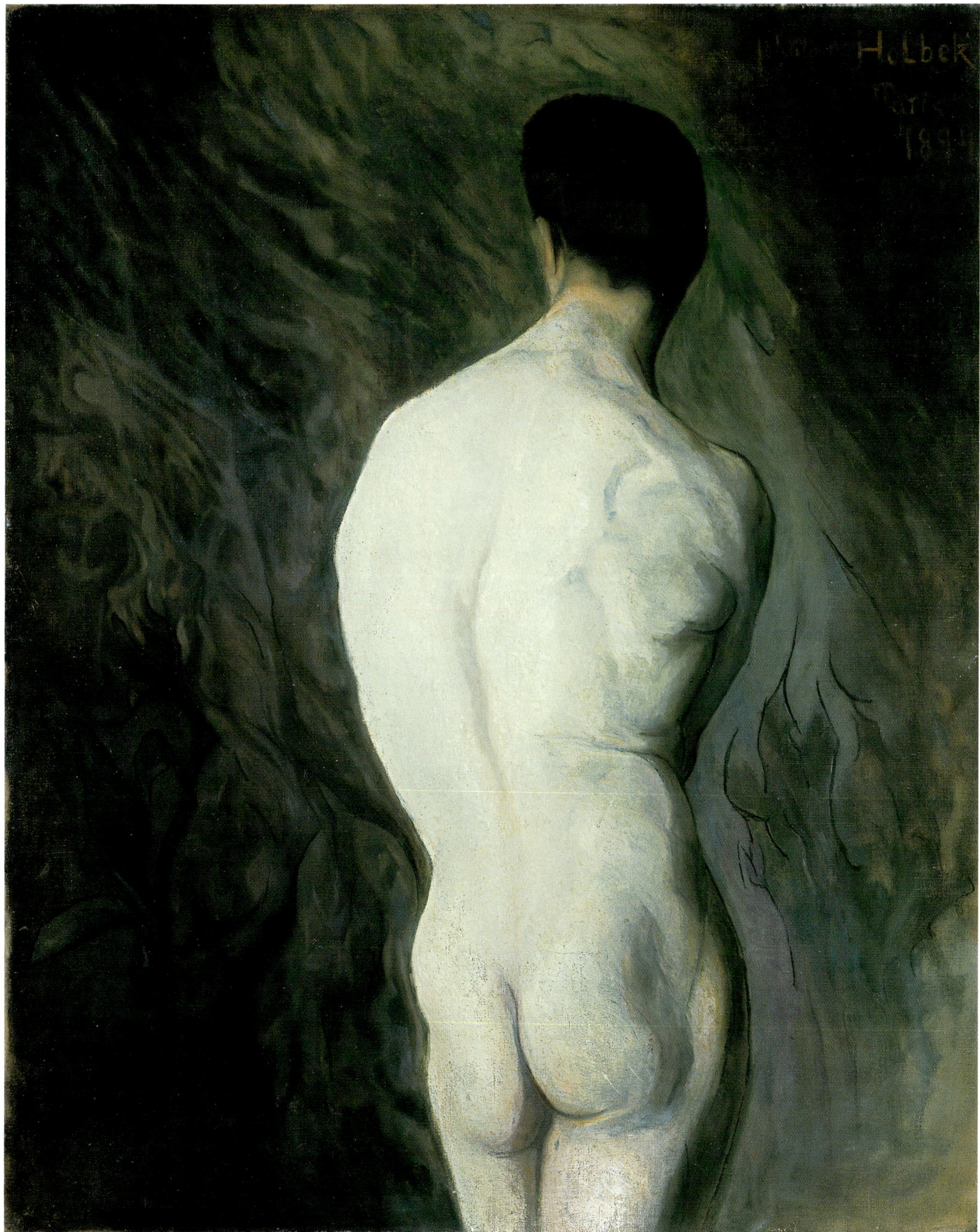

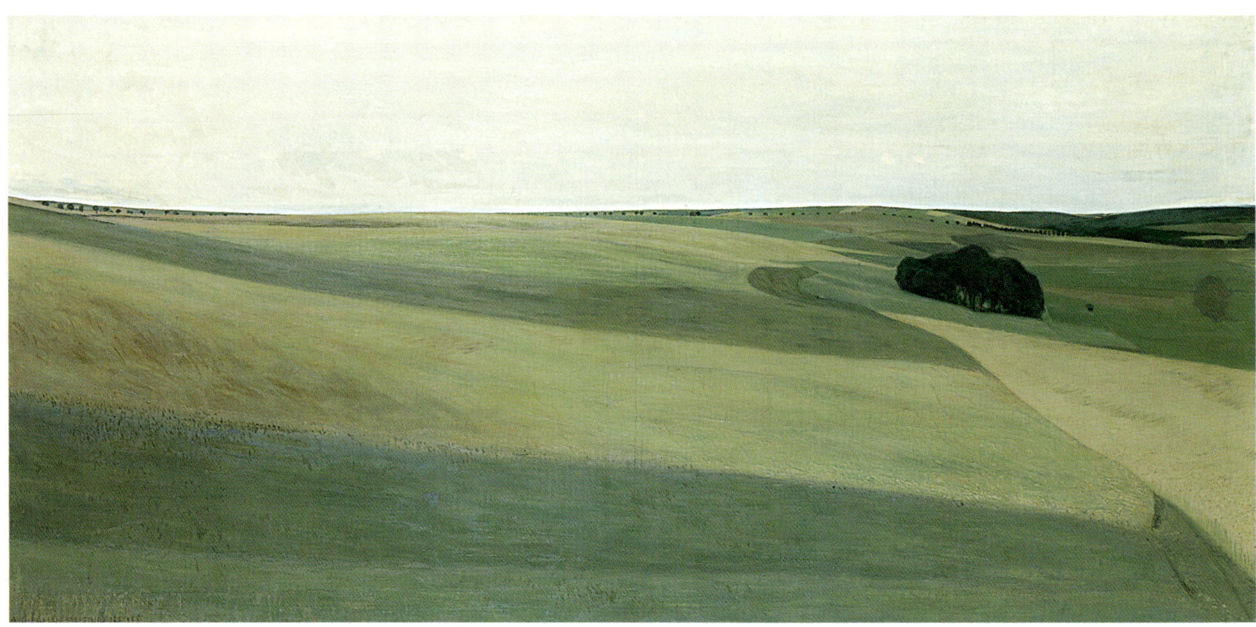

175.
Ejnar Nielsen
Landscape. Gjern, 1896–97
Oil on canvas, 43⅜ x 86⅝ in.
(110 x 220 cm)
Vejen Kunstmuseum

Nielsen's model died in 1898, the artist used the image of his body in *Death and the Cripple* of that year.[123] He explained his interest in representing such blunt images of the dead and dying by expressing a metaphysical belief in continuity: "Life interests us to a significant degree—Why doesn't death? After all, death is just as important: It serves life itself."[124]

Nielsen's *Blind Girl*, with which this chapter began, also depicted a local resident of Gjern, Dagmar Andersen. Born in 1874, she had been blind since the age of seven, the victim of an eye infection. Nielsen had described her as captivating: "She was no beauty in the classic sense, but her face held a sensitive and serious expression that fascinated me."[125] In his transformation of the "homely" peasant into an emblem for second sight, Nielsen invested Denmark's rural culture with transcendent meaning. Like the Slott-Møllers, Ring, Willumsen, and his other contemporaries, Nielsen engaged in international artistic practices only to reflect back on Denmark and its meaning as the nineteenth century drew to its close. His generation of artists, like the politicians who debated the direction of Denmark's material and temporal well-being, offered conflicting representations of its spiritual meaning. Rejecting Denmark's stable academic authority while nurtured by the new schools, exhibitions, patrons, and museums that offered models of independence, the artists of the 1890s forged disparate paths, many of which intersected at the Free Exhibition. Poised between material fidelity and decorative abstraction, description and symbolic evocation, and local culture and European-wide aesthetic revolutions, Nielsen's *Blind Girl* amplifies this complexity. In it, the journey outward made Denmark part of an international artistic community, while the inward-looking gaze of the artist yielded new worlds of spirit and imagination.

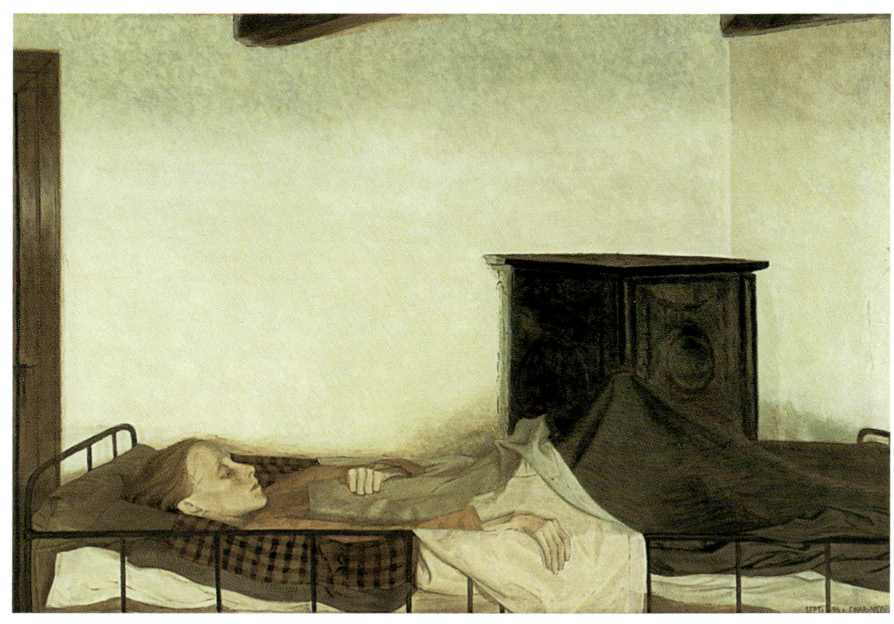

176.
Ejnar Nielsen
The Sick Girl, 1896
Oil on canvas, 43¾ x 64½ in.
(111 x 164 cm)
Statens Museum for Kunst,
Copenhagen

177. Ejnar Nielsen
And in His Eyes I Saw Death, 1897
Oil on canvas, 54 x 74 in.
(137 x 188 cm)
Statens Museum for Kunst,
Copenhagen

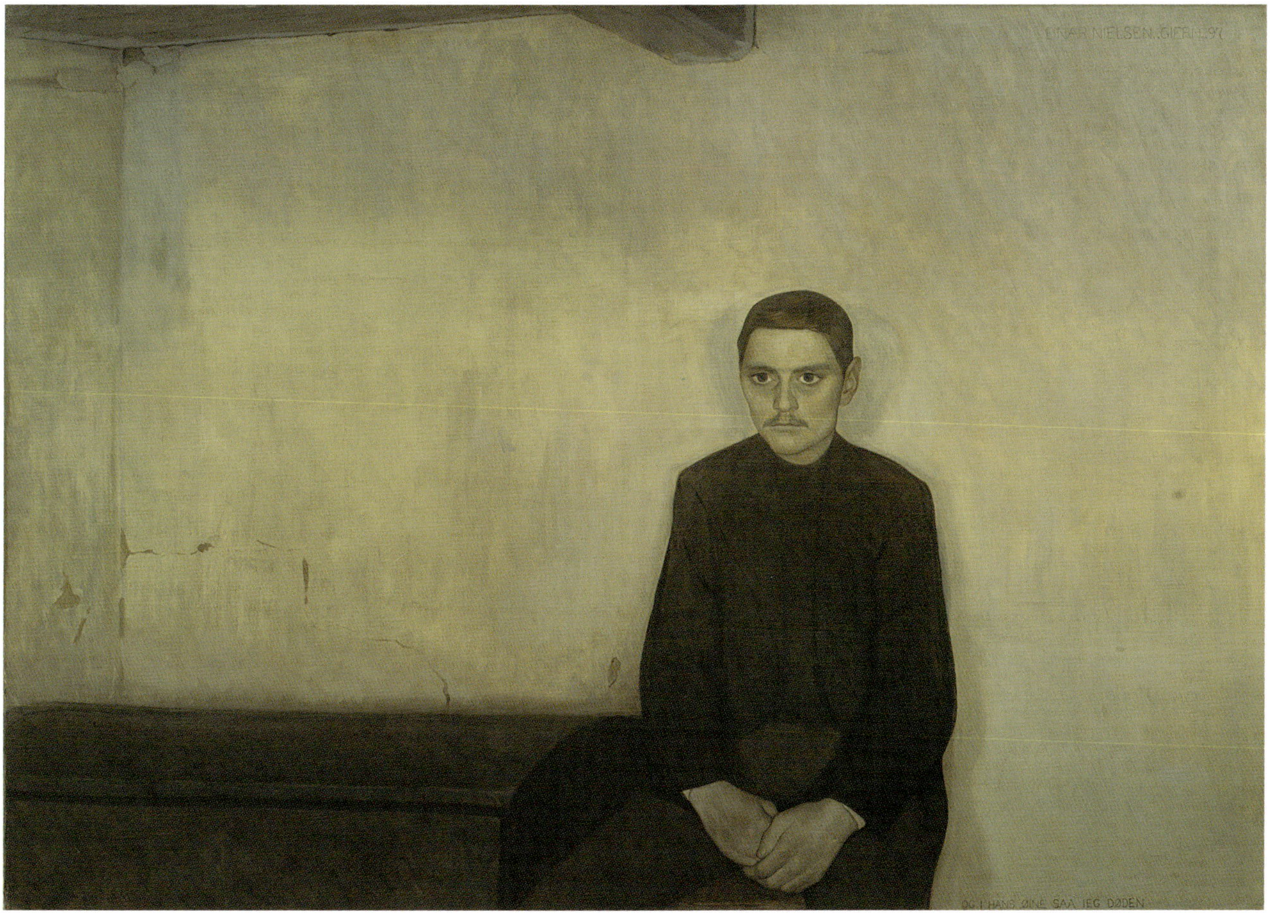

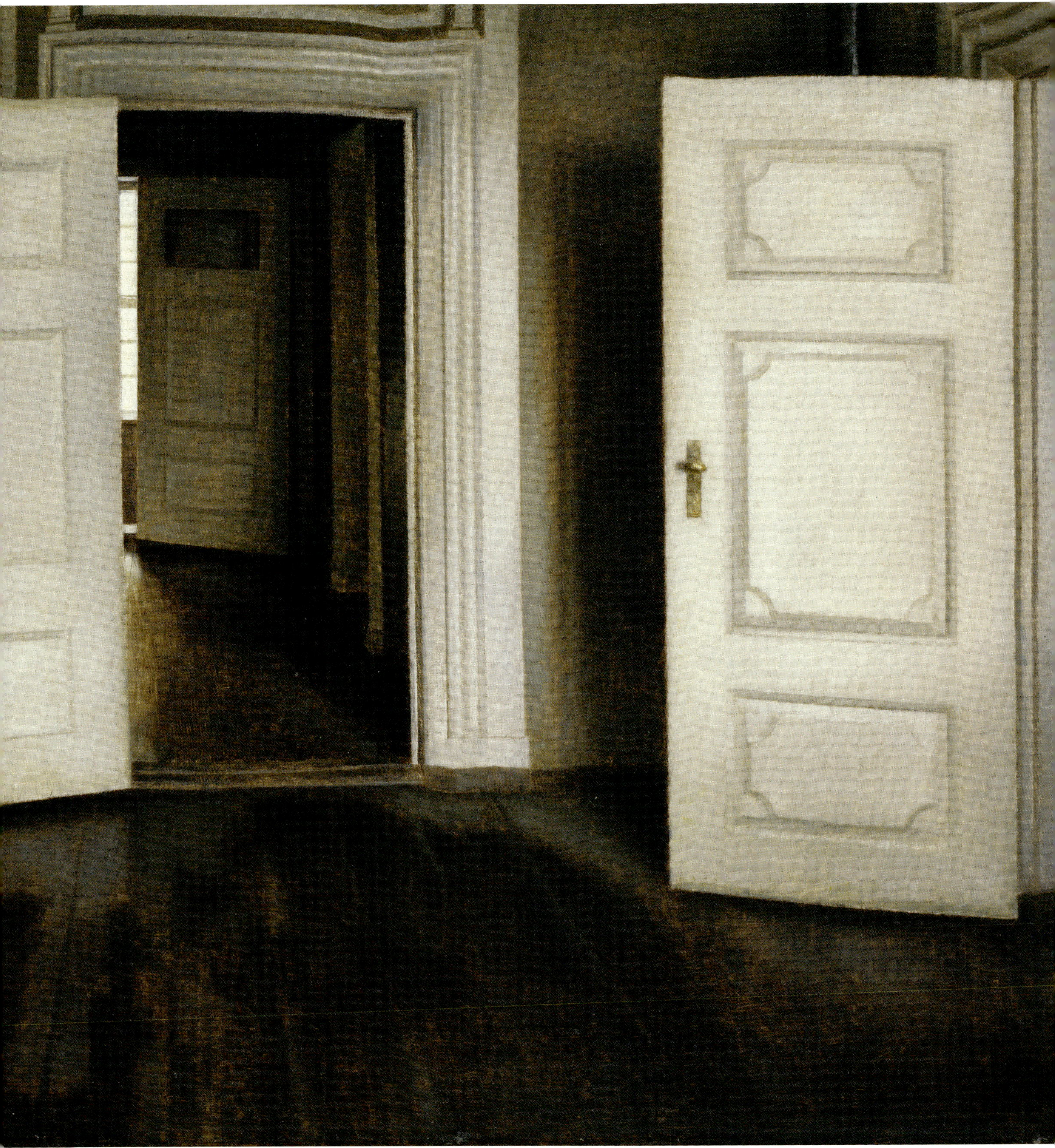

7

Hammershøi and Urban Places

The Danes stop in time; they avoid paradox or do not carry it to its logical
conclusion; they have the steadiness due to naturally well-balanced minds and
naturally phlegmatic dispositions; they are hardly ever indecent, audacious,
blasphemous, revolutionary, wildly fantastic, utterly sentimental, utterly unreal, or
utterly sensual; they seldom run amuck, they never tilt at clouds, and they never
fall into a well. This is what makes them so popular with their own countrymen.
Unerring taste and elegance . . . [and] vigorous healthy originality . . . will always
be prized by Danes as the expression of noble and self-controlled art.

— Georg Brandes [1872][1]

THROUGH SUCH DRY CHARACTERIZATION, THE CRITIC GEORG
Brandes distinguished the special sobriety of Danish Romantic literature of the early nineteenth century. In 1890, writer Valdemar Vedel retrospectively employed the term "Golden
Age" to characterize that period.[2] The Golden Age, derived from Greek mythology and
Roman poetry, refers to a pure, utopian state at the dawn of civilization that usually comes
to an end with a devastating event.[3] Artists of the 1890s responded with ambivalence to this
inheritance, perhaps none more so than Vilhelm Hammershøi, whose elegant work balanced
on the edge of Brandes's rhetoric. Hammershøi's work drew upon familiar Danish genres,
themes, and images only to drain them and offer them with a new meaning. In the words of
Kasper Monrad, Hammershøi "scraped the story away and left the core behind."[4]

Hammershøi's masterpiece, *Five Portraits* (1901–02; fig. 178), a huge canvas measuring
approximately six by twelve feet, performs in this way, invoking and then resisting the stability
and clarity of the Golden Age. In it, Hammershøi recalls artistic friendship paintings such as
Wilhelm Bendz's *Smoking Party* (fig. 42), Ditlev Conrad Blunck's *Danish Artists in the Osteria
La Gensola in Rome* (fig. 43), and P. S. Krøyer's *Hip, Hip, Hurrah!* (fig. 96),[5] only to transform
their conviviality and worldly pleasures into an emblem of austerity. Hammershøi himself is
physically absent from the painting, puncturing the tradition of picturing a cohesive collective.
Even the enigmatic title, *Five Portraits*, pointing to the individual sitters rather than the collective, suggests this.

179.
Vilhelm Hammershøi
*White Doors (Open Doors),
Strandgade 30*, 1905
(detail)

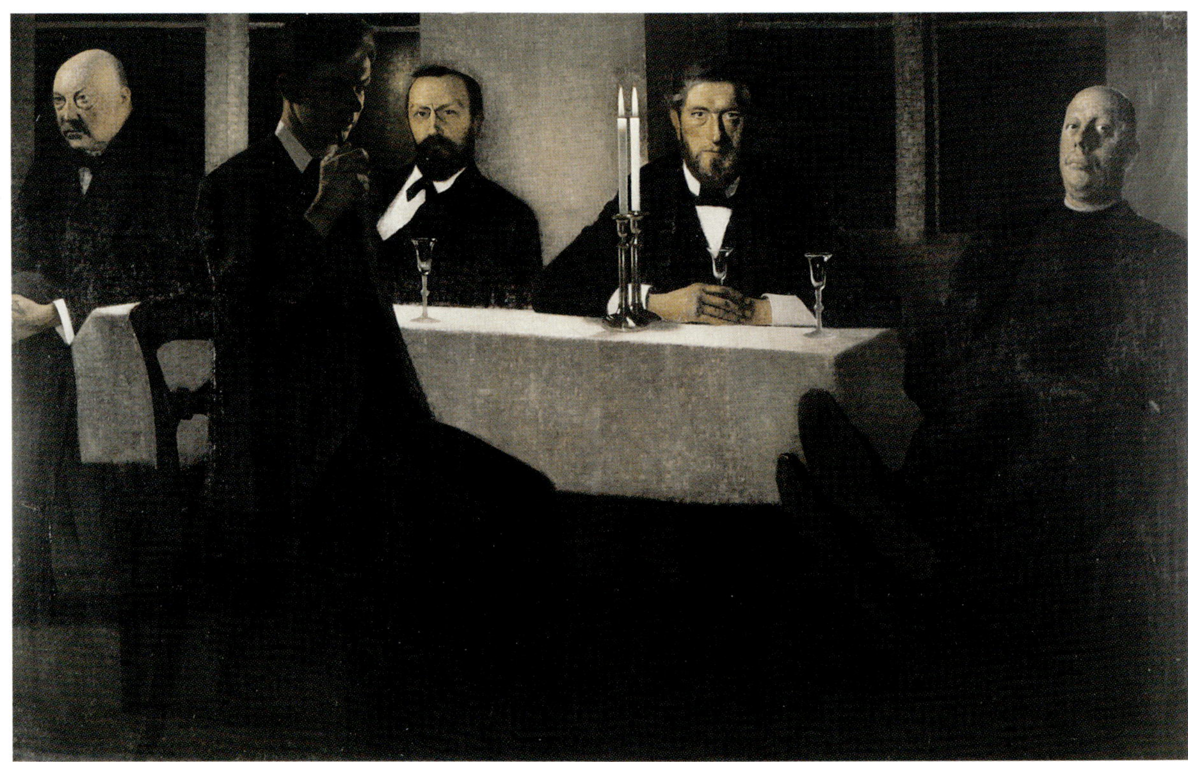

178.
Vilhelm Hammershøi
Five Portraits, 1901–02
Oil on canvas, 74¾ x 133⅞ in.
(190 x 340 cm)
Thielska Galleriet, Stockholm

Bathed in Georges de La Tour-like light radiating from two glowing candles, five men, all Hammershøi's intimate friends, sit at a table in Hammershøi's darkened apartment. On the far left, the architect and ceramicist Thorvald Bindesbøll turns away from his colleagues. On our side of the table, enrapt in his pipe and with his back turned to the introspective Bindesbøll, sits Svend Hammershøi (1873–1948), Vilhelm's younger brother, himself a painter, ceramicist, and printmaker. To the right of Hammershøi, art historian Karl Madsen and painter Jens Ferdinand Willumsen gaze directly at us, as does Carl Holsøe (1863–1935), sitting on the far right, an artist whom Hammershøi had met in his student days. The over life-size figures, compressed by the canvas's horizontal format and locked in place by the architectural background, communicate gravity through their firm gazes. At the same time, Hammershøi has given Holsøe enormous feet, which both help the viewer to track the spatial recession into the canvas from front to back and which lend an air of informality, even satire, to this otherwise sober composition.[6] These men were among the artists who had founded and supported the Free Exhibition. Madsen was the critic who gave voice to the organization, and Willumsen and Bindesbøll were the architects who designed the exhibition halls. This gathering therefore represents Denmark's leading voices in the promotion of free, advanced national art. In this regard, the painting seems manifesto-like, akin to similar contemporary assertions of artistic identity such as Finnish painter Akseli Gallen-Kallela's *Symposium (The Problem)* (1894, Helsinki). However, it offers no clear clues in that direction. Many historians have noted a similarity between this painting and scenes of the Last Supper, particularly C. W. Eckersberg's 1840 version of the motif from Frederiksberg Church, the Hammershøi family's parish church during the artist's childhood.[7] Nonetheless, the painting defies a clear interpretation and has been troubling and haunting in its ambiguity since it was first exhibited.[8]

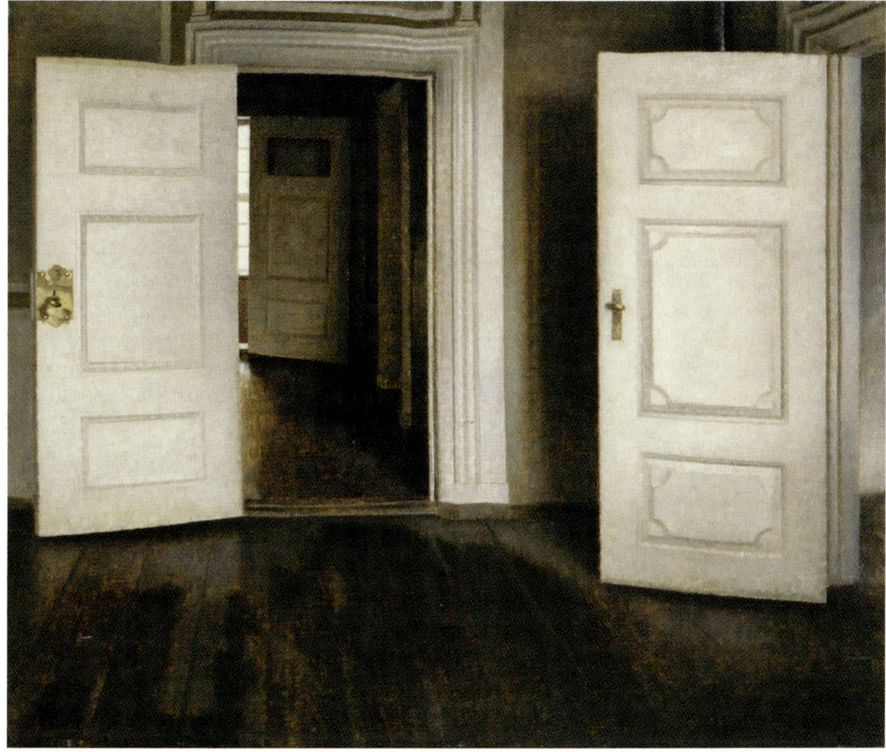

179.
Vilhelm Hammershøi
White Doors (Open Doors),
Strandgade 30, 1905
Oil on canvas, 20⅝ x 23⅝ x in.
(52.5 x 60 cm)
The David Collection, Copenhagen

Similarly, Hammershøi's best-known works, meticulously constructed views of the interiors of his homes, oscillate between Golden Age domesticity and abstract geometry. Like *Five Portraits,* Hammershøi's architectural works often invoke Golden Age themes and compositional gambits, but emptied of narrative content and comprehensibility. For example, *White Doors (Open Doors), Strandgade 30* (1905; fig. 179) reduces the genre of architectural painting, so admired and so widely practiced during Denmark's Golden Age, to a kind of enigmatic essence. The painting is rigorously ordered; the tilted floor, the angles of the open doorways, and the telescoping spatial recession culminate in a slice of whiteness in the distant window, nearly obstructed by a final, open door. The filtered light, creating muffled shadows, also emphasizes scuffed floor varnish and polished door handles, evidence of age and use. The painting is a nearly monochromatic world, a paean to architectural detailing and a subtle palimpsest of renovations—varying door panels and doorknobs perhaps narrate a history of taste that has inhabited and shaped the rooms. But perhaps not. In its emptiness and its central open door, the painting alludes to some kind of meaning but offers no specific narrative or anecdotal cues.

Kasper Monrad notes that since these paintings were created, Hammershøi's historians and biographers have attempted to fill the emptiness with projected stories.[9] Moreover, art historian Thor Mednick astutely identified Hammershøi's lack of anecdote itself as a strategy, "a disruption in the typical exchange between viewer and artwork: a subversion by Hammershøi that confounds the legibility of the work by failing to deliver the content-matter that the setting leads the viewer to expect." In this way, Mednick continues, "the Danish Golden Age [was] denuded by its own heir apparent. . . . He gave his viewers a world they were sure they had seen before, and then less sure, as they looked closer."[10] This observation strikes at the core of Hammershøi's curious and ambivalent modernity.

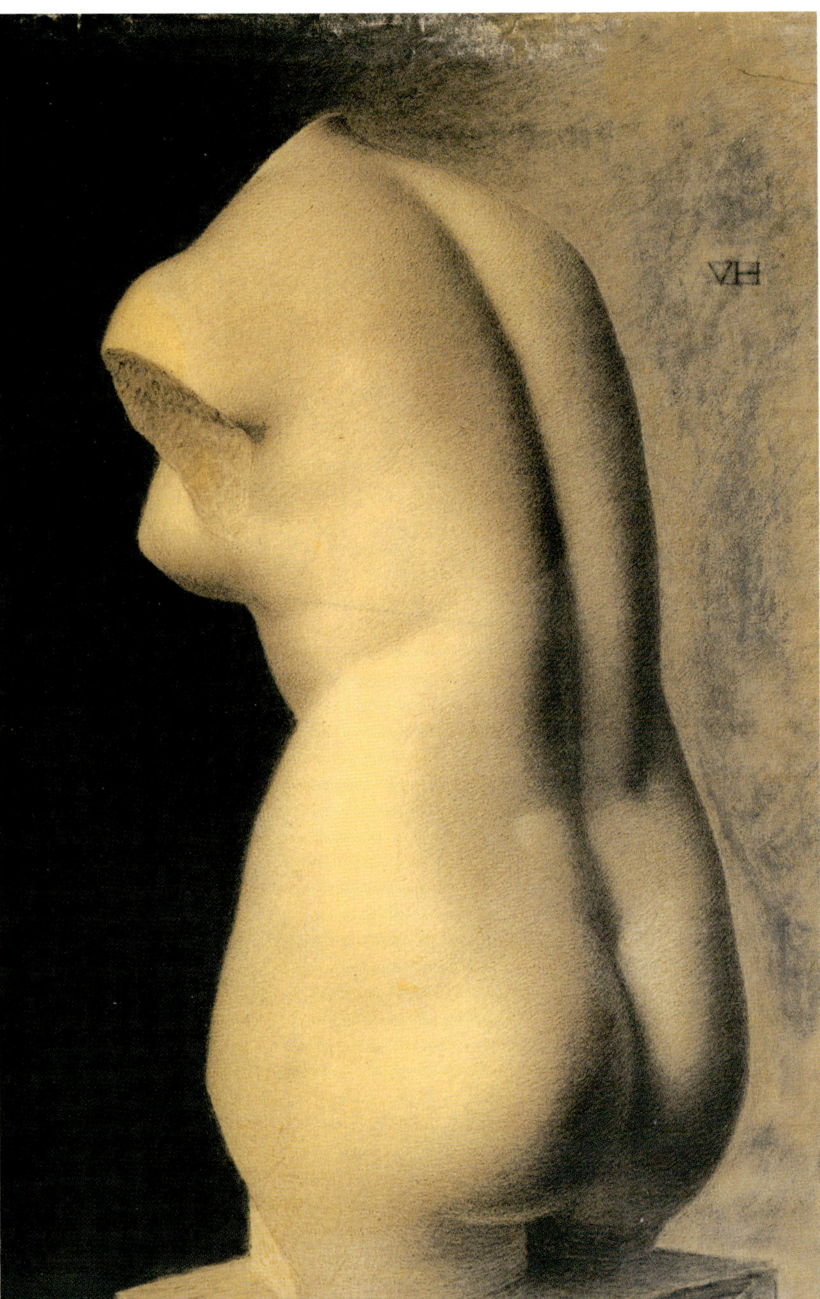

180.
Vilhelm Hammershøi
*Study Drawing after Plaster Cast
of Ancient Greek Aphrodite, Torso
from ca. 500 B.C.E.*, ca. 1880
Charcoal, 29½ x 18⅞ in.
(75 x 48 cm)
Collection of Ambassador John L. Loeb Jr.,
New York

181.
Vilhelm Hammershøi
*Study of Standing Woman,
Seen from Behind*, 1884–88
Oil on canvas, 20⅞ x 13¾ in.
(53 x 35 cm)
Collection of Ambassador John L. Loeb Jr.,
New York

Of all of the painters working in Denmark at the turn of the last century, Vilhelm Hammershøi was one of the most internationally celebrated.[11] Hammershøi was born in Copenhagen to a merchant family in 1864 and, with the exception of a few half-year periods spent in Paris (October 1891–March 1892), London (October 1897–May 1898), and Rome (October 1902–February 1903), and study trips to France, England, Germany, Belgium, Holland, and Italy, he spent his life in and around Copenhagen. Supported by a cultivated family, he began to take formal drawing lessons twice a week at the age of eight in 1872.[12] From 1879 to 1884 he studied at the Danish Academy of Art, initially also taking drawing instruction at the

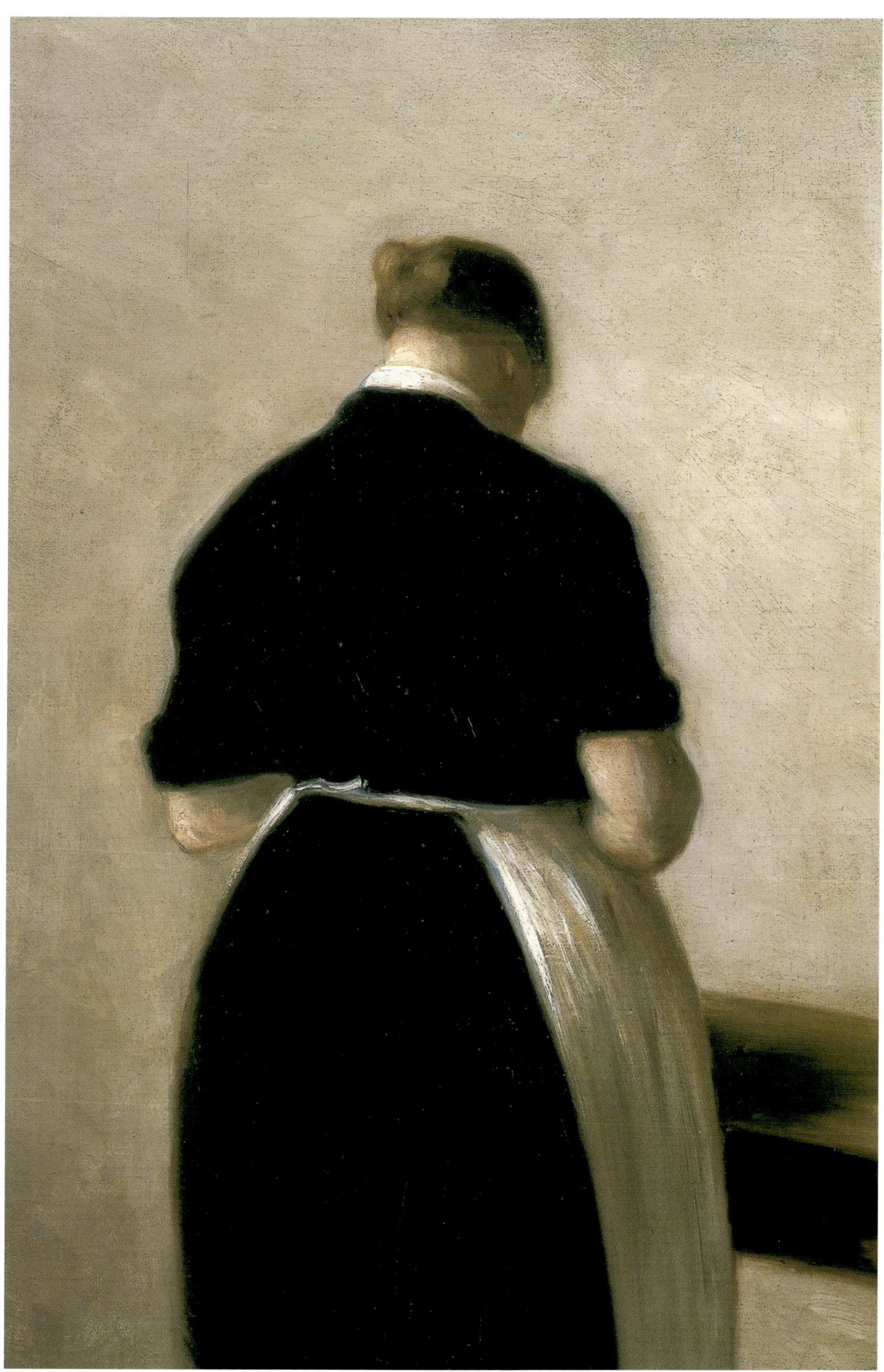

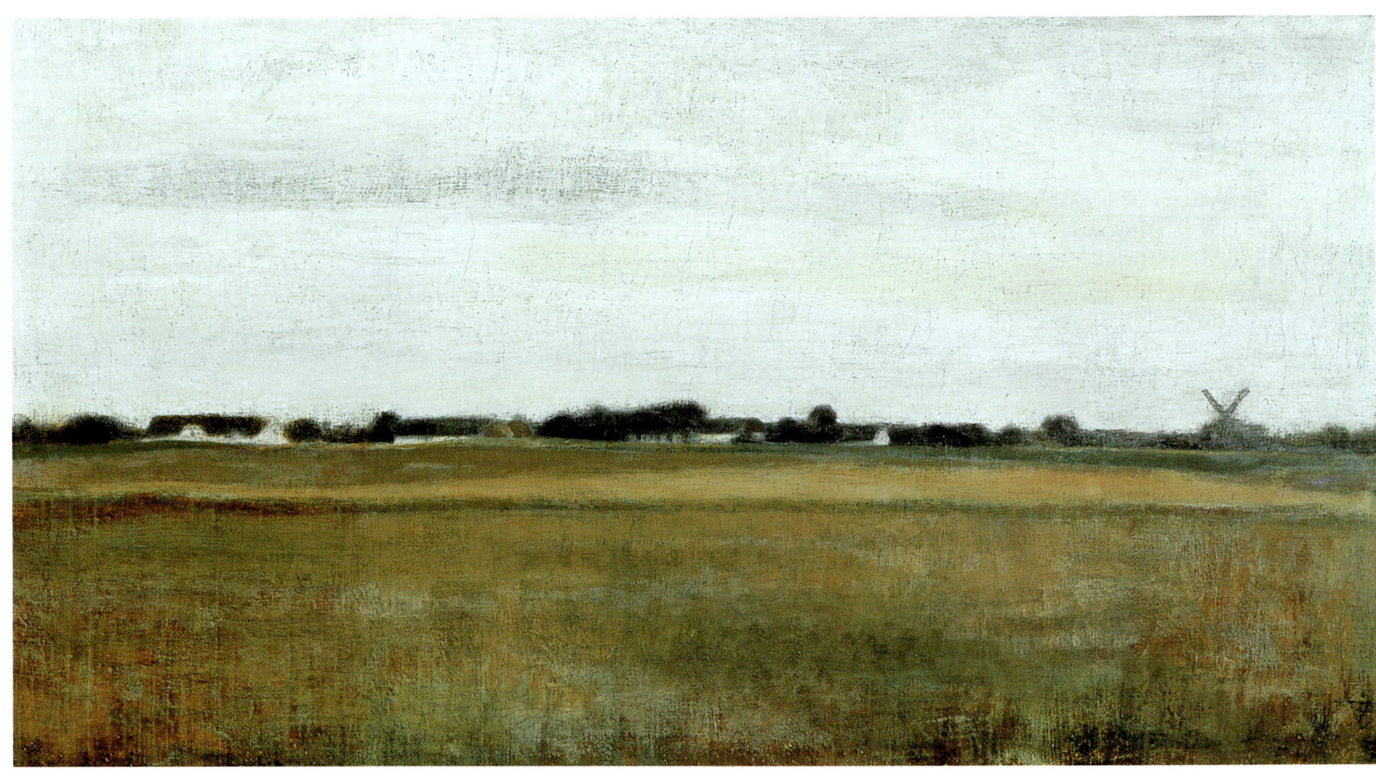

Technical School (a pre-academic training) from Holger Grønvold (1850–1923), a Parisian-trained artist in the tradition of David and Ingres. In these classes, Hammershøi was steeped in drawing pedagogy that stemmed from eighteenth-century classicism and was perpetuated by the academy.

Study Drawing after Plaster Cast of Ancient Greek Aphrodite, Torso from ca. 500 B.C.E. (ca. 1880; fig. 180) dates from this period. Like the training received by Danish artists since the eighteenth century (see chapter 3), Hammershøi commenced his studies by copying from prints and then plaster casts. However, clear outlining, one of the conventional stylistic markers of this procedure, is missing in Hammershøi's drawing. Instead, using a softened cross-hatching technique, Hammershøi invested in the torso a delicate pulchritude that was characteristic of his mature work.[13] Hammershøi's contemporaries attest to such an early and persistent vision, establishing a legend for the artist. Jens Ferdinand Willumsen, a fellow student at the Academy at the time, reported, "The plastic form in his life study was just as mature as the one he later had in his paintings. Actually, he was full-fledged."[14] Beginning in 1883, Hammershøi studied at the Artists' Study School under Peder Severin Krøyer, whose sun-drenched work could not have been more different from his pupil's: "I have a pupil who paints most oddly. I do not understand him, but believe he is going to be important and do not try to influence him."[15]

A modest oil sketch from Hammershøi's earlier years likewise suggests the artist's solidity of vision and approach. *Study of Standing Woman, Seen from Behind* (1884–88; fig. 181) represents a woman, her head bent in seeming concentration. Her activity or inactivity, unknown to us, is masked by her body. The painting's unified palette and gentle evocation of light falling from the painting's left edge soften the contours and enhance the sculptural effect

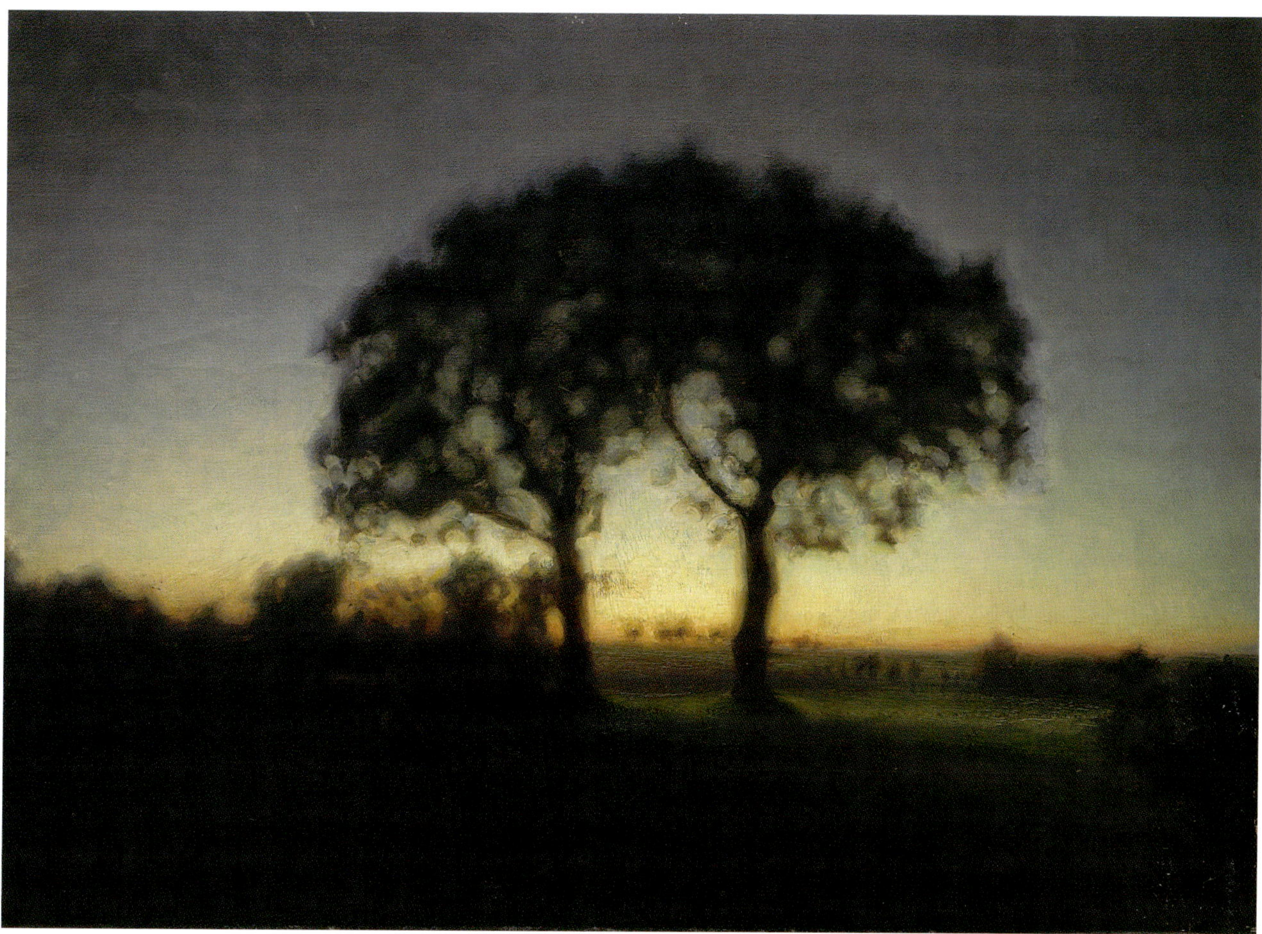

of the model's body. In its stasis, pearlescent light effects, and motif of a woman in an interior space, the painting suggests Hammershøi's interest in Dutch painting of the seventeenth century, examples of which he could see at the Royal Painting Collection or in Count Molkte's Collection (see chapter 2).

Hammershøi began to paint landscape views in the late 1880s, among them *Landscape from Virum Near Frederiksdal, Summer* (1888; fig. 182). Although this image appears isolated and emptied, it was painted while Hammershøi was the guest of Karl Madsen in suburban Lyngby, outside of Copenhagen. It was during this trip, as well, that Hammershøi began to paint images of empty rooms.[16] With its large, flat foreground and its representation of human habitation compressed and miniaturized between field and sky, *Landscape from Virum Near Frederiksdal, Summer* is a painting of the utmost eccentricity. The softly scuffed surface that melts details and emphasizes the texture of the underlying canvas and the insistent horizontal lines that define the composition suggest that this is a landscape based not on observation but on invention. Yet, in its careful depiction of light effects and topography and even in its unconventional composition, the work reaches back to Denmark's venerable landscape tradition of the earlier nineteenth century, as in paintings by Johan Thomas Lundbye (figs. 75–78, 80), only to "depopulate" and render them enigmatic.[17] The Hammershøi painting offers a near-ethnographic depiction of the local stuccoed hip-roofed buildings, but rather than

183.
Julius Paulsen
Sunset, 1893
Oil on canvas, 24 x 32¼ in.
(61 x 82 cm)
Randers Kunstmuseum

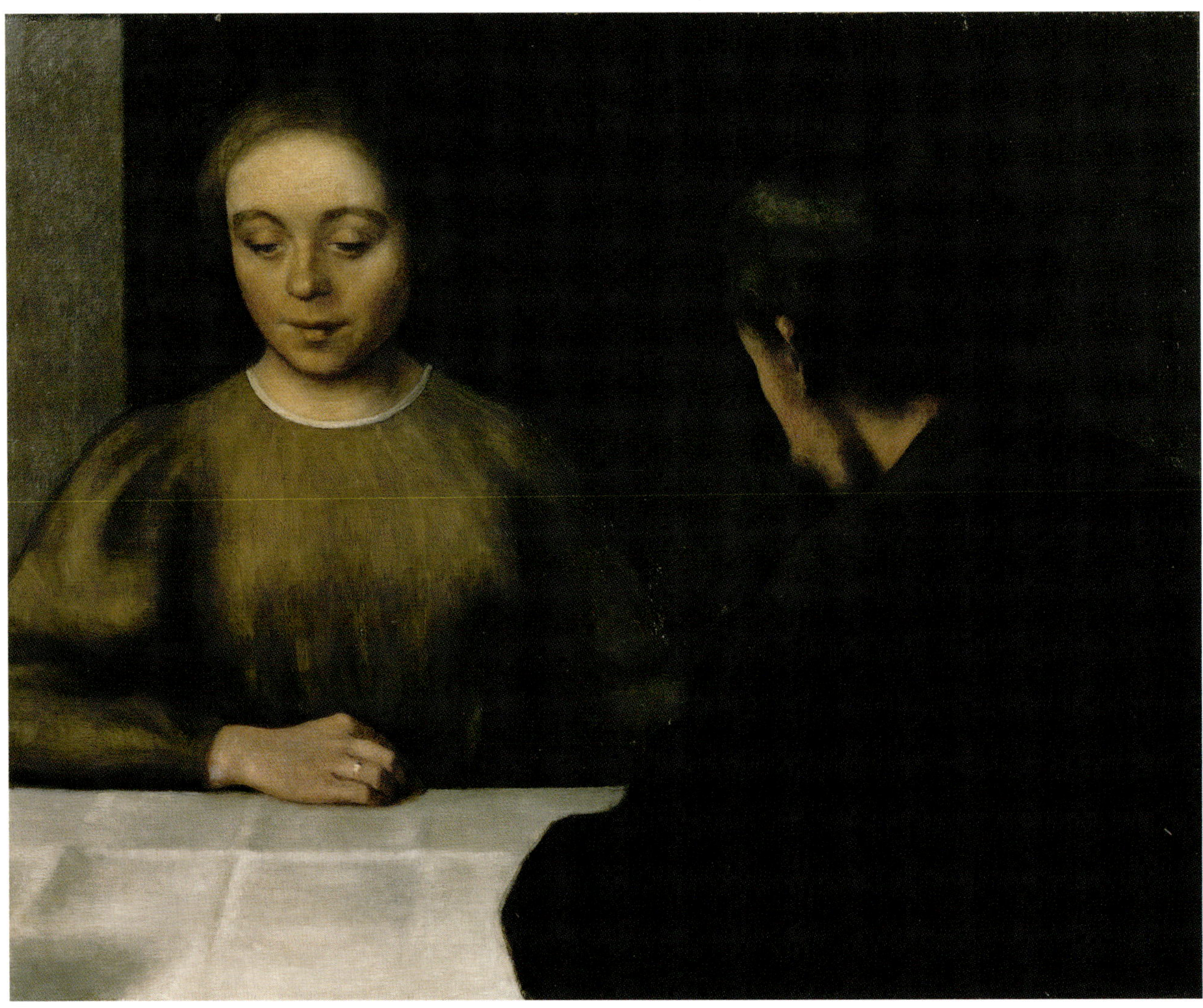

184.
Vilhelm Hammershøi
Two Figures. Double Portrait of the Artist and His Wife, 1898
Oil on canvas, 28¾ x 34 in.
(72 x 86.5 cm)
ARoS Aarhus Kunstmuseum

emphasizing material culture, as had his predecessors, it offers human habitation as though seen through the wrong end of a telescope. Hammershøi's effects of rendering familiar landscapes in an abstract manner had great resonance, in turn, with artists such as Julius Paulsen (fig. 183), whose moody works of the 1890s likewise suffused modest Danish scenes with a dreamy twilight quality. The lack of clear boundaries within such works, and the flattening of pictorial space, antithetical to Golden Age formulae, was at the heart of Symbolist practice (chapter 6).

In 1891, Hammershøi became one of the founding members of the Free Exhibition (chapter 6), the arts society that had been initiated in part because of Hammershøi's rejection from official exhibitions. It was there, in 1894, that Hammershøi caused a sensation with his painting *Artemis* (fig. 161). In 1891, Peter Ilsted (1861–1933), one of Hammershøi's fellow students, introduced Hammershøi to his younger sister Ida (1869–1949). They were married in the same year, honeymooning in Holland and Belgium, and then living in Paris. From the time they met until Hammershøi's untimely death in 1916, Ida was his chief model, appearing in the majority of his paintings.

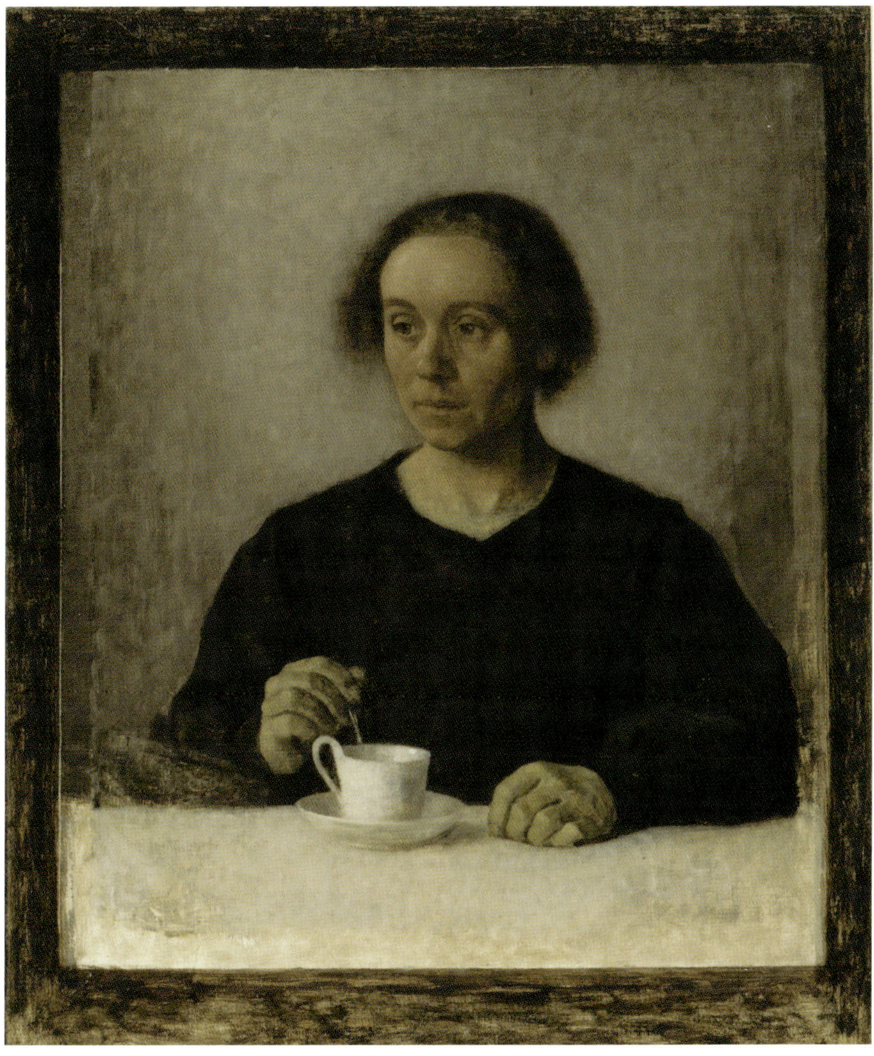

185.
Vilhelm Hammershøi
Portrait of Ida Ilsted, 1907
Oil on canvas, 35⅞ x 29 in.
(91 x 73.5 cm)
Statens Museum for Kunst,
Copenhagen

Born in a small rural Danish town, Ida quickly acclimated to Copenhagen and to a life of travel and modeling for her increasingly famous husband. In 1897–98, during the couple's first visit to London, Hammershøi portrayed himself and his wife in *Two Figures. Double Portrait of the Artist and His Wife* (1898; fig. 184), in which the artist is seen from the back and Ida viewed frontally. The two sit across from one another, separated by a starched white cloth that bisects Ida's torso, shaping her generalized form into a quattrocento Italian portrait bust. The artist is barely distinguishable, his looming form nearly blending with the darkened background. Hammershøi suggested the enigma of such a representation, in which a marriage portrait is at the same time an abstract study: "The one picture I am painting, and on which I have worked since we came back here after Christmas, is a kind of double portrait of Ida and myself. That is to say I am practically turning my back, nor is it supposed to be a portrait in the strictest sense. I am rather satisfied with it."[18] Suffusing Ida's features with a pale, glowing light and reforming her face into a gentle oval, the artist idealizes her beauty in a manner echoing P. S. Krøyer's idealization of Marie Triepcke (fig. 129).[19] The deadpan title, describing objectively what is represented, looks ahead to the particularity of *Five Portraits*.

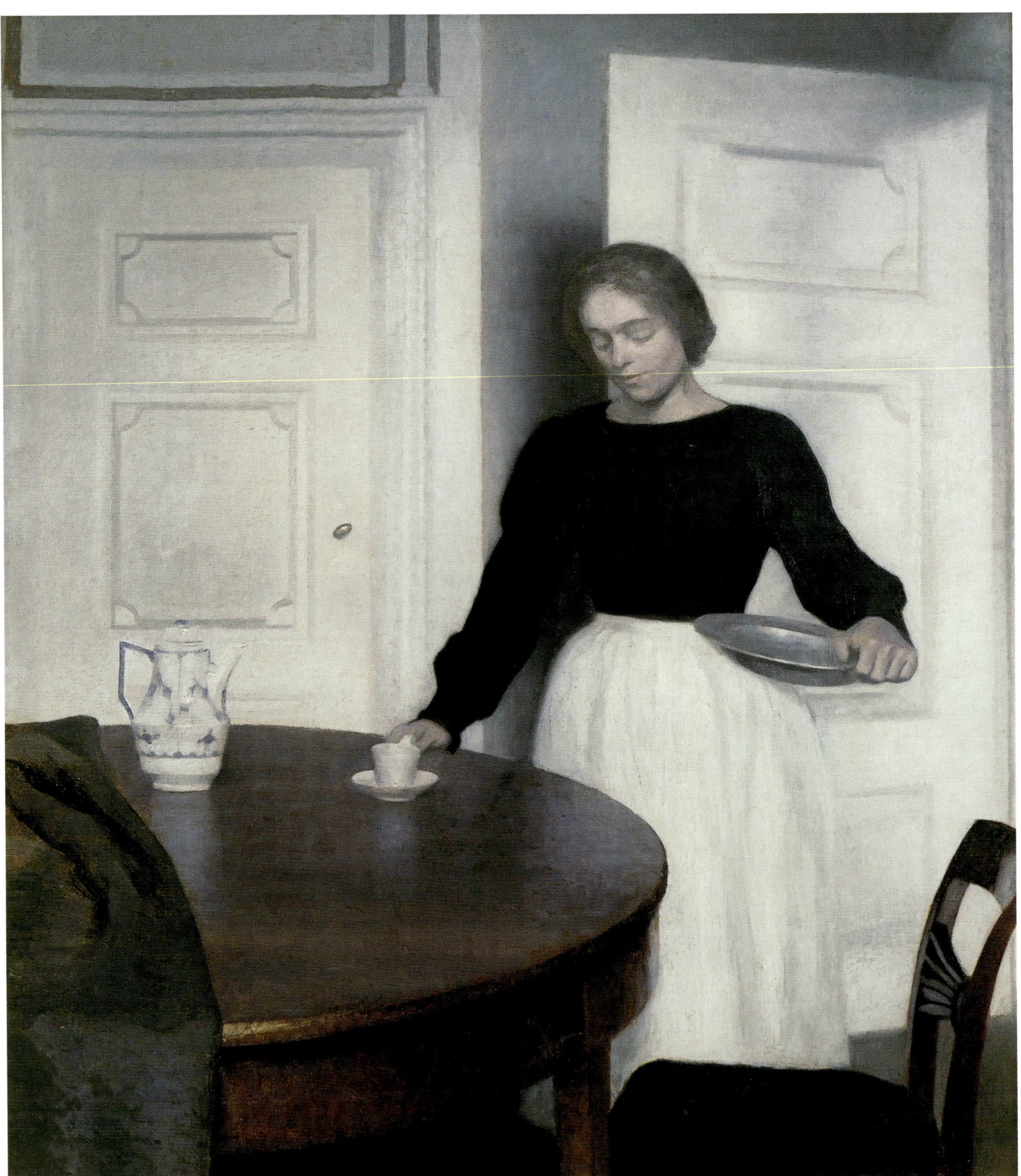

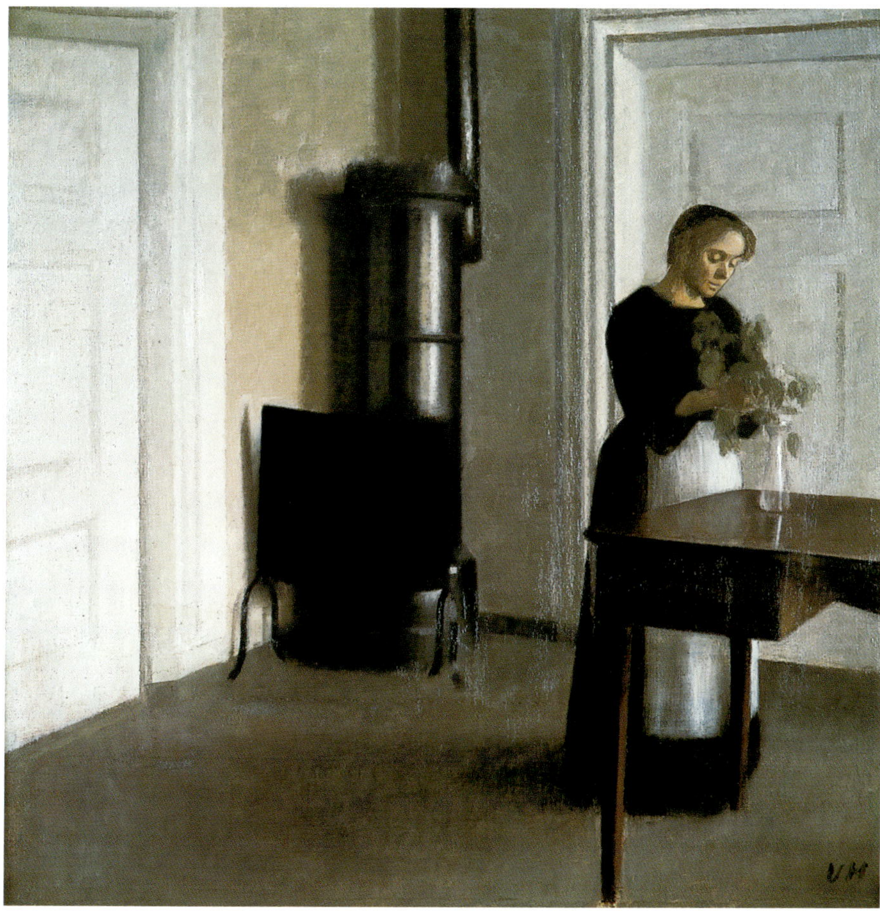

In 1907, Hammershøi again painted two versions of a close-up view of Ida's face and upper body, this time with great poignancy following an illness and operation from which the artist feared his wife would not recover (fig. 185).[20] Ida rests one hand on the cloth-covered table before her and with the other stirs the contents of a white porcelain cup. In the starkness of this rendering, the large darkened background, and the simplicity of the composition and gesture, the painting seems to acknowledge Constantin Hansen's *Portrait of a Little Girl, Elise Købke, with a Cup in Front of Her* (fig. 88).[21] At the same time, Ida Hammershøi's deflected gaze and softened contours, and the summary execution and painted framing device within the composition, marks the representation's psychological and formal distance from Købke's clarity and linear acuity.[22] It is in part this curious space between historical quotation (the composition, the gesture) and the departure from historical precedent (clarity, coloristic intensity) that Hammershøi's works resonate.

Hammershøi's tightly nuanced palette represents a reordering of sensual stimuli, the assertion of a closely reasoned range of hues that requires the viewer to engage in a slow reading of surface. Monochrome is itself a carrier of meaning, representing a kind of visual cleansing, an artistic invitation to open contemplation through a reduction in visual complexity.[23] Experiencing Hammershøi's surfaces requires time to register range and richness, somewhat like having to adjust one's vision in a darkened room after being in bright sunlight. Once accomplished, the paintings reveal richly worked surfaces, brocade-like in their woven brush

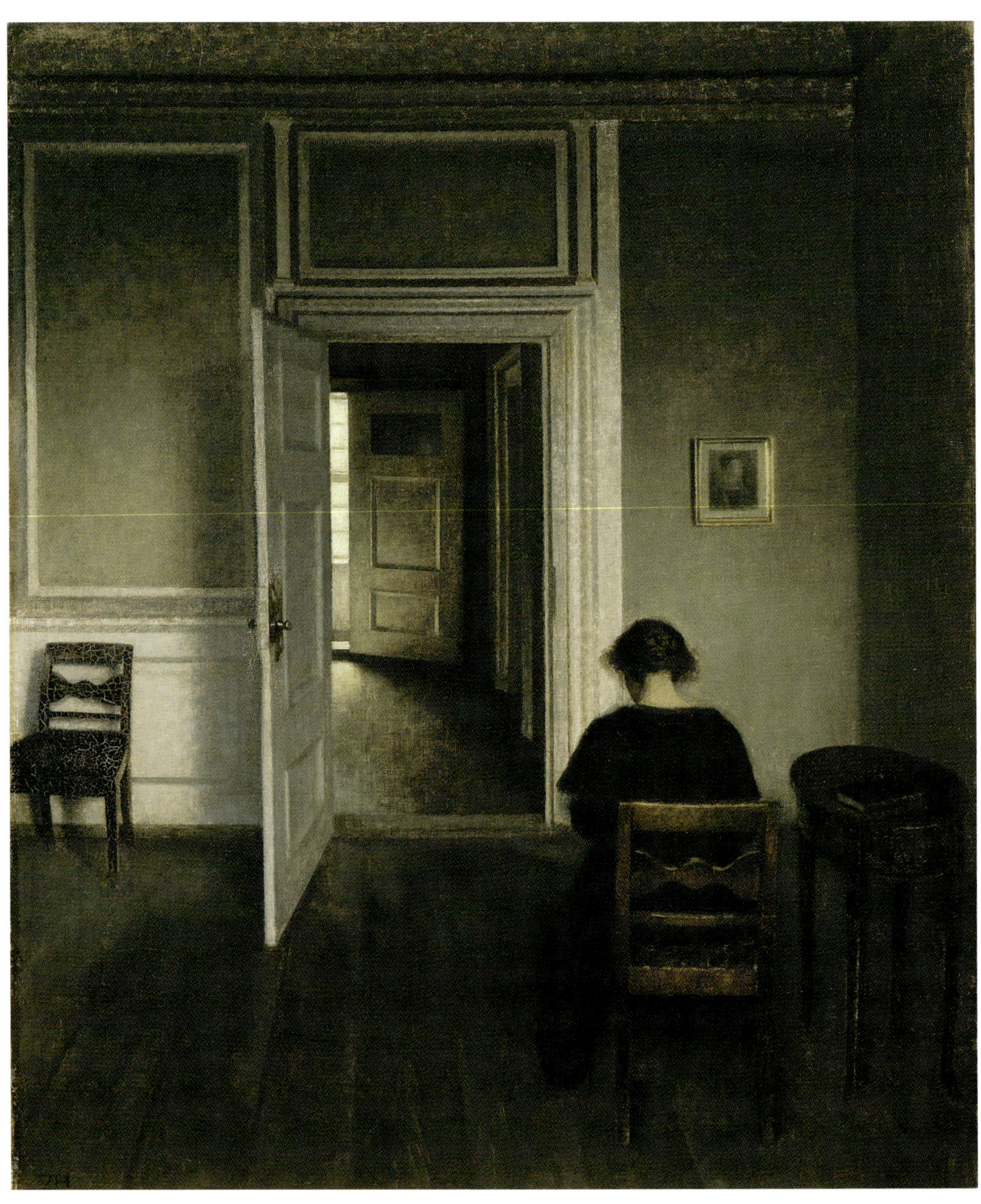

188.
Vilhelm Hammershøi
Interior, Strandgade 30, 1908
Oil on canvas, 31⅛ x 26 cm
(79 x 66 cm)
ARoS Aarhus Kunstmuseum

patterns, composed of plums, ochres, blues, siennas, umbers, greens, and charcoals, neutralized and yet infinitely varied. Critics early in Hammershøi's career commented on the curiosity of his color choices: "Possibly this washed-out color tone is a natural inclination in the artist . . . But it leaves us with the impression that the entire scene has been shrouded in this foggy veil intentionally, that the effect is calculated, and such a calculation, toward the 'modern,' is not a fortunate trait in a debutant."[24] In considering the artist's works, Karl Madsen made the claim at the turn of the century that Hammershøi was "the oddest, most peculiar, and private, painter among his Danish contemporaries," but also expressed the confidence that there was something receptive to his work in the Danish character. "As Danes we understand, perhaps better than most others, the human qualities that express themselves through color. And indeed, behind

Hammershøi´s colors, we sense an infinitely cautious person, a quiet, sad dreamer, the weird-
est soul ever to grace Danish painting."[25] Hammershøi's work has been interpreted through
this lens of "weirdness," melancholy, neurasthenia, and childlessness. As his biographer Poul
Vad noted, "Hammershøi changes with us and will change with those after us," the mirror of
our projected fantasies. For his part, Hammershøi made a different claim for his work: "the
best joy is that one experiences oneself when painting . . . and one is absorbed by it."[26]

Over the course of twenty-six years, Hammershøi represented his wife from a slight
distance, and often from behind, in the rooms of their Copenhagen apartments. When he
revealed Ida to be engaged in seemingly common domestic activities, he rendered her as static,
draining domestic genre of its accustomed themes of industry or comfort through his minute
adjustments of every pictorial element.[27] In *Interior, Strandgade 30* (1899; fig. 186), in which
Ida seems to be setting a table, and *Interior of Woman Placing Branches in Vase on Table* (1900;
fig. 187), the artist's wife stands in the central room of this apartment. A comparison of the two
works suggests the extent to which the artist selectively orchestrated
the setting, moving furniture, emphasizing or masking the corner
stove, and even transforming the color of the walls.[28] This marshaling
of detail establishes the framing devices that imbue Hammershøi's
works with such a profound sense of stasis. Such elements as the
brass doorknob in *Interior, Strandgade 30*, which extends an invisible
line of orchestration from the spout of the Royal Copenhagen pot on
the table to the highest peak of Ida's forehead, lock the model's figure
into an all-pervasive geometry.

Elisabeth Fabritius suggests that such views, which often include
eccentrically expanded foregrounds, are the result of Hammershøi's
use of optical devices such as a camera lucida or camera obscura. Both
devices create fugitive images of a scene by focusing light through a
lens and projecting it onto a flat surface.[29] Hammershøi both collected
photographs and relied on them in the construction of some of his
paintings.[30] Beyond that, art historian Gertrude Oelsner has proposed
that Hammershøi had a "photographic eye"—a habit of seeing that was
in the first instance shaped by the formal eccentricities of photographic
images, including exaggerations in perspective, abrupt cropping of
images, and distortions in value range, silhouette, or surface textures.[31]
This modern sight shaped Hammershøi's strategy of revisiting and
remaking interior genre painting.

In this regard, Hammershøi frequently depicted Ida from behind so that our desire
to understand human activity, whetted by our reception of older interior genre painting, is
deflected onto the room around her. *Interior, Strandgade 30* (1908; fig. 188) pictures her in the
central room of their apartment in a view similar to *White Doors (Open Doors)*, and in diminished light. A gilt-framed portrait, a table, book, and chair, and the open door, are the front
room's only other "occupants." Seated with her head inclined, Ida faces away from the viewer
so that her activity, or inactivity, is unidentifiable. In spatial structure, the painting repeats the
complex sequencing of Dutch painting of the seventeenth century, and particularly the paintings of Gerard ter Borch (1617–1681), Pieter de Hooch (1629–1683), and Johannes Vermeer
(1632–1675; fig. 189).

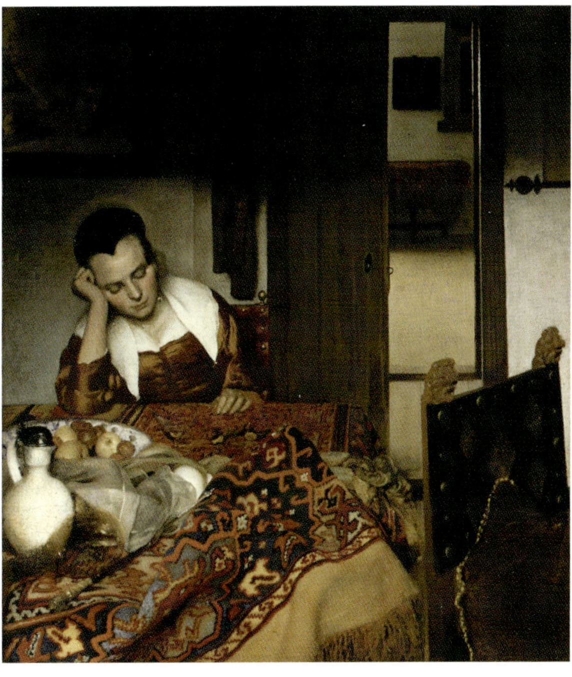

189.
Johannes Vermeer
A Woman Asleep, c. 1657
Oil on canvas, 34½ x 30⅛ in.
(87.6 x 76.5 cm)
The Metropolitan Museum of Art,
New York
Bequest of Benjamin Altman, 1913

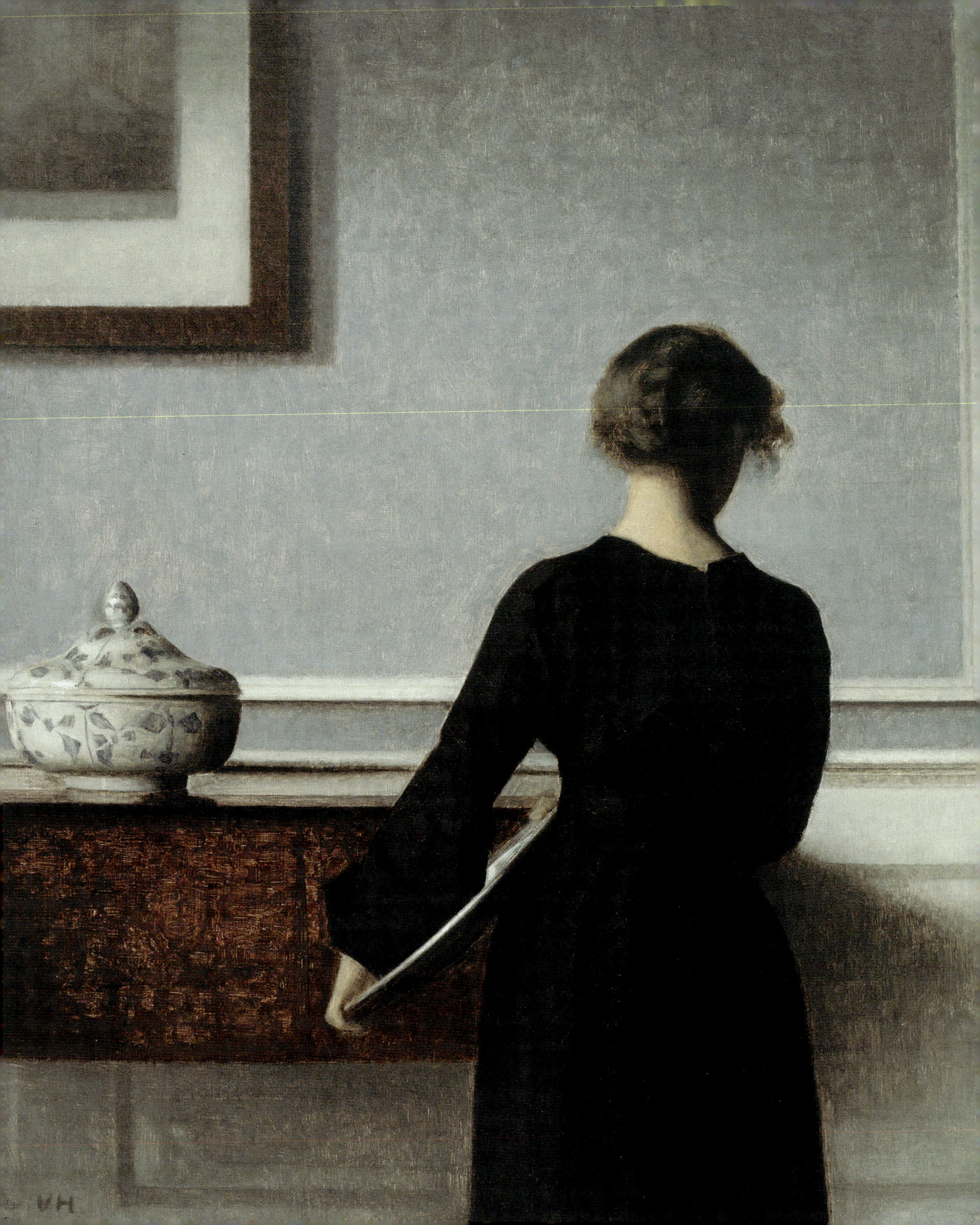

Like his Danish contemporary Anna Ancher, one of Hammershøi's strongest affinities was with Vermeer's interiors. He first encountered Vermeer's work during his initial study trip to Berlin in 1885, and then in the Netherlands in 1887.[32] It is hard to remember that Vermeer's work was virtually unknown until the 1870s. At that time, an influential monograph on the artist rekindled audiences' interest in his work while also introducing him to contemporary readers as mysterious, "a sphinx."[33] The paintings of Vermeer suggested to Hammershøi's contemporaries an uncanny inner meaning imbuing the spaces of domesticity, a static and ascetic geometric ordering of intimate spaces animated by masterful light effects. In turn, Hammershøi was identified as a kind of modern-day Vermeer.[34] Hammershøi's ability to conjure up associations simultaneously with old master art and with new technologies of seeing suggest both his complexity in the Danish contemporary art world and also the intricacies of his vision.

Interior with Young Woman Seen from Behind (1903–04; fig. 190) is an exceptionally rich example of Hammershøi's interplay between architectonic form, human presence, and the organizing function of sight. Like *Interior, Strandgade 30*, it offers a view of a dark-clad figure whose expression and activity are hidden and who stands against a wall formed of concentric squares radiating from the upper left corner. With the geometric rigor of Italian Renaissance master Piero della Francesca (1416–1492), whose work was much in vogue at the time, and of contemporary French painter Georges Seurat (1859–1891), and through the use of a harmonious, reduced palette, Hammershøi enmeshes the figure. Among the many interpretations that have been offered for this work, Henrik Wivel sees a profound eroticism in this painting, from the exposed neck of the model to the subtle curves of her silhouette in contrast to the room's geometry, the visual opening between her left arm and torso, and the pairing of her body with the porcelain vessel—her proposed double— that rests on the sideboard, engaging contemporary gender politics regarding the entrapment of women in domesticity.[35]

Hammershøi said little about his own work, and virtually nothing about any theory of art. Instead, he described himself as a kind of sensitive eye: "What makes me choose a motif is as much the lines in it, what I would call the architectural stance in the picture. And then the light, of course. It is naturally also very important, but the lines are almost what I am most taken by. Color is of secondary importance, I suppose; I am not indifferent to how it looks in color. I work very hard to make it harmonious. But when I choose a motif I think I mainly look at lines."[36]

Hammershøi exercised an antiquarian sensibility when seeking such architectural "lines." His biographer Poul Vad characterized him as a "house hunter, a space hunter."[37] Between 1898 and 1909, the Hammershøis lived in one of the oldest surviving houses in Copenhagen—where he painted these interiors. Their district, Christianshavn, was built in the early seventeenth century by Christian IV as a civil and commercial harbor to resemble a Dutch

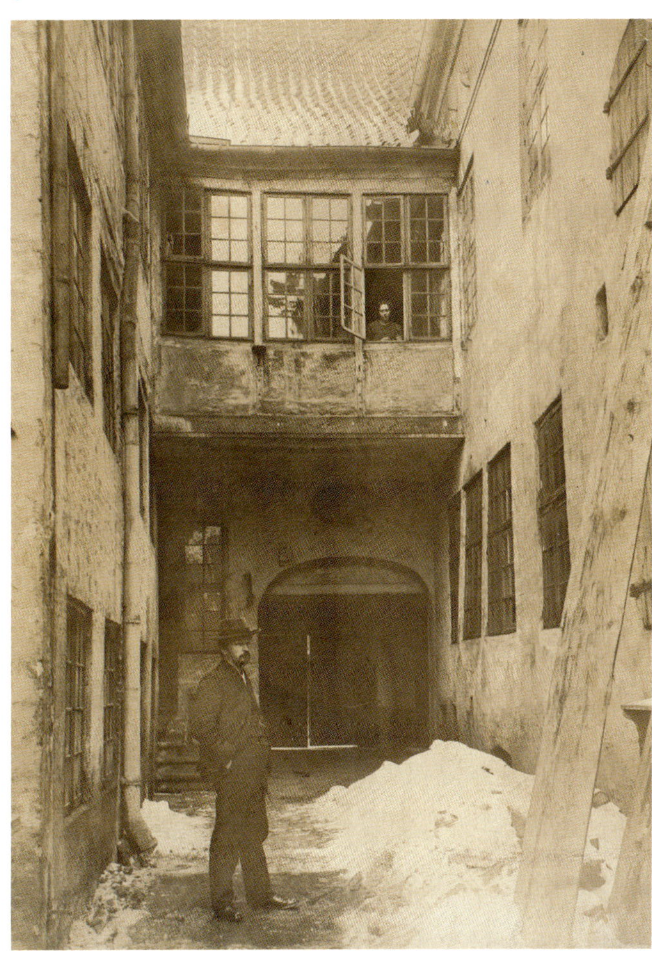

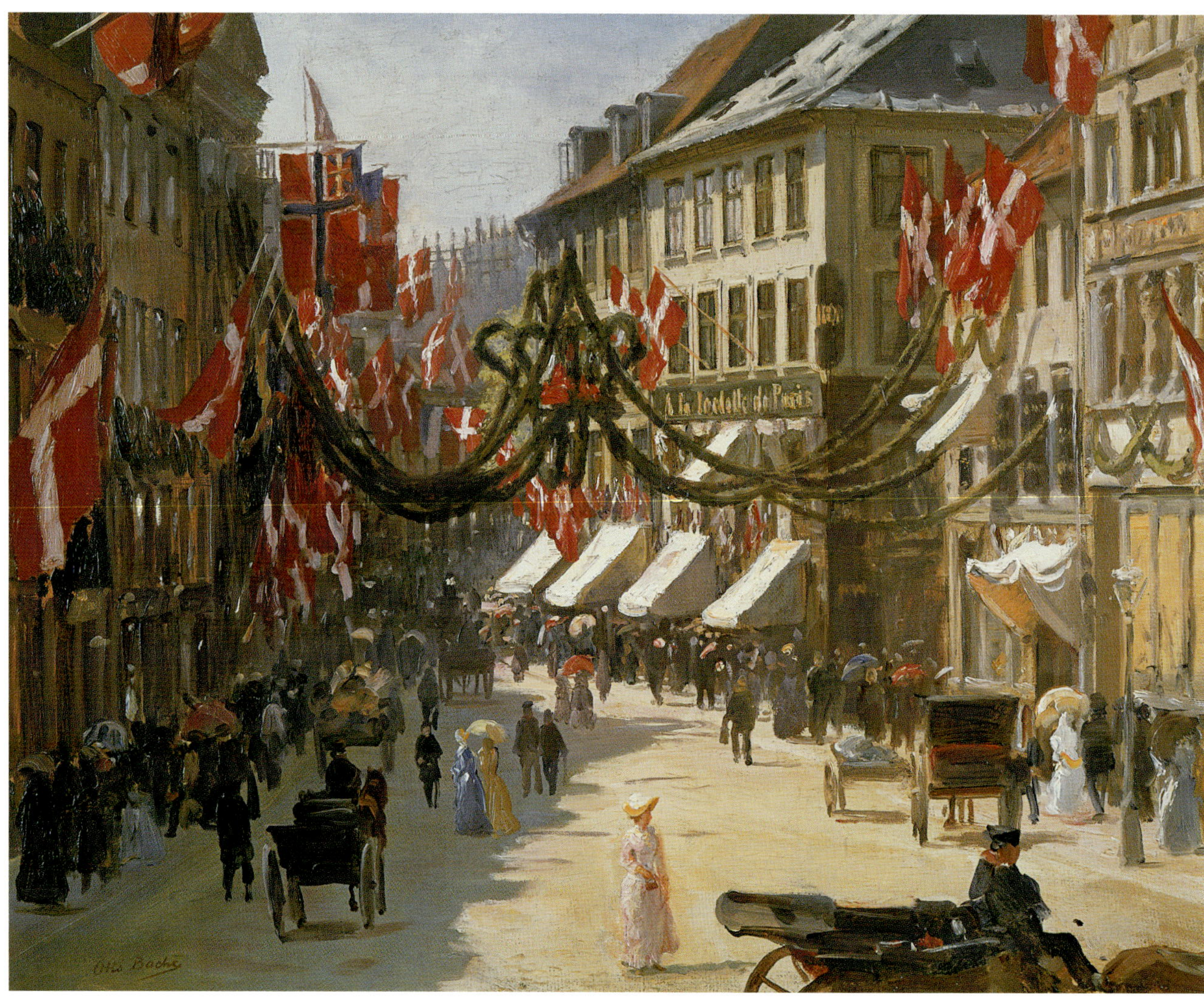

enclave. Originally laid out and built by Dutch engineers, the district included buildings that featured Dutch lifting hooks, familiar from houses in Holland. Among the oldest houses are those on Strandgade, including number 30, the Hammershøi's home, built by 1636 (fig. 191).[38] The district did not suffer the fires or bombings that ravaged Copenhagen proper (such as the bombardment of the harbor by the English in 1807) and it consequently retained some of its early Dutch character. It was an area of the city beloved of national preservationists in the late nineteenth century, when the center of Copenhagen had undergone great changes.

From the 1850s through the early twentieth century, the ramparts that had circumscribed the city were demolished, and Copenhagen's urban fabric was extended beyond the old walls.[39] Large public works projects, including axial boulevards, enhanced sanitation systems, and later electric lighting, museums (such as the Ny Carlberg Glyptotek), municipal buildings, and commercial establishments, some on a grand scale, transformed the former walled city into a modern metropolis, perhaps not quite on the order of Paris, but newly scaled and populous nonetheless. Hammershøi's paintings communicate nothing of this growth, nor does it engage any of its attendant problems or pleasures.

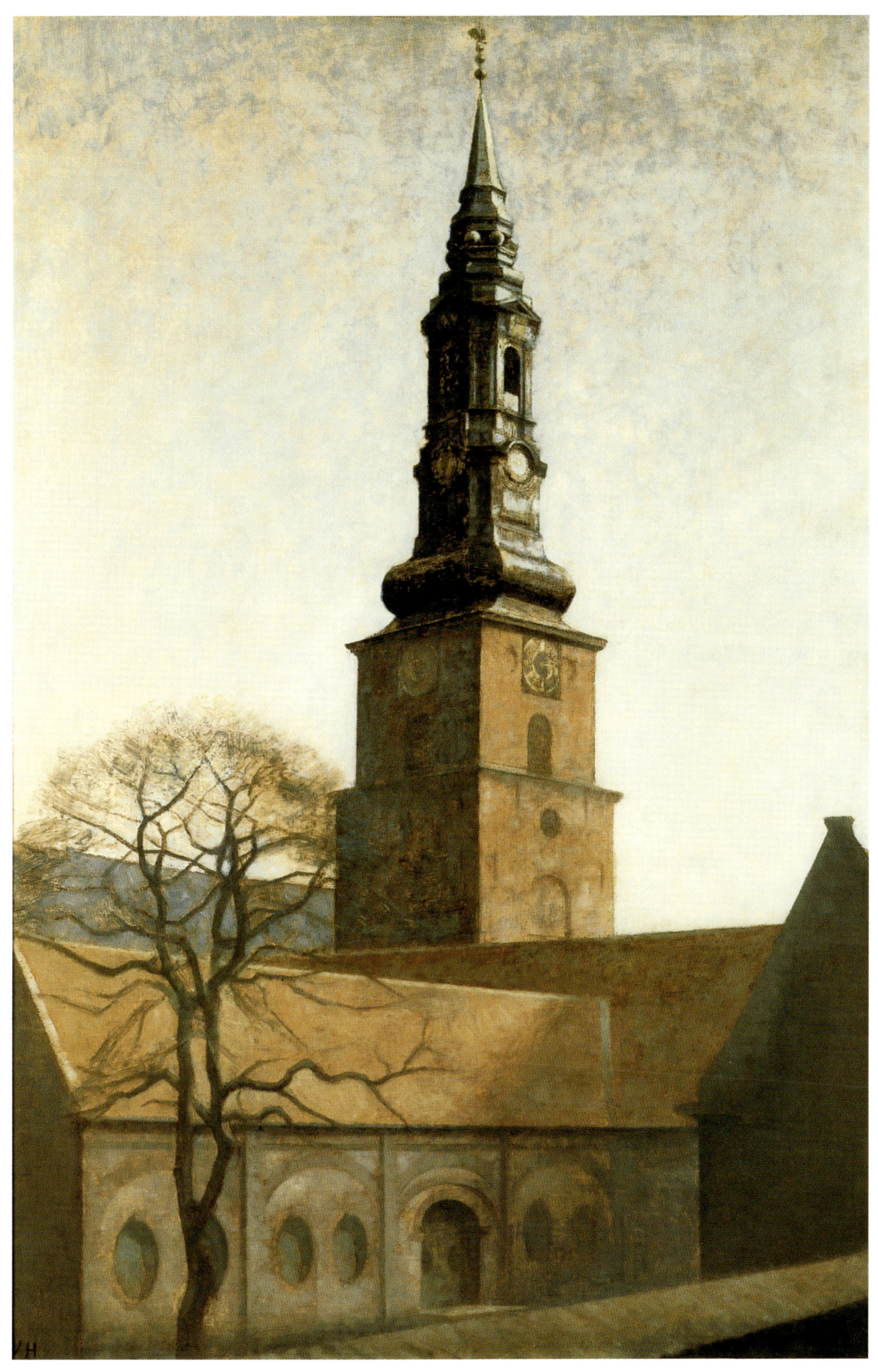

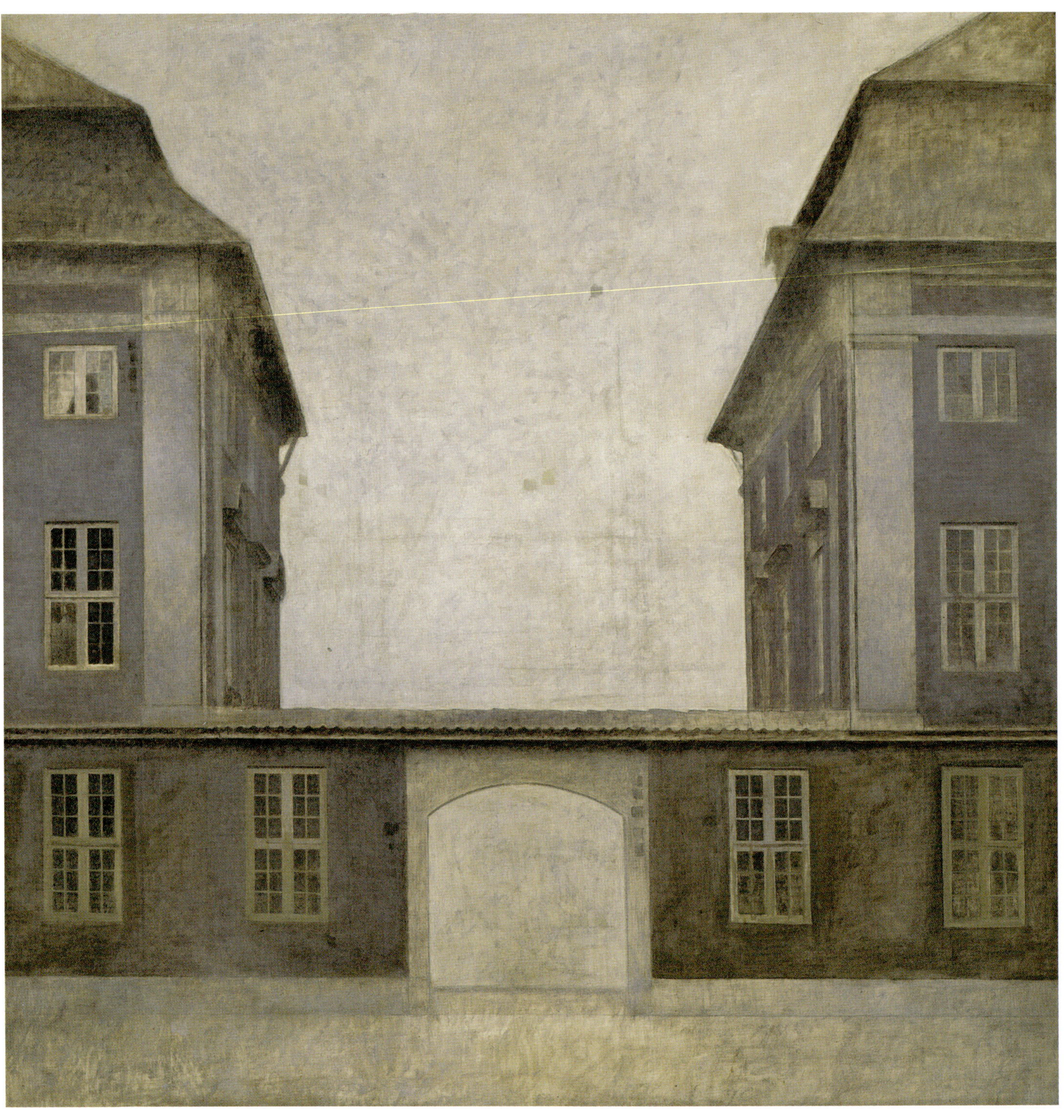

In contrast, Otto Bache's *Flag Day in Copenhagen on a Summer Day, in Vimmelskaftet* (after 1892; fig. 192) emphasizes the city's transformation. Bache used the golden anniversary of King Christian IX and Queen Louise in 1892 as an opportunity to depict Copenhagen as a Danish metropolis, its cosmopolitanism reinforced by the new spectacles of streetlights and shop signs, and through the inclusion of flags from other nations.[40] In the distance, the spires of the Church of the Holy Spirit rise above the rooflines, a reminder of the city's historical past, while the Danish flags that line this modern urban space, in tandem with the garlands gathered to form the royal crown over the street, suggest stability, continuity, and prosperity. The painting's relatively high viewing angle, expansive entry into the street in the foreground, and telescoping perspective recapitulate urban views of Paris first recorded by Parisian documentary photographers during the period of Haussmanization and recall paintings by Camille Pissarro (1830–1903), Claude Monet (1840–1926), and other members of the Impressionist generation during and after the radical transformation of Paris. For Bache, who had witnessed both the ongoing engineering of the city and its representation by the Impressionists in the mid-1860s and 1870s, this approach to recording urban experience was a valuable model.

Copenhagen's modernization and transformation is suggested in a vastly different manner—through negation—in Hammershøi's intimate views of the city. In *The Church of St. Peter, Copenhagen* (ca. 1906; fig. 193), the artist emphasizes the details of the medieval stonework and Baroque tower, erasing the urban fabric adjacent to the church, and inserting a wintry, denuded tree. In this way, Hammershøi suspends present time in order to evoke the tangible presence of history. In assuming an upwardly turned perspective that accentuates and isolates the tower, he also invokes associations with such well-known motifs by the Golden Age master Christen Købke, as *One of the Small Towers of Frederiksborg Castle* (fig. 63). In fact, there is a curious dialogue between Hammershøi's painting and Købke's canonical work, one which offers insights into Hammershøi's historical self-consciousness. Købke's painting represents the aspirations and technical achievements of Golden Age painters: clarity, brilliant light, and homey narrative details such as storks, populated paths, and a farm render the everyday extraordinary. Hammershøi's representation, like his view of *Amalienborg Square* (fig. 1), is indistinct, overcast, monochromatic, slightly blurred, and lacking in human anecdote. In other words, Hammershøi negated the very terms of Golden Age view paintings, while retaining vestiges of their form.

Similarly, *The Asiatic Company Buildings*, which Hammershøi painted in 1902 (fig. 194), is edited and reformulated to both erase modernity and resist historicism. The office building, which was constructed for the Asiatic Company in 1738, and its twin warehouse built nearly fifty years later, were located directly across the street from the Hammershøis' home on Strandgade. A photograph of the Asiatic Company buildings from Hammershøi's collection, taken from the same angle as the painting, shows a lamppost to the right of the gate, and the street to be populated and featuring the dirt and detritus suggestive of daily use.[41] Hammershøi edited out any

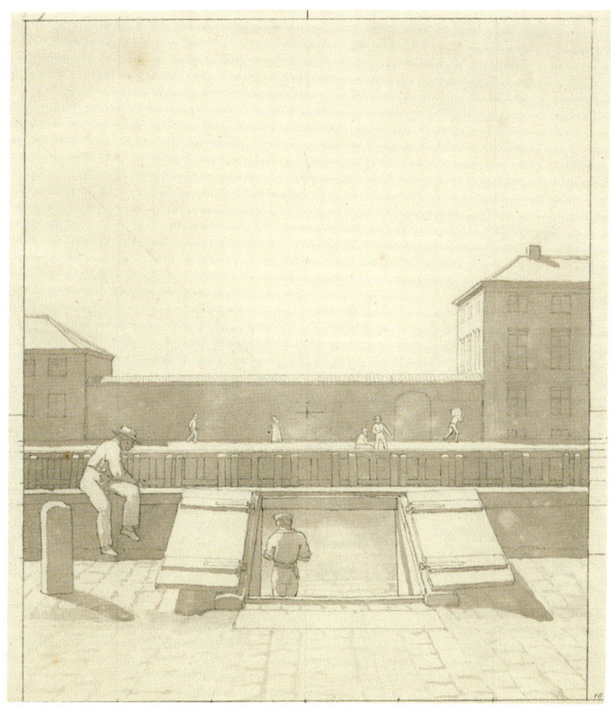

modern incursions into the setting, focusing exclusively on the buildings' mass and linearity, and inserting a grisaille emptiness to veil the harbor and sky beyond the gate.

In addition to its likely relationship to photography, *The Asiatic Company Buildings* may also have been rendered in dialogue with a drawing by C. W. Eckersberg, owned by Hammershøi, entitled *Ideal View of Charlottenborg and the Gardener's Lodge at the Botanical Garden* (1845; fig. 195).[42] Eckersberg's drawing, which employs the perspectival systems he published in 1840 (see chapter 4),[43] is a meticulously crafted study of more or less symmetrical elements balanced against a strong central axis. Similarly, Hammershøi locates his view of the buildings at ground level, offering paired structures on either side of two voids—the view through the arched gateway in the wall linking the buildings, and the empty sky above. The subtle asymmetries, as in Eckersberg's drawing, become more pronounced the longer one views the composition. The mansard roof on the right begins lower on the canvas and rises higher, to be cropped along the top edge, and the detailing of the facade and the glass covering the windows on the right gathering more reflected light. Tiny formal comparisons across the central axis, which multiply with each sideways glance, transform the buildings, monuments of Denmark's past global economic reach, into silent and abstract forms, distanced from the active city. Like *St. Peter's Church* and *Amalienborg Square* and his numerous other paintings of Danish official architecture, Hammershøi pictured the city and the architectural legacy of absolutism as realms of silence.

Hammershøi's representations of his own home operate in a similar manner. *Courtyard Interior at Strandgade 30* (ca. 1905; fig. 196), representing the light well of his apartment building, offers a lens onto his preservationist temperament. The painting's monochromatic palette and its emphasis on the subtly warped windows and the half-timbered framing displacing the aging plaster testify to a veneration of the past. However, this veneration is offered in an acutely vectored and constrained modern composition. Hammershøi's regard for the art and architecture of Denmark's—and Holland's—past had deep roots in elite Danish culture. In the first half of the nineteenth century, one of the means of forging a sense of a renewed Danish identity had been by reaching back to symbols of past eras of power and prestige, initially to Greece and Rome via the French academic model. The Danish Golden Age artists' admiration for Dutch and Flemish art mirrored and encouraged their growing interest in local landscape and genre painting. In the 1890s, Hammershøi's allusions recalled the heyday of Danish-Dutch relations in the seventeenth century.[44]

In 1909–10, the sale of their building forced the Hammershøis to move from their rented Strandgade apartment to central Copenhagen. On Bredgade, Hammershøi painted *Interior with the Artist's Easel* (1910; fig. 197), which shows one of the few views of this apartment that seems to have pleased the artist.[45] In a painting structured by almost unrelievedly vertical and horizontal elements, Hammershøi offers a series of visual dualities—two floor lines (lower in the front room and raised in the back), two doors, one open and one closed, and two works of art, the unseen canvas resting on Hammershøi's easel and J. F. Clemens's engraving of C. A. Lorentzen's painting *The Battle of Copenhagen, 2 April 1801* (see fig. 38). The canvas, turned away from our view, is strongly backlit with a shimmering, theatrical quality evoking the work of Rembrandt (fig. 198) and arousing the curiosity of the spectator as to what, if anything, is portrayed. With the view through the doorway, reminiscent of Vermeer's paintings, and the Golden Age print hanging high on the wall, the painting offers historical resonance.

196.
Vilhelm Hammershøi
*Courtyard Interior at
Strandgade 30*, ca. 1905
Oil on canvas, 29½ x 24¾ in.
(75 x 63 cm)
Collection of Ambassador John L. Loeb Jr.,
New York

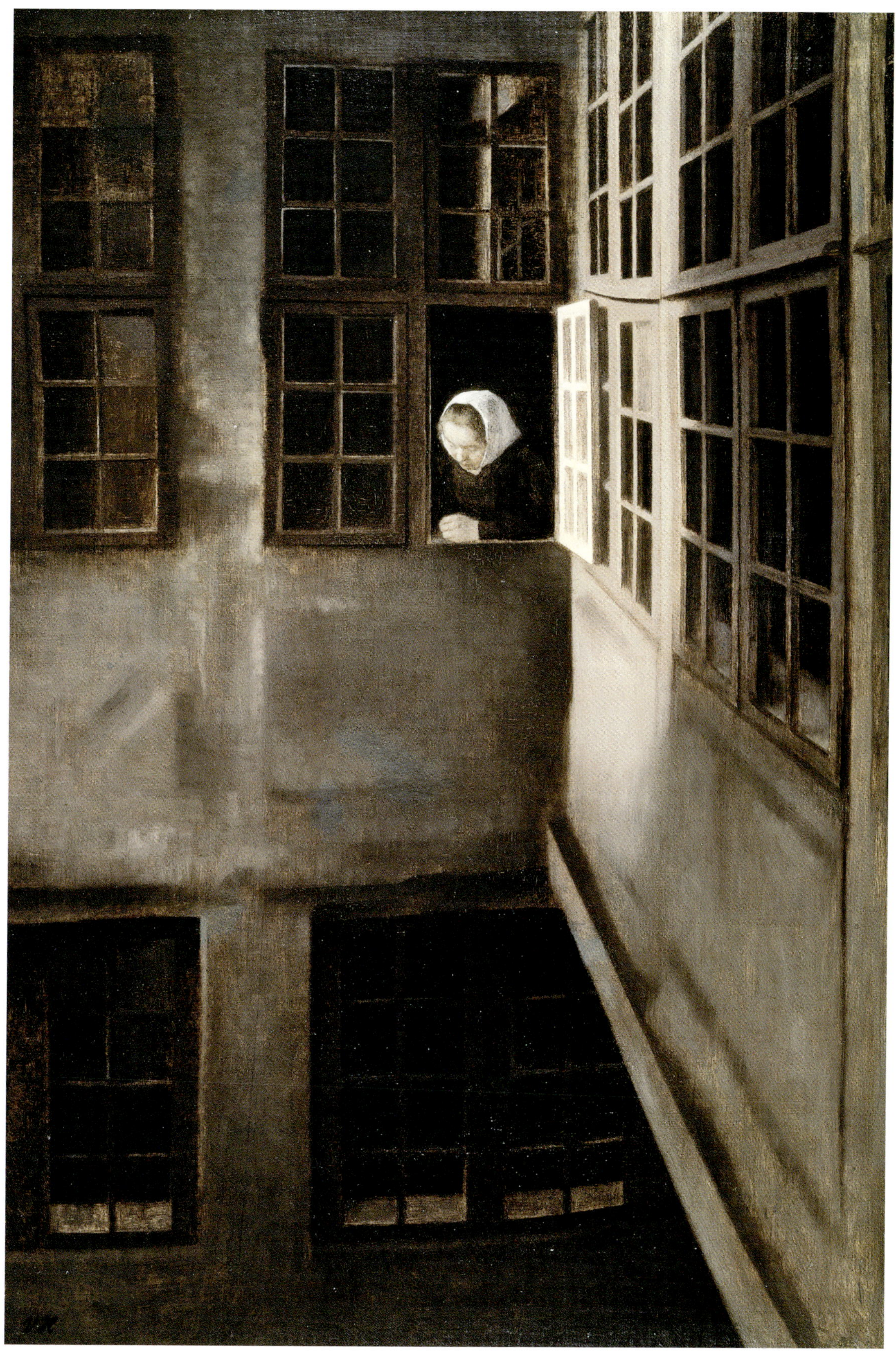

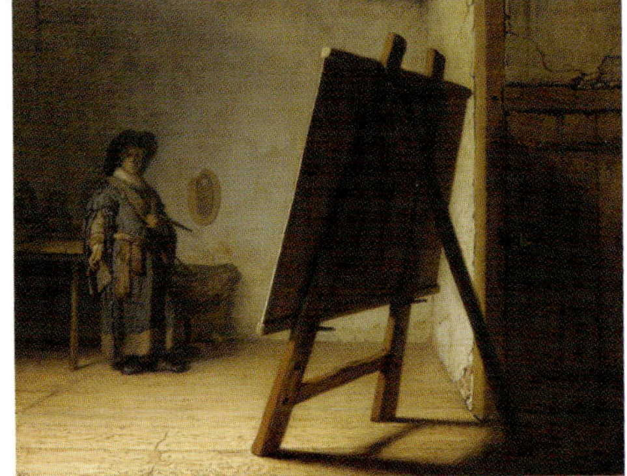

In 1913, the Hammershøis moved back to Christianshavn, occupying an apartment in Strandgade 25, the old Asiatic Company buildings, directly across from their earlier flat. In these high-ceilinged rooms, Hammershøi returned to motifs that he had painted in the 1890s, among them *Interior, the Tall Windows, Strandgade 25* (1913; fig. 199). Revising a Romantic formula familiar from the work of Caspar David Friedrich (fig. 200), a window offers both a view onto the exterior world and a barrier to proximity, the double of the yearning soul. A motif that continued to have potency into the late nineteenth century, poignantly in Edvard Munch's harmonious and elegiac *Night in St. Cloud* (1890; fig. 201), the window offers a pictorial inhabitant a view but inhibits ours, soliciting us to consider the consciousness of the viewer pictured.[46] The vast space, structured by the geometry of window sash, wainscoting, and enameled moldings, unfolds to reveal floor and ceiling, a repetition of the box-like space of Wilhelm Bendz's view of his family home from 1827 (fig. 41). In that canonical Golden Age painting, sunlight clarifies detail, acting as the agent of an

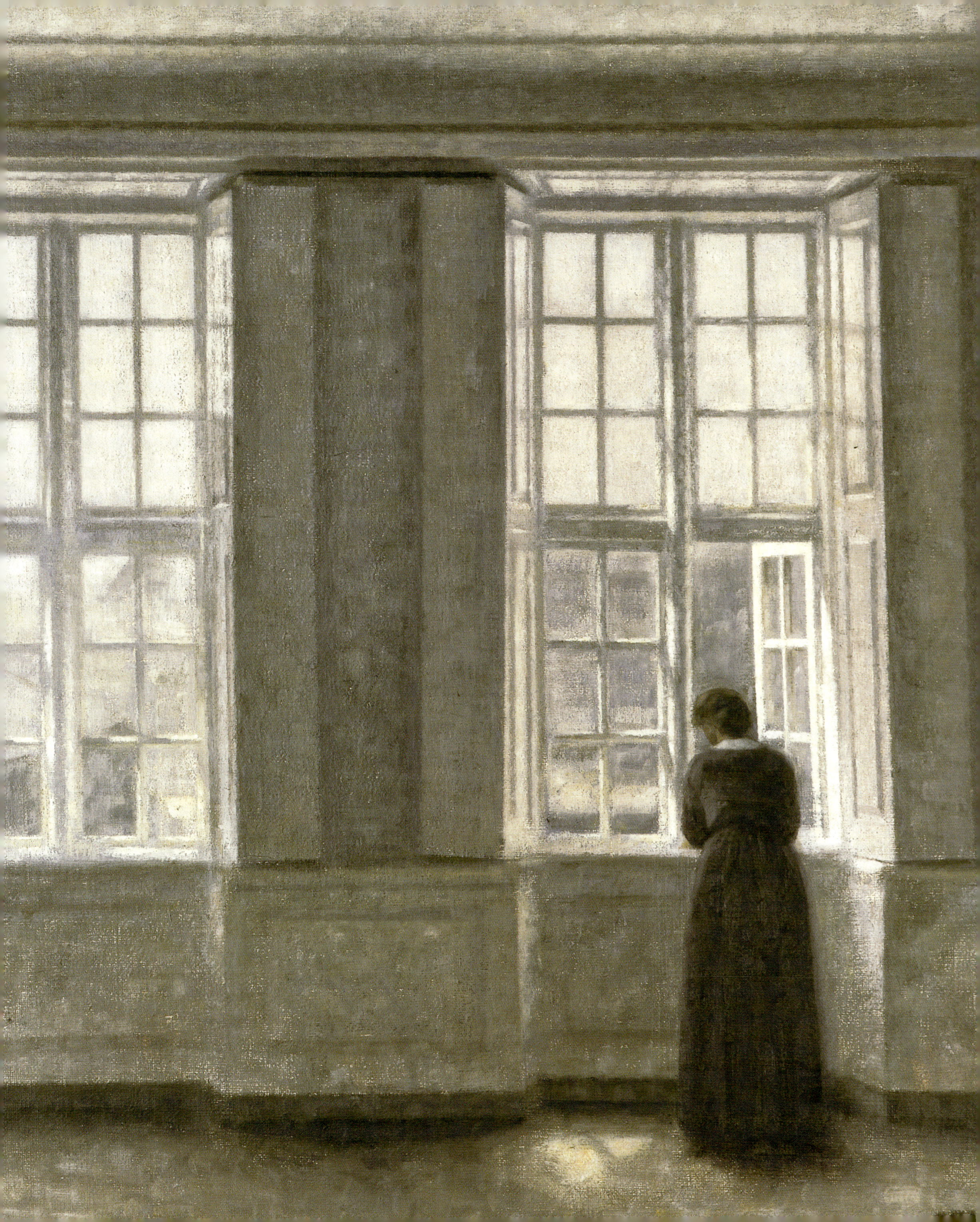

astringent visual clarity. Characteristically, Hammershøi reverses the function of light, controlling it to bleach the open window frame and puddle on the floor, but not to clarify the diminutive woman or her activity.

The views of his homes offer themselves as refuges, their silence and stasis operating as paradoxical tokens of urban life. Art historian Sharon Hirsh notes that such an emphatic rejection of the city reflected a position shared by artists of the Symbolist generation throughout industrialized Europe. In erasing urban and industrial modernity, as Willumsen, the Slott-Møllers, and Hammershøi seem to have done, these artists only strengthened their connection to it.[47] The home in particular became sacralized in the latter nineteenth century in direct proportion to a city's cosmopolitanism and growth, its industrialization, and its programmatic ordering.[48] British theorist John Ruskin, whose work was so important to the Pre-Raphaelites and the Symbolist generation, described the home in the 1870s as "the place of Peace; the shelter, not only from all injury, but from all terror, doubt, and division . . . it is a sacred place, a vestal temple, a temple of the hearth watched over by the Household Gods."[49]

Throughout late nineteenth-century literature and art, the city street was symbolically understood to be the space of maleness and public interaction, while the interior was the space inhabited by the new middle class woman.[50] However, social critics at the turn of the century suggested that men needed domesticity the most—the comfort, isolation, and spirituality of the home could reinvigorate the tired urban man worn down by the numbing effects of the city. As one Belgian critic noted: "Inside meant family and security, outside meant strangers and danger."[51] These are the messages conveyed by the harmonious middle-class domestic interiors by Peter Ilsted (fig. 202), Hammershøi's brother-in-law, and by Hammershøi's colleague Carl Holsøe (fig. 203). Indeed, the genre of interior painting gained in popularity in direct proportion to Denmark's industrialization, continuing the Danish tradition of picturing gemütlich bourgeois rooms from the Golden Age, but increasingly made static and moody.

The apartments where the Hammershøis lived seem spartan, suggestive at first glance of modesty or perhaps a lack of means. This impression is deceptive, however. Instead, what we witness is Hammershøi's selectiveness as a painter. Indeed, photographs of the couple's apartments reveal a greater variety of possessions (and of Ida's wardrobe, though invariably painted as black and almost timeless) than Hammershøi represented. In his paintings, we are privy to Hammershøi's elite vision of design. In an era in which many progressive artists, such as Marie Krøyer or the Slott-Møllers (see chapters 5 and 6), engaged in William Morris's Arts and Crafts aesthetic, designing or admiring interior decoration that spoke of medieval craftsmanship, the Hammershøis organized their environment in what we understand retrospectively to be modernist taste, paralleling that of Adolf Loos (1870–1933) in Austria.

In 1909, the Hammershøis' home at Kvæsthusgade 6, where they lived temporarily, was featured in the journal *Hjemmet*, accompanied by an interview with Vilhelm: "Strictly speaking, I am fond of the old, of old homes, old furniture, or the quite distinctive atmosphere which reposes in all of this. But at the same time I am not blind to the fact that there is something wrong in favoring the old at the expense of the new—at the expense of the good new, mind you. Modern people ought to live in modern, up-to-date homes. And far better to follow a modern style than to imitate the old. . . . One hundred years ago the craftsmen labored with a greater artistic understanding and far greater love for their work then nowadays when so much is factory work. . . . If only people would open their eyes to the fact that a few good things in a room give it a far more

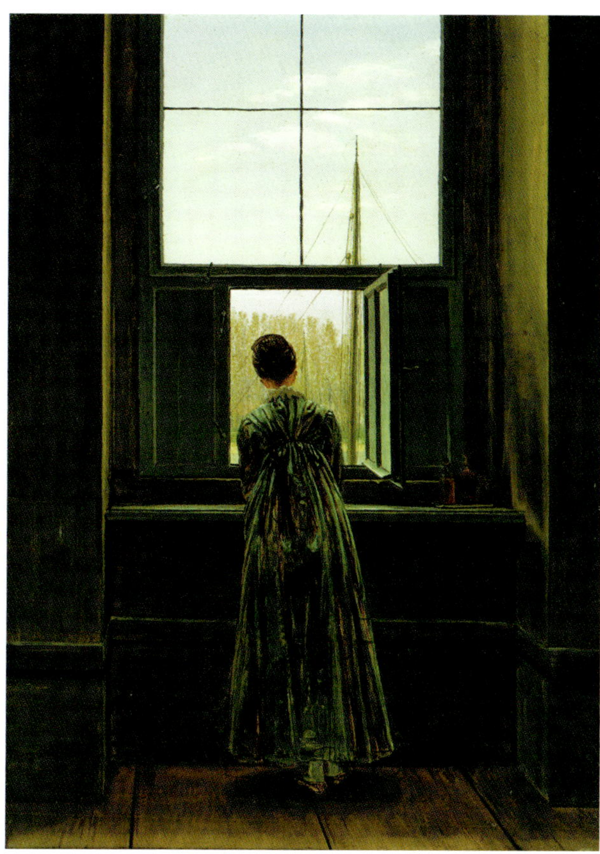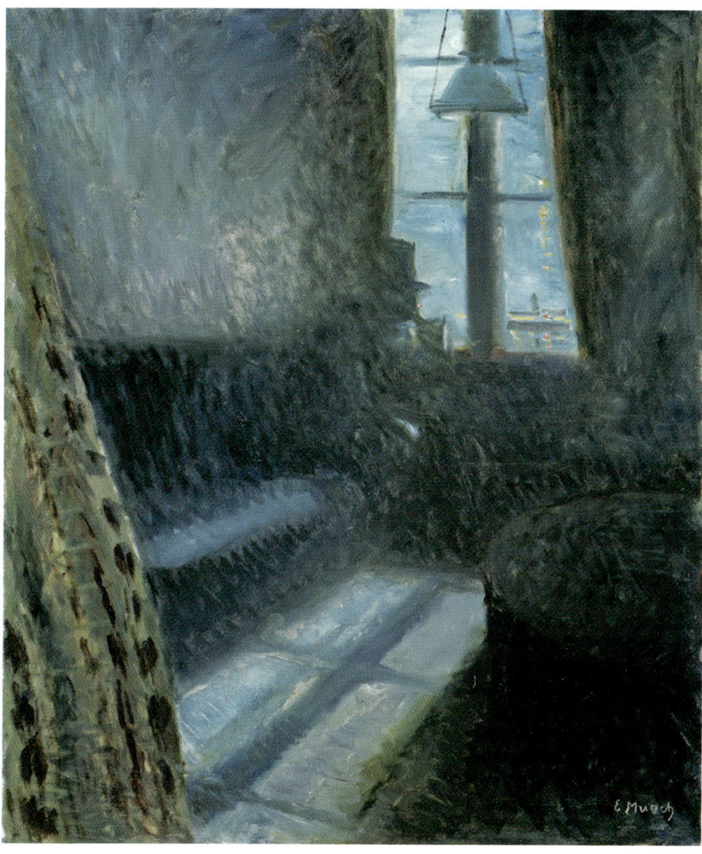

beautiful and finer quality than many mediocre things. . . . That every genuine object, even if it is of cheap materials, is better and handsomer than imitation expensive objects."[52]

The couple's successive apartments embodied this discerning sensibility—and the influence of Ruskin's and Morris's theories of authenticity and truth. On Strandgade, the walls were painted in a uniform pale gray and cream to highlight the Baroque and Neoclassical detailing, and the apartment contained a few pieces of furniture and was sparsely decorated with art from Denmark's Golden Age and reproductions of old master work.[53] The Hammershøis collected Empire and Biedermeier furniture, rare and artisanally designed books, and the few exquisite pieces of porcelain that appear in many of Hammershøi's paintings. By the 1890s, Biedermeier furniture was anachronistic in interior decoration. Biedermeier and Empire furniture was the stuff of the Hammershøis' parents' and grandparents' generation, the richly pared down forms of the post-Napoleonic period.

As Hammershøi had written home from Paris in 1891, the couple loved antiques: "After dinner . . . we go and wallow in Empire and Louis Seize furniture and old dishes and old silks," wrote Hammershøi from Paris in 1891.[54] With the rise of William Morris's Arts and Crafts Movement in England and its affiliates, and the appearance in the 1890s of architectural design magazines throughout Europe, the emphasis on decorated and hand-made things—and not on the industrially produced—within the home became influential among social progressives.[55] Most potent among these things were antiques, objects that represented older and better times,

200.
Caspar David Friedrich
Woman Before the Window, ca. 1822
Oil on canvas, 17⅜ x 14½ in.
(44 x 37 cm)
Nationalgalerie, Berlin

201.
Edvard Munch
Night in St. Cloud, 1890
Oil on canvas, 25⅜ x 21¼ in.
(64.5 x 54 cm)
The National Museum of Art,
Architecture, and Design, Oslo

objects that, according to Hirsh, became chic in the 1890s.[56] Within nationalist rhetoric, and as practiced by the open-air folk museums such as Denmark's Frilandsmuseet (see chapter 3), the inheritance of past generations offered stability and groundedness for the present industrialized generation anxious about the disappearance of pre-industrial culture.[57] Making the connection with "past perfect" societies,[58] such objects spoke of less corrupted times—of a Golden Age—carrying memory and meaning into the present. Things, suggested Belgian artist Xavier Mellery, had "lives." He vitalized the spaces of domesticity in his series of drawings, *The Life of Things*, later retitled *The Soul of Things*.[59]

The resonance of antique Danish furniture as well as the late nineteenth-century reassessment of Golden Age painting also underlie one of the most celebrated portraits of the Danish Symbolist generation, Ludvig Find's *Portrait of a Young Man. The Painter Thorvald Erichsen* (1897; fig. 204). The Norwegian Thorvald Erichsen (1868–1939), then a student at Zahrtmann's school, is seated on an Empire sofa. Behind him are reproductions of paintings by Taddeo Gaddi, Masaccio, and Duccio,[60] reminiscent in placement to Eckersberg's much-emulated portrait of Bertel Thorvaldsen (fig. 25). The precision of Find's brushwork and the theme of the artist's portrait also evoke associations with Eckersberg's students, particularly the friendship portraits of Bendz (figs. 39, 40) and Blunck (fig. 38). Like Hammershøi's work, Find's portrait of Erichsen is historically resonant without being strictly historicist as it is transformed by the closely nuanced palette and the tight coordination of compositional elements to suggest absolute inactivity and pictorial stasis. Hammershøi's refined aesthetic depictions of antique objects and spaces and his allusions to Golden Age painting operate in part as inquiries into Danish historical identity.

The end of the nineteenth century was a period of intensive research into the history of Danish art and literature and, consequently, of artistic genealogy construction. Among the most notable publications were Carl Frederik Bricka's *Dansk biografisk Lexikon* (1887–1905), the first of its nineteen volumes appearing in 1887, and Philip Weilbach's *Dansk Kunstnerlexikon*, the first volume of which was published in 1877.[61] The history of Danish art, seen from the perspective of fin-de-siècle scholars emerged with the advent of Eckersberg. Indeed, Eckersberg was hailed as the "father" of Danish painting, and the artists who followed him were understood to be his progeny.[62] The notion of a native school, a political strategy propounded by N. L. Høyen in the early part of the century, became naturalized in the writings of such figures as Emil Hannover, Karl Madsen, and Julius Lange, the three most influential and systematic art historians of their generation. Even when these writers disagreed with Høyen's emphasis on Denmark's nativism and cultural isolation, as Julius Lange had in his 1879 "Art in Denmark and Abroad" (chapter 5), they nonetheless helped to stabilize a narrative of Denmark's art in which generational influences and a sense of organic unity prevailed. In keeping with art-historical writing throughout Europe, the foundational studies of Danish art largely took the form of biographies, of which Emil Hannover's *Maleren C. W. Eckersberg: En Studie i Dansk Kunsthistorie* (1898) was a model. Typical of the form, Hannover's monograph begins with a genealogy: "The truth is, the name commonly ascribed to the father of Danish painting is of German origin: Thus 'Eckersberg' is German for 'Eggersberg' or 'Egersbjærg,' not the other way around."[63] In a single stroke, Eckersberg is introduced in the book as the progenitor of Danish art and the issue of his complex nationality is discharged.

202.
Peter Ilsted
Mother and Child, 1892
Oil on canvas, 22½ x 17¾ in.
(57 x 45 cm)
Collection of Ambassador John L. Loeb Jr.,
New York

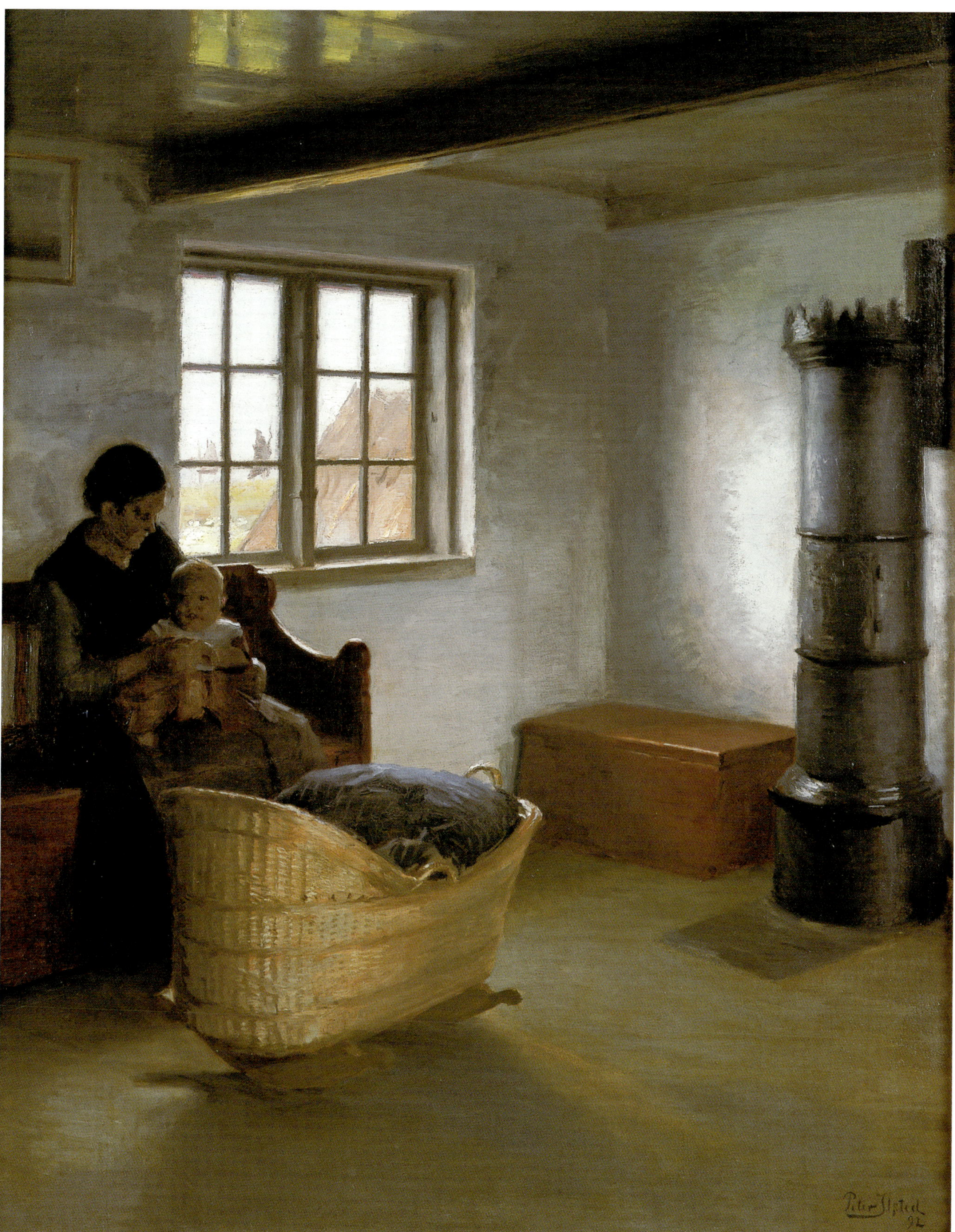

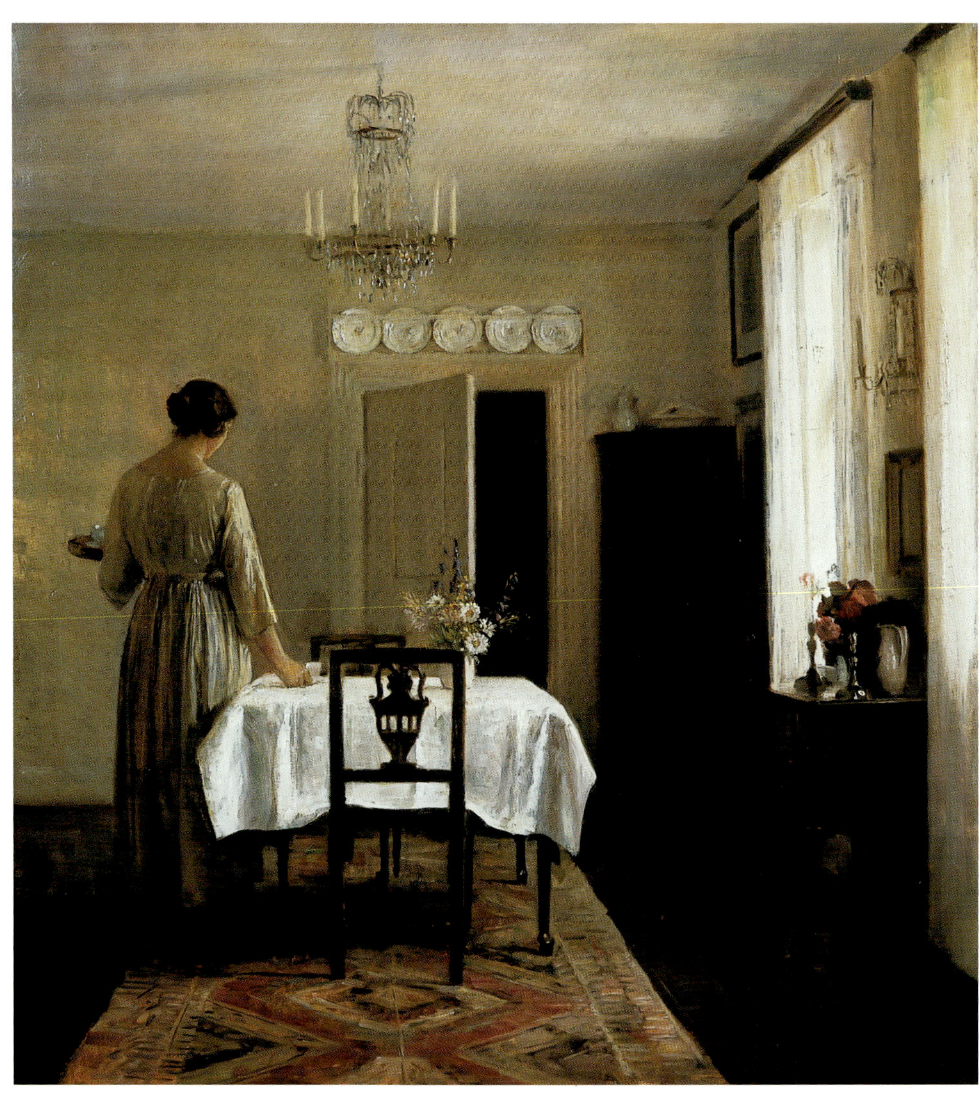

Agnes Slott-Møller's own reminiscences were shaped by this model of national genealogy construction. She reported that her early education occurred at the private school run by Eckersberg's daughters where "Eckersberg's paintings hung on the wall" and she was "nurtured with stories of Thorvaldsen and Marstrand."[64] Slott-Møller strongly supported the notion of an organic legacy, offering in a lecture entitled "On Patriotism": "We are born, so to speak, *into* a fatherland. It stands by our crib as we slowly become conscious of life itself. Its voice, our first lullaby, is blended into our mothers´ first words. Everything that is Danish is passed on to us by our mother country, as if poured from a precious piece of china. Its liquid contains memories that serve to give us strength and make us better. Like a grand picture book it reveals the figures upon whom all Danes wish to model themselves, and generates in them a desire to excel."[65] Artistic biography, modeled like genealogy, reinforced the notion of a primal Danish family.

As a painter who engaged in institution building in Copenhagen, at the Free Exhibition and later at the Kunstforeningen, and as a close friend of Denmark's leading critics, artists, and writers, Hammershøi was well aware of his and his generation's position within this imaginary

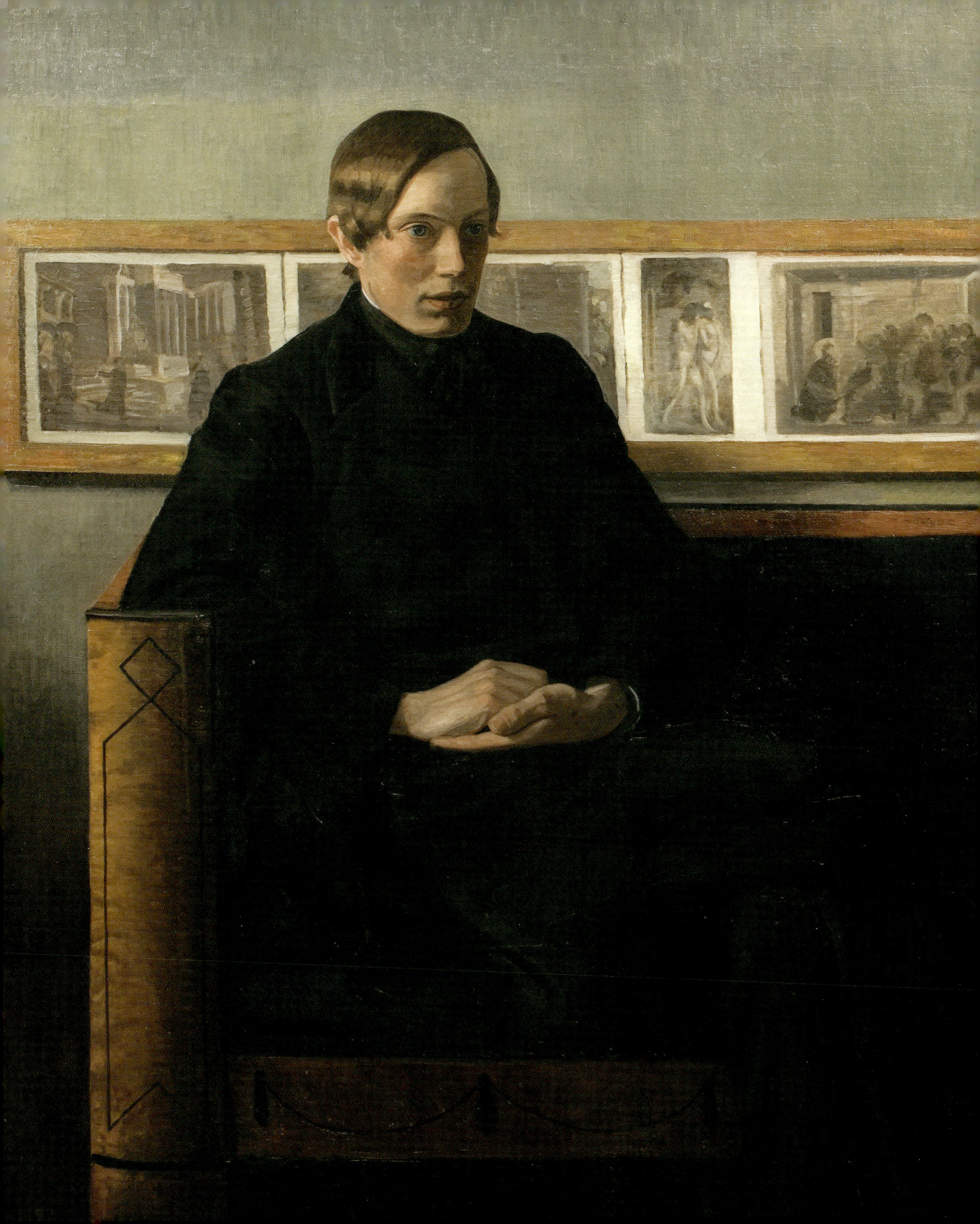

Danish family. Hammershøi's collector and biographer Alfred Bramsen reported that when *Five Portraits* (fig. 178) was sold to the Swedish collector Ernst Thiel in 1905, the artist was disappointed that it had not been purchased by the Statens Museum for Kunst. It was "a work he had put his whole soul, his whole talent into, which portrayed some of our most outstanding personalities within pictorial art, and which he naturally desired to be represented by his native country's art museum."[66]

In 1907, when an exhibition of Danish paintings was held at Guildhall in London, Hammershøi was described in the catalogue in terms that negated Georg Brandes's characterization of a steady, well-balanced Danish temperament: "The strangest development of all in recent years in Denmark has been the art of Hammershoj [sic]. Who would have ever thought of putting forward an empty room as the subject for a picture. Yet the sensitive gradations of light and their value in empty places, have aroused in him a curious kind of perception, which may in the future be repeated and practiced by others, but its originator is Hammershoj . . . To produce what he does with so limited a palette, to be content with that limit . . . suggests the possession of an uncommon power of restraint."[67]

In its restraint and refusal to narrate, and in its echoes and abjuration of a Golden Age inheritance, Hammershøi's work remains as enthralling and perplexing as it was to turn-of-the-century critics. Throughout the nineteenth century, light had permeated Danish painting, falling on material and rendering it knowable. Here, on the other hand, in a work by Hammershøi such as *Sunlight in the Room (Dust Motes)* (1906; fig. 205), light itself becomes constructive, architectonic. But whether it is "metaphysical" and "uncanny,"[68] or offers solace to the overwrought cosmopolitan, or is merely optical, is a question that Hammershøi resolutely avoided. Instead, he offered the spaces of his domesticity as, in a sense, a public mirror, reflecting the private fantasies of his viewers. In this sense, Hammershøi's work punctures Brandes's assessment of Danish art, as did much of the work of the Danish Symbolist generation. However, in Hammershøi, from *Artemis* to *Five Portraits*, paradox not only has its own logic, but it is the cornerstone of the Danish artistic culture of the twentieth century.

205.
Vilhelm Hammershøi
Sunlight in the Room (Dust Motes), 1906
Oil on canvas, 21½ x 18¼ in.
(54.5 x 46.5 cm)
The David Collection, Copenhagen

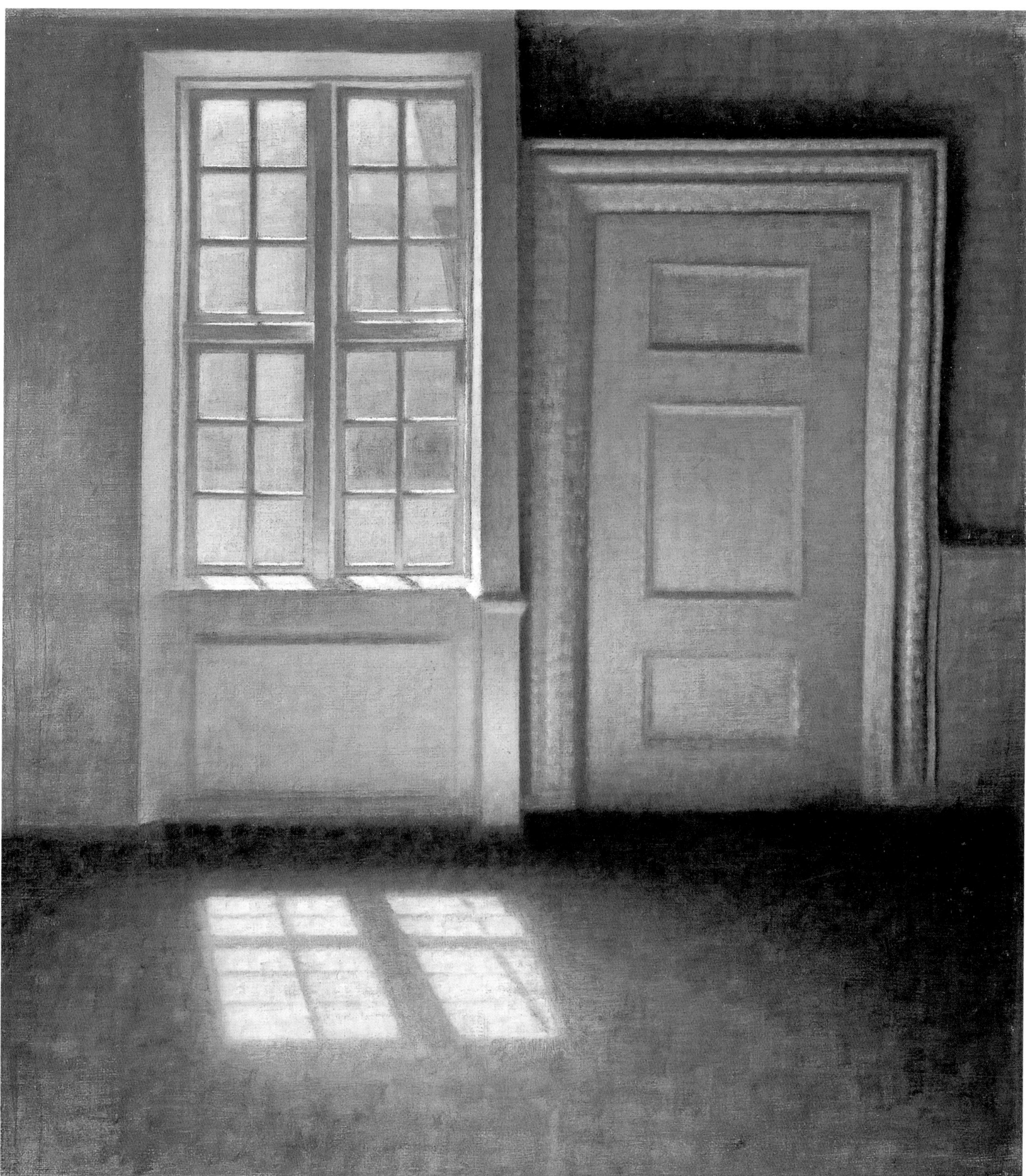

NOTES

INTRODUCTION

1 This term was used by Michael Kimmelman in "A Golden Age: New to America," *The New York Times*, February 11, 1994, a review of *The Golden Age of Danish Painting*, the survey exhibition held at the Los Angeles County Museum and the National Gallery in Washington in 1993–94 (see below).

2 The problem of defining an alternative, non-French, model of nineteenth-century production, and the particular conditions within Northern Europe, is taken up by Michelle Facos, *Nationalism and the Nordic Imagination: Swedish Art in the 1890s*, Berkeley: University of California Press, 1998, Introduction.

3 For a critical summary of Denmark's nation building efforts, and of its myths of coherence, see Knud J. V. Jespersen, *A History of Denmark* (trans. Ivan Hill), London: Palgrave Macmillan, 2004, chapter 8: "The Danes—A Tribe or a Nation?"

4 Christian Brinton, "Scandinavian Painters of Today," *Scribners*, Vol. LII, No. 6, December 1912, 654.

5 Vagn Poulsen, *Danish Painting and Sculpture*, Copenhagen: Det Danske Selskab, 1976

6 Among the most influential English-language survey exhibitions have been Kirk Varnedoe, *Northern Light: Realism and Symbolism in Scandinavian Art, 1880-1910* (exh. cat.), The Brooklyn Museum, 1982; Roald Nasgaard, *The Mystic North: Symbolist Landscape Painting in Northern Europe and North America, 1890–1940* (exh. cat.), Art Gallery of Ontario, Toronto, by the University of Toronto Press, 1984; *Dreams of a Summer Night: Scandinavian Painting at the Turn of the Century* (exh. cat.), The Hayward Gallery, London, 1986; Kasper Monrad, et al. *The Golden Age of Danish Painting* (exh. cat.), Los Angeles County Museum and Hudson Hills Press, 1993; Peter Nisbet, *Danish Paintings of the Nineteenth Century from the Collection of Ambassador John L. Loeb, Jr.* (exh. cat.), Busch-Reisinger Museum, Harvard University, 1994; Catherine Johnson, Helmut R. Leppien, and Kasper Monrad, *Baltic Light: Early Open-Air Painting in Denmark and North Germany* (exh. cat.), National Gallery of Canada, Ottawa and New Haven and London: Yale University Press, 1999; Peter Nørgaard Larsen, *Symbolism in Danish and European Painting 1870–1910* (exh. cat.), Statens Museum for Kunst, Copenhagen, 2000; and Kaspar Monrad, et al. *The Two Golden Ages: Masterpieces of Dutch and Danish Painting* (exh. cat.), Rijksmuseum, Amsterdam, Zwolle: Waanders Publishers, 2001.

7 Kirk Varnedoe, *Northern Light: Realism and Symbolism in Scandinavian Art, 1880-1910* (exh. cat.), The Brooklyn Museum, 1982. This catalogue was later revised and published as *Northern Light: Nordic Art at the Turn of the Century*, New Haven and London: Yale University Press, 1988 (also published as *Nordisk Gullalderkunst*, Oslo: Stenersens Forlag, 1988).

8 *Dreams of a Summer Night: Scandinavian Painting at the Turn of the Century* (exh. cat.), The Hayward Gallery, London and Kunstmuseum Düsseldorf, 1986; *1880-tal i nordisk måleri*, Stockholm Nationalmuseum and Oslo Nasjonalgalleriet, 1986; *Lumières du nord*, Paris, Musée du Petit Palais, 1987; and *Im Licht des Nordens*, Altonaer Museum, Hamburg, 1993.

9 Michelle Facos, op. cit. See also Michelle Facos and Sharon Hirsh, eds. *Art, Culture, and National Identity in Fin-de-Siècle Europe*, ed. N. Y.: Cambridge University Press, 2003.

10 Robert Rosenblum, *Transformations in Late Eighteenth-Century Art*, Princeton: Princeton University Press, 1967; and his *Modern Art and the Northern Romantic Tradition, Friedrich to Rothko*, New York: Harper and Row, 1975.

11 Robert Rosenblum and H. W. Janson, *Nineteenth Century Art*, New York: Abrams, 1984; and Robert Rosenblum, MaryAnne Stevens, and Ann Dumas, *1900: Art at the Crossroads* (exh. cat.), New York: Abrams, 2000.

12 Roald Nasgaard, op. cit.

13 Torsten Gunnarsson, *Nordic Landscape Painting in the Nineteenth Century* (trans. Nancy Adler), Cambridge and New York: Cambridge University Press, 1998; and Torsten Gunnarsson et al. *A Mirror of Nature: Nordic Landscape Painting 1840-1910* (exh. cat.) Ateneum Art Museum, Helsinki, Nationalmusuem, Stockholm, The National Museum of Art, Architecture and Design, Oslo, The Minneapolis Institute of Arts, Minneapolis, and Statens Museum for Kunst, Copenhagen, 2006. See also Gunnarsson, and Per Hedström, eds. *Impressisonism and the North* (exh. cat.), Nationalmuseum, Stockholm and Statens Museum for Kunst, Copenhagen, 2002–2003.

14 Barbara Miller Lane, *National Romanticism and Modern Architecture in Germany and the Scandinavian Countries*, London and New York: Cambridge University Press, 2000.

15 Suzanne Ludvigsen, et al. *The Ambassador John L. Loeb Jr. Danish Art Collection*, New York: John L. Loeb Jr., 2005.

CHAPTER 1

1 Knud J. V. Jespersen, 2004, 3.

2 See Hans Vammen, "A Small, Poor Nation": Danish Society during the Golden Age," in Kasper Monrad et al. *The Golden Age of Danish Painting* (exh. cat.), Los Angeles County Museum and Hudson Hills Press 1993, 20–27.

3 Jespersen, 142.

4 Philip Conisbee, "Eckersberg, An Original in His Time," in *Christopher Wilhelm Eckersberg 1783–1853* (exh. cat.), Washington: National Gallery of Art, 2003, 28. The term "Golden Age" (*guldalderen*) first appeared in Vedel's study of early-nineteenth-century poetry, *Studier over guldalderen i Dansk Digtning*, Copenhagen: P. G. Philipsens Forlag, 1890.

5 Sophus Michaëlis and Alfred Bramsen, *Vilhelm Hammershøi*, Copenhagen, 1918, 46, cited in Poul Vad, *Vilhelm Hammershøi and Danish Art at the Turn of the Century*, (trans. Kenneth Tindall), New Haven and London: Yale University Press, 1992, 149–150.

6 Poul Vad cites the source as "Undated press notice originating from Ida Hammershøi's estate, Private Collection," in Vad, 149. Vad's monograph on Hammershøi is authoritative. Many of the primary sources are derived from scrapbooks meticulously maintained by Hammershøi's family.

7 A series of reforms, forwarded by Johann Friedrich Struensee (1737–1772), royal physician and advisor to the mentally unstable Christian VII, were intended to rein in the Academy's budget, culminating in a new set of regulations issued in June 1771. They also emphasized craftsmanship in all areas of study, raising the level of manual skill and also effectively establishing a new court style. F. Meldahl and P. Johansen, *Det Kongelige Akademi for de Skjønne Kunster 1700–1904*, Copenhagen: H. Hagerups Boghandel, 1904, 79–88, esp. 83–84, and Emma Salling and Claus M. Smidt, "Fundamentet," in *Kunstakademiet 1754–2004*, Volume 1, ed. Anneli Fuchs and Emma Salling, Copenhagen: Det Kongelige Akademi for de Skønne Kunster and Arkitektens Forlag, 2004, 34.

8 Ellen Poulsen, *Jens Juel*, Volume 1: *Katalog/ Catalogue*, Copenhagen: Selskabet til udgivelse af danske mindesmærker; Christian Ejlers' Forlag, 1991, 258.

9 Letter dated September 14, 1772, translated in Ellen Poulsen, Vol. 1, 258.

10 Ellen Poulsen, Vol. 1, 259.

11 Kasper Monrad, et al., 1993, 137.

12 Colin J. Bailey, "Casper David Friedrich: An Introduktion til hans liv og arbejde," in *Caspar David Friedrich og Danmark / Caspar David Friedrich und Dänemark* (ed. Kasper Monrad and Colin J. Bailey), (exh. cat.), Statens Museum for Kunst, 1991, 21ff.

13 See Ellen Poulsen, Vol. 1, 24–25.

14 Monrad, et al. 1993, 137.

15 Vagn Poulsen, 1976, 32.

16 Ellen Poulsen, Vol. 1, 25.

17 Joseph Koerner, *Casper David Friedrich and the Subject of Landscape*, London: Reaktion Books, 1990, 83–84.

18 Ellen Poulsen, Vol. 1, 264.

19 Torben Holck Colding, "Jens Juel," in *Dansk Kunsthistorie: Billedkunst og Skulptur: Akademiet og Guldalderen, 1750–1850*, Copenhagen: Politikens Forlag, 1972, 178.

20 Ellen Poulsen, Vol. 1, 264, and Ellen Poulsen, "Jens Juel: Master Portrait Painter," *Connoisseur*, Vol. 149, No. 600, 1962, 71–75.

21 Monrad, et al. 1993, 142.

22 *Danish Painting of the Nineteenth Century from the Collection of Ambassador John L. Loeb Jr.* (exh. cat.), Greenwich, CT: Bruce Museum of Arts and Sciences, 2005, 32.

23 Vagn Poulsen calls this portrait "the starting point of modern art in Denmark," and Denmark's "first meeting with the great tradition in European painting." Vagn Poulsen, 10.

24 This observation was made By Elisabeth Fabritius in Suzanne Ludvigsen, et al. 2005, 111.

25 Ellen Poulsen, Vol. 1, 262.

26 Ellen Poulsen, Vol. 1, 253.

27 Art-historical sources for, and biographical meanings invested in, Fuseli's *Nightmare* are discussed in Jørgen Andersen, *De år i Rom*, Copenhagen: Christian Ejlers' Forlag, 1989, 200–207. First exhibited at the Royal Academy in London in 1782, *The Nightmare* was recreated by Fuseli in several variations, including one that appeared as an engraving in Erasmus Darwin, *Botanic Garden*, 1794, which Abildgaard owned. Andersen speculates that Abildgaard engaged this image following a visit by Sergel to Copenhagen in the 1790s. He also interprets the setting to be a throwback to a Rococo boudoir, precisely the kind of references that Sergel rejected. (Andersen, 205–206).

28 Charlotte Christensen, *Maleren Nicolai Abildgaard*, Copenhagen: Gyldendal, 1999, 173.

29 Abildgaard's library is analyzed in Patrick Kragelund, *Abildgaard: Kunstneren mellem oprørerne*, 2 Volumes, Copenhagen: Museum Tusculanums Forlag, København Universitet, 1999, vol. 1, chapter 5, and volume 2, 585ff.

30 Kragelund, Vol. 1, 214.

31 Else Kai Sass, *Lykkens Tempel: Et maleri af Nicolai Abildgaard*, Copenhagen: Christian Ejlers' Forlag, 1986, 9–14.

32 Kragelund, Vol. 1, 215.

33 His *Geschichte der Kunst des Altertums* (1764; *History of the Art of Antiquity*) offered a model of classicism as an organic development of growth, maturity, and decline and asserted a version of it as the definition of ideal beauty.

34 Lessing, *Laokoon: oder über die Grenzen der Malerei und Poesie* (1766; *Laocoon; or, On the Limits of Painting and Poetry*). See Alex Potts, *Flesh and the Ideal: Winckelmann and the Origins of Art History*, New Haven and London: Yale University Press, 1994, especially chapter IV, "The Sublime Fetish."

35 On the debates surrounding readings of the sculptural group Laocoon, and their implications for Abildgaard's work, see Kragelund, Volume 1, 209–224.

36 See Torben Holck Colding, "Nicolai Abildgaard, 1743–1809," in *Dansk Guldalderkunst. Maleri og skulptur, 1750–1850*, Copenhagen: Politikens Forlag, 1979, 143–157.

37 Kragelund, Vol. 1, 228–238.

38 Kragelund, 228 (English summary Volume 2, 695–696).

39 Kragelund, Vol. 1, 270ff. and English summary, Volume 2, 695–696.

40 Kragelund, Vol. 1, 243.

41 Both Kragelund and Monrad discuss the implications of Abildgaard's use of Baroque compositional formulae and iconography as a kind of intentional "throw-back" in support of this commission. See Kragelund, Vol. 1, chapter 7, and Monrad, *Hverdagsbilleder: Dansk Guldalder—Kunstnerne og deres vilkår*, Copenhagen: Christian Ejlers' Forlag, 1989, 17. A detailed analysis of this project, and of the architecture, is found in Christensen, 1999.

42 See Marina Belozerskaya, *Luxury Arts of the Renaissance*, London and New York: Thames & Hudson, 2005, on the propagandistic dimensions and strategic deployment of the sumptuous arts in Renaissance, and post-Renaissance, court life.

43 Kragelund, Vol. 1, 259ff.

44 Robert Rosenblum, "Danish Golden Age Painting: An International Perspective," *Thorvaldsen Museum Bulletin*, 1997, 47.

45 The phrase was written by the 14-year-old Adam Oehlenschläger, later one of the most influential poets in nineteenth-century Denmark, quoted in Thomas Kappel, "Christiansborg Palace Burned in 1794 and a Large Part of the City in 1795," in *Copenhagen as it was in 1796*, eds. Margrethe Floryan, et al. Thorvaldsens Museum, 1996, 13.

46 Rasmus Nyerup, *Kjøbenhavns Beskrivelse*, Copenhagen, 1800, 191–192, quoted in Thomas Kappel, "The King Moves to Amalienborg," in Margrethe Floryan, et al., 1996, 39.

47 Kragelund, Vol. 2, 422.

48 See Kragelund, Vol. 2, chapter 8, esp. 404–417.

49 The peasant freedom monument, which was erected in large measure through the efforts of Abildgaard, celebrated the abolition of adscription in 1788. See Kragelund, Volume 2, 377ff. The history and iconography of the *Freedom Monument* is traced in Karin Kryger, *Frihedsstøtten*, Odense: Landbohistorisk Selskab, 1986.

CHAPTER 2

1 Kasper Monrad, et al. 1993, 58.

2 This painting was exhibited at the Charlottenborg in the same year, 1826, and was purchased for the Royal Picture Gallery. Art historian Niels Laurits Høyen noted at the time that the painting was a source of gossip because every figure in it was identifiable. Monrad, 1993, 58.

3 Eckersberg, translated in Erik Fischer, et al. *Tegninger af C. W. Eckersberg* (exh. cat.), Statens Museum for Kunst, Copenhagen, 1983 (trans. Jan Smith), 16, and quoted in Conisbee, in Monrad, et al. 2003, 51.

4 Monrad, 1993, 54.

5 See Salling and Smidt, 23–30. The earliest attempt to establish an academy was in 1701, when Thomas Quellinus and a group of artists petitioned Frederik IV to establish a "Society for the Promotion of the Fine Arts." A more concerted effort was exerted under the reign of Christian VI, when a group of artists formed the Painting and Sculpture Academy in 1738. Since 1751 Niels Eigtved had been director of the "Old Academy," which was first organized in a private house.

6 These are listed in Nikolaus Pevsner, *Academies of Art Past and Present*, New York: Da Capo Press, 1973, 141–143.

7 This notion was supported by Johann Joachim Winckelmann's ideal that art reflected, and in turn shaped, an ideal society: "In order that the arts may flourish in a nation, it is necessary that the artists should be honored." Translated in Pevsner, 149.

8 Quoted from the original charter, *Fundation for Det Kongelig Danske Skildre—Bildhugger—og Bygnings—Academie i Kiøbenhavn*, 1854, in Fuchs and Salling, 30.

9 Thomas Le Brie Sloan, "Neoclassical and Romantic Painting in Denmark, 1754–1848," unpublished Ph.D. dissertation, Northwestern University, Evanston, Illinois, 1972, 13.

10 Sloan, 30.

11 *Tanker om Smagen udi Konsterne i Almindelighed* (1762, *Thoughts on Taste in the Arts in General*).

12 Pevsner, 179.

13 Leo Swane, "Abildgaard og Christian VIII's Palæ," *Kunstmuseets Aarsskrift*, III (1917), 94, quoted in Sloan, 62.

14 Originally built in the late 1670s, the Charlottenborg became a Royal residence under Charlotte Amalie, widow of Christian V. Part of the building was given over to the older academy in 1753, and after the fire of 1795, other institutions moved in to share the large Dutch Baroque-style building.

15 F. Meldahl, *Kunst Udstillingerne ved det Kongelige Akademie for de Skjønne Kunster*, Copenhagen: H. Hagerups Boghandel, 1906, 8.

16 Aug. Hennings, "Essai historique sur les arts et sur leur progrès en Dannemarc. Publié à l'occasion du Salon de l'Académie Royale de Charlottenbourg," Copenhagen, 1778, cited in Meldahl, 20.

17 Meldahl, 27–28.

18 N. L. Høyen, quoted in Meldahl, 29.

19 F. Meldahl and P. Johansen, *Det Kongelige Akademi for de Skjønne Kunstner 1700–1904*, Copenhagen: H. Hagerups Boghandel, 1904, 135.

20 Meldahl and Johansen, 147, Salling and Smidt, Vol. 1, 36–37.

21 Quoted in Salling and Smidt, Vol. 1, 37.

22 Emma Salling, *Kunstakademiets Guldmedalje Konkurrencer, 1755–1857*, Copenhagen: Kunstakademiets Bibliotek, 1975, 7. The revival of the regulations in 1814 provided for practical skill development as well, including color blending and brush techniques for painters, carving techniques for sculptors, and material analysis for architects. Salling, 8–9.

23 Francis Haskell and Nicholas Penny, *Taste and the Antique: The Lure of Classical Sculpture*, 1500–1900, New Haven and London: Yale University Press, 1981, 16. The establishment of plaster cast collections, and the academic use of plaster casts, is traced in 16ff. See also Carsten Thau, "The Right Cast: plaster as art, copy and doctrine," in *Afstøbningssamlingen—Død eller levende? / The Cast Collection—dead or alive?*, Ernst Jonas Bencard, Marie-Louise Berner, Rune Frederiksen, Anne Haslund Hansen, and Jan Zahle, eds. Copenhagen: Friends of the Copenhagen Cast Collection, 2005. The latter publication was issued when public access to the old cast collection (now in a separate museum) was under dispute.

24 Mogens Nykjær, *Kundskabens Billeder: Motiver i dansk kunst fra Eckersberg til Hammershøi*, Aarhus Universitetsforlag, 1991, 94–96. Hans Edvard Nørregård-Nielsen calls the gesture "almost worshipful" in *Christen Købke*, Vol. 1, *Omkring Kastellet*, Copenhagen: Gyldendal, 1996, 298.

25 Salling, 1975, 5.

26 Meldahl and Johansen, 1904, 150.

27 Koerner, 80.

28 Karl Privat, *Philipp Otto Runge: Sein Leben in Selbstzeugnissen Briefen und Berichten*, Berlin, 1942, 57, quoted in Sloan, 127.

29 Koerner, 82. Runge's published correspondence is a valuable source of information about the Academy at the turn of the eighteenth century. See Meldahl and Johansen, 138–142, Rudolf M. Bisanz, *German Romanticism and Philipp Otto Runge: A Study in Nineteenth-Century Art Theory and Iconography*, DeKalb, 1970, and Sloan, 127.

30 Sloan, 163: Eckersberg, in a letter to Prince Christian, 17 November 1811, in Henrik Bramsen, ed. *C. W. Eckersberg, Dagbog og Breve, Paris 1810–13*, Copenhagen, 1947, 70.

31 Bramsen, translated in Sloan, 164.

32 Kasper Monrad, "Fra Odysseus' borg til Langebro i København: Fire nyerhvervede malerier af C. W. Eckersberg," in *Kunstmuseets Årsskrift 1990*, Copenhagen: Statens Museum for Kunst, 1990, 84.

33 See Kasper Monrad, *Dansk Guldalder: Hovedværker på Statens Museum for Kunst*, Copenhagen, 1994, 46. A study of Homeric themes at the École des Beaux-Arts is provided in Emmanuel Schwartz, et al. *The Legacy of Homer: Four Centuries of Art from the École Nationale Supérieure des Beaux-Arts, Paris*, New Haven and London: Yale University Press, 2005.

34 The role that David's painting played in contemporary French revolutionary politics is found in Robert Herbert, *David, Brutus, and the French Revolution: An Essay in Art and Politics*, London: Allen Lane and The Penguin Press, 1972.

35 Eckersberg, in a letter to J. H. Clemens dated June 22, 1812, quoted in Bramsen, 90–93, and translated in Sloan, 165.

36 Torsten Gunnarsson, *Friluftsmåleri före friluftsmåleriet*, Uppsala: Acta Universitatis Upsaliensis. Ars Suetica 12, 1989, 62–63.

37 Valenciennes began to teach perspective at the École des Beaux-Arts in 1812. His influential book *Éléments de perspective pratique* (1799–1800), issued in a German edition of 1803, was owned by both Abildgaard and Thorvaldsen. The importance of this work is cited and discussed in Bente Skovgaard, "C. W. Eckersberg og hans billeder," in *C. W. Eckersberg og hans elever* (exh. cat.), Hanne Jönsson, ed. Copenhagen: Statens Museum for Kunst, 1983, 19. The significance of Valenciennes for open-air painting throughout Europe, and particularly for artists in Rome, is discussed in Conisbee, et al. 1996.

38 This observation is made in Monrad, 1993, 91.

39 Eckersberg's portrait of Thorvaldsen was one of the most copied in Denmark, both by his students and followers, but also by his own hand: he received commissions to copy the portrait in 1832 (Stockholm Nationalmuseum) and 1838 (Ny Carlsberg Gylptotek, Copenhagen).

40 Skovgaard, 22. English translation of the catalogue essays: *C. W. Eckersberg and His Pupils*, Statens Museum for Kunst, Copenhagen, 1984, 12.

41 A version of the complete painting, and technical studies of both the full composition and the fragment, may be found in Lone Bøgh, "Eksempler på udertegninger hos C. W. Eckersberg," in *De lyse Sale: Festskrift til Bente Skovgaard 30. Oktober 1990*, Hanne Jönsson, Kirsten Strømstad, and Hanne Westergaard, eds. Copenhagen: Christian Ejlers' Forlag, 1990.

42 Salling and Smidt, 45–48; Emma Salling, "Akademiet i København mellem det hjemlige og det internationale," in *Natur och nationalitet. Nordisk bildkonst 1800–1850 og deres europeiske bakgrund*, ed. Jörgen Weibull and Per Jonas Nordhagen, Höganäs: Wiken, 1992, 78–80. One of the most popular literary sources was James MacPherson's "discovery" of the Gaelic tales of Ossian, which he claimed to have translated. He first published *Fingal* in 1762, and the complete cycle, *The Works of Ossian*, in 1765. This was translated into Danish in 1790. An increasing interest in northern European histories, in part inspired by MacPherson's publications, had by the 1780s spurred a European-wide interest in Nordic themes. These were realized in a series of works on the theme of Ossian and Fingal by Nicolai Abildgaard in the 1780s (engraved by J. F. Clemens), and perhaps best known, by Jean-Auguste-Dominique Ingres' *Dream of Ossian* (1815, Musée Ingres, Montauban). On this, see Henry Okun, "Ossian in Painting," *Journal of the Warburg and Courtauld Institutes*, Vol. XXX, (1967), 327–356.

43 Julie Eckersberg, *Optegnelser om C. W. Eckersberg* (introduction by Emil Hannover), Copenhagen: Forening for Boghaandværk, 1917. Julie Eckersberg was the daughter of Eckersberg and his third wife, Susanne Juel, daughter of Jens Juel. Eckersberg's second wife, who died in 1827, was Susanne's sister Julie Juel (see chapter 4).

44 Salling, 1975, 8.

45 Meldahl and Johansen, 196.

46 Hanne Jönsson, "C. W. Eckersberg og hans elever," in Hanne Jönsson, 1983, 50–54.

47 *Forsög til en Veiledning i Anvendelse af Perspectivlæren for unge Malere*, Copenhagen: Thieles Bogtrykkeri 1833, and *Linearperspektiven, anvendt paa Malerkunsten en Række af perspektiviske Studier*. Copenhagen: Universitets-Boghandler C. A. Reitzel, 1841.

48 Marianne Saabye, "Mellem ideal og virkelighed," in *Den nøgne guldalder. Modelbilleder* (exh. cat.), Hirschsprung Collection, Copenhagen, 1994, 20. Emma Salling suggests that Frørup was likely related to Frederik Abraham

Frørup, the Academy's porter between the years 1835–1848. Salling, "Modelstudiet i Eckersbergs professortid," in Johansen, et al. 39.

49 The five life-size or over-life size nudes, donated after Eckersberg's death to the Royal Academy, are reproduced in Annette Johansen, et al. 100–107. They include two adult males, two adult females, and an 11-year-old girl, and they are all characterized by the specificity of their facial as well as bodily portrayals. They form a highly eroticized group: *Seated Male Model. Peter Kristrup* represents a man seated on a fur, regarding his bleeding hand. *Standing Female Model Against a Green Background* represents a woman who has a cloth wrapped just below her breasts, her brow compressed in elusive consternation or contemplation. In *Standing Model Against a Red Background*, the model touches her cheek in a gesture of apparent self-consciousness, and in *Model Study of an 11-year-old girl*, the naked pre-pubescent body contrasts with a carefully rendered adult coiffure.

50 On this theme, see Robert Rosenblum, "The Origin of Painting: A Problem in the Iconography of Romantic Classicism," *Art Bulletin*, XXXIX, December 1957, 279–290.

51 Saabye, in Johansen, et al. 22.

52 Johansen, et al. 112ff.

53 Ibid. 114.

54 Eckersberg's private students and those who attended the Academy of Art's plaster classes and model school between 1818 and 1853 are chronicled in Hanne Jönsson, "C. W. Eckersberg og hans elever," and in her summary lists, both in 1983, 48–70.

55 Eckersberg's diary entries that recall the modeling sessions are excerpted in Annette Johansen, et al. 1994, 134.

56 Suzanne Ludvigsen, "Joel John Ballin," in Ludvigsen et al. 2005, 45–49.

57 P. Johansen, *Den Danske Malerkunsts Fader: Christopher Wilhelm Eckersberg*, Copenhagen, 1925, 29, quoted in Sloan, 170.

58 See Monrad, 1989, 69.

59 Monrad, 1989, 91–92.

60 Monrad, 1989, 90–91.

61 Monrad, 1989, offers a close analysis of arts patronage and the class identity of the Golden Age painters' patrons, as a way of tracing the predominance of genre, landscape, and portrait painting in mid-nineteenth-century Denmark. See especially "København som kunstcentrum," 59–110 (summarized in English on pages 294–297). He provides a breakdown of Eckersberg's portrait patrons by class and occupation on page 62.

62 Hjorth's target was the first to carry an artist's signature. Jens Juel, Constantin Hansen, and Anton Melbye, among others, created such targets. The society owns approximately 2000 targets, dating

back to 1752. See Thorkild Kjærgaard, *Fremskridtets Mænd* (exh. cat.), National History Museum at Frederiksborg, 1997, 11. Niels Jul Nielsen offers the targets as subjects of social history in *København på kornet: Skydeskiver og fotografier fra 1890erne*, Bymuseum, Copenhagen, 2004.

63 Emil Hannover, *Maleren C. W. Eckersberg: En Studie i Dansk Kunsthistorie*, Copenhagen: Kunstforeningen i København, 1898, 64.

64 Hannover, 192. The idea was to commission Christian August Lorentzen to paint one scene from each of Holberg's plays as models for engravings by J. F. Clemens.

65 Nykjær, 2–23. See also Jørgen Bonde Jensen, "Guldalder: To familiebilleder af Eckersberg og Marstrand from 1818 og 1836," *Hug*, Vol. 1, No. 7, 1975, 18–28. Jensen calls attention to the ambiguities in the painting, such as the circumstances of the representation, the oddly directed gazes of the children away from their parents, and Mrs. Nathanson's fixity within the dynamism of the rest of the composition.

66 Harald Jørgensen, "M. L. Nathanson," *Dansk Biografisk Leksikon*, Volume 12, Povl Engelstoft, ed. Copenhagen: J. H. Schultz Forlag, 1939, 525–527.

67 Monrad, 1989, 116.

68 Conisbee, et al. 2003, 110.

69 Mogens Nykjær interprets the caged bird as an allegory of bourgeois containment, that the two girls of marriageable age are entrapped by the security of their parents' home and aspirations. See Nykjær, 27–28. Lene Rønberg in Monrad, Kasper et al. 2001, 126–136, interprets the parrot within the iconographic tradition of virtue, a view also asserted in Conisbee, et al. 2005, 110. In addition, she locates the image of a girl teaching a parrot to speak within the Dutch seventeenth-century iconography of industriousness.

70 Monrad suggests that the ivy that appears in the painting secures this meaning in 1993, 151. See also Munk, 1985

71 Monrad, et al. 1993, 151.

72 The conventional arrangement of colors on a palette was a disciplined practice within the French academy and its allied institutions throughout Europe. See Albert Boime, *The Academy and French Painting in the Nineteenth Century*, London: Phaidon, 1971, 37.

73 Monrad, 1989, 145ff.

74 Monrad, 1993, 68.

75 Kasper Monrad states that Blunck's painting of Sonne, which is in the collection of the Statens Museum for Kunst, gave Bendz the idea of representing Blunck in this manner. Monrad, 1989, 143.

76 Monrad, 1993, 143. Søren Kjørup interprets the double registered space and motifs in this painting in the light of Michael Fried's

notion of absorption in "Gulalderforskningens paradigmer—eksemplificeret på et maleri af Wilhelm Bendz," *Meddelelser fra Thorvaldsens Museum*, 1994, 122. Nykjær, 75ff. interprets this painting to be a demonstration piece of Bendz's interest in Platonic philosophy: the mirror reveals the canvas that is being worked on to the audience as a reflection—an idealized, flattened version—rather than the thing in itself. Blunck (1799–1845), born in Denmark's German duchy of Holstein, had first enrolled at the Royal Academy in 1814 and then traveled to Munich to study at the art academy in 1818. Returning in 1820, he became closely affiliated with Eckersberg's circle at the Academy. In the year after Bendz painted his portrait, Blunck won the great Gold Medal and was rewarded with the travel stipend from the Academy. He first visited J. C. Dahl and Caspar David Friedrich in Dresden, and in Munich the Nazarene painters Peter von Cornelius and Julius Schnorr von Carolsfeld. He then traveled to Rome where he became part of Bertel Thorvaldsen's circle, as we shall see in the next chapter, and became strongly influenced by the art of Friedrich Overbeck and the Nazarenes. Blunck returned to Copenhagen in 1838, but then left permanently in 1844, settling in Vienna and then Hamburg. During the Dano-Prussian War of 1848–50, he joined the Schleswig-Holsteiners and in this way seems to have severed his relations with his Danish artist colleagues.

77 Jens Peter Munk, "Kunstnerportræt— selvportræt. Om guldalderkunstnernes sociale og kulturelle selvforståelse, når de portrætterer sig selv og hinanden," *Meddelelser fra Thorvaldsens Museum*, 1994, 103–113.

78 Monrad 1989, 105.

79 The identities of the ten figures were noted in a protocol of the Fine Art Society from March 1833, when the painting was exhibited. They are listed in *Wilhelm Bendz 1804–1832. En ungt Kunstnerliv*, Hirschsprung Collection, Copenhagen, 1996, 100.

80 A. Røder, *Maleren W. Bendz*, Copenhagen: Karl Kløster, 1905, 26.

CHAPTER 3

1 Hans Christian Andersen, *The True Story of My Life*, (trans. Mary Howitt), New York: The American-Scandinavian Foundation, 1926, 285–287.

2 *H. C. Andersens Rom: Dagbogsnotater og tegninger*, Helge Topsøe-Jensen, ed. Copenhagen: Gyldendal, 1980.

3 Chloe Chard, "Crossing Boundaries and Exceeding Limits: Destabilization, Tourism, and the Sublime," in *Transports: Travel, Pleasure, and Imaginative Geography, 1600–1830* (ed. Chloe Chard and Helen Langdon), New Haven and London: Yale University Press, Studies in British Art 3, 1996, 117ff.

4 The first recorded Danish artist in Rome was Melchior Lorck (1526/7–1588), who was sent there by Christian III in the mid-sixteenth century. From the establishment of the academy in the mid-eighteenth century, an increasing number of Danes could be counted within the expatriate community in Rome. See Jørn Rubow, "Danske malere i Rom," in *Danske malere i Rom i det 19. århundrede*, Statens Museum for Kunst, Copenhagen, 1977, 19.

5 On the rhetoric of influence and its specific social and medical meanings in Rome of the early nineteenth century, see Richard Wrigley, "Infectious Enthusiasms: Influence, Contagion, and the Experience of Rome," in Chard and Langdon, 75–116.

6 On theories of social and artistic revelation as an aspect of tourism, see Ilaria Bignamini, "The Grand Tour: Open Issues," in *Grand Tour: The Lure of Italy in the Eighteenth Century*, ed. Andrew Wilton and Ilaria Bignamini, (exh. cat.), Tate Gallery, London, 1996, 31–36.

7 Monrad notes that elements of the first version of the motif, which belongs to the Thorvaldsen Museum, were not warmly received by Copenhagen critics, and in the second variation changes were made to accommodate those points of contention. Monrad, 1989, 198.

8 *Danske malere i Rom i det 19. århundrede*, Statens Museum for Kunst, Copenhagen, 1978, 24. Monrad noted the similarities in composition in 1989, 198–9.

9 There Thorvaldsen received his early encouragement from the Danish scholar Georg Zoëga (1755–1809) who had gone to Rome in 1775. He had catalogued the coin collection of Cardinal Stefano Borgia, and was patronized by, among others, Pope Pius VI.

10 See Fred Licht, "Canova und Thorvaldsen," in *Künstlerleben in Rom. Bertel Thorvaldsen: Der dänische Bildhauer und seine deutschen Freunde* (exh. cat.), ed. Gerhard Bott and Heinz Spielman, Germanisches Nationalmuseum, Nürnburg, 1991, 45ff.

11 The fragmentary works, discovered in 1810, had been acquired in 1813 by Crown Prince Ludwig of Bavaria (later King Ludwig I), an admirer of Thorvaldsen, and the commission was secured in part through the efforts of the noted archeologist Peter Oluf Brøndstad (1780–1842). See Lars Olof Larsson, "Thorvaldsens Restaurierung der Aegina-Skulpturen in Lichte zeitgenössischer Kunstkritik und Antikenauffassung," *Konsthistorisk tidskrift* 38 (1969), 23–46. One century later, Thorvaldsen's amendments would come under attack for their inaccuracies, and in the latter half of the twentieth century, they were removed. On the restoration and the politics of its reversal, see William J. Diebold, "The politics of derestoration: the Aegina pediments and the German confrontation with the past," *Art Journal*, Summer 1995, 60–66.

12 For a critical assessment of Thorvaldsen's studio practice, see Harald Tesan, *Thorvaldsen und seine Bildhauerschule in Rom*, Köln, Weimar, Wein, Böhlan Verlag, 1998.

13 Cited in Monrad, et al. 1993, cat. 44, 121. The other magnet for Scandinavian artists studying in Rome was Swedish sculptor Johan Niklas Byström (1783–1848), whose home near the Piazza di Spagna was a meeting place for Scandinavian expatriates. Torsten Gunnarsson, 1998, 57–59.

14 Henny Glarbo, "Martens og Thorvaldsen," *Meddelelser fra Thorvaldsens Museum*, 1944, 53ff. In a letter to Royal Academy in 1828, Martens stated his plan to emphasize the assembly of Thorvaldsen's works. A detailed description of the painting is included in Bott and Spielman, 529–532.

15 *H. C. Andersens Rom: Dagbogsnotater og tegninger*, (ed. Helge Topsøe-Jensen), Copenhagen: Gyldendal, 1980, 51–52.

16 Andersen, 174–175, 177.

17 The history of the gift and the fundraising is traced in Henrik Bramsen, *Gottlieb Bindesbøll. Liv og arbejder*, Copenhagen: Selskabet til udgivelse af skrifter om danske mindesmærker, 1959, 49ff., esp. 60ff.

18 Thorvaldsen collected work by the German and Austrian members of his circle in Rome, including Joseph Anton Koch, Franz Riepenhausen, Peter Cornelius, Wilhelm Schadow, and Friedrich Overbeck. He also owned works by Danish artists Constantin Hansen, Wilhelm Marstrand, Johan Thomas Lundbye, and the Norwegian J. C. Dahl. Thorvaldsen was, in fact, one of the major patrons of Danish art in the early and mid-nineteenth century. See Monrad, 1989, 94–96. Thorvaldsen was also an avid collector of antiquities, including Roman sculpture, Greek and Etruscan vases, and Etruscan bronzes, glass, gems and terracottas (Thorvaldsens Museum).

19 Rosenblum, 1997, 51.

20 Lisbet Balslev Jørgensen, "Arkitekturens frihed," in *På klassisk grund*, The Thorvaldsen Museum Bulletin, 1989, 178–184; see also Bramsen, 1959, 157.

21 Thorvaldsen's spectacular return to Copenhagen was also depicted in a painting by Eckersberg, *Thorvaldsens ankomst og modtagelse 17 September 1838* (1838, Thorvaldsens Museum B217).

22 *Constantin Hansen, 1804–1880*, (ed. Bjarne Jørnæs and Stig Miss), Thorvaldsens Museum, Copenhagen, 1991, 243.

23 Kasper Monrad, *Dansk Guldalder. Hovedværker på Statens Museum for Kunst*, Copenhagen: Statens Museum for Kunst, 1994, 114–115.

24 Søren Kaspersen, "Et Selskab af Danske Kunstnere i Rom," in Jørnæs and Miss, 54. Hansen seems to have used Bindesbøll's studio as his own for a period of time, rendering individual sketches of each of the artists as well as an oil sketch of the room, and then creating a united composition from the separate studies. The studies are reproduced on pp. 174–182 of the same publication.

25 Gunnarsson, 1998, 56.

26 Tone Brekke, "A Cosmopolitan Salon-Hostess: Friederike Brun's Revision of Schiller in *Idas ästhetische Entwickelung* (1824)," *Literature Compass* 1 (1), 2004.

27 Sloan, 129.

28 The paintings were removed to the National Gallery, Berlin. See Keith Andrews, *The Nazarenes: A Brotherhood of German Artists in Rome*, New York: Hacker Art Books, 1988, 33–37.

29 Joseph Anton Koch, *Moderne Kunstchronik*, and *Gedanken über ältere und neuere Malerei*, 1834 and 1862 respectively, excerpted and translated in Lorenz Eitner, ed. *Neoclassicism and Romanticism 1750–1850, An Anthology of Sources and Documents*, New York: Harper & Row, 1989, 119.

30 See Mitchell Benjamin Frank, *German Romantic Painting Redefined: Nazarene Tradition and the Narratives of Romanticism*, Burlington, Vt.: Ashgate Press, 2001, "Brotherhood," 11–35.

31 Hermann Mildenberger, "Wilhelm von Schadow," in *Künstlerleben in Rome. Bertel Thorvaldsen (1770–1844): Der dänische Bildhauer und seine deutschen Freunde*, ed. Gerhard Bott and Heiny Spielmann, Nürnberg, Germanisches Nationalmuseum, 1992, 521.

32 On the relationship between tourism and the representation of Rome in prints, see *Exploring Rome: Piranesi and His Contemporaries* (exh. cat.) ed. Cara D. Denison, Myra Nan Rosenfeld, and Stephanie Wiles, The Pierpont Morgan Library, New York, 1993. On the production of art, and of eighteenth-century tourist rhetoric that shaped northern Europeans' expectations of Rome, see Jeremy Black, *Italy and the Grand Tour*, New Haven and London: Yale University Press, 2003.

33 Gunnarsson (1989, 76 and 95) reports that the painting, which exists in two versions (the other version is in the C. L. David Collection in Copenhagen), was somewhat conventionalized at the time. An engraved version, rendered by Luigi Rossini, was included in *I monumenti piu interessanti di Roma 1818*, 76, 95.

34 Ludvigsen, et al. 2005, 271–2.

35 Karl Madsen, *Wilhelm Marstrand, 1810–1873*, Copenhagen: Kunstforeningen, 1905, 125.

36 See Chloe Chard, *Pleasure and Guilt on the Grand Tour: Travel Writing and Imaginative Geography 1600–1830*, Manchester: Manchester University Press, 1999.

37 Gunnarsson, 1998, 56.

38 Eckersberg, quoted in Monrad, et al. 1993, 88.

39 The category was most prominently articulated by William Gilpin's *Three Essays: On Picturesque Beauty; On Picturesque Travel; and on Sketching*

Landscape: to which is Added a Poem, On Landscape Painting, London, 1792.

40 Monrad, et al. 1993, 88.

41 Kasper Monrad, *Danish Painting: The Golden Age* (exh. cat.), National Gallery, London, 1984, 96.

42 Quoted in Monrad, et al. 1993, 95.

43 Robert Rosenblum, 1967, 114.

44 Kasper Monrad, "A View through Three Arches: Danish and German Artists in Denmark, Germany, and Italy," in Catherine Johnson, et al., 1999, 2.

45 Gunnarsson, 1989, 13.

46 See *Paysages d'Italie. Les Peintres du Plein Air, 1780–1830*. Galeries nationales du Grand Palais, 2001.

47 Eckersberg to J. F. Clemens, dated July 23, 1814, quoted in Gunnarsson, 1989, 72.

48 Gunnarsson, 1989, 70–71.

49 Eckersberg, in Bramsen, 1974, 78, quoted in Philip Conisbee, Sarah Faunce, and Jeremy Strick, "Introduction," *In the Light of Italy: Corot and Open-Air Painting*, (Peter Galassi, Guest Curator), National Gallery of Art, Washington and Yale University Press, New Haven, 1996, 20.

50 Gunnarsson, 1989, 29ff .

51 Monrad, 1993, 66, quoted in Conisbee, et al. 1996, 170.

52 S. Lang, "The Early Publications of the Temples at Paestum," *Journal of the Warburg and Courtauld Institutes* XIII, Jan-June, 1950, 48–64.

53 Monrad, 1993, 124.

54 See Richard Hamblyn, "Private Cabinets and Popular Geology: The British Audiences for Volcanoes in the Eighteenth Century," in Chard and Langdon, 1995, especially 190–200.

55 Koerner, 84.

CHAPTER 4

1 Købke's first view of Frederiksborg appeared in a portrait of C. W. Eckersberg's five-year-old son Julius (1831, Statens Museum for Kunst), rendered as a small black and white view held by the child. See Hans Tybjerg, *Omkring Købkes Frederiksborg Slot ved aftenbelysning*, Copenhagen: C. A. Reitzels Forlag, 1996, 8.

2 The other paintings included a second view from the roof of Frederiksborg Palace (Kunstindustrimuseum) and painted copies after Thorvaldsen's panels *Day* and *Night* (The David Collection, Copenhagen). See Monrad, 1993, 156.

3 *Niels Laurits Høyens Skrifter*, (ed. J. L. Ussing), Volume 1, Copenhagen: Den Gyldendalske Boghandel, 1871, 225–226.

4 Red brick architecture itself was in the process of being identified as a native phenomenon, promoted by N. L. Høyen and German architect Gustav Friedrich Hetsch (1788–1864). See

Barbara Miller Lane, *National Romanticism and Modern Architecture in Germany and the Scandinavian Countries*, New York and Cambridge: Cambridge University Press, 2000, 44–45.

5 Christian I. Molbech, *Ungdomsvandringer i mit Fødeland* (Youthful Travels in the Land of My Birth), 1811, 156, quoted in Gelius and Miss, 46.

6 Molbech, 171, quoted in Tybjerg, 73–7. Frederiksborg had been not only the focus of Høyen's adulation, but the subject of a full-scale book by author Johan Peter Rasbech and of a number of popular articles and poems. Tybjerg, 34, and footnote 50, which chronicles these publications.

7 Tybjerg, 12–14. Købke's friend Jørgen Roed won the competition with a painting of Frederiksborg. Tybjerg's monograph (op. cit.) is the most comprehensive study of this painting. Tybjerg also details and reproduces many sketches for the composition rendered on site. See also Monrad, et al. 1993, 158.

8 Kirsten Agerbæk, *Høyen mellem klassicisme og romantik*, Esbjerg: Sydjysk Universitetsforlag, 1984, 115.

9 Johann Gottlieb Fichte, "Thirteenth Address: Lectures to the German Nation," ed. George A. Kelly, *To the German People*, New York: Harper Torch Books, 1968, 197–198.

10 Agerbæk, 1984, 243ff.

11 See Høyen's essay "Aarhus Domkirke," in *Skrifter*, vol. 2, 181ff.

12 The first open-air museum in Denmark, the Frilandsmuseet, was established in 1897. On the phenomenon of open-air folk museums in the Nordic countries, and the politics of nation building through such popular spectacles, see Mark Sandberg, *Living Pictures/ Missing Persons: Mannequins, Museums, and Modernity*, Princeton and Oxford: Princeton University Press, 2003, chapters 6–9.

13 N. L. Høyen, *Konsten i Danmark til dette Aarhundredes Begyndelse. Konsten i Danmark i dette Aarhundrede*, Copenhagen 1876. Within a few years, Philip Weilbach first published his dictionary of Danish artistic biography in which Høyen had a hand, Dansk Konstnerleksikon (1877–8). In its revised editions, it has remained the authoritative dictionary of Danish art and artists.

14 Høyen, 351 and 361.

15 On Ørsted's role as a scientist and cultural figure, see Mogens Bencard, ed. *Intersections: Art and Science in the Golden Age*, Copenhagen: Gyldendal, 2000.

16 Facos, 4.

17 Meldahl and Johansen, 1904, 279–80.

18 Høyen, "Om Betingelserne for en skandinavisk Nationalkonsts Udvikling" (1844), in *Niels Laurits Høyens Skrifter*, Volume 1, 360.

19 Danish historical self-consciousness and the advent of "folk" histories of the country are chronicled in a publication celebrating the fiftieth anniversary of the founding of the Danish Historical Society in 1839. See Johannes C. H. R. Steenstrup, *Historieskrivningen i Danmark i det 19de Aarhundrede (1801–1863)*, Copenhagen: Bianco Lunos Kgl. Hof-Bogtrykkeri, 1889.

20 Høyen, "Nogle Bemærkninger over de paa Charlottenborg udstillede Konstsager," in *Skrifter*, Vol. 1, 61.

21 Working through the late summer and autumn of 1835, Købke rendered numerous studies in pencil and in oil, and he noted his dissatisfaction, as well as Høyen's pressureful presence, in letters to Roed. These are excerpted in Tybjerg, 22–27.

22 Monrad and Bailey, 81–82.

23 Høyen, "Konsten i Danmark i dette Aarhundrede," [1851], *Skrifter*, Vol. 3, 135, cited in Gelius and Miss, 48.

24 These works are examined in Marie Lødrup Bang, *J. C. Dahl: Life and Works*, Oslo: Norwegian University Press, 1987, Volume 2, 48 and 63–64, and Volume 3, 57, 103–106.

25 Gunnarsson, 1989, 160ff.

26 On Howard's influence, see Ludvigsen, et al. 2005, 266, and John Thomes, "Constable's Clouds," *Burlington Magazine*, Vol. 121, 1979, 697–704.

27 Gelius, in Gelius and Miss, 35–6.

28 Ludvigsen, et al. 2005, 365.

29 Ludvigsen, et al. 2005, in 366. For a full account, see Jens Peter Munk, *Købke, Sødring og atelieret på Toldbodvejen* (exh. cat.), Hirschsprung Collection, Copenhagen, 1985.

30 Monrad chronicles artistic interest in this motif in 1993, 220, and in 1994, 130. A comprehensive account of the church, its building history, patronage and politics, and a summary of the artists who created images of it, can be found in Claus M. Smidt, *Marmorkirken: Visioner og virkelighed*, Copenhagen: Selskabet for Arkitekturhistorie, 1994. On the views of the Marble Church, see "Et Københavnsk Forum Romanum," 21ff.

31 Monrad, et al. 1993, 145.

32 Eckersberg, *Linearperspectiven, anvendt paa Malerkunsten, en Række af perspectiviske Studier*, Copenhagen: Universitets-Boghandler C. A. Reitzel, 1841, text accompanying Plate 3.

33 Eckersberg, 1841.

34 Marine paintings constituted the largest body of work that Eckersberg produced in his later career. Eckersberg himself reported that his interest in the sea and in ships stemmed from his childhood on the Flensborg Fjord. Hannover, 1898, 211, cited in Monrad, et al. 1993, 122.

35 Ibid.

36 Eckersberg, 1841. The text accompanying Plate X offers this advice to students.

37 Peter Michael Hornung and Kasper Monrad. *C. W. Eckersberg—dansk malerkunsts fader*, Copenhagen: Palle Fogtdal, 2005, 236.

38 Monrad, 1993, 126. It has been noted that Eckersberg's naval and meteorological notations tally with those of the military observations of Three Crown Fort and on the guard ship. Frank Allan Rasmussen, "Virtue and Maternal Love," in Mogens Bencard, ed., 2000, 153.

39 Rasmussen, 160ff.

40 In the later 1830s, Eckersberg reprised the uncanny sense of the nocturnal city in a series of plates that he used to illustrate his 1841 *Linearperspektiven anvendt paa Malerkunsten*, especially plate IV, figures 1 and 2). See Monrad, 1990, 96–97.

41 On October 21, 1836, following one of his foot tours through the city, Eckerberg noted that he wished to paint Long Bridge. He completed it on November 10: "Worked on, and finished, the little painting of a moonlit night, full moon. The motif is Long Bridge with several running figures." Monrad, 1990, 94.

42 Jørgen Bonde Jensen, "Langebro i måneskin. Et billede af C. W. Eckersberg fra 1836" in *Forgyldning forgår: Gulalderlæsninger*, Copenhagen: Babette, 1998, 28.

43 Carl Bernhard, *Samlede Skrifter*. 2. udgave, Vol. II, 1869. According to Jørgen Bonde Jensen, the book was mentioned in *Dansk Literatur Tidende* on January 6, 1836. Bonde Jensen, 1998, 34–5, and summarized in English in Lene Bøgh Rønberg, catalogue entry for *Langebro Bridge in Copenhagen with Running Figures*, in *Christoffer Wilhelm Eckersberg, 1783–1853*, Washington, D.C.: National Gallery of Art, 2003, 146.

44 J. T. Lundbye, diary entry for 24 March 1842 in the Royal Library Copenhagen, published in *A Year in My Life*, Copenhagen, 1967, 47, and translated in *Danish Paintings of the Golden Age* (exh. cat.), catalogue based on research by Suzanne Ludvigsen, Artemis Fine Arts, Inc. New York, 1999, cat. 29.

45 Gunnarsson, 1998, 151–152.

46 See Gunnarsson, 1998, 155ff.

47 Karl Madsen, *Johan Thomas Lundbye, 1818–1848*, Copenhagen: Gyldendal Boghandel, Nordisk Forlag, 1949, 129. Lundbye was a prolific reader and writer, and his diaries from 1842 recount the evolution of this painting, and of the distinct roles and ambitions that studies after nature played in his work, in contrast with his large studio compositions. Gunnarsson, 1998, 157.

48 Lundbye was also an important innovator in the arena of book illustration in the 1840s. Along with his colleagues P. C. Skovgaard and Lorenz Frølich, Lundbye began to publish motifs in the popular, inexpensive collections of writings, folk tales, books of poetry, and didactic manuals that began to appear in that decade. Woodcuts representing rural peoples, accompanied by gothicized typography, were created by Lundbye to inspire a love of old stories and traditions in the contemporary public. H. P. Rohde, *Dansk bogillustration 1800–1890*, Copenhagen: Det Hoffensbergske Etablissement, 1949, 46–48. His National Romantic motifs and naturalizing style helped to replace the Neoclassical imagery that had prevailed previously in Danish publishing. Lundbye's images, accompanying H. C. Andersen's children's stories, among other widely circulated literatures, furnished the imaginations of the generations at mid-century.

49 Suzanne Ludvigsen reports that the site was memorialized in a popular novel of the 1880s entitled *Nytaarstid i Nøddebo Præstegaard* (New Year at Nøddebo Parsonage) by Henrik Scharling (1836–1920). She characterizes it as a humorous portrayal of life in the Danish parsonage, which nonetheless raised some of the social debates then ongoing in Denmark. The book was turned into a comic play that premiered in 1888 and is still performed at Christmas time throughout Denmark. Ludvigsen, et al. 2005, 239.

50 *Nyt Magazin for Kunstnere og Haandværkere* in 31 October and 7 November 1839, cited in Bjørn Ochsner, *Fotografer i og fra Danmark til og med år 1920*, Vol. 1 (parallel texts in Danish, English, German, and French), Copenhagen: Bibliotekscentralens Forlag, 1986, 18.

51 Ochsner, 18.

52 By 1843, a photographer working in Tivoli (Copenhagen's new pleasure garden) charged about 4 rix-dollars, or $48 currently, for a portrait. Ochsner, 19.

53 Marie-Louise Berner, *Bertel Thorvaldsen: A Daguerreotype Portrait from 1840*, Copenhagen: University of Copenhagen and Tusculanum Press, 2005, 6 and 86.

54 Ochsner, 19.

55 Mette Sandbye and Gitte Pedersen, eds. *Dansk fotografihistorie*, Copenhagen: Gyldendal, 2004, 71.

56 *Beretninger fra Dansk Fotografisk Forening*, 1881, nr. 15, quoted in Sandbye and Pedersen, 22–23.

57 A sequence of these views is published in Hans Edvard Nørregård-Nielsen, *Christen Købke: Volume 2, Dosseringen og Frederiksborg*, Copenhagen: Gyldendal, 1996, 178–195.

58 Exhibited in 1838 at the Charlottenborg, the painting was purchased in 1839 for the Royal Picture Gallery (now the Statens Museum for Kunst).

59 The flying of the flag was a symbol of reviving national pride in the early 1830s, but in 1834, the monarchy opposed such popular manifestations of nationalism and the raising of flags by private individuals was banned in 1834. London, 1984, 218.

60 Gunnarsson, 1998, 30.

61 Tybjerg, 42.

62 The fact of her pregnancy is noted by Emil Hannover, 1898, 140. See the description in Monrad, 1993, 97, and *Christoffer Wilhelm Eckersberg, 1783–1853*, ed. Philip Conisbee, Kasper Monrad, and Lene Bøgh Rønberg, Washington, D.C.: National Gallery of Art, 2003, 107.

63 The mother of six children, Julie Juel Eckersberg died in 1827 at the age of thirty-six. Following her death, Eckersberg married her sister, Suzanne, a practice not uncommon at the time, particularly among families whose children were left motherless.

64 Monrad, 1993, 192.

65 Monrad, 1993, 192, and Monrad, 1989, 121–122.

66 Hans Ottomeyer, Klaus Albrect Schröder, and Laurie Winters, *Biedermeier: The Invention of Simplicity* (exh. cat.), Milwaukee Art Museum; Albertina, Vienna; and Deutsches Historisches Museum, Berlin, 2006, 261.

67 Anne-Birgitte Fonsmark, "Udsigter og indsigter. Martinus Rørbye: 'Udsigt fra kunstnerens vindue, ca. 1825'" in *Kunstværkets krav. 27 fortolkninger af danske kunstværker*, ed. E. J. Bencard, A. Kold, and P. S. Meyer, Copenhagen; Palle Fogtdal, 1990, 67–77. An English summary is provided in Monrad, et al. 1993, 202.

68 Ludvigsen, et al. 2005, 52–53.

69 See Monrad, 1989, 61ff.

70 The 1906 self-portrait and a full inventory of this painting, are offered in Ludvigsen, et al. 2005, 89–90.

71 The Royal Anthem, Johannes Ewald's "King Christian Stood by the Lofty Mast," adapted in 1780, remains as well.

CHAPTER 5

1. *Murray's Handbook: A Handbook for Travellers in Denmark, Slesvig, and Holstein*, London: John Murray, 1875, 95.

2 In fact, Krøyer identified this as a painting of an artist's "gilde" or guild, as well as an artist's party. See Elisabeth Fabritius, *P. S. Krøyer's Hip, Hip, Hurra!: Et Kunstnergilde*, Copenhagen: Vandkunsten, 2005, 54. Fabritius also locates this painting within the European tradition of guild, corporation, and friendship paintings. Her book is the definitive synthetic study of this painting.

3 The term is drawn from sociologist Rob Shields's notion of a site that attains cachet and cult status through the repetition of stories and images that simplify and reformulate its meaning. *Places on the Margin: Alternative Geographies of Modernity*, London: Routledge, 1991. This model is used in Nina Lübbren, *Rural Artists' Colonies in Europe, 1870–1910*, New Brunswick: Rutgers University Press, 2001, 114ff.

4 Krøyer's *Hip, Hip, Hurrah!* is one of the most beloved of Denmark's immensely popular

Skagen paintings, and appears on mass-produced commodities, such as tea towels and greeting cards, and it occasioned the feature film about the Skagen artists' community, *Hip, Hip, Hurrah!*, directed by Kjell Grede, produced by Katinka Farago, and released in 1986 by the Norsk Filminstituttt.

5   Hanna Rönnberg, *Konstnärsliv i slutet av 1880-talet/ Konstnärskolonien på Åland*, Önningebymuseet, 1993, 10–11. Translated in Lübbren, 147.

6   Christian Krohg, "Skagen" [1894], in *Kampen for Tilværelsen*, Oslo: Gyldendal Norsk Forlag, 1954, 505–506, translated in Lübbren, 146.

7   H. C. Andersen, *The True Story of My Life*, 89–90. Steen Steensen Blicher had visited Skagen in 1839 and had written two novels about the "simple folk" and ravishing setting that he encountered there: *Vestlig Profil af den Cimbriske Halvøe* and *Trækfuglene* (1838).

8   "Skagen," was first published in *Folkekalender for Danmark*, Volume 9, 1860, 46–58 (issued December 1859), and then published in *Samlede Skrifter af H. C. Andersen*, Volume XXVIII, Copenhagen, 1868. "En historie fra Klitterne" was published in *Nye Eventyr og Historier*, published in December 1859, and then in *Samlede Skrifter af H. C. Andersen*, Volume XXVI, Copenhagen, 1868. "Jylland" was published in *Illustreret Tidende* on 18 March 1860.

9   H. C. Andersen, "Skagen" [1859], in *Skagen og En Historie fra Klitterne* (Afterword by Erik Dal), Copenhagen: P. Haase & Søns Forlag, 1967, 7.

10   Anna Ancher also recounts this incident in her memoirs: Andersen had apparently complained to the pregnant Ane Brøndum, one of the proprietors of the inn, about her cooking, and then stormed out of the hotel. The distraught Ane then went into early labor. Anna Ancher, "Barndoms Minder fra Skagen," [1911], in Ole Wivel, *Anna Ancher 1859–1935*, (parallel texts in English, Danish, and German), Lyngby: Stok-Art, 1994, 72.

11   Knud Voss, *Skagens malerne*, Lyngby: Stok-Art, 1994, 15.

12   Eva Henschen, "Rørbye og Jylland," in Dyveke Helstad, et al. *Martinus Rørbye 1803–1848* (exh. cat.), Thorvaldsens Museum, Copenhagen, 1981, 183–4.

13   Helstad, 204.

14   Karl Madsen identifies the setting as "The Spanish Sea," a sand dune that was hard to navigate, according to Madsen, after an evening of drinking. Helstad, 202.

15   Quoted in Wivel, *Skagen*, 31.

16   Walter Schwartz, *Skagen i Nordisk Kunst: Fra Michael Ancher til Ludvig Karsten*, Copenhagen: Gyldendal Norsk Forlag, 1952, 13.

17   Elisabeth Fabritius, *Michael Anchers Ungdom 1865–1880*, Skagen: Helga Anchers Fond and Poul Kristensens Forlag, 1992, 107.

18   Fabritius, 1992, 45–46.

19   Lise Svanholm, *Northern Light—The Skagen Painters* (trans. Walton Glyn Jones), Copenhagen: Gyldendal, [2001] 2004, 45.

20   Svanholm, 2004, 52–53.

21   Drachmann, 351.

22   Hanna Rönnberg reports the effect that the story had on the general public, and within the artists' community in Rönnberg, 18–19. The convergence of painting and story also helped to generate a mythic aura around Michael Ancher, whose identity as a painter began to coalesce with those of his subjects. Karl Madsen wrote of this painting: "The title is Drachmann's and is half symbolic. A group of fishermen is represented in an excellent composition in the tradition of Raphael's 'Watch my Sheep,' even in the form which derives directly form it…. The standing figures are all known to Ancher…. Ancher had the same determined will that he had found or saw among the Skagen fishermen. As well as they, he knew how hard the wind could blast against one." Karl Madsen, *Skagens Malere og Skagens Museum*, Copenhagen: Gyldendalske Boghandel, Nordisk Forlag, 1929, 26, translated in Inga Rocksvold Platou, *The Art Colony at Skagen: Its Contribution to Scandinavian Art* (unpublished Ph.D. dissertation), University of Minnesota, 1968, 56.

23   Holger Drachmann, "Lars Kruse. En Skildring fra Virkelighedens og—Sandets Regioner," [1879], in *Samlede Skrifter*, Volume 4, 305, 315 and 321.

24   Lübbren, 138–9.

25   Census returns show that Skagen had 2,323 residents in 1890, half of whom were active in fishing. The other half were largely invisible in Skagen painting—artisans, and those occupied by agriculture, shipping, and trade. In addition, there were increasing numbers of tourists, who are largely absent from the paintings. Lübbren, 55–56.

26   The writer Walter Schwartz, son of Skagen chronicler Alba Schwartz, recalls that "the real liberation of his [Ancher's] art came…when Christian Krohg came to Skagen in 1879. In the beginning, Ancher had little enthusiasm for Krohg, finding his painting technique dry and he could not fathom the intensity of his color handing and heavy impasto…. Krohg opened his eyes to a realm of motifs which Ancher had long ignored." Walter Schwartz, *Skagen in Nordisk Kunst*, Copenhagen: Carit Andersens Forlag, 1952, 58–60.

27   Krohg, "Skagen," 520–521.

28   Krohg, "Skagen," 523.

29   Krohg, "Skagen," 524.

30   Platou, 47.

31   See Oscar Thue, *Christian Krohg* (ed. Knut Berg), Oslo: Aschehoug, 1997, 72ff.

32   Michael Jacobs notes that a critical factor in establishing an artists' colony in the nineteenth century was the presence of just such an inn whose sympathetic host supported the artistic enterprise. Michael Jacobs, *The Good and Simple Life: Artist Colonies in Europe and America*, Oxford: Phaidon Press, 1985, 12.

33   Madsen, 1929, 79.

34   Madsen, 1929, 51.

35   Others included Anna's cousins Martha Møller (1860–1929), who married painter Viggo Johansen (1851–1938) and Henriette Møller (1859–1881), who married Karl Madsen, and her brother Degn Brøndum (1856–1935), who later ran the hotel and was a member of the artists' inner circle. Martha Møller Johansen is seated in the extreme foreground of *Hip, Hip, Hurrah!* and Degn Brøndum stands, fifth from the left.

36   The writer and critic Georg Brandes owned a version of this painting. Cited in Ole Wivel, 1987, 33.

37   Ancher had seen examples of advanced French painting in the brewer Carl Jacobsen's collection in Copenhagen (see chapter 6) and at the exhibition of French painting in Copenhagen in 1888. In Paris, during her study trip in 1888–89, Ancher visited numerous museums and galleries, as well as the Universal Exposition. On June 30, 1889, Michael Ancher wrote to Krøyer shortly after the couple's return to Denmark: "Don't miss the Impressionist exhibition on rue Lafitte—especially the large gallery with Degas's work." Claus Olsen, "Anna Ancher i Paris 1889," in *Anna Ancher 1859–1935: Malerin in Skagen* (exh. cat.), Heide Grape-Albers, ed. Hannover, 1994, 127.

38   Ole Wivel, 1987, 36.

39   Voss, 121.

40   They are listed in Peter Michael Hornung, "I Købmandens bod, når der ikke fiskes," in Lisa Svanholm, ed. *Skagen Leksikon: Malerne, Modellerne, Værkerne og Stederne*, Copenhagen: Gyldendal, 2003, 100–101.

41   Alison deLima Green, in Varnedoe, 156.

42   As Anna's husband and Degn's brother-in-law, Ancher seems to have felt proprietary toward the Brøndum family and its enterprise, and he wrote to Krøyer regarding his use of the shop: "It reminds me of the parable of the rich man who has many sheep but has slaughtered the poor man's only lamb." Ole Wivel, *Rejsen til Skagen: Erindringsmotiver og historiske digressioner*, Copenhagen: G. E. C. Gad, 1977, 97.

43   Hanna Rönnberg, *Konstnärsliv i slutet av 1880-talet/ Konstnärskolonien på Åland*, Önningebymuseet, 1993, 9.

44   Georg Brandes, in Svanholm, 2004, 75–76.

45   The motif is strongly reminiscent of his 1879 *Artists' Luncheon in Cernay-la-Ville* (Skagen Museum), representing the dining room of the inn where he stayed in that town.

46 Claus Olsen, "Krøyer and the Japanese
Print," in *Harmony in Blue: P. S. Krøyer's
Poetic Paintings from the 1890s* (exh. cat.),
Skagens Museum, Skagen, 2001, 77–83.

47 Elisabeth Fabritius, "Skagensmalerne," in
Ingrid Fischer Jonge and Gertrud With, eds.
*Verden set paa ny: Fotografi og Malerkunst
i Danmark 1840–1900*, Copenhagen: Det
Nationale Fotomuseum, 2002, 59–74.

48 See Elisabeth Fabritius, *P. S. Krøyer's
Photographs* (exh. cat.), Den Hirschsprungske
Samling, Copenhagen, 1990.

49 Fabritius, 2005, 14.

50 The story behind the painting, and Krøyer's
efforts to render it from live models,
is recounted in Fabritius, 2005.

51 Lübbren, 1.

52 Lübbren, 2.

53 Erik Mørstad, "Christian Krohg i Skagen:
Et Norsk Perspektiv," in *Christian Krohg og
Skagen* (exh. cat.), Skagens Museum and
Lillehammer Kunstmuseum, 2004, 15.

54 The words of Armond Dayot, "Anders Zorn,"
L'Art et les artistes, 3, 1906, 43, in a paraphrase
and summary of the review by Charles Blanc,
Les Beaux-arts à l'exposition universelle de 1878
(Paris: Librairie Renouard, 1878), 341–346,
quoted in Emily Braun, "Scandinavian Painting
and the French Critics," in Varnedoe, 1982, 67.

55 Julius Lange, *Vor Kunst og Udlandets: Et Foredrag*,
Copenhagen: P. G. Philipsens Forlag, 1879, 7.

56 Karl Madsen, "Impressionismen I–II,"
Dagsavisen, 22 and 23 October, 1882.

57 Madsen's extensive publications are listed in Merete
Bodelsen, *Karl Madsen Bibliografi*, Copenhagen:
Fischers Forlag, 1939. Madsen later became the
first director of the Skagen Museum and wrote a
book about the Skagen painters that remains the
authoritative source: *Skagens Malere og Skagens
Museum*, Copenhagen: Gyldendal, 1929.

58 On Brandes and other literary members of the
Skagen community, see Alba Schwartz, *Skagen:
før og nu*, vols. 1 and 2, Copenhagen, 1912–13;
and Knud Voss, *The Painters of Skagen* (trans.
Peter Shields), Copenhagen: Stok-Art, 1990.

59 Brandes´s *Main Currents in Nineteenth-Century
Literature* (*Hovedstrømninger i det 19de århundredes
Litteratur*, Volumes 1–6, Copenhagen, 1872–1890)
is a vast and synthetic examination of advanced
Realist and Naturalist literature and philosophy.

60 Because of his radical social proselytizing,
Brandes was forced to leave Denmark in 1877
and assumed residence in Berlin where he
established his international reputation as a writer.
At the behest of a prominent group of Danish
intellectuals, Brandes returned to Denmark
in 1883. Brandes again offered public lectures
despite the fact that the conservative government

would not grant him a professorship. Sven Møller
Kristensen, "Georg Brandes, Cultural Emissary,"
in Kirk Varnedoe, *Northern Light: Realism and
Symbolism in Scandinavian Painting 1880–1910*
(exh. cat.), The Brooklyn Museum, 1982, 54.

61 On Brandes' impact on Danish artists, see
Elisabeth Fabritius, *Michael Ancher og det
Moderne Gennembrud 1880–1890*, Skagen: Helga
Anchers Fond og Christian Ejlers' Forlag, 1999,
133–138. His influence on the European art
world is discussed in Robert Jensen, *Marketing
Modernism in Fin-de-Siècle Europe*, Princeton:
Princeton University Press, 1994, 215–7.

62 Georg Brandes, "Danskheden I Sønderjylland,"
[1989], in *Samlede Skrifter*, Volume 12,
Copenhagen: Gyldendalske Boghandels
Forlag, 1902, 213. A section is quoted in
Kristensen, in Varnedoe, 1982, 54.

63 Lise Svanholm, "The Artist Marie Krøyer," in
Portraits of a Marriage: Marie and P. S. Krøyer
(exh. cat.), ed. Jacob Thage, Gl. Holtegaard
and Skagens Museum, 1997, 111.

64 *De drogo till Paris: Nordiska konstnärinnor
på 1800-talet* (exh. cat.), ed. Lollo
Fogelström and Louise Robbert), Liljevalchs
Konsthall, Stockholm, 1988, 215.

65 Elisabeth Fabritius, in Ludvigsen, 2005, 401.

66 Fabritius, in Ludvigsen, 2005, 405: "I was a model
for Bertha Wegmann for a large portrait, which was
painted in Tivoli's Garden, down by the moat—at
that time, the setting was not part of the public
space for Tivoli's guests, but it was idyllic with
tall trees, water lilies, ducks, and where only a few
were allowed in. My sitting time stretched over
half a year, and I confided in Bertha Wegmann,
that my goal was to try to become a painter, and
she saw my work and motivated me and promised
me to write to Krøyer and ask him to teach me."

67 Svanholm, in Thage, 109–110. Johanne Krebs
had published articles in the newspaper *Politiken*
in 1888 requesting state-supported art schools
for women, continuing a cause that had been
debated publicly since the early 1870s. Birthe
Møller-Nielsen, "Två systrar i Paris. Emmy och
Ludovica Thornam, 1852–1935, 1853–1896,"
in Fogelström and Robbert, 1988, 210.

68 Diary entry dated 9 January 1889, translated in
Lise Svanholm, *Marie Krøyer, 1867–1940*, Skagen
Monografier 2, Skagens Museum, 1987, 44–47.

69 Anne Wichstrøm estimates that approximately
150 Nordic women artists studied in
Paris in the 1880s. I would like to thank
Dr. Wichstrøm for that information.

70 The Académie Julian was the school most
favored by Nordic women artists. Møller-
Nielsen, in Fogelström and Louise Robbert,
188. Gabriel Weisberg notes the by 1890,
the Académie Julian had opened four studios
for women in Gabriel P. Weisberg and Jane
R. Becker, eds. *Overcoming the Obstacles: The

Women of the Académie Julian* (exh. cat.) Rutgers
University Press and Dahesh Museum, 1999,
16. Weisberg, Becker, and Tamar Garb provide
a wide-ranging analysis of the academic training
and social environment for women, although
they do not focus on Danish painters.

71 The pattern of Scandinavian women's artistic
training and professional culture, and this all-
too-typical trajectory of married women artists,
is explored in *De drogo till Paris. Nordiska
konstnarinnor på 1880-talet* (exh. cat.), Liljevalchs
och Kulturhuset, Stockholm, 1988; Heide
Grape-Albers, et al. *Malerin Anna Ancher in
Skagen 1859–1935* (exh. cat.), Niedersächsisches
Landesmuseum, Hannover, 1994; and Anne
Wichstrøm, *Kvinneliv Kunstnerliv: Kvinnelige
malere I Norge før 1900*, Oslo: Gyldendal, 1997.
See also Helle Behrndt and Jorunn Veiteberg,
eds. *Når kvinder fortæller. Kvindelige malere i
Norden 1880–1900*, Copenhagen, 2002.

72 Tonni Arnold reports that there was much public
attention brought to the engagement, because of
Krøyer's fame as a painter and Triepcke's famous
beauty, but that Tripecke's closet friends brooded
over the news: The Slott-Møllers were certain that
it would be the "death of her art." Harald Slott-
Møller's unpublished memoirs, quoted in Tonni
Arnold, "A Life in Two Voices," in Thage, 1997, 81.

73 Among Key's most influential publications were
"Om småbarnslärarinnor för hem och skola"
[Teachers for Infants at Home and in School],
in *Tidskrift för hemmet* (Stockholm), 1876;
"Böckerna mot" läseböckerna [Books Versus
Schoolbooks] in *Verdandi* (Stockholm), No. 2,
1884; *Om yttrande- och tryckfrihet* [On Freedom
of Speech and Publishing]. Stockholm, 1889;
"Själamorden i skolorna" [Murdering the Soul in
Schools], in *Verdandi* (Stockholm), No. 2, 1891;
Missbrukad Kvinnokraft [Misused Female Power].
Stockholm, 1896; *Skönhet för alla* [Beauty for
All], Stockholm, 1899; and especially *Barnets
århundrade, I–II* [The Century of the Child],
Stockholm, 1900 (translated into English in 1909).

74 Gertrude Oelsner, "Mellan estetik och liv: Om
Marie Krøyers måleri och inredningskonst,"
in *Marie och P. S. Krøyer* (exh. cat.), ed.
Lena Böethius, Götheborg, 2006, 106.

75 Marie Krøyer subscribed to the primary organ of
the British arts-and-cafts movement, *The Studio*.
In Svanholm, in Thage, 114. She also designed and
decorated furniture as well as architectural elements
for their home, and also furniture for Brøndum's
Hotel and for Holger Drachmann's home in
1902. Some of her designs were reminiscent of
the work of Scottish architect Charles Rennie
Mackintosh. See Oelsner, 2006, 110–111.

76 Oelsner, 2006, 112.

77 Marie Krøyer had no significant place in Danish art
history until the mid-1980s, when the collection
of her paintings belonging to her daughter Vibeke
Krøyer Dahl (1895–1985) was discovered. Prior
to that time, historical opinion of Triepcke was

extremely negative, the result of her decision to leave the beloved P. S. Krøyer and their daughter to marry Alfvén. In recent years, however, Marie Krøyer has been the focus of serious scholarly and biographical attention. Among the recent publications are: the pioneering catalogue by Lise Svanholm, *Marie Krøyer*, Skagen Monografier 2, Copenhagen: Herluf Stockholms Forlag, 1987; Lisa Svanholm, *Agnes og Marie. Breve mellem Agnes Slott-Møller og Marie Krøyer 1885–1917*, Copenhagen, 1991; Anastasia Arnold, *Balladen om Marie*, Copenhagen, 1999; Tonni Arnold, *Kunsten i Marie Krøyers liv*, Copenhagen, 2002; Elisabeth Fabritius, *Skitser af Marie Krøyer og Anna Ancher*, Skagen, 2002; and Margrethe Loerges, *Marie Krøyer: Portræt af skagensmaleren P. S. Krøyers hustru*, Copenhagen, 2004. Several more studies have examined the Krøyers' marriage, among them Jacob Thage, ed. *Portraits of a Marriage: Marie and P. S. Krøyer*, Skagens Museum, 1997, and Lena Boëthius, ed. *Marie och P. S. Krøyer* (exh. cat.), Göteborgs Konstmuseum, 2005. These latter studies are part of a larger literature on Nordic artist couples, which includes Randi Nygaard Lium, ed. *Kunstnerektaparene på Skagen; Anna og Michael Ancher, Marie og P. S. Krøyer, Viggo Johansen* (exh. cat.), Trondheim Kunstmuseum, 2000; and Margareta Gynning, Annette Johansen and Mette Bøgh Jensen, *Konstnärspar kring sekelskiftet 1900* (exh. cat.), Nationalmuseum, Stockholm, 2006; and Margareta Gynning, et al. *Nordic Artist Couples around 1900* (exh. cat.), Skagens Museum, 2006 (translated and shortened version of Gynning's essay in *Konstnärspar kring sekelskiftet 1900*. These latter studies are indebted to the essays published in *Significant Others: Creativity and Intimate Partnership*, ed. Whitney Chadwick and Isabelle de Courtivron, New York: Thames & Hudson, 1993.

78 A large number of Whistler's "Nocturnes" had been exhibited in London in 1884 at Grosvenor Gallery, which Krøyer may have seen, and again at Galerie Georges Petit in 1887 in an exhibition in which Krøyer also participated. See Peter Michael Hornung, *Peder Severin Krøyer*, Copenhagen: Forlaget Palle Fogtdal, 2005, 266.

79 In his book on Japanese art (*Japansk Kunst*, Copenhagen: P. G. Philipsens Forlag, 1885), Karl Madsen had described such a meandering line arabesque line as Japan's "norm for beauty" (p. 41). He described 1868 not only as the revolutionary year in which Yokohama Harbor opened to the West, but also as a European revolution, when the visual world of Western art was transformed by Japanese visual culture, by its decorative character (p. 14) and lack of deep perspective, but also by its emphasis on change and transformation (p. 25). He devoted two chapters to Hokusai, whom he described as reveling in ecstasy over the beauty of nature.

80 Claus Olsen, "Krøyer and the Japanese Print," in *Harmony in Blue*, ed. Annette Johansen and Mette Bøgh Jensen, (exh. cat.), trans. W. Glyn Jones, Skagen: Skagens Museum, 2001. See also

Elisabeth Fabritius, "Hjemmet som kunstværk," in *P. S. Krøyers Photographs*, 1990, ft. 61.

81 *Baedeker's Norway, Sweden, and Denmark with Excursions to Iceland and Spitzbergen*, Karl Baedeker: Leipzig, 1912, 440–4.

82 Ole-Christian Munk Plum and Birger Wilcke, *Skagensbanen gennom 100 år*, Copenhagen: Dansk jernbane-klub, 1990.

83 Undated advertisement, Skagen Town Archives. With increasing public awareness of disease-causing micro-organisms and an allied anxiety about demographic changes in crowded European and North American cities, public hygiene became a practical as well as a political priority. Urban sanitation movements encouraged the growth of public bathing and open-air exercise movements. Accompanying these phenomena, a new rural "geography of tourism" emerged before the Great War—resort-based health spas, located in or near towns and villages with natural mineral springs, mountain topographies, or beaches. From the mid-eighteenth century to the end of the nineteenth century, the medical evidence that sea-cures and the drinking of seawater were beneficial for a host of illnesses (including tuberculosis) spurred the growth of seaside resorts. Consequently, sea spas exploded in number and complexity between the 1880s and the Great War. Water spas were initially the domain of the sick, but because of their promotion as fashionable locales, spas also began to attract healthy tourists in search the social life and the extra-urban experience of the spa. This was the case with Skagen. On the history of Skagen's bathing culture, see Bent Hardervig, *Det var en Herlig Tid: En uhøjtidelig historie om Jeckels i Gl.Skagen, et badehotel og dets mennesker*, Gl. Skagen: Jeckels, 1984, and his *Ferieliv gennem 100 år*, Skagen Turistforening, 2006.

CHAPTER 6

1 The phrase was coined by Karl Madsen to identify new subjectivist tendencies in Danish art in "Dansk Kunst i det sidste år," *Nordisk tidskrift för vetenskap, konst, och industri*, Stockholm, 1888, No. 1–2, 106, quoted in Vad, 1992, 63.

2 Ulla Sjöström, *Maleren Ejnar Nielsen 1872–1956*, Copenhagen: Christian Ejlers' Forlag, 2000, 34. Sjöström reports that Maeterlinck's symbolist plays, including *L'Intruse* (*The Intruder*, 1890) and *Les Aveugles* (*The Blind*, 1890), were translated into Danish into 1891.

3 Sasha M. Newman, in Varnedoe, 1988, 199, linked this painting with the notion of "second sight," gleaned from the writings of eighteenth-century theologian and mystic Emmanuel Swedenborg (1688–1772).

4 Merete Bodelsen identifies this work as a breakthrough in Gauguin's sculptural works, influenced in part by Inca portrait-vases, and related formally to his programmatic *Self-Portrait "les misérables"* dedicated to Vincent van Gogh (1888; Stedelijk Museum, Amsterdam). This

ceramic work was exhibited at the Free Exhibition in the van Gogh and Gauguin exhibition in 1893 (see below). See Bodelsen, *Gauguin's Ceramics: A Study in the Development of his Art*, London: Faber and Faber Limited, 1964, 111–120, and Merete Bodelsen, *Gauguin og van Gogh i København i 1893/ Gauguin and van Gogh in Copenhagen in 1893* (exh. cat.), Ordrupgaard Collection, Copenhagen, 1984, 74–76.

5 See Jespersen, 200–213.

6 Grundtvig's formal training was in Enlightenment and Romantic philosophies, and in Icelandic sagas. His early publications focused on Nordic mythology. In 1810, he underwent a religious conversion, and he subsequently wrote theological tracts, histories, secular poetry, and psalms. See A.M. Allchin, *N.F.S. Grundtvig. An Introduction to His Life and Work*. London: Darton, Longman and Todd, 1998. His works are collected in Holger Begtrup, ed. *Udvalgte Skrifter*, 1–10. Copenhagen: Gyldendal, 1904–1909.

7 On Edvard Brandes and *Politiken*, see Kristian Hvidt, *Edvard Brandes. Portræt af en radikal blæksprutte* (3rd edition) Copenhagen: Gyldendal, 2005.

8 Peter Nørgaard Larsen, *L. A. Ring: On the Edge of the World* (exh. cat.), Statens Museum for Kunst, Copenhagen, 2006, 23.

9 Larsen, 2006, 26.

10 Larsen, 2006, 19–22.

11 On Bastien-Lepage's impact on European-wide Naturalist art, see Gabriel P. Weisberg, *Beyond Impressionism : The Naturalist Impulse*, New York: Abrams, 1992, chapter 9: "Scandinavian Naturalism," 242–273.

12 See Sandberg, 157–158.

13 Larsen, 2006, 22 and 221.

14 Larsen, 2006, 26.

15 The figure of the Grim Reaper was based on Ring's studies of a skeleton in P. S. Krøyer's school (Larsen, 2006, 44).

16 See Finn Terman Frederiksen, "Ring's Roads," in Larsen, 2006, 149ff.

17 Larsen, 2006, 51.

18 Poul Uttenreitter, *Maleren Niels Bjerre*, Copenhagen: Kuntforeningen, 1949, 58.

19 Uttenreitter, 90–91.

20 Patricia G. Berman, in Varnedoe, 1988, 56–57.

21 Bjerre wrote "Fiskere" in 1891 and published it under the pseudonym J. G. Pinholt in *Illustreret Tidende* 17 July 1892. Uttenreitter, 61. His story, "The Sacred Congregation" was written in 1892 and published in 1932. He also translated Friedrich Nietzsche's *Thus Spake Zarathustra* in 1890 (unpublished).

22 Quoted in Kasper Monrad and Peter Michael Hornung, *The Modern Breakthrough in Danish Painting 1870–1890* (exh. cat.), Golden Days in Copenhagen, 2002, 1.

23 Adna Ferrin Weber, *The Growth of Cities in the Nineteenth Century: A Study in Statistics*, Ithaca: Cornell University Press, [1899] 1963, 112–113. See also statistics maintained by the City of Copenhagen: http://www.sk.kk. dk/english/tal_faktaUK/befolkning1a.html

24 Sys Hartmann and Villads Villadsen, *Danmarks Arkitektur: Byens huse, byens plan*, Copenhagen: Gyldendal, 1979, 33.

25 Patricia G. Berman and Kasper Monrad, in Varnedoe, 1988, 222–223.

26 Valdemar Vedel, "Modern Digtning: Tilbageblik og Fremblik," *Ny Jord*, 1888, No. 2, 155–164, translated in Peter Nørgaard Larsen, ed. *Symbolism in Danish and European Painting 1870–1910* (exh. cat.), Statens Museum for Kunst, 2000, 15.

27 Westergaard, in *Nordiske stemninger: Nordisk maleri fra århundreskiftet* (exh. cat.), Nasjonalgalleriet, Oslo, 1987, 256, quoted in Larsen, 2006, 90.

28 Wivel, 1997, 17.

29 Larsen, 2006, 90.

30 This painting is described and analyzed in light of Ring's biography and the literature of the period in Finn Terman Frederiksen, *Før Solopgang. Omkring et billede af L. A. Ring*, Randers: Randers Kunstmuseumsforlag, 2006.

31 Their writings are summarized in Larsen, 2006, 80.

32 Frederiksen, 2006, 40ff. and 54.

33 Jean Moréas, "A Literary Manifesto—Symbolism," *Le Figaro Littéraire*, 18 September 1886, 150, translated in Henri Dorra, *Symbolist Art Theories: A Critical Anthology*, Berkeley: University of California Press, 1994, 151–2; and G.-Albert Aurier, "Le Symbolisme en peinture: Paul Gauguin," *Mercure de France*, March 1891, 155–165.

34 See Debra Silverman, *Art Nouveau in Fin-de-Siècle France: Politics, Psychology, and Style*, Berkeley: University of California Press, 1989, chapter 5, 75ff.

35 Larsen, 2000, 11.

36 Johannes Jørgensen, "Symbolismen," *Taarnet*, 1893, 51–56, translated in Østermark-Johansen, 179–180.

37 Historians continue to grapple with the definitions of Symbolism as a movement in the visual arts, variously and problematically distinguishing Symbolist art from other contemporaneous manifestations by emphasizing either theme or style. A compendium of Symbolist theoretical writings is provided in Dorra, 1994. Broader histories of Symbolism, and attempts to define the movement, include Anna Balakian, *The Symbolist Movement: A Critical Appraisal*, New York: Random House, 1967; *The Sacred and Profane in Symbolist Art* (exh. cat.), Art Gallery of Ontario, Toronto and Turin, Associazione Amici torinesi dell'arte contemporanea, 1969; David L. Anderson, et al. *Symbolism: A Bibliography of Symbolism as an International and Multi-Disciplinary Movement*, New York: New York University Press, 1975; Phillipe Julian, *The Symbolists*, New York: E. P. Dutton, 1977; Robert Goldwater, *Symbolism*, New York: Harper & Row, ca. 1979; Reinhold Heller, "Concerning Symbolism and the Structure of Surface," in *Art Journal*, Vol. 45, No. 2, (Summer, 1985), 146–153; Pierre Théberge and Jean Clair, eds. *Lost Paradise: Symbolist Europe* (exh. cat.), Montreal: Montreal Museum of Fine Arts, 1995; and Patricia Mathews, *Passionate Discontent: Creativity, Gender, and French Symbolist Art*, Chicago: University of Chicago Press, 1999.

The same problems with the literature on Symbolism throughout Europe are manifest in the literature on Danish Symbolism. General studies of Symbolism, which attempt to define a broad term in which the eclectic arts of fin-de-siècle Denmark can rest, include Leila Krogh, et al. *J. F. Willumsen og Den frie Udstillings først år 1891–1898* (exh. cat.), J. F. Willumsens Museum, Frederikssund, 1982; Varnedoe, 1982 [1988]; Nasgaard, 1984; Hanne Honnens de Lichtenberg, *Symbolismen i dansk Kunst* (exh. cat.), Nivaagaards Malerisamling, 1993; Jens Peter Munk and Kirsten Olesen, *Postimpressionisme* (exh. cat.) Ny Carlsberg Glyptotek, Copenhagen, 1993; Henrik Wivel, *Symbolisme og Impressionisme*, Ny Dansk Kunsthistorie, Vol. 5, Copenhagen: Palle Fogtdal, 1994, also published as *Den Store Stil: Dansk symblisme og impressionisme omkring år 1900*, Copenhagen: Palle Fogtdal, 1995; *Landschaft als Kosmos der Seele. Malerei des nordischen Symbolismus bis Munch*, Götz Czymmek, ed. (exh. cat.), Wallraf-Richartz-Museum, Cologne, 1998; and Larsen, 2000. Larsen's catalogue includes several essays on the historiography of Symbolism in Denmark, and on the designation's instability, inclusions, and exclusions. Excellent studies of individual artists, including Jens Ferdinand Willumsen, L. A. Ring and Vilhelm Hammershøi, noted elsewhere in the footnotes, take up the question of Symbolism and its limits. Particularly helpful in this regard is Larsen, 2006.

38 Johannes Jørgensen, *Taarnet*, February 1894, 218–222, translated in Charlotte Christensen, "The Noble is Simple." in Larsen, 2000, 187.

39 Leila Krogh, "Den frie Udstillings tilblivelse," in *J. F. Willumsen og Den frie Udstillings Første år 1891–1898* (exh. cat.), J. F. Willumsens Museum, Frederikssund, 1982, 8–9.

40 A new exhibition locale had been opened in 1883 to provide better space and light than the "old dark brown palace." Peter Nørgaard Larsen, "Med Ryggen mod Fremtiden: Billedkunst i anden halvdel af 1800-tallet," in Fuchs and Salling, Vol. 2, 2004, 147. At the opening of this new space, its architect, Ferdinand Mehldahl, offered, "the rising generation must learn to love everything noble and good and sacrifice itself for its country." Mehldahl is quoted in Kjeld Heltoft, "Exhibition Life and Associations," in Marianne Barbusse and Nanna Hertoft, eds. *Danske kunstnersammenslutninger/ Danish Artists' Associations*, Copenhagen: Gyldendal, 1996, 27.

41 Around 1879, a group of younger artists, among them Laurits Tuxen, Niels Skovgaard, and Kristian Zahrtmann, had wished to open an art school to supplement the Academy's training, with particular emphasis on drawing from live models. In the following year, the Artists' Model School was established. See Larsen, in Fuchs and Salling, Vol. 2, 2004, 159ff. Larsen notes that the most significant model for this system was Léon Bonnat, whose studio was popular was a popular among Nordic students. On Bonnat's Nordic students, see Siulolovao Challons-Lipton, *The Scandinavian Pupils of the Atelier Bonnat, 1867–1894*, Lewiston, NY: Edwin Mellen Press, 2002.

42 Krogh, 1982, 9.

43 Gunnar Sörensen, "Zahrtmanns Malerskole 1885–1908 sett i relasjon til samtidens kunstmiljö og med hovedvekten på de norske elevene," unpublished Magistergradsavhandling, University of Oslo, 1976, 8.

44 Ernst Goldschmidt, "Ved Kunstakademiets 150 Aars Jubilæum," *Tilskueren*, 1904, 563, quoted in Larsen, in Fuchs and Salling, Vol. 2, 2004, 166.

45 Hanne Honnens de Lichtenberg, *Zahrtmanns Skole*, Copenhagen: Forum, 1979, 54–55.

46 Translated in Heltoft, in Barbusse and Hertoft, 29.

47 Krogh, 1982, 12.

48 Krogh, 1982, 13.

49 See Krogh, 1982, 17–19.

50 "Danske kunstnere på Den frie Udstilling 1891–1898," in Krogh, 1982, 36.

51 Loa Haagen Pictet, "J. F. Willlumsen, The European: Views on Art and Self-Understanding at the Start of the Twentieth Century," in Larsen, 2000, 199.

52 Charlotte Christensen, "The Noble is Simple," in Larsen, 2000, 188.

53 Gauguin's winter spent in Copenhagen is examined in detail in Anne Birgitte Fonsmark, *Gauguin og Danmark* (exh. cat.), Ny Carlsberg Glyptotek, Copenhagen, 1985.

54 Mette Gad Gauguin became an important conduit for Impressionist art in Denmark. Remaining in Copenhagen after her husband departed for France and the South Pacific, she functioned as his sales manager, opened her collection to younger artists, and helped them to secure contacts in France.

55 See Bodelsen, 1984. A facsimile of the exhibition catalogue appears on pp. 31–42.

56 The controversy in Berlin eventually impelled Berlin's *Verein Berliner Künstler* to found the Berlin Secession. See Reinhold Heller, "Affæren Munch. Berlin 1892–1893," *Kunst og Kultur*, 1969, 175–191.

57 Emil Hannover, *Politiken*, February 24, 1893, cited in Jan Kneher, *Edvard Munch in seinen Ausstellungen zwischen 1892 und 1912: Ein Dokumentation der Austellungen und Studie zur*

Rezeptionsgeschichte von Munchs Kunst, Worms: Wernersche Verlagsgesellschaft, 1994, 25–26.

58 "Our Reporter" in the *Aalborg Stiftstidende*, April 29, 1893, in Kirsten Olesen, "From Amsterdam to Copenhagen," in Bodelsen, 1984, 30.

59 Karl Madsen, review in *Tilskueren*, 1893, translated in Olesen, in Bodelsen, 1984, 30. The phrases are taken from a selection of reviews that are summarized or quoted in Olesen.

60 See Peter Nørgaard Larsen, "Malerisk sansning og sjælens syner. Impressionismen og postimpressionismen i Danmark," in Torsten Gunnarsson, ed. *Impressionismen og Norden. Fransk avantgarde i det sene 1800-tal og kunsten i Norden 1870–1920* (exh. cat.), Nationalmuseum, Stockholm and Statens Museum for Kunst, 2003, 159ff.

61 Larsen, 2000, 84.

62 Johan Rohde, *Journal fra en Rejse i 1892*, Copenhagen: Forening for Boghaandværk Erik Paludan, 1955, 113.

63 See Hanne Honnens de Lichtenberg, 1993, 25–41. Ballin had studied French with Mette Gauguin, who had also introduced him to the work of her husband and then provided him with a letter of introduction to Émile Schuffenecker in Paris. Charlotte Christensen, "The Noble is Simple," in Larsen, 2000, 189.

64 Hannover, quoted in Larsen, 2000, 313.

65 Mogens Ballin to Johannes Jørgensen, quoted in Peter Schindler, *Mogens Francesco Ballin*, Copenhagen, 1936, 43ff., and translated in Christensen, in Larsen, 2000, 189–90.

66 Pierre Louis [Maurice Denis], "Définition du néo-traditionalisme," *Art et critique*, August 12, 1890, 540–542, and August 30, 1890, 556–558, quoted in Dorra, 1994, 235.

67 Simon Koch, "Ludvig Find," in *Taarnet* [October 1893], (facsimile edition, Copenhagen: Det Danske Sprog- og Litteraturselskab, 1981, 26.

68 Simon Koch, "Ludvig Find," *Taarnet*, October 1893, 22, translated in Christensen, in Larsen, 187.

69 Christensen, in Larsen, 2000, 192. The painting, which was subsequently purchased by Mogens Ballin, changed hands several times in the early twentieth century, and was seized as "Degenerate Art" by the National Socialists in Germany, is now in an unknown private collection after fetching record price at auction in 1990. The story is recounted in Cynthia Salzman, *Portrait of Dr. Gachet. The Story of a van Gogh Masterpiece, Modernism, Money, Politics, Collectors, Dealers, Taste, Greed, and Loss*. New York: Viking, 1998.

70 Larsen, 2000, 18.

71 Henrik Wivel, "The Metaphysical Body: Examples of Non-Being and the Incorporeal in Figure Painting around 1900," in Larsen, 2000, 272.

72 Mogens Ballin, *Taarnet*, 1894, in Larsen, 2000, 24.

73 Larsen, 2000, 142, footnote 8.

74 J. F. Willumsen reports that Puvis had been of exceptional interest as a painter of "Naturpoesi" for the Nordic community in 1888, when *Poor Fisherman* went on exhibition at the Musée Luxembourg. Claus Olsen, 1994, 125. On Puvis's importance for Danish vanguard art, see Peter Nørgaard Larsen, "Beauty and Death," in 2000, 22–23.

75 Hammershøi had also seen Puvis's work at the 1889 Universal Exposition in Paris, and had likely viewed Puvis's much-debated murals for the Sorbonne while living in Paris in 1891–2. Larsen, 2000, 23, reports that Puvis's murals for the Sorbonne were much visited by Danish artists, as they were for artists internationally.

76 Peter Nørgaard Larsen, "Joakim Skovgaard: Christ in the Realm of the Dead," in Larsen, 2000, 287.

77 Verner von Heidenstam, "The Logic of the Imagination" [1896], in *Verner von Heidenstam*, Stockholm, 1965, 11–26, translated in Larsen, 2000, 239.

78 Larsen, "Joakim Skovgaard: Christ in the Realm of the Dead," 228 and footnote 2, Grundvig's 1837 poem is translated in full on p. 234. Skovgaard, Denmark's foremost religious painter of the period, and an artist who had been intimately involved in architectural renovation projects (the legacy of Høyen's ecclesiastical preservation movement), likened Jesus to "an immovable, mighty tower standing in the midst of tempestuous waves," and noted that he had structured the composition so that its underlying geometry would communicate the content directly. Quoted in Vilhelm Wanscher, "Joakim Skovgaard, by Vilhelm Wanscher, with letters on Art of the Master Himself, and an introduction in French by his intimate Friend Karl Madsen," *Artes*, Vol. 2, 1933, 174, translated in Larsen, 2006, 228.

79 Mogens Ballin, *Taarnet*, 1894, quoted in Larsen, 2000, 227. The day after the painting was unveiled, a critic in the newspaper *Socialdemokraten* claimed that it reanimated "monumental art," and art historian Emil Hannover declared it a troubling masterpiece, filled with ecstasy as well as pathos. *Socialdemokraten* March 25, 1894, cited in Bente Scavenius, "Et omstridt gigantbillede. Joakim Skovgaard: "Kristus i de Dødes Rige, 1891–1894," in Ernst Jonas Bencard, Anders Kold, and Peter S. Meyer, *Kunstværkets Krav: 27 fortolkninger af danske kunstværker*, Copenhagen: Palle Fogtdal, 1990, 149 and 150. The painting also had its detractors, most powerful among them the art historian Julius Lange who expressed the opinion that it was a well meaning but misconceived effort, and who blocked its purchase by the Statens Museum for Kunst. Scavenius, 151ff. Hannover and Lange engaged in a polemical debate over the painting, a retrenching of on-going debates between the two about the meaning and needs of Danish art in the late nineteenth century. The painting was in the end purchased for the Statens Museum for Kunst at the initiative of Karl Madsen. Placed in

storage for much of the twentieth century, it now has pride of place in the museum's new installation (2006), a monument to changing tastes.

80 Wivel, 1994, 65ff. The rise in popularity of art ceramics was buoyed by the same anti-academic tendencies that gave rise to the Artists' Studio Schools and the Free Exhibitions, a desire to express freedom by embracing non-traditional methods and motifs.

81 Larsen, 2006, 65–67.

82 On Bindesbøll's sources, see Vibeke Woldbye, "Keramik," and Charlotte Christensen, "Bindesbøll og de ideale fordringer," in Bodil Busk Laursen, ed. *Thorvald Bindesbøll: En dansk pioner* (exh. cat.), Kunstindustrimuseum, Copenhagen, 1996, 58–91, and 92–101. The catalogue provides a survey of his production in ceramics, silver, and interior design. See also Wivel, 1994, 58–71.

83 Carl Jacobsen was also a master of marketing, including the reminder that Ny Carlsberg brewery was purveyor to the court printed on Bindesbøll's "Hof Pilsner" label. As Henrik Wivel observes, the term "hof" or royal, that appears in Bindesbøll's beer label is also a characterization of the art nouveau aesthetic espoused by Bindesbøll, the Slott-Møllers, and Marie Krøyer, all followers of the British Arts and Crafts Movement. Wivel, 1994, 55. On the relationship between Carlsberg's art collection and his commitment to modern industry, see Kristof Glamann, *Beer and Marble: Carl Jacobsen of New Carlsberg* (research by Kirsten Glamann, trans. Geoffrey French), Gyldendal, 1996, 237.

84 Jacobsen's father, J. C. Jacobsen, who founded the "old" Carlsberg Brewery, and with whom Carl competed in business, had likewise been an important philanthropist, art collector, and patron. In the 1870s, he also financed the renovation of Frederiksborg Castle, responding to the wish expressed by Høyen early in the century that the national monument required attention, and rescuing the building, and the national painting collection, after a disastrous fire in 1859. See Mette Bligaard, *J. C. Jacobsen and Frederiksborg Castle*, Hillerød: Frederiksborg Museum, 1997.

85 *Officiel Fører paa den nordiske Industri-, Landbrugs- og Kunstudstillingen i Kjøbenhavn*, 1888, Hagerups Forlag, Copenhagen,1888, 97.

86 C. F. Bricka, ed. *Dansk Biografisk Leksikon*, Vol. 4, Copenhagen: Gyldendalske Boghandels Forlag, 1890, 393–396. Ebbesen's mythology and transformation into a national symbol is traced in "Niels Ebbesen," in Inge Adriansen, ed. *Nationale symboler i Det Danske Rige 1830–2000*, Vol. 2, Copenhagen: Museum Tusculanums Forlag, Københavns Universitet, 2003, 481–500.

87 The text is reproduced in Adriansen, 486–487. In the visual arts, Ebbesen was the subject of history painting, an ongoing debate about a monument in Randers (completed in 1882), and a theme promoted by Carl Bloch at the Academy shortly after the 1864.

88 Agnes Slott-Møller, *Folkevisebilleder*, Copenhagen: Aschehoug, 1923, 31, quoted in Adriansen, 492. She also hoped that that the painting would enter the National History Museum at Frederiksborg, but it was rejected because the crossbow in Ebbesen's hand was not seen as historically accurate. Critic Julius Lange, however, deemed the painting "properly and characteristically Danish," and it was purchased, by subscription, for the Randers Art Museum.

89 Slott-Møller had previously submitted medievalizing representations of historical Danish royalty, King Oluf and Queen Dagmar, to the first Free Exhibition in 1891, and these had been well received. See Bente Scavenius, "Udpluk af de først års kunstkritik," in *Agnes and Harald Slott-Møller: Mellem kunst og idealer* (exh. cat.), Copenhagen Kunstforening, 1988, 34–35. In its emblematic simplicity and scale, however, *Niels Ebbesen* signalled a more ambitious type of history painting.

90 The tragic ballad recounts the story of the youth Tidemand who yearns for the maiden Blidelil. He is instructed to inscribe runes on two roses, which the maiden finds on a beach. Awakened from sleep by the mysterious power of the runes, and against the wishes of her sister, Blidelil dons a cloak of feathers and flies over the water to Tidemand. She alights on his ship and then drowns herself when he will not acknowledge her. He, in turn, casts himself into the water and the two die side by side. Slott-Møller explains the ballad in 1923, 78–80.

91 Agnes Slott-Møller, 1923, 78–80.

92 Agnes Slott-Møller, 1923, 78ff., translated in Larsen, 2000, 300.

93 A brief historiography of ballad collecting is offered in Jens Henrik Koudal, "Ethnomusicology and Folk Music Research in Denmark," in *Yearbook for Traditional Music*, Volume 25, 1993, 300–303.

94 Christian Molbech, *Eventyr og udvalgte og Fortællinger: En Lærebog for Folket og for den barnlige Verden*, Copenhagen: Reitzel, 1843, vi.

95 See "Fædrelandssange," in Adriansen, 59–98.

96 Agnes Slott-Møller, *Nationale Værdier*, Copenhagen: Græbes Bogtrykkeri, 1917, 155.

97 "Jeg vilde dennegang prøve at samle flere Billeder til den same Vise indenfor en fælles samme, som jeg paa mangen en gammel, gotisk Altertavle havde set en Helgens Livstildragelser fortalt gennem flere Billeder, og dekorere Rammen med Bogstaver, hvor Visens Vers stod at læse, som den hellige Tekst jo tidt stod at læse paa Altertavlernes Rammer i Middelalderens Minuskelbogstaver."

98 Lene Østermark-Johansen, "Reading and the Pleasures of the Eye: Text and Image in English and Danish Symbolism," in Larsen, 2000, 172.

99 Honnens de Lichtenberg, 1993, 67–68.

100 Reviewing the 1894 Free Exhibition, Emil Hannover stated that Slott-Møller's cradle captivated him the most of any decorative composition. Bente Scavenius, "De første års anmeldelser," in Krogh, 1982, 54.

101 Harald Slott-Møller, "Foraarudstillingerne 1909," *Tilskueren*, 1990, 471–87, 472, translated in Østermark-Johansen, 179.

102 Harald Slott-Møller, *Kunstens Kilder*, Copenhagen: H. Hagerup's Forlag, 1917.

103 Agnes Slott-Møller, "Om fædrelandkærlighed, 1917, 124. (Lecture at the Dansk Kvinders Forsvarsforening.)

104 Pictet, in Larsen, 2000, 211.

105 Willumsen's years spent in France, his intellectual and aesthetic education, and his social and institutional relations, are traced in Merete Bodelsen, *Willumsen i Halvfemsernes Paris*, 1957, which offers a summary in English. This is a foundational study of Willumsen's work.

106 See Roald Nasgaard, "Willumsen and Symbolist Art, 1880–1910," unpublished Ph.D. dissertation, New York University Institute of Fine Arts, 1973.

107 Troels Branth Pedersen, *Bjergtaget: J. F. Willumsen i Norge 1892*, Århus: Klim, 2006.

108 Translated in Larsen, 2000, 65.

109 Bodelsen, 1957, 36–46, Cited in Larsen, 2000, 63.

110 Johannes Jørgensen, "Symbolism," *Taarnet*, 1893, facsimile edition 1981, 51–56, translated in Henrik Wivel, in Larsen, 2000, 269–270.

111 The artist manipulated the distance of Mt. Blanc from the edge of the lake, as observed by Pictet, in Larsen, 2000, 202.

112 Pictet, in Larsen, 2000, 201. The Vitalist movement in literature and philosophy has been analyzed by Sven Halse, "Vitalisme—Fænomen og begrip," *Kritik*, 171, 1–7. On Vitalism and the visual arts, see Karen E. Lerheim and Ingebjørg Ydstie, eds. *Livskraft: Vitalismen som Kunstnerisk Impuls 1900–1930* (exh. cat.), Oslo: Munch Museum, 2006.
   On Haeckel and turn-of-the-century artists, see Patricia G. Berman, "Edvard Munch's 'Modern Life of the Soul,'" in *Edvard Munch and the Modern Life of the Soul* (exh. cat.), ed. Kynaston McShine, Museum of Modern Art, New York, 2006, 34ff.

113 See Sharon L. Hirsh, "Swiss Art and National Identity at the Turn of the Twentieth Century," in *Art, Culture, and National Identity in Fin-de-Siècle Europe*, ed. Michelle Facos and Sharon Hirsh, N. Y.: Cambridge University Press, 2003, 250–285.

114 See Gunnar Sørensen, "Vitalismens år," in Lerheim and Ydstie, 2006, 13–41.

115 Holbek died in 1903, leaving behind voluminous writings and a body of fantastical decorative work. His aubiographical writings were published posthumously in three volumes. Larsen, 2000, 101.

116 Translated in Larsen, 2000, 78.

117 Letter to Marie Thaarup, dated 25 December 1898, translated in Larsen, 2000, 50. Böcklin's *Island of the Dead* (first version 1880) was described by Emil Hannover in article in *Tilskueren*: "It is scarcely an exaggeration to say that this picture is one of the small number of works of art which it is difficult to understand as having been born of human brains and fashioned by human hands.… Words cannot convey the artistic beauty and the indescribably powerful concentrated mood of bitter solemnity and boundless sorrow." *Tilskueren*, 1892, 118–134, 128, translated in Larsen, 50

118 Ejnar Nielsen , to Marie Thaarup, quoted in Sjöström, 2000, 15.

119 Sjöström, 16–17.

120 See Thomas Dormandy, *The White Death: A History of Tuberculosis*, London: Hambledon and London, Ltd. 1999.

121 Alena Marchwinski, "Idyllen og den dødsmærkede verden," *Statens Museum for Kunst Årsskrift*, 1990, 164–173.

122 Nielsen wrote of Puvis, "the remarkable thing about [Puvis de Chavannes] is that he was and even after his death remains the greatest modern painter in France and then that he was E.N.'s and still is E.N.'s great, beloved artist." Letter to Marie Thaarup, quoted in Larsen, 2000, 28.

123 Larsen, 2000, 31.

124 Ejnar Nielsen, in an interview in 1927, in Steffen Lange, *Eneren. Maleren Ejnar Nielsen*, Copenhagen: Poul Kristensens Forlag, 1998, 53.

125 Sjöströom, 2000, 34.

CHAPTER 7

1 Georg Brandes, *Main Currents in Nineteenth Century Literature*, Vol. 2. "The Romantic School in German," London: William Heinemann Ltd., 1923, 9.

2 As noted in Conisbee, 2003, 28. In the foreword to his study, Vedel noted, "The survey's title is chosen for lack of a better name, though its almost *reverent* tone personally offends me." Vedel, *Studier over Guldalderen i Dansk Digtning*, Copenhagen: P. G. Philipsens Forlag, 1890, [i], unpaginated foreword.

3 Klaus P. Mortensen, "Demons of the Golden Age: Hans Christian Andersen and Søren Kierkegaard," in *Thorvaldsen Museum Bulletin*, 1997, calls attention to the high degree of mythification that underlay this reading of the period and examines the complexity of Danish society in the period that was selectively remembered as "golden."

4 Kasper Monrad, "Stories that are not Told: The Narrative Element in Hammershøi's Work," in Larsen, 2000, 248.

5 Henrik Wivel notes that Constantin Hansen's *A Party of Danish Artists in Rome* (fig. 49) had also recently been in exhibited twice in Copenhagen. See his catalogue entry for this painting in *Nordiske Stemninger: Nordisk maleri fra århundreskiftet* (exh. cat.), Nasjonalgalleriet, Oslo, 1987, 146. (Norwegian version of Lena Ahtola-Moorhouse, et al. *Dreams of a Summer Night: Scandinavian*

Painting at the Turn of the Century (exh. cat.), The Hayward Gallery, London, 1986.

6   These greatly enlarged feet correspond to the accidents and distortions typical of wide-angle photography, in which objects close to the lens are exaggerated in scale. This odd effect in the painting disquieted Hammershøi's audience when it was first exhibited in Copenhagen. A local shoe store capitalized on the scandal by caricaturing the painting in an advertisement from 1902: "Hammershøi paints it; Oettinger sells it—a good Shoe." Published in Felix Krämer and Ulrich Luckhart, eds. *Vilhelm Hammershøi* (exh. cat.), Hamburger Kunsthalle, 2003, 144. Hammershøi took legal action to remove the advertisement.

7   Vad, 1992, 225–226.

8   Vad, 1992, 230–232, summarizes the very strong and often negative reactions this ambitious painting elicited upon its exhibition in Copenhagen. Exhibited several times in the first years of the twentieth century, it was purchased in 1905 by Ernst Thiel, Sweden's foremost collector of progressive Nordic art.

9   Monrad, in Larsen, 2000, 247.

10   Thor Mednick, "On the Question of Content on Vilhelm Hammershøi's Interiors," unpublished manuscript. I would like to thank Thor Mednick for allowing me access to this article.

11   By the time of his death in 1916, Hammershøi was hailed as one of the most important figurative painters in Europe, celebrated throughout Germany, France, and the Nordic nations and receiving, among other accolades, the grand prix at the International Exhibition in Rome in 1911. After the French critic Théodore Duret (1838–1927) viewed the artist's work at the Universal Exposition in Paris, he traveled to Copenhagen, believing, as it was reported in 1890, "youngest Danish art . . . has a first-class master in Hammershøi, a few pictures by whom he wants to acquire for his choice collection of modern art." *Dagbladet*, 16 July 1890, translated in Vad, 74, ft. 89. The poet Rainer Maria Rilke was likewise struck by Hammershøi's work, expressing a desire in 1904 (never requited) to write about it: "The work of this great artist has not ceased to occupy me." Rainer Maria Rilke, letter to Alfred Bramsen, dated 22 November 1904, translated in Vad, 404. Recently, again, Hammershøi has been the subject of major museum exhibitions throughout Europe and North America, including two in the United States, at the Phillips Collection in Washington in 1983 and at the Solomon R. Guggenheim Museum in New York in 1998.

12   Hammershøi's mother, Frederikke (née Rentzmann, 1838–1914) diligently collected his juvenilia, as well as scrapbooks of his press clippings. Vad, 14ff.

13   This observation made by Elisabeth Fabritius, in Ludvigsen, 2005, 111–112.

14   Jens Ferdinand Willumsen, unpublished recollections. Volume 2, p. 202 recto and verso, J. F. Willumsen Museum, Frederikssund, translated in Vad, 23.

15   P. S. Krøyer, quoted by Kristian Zahrtmann, words of tribute at Hammershøi's death, *Berlingske Tidende*, 14 February 1916, in Vad, 24.

16   Vad, 1992, 62–63.

17   Monrad, in Larsen, 253.

18   Vad, 1992, 176.

19   See Mogens Nykjær, "Kærligheds Natur," in Nykjær, 1991, 121–157. Nykjær locates Hammershøi's double portraits within a tradition of marriage or love portrayals in Danish art, allying this painting with Hammershøi's *Artemis* (fig. 161) and suggesting a Symbolist, transcendent, reading of it, see esp. pp. 145–149. Many interpreters of this painting view it as "filled with melancholy," comparing to a double portrait that Hammershøi had painted in 1892, which has a greater freshness and brighter values than the present painting. The 1892 canvas has been allied to the Krøyers' mutual rendering by Felix Krämer, 2003, 20–21, who in turn finds the 1898 painting to be melancholic in comparison.

20   Vad, 1992, 291.

21   See Lena Boëthius and Görel Cavalli-Björkman, eds. *Vilhelm Hammershøi* (exh. cat.) Gothenburg Art Museum, 1999, 128.

22   Vad, 1992, 291–292 interprets the paintings as signs of devotion following the distress of Ida's condition. In contrast, Henrik Wivel reads them as "illusionless," melancholic, any references to Ida's earlier sensuality drained away, leaving an unsentimental representation of a middle-aged woman, now a partner rather than a love object. See Wivel, *Vilhelm Hammershøi*, Copenhagen: Forlaget Søren Fogtdal, 1996, 53–55.

23   See Beate Epperlein, *Monochrome Malerei: zur Unterschiedlichleit des vermeintlich Ähnlichen, Nürnberg: Verlag für moderne Kunst,* 1997; and Denys Riout, *La peinture monochrome: histoire et archéologie d'un genre*, Nîmes: Editions J. Chambon, 1996.

24   Carl Hartmann in *Nationaltidende*, 30 April 1885, translated in Anne Rosenvold Hvidt, "The Strange Thing about Hammerhøi," in *Hammershøi/Dreyer: The Magic of Images* (exh. cat.), ed. Anne Rosenvold Hvidt, Ordrupgaard Collection, Charlottenlund, 2006, 48.

25   Karl Madsen, "Vor tids malerkunst," in *Kunstens Historie i Danmark* (Karl Madsen, ed.), Copenhagen: Alfred Jacobsen, 1901–1907, 414.

26   Letter to Svend Hammershøi, from Rome, 20 December 2002, translated in Vad, 1992, 392.

27   Kirk Varnedoe discussed the body of Hammershøi's domestic paintings and located them within turn-of-the-century domestic representation, linking their theme and aesthetics to pan-European and North American currents, in Varnedoe, "Private Light," *Art in America*, Vol. 71, No. 3, 1983, 110–116.

28   The observation made by Elisabeth Fabritius in Ludvigsen, 2005, 131.

29   Fabritius, in Ludvigsen, 2005, 129–131. She further suggests that there are no sketches for these scenes because they were rendered directly onto the canvas or to a glass plate by cast light. See also Elisabth Fabritius, "Vejen ud af fotografiets perspektiviske rum," in *Verden set på ny: Fotografi og malerkunst i Danmark 1840–1900* (exh. cat.), Det Nationale Fotomuseum, 2002, esp. 80–81.

30   See Vad, 1992, 369–372, and Fabritius, 2002.

31   Gertrud Oelsner Hansen, "Snapshots: On P. S. Krøyer, Julius Paulsen, and Vilhelm Hammershøi," in Johansen and Jensen, 2001, 85–94; Gertrud Oelsner, "Photographic Strategies, Perceptual Reflections and Introvert Tendencies in Painting around 1900," in *Statens Museum for Kunst Journal*, Vol. 6, 2002, 25–43; and Hvidt, esp. 43–60.

32   This modest sketch is related to larger compositions from 1884 entitled *A Young Girl Pouring Tea* (1884, Private Collection) and *From a Baker's Shop* (1888, Vejen Kunstmuseum), and to the nearly identical *Female Figure* (1888, Statens Museum for Kunst). The date of 1884/1888 is offered by Fabritius, in Ludvigsen, 2005, 117–119.

33   Étienne-Joseph-Théophile Thoré, writing under the name W. Bürger, published the first major monograph on Vermeer: "Van der Meer de Delft," *Gazette des Beaux-Arts* 21 (October–December 1866): 297–330, 458–470, 542–575. See Elizabeth E. Gardner, "Thoré's Sphinx," *The Metropolitan Museum of Art Bulletin*, New Series, Vol. 7, No. 3, November 1948, 73–78; and Frances Suzman Jowell, "Vermeer and Thoré-Bürger: Recoveries of Reputation," in *Vermeer Studies*, by Ivan Gaskell and Michael Jonkers, eds. London and New Haven: Yale University Press, 1998, 35–57.

34   See Arthur Clutton Brock, "Danish Pictures at the Guildhall: A New Master," London, 1907, translated in Vad, 1992, 407–408.

35   Henrik Wivel, "Ånnernes rige," in *Symbolismen og impressionisme, Volume 5 of Ny Dansk Kunsthistorie*, Copenhagen: Kunstbogklubben, 1994, 104–105. See also Larsen, 2000.

36   "With the Exhibition Approaching (II. Vilhelm Hammershøi)" [interview recorded by C. C. Clausen], *Hver 8. Dag*, 1907, 437–438, in Vad, 1992, 401.

37   Vad, 1992, 58.

38   Hartmann and Villadsen, 66.

39   Hartmann and Villadsen, 35.

40   See Ludvigsen, 2005, 41–42.

41   The photograph is published in Vad, 1992, 242.

42   Michaëlis and Bramsen, 1918, 303. See also Vad, 1992, 241–246.

43 Analyses of this drawing are provided in
Erik Fischer, *Tegninger af C. W. Eckersberg*,
Statens Museum for Kunst, Copenhagen,
1983, catalogue no. 140, pp. 200–204.

44 On the cultural parallels and conscious ties between
the art of Baroque Holland and nineteenth-
century Denmark, see Kaspar Monrad, et al.
*The Two Golden Ages: Masterpieces of Dutch
and Danish Painting* (exh. cat.), Rijksmuseum,
Amsterdam, Zwolle: Waanders Publishers, 2001.

45 *Vilhelm Hammershøi 1864–1916: Danish
Painter of Solitude and Light*, ed. Anne-Birgitte
Fonsmark and Mikael Wivel, eds. (exh. cat.),
Ordrupgaard Collection and Solomon R.
Guggenheim Museum, New York, 1997, 176.

46 On Munch's painting, see Reinhold
Heller, "Munch's *Night*, the Aesthetics of
Decadence, and the Content of Biography,"
Arts Magazine, 1878, no. 2: 80–105.

47 Sharon Hirsh, *Symbolism and Modern
Urban Society*, Cambridge and New York:
Cambridge University Press, 2004.

48 See Richard Sennett's books *Flesh and Stone: The
Body and the City in Western Civilization*, New
York: Norton, 1994, and particularly *The Conscience
of the Eye: The Design and Social Life of Cities*, New
York: W. W. Norton, 1990, chapter 1, "The Refuge."

49 Ruskin, *Sesame and Lillies*, 108,
quoted in Hirsh, 221.

50 See for example Debra Silverman, *Art Nouveau in
Fin-de-Siècle France: Politics, Psychology and Style*,
Berkeley: University of California Press, 1989, and
Suzanna Barrows, *Distorting Mirrors: Visions of
the Crowd in Late Nineteenth-Century France*, New
Haven and London: Yale University Press, 1981.

51 François Bédarida, "La Vie de quartier en
Angleterre, Enquêtes empiriques et approches
théoriques," *Le Mouvement social* I, 1892, 14,
as cited in Perrot, 361, and in Hirsh, 227.

52 "Interview with the painter Vilh. Hammershøi
about 'Our Home's Arrangement,'" *Hjemmet*,
1909, 268, translated in Vad, 1992, 403–404.

53 Descriptions and plans of the apartment, and of
the Hammershøis' other apartments are found in
Vad, 1992, 186–190; Kasper Monrad, et al. *Vilhelm
Hammershøi* (exh. cat.), Hamburger Kunsthalle,
2003, 16ff.; and Dan Hofstader, "Hammershøi's
Rooms," *Art and Antiques*, December 1985,
71–5. See especially Hammershøi's interview, "Our
Home's Arrangement," in the Danish magazine
Hjemmet (1909), translated in Vad, 1992, 402–403.

54 Vad, 1992, 100.

55 See for example Charlotte Gere and Lesley
Hoskins, *The House Beautiful. Oscar Wilde
and the Aesthetic Interior*. London: Lund
Humphries and Geffrye Museum, 2000.

56 Hirsh, 2004, 228–229.

57 Sandberg, 155–6. See also Jonas Frykman and Sven
Löfgren, *Culture Builders: A Historical Anthropology
of Middle-Class Life* (trans. Alan Crozier), New
Brunswick, N.J.: Rutgers University Press, 1987.

58 Hirsh, 2004, 229.

59 Sharon Hirsh explores the implications of these
titles, and of Mellery's domestic iconography in
2004, 217ff. Mellery's series of drawings was first
exhibited in 1889 in the Brussels exhibition of
Aquarellistes, in 1890 at the exhibition of *Les XX*,
and in 1895 under the title " Emotions d'Art, l'âme
des choses" (Emotions in Art, the Soul of Things)
at the 1895 exhibition of *La Libre Esthetique*.

60 Emily Braun in Varnedoe, 1988, 76.

61 This was also the period in which two major
systematic studies were published about the
Royal Academy, coinciding roughly with
its 150-year celebration: F. Meldahl and
P. Johansen, *Det Kongelige Akademi for de
Skjønne Kunster 1700–1904* (1904) and F.
Meldahl, *Kunstudstillingerne ved det Kongelige
Akademie for de Skjønne Kunster* (1906).

62 Philip Weilbach's biography of Eckersberg,
published in 1872, identifies Eckersberg's students
in this way, as inheriting his characteristics.
Weilbach, *Maleren Eckersbergs Levned og
Værker*, Copenhagen: Th. Lind, 1872, 162.

63 Emil Hannover, *C. W. Eckersberg: En studie i Dansk
Kunsthistorie*, Copenhagen: Kunstforeningen,
1898, 1. In Hannover's work, Eckersberg himself
coalesced with the characteristics that Brandes had
identified as typically Danish: "Entirely devoid of
nervousness, he received all impressions calmly and
imperturbably, nothing could give him a shock,
nothing could influence him or color what he
saw or obscure it or warp it to fit some subjective
impression rather than the objective reality. This
fixity was so intense that it amounted almost
to genius. Yet Eckersberg did not really attain
genius.... It was the homely virtues, amiability,
righteousness, diligence, and sense of duty, which
throve best in the quiet atmosphere of his sitting
room. To his brush nothing was insignificant. For
fear of missing something, he avoided half-lights
and chiaroscuro. Only in the clear, sober light of
day could Eckersberg satisfy his keenest passion as
an artist." Emil Hannover, *Scandinavian Art*, New
York: The American-Scandinavian Foundation and
London: Oxford University Press, 1922, 247–248.

64 Agnes Slott-Møller, "Nationale Værdier
som Grundlag for en kunstnerisk
Udvikling" in 1917, 156.

65 Slott-Møller, 1917, 124.

66 Michaëlis and Bramsen, 1918, 48,
translated in Vad, 1992, 234.

67 A. G. Temple, *Catalogue of the Exhibition of
Works by Danish Painters*, London: Art Gallery
of the Corporation of London, 1907, 14.

68 Wivel, 1996, 36 and 39.

SELECTED BIBLIOGRAPHY

Agerbæk, Kirsten. *Høyen Mellem Klassicisme og Romantik*. Esbjerg: Sydjysk Universitetsforlag, 1984.

Behrndt, Helle, and Jorunn Veiteberg, eds. *Når kvinder fortæller. Kvindelige malere i Norden 1880–1900* (exh. cat.). Copenhagen: Kunstforeningen, 2002.

Bencard, Ernst Jonas, Anders Kold, and Peter S. Meyer. *Kunstværkets Krav: 27 fortolkninger af danske kunstværke*. Copenhagen: Palle Fogtdal, 1990.

Bencard, Mogens, ed. *Intersections: Art and Science in the Golden Age*. Copenhagen: Gyldendal, 2000.

Berman, Patricia G. "Lines of Solitude, Circles of Alliance: Danish Painting in the Nineteenth Century." In *Danish Painting of the Nineteenth Century from the Collection of Ambassador John L. Loeb Jr.* (exh. cat.). Greenwich, Conn.: Bruce Museum of Arts and Sciences, 2005.

Bodelsen, Merete, and Aage Marcus. *Dansk kunsthistorisk Bibliografi*. Copenhagen: C. A. Reitzels Forlag, 1935.

Bodelsen, Merete. *Gauguin og van Gogh i København i 1893 / Gauguin and van Gogh in Copenhagen in 1893* (exh. cat.). Copenhagen: Ordrupgaard, 1984.

Colding, Torben Holck. "Nikolai Abildgaard, 1743–1809." In *Dansk Guldalderkunst Maleri og Skulptur, 1750–1850*. Copenhagen: Politikens Forlag, 1979.

Conisbee, Philip, et al. *Christopher Wilhelm Eckersberg 1783–1853* (exh. cat.). Washington: National Gallery of Art, 2003.

Conisbee, Philip, Sarah Faunce, and Jeremy Strick; with Peter Galassi, guest curator. *In the Light of Italy: Corot and Early Open-Air Painting*. Washington: National Gallery of Art; New Haven and London: Yale University Press, 1996.

Constantin Hansen, 1804–1880 (exh. cat.). Copenhagen: Thorvaldsens Museum; Aarhus: Aarhus Kunstmuseum, 1991.

Czymmek, Götz, ed. *Landschaft als Kosmos der Seele. Malerei des nordischen Symbolismus bis Munch 1880–1910* (exh. cat.). Cologne: Wallraf-Richartz-Museum; Heidelberg: Braus, 1998.

Danish Paintings of the Golden Age (exh. cat.). Catalogue based on research by Suzanne Ludvigsen. New York: Artemis Fine Arts, Inc., 1999.

Danske malere i Rom i det 19. århundrede. Copenhagen: Statens Museum for Kunst, 1978.

De drogo till Paris. Nordiska konstnarinnor på 1880-talet (exh. cat.). Stockholm: Liljevalchs och Kulturhuset, 1988.

Dreams of a Summer Night: Scandinavian Painting at the Turn of the Century (exh. cat.). Ahtola-

Moorhouse, Lena, ed. et al. The Hayward Gallery; London: Arts Council of Great Britain, 1986.

Eitner, Lorenz, ed. *Neoclassicism and Romanticism 1750–1850, An Anthology of Sources and Documents*. New York: Harper & Row, 1989.

Fabritius, Elisabeth. *Michael Ancher og det Moderne Gennembrud 1880–1890*, Skagen: Helga Anchers Fond og Christian Ejlers' Forlag, 1999.

Fabritius, Elisabeth. *P. S. Krøyers Fotografier/ P. S. Krøyer's Photographs*. Trans. David Hohnen (exh. cat.). Copenhagen: Den Hirschsprungske Samling, 1990.

Facos, Michelle. *Nationalism and the Nordic Imagination: Swedish Art in the 1890s*. Berkeley: University of California Press, 1998.

Fischer, Erik, et al. *Tegninger af C. W. Eckersberg* (exh. cat.). Trans. Jan Smith. Copenhagen: Statens Museum for Kunst, 1983.

Floryan, Margrethe, Thomas Kappel, Torben Melander, and Stig Miss, eds. *Copenhagen as it was in 1796*. Copenhagen: Thorvaldsens Museum, 1996.

Fonsmark, Anne-Birgitte, and Mikael Wivel, et al. *Vilhelm Hammershøi 1864–1916: Danish Painter of Solitude and Light* (exh. cat.). Copenhagen: Ordrupgaard; New York: Solomon R. Guggenheim Museum, New York, 1998.

Galassi, Peter. *Before Photography: Painting and the Invention of Photography* (exh. cat.). New York: The Museum of Modern Art, 1981.

Grape-Albers, Heide, et al. *Anna Ancher 1859–1935. Malerin in Skagen* (exh. cat.). Hannover: Niedersächsisches Landesmuseum, 1994.

Gunnarsson, Torsten, et al. *A Mirror of Nature: Nordic Landscape Painting 1840–1910* (exh. cat.). Helsinki: Ateneum Art Museum; Stockholm: Nationalmusuem; Oslo: The National Museum of Art, Architecture and Design; Minneapolis: The Minneapolis Institute of Arts; Copenhagen: Statens Museum for Kunst, 2006.

Gunnarsson, Torsten. *Nordic Landscape Painting in the Nineteenth Century*. Trans. Nancy Adler. Cambridge and New York: Cambridge University Press, 1998.

Gunnarsson, Torsten, and Per Hedström, eds. *Impressionism and the North* (exh. cat.). Stockholm: Nationalmuseum; Copenhagen: Statens Museum for Kunst, 2002–2003.

Harmony in Blue: P. S. Krøyer's Poetic Paintings from the 1890s (exh. cat.). Skagen: Skagens Museum, 2001.

Helsted, Dyveke, et al. *Martinus Rørbye 1803–1848* (exh. cat.). Copenhagen: Thorvaldsens Museum, 1981.

Henschen, Eva, Torben Melander, and Stig Miss, eds. *Johan Thomas Lundbye 1818–1848: at male det kjære Danmark*. Copenhagen: Thorvaldsens Museum, 1994.

Hirsh, Sharon. *Symbolism and Modern Urban Society*. Cambridge and New York: Cambridge University Press, 2004.

Hofstader, Dan. "Hammershøi's Rooms." *Art and Antiques*, December 1985, 71–75.

Honnens de Lichtenberg, Hanne. *Symbolismen i dansk kunst* (exh. cat.). Nivaagaards Malerisamling, 1993.

Hornung, Peter Michael. *Peder Severin Krøyer*. Copenhagen: Forlaget Palle Fogtdal, 2005.

Høyen, N. L. *Konsten i Danmark til dette Aarhundredes Begyndelse. Konsten i Danmark i dette Aarhundrede*. 3 volumes. Copenhagen, 1876.

Jacobs, Michael. *The Good and Simple Life: Artist Colonies in Europe and America*. Oxford: Phaidon, 1985.

Jensen, Mona, ed. *Danske Kunstnerkolonier Skagen, Fyn, Bornholm* (exh. cat.). Aarhus: Aarhus Kunstmuseum, 2000.

Jensen, Robert. *Marketing Modernism in Fin-de-Siècle Europe*. Princeton: Princeton University Press, 1994.

Jespersen, Knud J. V. *A History of Denmark*. Trans. Ivan Hill. London: Palgrave Macmillan, 2004.

Johansen, Annette, et al. *Den Nøgne guldalder. Modelbilleder. C. W. Eckersberg og hans elever* (exh. cat.). Copenhagen: Den Hirschsprungske Samling, 1994.

Johnston, Catherine, et al. *Baltic Light: Early Open-Air Painting in Denmark and Germany* (exh. cat.). Ottawa: National Gallery of Canada in association with Yale University Press, 2000.

Jones, Benedicte. "Skagen, Denmark: Unspoiled Motifs and Blue Northern Skies," unpublished Master's thesis, Harvard University, 1993.

Jonge, Ingrid Fischer, and Gertrud With, eds. *Verden set på ny: Fotografi og Malerkunst i Danmark 1840–1900*. Copenhagen: Det Nationale Fotomuseum, 2002.

Jönsson, Hanne. "C. W. Eckersberg og hans elever," in *C. W. Eckersberg og hans elever* (exh. cat.). Copenhagen: Statens Museum for Kunst, 1983.

Krogh, Leila, et al. *J. F. Willumsen og Den frie Udstillings første år 1891–1898* (exh. cat.). Frederikssund: J. F. Willumsens Museum, 1982.

Kragelund, Patrick. *Abildgaard: Kunstneren mellem oprørerne*. Volume 1 and 2. Copenhagen: Museum Tusculanums Forlag, 1999.

Larsen, Peter Nørgaard. *Symbolism in Danish and European Painting 1870–1910* (exh. cat.). Copenhagen: Statens Museum for Kunst, 2000.

Larsen, Peter Nørgaard, ed. *L. A. Ring: On the Edge of the World* (exh. cat.). Copenhagen: Statens Museum for Kunst, 2006.

Ludvigsen, Suzanne, et al. *The Ambassador John L. Loeb Jr. Danish Art Collection*, New York: John L. Loeb Jr., 2005.

Lübbren, Nina. *Rural Artists' Colonies in Europe, 1870–1910*. New Brunswick: Rutgers University Press, 2001.

Madsen, Karl. *Skagens Malere og Skagens Museum*. Copenhagen: Gyldendalske Boghandel, 1929.

Michaëlis, Sophus, and Alfred Bramsen. *Vilhelm Hammershøi: Kunstneren og hans Værk*. Copenhagen-Christiania (Oslo): Gyldendalske Boghandel, Nordisk Forlag, 1918.

Monrad, Kasper. *Dansk Guldalder. Hovedværker på Statens Museum for Kunst*, Copenhagen: Statens Museum for Kunst, 1994.

Monrad, Kasper, et al. *The Golden Age of Danish Painting* (exh. cat.). New York: Hudson Hills Press in association with Los Angeles County Museum, 1993.

Monrad, Kasper, et al. *The Two Golden Ages: Masterpieces of Dutch and Danish Painting* (exh. cat.). Amsterdam: Rijksmuseum; Zwolle: Waanders Publishers; Copenhagen: Statens Museum for Kunst, 2001.

Monrad, Kasper, et al., *Vilhelm Hammershøi* (exh. cat.), Hamburg: Hamburger Kunsthalle, 2003.

Munk, Jens Peter and Kirsten Olesen, *Postimpressionisme* (exh. cat.). Copenhagen: Ny Carlsberg Glyptotek, 1993.

Nasgaard, Roald. *The Mystic North: Symbolist Landscape Painting in Northern Europe and North America, 1890–1940* (exh. cat.). Toronto: University of Toronto Press in association with Art Gallery of Ontario, 1984.

Nisbet, Peter. *Danish Paintings of the Nineteenth Century from the Collection of Ambassador John L. Loeb Jr.* (exh. cat.). Cambridge: Busch-Reisinger Museum, Harvard University, 1994.

Nørregård-Nielsen, Hans Edvard. *Christen Købke*. 3 volumes. Copenhagen: Gyldendal, 1996.

Nørregård-Nielsen, Hans Edvard. *Dansk Kunst: Tusind års kunsthistorie*. 6th edition. Copenhagen: Gyldendal, 2003.

Nørregård-Nielsen, Hans Edvard, and Kasper Monrad, eds. *Christian Købke 1810–1848* (exh. cat.). Copenhagen: Statens Museum for Kunst, 1996.

Pese, Claus. *Künstlerkolonien in Europa: In Zeichen der Ebene des Himmels* (exh. cat.). Nürnberg: Germanisches Nationalmuseum, 2002.

Platou, Inga Rockswold. *The Art Colony at Skagen: Its Contribution to Scandinavian Art* (unpublished Ph.D. dissertation), University of Minnesota, 1968.

Poulsen, Vagn. *Danish Painting and Sculpture*. Copenhagen: Det Danske Selskab, 1976.

Poulsen, Vagn, Erik Lassen, and Jan Danielsen. *Dansk Kunst Historie: Billedkunst og Skulptur*. 5 volumes. Copenhagen: Politikens Forlag, 1972–1974.

Rosenblum, Robert. "Danish Golden Age Painting: An International Perspective," in *Thorvaldsens Museum Bulletin*, 1997, 45–58.

Rosenblum, Robert. *Transformations in Late Eighteenth Century Art*. Princeton: Princeton University Press, 1967.

Schwartz, Alba. *Skagen: før og nu*. Volumes 1 and 2. Copenhagen, 1912–13.

Sloan, Thomas Le Brie. "Neoclassical and Romantic Painting in Denmark, 1754–1848," (unpublished Ph.D. dissertation), Northwestern University, Evanston, Illinois, 1972.

Svanholm, Lise. *Marie Krøyer, 1867–1940*. Skagen Monografier 2, Skagens Museum, 1987.

Svanholm, Lise. *Northern Light—The Skagen Painters*. Trans. Walton Glyn Jones. Copenhagen: Gyldendal, 2004.

Svanholm, Lise, ed. *Skagen Leksikon: Malerne, Modellerne, Værkerne og Stederne*, Copenhagen: Gyldendal, 2003.

Sørensen, Jens Erik. *P. S. Krøyer: Tradition. Modernity*. Aarhus: Aarhus Kunstmuseum, 1992.

Thage, Jacob. *Portraits of a Marriage: Marie and P. S. Krøyer*. Skagen: Skagens Museum, 1997.

Vad, Poul. *Vilhelm Hammershøi and Danish Art at the Turn of the Century*. Trans. Kenneth Tindall. New Haven: Yale University Press, 1992.

Varnedoe, Kirk, et al. *Northern Light: Realism and Symbolism in Scandinavian Art, 1880–1910* (exh. cat.). Brooklyn, N.Y.: The Brooklyn Museum, 1982.

Varnedoe, Kirk, et al. *Northern Light: Nordic Art at the Turn of the Century*. New Haven and London: Yale University Press, 1988.

Voss, Knud. *The Painters of Skagen*. Trans. Peter Shields. Copenhagen: Stok-Art, 1990.

Wivel, Henrik. *Den Store Stil: Dansk symbolisme og impressionisme omkring år 1900*. Copenhagen: Palle Fogtdal, 1995.

CREDITS

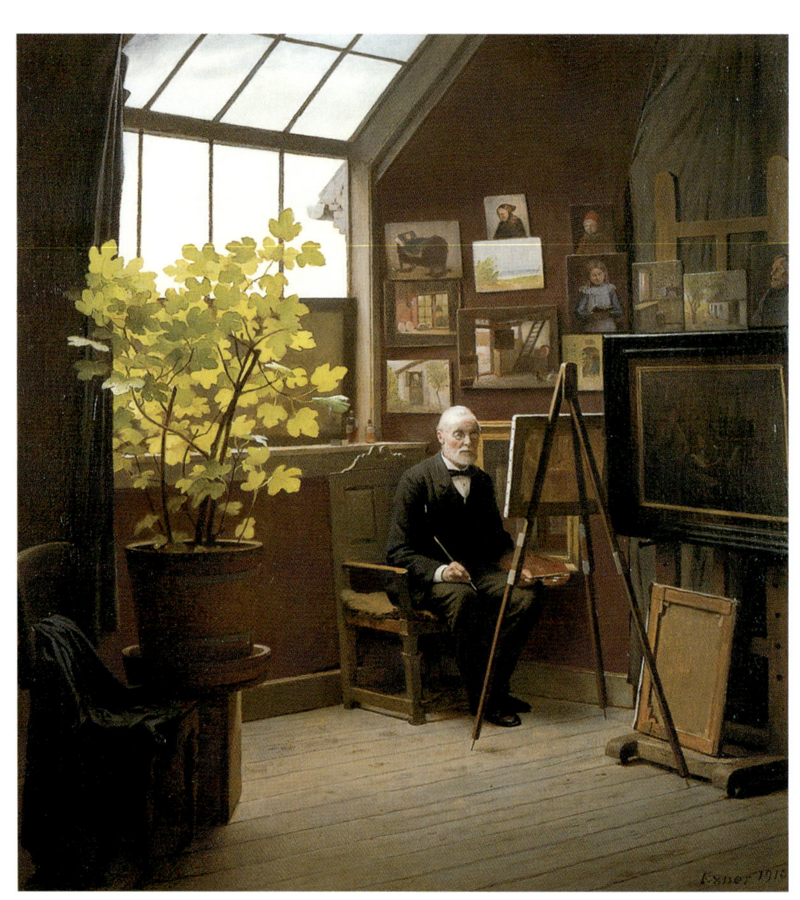